Anything, Ar

Tactical Airlift in the US Army Air Forces and US Air Force from World War II to Vietnam

Sam McGowan

Fourth Edition

Anything, Anywhere, Anytime

Copyright 2002 by Sam McGowan

ISBN-13:
978-1979171274

ISBN-10:
1979171270

Sam McGowan

Other Books by Sam McGowan
The C-130 Hercules, Tactical Airlift Missions, 1956-1975, Tab/Aero, 1988
The Cave, 1st Books Library, 2000
Trash Haulers, Author House, 2010 (A revision of the Tab/Aero release)
Anything, Anywhere, Anytime, Author House, 2011
Hauling Trash, Create Space, September 2012 (Sam McGowan's personal memoir of his military experiences) World War II, the World War II Articles of Sam McGowan, Volume 1, CreateSpace, December 2012
The Cave, Second Edition, CreateSpace, December 2012 (A novel of the Vietnam War)
Two years in the Sky, CreateSpace, January 2013 (Sam McGowan's memoir of his aviation career)
Anything, Anywhere, Anytime, Second Edition, CreateSpace, May 2013 (An informal history of the US Air Force tactical airlift mission)
West Tennessee, the Land Between the Rivers, CreateSpace, July 2013
Mortar Magnets, (A novel of the Vietnam War), Create Space, 2014
The Scout, A novel of the War of Secession), Create Space, 2014
Raleigh Bear, the Best of Dogs, Create Space, 2015
Orange Grove Road, (A novel of the Vietnam War), Create Space, 2015
The Trash Hauler, Create Space, 2016
Pappy Gunn, Southwest Pacific Hero, Create Space, 2017
A Norwegian Girl, Create Space, 2017
Naha Story, Create Space, 2017

Anything, Anywhere, Anytime

Dedicated to Ronda Ann McGowan, my partner and Muse

All photographs are from government sources unless otherwise noted.

Sam McGowan

Contents

Introduction	9
Prologue	11
Chapter One - "The Beginning"	13
Chapter Two - "WAR!!!"	29
Chapter Three - "New Guinea"	57
Chapter Four - "China-Burma-India"	83
Chapter Five - "The Pacific"	109
Chapter Six - "North Africa and the Mediterranean"	150
Chapter Seven - "The Continent"	179
Chapter Eight - "Logistics and ATC"	213
Chapter Nine - "Postwar"	243
Chapter Ten - "Korea"	273
Chapter Eleven - "INDOCHINA"	297
Chapter Twelve - "A NEW FACE"	317
Chapter Thirteen - "PUT TO THE TEST"	355
Chapter Fourteen - "Farmers, Cowboys, Mule Skinners and the Dirty Thirty"	369
Chapter Fifteen - "The Troubled Sixties"	389
Chapter Sixteen - "The Cold War Turns Hot"	411
Chapter Seventeen - "MORTAR MAGNETS"	445
Chapter Eighteen - "KHAM DUC"	467
Chapter Nineteen - "THE NEVER-ENDING WAR"	497
Chapter Twenty - "THE MILITARY AIRLIFT COMMAND"	529
Chapter Twenty One - "Special Applications and Operations"	561
Chapter Twenty Two - "SECRET WAR"	587
Chapter Twenty Three - "A Disastrous End and a Dismal New Beginning"	603
Epilogue	615

Anything, Anywhere, Anytime

Works Cited   657

About the Author   661

Sam McGowan

Preface to Fourth Edition

The Air Force troop carrier mission, or tactical airlift if you will, has been dear to my heart since I left the US Air Force in disgust in July 1975. I became even more disgusted when I made a trip to the National Air & Space Museum in Washington, DC and noticed that although there was an exhibit devoted to military air transportation, it was all about the Air Transport Command, Military Air Transport Service and Military Airlift Command. The troop carrier mission was barely mentioned even though it was the dominant air transport mission in all of the three principal wars in which air forces have played a major part. Over the years, I have been attempting to tell the real story of the military airlift mission. This book is the culmination of that effort.

I wrote Anything, Anywhere, Anytime over a period of time ranging from 1994 to 2011. After the first edition was published, I obtained access to additional information about air taxi operations in the Philippines during the early months of World War II and felt that the book should be revised for that reason alone. As I read through it, I discovered other things that needed to be changed for clarity and to provide new information and published the book in a larger format with the addition of photographs. In this edition, the main changes is a version with a smaller format.

Sam McGowan
October 2017

Anything, Anywhere, Anytime

Sam McGowan

Introduction

The most neglected aspect of military aviation history has long been what is known today as "combat airlift;" a mission that started out in the dark days of World War II as the "air transport" mission then was redesignated in April 1942 as "troop carrier" when the US Army Air Forces reorganized. For the next twenty-three years, it remained troop carrier. In 1967, the Air Force Staff decided "troop carrier" was out of date and redesignated all troop carrier units as "tactical airlift," using a term that came into use in the 1950s when the words "air" and "lift" used to describe the resupply of Berlin were combined into one word. From December 1941 to July 1975, when all US Air Force tactical airlift was rolled into the Military Airlift Command, troop carrier crews and their tactical airlift successors performed vital missions that sometimes went well into the realm of heroism; missions that often saw flight crews in grave danger from hostile fire as they flew through intense small arms and antiaircraft fire to drop paratroops and deliver loads of vital supplies to troops engaged in combat in the field. In some instances, the fire was from their own side. During World War II and in the early months of the Korean War, troop carrier crews often flew through hostile skies over enemy-occupied territory and were subject to interception by enemy fighters.

Yet even though the troop carrier mission and the tactical airlift mission that followed it were vital, often dangerous missions, very little attention has been paid to it by authors and historians who have been more attracted to the glamour of fighters and bombers. Except for a few personal memoirs, all recently published books on airlift have been devoted to the Air Transport Command and its descendants,

Anything, Anywhere, Anytime

morning of October 6 and dropped bundles of supplies but they were not satisfied with their accuracy. In fact, although several 50th AS crews dropped supplies, the combination of dense forest and intense ground fire caused most of them to fall into areas where they could not be retrieved. The situation on the ground had become desperate as the battalion was running out of ammunition.

After their first mission, Goettler and Bleckley volunteered for a second, even though their commanding officer told them that the second mission would be more difficult and dangerous than the first since the Germans now knew that the Allies were attempting to drop supplies. Bleckley was heard to remark that they would get their load to the trapped Americans "or die trying." The two young officers took off from Remicourt Aerodrome late in the day and headed for the Argonne Forest. As they came over the German forces surrounding the trapped unit, their fragile DH-4 encountered a barrage of rifle and machinegun fire. Still, they continued over the position to drop their bundles. More ground fire struck the airplane during and after the drop. Both pilots were wounded but Goettler managed to reach Allied lines where the DH-4 made a precarious, but successful landing. As Allied troops reached the shot-up airplane, they discovered that Goettler was dead from a head wound, having evidently devoted his last efforts to getting the airplane on the ground. Beckler, a member of the Kansas National Guard who was flying as an observer, was badly wounded. He died in the ambulance.

The resupply of The Lost Battalion was the first time airplanes were used to resupply ground troops by American forces and is one of the most heroic missions in aviation history. Goettler and Beckler were recommended for and awarded the Distinguished Service Cross. In 1922, the two airmen's heroism was recognized with the award of the Congressional Medal of Honor.[2] Their mission and the efforts of other 50th AS crews to resupply The Lost Battalion is now recognized by the US Air Force as the first combat airlift mission in history. Yet, even though the resupply effort demonstrated the need for dedicated air transport units with combat capabilities, it wasn't until 1941 that such units finally came into existence. Their heroism, however, is not unique.

---

[2] Modern wannabe purists insist that the correct title is Medal of Honor, but from World War I through World War II, the senior officers who were responsible for awarding it always referred to it as the Congressional Medal of Honor, sometimes shortened to the Congressional Medal.

Sam McGowan

Chapter One - "The Beginning"

Brig. Gen. William L. Mitchell

If there was a true visionary in the US military in World War I, it was Brigadier General William Landrum "Billy" Mitchell of the US Army Air Service. Already in Europe as an observer when the US declared war on Germany in 1917, Mitchell transferred to Paris to take his place as chief of staff for air on General John "Blackjack" Pershing's American Expeditionary Force staff. He studied the role the airplane had already played in the war so far and paid particular attention to the ideas of British Major General Hugh M. Trenchard, the chief of the Royal Flying Corps, and adopted his philosophy that the airplane is an offensive, rather than a defensive, weapon. At a time when few people were willing to listen to his message, Mitchell recognized that not only was the airplane going to be important to modern warfare, it would revolutionize the very nature of war itself. He envisioned the airplane as a weapon that would take warfare into the very heart of the enemy's homeland; an airborne military vehicle unencumbered by the barriers of mountains, jungles, swamps, rivers and oceans. In Mitchell's mind, the airplane offered potential as a new weapon that could strike anywhere at will and a vehicle that would provide unprecedented mobility to ground forces. He believed that air forces would soon replace the Navy's battleships as America's first line of defense and would enable ground armies to move deep into enemy territory and wage war from behind the lines. Mitchell's ideas and

Anything, Anywhere, Anytime

outspoken personality would eventually get him into trouble with his superiors and lead to his court martial but his ideas form the basis for the present-day military forces of the United States.

In the fall of 1918, Mitchell approached his boss, General Pershing, with one of his revolutionary ideas. He wanted to establish a special force of infantrymen trained to parachute from airplanes; an idea made even more remarkable by the fact that few Army personnel had ever used a parachute. As he envisioned them, these airborne soldiers would assault the Germans from their rear and create havoc well forward of the Allied lines. The resulting disruption would allow conventional infantry troops to advance. Although many senior US Army officers detested Mitchell, Pershing was impressed with the airman and accepted many, if not most, of his ideas. After reviewing the plan with his staff, he gave it the go-ahead. Pershing authorized Mitchell to begin the formation of an airborne infantry force that would strike from the skies under a timetable commencing in early 1919. Major Lewis H. Brereton, who had just joined Mitchell's staff as operations officer, was given responsibility for developing the plan.(Brereton, 1946) Brereton developed a plan and Mitchell presented it to Pershing, who approved it. However, it would take time to implement and the war was nearing its end. World War I ended only a few weeks after Mitchell's plan was approved so it was never implemented but the concept was not forgotten by either Mitchell or Brereton, who would command the massive First Allied Airborne Army in Europe 26 years later.

Lt Gen. Lewis H. Brereton

With the war over, the American military returned to its former ways of thinking and the ideas put forth by Brereton and Mitchell were put aside as the US Army shrank back into its prewar boundaries. While many younger officers thought his ideas had merit, none of the senior officers in the War Department wanted to hear such nonsense, with the possible exception of Major General Douglas MacArthur, who had been Mitchell's friend since childhood.[3] Mitchell himself became a very outspoken prophet of air power. While he later proved some of his theories – particularly the vulnerability of ships to attack from the air – his superiors felt he was stepping out of line when he criticized senior generals and admirals for failing to grasp the lessons of World War I.[4] When he publically criticized senior Army and Navy officers after the Navy airship *SHENENDOAH* flew into a thunderstorm and crashed, Mitchell was court martialed for insubordination and forced to retire. The single dissenting vote on the court that convicted him was Douglas MacArthur.[5] Mitchell soon succumbed to stress and died of heart disease without seeing his ideas come to fruition. Still, they lived on in the minds of officers such as Brereton and Captain George C. Kenney – and Douglas MacArthur – and eventually these men would put Mitchell's ideas to work in a war that was fought largely with airplanes playing roles which varied from bombardment to logistical air transportation.

Although Mitchell was forced out of the Army, the publicity surrounding his court martial led Congress to finally do something about the Air Service. Prior to World War I, all Army aviation had been part of the Signal Corps. In 1918, President Woodrow Wilson used special wartime powers granted to him by Congress to separate aviation from the Signal Corps and created the Air Service as an adjunct to Army ground units. The wartime Air Service was not authorized by Congress and thus had no budget of its own, but was dependent on the office of the Chief of Staff to fund its needs from the overall US Army budget. No air officers were assigned to the office of the Army Chief. In 1926, Congress passed the Air Corps Act which established the US Army Air Corps as a combatant force although combat air units remained under the control of the field army

---

[3] Mitchell's and MacArthur's fathers were both Wisconsin Civil War veterans and the boys had gone with them to reunions.

[4] When tests arranged by Mitchell sank several German and surplus Navy ships after World War I, the Navy criticized the tests because the ships were at anchor and not able to maneuver. In March 1943, an air force under MacArthur's command wiped out a Japanese convoy in the Battle of the Bismarck Sea and proved Mitchell's theories beyond a shadow of a doubt, much to the Navy's chagrin.

[5] There is some controversy as to MacArthur's vote but Fiorello La Guardia reported that MacArthur's "no" vote was found in a wastebasket after the trial.

commanders in whose districts they were assigned. Airmen were still not represented in the office of the Chief of Staff.

Lt. Gen. Frank M. Andrews

A decade later, General Douglas MacArthur, who was now Chief of Staff, created the GHQ Air Force, a unit technically under the Chief of the Air Corps but reporting directly to him. Its purpose was to support the Army's General Headquarters, an organization that would be responsible for fighting the next war. Lt. Col. Frank Andrews, who had been in charge of developing the plan for the new organization, was jumped two ranks to temporary brigadier general and given command. One of his staff was Captain George C. Kenney. All combat squadrons transferred into the GHQ Air Force but support functions remained under the Air Corps, whose mission was to procure aircraft and parts, provide training of personnel and to otherwise support the GHQ AF. The few transport aircraft that the Army had purchased were assigned to the Air Corps as no combat air transport mission had yet developed.

During the 1920s and 1930s the United States saw no role for airborne and air transported forces in its army, but such was not the case in Europe. In 1930, the Soviet Army revealed their new parachute troops to the world during a public demonstration in which a lieutenant and eight enlisted men parachuted from a cargo plane and assaulted a simulated objective. The Russians were also experimenting with the use of airplanes to transport infantry. By 1935, they had formed an air landing corps and proven its mobility by flying the unit across the country from Moscow to Vladivostok. They had also demonstrated that large items such as artillery and trucks could be delivered safely by parachute. Some American officers were impressed by the Soviet accomplishments but the War Department made no move to consider copying them. The only American recognition of the possibility of such tactics was the inclusion of the concept in courses taught to field grade officers at the Army Command and General Staff School at Ft. Leavenworth, Kansas.

Yet while the Army as a whole failed to get the message put forth by the Russian accomplishment, the Army Air Corps did, in fact, establish an air transport group within its organization although its initial constitution was in an inactive status and it never became fully operational. The 1st Transport Group was consolidated with the 10th Observation Group on 1 October, 1933 and became the 10th Transport Group in May 1937; its base was at Wright Field, Dayton, Ohio where the Air Corps had its principal logistical base. As the US Army's first transport organization, the 10th Group was assigned directly under the office of the Chief of the Air Corps with the mission of providing logistical support to GHQ Air Force combat units using C-27 and C-33 transports to do the job.(Maurer, 1961) The C-27 was a large single-engine biplane built by Bellanca while the C-33 was a militarized version of the Douglas DC-2 airliner.[6] At this time, the role of Army air transport was confined solely to logistical support of air combat squadrons; no preparations were made for the use of airplanes to transport and support ground troops.

While America paid only slight attention to the Soviet accomplishments, the military leaders of Adolph Hitler's Germany sat up and took notice as they were taking steps to develop their own air transportable infantry units. Within five years, the German paratroop corps of the Luftwaffe would demonstrate to the world just how well they had learned lessons first taught by the Soviets – and how they had improved on them. On May 10, 1940 German paratroops jumped from troop-carrying transports over the Netherlands and captured several bridges in the vicinity of Rotterdam and The Hague. Simultaneous assaults by other Luftwaffe troopers seized several airfields near the two cities, thus providing landing strips for Junkers 52 transports. As soon as the airfields were in German hands, the Ju 52s began landing with reinforcements and equipment too large to be dropped by parachute. For the first time in history, the Germans had established an "airhead" behind the lines; a landing zone into which transports could bring reinforcements and supplies for troops in combat.

---

[6] Several versions of the DC-2 were purchased by the Army, and were given different designations depending on how they were configured. There were different versions of the DC-3 as well.

Anything, Anywhere, Anytime

Bellanca C-27

In Belgium, German paratroops quickly overcame the elaborate defensive positions that were supposed to hold their infantry counterparts at bay. Fort Eban Emael was the center point and most powerful of a series of Belgian fortresses that had been constructed along a line adjacent to the Meuse River. While Luftwaffe paratroops were jumping into Holland, ten gliders landed smack on top of the underground Eban Emael and discharged 78 troops laden with explosives. The glider troops quickly blasted their way into the fortress and thus ended forever the idea of fortified warfare. Simultaneously with the assault on Eban Emael, a thirty-glider force landed with 350 troops in fields around three Meuse River bridges. The gliderborne troops quickly captured the bridges, thus providing avenues for Wermacht tanks and motorized infantry to roll out of Germany and take Belgium practically overnight.

The outbreak of war found the United States virtually unprepared militarily, but the country had an industrial base that had been idled due to the economic depression that gripped the nation that had the capacity to produce large quantities of military hardware and to do it in a hurry. President Franklin Roosevelt saw the war in Europe as a golden opportunity not only to put jobless Americans back to work, but also as justification for putting thousands of unemployed young men into uniform and out of the unemployment lines that characterized the country during the Depression. Because airplanes were playing such a large role in the war in Europe, the American aviation industry rebounded very quickly when the country began providing new aircraft to its European allies. In January 1939, President Roosevelt ordered an increase in aircraft production for sale overseas. Although he did not specifically order a US military buildup at that time, one was inevitable and by 1940 the US military was undergoing a dramatic increase in size including an increase in Air Corps combat groups, some of which were dedicated to air transport.

Even though the United States was technically still neutral, several American military officers went to Europe as observers. Major George Kenney, a fighter pilot in World War I and a former member of the GHQ AF staff, was a firm believer in the airplane as an offensive weapon and what he saw in Europe reinforced his opinions. Unlike many of his peers, who thought only in terms of pursuit ships and bombers, Kenney recognized the possibilities offered by transport airplanes, both to support combat squadrons and to provide mobility for ground troops. He would later prove his ideas in New Guinea. The German successes also convinced Kenney that his country was inadequately prepared to fight a modern war and he returned to the United States to say so. The testimony of Kenney and other observers was enough to convince President Franklin D. Roosevelt. The United States began a massive military buildup in an attempt to bring the US Army and Navy up to par with those of Europe, with a major focus on developing air forces. Some twenty years after having been forewarned by Billy Mitchell, the US War and Navy Departments finally recognized that the airplane was the weapon of a future that had suddenly become the present.

Almost exactly one year after the invasion of Belgium, the Luftwaffe demonstrated that airborne forces could invade a country alone when they assaulted the Mediterranean island of Crete. German paratroops and gliderborne infantry landed on Crete and secured airfields into which the trimotored Junker's transports began an air bridge bringing troops in from Greece. The Cretin invasion was solely an airborne operation; every German soldier arrived on the island either by parachute or in the cargo compartment of a Junkers 52 or glider. Yet, although the invasion of Crete was a success, the German inability to control the seas around the island made the operation very costly and led Hitler to rule out the use of his crack paratroop units in such attacks in the future, perhaps to his eventual dismay as the war turned in the Allies' favor. Allied airborne operations would turn out to be costly too, but superior Allied logistics allowed troops delivered by air to be resupplied and reinforced.

Germany's success with airborne and air transported ground troops caused the US War Department to take another look at the idea of establishing a parachute corps of its own. While some officers, including Kenney, believed the airplane could be valuable as a means of transporting and supplying conventional forces, no move was made to achieve this end; the original US effort was oriented solely toward paratroops. In April 1940, the War Department approved tests for a platoon of parachute infantry. Tests carried out at Lawson Field at Fort Benning, Georgia proved so successful that the test platoon was expanded to become the 1st Parachute Battalion. Their jump planes were twin-engine Douglas C-39s and C-47s, essentially olive-drab painted DC-2 and DC-3 airliners that had been stripped of passenger-carrying amenities and modified to carry cargo.

Assigned to the Air Corps's only air transport wing, the C-39s and C-47s had originally been purchased to replace the outdated C-27s and C-33s to provide logistical support for the Army's aviation units in the United States and Alaska. Fortunately, the versatile Douglas proved adaptable to paratroop operations as well. A new version, the C-53, was developed specifically for paratroop and troop carrier operations. "Bucket" seats were installed along the sides of the cargo compartment. The C-53 *Trooper* differed from the cargo C-47 *Skytrain* in that the latter featured a wider entrance door to allow easier loading of cargo and a reinforced floor, but other than that they were the same.[7] While the Douglas transports were adequate for military use, their military capabilities were limited. They could only carry small vehicles and were incapable of dropping military equipment larger than small pack howitzers. Consequently, the Army sought new aircraft designs with true military capabilities. In November 1941, the Air Corps issued a requirement for a military transport that became the Fairchild C-82 *Packet*, but it had just entered production when the war ended. Other designs were studied, but the C-82 was the only wartime military transport that entered production before war's end. However, it entered service too late to for overseas duty.

Partially to accommodate the transportation needs of the new airborne troops, but primarily to provide logistical transport for its expanding combat squadrons, the Army Air Corps activated five new groups dedicated to air transport in November and December 1940: the 60th and 61st Transport Groups at Olmsted Field, Harrisburg, Pennsylvania, the 62nd at McClellan Field, Sacramento, California, the 63rd at Wright Field, Ohio and the 64th at Duncan Field, San Antonio, Texas. Assigned to the Air Corps Maintenance Command, all five groups were located at Air Corps maintenance depots and were tasked to deliver parts to combat squadrons. They started out using existing transports, including Ford Trimotors and militarized Douglas DC-2s – C-39s – but they all eventually received C-47s. While these groups were the forerunners of the many that would perform valiantly in World War II, in 1941 they initially existed primarily on paper. The

---

[7] The DC-3 was adapted for military use in several variations, with each given its own designation. By the war's end, the C-47 designation had been given to all of them.

five groups were later assigned to the 50th Transport Wing, a new unit that activated at Wright Field a few months before Pearl Harbor.

By the spring of 1941, a jump school was in full swing at Fort Benning where several new paratroop battalions were being formed. Plans had been made for two paratroop divisions, the 82nd and 101st Airborne Divisions, both to be formed out of the famous 82nd Infantry, the All-American Division of World War I which had included Medal of Honor winner Alvin C. York among its ranks.[8] To transport the paratroop divisions and perform other air transportation tasks, the War Department increased its purchasing of Douglas C-47s and C-53s. Other civilian aircraft were also pressed into military service, including Beechcraft's twin-engine D-18, a light transport commonly known as the Twin Beech which became the C-45, and the larger Lockheed Lodestar which was designated as the C-60. Obsolete or inadequate bombers were converted into transports, particularly the Douglas B-18 and B-23, which were based on the DC-2 and DC-3 airliners respectively.

Douglas C-39

Original Army doctrine saw paratroops as a means of securing landing zones for conventional infantry who would come in by glider, but in 1941 no military gliders had yet entered production in the United States. The German model included conventional infantry who would be transported to airfields that had been captured by paratroops, but US thinking had yet to progress to that level, at least not officially, when war broke out. The role of transports was to support the Army's combat squadrons by delivering spare parts and providing transportation for high-ranking officers. Supporting infantry

---

[8] York, a Tennessee native, was the most decorated American soldier of The Great War.

was an afterthought, even though the Army was built around the infantry. Few in the Army had yet to realize that the airplane provided a means of avoiding obstacles such as mountains, rivers and even oceans thus providing unprecedented mobility to infantry. It was only when they saw what the Germans were doing that Army leaders began paying attention to the possibilities afforded by air transportation for transport and resupply of combat forces. With one exception, no transport squadrons had yet been assigned overseas; not even in the Philippines where the US began a major military buildup in the summer of 1941.

Douglas C-47 Skytrain

Lockheed C-60 Lodestar

The single exception was the Panama Canal Zone, which was considered highly vulnerable to attack. The Panamanian president was pro-Nazi, which placed the US-administered Canal Zone in a precarious position. Maj. Gen. Frank Andrews, who had formerly commanded the GHQ Air Force and served on the Army Staff, was sent to Panama to organize the Air Corps[9] squadrons then was placed in command of all US Army forces in the Caribbean. The far-thinking officer had greatly impressed General George C. Marshall, who had come to believe the Tennessee native was the most capable officer in the US Army.[10] Andrews requested paratroopers and transports and got them. (Craven & Cate, 1956) Air transport needs in the Philippines were initially met with the reassignment of Douglas B-18 bombers to transport duty as they were replaced by Boeing B-17s.[11]

Because of the emphasis on speed in prewar aviation circles, the aviation industry had several new ideas for pursuit-type airplanes on the drawing boards. An Air Corps contract for a new bomber in the mid-thirties led several manufacturers to come up with their own designs which, while they failed to win the competition and lost out to the Douglas B-18 before the war, were dusted off and redesigned to fill overseas requirements and meet US government needs. The same competition also led Boeing to develop a four-engine bomber that the Army designated the B-17 but the purchase and operating costs were considerably higher than the B-18 and the War Department only purchased thirteen prior to 1939. To correct the B-17's short-comings, the Air Corps contracted with Consolidated Aircraft for a new four-engine bomber and designated it as the B-24. In order to fill transportation requirements created by the assignment of Air Corps and other Army personnel overseas as advisors and logisticians, the Army Ferrying Command received the first eleven B-24As as they were delivered in the summer of 1941 to use for long-range transport duty. What was lacking was a truly military transport. The C-82 was on the drawing board but there were no military transport aircraft available. To fill the gap, the Army turned to the adaptation of airplanes that had been designed for airline use, including large seaplanes, and converted bombers.

The eleven Liberators proved to be a Godsend as they were the first transports capable of transoceanic operations. They opened up

---

[9] The terms "Air Corps" and "Army Air Forces" are misleading. Although the US Army Air Forces was established in 1941, then reorganized a few months later after the outbreak of war, it did not replace the Air Corps, which was authorized by Congress in the Air Corps Act of 1926. In fact, the USAAF was actually a training and support organization and had no command over combat units overseas, which were under the command of the theater commander. Army Air Forces became a generic term for all of the Army's Air Corps units, but it was not official except in the case of training units and units assigned to Zone of the Interior forces of the First, Second, Third and Fourth Air Forces and the Air Transport Command.

[10] Marshall indicated that he intended for Marshall to be the senior officer in the European Theater and only chose Eisenhower after Marshall's untimely death.

[11] Like the C-39, the B-18 was based on the Douglas DC-2.

nucleus for an organization that was yet in the future, and which would come to be known as the Air Transport Command. By the end of the war, ATC would evolve into a military airline with global air transport capabilities. The troop carrier mission, as it developed, was entirely different from the long-range air transport mission that would eventually be incorporated into the ATC. There was no connection between them and the only similarity was that they operated transports.

Troop carrier squadrons were planned for a combat role and would be part of the overseas combat commands although they didn't start out that way. During the prewar military buildup, several new commands were created, including the Air Corps Maintenance Command, which became the Air Service Command in early 1942. In January 1941, the 50th Transport Wing was organized under the Maintenance Command to transport Air Corps technical supplies between the maintenance and supply depots and combat squadrons around the country and in Alaska and Panama. (Craven & Cate, 1956) As the new paratroop battalions increased in prominence and size, the 50th was given the additional task of providing airplanes and crews for airborne training. Plans were made for the activation of new air transport groups but most were still on paper when the United States went to war.

After the US entered the war, the US Army reorganized. Part of the reorganization was a change in status of the US Army Air Forces, a new organization that had been established a year earlier. The Army Air Forces were elevated to equal status with the Army Ground Forces. Maj. General Henry H. Arnold, who had previously been chief of the Army Air Corps, was placed in command. Maj. General George Brett was given command of the Army Air Corps but the office was abolished in April 1942 during the reorganization. However, the Army Air Corps remained in existence as the statutory US Army air arm. The AAF was NOT, however, in command of all Army aviation. It was a US-based organization with responsibility for procurement and training, including the development of tactics. Combat units were under the respective theater commander where they were assigned.

During the reorganization, the 50th Transport Wing left the Air Service Command and became part of a new organization the Army created as the Air Transport Command and given responsibility for the transport of troops. A few weeks later, the 50th was joined by the 51st and 52nd Transport Wings as America geared up to fight the war. At the time, both wings existed primarily on paper. The Air Transport Command designation was short-lived, however. Plans were made for the creation of a new military airline from the Ferrying Command and the "transport" designation was taken away from the existing command and given to the new one although the units were left intact. The former Air Transport Command became the I Troop Carrier Command, and in that capacity began building a troop carrier force for overseas duty. Its groups and squadrons retained their transport identity until July, 1942 when they were redesignated as "troop carrier." By that time, the country was at war.

Anything, Anywhere, Anytime

Sam McGowan

Chapter Two - "WAR!!!"

Col. Paul I. "Pappy" Gunn

By the time the I Troop Carrier Command was established, the United States was already at war and transport airplanes and crews were heavily involved. As it turned out, the first blow did not fall in the Panama Canal Zone as so many Americans had expected, but came down in the Pacific in Hawaii and the Philippines. The attack on Hawaii was just that, an attack aimed at the US Pacific Fleet at Pearl Harbor,[13] but the Japanese' objective in the Philippines was to defeat the US forces there and capture the islands, then use them as a base for operations further south in the East Indies. It was in the Philippines that American transport pilots would first see action.

Within a week after war came to the Philippines, a newly created provisional transport squadron was in action, flying under the command of a man who would become a legend in the Pacific and one of the true characters of World War II. Paul Irvin "P.I." Gunn, an Arkansas native who had grown up in the foothills of the Ozarks north of Little Rock, had already served one career as a US Navy enlisted fighter and seaplane pilot and flight instructor. After his retirement from the Navy in 1937, Gunn took his family to the Philippines where he had found employment in Manila as the personal pilot for Filipino industrialist Andres Soriano[14]. Shortly after he arrived in Manila, Gunn

---

[13] If the fleet had been at sea as it should have been considering that US leaders were expecting war, there would have been nothing in the harbor for the Japanese to attack.

[14] Soriano's holdings included the San Miguel Brewing Company. A popular myth developed among US military personnel who served in the Philippines after

Anything, Anywhere, Anytime

convinced Soriano to start an interisland airline. By December 1941, the airline was operating several Beech 18s and a trio of Lockheed Lodestars were on their way to Manila by ship. The Lodestars never made it. The ship that was carrying them was diverted to Australia when war broke out and they were appropriated by the military when they arrived in Brisbane.

Gunn and his airline attracted the attention of the senior air officer in the Philippines, the same Louis H. Brereton who had served under Billy Mitchell in France and was now a major general and commander of Far East Air Force in Manila. Shortly after the Japanese attacked Clark Field, Brereton called Gunn to his office and told him that he and his airline were now part of the US Army and that he held the rank of captain and was in command of a transport squadron. Gunn would later say that while he had intended to go back into the Navy, it made little difference to him. War had come and he was in it.(Kenney G. C.)(Gunn)(Edmonds, They Fought With What They Had) He approached the Navy immediately after the outbreak of war but was told that all it had in the islands were some PBY patrol aircraft and that the Army could make better use of him.[15]

Along with Gunn, the Beech 18's also came into the Army as did his chief mechanic, Dan Strickland, who was also a Navy veteran who had come to Manila from Hawaii. The two former naval aviators joined a handful of other American and Filipino civilian pilots and mechanics to make up a small transport squadron. To hide the airplanes, Gunn moved them off of Nichols Field and began operating from a Chinese cemetery called Grace Park on the outskirts of Manila. The cemetery was adjacent to an airfield that had been used by an air taxi company until a year or so before. They parked the airplanes under the shelter of trees and knocked down a few tombstones along a driveway to turn it into a taxiway. The Japanese never realized that the cemetery was being used as an airfield. In addition to the Beechcraft, the squadron was expanded to include a WACO, an amphibious Grumman Duck and two obsolete Seversky P-35s that were not suitable as fighters but were adaptable for courier work. In addition to Gunn's PAL pilots, Army pilots from Far East Headquarters flew transport missions. The new squadron, along with an assortment of other aircraft that served as transports in the dark days of early 1942, was quickly dubbed the

---

the war that the company was owned by General Douglas MacArthur, but it was just that, a myth. Soriano held US citizenship and was commissioned as a colonel on MacArthur's staff. He would rise to the rank of major general.

[15] Gunn's commissioning orders are dated a week after the Japanese attacks but he had been flying transport missions for the Army in the interim. In fact, he was shot up over Cebu and crash-landed at Nichols Field before the date of the order.

"Bamboo Fleet."[16] Gunn went into service flying his Beechcraft throughout the islands, transporting supplies, personnel and dispatches to various military installations. He and his men flew through skies that were controlled by the Japanese and were susceptible to attack both in the air and on the ground. The pilots flew as close to the tops of the trees as they could to elude the Japanese fighters that prowled the skies. They were joined in the transport effort by several Douglas B-18s that had been replaced by B-17s as bombers and converted into transports. The B-18s operated under the 19th Bombardment Group to which they were officially assigned rather than as part of Gunn's ad hoc transport operation.

Twin Beech 18/C-45

P.I. Gunn would become a legend in the Fifth Air Force in the Southwest Pacific, and the subject of a book by General George Kenney. Later on, in Australia and New Guinea he would regale younger audiences with tales of his exploits in his long and colorful

---

[16] The "Bamboo Fleet" nickname is most commonly associated with the assortment of single-engine airplanes that remained in the Philippines after Pappy Gunn was ordered to Australia with his three Twin Beeches. Gunn flew out with a load of Far East Air Force staff officers around Christmas. The second Beech left a few days later with part of a group of fighter pilots from the 17th Pursuit Group who had been ordered to Australia. The third Beech left in early January with another group of fighter pilots, one of whom was Captain Boyd "Buzz" Wagner, the first American ace of World War II. The airplane was in terrible shape and was literally held together with baling wire, but it made it to Java!

Anything, Anywhere, Anytime

career. But the tales he told were tall, and he purposely left out what he had really done in the Philippines and Java – and he had done a lot. Until he was ordered out of the islands on Christmas Eve, Captain Gunn and his pilots flew all over the Philippines on a daily basis transporting whatever needed to be carried to wherever it needed to go. They were shot at nearly every time they flew, both by ground fire and the Japanese fighters that prowled the skies – and often by American and Filipino troops who mistook them for Japanese. A few days after the outbreak of war, Gunn was flying over the island of Cebu when he was attacked by a Japanese fighter. Fortunately, it was just before nightfall and Gunn was able to elude his pursuer by flying low in the shadows. He flew the damaged airplane back to Manila but he had to fly over a Philippines Air Force field and was shot at by Filipino soldiers. He managed to crash-land the badly damaged airplane at Nichols Field. Gunn walked away from the crash, but the airplane was only good for parts.[17] One of the last missions he flew before he was sent to Australia was to Mindanao to deliver a load of turkeys for Christmas dinner.

But the Philippines were doomed to fall, and when President Roosevelt decided to abandon the American and Filipino soldiers, sailors and airmen to their fate, Gunn was ordered to fly a load of Far East Air Force staff officers to Australia.[18] When he got there, he was told to remain. Not knowing when he could come back, before he left Manila he rounded up as much cash as he could and gave it to his wife Clara. He told her to not let the Japanese know who they were and to never discuss him. She was to tell them that her husband was a sailor who had been killed during the bombing of Cavite. Clara Gunn was interned in Santo Thomas University in Manila along with their four children and their status served as an inspiration for their husband and father to fight his own personal war to gain their release.[19] Gunn's family would remain in Japanese hands until early 1945 when the camp was liberated by a special force from the 1st Cavalry Division that had been dispatched on MacArthur's personal command.

In the chaos of the early days of the war there was little command and control in the Southwest Pacific and there were pilots and other aviation personnel still in the Philippines. Gunn knew they would be

---

[17] There is some question as to whether the airplane was scrapped or returned to a semblance of flying condition.

[18] Roosevelt made the decision only reluctantly, primarily because of advice from the Navy. Even as late as February 1942, convoys were still being made up for Manila although they were all diverted to Brisbane.

[19] Dan Strickland, Gunn's chief mechanic, was also interned. Although he had been commissioned as a lieutenant, Strickland wore no rank and managed to convince the Japanese that he was a civilian.

Sam McGowan

invaluable as the Americans set out to defeat the Japanese. He flew a number of trips to Mindanao carrying cargo for the US and Filipino forces still in the islands, then brought out pilots and other military personnel who had escaped from Luzon and made their way south. On at least a few occasions Gunn flew on to Bataan with badly needed supplies, and after being told by a Filipino soldier that he might be able to bring his family to safety for a price, he once landed on Quezon Boulevard in Japanese-occupied Manila. After waiting fifteen minutes, he took off again when his family failed to appear. He personally brought a number of pilots and maintenance personnel out of the Philippines. On one occasion he flew a damaged B-17 that had been abandoned on Mindanao because an engine wouldn't start. Gunn and a team of mechanics repaired the engine and he flew it to Australia with a load of pilots and aircraft mechanics on board. Captain Paul I. Gunn was very active after his arrival in Australia, both behind the controls of a transport and also reportedly in the cockpit of an Australian Whirraway[20] fighter when Japanese forces attacked Rabaul in New Britain. He was allegedly shot down and spent several days in the jungle before he walked out to rejoin the Allied forces. During his ordeal, Gunn's hair turned snow white (although it later returned to its original brown) and the young pilots and mechanics began calling him "Pappy."

Gunn and two of his pilots[21] were ordered out of the Philippines to Australia with the Beeches but after they departed, air taxi operations continued under the command of Major William "Jitter Bill" Bradford. Bradford was a World War I pilot who went to Manila in the early 1930s to take a job as chief pilot for Philippine Air Taxi Company, a charter company that operated a small fleet of single-engine airplanes on scheduled and nonscheduled flights around the islands. A Texas native, he was heavily involved in the American Legion and when he wasn't flying, he spent much of his time at the Manila Post.

---

[20] The Whirraway was an Australian fighter based on the North American AT-6 advanced trainer airframe. Only lightly armed, they were no match for the Japanese fighters. Whirraways played a role in troop carrier operations in New Guinea, serving as spotters for troop carrier aircraft on airdrops. There is some question as to whether or not he was at Rabaul. Australian official records make no mention of him being there but there were rumors in the Southwest Pacific that he was. His son Nat says he was.

[21] The two pilots who went to the Philippines were Captains Harold Slingsby and Lewis Connelly. A fourth Beechcraft was flown out by Captain Cecil McFarland, who was officially the fuels officer for Far East Air Force. McFarland returned to the Philippines with Gunn on the flight when he was shot down and remained on Mindanao and was either killed or died as a POW. Connelly later joined a bomber squadron and was killed on a mission over the Japanese installation at Lae, on Papau New Guinea.

Anything, Anywhere, Anytime

Bradford was one of the first Americans in the Philippines to recognize the threat to the islands presented by Japan's Asian ambitions, and he often held forth his opinions of the danger in the Legion. PATCO operated out of a grass strip at Grace Park, the same strip that Gunn moved his operations to when the war broke out. PATCO's owners were making plans to expand their operation but Bradford advised against it. He told them that they were likely to lose their investment when the inevitable war came to the islands. Soriano bought PATCO's charter certificate and the company shut down its operation at Grace Park. Philippine Airlines started operating out of Nielsen Field on the other side of Manila. Since PAL was using multiengine airplanes, PATCO's single-engine airplanes were sold.

Bellanca Skyrocket

For some reason, Bradford chose not to go to work for Soriano when he purchased PATCO's business. Instead, he decided to volunteer to return to active duty with the Army, in which he held a reserve commission as a captain. By this time Bradford was in his forties and too old to be a combat pilot so he went back into the Air Corps as an engineering officer. When General Brereton activated Far East Air Force, he put Bradford in command of the maintenance depot at Nichols Field in Manila. Soriano and Gunn, who was his chief pilot, weren't interested in the use of single-engine airplanes but preferred to use multiengine airplanes. One of PATCOs airplanes, a Beechcraft Staggerwing, was at Neilsen Field in Manila when war broke out. When Gunn formed his provisional air transport squadron right after December 8, Bradford was not assigned to it but he flew some flights, as did Major Cecil MacFarland, the fuels officer for Far East Air Force. Col. Harold George, who was acting commander of V Interceptor Command, sent Bradford to southern Luzon to supervise construction

Sam McGowan

of an airfield. He was there when Gunn and his pilots left for Australia. When MacArthur ordered all US and Filipino troops on Luzon to retreat to Bataan, Bradford went to the peninsula along with everyone else.

Shortly after the retreat to Bataan, Col. George sent word to Bradford that he needed someone to fly a new code to the US commander on Panay, an island in the central Philippines. Once the code was delivered, Bradford was to undertake a survey of the airfields on the island, including some that were under construction in anticipation of the arrival of aircraft from Australia. Captain Hervy H. Whitfield was sent out at the same time in the Beechcraft with a code for the commander on Mindanao. There were several Philippine Air Force Stearman trainers on Bataan and Corregidor that had been converted into observation airplanes and armed with .30-caliber machineguns. Although there was no official designation for them, they were called O-1s. Bradford delivered the code then went out to check the airfields. He discovered that the old Bellanca Skyrocket that he had flown for PATCO was on the island, and the regional commander, Brigadier General Bradford Chenowyeth, was using it as an observation airplane.

Bradford saw the possibility of using the Bellanca for what it was intended to be; as a light transport. It was ill suited for observation work due to the lack of rearward visibility. On the other hand, the open cockpit O-1 made an ideal observation platform. Bradford talked to Chenowyeth and they worked out a trade, under the condition that it would have to be approved by MacArthur's headquarters. When he got back to Bataan, Bradford informed George, who had just been promoted to brigadier general, that the Bellanca was on Panay and suggested they swap one of the O-1s for it and use it to carry supplies to Bataan. George was enthusiastic about the plan, as was MacArthur when he learned about it. Bradford left immediately in an O-1 to trade.

The Bellanca wasn't in the best of shape but it would fly.[22] On the way back to Bataan, Bradford brought a load of vegetables and other foodstuffs. He had also brought what food he could carry back in the rear cockpit of the Stearman on his first flight but the Bellanca could carry a sizeable load. When he got back, George told Bradford to take the Bellanca and fly it to the Del Monte Pineapple Plantation on Mindanao where a complex of airfields had been constructed just before the outbreak of war. The general told Bradford that he would meet him there.[23] Whitfield had also been ordered to Mindanao as had

---

[22] Bradford would tell an Army Air Forces interviewer that the airplanes were in pretty bad shape, but no baling wire was used to hold them together.

[23] George also told him that there was no way he was going to fly in that old rattletrap of an airplane!

Anything, Anywhere, Anytime

Captain Joe Moore, who had retrieved a sunken US Navy Duck amphibian, and several Filipino pilots, one of whom brought in a WACO that had been part of PATCO. Their orders were to wait for General George. A few days later George showed up, along with General Douglas MacArthur, his wife and son and his staff. George told Bradford that he and the others had been sent to Del Monte in case the party had to be evacuated to secret bases if the Japanese attacked before their transport arrived from Australia. He also said that when he arrived in Brisbane, he was going to organize "a supply train" to bring supplies to Mindanao from Darwin. He was putting Bradford in charge of a small squadron made up of the Bellanca, the Beechcraft, the WACO and the Duck whose mission would be to deliver the supplies on to Bataan, where they were badly needed.

B-24A Transport[24]

Sometime in mid-to-late December or early January three or possibly four B-24A bombers that had been converted for transport use were sent to the Far East by the Army Ferrying Command. One was being used by Air Corps chief Maj. Gen. George Brett, who was on a worldwide inspection trip at the outbreak of war and was sent to Australia to take command of the newly organized US Army in Australia. Two (or three) others were sent out to fly a supply of .50-caliber ammunition to the Philippines. A Pan American Airways Clipper was sent from New York bound for Manila with the ammunition, but when it reached Calcutta, it was turned around and sent back to Karachi to offload its cargo. The B-24s picked the load up at Karachi and delivered it to the Philippines, although it is unclear if

---

[24] Artist's conception of the last airplane to fly into the Philippines. It probably was no longer wearing that huge flag by that time!

they went into Bataan[25] or Mindanao. The B-24s were still under Ferrying Command and were originally intended to return to India but were ordered to remain in the Far East instead.

On January 22 while Captain Gunn was incognito, General Brereton's Far East Air Force headquarters activated a new unit at Amberly Field near Brisbane, Australia to be responsible for air transportation operations in the Southwest Pacific. The new unit was designated as the Far East Air Force Air Transport Command and was initially commanded by 1st Lieutenant Edgar W. Hampton, Brereton's former aide.[26] Command personnel consisted of ten officers and fifteen enlisted men who had arrived in Australia on December 22 and were originally assigned to the 7th Bombardment Group, whose air echelon was still enroute to Australia, and the 35th Pursuit Group. Both groups had been in a convoy bound for the Philippines when war broke out, but were diverted to Australia. The command was organized "to control all United States transport planes in Australia and all combat airplanes that were flyable, but unfit for combat."(Gunn)

Although it was optimistically a "command," the new unit really consisted of only one under-strength squadron. The ATC was initially equipped with Gunn's Beech D-18/C-45s, a pair of Douglas B-18 bombers and a single C-39 that had come out of the Philippines, along with the three Lockheed Lodestars that had been on their way to join Philippines Airlines and had arrived in Brisbane in the same convoy with the initial contingent of personnel. The command began to flesh out with the arrival of five factory-fresh C-53s that arrived from the United States.[27] On February 4, after he returned from Darwin, Captain Gunn was officially placed in command of the Air Transport Command and the headquarters moved to Archerfield, near Brisbane.[28] Four days later the ATC increased in size and capabilities when the trio of Ferrying Command B-24s joined the command, along with ten aircrew members with transport experience. FEAF ATC was the US component of the Directorate of Air Transport, a multi-national organization that was set up under Royal Australian Air Force Air Marshall Sir Harold Gatty, who had achieved fame as a long-distance air racer before the war.

---

[25] Air Corps personnel at the airfields on Luzon began withdrawing to Bataan on Christmas Day. Several airfields were constructed on the peninsula and it's possible the transports delivered the ammunition there.

[26] Hampton would spend the rest of his military career in airlift, and would retire as a brigadier general.

[27] Some sources indicate that the C-53s arrived by ship, and were intended to support the 7th Bombardment Group, which had started moving to the Far East in late December.

[28] The airfield was actually Archer Field but the Australians followed the English style of combining names of places into one word.

Anything, Anywhere, Anytime

The first task of the fledgling air transport organization was to provide air transportation for the Allied troops who went to Java to fight the Japanese. They transported mechanics and supplies for a squadron of P-40s that were sent north to Darwin, then across the Timor Sea to Java. That the P-40s were operational was largely thanks to Pappy Gunn – he had found the airplanes sitting on the docks and had organized a team of mechanics to assemble them then located pilots who had been flown out of the Philippines and took them to Brisbane to staff the squadron. As soon as they were assembled, Gunn led the P-40s north across Australia to Darwin, then over the water to Java in his C-45.

Early Model B-17

It was shortly after this that Gunn was involved in one of the most amazing events of his career. When he came back to Darwin from Java, he was told that there were some B-17s there that General Brereton had decided should be assigned to his ad hoc air transport squadron. These particular B-17s were older models that had transferred to the Philippines before the war with the 19th Bombardment Group.[29] New B-17Es had just arrived from the States with the 7th Bombardment Group and the older airplanes were being withdrawn from combat operations so Brereton decided to have them converted for transport use. This was in early 1942 and the Japanese had yet to advance into the Netherlands East Indies. In late January the Allies learned that a Japanese invasion fleet was headed into the Makassar Straits, apparently in preparation for an invasion of Java. Whether he was told to or he decided to do it on his own is uncertain, but Gunn decided that he had a heavy bomber and there was a war to fight. He rounded up a crew and loaded one of his B-17s with bombs and set out for the Makassar Straits. When Gunn's son Nathaniel was researching such of

---

[29] The lineage of the 19th BG was bestowed on the current 19th Airlift Group at Little Rock.

Sam McGowan

his father's military records as he could find, he came across a citation that had been written up requesting the award of the Distinguished Service Cross to Colonel Gunn for his actions against the Japanese ships. He made not one but several attacks that day and claimed hits and possible sinkings. He was never awarded the DSC however; Gunn's highest combat award was the Silver Star which he got for participation in the Royce Raid the following April.

The first air transport[30] operation in the theater – the first operational air transport mission in US history – was the movement of the guns and personnel of a US Army antiaircraft unit from Brisbane to Darwin, which had become a target for Japanese carrier aircraft. During the battle for Java, the transports continued to operate; flying men and supplies into the islands then evacuating them when the Japanese gained the upper hand. Two transports were lost during the Java Campaign, one when it found the weather too bad to land at Darwin and suffered irreparable damage during a landing at an emergency strip. The other ran out of fuel while enroute from Perth to Broome.

The three B-24s were very active during the Java operation and were the last Allied airplanes out of the islands. Two were lost to enemy action against Broome, a coastal town in northwestern Australia, including one that was shot down immediately after taking off from Broome with a load of thirty wounded on board and went into the sea. One person survived. The other B-24 was still on the ground when a formation of Japanese fighters appeared and began strafing. It was set on fire and destroyed. The third had departed Broome the afternoon before and had already reached Melbourne. It was lost two months later after it made the last flight to Del Monte airfield in Mindanao just before the Philippines fell then ran out of fuel on the way back to Australia and was forced to ditch.

Gunn's transports and a few submarines provided the only lifeline between Australia and the beleaguered American and Filipino troops still in the Philippines.[31] His squadron was augmented by bomber crews from the 7th Bombardment Group, which has lost some of its B-17s to the 19th.

---

[30] The term "airlift" did not exist during World War II. It came into use after the Berlin Airlift, which was known at the time as an "air lift."

[31] Attempts to send supplies to the islands by ship were met mostly with frustration. US Army Col. John Robeson was given $10,000,000 to purchase supplies and hire ships, but had a hard time finding crews willing to take the risk. A few ships managed to get through to Mindanao and Cebu, but most were intercepted by the Japanese. No surface ships reached Bataan or Corregidor from Australia, but local island vessels brought in some supplies from the south.

Anything, Anywhere, Anytime

After the Japanese occupied the Netherlands East Indies, most of the refueling stops were no longer available. The remaining B-24 had the range to make the round trip nonstop. It was joined by an occasional war-weary B-17 from the 19th Bombardment Group and several LB-30s[32] that had formerly belonged to the 7th Bombardment Group, which had moved to India to join Tenth Air Force but had left most of its personnel and airplanes behind. They flew north carrying badly needed ammunition, medicines and other supplies then returned with key personnel who had been identified by the War Department as crucial to the defense of Australia and the Allied military buildup in the Southwest Pacific. A 7th Bombardment Group crew flew General Douglas MacArthur and his family and staff out of Darwin in one of the C-47s after they arrived from Mindanao in a specially appropriated B-17.[33] MacArthur was initially disturbed when the crew made a hasty takeoff as soon as the passengers were aboard but his anger subsided when he was told that Japanese aircraft were on their way to attack the airstrip. The flight over the Australian Outback made his wife Jean airsick and he refused to continue the journey by air when the crew landed for fuel at a remote airstrip. He and his party made the rest of the trip to Melbourne by train.

On March 25, Gunn and Maj. Cecil MacFarland departed Darwin in Gunn's C-45, which he had modified considerably to carry additional fuel, bound for Del Monte. Although the purpose of the flight is not recorded, it is probable that they were sent to Mindanao on orders from General George to join Bradford in the resupply effort to Bataan. They were flying at night to avoid detection but when they neared the vicinity of Davao, a Japanese floatplane evidently spotted the C-45's exhaust flames and came in for an attack. One of the C-45's engines was knocked out. Rather than risk being shot down, Gunn decided to crash-land on the beach on one of the outlying islands. The next day he arranged for transportation by boat for himself, MacFarland and their

---

[32] The LB-30 designation was given to B-24As that were built to British specifications. They were essentially identical to B-24s except for smaller caliber guns and the lack of superchargers. Eleven arrived in Java in early 1942.

[33] MacArthur and his family and staff made their way to Mindanao on Navy PT boats then were picked up by B-17s that had previously been under Navy control. They belonged to a reconnaissance squadron that had been on the way to the Philippines when war broke out and were held in Hawaii by the Navy, and transferred to Australia while still under Navy control. The 19th BG B-17s were worn out and Gen. Brett prevailed in a fight with the Navy over the B-17s from the 14th Reconnaissance Squadron and they were transferred to Army control and used to evacuate the MacArthur party. Why one of the remaining LB-30s or the ATC B-24 wasn't used – the B-24 made several trips between Darwin and Mindanao – has never been explained.

cargo to Mindanao. The supplies were picked up by truck and transported to Del Monte where Gunn discovered a B-17 that had been abandoned due to an engine problem. He rounded up a crew of mechanics to help him repair the engine then flew the Flying Fortress back to Darwin with a load of Air Corps personnel on board.[34] He and MacFarland were awarded the Distinguished Flying Cross for the flight. McFarland remained on Mindanao and became a POW. He died while a prisoner, possibly when a ship carrying POWs to Japan was torpedoed by an American submarine.

Major Gunn remained in command of the first troop carrier organization to see combat until April when he transferred to the 3rd Bombardment Group[35], a unit that had recently arrived in Australia. When he was not flying, he put his talents as an aircraft maintenance expert to good use. Shortly after arriving in Australia he became friends with the pilots of the 27th Bombardment Group, a light bomber unit that had just arrived in Australia when war broke out. Some two dozen of the group's pilots were flown out of the Philippines to Australia in mid-December 1941 in a C-39 and a pair of B-18s. Their Douglas A-24 dive-bombers were on the same ship with the P-40s Gunn assembled and he helped the 27th pilots ready their airplanes for combat. After the Java campaign the 27th was rolled into the newly arrived 3rd Bombardment Group, commonly known by its pre-war designation as the 3rd Attack Group, which arrived in Australia without its airplanes and was given the A-24s. Experienced 27th personnel assumed key roles in the reorganized unit. Some of the 3rd and 27th pilots flew transport missions with Gunn's Air Transport Command while they were waiting for more light and medium bombers to arrive.

When he wasn't flying transport missions, Gunn spent much of his time with the men of the 3rd, helping them keep their A-24s in operational condition. In late March he "appropriated" a couple of dozen B-25s that had been consigned to the Netherlands East Indies Air Force for his friends in the 3rd and was officially transferred out of the Air Transport Command to the group. He then led ten B-25s and

---

[34] A recent Gunn biography claims that he came out of Del Monte on a B-17 that had been sent up to pick up Philippine President Manuel Quezon, but there are some discrepancies since Quezon's airplane didn't leave until the night after Gunn is reported to have been back in Australia. There is no doubt that Gunn flew an abandoned B-17 out of Del Monte at some point. The incident was well known and some of the enlisted men who flew out with him have written about it.

[35] The 3rd produced three senior officers who would make their mark in troop carrier aviation in the 1950s and 60s.

Anything, Anywhere, Anytime

three B-17s to Mindanao on a mission commanded by Brig. Gen. Ralph Royce to bomb Japanese targets in the Philippines in early April 1942. Gunn and his crew remained behind on Mindanao when the rest of the force returned to Australia and were sent on a special mission to pick up a Japanese-American intelligence specialist who had escaped from Manila after infiltrating the Japanese headquarters.[36] The agent and three other passengers had been flown out of Corregidor in the WACO and an O-1. They flew to Panay, where they were picked up by Pappy Gunn in his B-25.

As it turned out, Bill Bradford flew into Panay in the Bellanca with a load of .50-caliber ammunition for a P-40 that was being used for armed reconnaissance while the passengers were waiting to be picked up, but his engine was acting up and he had to work on it. He and the three pilots who had made the dangerous trip to Corregidor were joined by three other officers who had flown an O-1 out of Bataan just before it fell, but had cracked up off of a tiny island. That night they attended a farewell party hosted by Pablo Meng, an American pilot and friend of Bradford's who lived on Panay, but was preparing to depart the next day. Early the next morning, Bradford received a message that Japanese ships were just off of Panay and were believed to be preparing to land an invading party. Bradford got off with the Bellanca and another pilot flew the WACO out, but it was shot down as it was approaching to land at one of the airfields on the Del Monte Plantation. (The other two pilots got out later.) (Edmonds, Notes from Bradford Interview, 1943)

The Beechcraft was lost during a Japanese attack on an airfield in Central Mindanao and the Duck cracked-up on Panay after it came out of Bataan with a load of pursuit pilots, so Bradford's Bellanca was the last of the Bamboo Fleet. Bataan had fallen and Bradford and some other pilots were expecting to be flown out on one of the Royce

---

[36] That there were Japanese-American agents operating in Manila was classified and their existence was not revealed until years after the war. Col. P.I. Gunn's military records were also classified due to the nature of some of the operations he was involved in during the war, and also because of his role in covert operations in the postwar period. The story of the rescue of the intelligence agents has only been revealed piecemeal, partly through accounts from the agents themselves and partly through information discovered by Gunn's son Nathaniel. One of the Nisei intelligence NCOs remained on Corregidor so a Nisei civilian who had been spying for the Americans in Manila could be evacuated. The other agent joined MacArthur's staff in Australia and remained with him until he was fired in Korea by Truman. Richard Sakikida, the agent who remained behind, was captured by the Japanese but managed to convince them he was a civilian who had been forced to work for the Americans. After the war, he went into the Army Air Forces and transferred into the US Air Force in 1947. He retired as a lieutenant colonel in the Air Force Office of Special Investigations.

Mission airplanes, probably Pappy Gunn's B-25. The Japanese had captured most of the airfields between Mindanao and Corregidor. But then a message came in from Gen. Jonathon Wainwright's headquarters requesting a flight. The senior Air Corps officer at Del Monte discussed the mission with Bradford and they both agreed it was suicidal. A message was sent to Corregidor that the flight was impossible but the reply came back "try it."

There were "about a score" of pilots assembled in the club in the jungle at the airfield at Maramag. They agreed to cut cards with the pilot with the lowest card making the trip. Bradford drew a Deuce of Diamonds. The other pilots thought he had palmed the card but he denied that he did, and insisted it was "just the luck of the draw." Due to the urgency of the mission and the distance to the main airfield at Del Monte where supplies were stockpiled, he was unable to round up a load of medical supplies, but finally found a supply of quinine tablets and sulfa drugs at the local dispensary. He took off in the afternoon so as to make the final leg of the flight in darkness and arrive right at dawn. He had decided to stop at an airfield on Negros, where he knew there were 1,400 gallons of gasoline available. Miraculously, he made the trip into Corregidor without incident. However, the flight out wasn't so successful. As he was taking off, one of the wheels drifted off of the narrow runway and the rocks on the side slowed it down, and caused the airplane to crack up.

Bradford was stuck on Corregidor with no way out. He reconciled himself to his fate but fate had a surprise in store. Two US Navy PBYs were sent up from Darwin with supplies and instructions to bring out personnel, including a number of nurses. Bradford was picked to go out on the flight.[37] Although one of the PBYs struck a rock while landing on a lake on Mindanao and had to leave its passengers behind, Bradford's airplane made it to Australia without incident. He soon returned to the United States to an assignment at Hondo Field, a training base just southwest of San Antonio. The other PBY's passengers had gone to the main airfield and the crew was unable to wait for them because the airplane was taking on water. The nurses were left behind to become prisoners but some PT boat crewmembers came out with it.(Bradford, 1943)

The last Army flight was made on the night of May 4-5 in the remaining B-24 by a crew commanded by Captain A.J. Mueller, who had originally been with the 19th Bombardment Group. Mueller had made the last landing at Del Monte on the night of April 29. His crew and another commanded by Captain Arthur Fletcher were told to

---

[37] It is probable that General Harold George requested that Bradford be brought out because of his transport experience and knowledge of the Philippines. Tragically, the general was killed a few days later in a freak accident.

Anything, Anywhere, Anytime

maintain an around the clock operation between Darwin and Mindanao with the Liberator. The two pilots had worked out a plan that in the event they were unable to land at Del Monte, they would proceed to Pulau Yu, a tiny island in the Moluccas, and ditch in a lagoon. Mueller arrived over the airfield that night and circled for an hour, but received no signal that it was safe to land. He then went to the alternate plan, of which only he and Fletcher were privy. He had his radio operator transmit the code word only they had decided to use. The ditching was successful and the crew was rescued by submarine a week later. The Philippines supply effort had ended, and the islands were now in Japanese hands.

When the 3rd Attack Group's Douglas A-20s finally arrived, the 3rd's commander, Lt. Col. John Davies, turned to Gunn for advice on how to make them ready for combat. Gunn conceived the idea of packing the nose of the A-20s with machineguns for low-level strafing attacks, an idea that became standard practice for light and medium bombers in the Pacific. When Major General George Kenney took command of the Army Air Forces in Australia, he found Gunn working on the A-20 conversion. Kenney was impressed by Pappy Gunn's talents and transferred the colorful officer to his staff, although he still filled the pilot's seat on a transport or bomber when he was needed (or whenever he was able to talk his way onto a mission.) Gunn's primary job was special engineering projects, and his most famous was the conversion of a squadron of B-25s into strafers by packing the noses full of .50-caliber machineguns as he had done with the A-20s. The two squadrons, one of A-20s and one of B-25s, would play the crucial role in the Battle of the Bismarck Sea as they literally wiped out a convoy of Japanese troop transports.

Because his family was interned in the Philippines, Gunn was anxious for the recapture of the islands and did everything he could to hasten the day. He would finish the war as a colonel on General Kenney's staff, after being wounded in the invasion of Leyte. When US troops landed on Luzon, General MacArthur dispatched a special mission by elements of the 1st Cavalry Division to liberate the American internees at Santo Thomas University and flew there himself to greet Gunn's family, then had them flown to Australia to join their husband and father. Gunn's son Nat, who was a young teenager at the time, says the family had no idea what Pappy had done but they were greeted like VIP's at every stop along the way.[38]

In April 1942, about the time that Pappy Gunn transferred from the Air Transport Command to the 3rd Bombardment Group, the Army

---

[38] The author is acquainted with Nat Gunn.

reorganized its air force in preparation for wartime operations. Included within the reorganization was the redesignation of its units. The former pursuit units were designated as "fighter" and the air transport units that had been organized prior to the outbreak of war were redesignated as "troop carrier" although that name change didn't officially take place until a few weeks later in July and some squadrons weren't notified for several weeks and even months. Major Gunn was replaced as commander of the FEAF ATC by Lt. Col. Erickson S. Nichols. The Air Transport Command became a squadron and was designated as the 21st Transport Squadron with Lt. Wade Hampton in command.[39] It would go on to become one of the most decorated units in Army Air Forces and Air Force history. The Directorate of Air Transport was reinforced by airplanes and Dutch civilian pilots from Netherlands East Indies Airways who flew for the military under contract. The arrival of new pilots and mechanics from the United States allowed the Army to buy the NEIA transports outright and staff them with military crews of mixed nationality.[40] With the additional aircraft and personnel, a second squadron was activated as the 22nd Transport Squadron on April 3, 1942. The transport designation was short-lived, however. Within a few weeks, the two squadrons were redesignated as "troop carrier."[41] They went on to pioneer procedures that became standard in troop carrier operations.

Shortly after it began operations, the DAT recognized the need for qualified transport personnel to plan loading of aircraft to achieve maximum payload, to maintain proper weight and balance and to supervise loading of cargo. Station control teams consisting of American and Australian load planning officers and enlisted men qualified to supervise cargo loading were trained. Their duties included evaluating requests for air transportation, assigning priorities, planning loads and routing transport missions so as to achieve maximum efficiency. In mid-1943, the teams were organized into an Airways Control Squadron; it was later redesignated as the 1st Air Cargo Control Squadron. The station control teams were responsible for teaching Australian – and later American – ground personnel how to plan loads and how to load the cargo into the

---

[39] Hampton's name was Edgar Wade but he was commonly known by his middle name.

[40] Due to the lack of aircraft for the Australian squadrons, RAAF pilots and mechanics were assigned to the American squadrons to supplement their assigned crewmembers and maintenance personnel. This practice continued well into 1943. Due to a shortage of qualified C-47 first pilots, Australian copilots were assigned to troop carrier squadrons so the more experienced Americans could fly as first pilots.

[41] The Army replaced the transport designation with "troop carrier" in July 1942, but it took some time for word of the redesignation to reach the field. It wasn't until October that some units were officially notified of the redesignation.

Anything, Anywhere, Anytime

airplane and secure it, and how to kick out bundles in the air.(Ford, 2010) Ground personnel from the unit that owned the cargo loaded the airplanes under the supervision of a station control team officer or NCO, then flew along on the mission to kick the bundles out over the designated drop zone. Troop carrier crews didn't include navigators so the NCO in charge of the kickers showed the pilots the way to the drop zone. When the airplane returned to Moresby, the ground personnel as often as not would start their trek into the jungle to join their comrades!

After the Americans were run out of the Philippines, they established a new base of operations in Australia, with General Douglas MacArthur as the commander of the Southwest Pacific Area of Operations. MacArthur had been personal friends with Billy Mitchell and had been receptive to his ideas about the use of airplanes to fight wars but he was not happy with the way airpower had been used in the Philippines and was less so when he arrived in Australia and found a generally defeated Allied command. The Australian high command was prepared to lose half the continent and fight along a line drawn halfway between the Northern Territories and Sidney but MacArthur had other ideas – he would hold in New Guinea. The Japanese were steadily advancing southward until only Papua New Guinea stood between them and Australia. MacArthur decided to defeat the Japanese advance and drive them northward away from Australia.

It would be in New Guinea that the Allies would make their stand and ultimately turn the war around, thanks largely to airpower, particularly the troop carrier squadrons which provided unprecedented mobility to the ground troops. While it is essentially an island, New Guinea is a big island that was still largely unexplored in early 1942. Like most of the subtropical regions of the world, it is a rugged land, characterized by dense, nearly impenetrable jungles. The island features a special set of obstacles, the rugged Owen Stanley Mountains that rise more than 13,000 feet from sea level into the sky, almost as high as the American Rockies. To reach Australian positions on the Owen Stanley's north slopes, the troop carrier pilots were forced to fly through a narrow pass where the tops of the ridges dropped to 7,000-9,000 feet. They began referring to the pass as "The Hump" and to missions through it as "flying the Hump" long before the term was identified with operations out of India into China. (54th TCW Historians) In 1942, the region's few villages and settlements were connected by primitive jungle trails, some of which wound their way through the mountains. The trails were too narrow and treacherous for trucks and other vehicles; all supplies moving north had to be transported by native porters or by air. It very quickly became apparent that the airplane was going to play a crucial role in the battle for New Guinea.

The transport force was a mixed-bag of airplanes. In addition to C-47s and C-53s, it also included C-56s and C-60s, both of which were derivations of the Lockheed Lodestar, and even a Douglas DC-5 that was one of three that had been appropriated from the Dutch and given the US Army designation of C-110.[42] A number of combat aircraft that had been replaced with newer models found their way into the troop carrier squadrons, particularly older B-17s that had been in the Philippines when the war broke out, and a few LB-30s and B-24As that arrived from the US. Maintaining such a menagerie of aircraft produced headaches for the understaffed maintenance shops, which were overworked already. For several weeks, there were only eight enlisted aircraft mechanics available to maintain the entire force! Yet the men worked miracles; when no parts were available to make repairs, the pilots flew the airplanes anyway. Engines from one type were used on another and when the wing on a DC-3 was damaged, the maintenance men replaced it with one from a wrecked DC-2 and called it a DC-2½. (54th TCW Historians)

In mid-July 1942, a Japanese force landed near Buna on the north coast of the Lae Peninsula across the Owen Stanleys from Port Moresby. Buna was a former government station where the Allies were planning to establish their own forward base but the Japanese beat them to it. An Australian force was on its way north to occupy Buna along the Kokoda Track, a rugged trail that ran through the forbidding Owen Stanleys, and were within three days of Buna when the Japanese landed. Immediately, the Japanese dispatched a force southward along the track in a drive to take Port Moresby.Within four days, the two opposing forces met near the village of Kokoda and the battle for Moresby began.

Because of the primitive nature of the jungle trail, the only reliable means of supplying the Australians was by air. The 21st and 22nd squadrons were given the task. They started out flying supplies into Kokoda airstrip, which was nothing but a runway located in a valley in the shadow of the mountains. The fighting was so close to the airfield that the pilots often weren't sure who had control of the field as they approached to land. Still, they landed – and kept the Australians supplied. On August 9 the Australians began pulling back southward along the Kokoda Track toward Port Moresby until they were only a few miles from the city itself. As they fought their way south, the Aussies depended on the US Army and RAAF troop carrier crews for their daily needs. Then, beginning in October 1942, with the arrival of the 6th Troop Carrier Squadron at Port Moresby, they

---

[42] Only a handful of DC-5s were ever built and they were all sold to the Dutch.

Anything, Anywhere, Anytime

depended on troop carrier crews as they began counterattacking back up the track toward Buna.

The Papuan Campaign severely taxed the limits of the capabilities of the two troop carrier squadrons. The campaign began in mid-July and continued into September when a Japanese landing at Milne Bay was defeated. The aerial resupply continued on a day-to-day basis throughout the campaign without letup. High, mountainous terrain coupled with fierce tropical thunderstorms made flying extremely hazardous – and the Japanese had air superiority in the skies. When they were available, Bell P-39 Airacobras flew escort. Although the little P-39s lacked the performance to serve as high altitude interceptors, they were in some ways superior to the Japanese Zeros and other fighters at low altitude and were effective in the escort role. Drop formations were accompanied by Australian Whirraways, whose pilots watched the skies for Japanese fighters. If they appeared, the Whirraway[43] pilot dove for the treetops and the transport pilots followed their lead. American and Australian P-39s, P-40s, B-25s and A-20s attacked the Japanese airfields on an almost daily basis and took a heavy toll of the aircraft they caught on the ground.

The 21st and 22nd, like the heavy, light and medium bomber squadrons, were not actually based in New Guinea. Their bases were in Australia, but crews flew north to Port Moresby to fly missions to deliver cargo to Australian units operating along the Kokoda Track. They did not remain on the ground at Moresby due to the constant threat of air attack, but were there only long enough to load up with cargo. They flew up early in the morning or late the evening before then, as soon as the airplane was loaded, took off at first light for their missions. As often as not, the airfields around Moresby were attacked while the transports were out on their missions. The two squadrons' airplanes were of mixed manufacture, which compounded maintenance and supply problems, and there were nowhere near enough skilled maintenance personnel to keep them in proper repair.

In spite of the difficulties, the men of the 21st and 22nd Troop Carrier Squadrons shouldered the load and kept the Australians supplied. When possible, pilots landed on the nearest airstrip. When no landing strip was available, supplies were dropped from the air. When necessary, parachutes were used but as often as not supplies were dropped free. An American supply officer in Australia named Bill Bentson[44] came up with the idea of using 5-gallon ice cream containers

---

[43] Whirraways were an armed version of the North American AT-6 trainer that had been developed and were produced in Australia. They were lightly armed and were no match for Japanese fighters, but they were ideal observation aircraft.

[44] Bill Bentson originally went to Australia as an enlisted man but became a warrant officer shortly after his arrival. He remained in Australia and married an

Sam McGowan

lined with straw to drop supplies, including small arms ammunition and rations. Because they were their main source of their daily rations, Australian troops soon were referring to the American troop carrier planes as "Biscuit Bombers." The Biscuit Bombers' daily airdrops kept the Australian troops from going hungry and running out of ammunition.

6th TCS C-47 Crew (Jack Heyn)[45]

Eventually, the Japanese abandoned their plan to take Moresby along the Kokoda Track. An Allied victory in Milne Bay, combined with the sudden and timely appearance of the A-20s modified by Pappy Gunn as they were on the outskirts of the city, caused the Japanese to break off their attack to retreat and regroup on the north side of the Owen Stanleys. The Australians could thank the American troop carrier crews for keeping them supplied as they held the line against the Japanese. The Papuan resupply operation was the first time American troop carriers had supported a combat operation and the first time their presence was crucial to military success. The 21st and 22nd TCS crews had set a precedent, and they would see even more involvement in combat operations in coming months and years in the Southwest Pacific. Their efforts in the campaign earned the two

---

Australian girl. After retiring from the US Air Force as a major, he returned to Australia where he was active in military history circles. In the 1990s he and the author were members of an Internet Email group devoted to the B-24 and frequently corresponded with each other.

[45] Heyn was a US Army photographer who served with Fifth Air Force.

Anything, Anywhere, Anytime

squadrons a Distinguished Unit Citation, the first of several they would earn over the coming years.

While the crews of the 21st and 22nd squadrons were beginning offensive combat air transport operations in New Guinea, their counterparts in the China-Burma-India area of operations were in the process of initiating another major theater air transport operation. In February 1942, when a Japanese victory in Java became apparent, General Brereton left Java and flew to Calcutta to organize a new command with the designation of Tenth Air Force. Tenth Air Force's original purpose was to organize an air campaign against the Japanese home islands from bases in China, but the region where the bases were planned to be constructed was lost when the Japanese went on the offensive in retaliation for the Doolittle raid on Japan.[46] A primary Tenth Air Force responsibility then became providing air transportation for Chinese and British troops fighting in China and Burma, and delivering supplies to Claire Chennault's American Volunteer Group, which was planned to be brought into the US Army as a fighter group.

Shortly after he arrived in India, Brereton was given the task of developing an air ferry of supplies across the Himalayas from Assam Province in India to Burma, where the Japanese were quickly gaining supremacy. Brig. Gen. Earl Naiden was instructed to plan an air transport service from India to China. By the end of March 1942, Naiden had drafted a plan calling for two theater transport routes – a Trans-India route between Karachi and Dinjan in Assam Province, India and the Assam-Burma-China route from Dinjan to Myitkyina in Burma, with occasional flights on to Loiwing in China proper. At the time, Burma was still in Allied hands and plans were for supplies to continue their journey into China by truck and barge but the ultimate goal of Naiden's plan was the establishment of routes all the way to Kunming and Chunking. While air transport operations in New Guinea involved direct combat operations delivering supplies to ground

---

[46] Although the Doolittle Raid on Tokyo is hailed as an American victory, it was actually a military disaster. Fifteen of the sixteen B-25s dropped bombs on Japan but all were lost when they arrived over China at night. The US hadn't informed the Chinese that the B-25s were coming earlier than expected – the mission had been planned to be over Japan during darkness and arrive over China after daybreak – and no signals had been set up and the airfields had not been lit. The B-25s were intended to join Tenth Air Force to form the nucleus of a medium bomber group. Even worse than the loss of all of the B-25s was the loss of the Chinese territory where Tenth Air Force commander Brereton had planned to establish advanced bases for B-17s and B-24s to attack the Japanese home islands. The Chinese suffered even worse losses as an estimated 250,000 Chinese, mostly civilians, died at the hands of the Japanese in retaliation for the raid.

Sam McGowan

troops in combat, the CBI operation was initially more logistical in nature. But it was not long before transport crews in the CBI were flying combat operations as well. By 1944 the war in the CBI had become heavily dependent upon air transportation to support ground operations. (Craven & Cate, 1956)

However, due to military politics, the development of an air transport capability in the CBI would be piecemeal and it would take more than a year before any troop carrier squadrons were actually assigned to the theater and when they were, they were made up of airplanes and personnel that had already arrive in the theater. Still, the two squadrons proved to be highly effective. The delay was due to the assignment of a special unit that had been set up by the Air Corps Ferrying Command before the command was elevated to become the Air Transport Command. The 1st Ferrying Group was organized at Pope Field, North Carolina with Army reserve pilots, most of whom had been employed by the airlines. Although Ferrying Command "owned" the group, Brereton argued that the assignment of a unit to his area of responsibility but not under his command was a violation of Army doctrine. Arnold and Marshall agreed and the group transferred to Tenth Air Force but would later return to the Air Transport Command.

Loading C-47 in the CBI

On the other side of the world in the European War, air transportation was playing only a small role in the ground war, although the logistical mission was growing at a phenomenal rate. For

Anything, Anywhere, Anytime

nearly a year, no American ground troops saw combat in the ETO, but each passing day saw the arrival of more and more US troops in the British Isles. Troop carrier squadrons went to England, but their mission remained logistical and training for airborne operations until the invasion of North Africa in November 1942. A few C-47s – including some that went from India to Egypt with Brereton – operated independently in North Africa in support of the British Eighth Army until the 316th Troop Carrier Group arrived in Egypt in November 1942.

Ryan PT-22 Primary Trainer

During the first months and years of the war, a massive training operation was underway in the United States. A million-man Army air force[47] was planned, and pilots and crews were at various points in the training pipeline to fill the seats of the fighters, bombers and transports that were coming off of the assembly lines. The Air Corps established new air bases and technical training centers all around the country to meet its needs as it geared up for war. Contract training bases operated by civilian flight schools were established for primary pilot training. Young men fresh from the cities and farms of America were assigned to courses that would turn them into pilots, navigators, aerial engineers, radio operators, gunners and mechanics. Within the

---

[47] At its highest level, the Army's air forces included 2.3 million men and women, but less than a million were actually combat personnel. The rest belonged to support functions – including the Air Transport Command – and a large percentage were from the Quartermasters, Signal Corps and Medical Corps.

Sam McGowan

pilot training schools, a system was developed in which the most promising students went to fighters, the next group to bombers and the remainder to transports, where duties were thought to be "less demanding."

Before the war, aviation cadets were required to have at least two years of college but the demand for pilots led to the removal of the requirement and applications were accepted based on aptitude testing. Immediately before the US entered the war, some enlisted men were given pilot training and awarded flight status as sergeant-pilots. Although some sergeant-pilots saw action in fighters and bombers, most were assigned to the newly created troop carrier squadrons. Most of the enlisted pilots were eventually either commissioned or given warrants as flight officers.(Ford, 2010) Some civilian pilots were given limited-duty ratings as "service pilots;" most were assigned to duty as ferry and transport pilots in the Air Transport Command.

After the war broke out, the new Army Air Forces developed a system for training entire combat units. Pilots and other crew members were sent to operational training units, or OTUs, where they were assigned to crews and squadrons and groups. An entire group would go through training at the same time then when it had been declared operationally ready, it would depart for overseas. Tiny Pope Field adjacent to Fort Bragg, North Carolina was one of the first OTU bases for troop carrier groups. Bowman Field at Louisville, Kentucky became an Army air base and troop carrier training facility. Bowman also became the training center for air evacuation medical personnel and flight surgeons. Some personnel were assigned to replacement training units, or RTUs where they trained as individual crews. Upon completion of their training, the new crews were sent overseas to join units that were already in combat. Some personnel went overseas as individuals.

While in New Guinea and the CBI the primary concern of the men in the combat commands – including troop carrier squadrons – was to hold off the Japanese long enough to build-up a sufficient force to begin pushing them back, in far-away Washington, DC new, more political, concerns arose. This was particularly true in the area of air transportation in which several prominent members of the airline industry had been commissioned as high ranking officers. As the military buildup began, several air transport services came into being. In Australia, new troop carrier squadrons were organized, while in England an Air Service Command was established to service the bomber squadrons that began arriving in mid-1942 to conduct the daylight bombing campaigns against Germany. In India, Tenth Air Force began air transport operations using both civilian contract crews from China National Airways Corporation and former airline

Anything, Anywhere, Anytime

pilots who had been called out of the reserves. The Navy established its own air transport service, while the Army had the Ferrying Command, which had begun overseas transport operations in the summer of 1941 using modified B-24s. Each organization was issuing contracts for airline services under its own authority, as were a myriad of other government organizations although the Air Corps had set up an airline contract office in its Maintenance Command. The Chairman of the Civil Aeronautics Board, Mr. L. W. Pogue, out of fear that confusion of command would disrupt the nation's airline industry, proposed the establishment of a single air transportation service to meet all government air transportation needs. The command proposed by Pogue would be separate from both the Army and the Navy and report directly to the President of the United States. In essence, he was proposing a government-owned and operated quasi-military airline to meet the government's air transportation needs. There was precedent in the Merchant Marine, which was considered part of the Navy but was actually civilian.

While Pogue's suggestion was not followed completely, both the War Department and the Navy Department each established their own air transport commands, each of which operated essentially as an airline in military garb. The headquarters of the Army Ferrying Command was elevated to become a new Air Transport Command[40], using the designation that had formerly belonged to the units that had recently been redesignated as "troop carrier." The former Air Transport Command was redesignated as I Troop Carrier Command and was given responsibility for training troop carrier crews and units for overseas duty. The USAAF executive order that established the ATC exempted all troop carrier and theater air transport functions, including those of the air force service commands.

As the United States built up for war, the troop carrier mission assumed a more and more prominent role and troop carrier units were planned for assignment to each theater. Although support of airborne forces was a primary troop carrier mission, the experience in New Guinea and Burma illustrated that highly motivated transport crews could perform valuable service transporting and resupplying conventional ground forces operating in forward areas in contact with the enemy. By early 1944, senior Army officers in the War Department

---

[48] The creation of a separate Air Transport Command solely for logistical purposes led to considerable confusion on the part of senior military officials. Senior commanders such as General Dwight Eisenhower frequently referred to troop carrier operations as Air Transport Command operations. When Eisenhower addressed paratroopers in 1944 after the First Allied Airborne Army was formed, he referred to the IX Troop Carrier Command as the Air Transport Command.

Sam McGowan

in Washington and in Eisenhower's headquarters in England and MacArthur's in the Far East had recognized that troop carrier aircraft offered unprecedented mobility to ground forces.

Anything, Anywhere, Anytime

Chapter Three - "New Guinea"

Generals McArthur (L) and Kenney (R)

In July 1942, just after the Japanese landed at Buna, General Douglas MacArthur's new chief of staff for air arrived in Australia. Army Chief of Staff Gen. George Marshall had personally selected Maj. Gen. George C. Kenney to replace Lt. Gen. George Brett, who had fallen into disfavor with the new commander of the Southwest Pacific Area of Operations. MacArthur asked for Lt. Gen. Frank Andrews, who at the time was in command of the Army's Caribbean Command and also a theater commander and thus equal to MacArthur in responsibility even though he was junior in rank. Andrews was somewhat offended by the request and turned the job down so Marshall focused his attention elsewhere.[49]

Kenney worked with Andrews during the formation of the GHQ Air Force and served on its staff as Director of Operations and Plans (G-3) and was thus well known to both MacArthur and Marshall.(Copp, 2002) Marshall also knew that Kenney was very forthright and not a "yes man" and that he would be able to deal with MacArthur. He was the kind of man who would advise his superiors when a task was impossible, yet strive to do as much as possible with the resources at his command. The War Department's priorities were directed toward

---

[49] Although Andrews had been MacArthur's direct subordinate when he was commander of the GHQ Air Force, he had been offended by something MacArthur did and wasn't comfortable with the idea of working for him again.

Anything, Anywhere, Anytime

winning the war in Europe and the Pacific, especially the Southwest Pacific, was slated to get what was left over to defend Australia. Although several combat squadrons, mostly fighter and bomber units, were dispatched to Australia at the beginning of the war after the fall of the Philippines, the emphasis turned to Europe in accordance with agreements worked out between President Franklin Roosevelt and British Prime Minister Sir Winston Churchill. Marshall knew that the difficult situation, combined with the low priorities for the Southwest Pacific Theater, dictated the presence of a man who could make do as best he could with what he had. He felt that the gruff, diminutive New Englander was his best candidate to get along with General MacArthur.

Some historians writing about General James H. Doolittle imply that he was Marshall's first choice for the job as "air boss" in the Southwest Pacific but this is not true. Doolittle's name was submitted along with Kenney's as an alternate choice. MacArthur sent back a message stating he did not chose the flamboyant air racer because he lacked experience for a job that would involve working with senior Australian officers. In truth, there was nothing in Doolittle's background to indicate that he would be a competent combat commander. His entire military background was in research and development and his reserve commission was as a technical (engineering) officer. He had gained notoriety for his role in planning and participating in the raid on Japan and had been jumped two ranks and awarded the Medal of Honor.[50] As it turned out, although Doolittle later commanded the Twelfth and Eighth Air Forces in Europe, he was a mediocre commander.[51] Kenney, however, is considered by many to have been the most effective air commander of World War II. He ultimately became commander of all Army Air Forces groups in the Pacific except for the B-29-equipped very heavy bomber units.

A Massachusetts Institute of Technology graduate with an engineering degree, Kenney was one of the forward-thinking air officers of the prewar days who firmly believed that the airplane

---

[50] Doolittle knew that he didn't deserve the prestigious medal and protested to Arnold that he didn't but was told to keep his mouth shut, President Roosevelt wanted him to have it. He was the first member of the Air Corps to receive the award although by this time several Army ground, Navy and Marine personnel had been awarded it. Doolittle was valuable to FDR because of his name. Prior to the war, he had been heavily involved in air racing.

[51] Immediately after Doolittle took command of Eighth Air Force, he became extremely unpopular with his officers and men. After he got permission to attack Berlin and took heavy casualties (over 1,000 men lost on two missions), Eighth Air Force personnel came to believe he was using them as pawns to further his own ambitions. Doolittle planned to lead the mission so he could claim he led the first missions against all three Axis capitals but General Carl Spaatz ordered him to stay on the ground.

would be the major weapon of World War II. As an engineering officer who spent much of his prewar time in research and development, Kenney developed several new features that became part of the modern combat airplane including mounting machineguns in the wings instead of having them fire through the propeller. He developed the delivery of fragmentation bombs by parachute, a concept that his men would use with great success against the Japanese. Before the war he worked with Frank Andrews in developing the plans for the GHQ Air Force and was well schooled in air force doctrine. As the GHQ Air Force G3, he had been instrumental in developing the plans that formed the foundation for the employment of air forces.[52] And, while some officers were oriented toward one particular aspect of aviation, Kenney's ideas were not confined. He saw air power as a multifunctional force that could first defeat an enemy's air force then support ground forces on the battlefield and had no grandiose ideas about the use of airpower to defeat an enemy nation. His ideas for support of ground forces included moving troops around on the battlefield and keeping them supplied. Air transportation of combat troops was an idea that was in the forefront of his mind when he arrived in Australia.

Kenney's ideas regarding air transport were going to have to wait until the right opportunity. First, he had to bring order out of the chaos that characterized the Allied air force in Australia in those early months of the war. He arrived in Australia to discover that the airmen who had been in the Philippines and Java were worn out, both physically and emotionally, and that their tasks had been made even more difficult by a complicated supply system that seemed more interested in paperwork than in defeating the Japanese. He immediately began a reorganization of the Allied air forces in Australia and the Southwest Pacific; he sent home officers who had a reputation for sluggishness and replaced them with men he knew to be "operators" like himself. He implemented a policy that no support personnel would be promoted until the rank structure in the combat squadrons was increased. Promotions would be based on performance in combat rather than time in service. As a result of Kenney's reorganization, Fifth Air Force gained a reputation as the most effective and efficient of all of the Army's numbered air forces, an air force that could consistently do more with less.

One of his first acts was to re-staff the office of Fifth Air Force which had been activated in the Philippines before Pearl Harbor but had not been functional prior to his arrival. While serving as MacArthur's senior air advisor, Kenney also initially wore the hat of

---

[52] G3 was the US Army's term for the operations and plans branch of an organization. George Kenney was GHQ Air Force director of ops and plans.

Anything, Anywhere, Anytime

Fifth Air Force commander, although operational command was given to Brig. Gen. Ennis Whitehead, who Kenney placed in command of an advanced echelon operating in New Guinea.[53] Under Fifth Air Force, he organized new combat units, including the 374th Troop Carrier Group, which activated in November 1942 with four squadrons; two new squadrons, the 6th and 33rd, had flown across the Pacific to join the battle-tested 21st and 22nd Troop Carrier Squadrons in October and November although most of the 33rd had been detained in New Caledonia for operations into Guadalcanal. The 33rd wouldn't join the 374th in its entirety until the end of December.

Before the arrival of the new squadrons and the activation of the 374th group, Kenney put the two existing squadrons to work in the dual role of providing logistical support for the fighter and bomber squadrons and resupplying ground forces in New Guinea, a mission they had already begun prior to his arrival. Kenney believed the transport airplane had almost unlimited potential, and as he became acquainted with the rugged terrain and conditions in his theater, he realized that air transportation would play a major role in the ground war – that is, it would if MacArthur's ground staff would allow it to. Lt. Gen. Richard Sutherland, MacArthur's chief of staff, opposed nearly every plan Kenney submitted until his boss overrode him.

In September 1942, Kenney finally got an opportunity to implement an idea he had been carrying around in his mind since his arrival in Australia in late July. General MacArthur had decided to deploy the US 32nd Division to New Guinea from Australia, where it had been in training. Even though the division was still not fully trained, the situation in New Guinea called for reinforcement. There was also a political issue – the Australian troops in New Guinea were not happy that the Yanks were in Australia while they were in the jungle fighting the Japanese. The Aussies were bearing the brunt of the ground combat while the "overpaid and oversexed" Americans were enjoying the comforts of their homeland – including the charms of Australia's female population – while they were enduring the deprivations of combat in New Guinea.

Two American regiments, the 126th and 128th Infantry Combat Teams, were slated for movement to Port Moresby by sea. Kenney proposed to MacArthur that he be allowed to make the move by air. MacArthur's chief of staff, Gen. Richard Sutherland, thought Kenney was out of his mind but his boss overruled him and gave the air force

---

[53] When the South Pacific Area was combined with the Southwest Pacific Area, a new Far East Air Forces headquarters activated with Kenney in command. Whitehead became Fifth Air Force commander.

Sam McGowan

permission to try their hand at the move.[54] Kenney was told to transport one regiment while the other would go by sea as originally planned. In coming months and years General Sutherland and the rest of MacArthur's staff often thought Kenney's ideas were ill-advised but they proceeded to make them work when General MacArthur thought otherwise. MacArthur had developed complete faith in Kenney and usually gave his assent to his chief airman's ideas. He gave permission to move one regiment by air while the other went by sea.

C-47 at Port Moresby (Army photo by Jack Heyn)

While Kenney's idea definitely had merit, the question was whether he had the resources to carry it out. He had an air force under his command that was severely lacking in everything, including and particularly transports. The two ill-equipped troop carrier squadrons and an RAAF transport squadron that made up the sole resources of the Directorate of Air Transport were already over-committed. But Kenney had a reputation for resourcefulness and he set out to make his idea bear fruit. He put his staff to work assembling every airplane that resembled a transport in the theater. Soon Australian airliners and military transports, US transports that weren't committed elsewhere – even some new B-17s that had just arrived in the theater with civilian ferry crews – were put to work flying combat-equipped American infantrymen to Port Moresby. In spite of a lack of airplanes, the move went so well that MacArthur gave his new air boss permission to transport the second regiment as well. Both combat teams were in position at Port Moresby by the end of September, a

---

[54] Modern "historians" become apoplectic over the use of the phrase "air force" in relation to World War II air units, but in truth the term is perfectly valid and was in common use within the military prior to and throughout World War II. The US Army Air Forces, plural, was the official term for the Army's stateside training and support organization while combat units overseas were assigned to a numbered air force reporting to the theater commander. Many airmen, particular those who had prewar service – including senior commanders – commonly referred to the "air force" or "Air Force."

Anything, Anywhere, Anytime

good two weeks sooner than they would have been had they gone by ship and several weeks before elements that had already left by sea arrived at Moresby. Air movement had also saved the infantrymen a long march through difficult jungle terrain from Milne Bay to Moresby. The move had set a precedent; air transportation would become the crucial element to drive the Japanese out of New Guinea.

Having demonstrated that air transportation could move fully equipped ground troops onto the battlefield, Kenney's next objective was to use his transports to move troops upon the battlefield itself. Prior to the Japanese landings at Buna, Kenney's predecessors had identified several flat areas not far from there as suitable for airstrips. Kenney believed that his troop carriers could land on these flat places and establish an airhead from which the Allies could begin a campaign to retake Buna and, ultimately, gain control of New Guinea. RAAF Captain Norman Wilde, who was serving as the Australian/New Zealand liaison officer with the troop carrier command, flew up in a light plane to check them out. Kenney's plan called for flying troops onto the north shore of the Lae Peninsula south of Buna some sixty-five miles. Wanigela Mission, on the northwestern shore of Collingwood Bay, was selected as the spot to commence the campaign. Australian officers flew in aboard light observation planes and supervised Papuan natives as they used machetes to clear landing strips in the tall kunai grass in preparation for test landings by transports.

In spite of the proven feasibility of transporting ground forces by air, some of MacArthur's staff members (i.e. his chief of staff, Maj. General Richard Sutherland) believed the operation was too risky. Such a military operation had never before been mounted by US forces, while at the same time the two troop carrier squadrons were still heavily involved in the resupply of the Australian troops on the Kokoda Track. Furthermore, the staff had just approved the movement of a small force into Wau, a remote airstrip in the New Guinea interior southwest of Lae. Prior to the war, Wau had been a gold mining town and the mining company had built the airstrip at the base of a mountain. It would serve as a base for the Kanga Force, an independent unit made up of Australian troops and local New Guinea militia whose mission would be to function as a guerrilla force operating against the Japanese rear. The Wau operation would be entirely dependent on air transport for resupply, but there were only two American and one Australian squadrons in the entire theater. Two other squadrons were enroute, but the first would not arrive in Australia in time for the operation.

Sam McGowan

Troops loading in Australia for movement to New Guinea

Over his staff's protest, MacArthur approved Operation *HATRACK*, subject to Kenney's approval of the plan when he arrived at Port Moresby later that same day, October 2, 1942. By October 5, the details had been worked out and *HATRACK* was on. Immediately, the 21st and 22nd squadrons went to work moving troops into Wanigela Mission. Within two days, Kenney's troop carriers had moved an Australian battalion into an airhead far in advance of the Allied lines. The move involved twelve C-47s making seventy-one flights into the hastily carved-out landing strip. The operation went off so smoothly that General E.F. Harding, the ground commander in New Guinea, decided to investigate the possibility of establishing other landing fields even closer to Buna. A missionary named Cecil Ables, who had been born in New Guinea, was flown to the area to look for sites. Aided by natives, Ables completed another landing strip near Mt. Sapia.[55] Two days later, American engineers arrived and began clearing a series of primitive landing strips along the coast. By November 4, a strip had been cleared at Pongani, only twenty-three miles south of Buna.

Meanwhile, the C-47s continued the movement into Wanigela Mission until heavy tropical rains turned the region into a sea of mud and put a halt to operations. When the weather cleared, the movement of the American 128th regiment continued while the 126th was transported further north to Pongani.[56] With the troops in place, the operation continued as transports kept the Allied forces supplied with

---

[55] Construction of a landing strip consisted of simply using machetes to cut down the tall Kunia grass and construct a strip long enough and wide enough for a transport to land.

[56] While the two regiments were entering combat, the third regiment, the 127th, had yet to arrive in New Guinea. It would not arrive until November 26.

Anything, Anywhere, Anytime

rations and ammunition. The original plan called for resupply by sea if at all possible, but the presence of Japanese aircraft posed a threat to the small coastal boats and barges that resulted in their virtual elimination as a source of supply. At the time, the Allies had yet to achieve complete air superiority over southern New Guinea. With the boats temporarily out of the picture, the troop carriers took up the slack as new airstrips were constructed right on the Japanese' doorstep at Dobodura, only fifteen miles from Buna. When the airstrips were all completed and handling aircraft, General MacArthur ordered operation *GULLIVER*, an attack on Buna, to commence in mid-November. The battle for "Bloody Buna" continued through the remainder of November and all of December until the entire area fell into Allied hands on January 3. The troops in battle at Buna were resupplied and reinforced by the troop carriers, with the transports either landing on the airstrips around Buna or airdropping supplies to units in the field.

During the Buna campaign, troop carriers evacuated casualties on their return flights from the forward airstrips. At the time, no formal air evacuation procedures had been established and there were no medical personnel to attend to the patients while in flight. They were simply loaded onto transports in stretchers – if there were stretchers available – and flown back to Moresby. During December and January, the troop carriers brought out an average of 100 patients per day, with the peak of 280 reached on December 8. The speedy movement of the men to rear-area hospitals allowed men to be treated and returned to combat while reducing the number of deaths from wounds and subsequent disease. The success of such operations led the Army Air Forces to establish a formal air evacuation mission and training of medical personnel began at Bowman Field at Louisville, Kentucky, although it would be nearly a year before the first squadron arrived in the Southwest Pacific. Air evacuation would become a major troop carrier mission and would save thousands of lives in coming years.

Sam McGowan

32nd Division troops loading for Buna

The Papua New Guinea operation set several precedents for the use of troop carrier aircraft and served as a model for the tactical airlift mission as it has developed over the past seven decades. When possible, the transports landed on established and hastily constructed landing strips; when none was available, they turned to airdrop to deliver their loads. The versatility of the troop carrier transport was exploited as the transports were reconfigured for casualty evacuation, which led to medical personnel being trained for air evacuation duties. Air land, airdrop and air evacuation of casualties would become, and remain, the primary mission of tactical airlifters.

Until October 1942, the air transport burden in the Southwest Pacific was borne by the 21st and 22nd squadrons, both of which had been activated in the theater using local resources. General Kenney had stressed a need to Army Air Forces headquarters for troop carrier squadrons in the theater and by November their strength was beginning to increase as the War Department diverted some transports and crews to Fifth Air Force that had originally been intended for service in Europe. In November, the 374th Troop Carrier Group was activated at Brisbane with four squadrons, including the 6th and 33rd Troop Carrier Squadrons along with the veteran 21st and 22nd. Less than a month later, the group moved its base forward to Port Moresby, from which the four squadrons kept busy supporting the campaign to drive the Japanese out of New Guinea. By the end of the

Anything, Anywhere, Anytime

war, the 374th had established a combat record that was second to none; it had earned no less than three Distinguished Unit Citations.[57]

The first troop carrier reinforcements were the 6th and 33rd Troop Carrier Squadrons, which had both originally started out at Olmsted Field at Middletown, Pennsylvania. The 6th was one of the original transport squadrons. In July 1942, the squadron was strengthened with the assignment of a number of new pilots, many of whom were recently rated staff sergeant pilots who had just completed the Army pilot training course as part of a special program that commenced in late 1940.[58] Thirteen of the squadron's 26 pilots, including two first pilots,[59] were NCOs. In September 1942, the men from the 6th Transport Squadron were sent by train to the Air Material Command depot at Mobile, Alabama to pick up a full complement of brand new C-47s that were fresh off of the assembly lines. After picking up their airplanes, the squadron flew to Hamilton Field at Sacramento, California where long-range fuel tanks were installed. The crews, which consisted of two pilots, a crew chief and a radio operator, were joined by navigators whose task was to take them across the Pacific to Hawaii, and then to Australia after enroute stops in the South Pacific. The navigators left the crews when they arrived in Brisbane. The squadron arrived at Brisbane during *HATRACK*.

After less than a week of orientation, the thirteen crews left Brisbane for a classified destination, which turned out to be Port Moresby. Immediately after their arrival, the crews were briefed by RAAF Captain Norman Wilde[60] on every aspect of how they would be

---

[57] The group's successor, the 374th Troop Carrier Wing, would earn additional unit citations in Korea and Vietnam, making it one of the most decorated units in US Air Force history.

[58] Army Air Corps policy was that only officers would be trained as pilots but as the War Department began gearing up in response to events in Europe, it became apparent that there weren't enough qualified applicants for the Aviation Cadet Program, which required a minimum of two years of college. Consequently, the Army relaxed its standards and allowed the training of enlisted men to become pilots. They went through the program in enlisted status and graduated as staff sergeants, regardless of their previous military rank. Although most of the new NCO pilots were trained to fly fighters, many were assigned to the transport squadrons which were in the process of forming in 1942. In mid-1943 most of the NCO pilots were either commissioned as second lieutenants or given warrants as flight officers when the college requirement for aviation cadets was deleted.

[59] In World War II, the command pilot on a crew was designated as a first pilot. The term was later changed to aircraft commander.

[60] Prior to the war Wilde had lived in New Guinea and knew the country inside and out. He used an airplane for his company travels, and when he went into the RAAF, he became a valuable asset because of his knowledge of the country. If someone needed to go into the New Guinea interior, Wilde frequently was the pilot who flew him into one of the prewar landing strips.

operating, from how the Australian ground troops would load the airplanes and eject the loads to the procedures for detecting the presence of enemy aircraft; an Australian pilot in a militarized AT-6 which the Australians called a *Whirraway* would accompany each mission and when the transport pilots saw him dive for the trees, they were to follow his lead because it meant he had sighted Japanese fighters. The 6th was the first troop carrier squadron to be physically based in New Guinea and squadron personnel found themselves in the middle of a combat zone where Japanese bombers came over every night and fighters came in to bomb and strafe the field nearly every day. The first thing the men did when they arrived at Seven Mile Aerodrome was dig slit trenches next to their quarters. Missions were actually scheduled so that the C-47s would be in the air when the Japanese came over on their daily bombing and strafing missions and would return after the enemy had left!

Army Quartermaster kickers

An Australian NCO who was in charge of the loading and kicking crew served as the "navigator" for the drop missions delivering supplies to Australian teams operating in the mountains just north of Port Moresby. The NCOs knew the location of the drop zones and pointed them out to the pilots. After the mission, the loading crew left the airplane to begin their trek to join their comrades at the point where they had just dropped their load. With the support of the 6th TCS crews, the Australians began pushing the Japanese further and further north. When the squadron first arrived at Moresby, they were dropping into drop zones within sight of their airfield, but within a few weeks the Japanese had been pushed more than sixty miles north to the other side of the Owen Stanleys. The 6th TCS remained in New

Anything, Anywhere, Anytime

Guinea for almost a year, the entire time in constant combat, until it was withdrawn to Australia for a rest and assigned to logistical resupply flights between rear area supply depots in Australia and forward airfields in New Guinea.(Ford, 2010)

When they were replaced in bomber squadrons, B-17s were reassigned to troop carrier squadron for transport duty.

Although the troop carrier squadrons were American units, most (if not all) US air combat units in the Southwest Pacific included Allied personnel, particularly Australians. The RAAF was short on aircraft at the beginning of the war and came to depend on US-supplied aircraft for its squadrons. For at least the first two years of the war, RAAF personnel were assigned to US squadrons as pilots, mechanics and gunners. Shortly after the 6th TCS arrived at Moresby, all of its American copilots were replaced by RAAF NCO pilots. Just where the American pilots went is unclear, but they most likely went to the 21st and 22nd squadrons as replacements for men who were flying transports on temporary duty from their assigned duties as bomber and fighter pilots.

The 33rd TCS made a journey to the Pacific similar to the one made by the 6th but part of the squadron was diverted to New Caledonia for several weeks to fly missions in support of combat operations on Guadalcanal. Most of the missions were to evacuate casualties. The 33rd didn't officially arrive in Australia until December 1 and it wasn't until December 28 that it joined the 6th at Moresby, where a complex of airfields, each identified by number by its distance from the town, had been built. Living conditions for the two squadrons at Moresby were dismal at best. Until early January 1943, and the appearance of the Lockheed P-38 *Lightning* as the predominant Allied fighter, the Japanese had control of the skies over the region and

American and Australian aircraft were subject to interception while the airfields were subject to frequent attack. The first thing the men did when they arrived at their new base was dig slit trenches right by their huts where they could take shelter during attacks. Fighter defenses consisted of Bell P-39s and P-400s[61] along with Curtis P-40s, some of which were operated by RAAF squadrons.

Weather conditions in the Owen Stanley's featured low clouds accompanied by frequent rain and fog which reduced visibilities to two miles or less on most days. Before the C-47 crews could make their drops, they had to find the narrow slot in the mountains which allowed them to get through to the other side where the drop zones were located. Maps of the region were nonexistent, and there were no radio navigational aids to help the pilots find their way. Navigators were not assigned to troop carrier crews and the pilots navigated by a combination of dead reckoning and pilotage using known landmarks for reference points.[62] Troop carrier operations in Papua, New Guinea in 1943 were basically hit and miss.

Troop carrier operations in New Guinea were as difficult as any flown anywhere in the world and would set the standard used in the postwar Army Air Forces and US Air Force into the 1970s. They involved flying unarmed transports deep into contested territory in skies that were often patrolled by Japanese fighters. The one consolation the troop carrier crews had was that their fighter protection was made up of the best pilots in the Air Corps. Fifth Air Force included four of the top-scoring fighter aces of the war, Majors Richard I. Bong and Thomas McGuire and Lieutenant Colonels Thomas Lynch and Gerald Johnson. Lynch, in particular, was with the troop carrier squadrons from the beginning; he worked with troop carriers while flying P-39s with the 39th Fighter Squadron. Troop carrier operations were always escorted by fighters if possible, usually by P-39s since transport operations were conducted at the lower altitudes where the often maligned Airacobra truly shined. Until the very end of 1942, the only fighters available were P-39s and P-40s. On December 27, 1942, Lockheed P-38s made their appearance in the skies over New Guinea and the entire equation changed literally overnight as the

---

[61] The Bell P-400 was an export version of the P-39 that had originally been developed for sale to the British. It differed from the P-39 primarily in armament. The RAF was unhappy with the P-400 and refused to accept them. When the US entered the war, dozens of P-400s were available and were shipped to Australia. As it turned out, although both the P-39 and P-400 were inadequate as high altitude interceptors, they were excellent ground attack aircraft and could more than hold their own with Japanese fighters at lower altitudes.

[62] Dead reckoning is based on time. A pilot lays out his course and calculates the time between checkpoints based on airspeed and forecast winds aloft. Pilotage is navigation based on visual recognition of landmarks.

Anything, Anywhere, Anytime

previously superior Japanese fighter pilots suddenly found the odds had turned against them. Few Japanese pilots who fought in the Southwest Pacific survived the war.

Enemy aircraft were not the only hazards faced by troop carrier crews in the Southwest Pacific. The rugged Owen Stanleys presented a formidable obstacle as many missions were flown into remote airfields lying in valleys in their shadow. The mountains were frequently obscured by clouds that developed due to up-slope conditions as warm moisture from the nearby Coral Sea made its way up the sides of the mountains and condensed into clouds and fog. Frequent tropical thunderstorms added to the hazards. The tropics are characterized by severe thunderstorms which build up over mountains on the islands and produce heavy rain and turbulence so severe it can tear an airplane apart. The transports operated into airstrips that were nothing but clearings in the rough kunai grass; they were often surrounded by jungles so dense they were nearly impenetrable. A man could get lost only a few feet from the jungle's edge. Jungle canopies as high as 300 feet completely obscured the sky and little sunlight ever reached the jungle floor. The jungles were populated by animals, snakes – many deadly poisonous – and clouds of insects while the rivers and coastal waters teemed with man-eating crocodiles. The people of New Guinea were beyond primitive; they were the most primitive people in the world. Cannibalism was still practiced in some parts of the country, which was largely unexplored and had never been charted. Not even Africa presented the kind of obstacles that had kept Europeans from exploring the country and making contact with the tribes. Still, the people were generally friendly enough, at least the ones around the coastal areas where the air bases were established.

Shortly before the loss of Buna to the Allies, the Japanese mounted a new effort to take Port Moresby. In early January 1943 3,000 Japanese troops landed at Lae by ship then headed overland to attack the little mining town of Wau where the Allies had established an outpost a few months before. Two Australian commando companies and a small band of native militia, the Kanga Force, made up the defense of Wau. They were kept supplied entirely by air. After learning of the Japanese landings, the Allies determined to defend the outpost. Troops were flown into the rugged mountain airstrip outside the town to reinforce the garrison but heavy cloud cover and turbulence delayed the operation. Meanwhile, the Japanese continued their advance until, by January 28, they were within four miles of the outpost. Four inches of rain fell on Wau the evening of January 28, with more following the next day. On January 29, heavy thunderstorms were building over the mountains but the clouds fortunately remained clear of the valley and the C-47 pilots were able to find the airstrip. After nearly a year of combat, the Fifth Air Force troop carrier pilots

Sam McGowan

were veterans; men who had learned to handle their C-47s "like fighters." Fortunately, the troop carrier pilots were also accustomed to landing at Wau, where the 3,000-foot landing strip ran uphill straight into a mountain! There was one way in and one way out.

With Japanese troops on the airfield perimeter, the troop carrier pilots brought their loaded C-47s into the wet, muddy runway and discharged their troops; some literally came out of the airplane with their weapons firing from the hip! One end of the runway was under constant mortar attack and, in some cases, Japanese troops were so close to the field that the airplanes had to circle while the Australians pushed them far enough back with grenades that the transports were able to land and offload their troops. By the time operations were halted by darkness, the troop carriers had made fifty-seven landings. The next day, the reinforcement continued as the Australians began pushing the Japanese forces further and further away from the airstrip. By noon, the Japanese had started retreating. For the first time in history, American air transportation had decided a battle and, combined with the Buna battle which had just concluded, the outcome of a military campaign.

On February 6, a few days after the successful reinforcement of Wau, the Japanese launched an air attack on the outpost with fighters and dive-bombers. Although one transport was destroyed on the ground, the Japanese paid dearly. Australian antiaircraft inflicted heavy casualties then, as the Japanese began departing, they were intercepted by Allied fighters that had been escorting bombers attacking the airfields at Lae. The fighters had a field day. They shot down twenty-five Japanese and claimed ten probables and five damaged, with no losses of their own.

In January 1943, while the 374th was involved in the battle for Wau, a new troop carrier group arrived in Australia. The 317th Troop Carrier Group had activated in the United States six months earlier and, after training at several fields in the southern United States, left for Australia from Bowman Field, Kentucky in factory-fresh airplanes. With four squadrons – the 39th, 40th, 41st and 46th – the group arrived in Australia only to have its new C-47s taken away and given to the veteran 374th! Initially, the group was assigned to combat operations in New Guinea, but once the situation at Wau stabilized, the 317th was withdrawn to Australia and assigned to logistical operations. The 317th squadrons were then assigned the war-weary mixture of C-39s, C-47s, C-53s, C-60s, B-17s and LB-30s that had been servicing the needs of the combat units for nearly a year. From its new base in Townsville, the 317th took over the logistics role of delivering troops and cargo to New Guinea from rear area depots and resupplying airfields in the Australian Northwest Territories. The veteran 374th was relieved of

Anything, Anywhere, Anytime

logistical support responsibilities for the more demanding combat air transport duties and the new arrivals were allowed a chance to get their feet wet before jumping in to assume their own share of the combat burden.

Shortly after the arrival of the 317th group, General Kenney activated the 54th Troop Carrier Wing at Brisbane as a command organization over the two groups that now constituted US troop carrier strength in the theater. Within a year, the wing would control four groups. With two full troop carrier groups under his command, Kenney was now in a position to develop a more ambitious plan. The aggressive airman had his eye on Nadzab, a Japanese airfield in the Markham Valley northwest of the city of Lae at the upper end of the Lae Peninsula. Kenney wanted to capture the airfield in a combined airborne and air transport assault timed to coincide with the advancement of ground forces moving north from Buna. His plan was contingent on the arrival of a paratroop unit and additional troop carrier squadrons from the States. There was still work to be done in preparation for the attack while he awaited the arrival of the paratroopers.

In preparation for the assault on Nadzab, Kenney ordered the establishment of a forward base on the north side of the Owen Stanleys at a place with the unlikely name of Tsili-Tsili, pronounced "silly-silly." Because the airfield would be established entirely by air transport, plans were made to bring jeeps and trailers into an existing strip at Marlinan where C-47s could land, then use them to move supplies the four miles to the construction site. To speed up the ground movement, someone came up with the idea of sawing two and a half ton truck chassis in half and loading each half into a transport for the flight across the mountains. When the halves were unloaded, they were bolted back together and the cab and body reinstalled. The idea worked; soon larger trucks joined the jeeps and trailers in the task of moving supplies to the construction site. Consequently, every "deuce and a half" truck in the theater was subsequently modified so that it could be transported by air. The practice was a source of great amusement when Kenney told General Arnold about it during a visit to the United States, but Arnold passed it on to other theater commanders who copied the procedure to move trucks in their own theaters. He also advised the Air Transport Command of the procedure, and it was used on the India-China Ferry.

The selection of Tsili-Tsili is a story in itself. Lt. Everett Frazier, a Fifth Air Force aviation engineer, was flown to Bulolo where he set out on foot into enemy territory accompanied by an Australian officer and a native escort. Captain Norman Wilde, who was familiar with the area after living in New Guinea as a mining engineer before the war, flew him in. Frazier and his team trekked fifty miles into the rugged

Sam McGowan

mountainous jungle to inspect the old airfield at Marlinan. He found it suitable for some operations and put the natives to work clearing the runway. When his plans to be picked up there went awry, Frazier made his way through the bush to Wau to catch a C-47 bound for Moresby. He reported that while Marlinan was suitable as a temporary base in dry weather, heavy rains would turn it into a quagmire and make it unsuitable for sustained fighter and bomber operations. Brig. Gen. Paul Wurtsmith, commander of V Fighter Command, flew into Marlinan and decided that an old strip at Tsili-Tsili was better suited for combat operations, but would require extensive work to prepare it to handle aircraft. The end result was that the troop carriers flew the supplies into Marlinan; they were then transported to the site of the new field by Jeeps and trucks until it had been developed to the point that C-47s could begin landing.

The Tsili-Tsili operation was not without cost. For some time, Kenney's men managed to keep the base's existence secret from the Japanese, but eventually they learned of its presence. The facilities were camouflaged to avoid detection from the air, while the troop carrier pilots used "clever flying techniques" to confuse the Japanese as to their destination.[63] The base could not remain secret forever and it was eventually discovered. On August 15, a Japanese attack caught a flight of transports as they were about to land with the ground echelons of the first fighter squadrons to be based at the remote strip. One C-47 flight had just landed when a dozen Sally bombers attacked the strip after flying low and taking advantage of the terrain to avoid the American radar. An equal number of fighters accompanied the Japanese bombers. One C-47 was shot down with the loss of all aboard, while a second disappeared into the mountains and was never found. American P-39s responded to the low-level attack and shot down all but one of the Sallys and at least two or three of their fighter escort.

By early August, the buildup at Tsili-Tsili was well underway. Troop carriers were bringing in both combat and support troops. In mid-August, a fighter control radar unit became operational at the base. The entire operation had been carried out solely by air transportation, and by this time the Allied command had become well aware that the troop carrier crews were the key element in the New Guinea campaign. For it was they who brought in the troops to secure the area and establish the base that would be home for the fighters and light and medium bombers that would assist the four-engine B-24s in carrying the war to the enemy's more distant bases.

---

[63] The "clever flying techniques" consisted of staying low to the ground and following the contours of the earth to avoid detection by radar. The olive drab transports blended into the green jungle foliage and were difficult to see from the air.

Anything, Anywhere, Anytime

After Kenney arrived in Australia, he made plans to gradually phase out the B-17s that had served as the mainstay of heavy bomber operations in the Far East since the beginning of the war. Although Kenney had had some reservations about the Liberator when he found out that he would be getting them just before he left the US, by 1943 they had proven to be ideally suited for the kind of operations found in the Southwest Pacific, where missions were flown over long expanses of water. As the war-weary B-17s were replaced, they were reassigned to the 54th Troop Carrier Wing, which assigned some to squadrons and placed others in a special airdrop unit. Because they were combat airplanes, the B-17s had an advantage over the unarmed C-47s. When the Boeings were converted for transport use, some of the gun positions were left intact. The armament allowed the converted bombers to operate into more hostile areas than the defenseless C-47s. After dropping their loads to troops operating in contested areas, the B-17s remained in the area strafing Japanese positions. The 54th Wing set up a special airdrop unit using B-17s to support Australian commandos operating in the vicinity of the Japanese stronghold at Rabaul. (54th TCW Historians)

During a visit to the United States, General Kenney stressed the success of his troop carriers to General Arnold. Along with more fighters, light, medium and heavy bombers – which turned out to be B-24s because they were (1) available and (2) better suited for the long overwater flights that constituted Pacific missions, Kenny also requested more transports and crews. He also asked for a division of paratroops and advised Arnold that, with them, he would be able to seize Japanese bases much further forward than would be possible with the infantry troops then in New Guinea. Arnold listened to Kenney, and while he was unable to meet all of the Southwest Pacific air boss' requests in view of the world situation and the demands of the European theater, he did promise new transports and the assignment of an airborne regiment to the Southwest Pacific.

Until October 1944, when it was deactivated and replaced by the 5298th Troop Carrier Wing (Provisional), all air transport operations in the Southwest Pacific were under the control of the Directorate of Air Transport, which was formed in early 1942. (The 5298th Troop Carrier Wing was a provisional unit and was of short duration. It was replaced by the 322nd Troop Carrier Wing.) The DAT was originally the Air Transport Command, but when the Army Air Forces in the US established the US Army Air Transport Command, the title was changed to avoid confusion. Essentially a command and control headquarters, the DAT was responsible for the movement of personnel and cargo throughout the Southwest Pacific. However, it was not responsible for combat operations; troop carrier operations in combat

Sam McGowan

were the responsibility of the 54th Troop Carrier Wing. Many of DAT's officers were former airline executives who had been called to active duty with the Air Corps before or at the beginning of the war. One former airline executive was commissioned as a supply officer in the US Army Services of Supply and went to Australia in that capacity. He was initially detached to the DAT but eventually transferred to the Air Corps as a service pilot.[64]

To exercise some control over passenger and cargo operations, the DAT organized its own Airways Control Squadron to process cargo and passengers and supervise loading operations. The ACS had detachments at bases throughout the region. In November 1943 the Airways Control Squadron, which wasn't an authorized US Army unit, deactivated and the 1st Air Cargo Control Squadron activated to take its place. DAT personnel and Gen. Kenney had been pressing the Army to train personnel for air cargo duty and when the squadron was authorized, training began in the States for additional air cargo control squadrons. In August 1944, the 2nd Air Cargo Control Squadron arrived at Finschaven.

The DAT was part of the Allied Air Forces in Australia and included Royal Australian Air Force personnel as well as Americans. At various periods in the war, different troop carrier squadrons were assigned directly to it for logistical operations. Several RAAF squadrons operated under DAT control. Initially, the RAAF units operated antiquated Dehavilland DH 84 and DH 85 transports. The DH 84 was a multiengine biplane and the DH 85 was a light single engine airplane.

In the summer of 1943, the 375th Troop Carrier Group arrived at Brisbane with its 55th, 56th, 57th and 58th squadrons to become the third transport group in the theater. The group's stay in Australia was short and sweet; within two weeks of their arrival, the men of the 375th moved north to Port Moresby to join the 374th. Once again, the new arrivals gave up some of their brand new C-47s to the older group and received worn-out B-17s in return. A few weeks after the arrival of the 375th, the 317th TCG, which had been enjoying the easy life flying logistical support flights in Australia for the DAT, also moved to Moresby as the war moved further north and away from the Land Down Under. Ships laden with supplies were now docking at Moresby and Air Transport Command transports coming from the US were beginning to land there as well. In late August 1943, the 433rd Troop Carrier Group arrived with its five squadrons, the 65th, 66th, 67th, 68th

---

[64] Service pilots were Army pilots who were awarded flight status based on their civilian flying experience. They were restricted from combat flying but were authorized to fly transports.

Anything, Anywhere, Anytime

and 69th. The new arrivals came at an opportune time, for General Kenney was preparing to launch his "big show."

The real apple in George Kenney's eye was not Marlinan, but rather Nadzab, a Japanese airfield just northwest of the city of Lae in the Markham Valley, a valley on the upper end of the Lae Peninsula. Kenny planned to use the recently arrived 503rd Parachute Infantry Regiment[65] to take the airfield and establish an airhead into which conventional troops could be flown to attack the Japanese at Lae from the rear, just as Billy Mitchell had envisioned more than two decades before. With their escape route cut off, the Allies could catch the Japanese between two forces as Allied troops moved up from the south. With the capture of Lae, the Allies would have control of the Markham River Valley and, ultimately, all of Papua New Guinea. In preparation for the attack, Australian infantrymen were airlifted into Tsili-Tsili, where they would be in position for further movement into the airfield at Nadzab after it had been seized by the 503rd.

On the morning of September 5, 1943, the 54th Troop Carrier Wing went on alert at Moresby. Men of the 503rd loaded aboard eighty-four C-47s from the three veteran groups of the wing – the 374th, 317th and 375th. At 0825, the first C-47 rolled down the runway. Within fifteen minutes, the entire flight was airborne. Over Thirty-Mile Aerodrome they picked up their fighter escort then continued to a rendezvous point over Marlinan. The drop formation moved into six-plane elements in right echelon. The C-47 pilots then dropped from thirty-five hundred feet down to their run-in altitudes, stacked between four and five hundred feet above the ground. At 0948 the pilots signaled that the formation was twenty minutes from the drop zone.

---

[65] There is considerable confusion over the identity of various units bearing the designation 503rd Parachute Infantry. The original 503rd formed at Ft. Benning, GA in early 1942. Later that year the regiment's 2nd Battalion moved to England. In November the 2nd Battalion, 503rd Infantry flew to North Africa to participate in operations in conjunction with the TORCH landings. However, only a day or so before the operation, the 2nd of the 503rd became the 509th Parachute Infantry although the designation took awhile to get into the Army's records. Consequently, airborne operations in North Africa are identified as performed by the 503rd, with the resulting implication that the regiment fought in both Europe and the Pacific. However, the rest of the 503rd had remained at Ft. Benning and was later deployed to Australia to join MacArthur.

503rd Parachute Infantry jumping at Nadzab

As the fleet of C-47s approached Nadzab, six squadrons of B-25s, each equipped with a nose full of .50-caliber machineguns that had been developed by Pappy Gunn, hit the field at treetop altitudes in a fierce strafing attack. The Mitchells strafed the field then released their loads of deadly parafragmentation bombs.[66] Thousands of .50-caliber rounds and hundreds of exploding fragmentation bombs rained onto Nadzab airfield during one of the most ferocious aerial attacks of the war. On the heels of the strafing B-25s, a flight of six A-20s laid down a smoke screen to obscure the sky and hide the arrival of the drop formation. At 1022, the first paratrooper hit the sky over Nadzab and, within minutes, the field was in Allied hands. General MacArthur and his staff, including General Kenney, observed the entire operation from over the objective as they circled in a B-17. The strafing attack was so fierce and the airborne assault so surprising that the Japanese offered little resistance. General MacArthur was so impressed by the performance that Kenney later reported he "jumped up and down like a kid" as the operation unfolded beneath them.

With the airfield in Allied hands, the C-47s and other transports of the 54th Troop Carrier Wing began arriving with troops of the Australian 7th Division who had been propositioned at Tsili-Tsili for the assault. The operation continued as more troops were brought in, along with communications and engineering personnel to establish an airbase. Within a week, three hundred and thirty-three transport loads

---

[66] Parafragmentation bombs were small 27-pound bombs suspended beneath parachute that were designed to be dropped from low-flying airplanes. They had been invented by General Kenney when he was with the Air Corps research and development laboratory in Florida before the war.

Anything, Anywhere, Anytime

had been brought in from Tsili-Tsili and another eighty-seven from Moresby and bases further south. As the troops came into the airfield, they moved out again to attack the Japanese defenders of Lae from the northwest, even as Allied troops were assaulting the city from the southeast, from Buna. The entire operation against Lae depended heavily on troop carrier transport from the very beginning.

  Nadzab is a classic example of the modern military concept known as "vertical envelopment." A combination of heavy aerial firepower and a massive airborne assault overwhelmed the defenses of an enemy airfield. Once the field was in friendly hands, troop carrier transports began landing with reinforcements to exploit the advantage, then the field was expanded to allow the arrival of fighters and bombers which would carry the war deeper into enemy territory. Such operations are the very crux of the troop carrier mission and the tactical airlift mission that followed it as it existed in World War II, as it has existed in the seven decades since the war and as it is conceived today. Australian and US engineers began work immediately to turn Nadzab into a major base of operations, with five runways. The airbase complex became home to a number of organizations, including the 54th Troop Carrier Wing and three of its groups. The Australians used Nadzab as a forward base for an attack on Lae, with the air transported troops advancing on the city from the northwest while troops that had landed by sea came in to catch the defenders in a pinschers movement. When the Japanese realized that they were not going to be able to hold their positions, they began withdrawing to the north, crossing over the rugged Surawaged Mountain Range. Australian troops advanced up the Markham and Ramu Valleys northwest of Nadzab and into the Finisetere Mountains. Engineers constructed airstrips as fast as suitable sites could be secured. Troop carrier transports supplied Australian patrols operating away from their main bases. An article in a Brisbane newspaper described the minute nature of troop carrier operations, relating how that Australian supply experts weighed even single rounds of ammunition in order to insure that the transports were not overloaded. Ammunition crates with differing kinds of wood were weighed so as to determine standard weights. The article pointed out that it was the first time an Australian division had ever been supplied entirely by air.

  After more than a year of combat operations, the Australian ground troops and American troop carriers had worked out operations to a science. Parachutes were dyed to reflect color codes that would allow troops on the ground to determine what each bundle contained before it hit the ground, and allow them to recover the most needed supplies first. The Australians recorded their lessons in a "blueprint," a seventy-five page manual that had become the "air supply Bible" for New Guinea. The aerial resupply effort was being watched closely by British and American commanders all over the world for possible application in their own theaters. Air evacuation of casualties had become routine. They became an official part of the troop carrier mission in the Southwest Pacific when the 804th Medical Air Evacuation Transport Squadron became operational in New Guinea in October 1943 and medical teams were assigned to casualty evacuation missions to tend to the patients.

Ambulances meeting C-47s

Until November 1942, the Army had made no provisions for the training of medical personnel to fly on transport aircraft to tend to casualties. The success of casualty evacuation in New Guinea led the Air Corps to establish a medical training school at Bowman Field, Kentucky where corpsmen, surgeons and nurses were trained to set up evacuation hospitals and to load and tend to patients in flight. Inexplicably, even though casualty evacuation was pioneered in the Southwest Pacific, it took almost a year before an air evacuation squadron was sent there. The first trained medical personnel went to North Africa, which was in the European Theater[67] and part of Churchill and Roosevelt's "Germany First" strategy. The 804th MAES finally arrived in Australia in September 1943, and its personnel began flying on troop carrier missions the following month.

---

[67] Contrary to popular belief and assertions by some historians, there were only three theaters of war during World War II, the American, Asiatic and European Theaters of war. Each theater was divided into Areas of Operations. For example, The Asiatic-Pacific Theater was divided into the Pacific Ocean Area, China-Burma-India Area, South Pacific Area and Southwest Pacific Area.

Anything, Anywhere, Anytime

In just over a year, General Kenney demonstrated that the airplane was indeed an offensive weapon in all its forms, and that air power could win battles – and even campaigns – against a numerically stronger enemy with shorter supply lines. He later described the entire strategy of the New Guinea Campaign as based upon the concept of rapid mobility. He and his boss, General Douglas MacArthur, saw no need for tanks and heavy armor in the jungle, but instead relied on highly mobile ground forces whose entire units would be moved at a moment's notice entirely by air then kept supplied by the same medium. Kenney recognized the true importance of air transportation as a vehicle to move ground and air forces quickly, on and in the vicinity of a battlefield, in a manner that escaped the minds of the leadership of the Air Transport Command.(Kenney G. C.) During and for years after the war, ATC senior officers would rant about the importance of air transportation to the military, but they never carried out a single combat operation.

In addition to their combat transport role, the troop carrier crews were also heavily involved in logistical support as they flew supplies to the combat squadrons from the rear area depots in Australia, and later in New Guinea as the war moved further north. Logistical operations were the responsibility of the DAT and various squadrons and groups were assigned to it directly. Newly arrived troop carrier squadrons were assigned to logistical support with the DAT to give the flight crews an opportunity to become theater oriented. Due to their lesser demands, veteran combat squadrons transferred to the DAT and were assigned to logistical operations when they were sent back to Australia for a rest. Not all logistical flying fell under the DAT, however. Transport operations into the forward airfields in New Guinea were the responsibility of the 54th Wing. When advanced airfields were established in the New Guinea interior and combat squadrons moved in, air transport was their only means of supply.

Flying in New Guinea was under some of the most difficult conditions found anywhere in the world. Not only were Japanese fighters still patrolling the skies in 1943, the high elevations of the Owen Stanleys presented a formidable obstacle, especially considering that many of the forward airfields were on their slopes. The tropical climate spawned fierce thunderstorms that could rip the fragile aluminum frame of an airplane to pieces, while the thick jungles were a forbidding prospect for the unfortunate airman who was forced down over them. The prospect of rescue from the jungles of New Guinea was very slim. Overwater flying was equally threatening. The warm, tropical waters teemed with sharks and few airmen who had the misfortune to parachute into or ditch in the ocean were ever seen again. It was a terrible and dangerous environment but "Kenney's Kids" kept on flying – and dying.

C-47s dropping troops at Noemfoor

Living conditions for aircrews in New Guinea were primitive. Men slept in tents and were constantly on the alert to scramble into their nearby slit trenches when Japanese bombers approached. The heat and humidity of the jungle environment made life almost unbearable, and the constant presence of swarming clouds of insects tipped the balance. Malaria and other tropical diseases affected aircrew and ground personnel alike. Heat rash and fungus infections were part of everyday life for military personnel in New Guinea. Marine Corps fighter pilot Major Gregory Boyington, who flew in the nearby Solomon Islands, told in his memoir how that he flew with fungus growth in his ears so bad that he had to periodically have them scraped out by the flight surgeon so he could hear.(Boyington, 1977) Heavy tropical downpours turned the airfields into quagmires of mud. For the airmen, some respite came in the form of logistics missions to

Anything, Anywhere, Anytime

the rear area depots at Townsville and Brisbane, but when their short sojourn in civilization was over, the crews returned to the mud, heat, humidity, insects and general deprivation of New Guinea.

In spite of the dangers and adverse living conditions, the airmen in New Guinea were making history. In one year's time, General Kenney's "kids" had turned what had been conceived in Washington as a prolonged holding action while the Allies fought the Germans into a major offensive against the Japanese. The Allied successes in the Southwest Pacific came about in spite of being on the bottom of the list for replacements, reinforcement and supply. The crucial element that turned the tide in the region was air transportation provided by the Fifth Air Force troop carrier squadrons. Commanders in other theaters were quick to take notice of the heretofore unprecedented mobility the transport airplane had provided to the outnumbered American and Australian ground forces in New Guinea. Soon, the tactics and methods used by the troop carrier squadrons under their command would be incorporated into the strategies in other part of the Pacific, and eventually in Europe as well. Kenney and the squadrons that served under him were teaching the world a lesson, a lesson that shortened the war in the Pacific by at least two years.

An important factor in the New Guinea campaign was the attitude of resourcefulness that permeated the entire Fifth Air Force, especially in the troop carrier squadrons. In other air forces, fighter and bomber pilots sometimes looked down upon their peers who flew transports. This was not true in New Guinea, where troop carrier pilots displayed the same aggressive attitude that is commonly attributed to fighter pilots. The transport crews were well aware of the importance of their role and that Allied infantrymen in the jungles were dependent upon them for their very existence. No less than three senior US Air Force troop carrier commanders from Korea to Vietnam came from one of General Kenney's favorite New Guinea combat groups, the 3rd Attack Group. It has been said that US Air Force transport pilots can "deliver a load of toothpicks to the gates of hell without losing their cool." This attitude was developed in the green hell that was New Guinea.

Sam McGowan

Chapter Four - "China-Burma-India"

Glider tow over Burma

Without doubt, the most famous World War II air transportation activities are those that took place within the China-Burma-India Area of Operations, commonly known as the CBI. This is not because they were the most important – they weren't – but because the Air Transport Command was heavily involved after February 1943, and they have become closely associated with the modern day Air Mobility Command and also because some CBI operations are pointed to by the Air Force Special Operations Command as part of its heritage. Throughout the war, a major air force mission in the CBI was simply getting supplies out of rear-area bases in India and across "the Hump" of the lower reaches of the Himalayas to China. The Hump Airlift as it is known today, or the India-China Ferry as it was officially known during World War II, has become famous largely because, for most of the war, it was the responsibility of the Air Transport Command, an organization based largely on the national airlines and consequently very publicity conscious. The ATC was also assigned directly to US Army Air Forces headquarters in Washington, DC and, unlike troop carrier commands overseas, had easy access to members of the press. In 1943, ATC contracted with noted photographer Ivan Dimitri to document its world-wide activities, including those in the CBI.

But there is more to the air transportation story in the CBI than the ATC role. While ATC was involved with the movement of supplies from India to China, the Tenth Air Force Troop Carrier Command was performing the same tasks as that of the Fifth Air Force troop carrier units in the New Guinea campaign. As their peers in the Air Transport Command flew supplies into China, troop carrier crews were moving men and equipment into position to fight the Japanese and keeping them supplied while they were under fire. By the last year of the war, ground and, to some extent, air combat operations in the CBI were built around troop carrier aviation just as they were in New Guinea. The difference was that, with one exception, few of the troops carried in the CBI were American.

In early 1942, the Japanese drove south and captured the Netherlands East Indies and the Malay Peninsula, in effect driving a wedge between what remained of Allied territory in the Pacific and East Asia to just a few miles from Australia in the south and to the Burmese border in the west. As the situation in the NEI deteriorated, Generals Brett and Brereton concluded that the route to defeat Japan lay in China, starting with the establishment of a large force of heavy bombers there. They proposed to General Marshall that the Allies should establish a large air force in India and China to wage war against the Japanese home islands and another in Australia to defend the Land Down Under. Japanese forces occupied part of China, mostly the coastal regions in the south, but much of the country was unoccupied. They proposed the construction of several airfields in China, combined with the buildup of a large air force in India to support an air campaign against Japan from Chinese airfields while also conducting operations against Japanese occupying forces in China proper. Another major concern was the defense of Australia. General Marshall notified the two generals that one would go to India while the other would return to Australia and the choice was up to them. Since Brett was already in command of US Army Forces in Australia, it was logical for him to go there and Brereton to India. In anticipation of Brereton's move, Tenth Air Force activated in the US but transferred to India a few days later.[68] His first task would be to develop a system of supply routes into China. At about the same time, Lt. Gen. Joseph Stillwell was ordered to India to command US military forces in the region.

---

[68] Military unit transfers are often mere paperwork. Such was the case in the transfer of Tenth Air Force.

Sam McGowan

Except for the Philippines, China was the one Asian country in which the United States had established a military presence prior to the war although the presence was entirely unofficial. In fact, it was what later came to be known as a covert operation. US neutrality laws prevented the assignment of military forces in the warring nations except in an advisory capacity but President Roosevelt got around the laws by allowing retired Air Corps Captain Claire Chennault to recruit a mercenary air force from Army and Navy personnel (including Marines.) Under the arrangement, men who volunteered to go to China were discharged from their respective branch of service regardless of whether they had fulfilled their commission or enlistment contract or not. They were then employed by a Chinese-American corporation with the initials CAMCO that had been organized in China in the 1930s by William D. Pawley of Curtis Aircraft.[69] The entire operation was covert, and was authorized by a confidential presidential executive order. Although the plan called for what were essentially two combat groups, one of fighters and one of light and medium bombers, only the fighter group had become operational by the outbreak of war. Tenth Air Force planned to absorb the two groups, which were unofficially known as the American Volunteer Group, and activate them as US Army air combat groups.

The supply lines to China were the longest in the world. With sea routes to China ruled out since the Japanese controlled the China Sea and much of the Pacific, the only means of getting supplies into the country was by rail from Rangoon in southern Burma, or by air from India to points on the Chinese border, where they could be loaded onto barges and trucks for the remainder of their journey. Just getting supplies to Burma and India was a major logistical problem. Ships had to take the long way around the Horn of Africa and up through the Indian Ocean, while the air routes that were eventually established also led east by way of Africa and the Middle East before finally reaching the Orient.

The China-Burma-India Theater covered a wide expanse of territory characterized by terrain that ranged from dense jungles to the lower reaches of the Himalayas, the highest mountains in the world[70]. India lay on one side of the Himalayas while China was on the other, with Burma to the south. Tibet is further to the west and Nepal

---

[69] The initials stood for Central Aircraft Manufacturing Company.

[70] The high Himalayas are actually some distance to the west of the route from India to China, in Nepal. The route used for the famous Hump Airlift, properly called the India-China Ferry, was across the lower reaches of the range where elevations are in the 15,000 foot range, around 1,000 feet higher than the Colorado Rockies.

Anything, Anywhere, Anytime

west of it. Until mid-1942, Burma was still in Allied hands, but after it fell to the Japanese the only safe way into China was over what would come to be known as "The Hump" out of India's Assam Valley. Air transportation would be America's sole line of communication with Allied forces in China for almost two years. Although the most direct route was across Burma, the threat of Japanese fighters led to the establishment of an indirect route northwest across the eastern reaches of the Himalayas then back to the southeast to Kunming and Chunking.

Transportation of supplies to China was a major Tenth Air Force responsibility; immediately after he arrived in Calcutta, Gen. Brereton was told to open up and maintain an air route out of India into China through Burma, which was still in Allied hands at the time. The Tenth Air Force chief of staff, Brig. Gen. Earl Naiden, was instructed to come up with a plan. Naiden determined that there should be two air routes in the CBI; one to bring supplies into India's Assam Valley from New Delhi and points west as far as Karachi, with another taking them out of the valley and into Myitkyina in eastern Burma, and ultimately on into the Chinese interior once the aircraft and crews were available to support such a route. Tenth Air Force came into being without any air transport resources of its own. The first transports in the region were ten Pan American Airways DC-3s working under the auspices of the Army Ferrying Command which were sent to India in preparation for the arrival of Lt. Col. James H. Doolittle's Tokyo Raiders. The Pan Am crews were dispatched to China from the Middle East, where they had been carrying supplies for the British, to haul 30,000 gallons of aviation fuel and 500 gallons of oil to China to service the B-25s so they could continue on to India. None of the raiders arrived in China in a flyable airplane so the DC-3s were turned to other chores when the first military transports arrived in India later in April.

The initial military air transport effort in the CBI began when Col. Caleb V. Haynes arrived in India with a squadron of B-17s and a few C-47s as Project *AQUILA*.[71] The crews believed they had been sent to India for a special mission to bomb Tokyo but the after affects of the Doolittle Raid and the impending Japanese conquest of Burma ruled out further attacks on the Japanese home islands. The B-17s were reassigned to the 9th Bombardment Squadron, which consisted of a handful of B-17s and a couple of LB-30s that had been brought to India from Java while the C-47s operated directly under Tenth Air Force

---

[71] *AQUILA* was the advance echelon for Brereton's Tenth Air Force, which had the mission of commencing a bombing campaign against Japan. They were to be joined by a larger force of B-24s under Col. Harry Halverson, but the B-24s were halted in the Middle East.

headquarters. Some of the pilots were older, field-grade officers and were not needed in the new bomber squadron. Since the *AQUILA* pilots were multiengine qualified, the older pilots were reassigned to transport duty and put to work supporting the Allied effort in Burma, with occasional trips into China. Colonel Haynes was placed in command of the Assam-Burma-China route with Col. Robert L. Scott, the author of the book *God is My Co-Pilot*, as his executive officer. Scott would eventually transfer to China to take command of the 23rd Fighter Group while Haynes would go back to bombers, but in the spring of 1942 they were transport pilots. Although fighter pilot Scott was less than enthusiastic about his new job – he referred to it as "insignificant" in comparison to his former mission of bombing Japan – he threw himself into his new task of flying supplies out of India and across the Himalayas to Burma and China.[72]

Immediately upon the arrival of the military transports, the crews were pressed into duty for an emergency effort to prevent Burma from falling into Japanese hands. After delivering their loads of ammunition, fuel and other supplies to Allied airfields in Burma, the transports returned to India carrying wounded soldiers and civilians who were being evacuated from territory in the line of Japanese advance. When it became apparent that Myitkyina and Loiwing were going to be captured, the Army pilots "threw away the book" and ignored published load limits for their airplanes to bring out the British troops. Pilots crammed as many people into their planes as they could then took-off, sometimes with more than seventy people aboard an airplane that had been designed for only twenty-four. At first, the Pan Am pilots were incensed that the Army pilots would be so reckless, but as they witnessed the incredible loads coming out of Burma without mishap, they also began carrying larger loads and threw their own best efforts into the task.

The situation in Burma was becoming even more perilous because the Japanese had occupied territory with airfields and brought in their own fighters and bombers. On one of their first missions, a Japanese fighter attacked a C-47. No friendly fighters were anywhere around. Scott was flying and Col. Haynes was in the copilot's seat.

---

[72] Scott's entire career had been spent in fighters. He was only in India because of a chance encounter with Marion Cooper at a cocktail party, Cooper, who had just been brought back into the Army, had hinted that he was going overseas on a secret mission and Scott managed to convince him that he should be a part. Scott and the other AQUILA pilots were convinced they were on a mission to bomb Tokyo and they were partially right. However, the transport missions they were flying had become even more important because they were supporting troops who would form the nucleus of the army that would eventually drive the Japanese out of Burma.

Anything, Anywhere, Anytime

Haynes went in back to grab a Thompson submachine gun to fight off the attack. Along with Col. Merian Cooper[73], a former World War I pilot, soldier of fortune and Hollywood movie producer who was on board, Haynes fought the attacker while Col. Don Old[74], dove the C-47 to the tops of the trees to keep the fighter from getting to them. Fortunately, the enemy pilot either gave up or lost sight of the transport because they eventually found themselves alone in the skies.

In spite of his temporary disappointment at not flying fighters, Scott praised the pilots of his squadron in his aviation classic *God is My Copilot*, referring to them as "the best transport pilots I have ever seen." One pilot, a Major Joplin, supervised the repairs on a damaged Pan Am DC-3 that had been belly-landed in a rice paddy then, after using a system of ropes and poles to move it to higher ground, flew the airplane out. Joplin often boasted that he was "born in a DC-2 and weaned in a C-47." After the retrieval of the written-off DC-3, Scott believed him!(Scott)

In mid-May, Haynes and Scott were on a mission together when they got word to leave immediately for Shwebo, a Burmese town on the Mandalay-Rangoon Railway, to evacuate General Stilwell and his staff. They flew south from Lashio through heavy thunderstorms, but managed to land at Myitkyina for fuel. After taking off again, they flew "as low as we could'" along the Myitkyina-Mandalay railroad into territory they knew was probably already in enemy hands. Although

---

[73] Cooper is a leading character of World War II in the Pacific. A bomber pilot during World War I, he was shot down and became a POW. He remained in Europe after the war and organized a group of mercenary pilots to fight the Bolsheviks in Poland and was captured again. After returning to the US he set forth on a life of adventure and became one of the first American documentary film makers. He created, produced and directed the movie King Kong, which was based on his own life. As a reserve officer, he returned to the Army Air Corps at the beginning of World War II and was sent to India as the project officer and intelligence officer for the AQUILA project, then was assigned to the Tenth Air Force staff. When Claire Chennault's American Volunteer Group was brought into the Army, Cooper went to China to serve as Chennault's chief of staff. Friction between Chennault, Cooper and Tenth Air Force commander Brig. Gen. Clayton Bissell led to his involuntary return to the US, where he told General Marshall that the senior US officer in the theater, General Joseph Stillwell, was a communist sympathizer and was doing more harm to the conduct of the war than good. Incensed at the comments, Marshall refused to allow Cooper to return to China and reportedly told him that he'd never see a promotion or decoration as long as he was in command of the Army. Exiled in Washington, Cooper was requested by General George Kenney for assignment to his staff, and he went to the Southwest Pacific and was assigned as chief of staff of V Bomber Command. When Marshall retired from the Army, Cooper was promoted to Brigadier General in the Air Force Reserve.

[74] Old, who was promoted to brigadier general, was a key figure in troop carrier operations in the CBI.

Sam McGowan

they encountered no fighters, they spotted a trio of Japanese bombers as they were circling over what they thought was Shwebo, looking for an airstrip a British pilot had told them was just southeast of town. Finally, they located their position on a map and realized they were ten miles north of Shwebo. They were told when they landed that Japanese fighters had been over the town only a few minutes before – the delay had saved them! As it turned out, the stubborn Stilwell refused to be flown out of Burma and stated his intention to walk out. Haynes and Scott considered knocking the recalcitrant general in the head and taking him out against his will but decided against the idea. Stilwell did walk out of Burma, but it took him several precious weeks to do it. As soon as he reached Indian territory, he called for a C-47 to pick him up.

Although the Allies put out their best efforts to save Burma, the Japanese ran the British out of Rangoon and occupied most of the country, except for the rugged Naga Hills on the Burma-Indian border and the northern mountains. However, even though the Japanese occupied the southern half of the country, British troops still controlled much of the northern half of the country, which is largely mountainous. In early July 1942, a force of British paratroopers jumped into Burma to investigate the military situation in the Myitkyina area than march overland 150 miles to Fort Hertz, a British installation in the northeast corner of the country. At the time, there was no communication with the fort and its status wasn't known. In early August the paratroops reached the fort, and discovered that it had been occupied by British and Burmese troops.

Fort Hertz had an airstrip but when the British reestablished contact with the fort, they learned that it was unusable. A party of British airborne engineers jumped into the fort the day after contact was established to refurbish the airstrip. Within a week, the strip was useable for transports. The British paratroops who had jumped into Burma in July were flown out after they were replaced by British Indian Army and Burmese troops. With communications reestablished, Fort Hertz became a base for British intelligence gathering patrols. The airstrip served both as a delivery point for supplies flown into Northern Burma as an emergency landing strip for aircraft operating over the area. Later in the war, American and British troops trained Burmese troops at the fort.

Anything, Anywhere, Anytime

Chinese troops awaiting transportation

Another project that departed for India was *AMMISCA*, an abbreviation for "American Military Mission to China." *AMMISCA* included a force of twenty-five C-47s that had been appropriated from the airlines and manned by pilots who were mostly recalled Army reservists who had been employed as airline pilots before the war. The new unit had been formed at Pope Field, North Carolina under presidential orders to operate a "ferry'" of supplies into China. It was designated as the 1st Ferrying Group. The pilots and crews had been trained under the auspices of the Ferrying Command and the Ferrying Command commander, Brigadier General Robert Olds[75], protested when General Brereton insisted that all transports assigned to his area be assigned to Tenth Air Force. Olds' objection was based on the premise that if the transports were assigned to Tenth Air Force, they would be diverted to combat operations from their primary duty of flying supplies to China. Brereton protested that such an arrangement was a violation of Army doctrine and that the unit would require massive support and security from Tenth Air Force and should thus be part of it. Arnold agreed with Brereton, at least in principle, and Olds was overruled.[76] When it arrived in India, the 1st Ferrying Group came

---

[75] General Olds was the father of Vietnam fighter commander Col. Robin Olds.

[76] General Henry H. Arnold was commander of the US Army Air Forces, but had no direct command over air commanders in the field. Air commanders reported

Page 90

under Tenth Air Force control and went into training at Karachi where Brereton had set up theater orientation training units. It wasn't until June that the group became operational. Their presence was extremely valuable because Tenth Air Force only had a small transport organization equipped with thirteen Pan Am DC-3s and Army C-47s before they arrived, and the military situation in the region had become desperate.

After the fall of Burma, the major Tenth Air Force mission was simply keeping the Japanese out of India, while at the same time keeping Allied forces in China and northern Burma alive and supplied. India itself was threatened by Japanese invasion and troops were stationed along the Burmese border to prevent it. The 1st Ferrying Group had been sent to India specifically to ferry cargo to China, but tactical considerations often led to diversions to support combat operations. A China Air Task Force was established under Brig Gen. Claire Chennault with a few personnel and the airplanes of the old American Volunteer Group after it became part of the Army in July 1942. The CTAF was supplemented by a newly arrived medium bomber group equipped with twin-engine B-25s.[77] Supporting the CATF was a logistical nightmare. After Burma fell, every drop of fuel, every bean, every bullet and every bomb used by Chennault had to be flown into China over the Himalayas from India. At the same time, the 1st Ferrying Group was also responsible for transporting supplies for the Chinese military. The India-China Ferry the group began was to become the major logistical air operation of the war, and the most publicized. However, it was not a combat operation.

In addition to the 1st Ferrying Group, the China National Aviation Corporation, owned in part by Pan American, operated a civilian airline in China and carried cargo under military contract. CNAC had actually begun the air ferry under contract to Tenth Air Force while the 1st Ferrying Group was undergoing training at Karachi. As efforts to develop a military air cargo route into China got off to a slow start, Gen. Stilwell conceded to a Washington-derived plan to give CNAC responsibility for all flights from India to China. This move released

---

to the theater commanders, who reported to Chief of Staff Marshall. However, Arnold also occupied seats on the Allied Combined Staff and the US Joint Chiefs, and in that capacity exercised some control over aviation units overseas, although his role was primarily in an advisory capacity. The Ferrying Command, however, and the Air Transport Command which followed it, were directly under USAAF and thus under Arnold's personal command.

[77] The loss of Doolittle's B-25s severely delayed medium bomber operations in the CBI. A number of pilots on the mission remained in China after the raid rather than returning to the US as Doolittle did.

Anything, Anywhere, Anytime

the US Army transports for combat operations in northern Burma and in defense of India. After some initial balking on the part of the Chinese, Stilwell finally secured their agreement to abide by US wishes regarding the ferry. When Burma fell, the US Army transports returned to missions to China while continuing to support combat operations in India east of the Assam Valley and in northern Burma, where Chinese and native troops under British command maintained outposts.

Prior to the fall of Burma, flights from Assam to Kunming could be made at low altitudes, with the transports stopping for fuel at Myitkyina airfield. With much of Burma in Japanese hands, the transports were forced to fly a more northerly route across the southern reaches of the Himalayas to avoid interception. The really high mountains were hundreds of miles to the west but the 15,000-foot elevations in the foothills were still as high as the North American Rockies. The heavily laden transports required significantly more fuel to climb to the altitudes needed to cross the mountains. The sudden temperature changes as the transports rose from the steamy humidity along the Brahmaputra to the sub-freezing temperatures over the mountains were hard on airplanes and crews alike. Frequently changing weather in the mountains often brought reduced visibilities in snow and rain in clouds that were lower than the mountain peaks. Storms caused violent turbulence. Some transports were not equipped for instrument flying while there was little instrument maintenance available for those that were. The summer monsoon season brought heavy rains to the Assam Valley which caused more problems for both flight and ground crews. To make matters worse, there just weren't enough airfields in Assam Province in 1942 to accommodate the volume of transport traffic needed to maintain the desired flow of supplies. There were few suitable emergency landing strips in the region the transports flew across. And, there weren't enough transports.

The problem of lack of air transport in the CBI was compounded when Tenth Air Force was ordered to transfer some of its assets – including much of its transport capability – to the Middle East to support the British in June 1942. The transfer was sudden and immediate, and came about as a result of the defeat of British forces at Tobruk in Libya's Western Desert. General Brereton received a message from the War Department ordering him to leave for temporary duty in the Middle East immediately, and to take every available heavy bomber and as many transports with him as were necessary to make the move. Elements of the 1st Ferrying Group had just arrived in India and Brereton took some of the group's C-47s with him. He and the B-17s that went with him ended up staying in the Middle East. Most of the transports returned to India after several weeks of operations in support of the British in western Egypt. In spite of the reduction in air transport capability, Tenth Air Force was expected to keep up with the supply demands of China, a responsibility that was rarely met until the final months of the war when a larger effort could be devoted solely to Hump air transport operations. Throughout 1942, the ferry to China failed to live up to expectations, although when the monsoon ended in the fall, tonnage levels began increasing.

CNAC maintenance facility

Just as Tenth Air Force was beginning to get a handle on the China operation, General Stilwell received word that the mission was to be taken over by the recently created Air Transport Command. Back in Washington, the ATC chief of staff, Colonel C.R. Smith, the former president of American Airlines, had suggested to General Arnold that ATC should be given the mission because Tenth Air Force "lacked singleness of purpose." Because ATC was not controlled by the theater command, Smith, whose background was in business and who had no significant military training or experience, reasoned that his command could do a more effective job by devoting all of its attention in the region to the China Ferry operation. While Smith's logic seemed sound, the reality of the situation in the theater was far different than that assumed by the ATC staff. Tenth Air Force was concerned with preventing the Japanese from occupying India, particularly the region where its transport airfields were located. Smith found ammunition for his proposal in the form of a letter written by a civilian war materials company executive who visited the region. The company was concerned because the condition for its China sales was that they would be paid for only on delivery and the transit delays were costing the company money.

The assumption of the ferry operation by ATC was actually a violation of the orders under which the USAAF had been formed. The USAAF mission was stipulated as procuring aircraft and supplies

Anything, Anywhere, Anytime

unique to the air force and providing trained combat units for overseas duty. It did not include theater operations which were a responsibility of air forces under theater command. The India-China Ferry was a theater operation and should have been under the theater commander. The ATC was a USAAF organization controlled directly from Arnold's headquarters in Washington. The transfer was justified by ATC's status as a non-combat logistical organization responsible for overseas deliveries of cargo from the United States. As it turned out, the arrangement presented considerable problems.

The 1st Ferrying Group was transferred from Tenth Air Force to Air Transport Command[78] control for the ferry operation in early 1943 while two troop carrier squadrons, the 1st and 2nd, were organized in India for combat operations. Both squadrons transferred, on paper, from their Stateside bases where they had been serving as training squadrons, and were staffed and equipped with personnel and airplanes already in the theater supplemented by new arrivals from the United States. ATC started the India-China ferry with the 1st Ferrying Group's C-47s but they were soon replaced by larger, faster Curtis C-46s and a dozen Consolidated C-87s flown by contract crews from American Airlines, C.R. Smith's own company.[79] A cargo version of Consolidated's B-24 Liberator bomber capable of carrying 10,000 pounds, the C-87 featured four turbocharged engines and a payload twice that of a C-47. With the increased payload of the larger transports, tonnage levels over the Hump should have increased immediately; instead they actually declined. The initial ATC monthly goal was 4,000 tons but it was not until August 1943 – more than eight months after ATC assumed control of the air ferry – that the goal was finally met. In June 1943, six months after ATC took over the operation, only 2,200 tons were carried. Yet at the same time using smaller DC-3s, CNAC was carrying substantially more cargo over the same route as ATC, yet with fewer airplanes. The newly organized troop carrier squadrons also exceeded ATC tonnages on their own missions into China from India.

Part of the blame for the ATC failure was due to a lack of adequate airdrome facilities in Assam to accommodate the necessary transports. Other problems stemmed from design deficiencies in the C-46, which led to their eventual grounding for modification. However, the fact that CNAC was lifting twice the tonnage per plane over the same route in

---

[78] 1st Ferrying Group was inactivated and replaced by an Air Transport Command "Army Air Forces Airbase Unit." Airbase units were established at ATC bases all over the world to handle the command's transports and provide services such as maintenance and handling of cargo and passengers.

[79] This was clearly a conflict of interest considering the role Smith had played in getting the mission transferred to ATC but the War Department let it go.

their DC-3s caused the chief of the Air Staff, Maj. Gen. George Stratemyer, to visit the CBI to take a look at the operation. World War I ace Eddie Rickenbacker, the president of Eastern Airlines, accompanied Stratemyer.[80] Rickenbacker and Stratemyer determined that the problem lay in the relative inexperience of the ATC pilots, few of whom were military trained[81], coupled with shortages in other personnel areas and a lack of sufficient airfields to handle the mission. Low morale was also identified as a problem, especially when the performance of the ATC crews was compared with that of recently arrived troop carrier crews who flew under the same conditions in the same region of the world. While the troop carrier pilots and crewmembers took readily to their task, the ATC crews seemed lost in a fog. Rickenbacker departed from the conventional wisdom of his peers in airline management and recommended that control of the ferry be removed from ATC and placed back under the theater command, a view shared by Tenth Air Force commander Brig. Gen. Richard Bissell. Instead of following his recommendations, the ATC leadership resorted to political maneuvering in Washington to fight it and kept control of the operation. (Craven & Cate, 1956)

Although Tenth Air Force was relieved of responsibility for the logistical mission over the Hump, X Troop Carrier Command assumed other, more militarily important, duties. Scattered throughout western China and northern Burma were several Chinese and British ground units operating far beyond the limits of ground supply. Furthermore, the rugged terrain and lack of roads and railroads in the region made ground transportation nearly impossible. While the Japanese never seemed to grasp the potential of air supply, the Allies slowly came to realize that it opened up a new set of possibilities as a line of communications. As early as 1941, the British had used airplanes to move troops from India to Iraq. During their failed Burma Campaign, the RAF's 31 squadron flew supplies to Rangoon and evacuated refugees and casualties while the meager *AQUILA* and Pan American force did likewise further north. Prompted in part by General Kenney's

---

[80] During an earlier inspection trip, Rickenbacker's B-17 ran out of fuel and ditched in the Pacific Ocean. Rickenbacker and the surviving crew members survived three weeks at sea in a life raft before they were finally spotted and rescued.

[81] ATC relied heavily on "service pilots," men with considerable civilian flying experience who were brought into the Army and given pilot ratings based on their previous flyiung experience. Their duties were limited to non-combat operations, including aircraft ferrying and transport operations. Since they had been recruited based on their previous flying experience, they were older than the military pilots who adapted more readily to the austere conditions in which they lived.

Anything, Anywhere, Anytime

efforts in New Guinea, the Allied command in the CBI soon recognized the importance of their air transport resources.

C-87 transport, built using B-24 airframe

For the troop carrier crews, a mission into either northern Burma or China meant crossing the same mountains that the ATC crews were crossing except they were crossing further south, closer to the Japanese airfield at Myitkyina. They then dropped down to low altitude over terrain that was often occupied by Japanese ground forces to drop supplies into remote drop zones that were nearly impossible to find. When there was an airfield available that was not in enemy hands, the troop carriers landed with their cargo. Their efforts were essential to the conduct of the war in the region, both because of terrain and natural obstacles and because the Japanese had occupied much of the country. In September 1943, Gen. Stratemyer, who had recently assumed command of the CBI Army Air Forces units, wrote Major Gen. Barney Giles who had taken his place as chief of the Air Staff that; "the only way we can supply any force that advances into Burma is by air. We MUST have troop carrier squadrons!"

Sam McGowan

C-46s were capable of substantial payloads but they were plagued with design problems

For some reason, Tenth Air Force was slow in organizing its own troop carrier operations and no troop carrier units were transferred intact to the region from the US until early 1944. Until February 1943, the 1st Ferrying Group was directly under Tenth Air Force and was responsible for most of the air transport operations in the region but there were also independent provisional units under Tenth Air Force control. One of the conditions for the transfer of the 1st Ferrying Group to Air Transport Command control was that Tenth Air Force would receive its own troop carrier assets. However, instead of transferring squadrons from the United States, the Army organized two squadrons in the theater and gave them the designations of existing units. Both squadrons dated back to the mid-1930s when they were part of the 10th Transport Group, with the 1st Transport Squadron operating out of Wright Field, Ohio while the 2nd was at Olmsted Field, Pennsylvania. After the outbreak of war, the two squadrons became responsible for training new troop carrier personnel as part of I Troop Carrier Command and moved to Pope Field at Ft. Bragg, North Carolina. In early 1943, the designations were given to the new squadrons that organized in India with existing personnel and aircraft. Although they were assigned to Tenth Air Force, the two squadrons were sometimes attached to Air Transport Command for operations into China until ATC resources in the region were built up.

Anything, Anywhere, Anytime

During the late spring and summer of 1942, Tenth Air Force transports flew supplies into northern Burma to support retreating Chinese troops. When Japanese forces halted their advance south of Fort Hertz, the fort's garrison was supplied entirely by air when ground resupply efforts failed. Transport crews airdropped supplies to remote aircraft early warning stations deep in the Burmese hills. In early 1943, General Stilwell realized that Chinese troops operating in the Naga Hills could not be adequately supplied by either native porters or with pack mules and ordered Tenth Air Force to mount a supply effort. He was aware of the importance of air transport to the recent Allied advances in New Guinea so he instructed Tenth Air Force to keep British and Chinese units in his theater supplied.

By the end of 1943, air transportation had become a way of life for Allied forces in the CBI. In December, Eastern Air Command was established as the command and control organization for all Allied air forces in the region except the ATC units, which were independent of theater control. Within the EAC, an Allied Troop Carrier Command was formed to integrate American and British squadrons into a single command. American Brig. Gen. William D. Old was designated as commander and given responsibility for providing air transportation for airborne and air transit forces and other land and air forces involved in operations in Burma. Old was a veteran of transport operations in the theater dating back to early 1942 when he had been part of the AQUILA force.

In February 1944, the 443rd Troop Carrier Group was established at Sylhet, India. Like the two squadrons which preceded it, the 443rd designation transferred from the United States and was given to a new unit that was organized from assets already in the CBI. The 1st and 2nd Troop Carrier Squadrons became part of the 443rd, along with the 27th and 315th, which also transferred to India from the US in name only. Additional air transport came to India in the form of the 3rd Combat Cargo Group, which activated at Sylhet in early June when a contingent of C-47s and C-53s arrived from the US as Project *BOND*. The group was organized to command four new squadrons formed from the *BOND* aircraft and personnel. The new group's leadership, including at the squadron level, came from the 443rd TCG. Three additional combat cargo groups, the 1st, 2nd and 4th, had begun training in the US.

The new combat cargo squadrons were basically the same as a troop carrier squadron except they had fewer support personnel and the crews weren't trained for large-scale paratroop operations. They were evidently formed as a means of gaining additional air transport capability while maintaining the number of authorized troop carrier units that had previously been mandated by Congress. A troop carrier squadron, the 319th, was also part of the 1st Air Commando Group, a special operations unit that activated in India in early 1944.

The 1st Air Commando Group, which was originally designated as the 5318th Provisional Air Unit, was the outgrowth of a meeting held in Quebec in August 1943 when President Franklin Roosevelt met with British Prime Minister Winston Churchill. British Brigadier Orde Wingate attended the meeting as did Lord Louis Mountbatten, who had just been appointed commander of the South East Asia Command. Earlier in the year, Wingate had led his "special force" of British Empire troops that had been recruited in India on a long-range mission into Burma. Wingate's "Chindits" were supplied by air by American and British transports during the expedition but had no means of evacuating wounded. The expedition met with mixed success and Wingate returned to England to lobby for increased support. He was invited to attend the Quebec Conference with Churchill. Wingate presented his plan for an aerial invasion of Burma to President Roosevelt, who was intrigued by the idea of long-range teams operating behind enemy lines. The British brigadier convinced Roosevelt of the need for US air support, and the president told General Henry H. Arnold to give him whatever he wanted.[82]

What Wingate wanted was essentially his own air force; a force to be made up of transports and gliders to move his men into battle along with fighters and medium bombers to provide air support. He also sought a means of evacuating his wounded by air. Arnold picked two of his staff officers, Lieutenant Colonels Philip Cochran and John Alison, to form the new organization and sent them to London to meet with the British. Both men were capable officers with considerable combat experience. Cochran had served in North Africa as a fighter squadron commander until the previous June and had participated in the first US special operation the previous year. Although he was a fighter pilot, Cochran flew the lead airplane in a two-airplane element of C-47s on a flight to drop paratroops whose mission was to blow up a key railroad bridge. Cochran went on the mission because he knew the location of the bridge after having attempted to destroy it by dive-bombing. As it turned out, he dropped the troops on the wrong side of the bridge and they spent several hours marching in the opposite direction before they realized the mistake. Although they managed to blow up the bridge, most of the paratroops were killed or captured. Cochran's squadron, the 58th Fighter Squadron, carried out "guerrilla air warfare" from an advanced base at Thelepte, Tunisia in December 1942. Alison also had an impressive record. He had previously served in China with Col. Robert L. Scott in the 23rd Fighter Group. Both men were capable leaders and eager to put together an air force that would

---

[82] Mountbatten also met with Arnold and advised him of the need for additional air power in his theater. He would later say that he never asked for specially trained units; he merely wanted additional combat squadrons.

meet Wingate's expectations. Immediately after they received their new assignment, they departed for London to meet with the British and determine how their new unit should be organized and equipped.

The new unit initially consisted of sections rather than squadrons: one bomber, one fighter, one liaison and one troop carrier. Since Wingate intended to rely on gliders to insert his men into enemy-occupied territory, Cochran and Alison placed heavy emphasis on glider training for themselves as well as for their men. They evidently also introduced a new concept by training a certain number of glider pilots to act as controllers once they were on the ground to bring in the rest of the force. General Arnold mentions this new technique in an article he wrote about the group for National Geographic. They may have borrowed this technique from the British when they visited the UK to discuss glider tactics when the group was forming. The liaison section was equipped with Canadian-built single-engine UC-64 Norseman transports capable of landing on short, unimproved runways to deliver supplies and evacuate casualties. In March 1944, the group was redesignated as the 1st Air Commando Group and the sections became squadrons, with the troop carrier section becoming the 319th Troop Carrier Squadron.(Arnold, 1944)

319th TCS C-47 over The Hump

The 1st and 2nd Troop Carrier Squadrons were already involved in the resupply of Allied forces which had remained in northern and western Burma after the fall of Rangoon, but their workload was slated to increase. In January 1944, British troops moved into the Arakan region of Burma and also required aerial resupply. In early February, the British force was cut-off, leaving 22,000 troops with only two days rations. The emergency led to the temporary transfer of 25 C-46s from the ATC India-China Ferry force to Troop Carrier Command to assist with the resupply effort. Japanese opposition was intense, both in terms of antiaircraft and fighter attack. In spite of the opposition, the American and British troop carriers pressed on with their mission, escorted by fighters from III Tactical Air Force. The airdropped supplies kept the British troops in the battle; by the end of February the attacking Japanese had been beaten back. Commanders in the region were quick to give credit for the success of the operation to the Troop Carrier Command.

UC-64 Norseman

While the battle was taking place in the Arakan, Brigadier Wingate was training his Special Force, an elite unit made up of highly trained British Empire and Indian troops who would win fame as "Chindits." Wingate's troops were trained for long-range glider penetrations deep into Japanese territory. To support the Chindits, the US Army Air Forces committed the 5318th Provisional Air Unit, the new organization commanded by Col. Phillip Cochran with Col. John Alison as his deputy. The group operated a mixed bag of aircraft, including B-25s, P-51s and light liaison aircraft as well as a troop carrier section of C-47s and WACO gliders. The liaison section even had a few helicopters for search and rescue. Air transport was a major responsibility of the provisional unit; Cochran's crews were responsible for towing Wingate's gliders into Burma, keeping the far-

Anything, Anywhere, Anytime

ranging troops supplied then evacuating them by air when their mission was over. However, once the aerial invasion of Burma commenced, Troop Carrier Command bore most of the burden.

Glider Troops in Burma

On March 5, 1944, Wingate's troops penetrated Burma in a gliderborne operation into a landing zone identified as *BROADWAY* in Operation *THURSDAY*. The success of the glider mission can only be termed as dubious. The first gliders to land encountered ditches, logging roads and water buffalo wallows that ripped off their landing gear. Out of seventy-seven gliders dispatched, only thirty-two landed on *BROADWAY,* and all of those were so badly damaged that only three were ever recovered. Nine gliders landed in enemy territory, nine others in territory held by friendlies, and two were never heard from again while fifteen turned back to their takeoff points after the first arrivals reported the field unsuitable for landings. Nevertheless, 539 men, three mules and 65,972 pounds of cargo were landed, including heavy construction equipment and runway lighting materials. Within twenty-five hours, the Special Force had constructed a 5,000-foot runway. Once the field had been leveled, reinforcements began arriving in C-47s. Over the next five days, troops, cargo and mules were brought in aboard C-47s and additional gliders.

Once they were on Burmese soil, the troops of the Special Force were solely dependent upon aerial resupply. The American 27th and 315th squadrons and the RAF 117 Transport Squadron were responsible for the effort, most of which involved airdropping supplies to the advancing columns. To prevent the Japanese from detecting the supply drops and pinpointing the Chindit positions, all missions were flown at night without fighter escort with the transport crews maintaining radio silence to avoid detection. The ground forces identified the drop zones with fires, flares and radio homing signals sent out by GP 1083 direction finder sets that could be picked up by the C-47s. To keep the enemy from triangulating their positions, the signals were not activated until fifteen minutes prior to drop time.

Burma is often touted as the first "aerial invasion" by Allied forces but it really wasn't. American and Australian troops had invaded the Markham Valley on the Lae Peninsula the previous September. Both operations also involved ground troops, although the British troops who walked into Burma are often glossed over. The Special Force's efforts were also undermined by a Japanese invasion of India that started immediately after the operation was launched. Japanese troops crossed the Chindwin River on March 9, and advanced toward Imphal, where Wingate had his headquarters and resupply and reinforcement missions originated. Supplies for Wingate's Special Force were delivered to Imphal then delivered by air to Burma. Fortunately, the Japanese ran out of supplies and were forced to retreat without overrunning the Allied air bases but the threat was enough to cause Wingate to evacuate his headquarters to Slyhet, an Indian town more than 100 miles to the west. The troop carriers were resupplying both the Special Force and the British troops fighting just east of Imphal.

Along with Wingate's Chindits, a special American force was also assigned to the CBI. Commanded by Brig. Gen. Frank Merrill, the 5307th Composite Unit would become famous as "Merrill's Marauders." The 5307th performed valuable duty in Northern Burma, where they were solely dependent on air transport for their resupply once they walked out of India into Burma. In fact, the Marauders were more successful than the THURSDAY force, which failed to accomplish its objective of capturing Myitkyina. The 5307th was also supported by the 71st Liaison Squadron, a unit staffed by mostly enlisted pilots who flew Stinson L-5s to pick up wounded when C-47 landings weren't possible. With both the Chindits and the Marauders depending on air transport, practical considerations led to Troop Carrier Command involvement, with both the provisional air unit and conventional troop carrier squadrons sharing the burden of operations in Burma. Control was divided, with the provisional unit responsible for glider operations and Troop Carrier Command having charge of transport. (Craven & Cate, 1956) The provisional unit P-51 and B-25 crews were also trained for resupply missions. Precious water was delivered to the

Anything, Anywhere, Anytime

long-range forces in drop tanks carried by fighters while B-25 crews parachuted supplies to teams on the ground.[83]

Troop carrier strength in the CBI was temporarily bolstered in early April with the arrival of the American 64th Troop Carrier Group from the Mediterranean, with its 4th, 16th, 17th, 18th and 35th squadrons. The British 216 Transport Squadron was also brought into the CBI from the ETO. The additional troop carrier forces remained in the theater throughout the Chindit operation in Burma, providing vastly increased air transport capability and allowing time for arrival of Project *BOND* and the activation of the 3rd Combat Cargo Group.

C-47 dropping to Merrill's Marauders near Myitkyina

Air transport of reinforcements into Burma continued. On the night of March 24, advance elements of 14 Brigade were flown into a just-constructed airstrip designated as *ABERDEEN*. The entire brigade was on the ground in Burma by April 4. In early April, troop carrier and provisional unit crews flew the West African 3 Division into Burma, while 16 Brigade came in overland from Ledo after starting their trek in February. General Wingate was killed in the crash of his personal B-25 in late March and was replaced by his subordinate, Maj. Gen Walter D.A. Lentaigne. Although the operation met with limited success, the primary mission objective of isolating the Japanese 18th division and capturing Myitkyina was not accomplished. Special Force

---

[83] The use of bombers to deliver cargo was common in both the Asian and European theaters.

units were never closer to the important airfield than fifty miles. Withdrawal of the force by air began on April 29 but some elements of the Special Force remained in Burma until well into August.

When the Chindit operation ended, the mission for which the provisional unit had been formed ended with it. Wingate was dead and the British had lost their enthusiasm for deep penetration missions. The Chindits withdrew to India and were retrained to become an airborne regiment. The provisional unit was redesignated as the 1st Air Commando Group, but it was soon broken up with its squadrons operating under the respective Eastern Air Command fighter, bomber and troop carrier commands. Col. Cochran went back to Washington for debriefing then went to England to join the First Allied Airborne Army staff. Alison also went back to the US to debrief then went to Florida to organize a new air commando group. He then went to the Southwest Pacific to join General George Kenney's staff. A second air commando group went to the CBI and a third to the Southwest Pacific, but neither ever functioned in the role for which they had been envisioned. Their troop carrier squadrons operated under the local troop carrier organization.

An innovation that Allison and Cochran introduced – they may have got it from the British – was the use of highly qualified troop carrier pilots to go in on the first glider with radio equipment to advise pilots on conditions at the landing zones. Cochran evidently recommended the practice to Brereton because combat controllers, as the pilots were called, were used in Europe during airborne and glider operations in support of British Field Marshall Montgomery's crossing of the Rhine the following March.

While the Chindits were operating in south Burma, "Merrill's Marauders'" were engaged in similar operations in the north. They would succeed where THURSDAY failed. Like the Chindits, the rugged Marauders – most were veterans of combat in the jungles of New Guinea and Guadalcanal and the rest had served and trained in Panama – were entirely dependent upon timely airdrop for their sustenance and resupply throughout the campaign as they penetrated more than 800 miles into Burma on foot. After accomplishing the first of their goals, the cutting of Japanese supply lines into northern Burma, the exhausted, under-nourished, diseased and demoralized Marauders learned that General Stilwell had other plans for them. The THURSDAY force had failed and was being withdrawn so Stillwell decided to use the Marauders in their stead. His plan was for them to march overland and capture the airstrip at Myitkyina and then the town itself once they were reinforced by Chinese troops, who would be brought in by air. Wingate's Special Force was supposed to have captured the airfield and town, but never reached it. The closest the Special Force came to Myitkyina, their main objective, was fifty miles.

Anything, Anywhere, Anytime

Exhausted, demoralized and suffering from various jungle maladies, with some soldiers on the verge of collapse, the Marauders set out through the Burmese jungle on a march of some sixty-five miles in jungle-covered mountainous terrain.

Evacuating injured glider pilots from Burma

The Marauders succeeded in capturing the airfield and securing it for C-47 landings on May 17, but the attack on the town itself turned sour when the Chinese troops became confused and their confusion turned to panic.[84] Stilwell was forced to turn the attack on the town into a siege, while still depending entirely upon air resupply to maintain his lines of communications. He feared that the monsoon rains would prevent the transports from landing but the rains were late that year and even when they did come and the airfield turned into a sea of mud, the C-47 pilots continued landing. The resupply effort was costly, with as many as a dozen transports lost at Myitkyina as a result of accidents caused by the muddy landing strip. The siege lasted until August 1944, when the town finally fell into Allied hands. The surviving Marauders were worn out. After a rest, they became the foundation for a new American unit called the MARS Brigade. The Marauders and the MARS Brigade were the only American ground combat troops to serve in the CBI. They were also supplied by air when they went back into Burma, this time to stay.

---

[84] Most of the British troops had already been withdrawn from Burma by this time.

Sam McGowan

According to the official US Army Air Forces history of World War II, "the most significant feature of the campaigns in Burma in early 1944 lay in the air transportation of large bodies of troops and their sustenance by air supply." (Craven & Cate, 1956)

Just as they were in New Guinea and everywhere else during the war, when the CBI troop carrier crews were not involved in combat operations, they were put to work in logistical flying, which in the CBI usually meant flying the Himalayan Hump. Except for missions from Karachi, all CBI air transport work involved some Hump flying. After ATC took over the India-China Ferry, the troop carrier squadrons were based further south in the vicinity of Sylhet and later 100 miles to the east around Imphal, leaving the Assam Valley bases for ATC since they were closer to China. The higher Himalayan peaks were much further north in Tibet and Nepal but the Naga Hills east of the Assam averaged 10,000 feet, with some peaks as high as 15,000. It was into the Naga Hills on the Indian/Burmese border that many of the troop carrier missions were flown, delivering supplies to Chinese and British troops who had retreated there from Burma. The high altitudes made flight operations very dangerous, especially for the C-47s, which were the mainstay of troop carrier operations. The C-87s and C-46s had turbocharged engines and were designed for high altitude operations but C-47s were low altitude aircraft.

Loading mule for Burma

While the mountains presented formidable obstacles and the threat from Japanese planes made all operations very dangerous, the threats were compounded by the difficult terrain below and the uncertainty of the loyalties of the indigenous personnel with whom a

Anything, Anywhere, Anytime

downed airman might come into contact. China and Burma were filled with many tribes of differing loyalties. Many were bandits, men who were as likely to kill a downed airman for the gold in his teeth as to deliver him to safety. In spite of the dangers, the troop carrier crews in the CBI soldiered on, flying their assigned missions in some of the most difficult terrain in the world, and doing so without recognition and with few comforts. Such is troop carrier life!

Sam McGowan

Chapter Five - "The Pacific"

While General Kenney's Fifth Air Force was turning the tide of war in New Guinea and Tenth Air Force was supporting Allied operations in Burma, a third campaign was underway in the South Pacific. Across the Solomon Sea from New Guinea lie the Solomon Islands, a chain of islands with names like Guadalcanal, New Georgia and Bougainville, all names that would soon become household words in the United States as the Allies began wresting them from Japanese control an island at a time. Further to the east were other island chains, the Gilberts and the Marshalls, which had Japanese garrisons ranging in size from a few troops to thousands. However, unlike operations on Papua New Guinea, where combat operations were heavily dependent on troop carrier squadrons to provide mobility and resupply to ground forces, Central and South Pacific forces could be supported by surface ships. However, even though it was limited, troop carrier squadrons played a role in the island campaigns.

Under the original war plan for the Asiatic-Pacific Theater, the theater was divided into three separate areas, the Pacific Ocean Area, the Southwest Pacific Area and the Southeast Asia Area. The Pacific Ocean Area was further divided into three areas – the North Pacific Area, the Central Pacific Area and the South Pacific Area. Because the POA consisted mostly of water, it was placed under Navy command with Admiral Chester Nimitz as the Commander in Chief. However, Southwest Pacific consisted mostly of land so an Army commander was appointed, General Douglas MacArthur. The most southern region of Nimitz' POA, the South Pacific Area, lay east of a line that ran to the east of Guadalcanal, but since there were no significant land masses and few Japanese in the South Pacific east of the line of demarcation between MacArthur's Southwest Pacific Area of Operations and Nimitz' Pacific Ocean Area, the Joint Chiefs shifted the line a little to the west so that Nimitz would have a role to play. Consequently, Guadalcanal shifted to Nimitz while the rest of the Solomons remained in MacArthur's area of responsibility.

The South Pacific was still mostly ocean but the Japanese had occupied the Solomon Islands and Guadalcanal. Although the islands were almost 1,000 miles from Australia, Guadalcanal was far enough to the south that Japanese aircraft could operate from there against the Allied supply lines that stretched from the American West Coast and Hawaii to Brisbane. Nimitz conducted a few small scale operations in the Gilberts before he was given permission to invade Guadalcanal and interrupt Japanese plans to use it as a major air base. The relatively

Anything, Anywhere, Anytime

small landmass of Guadalcanal and the other islands ruled out the need for air transportation to provide mobility for the ground forces, who slogged their way ashore from landing craft during amphibious landing operations. The same landing craft could bring in supplies from ships anchored offshore. Nevertheless, troop carrier squadrons had a role to play in Guadalcanal, the Solomons and other South and Central Pacific locations, even if they were not involved directly in combat as they were in New Guinea and the CBI.

Flight nurse and medic tending patients

Once airfields that had been built by the Japanese had been captured and secured, Army, Navy and Marine Corps transports began operating into them. However, instead of delivering reinforcements and supplies for the soldiers and Marines that had landed from the sea, their role was primarily logistical support of the air combat squadrons that moved onto the airfields to provide air cover and close air support for ground troops. A major objective of the Guadalcanal landings in August 1942 was the capture of the airfield, which was still under construction. It was named Henderson Field after a Marine aviator killed at Midway and used to establish a US aviation presence on the

Sam McGowan

island. Because the initial Guadalcanal invasion was a Navy and Marine Corps operation, the first aircraft to arrive were Marine fighters, but they were quickly joined by Army P-39s and P-400s. Whenever fighters and bombers arrived at a forward airfield, at least a portion of their resupply needs were often met by transports, usually C-47s or the Navy version, the R4D. Transports also brought in their mechanics and other support personnel.

There was one important role the transports could provide for the ground forces; the evacuation of casualties. Transports came in to island airfields with aircraft parts and other logistical supplies and returned with casualties. The Navy had hospital ships offshore, but air transport allowed the removal of the more serious casualties to rear area hospitals hundreds of miles to the south of the action.

No troop carrier squadrons had been formed in the South Pacific, so C-47s and their crews, who were on their way to Fifth Air Force in Australia, were often held in the South Pacific Area for transport duty. The 33rd Troop Carrier Squadron was on its way to Australia when it was notified to give up six airplanes and their crews for a month's duty flying out of New Caledonia carrying supplies and personnel to Guadalcanal. The detachment was heavily involved in air evacuation of casualties from the fierce fighting on the island.

Guadalcanal was secured in early 1943 and Nimitz obtained permission from MacArthur to continue operations in the Solomons which extend northwest from Guadalcanal to Bougainville.[85] Under the terms of their agreement, South Pacific forces would move north through the Solomons Chain while Southwest Pacific troops moved northward on New Guinea and eastward on New Britain, a large island in the Bismarck Archipelago that is part of Papua New Guinea. Once the Solomons had been secured, South Pacific air and ground forces would assist Southwest Pacific forces in an attack on Rabaul, a city on New Britain with a large natural harbor that the Japanese had turned into a major supply base. Some troop carrier missions involved providing navigation for flights of Army and Marine fighters on long overwater flights between islands. In addition to troop carrier C-47s, the Navy and Marine Corps had their own transport squadrons and it wasn't long before they established a presence in the Pacific War.

Like the Army, the Navy Department depended on modified airline-type aircraft for its transports. The most prevalent was a variation of the versatile Douglas DC-3, which the Navy designated as the R4D. The Navy also operated a number of amphibious transports and flying boats, including Martin PBM Mariner and four-engine Mars.

---

[85] Nimitz' area of responsibility was the Pacific Ocean Area, which did not include the Solomons, which were in MacArthur's Southwest Pacific Area. Nimitz' area was primarily open ocean with a few islands large enough to be occupied.

Anything, Anywhere, Anytime

When the Douglas C-54 came into use in the Army's Air Transport Command, a number were transferred to the Navy where they became R5Ds. Navy and Marine Corps transport operations were almost entirely logistical.

Flying in the Solomons and in support of other Pacific operations was almost entirely logistical, which is not to say it wasn't dangerous. Japanese fighters were active in the area and they made no distinction between transports on logistical missions and those involved in direct combat operations. Forward airfields were often within Japanese artillery range and sometimes snipers came close enough to pick off the occasional crewmember or mechanic. The islands themselves, except for the larger ones around New Guinea and in the Philippines, were too small to require the kind of deep penetration missions that would have required the extensive parachute resupply that proved so valuable in New Guinea and Burma. Troop carrier operations in the Central and South Pacific were mostly in support of air combat squadrons and evacuation of casualties.

39th TCS C-47

In January 1943, the 13th Troop Carrier Squadron arrived in the South Pacific and was assigned to Thirteenth Air Force, which had activated a few weeks previously. For the next eight months, it operated as an independent squadron. Until August, it was the only troop carrier squadron in the theater. Two additional squadrons arrived in August, the 63rd and 64th. In September, more than six months after combat ended on Guadalcanal, the 403rd Troop Carrier Group arrived in the South Pacific and joined Thirteenth Air Force as the command organization for transport operations from its base on Espiritu Santo. The South Pacific was a Navy area and troop movements and resupply were from the sea. The 403rd was a troop carrier unit, but its operations were primarily logistical and evacuation of casualties at the time. Its squadrons operated throughout the South Pacific and also to Australia, New Zealand and New Guinea. Army, Marine and Navy fighter squadrons operated as close to the lines as possible. The fastest means of bringing in aircraft parts and other supplies was by air. Troop carriers took wounded and other patients to rear area hospitals on their return flights.

After the capture of Bougainville in late 1943, Generals MacArthur and Kenney convinced the Joint Chiefs to disband the South Pacific Area since it was no longer needed and transfer Thirteenth Air Force into a new theater air force consisting of it and Fifth Air Force. Kenney was given command of the new Far East Air Forces. Even though it became part of the FEAF, the 403rd Troop Carrier Group did not join the 54th Troop Carrier Wing, a Fifth Air Force organization. It was instead assigned to XIII Service Command and served primarily as a logistical transport group supporting Thirteenth Air Force combat groups. Later in the war, the 403rd entered combat operations in support of operations in New Guinea from its new base on Los Negros in the Admiralties. The group moved to Biak in what is now Indonesia then to the Philippines where it was initially based on Leyte. 403rd TCG C-47s dropped a platoon of paratroops as part of the operation to free civilian internees at the camp at Los Banos in February 1945. The group remained in the Philippines after the war until October 1946, when it inactivated.

Army flight nurse posing by C-47 in South Pacific

Anything, Anywhere, Anytime

No troop carrier groups were assigned to the Central Pacific Area until January 1945 when the 419th TCG activated on Guam. However, the group had no squadrons or aircraft assigned and was primarily responsible for operating air terminals in the Marianas. The group was also responsible for air rescue operations in the Central Pacific. Air transport in the region was provided by Navy and Marine squadrons, by the Army Air Transport Command and by Twentieth Air Force intrinsic units.

One area of the Pacific where troop carrier operations are often overlooked is Alaska and the Aleutians. Early in the war, the Japanese occupied some small islands in the western Aleutian Islands, a chain west of Alaska that stretches nearly all the way to Japan where they become the Kuriles. In the spring of 1943, the Allies began a campaign to recapture the primary islands of Attu and Kiska, which had been occupied in June 1942, in conjunction with the attempted invasion of Midway. Along with B-24s and fighters, the Eleventh Air Force in Alaska included two troop carrier squadrons, the 42nd and 54th. Throughout the Aleutian campaign, the two squadrons provided the same air transportation services characterized by their peers elsewhere in the world. On flights originating from Elmendorf Field outside Anchorage, the two squadrons delivered an average of 7,500 tons of freight and 15,000 passengers to bases throughout the Aleutians in support of combat operations although they were not involved in combat themselves. Eleventh Air Force C-47s flew air evacuation missions bringing casualties out of Attu as soon as a suitable strip was opened.[86]

After the Japanese abandoned Kiska, ground combat operations in the Aleutians came to an end. However, there were a number of airfields and naval bases along the island chain and the two troop carrier squadrons provided logistical support for the units based on them. In 1944, the 42nd TCS was inactivated and the 54th assumed all transport duties in the Alaska Area other than those assigned to the Air Transport Command. There were B-24, B-25 and US Navy PV-1 squadrons operating from Attu and other islands along the Aleutians Chain. The 54th TCS supported them by bringing in supplies from Alaska. Although ground combat in the theater had ceased, there was still a need for air evacuation flights from the remote islands.

Flying in the Aleutians was as difficult as anywhere in the world, including the Himalayas. Although the temperatures in the islands are usually right around freezing in the winter, the climate is characterized by frequent rain and fog caused by the cool air moving over the warmer waters of the Pacific. Frequent high winds added to

---

[86] The Japanese abandoned Kiska after Allied troops landed on Attu.

the hazards. The 54th TCS also operated across Alaska, where extreme cold was one more factor that the airmen had to deal with. Fortunately, after the capture of Attu and Kiska, they didn't have to contend with the threat of enemy action.

While the Solomons and Aleutian campaigns were very important to the overall war effort and the role of troop carrier crews was consequential, the Pacific War was pretty much a naval show, and resupply and troop movements were by sea. It was in the Southwest Pacific and the CBI, where there were large landmasses, that the transport airplane was crucial to the conduct of the war. Largely thanks to the resourcefulness of the Fifth Air Force transport crews in 1943, the New Guinea Campaign – and therefore the war in the Pacific – was well in advance of the planned schedule in early 1944. General Kenney's successful airborne assault on Nadzab allowed the Allies to catch the Japanese at Lae in a pincers movement and secure Papua New Guinea, although the entire island would not be free of Japanese until the end of the war. As a result of the Allied victory in New Guinea and the loss of Guadalcanal, Japan moved its line of defense several hundred miles northward. MacArthur's strategy was to defeat the Japanese in the eastern half of the island and establish bomber bases further and further north toward the Philippines, and ultimately Japan, a strategy that came to be known as "island hopping." The western half of New Guinea and the Netherlands East Indies would be bypassed and left to Australian troops to mop-up, while the Americans continued moving north toward Japan. The new strategy was developed by MacArthur's headquarters to isolate Japanese garrisons in eastern New Guinea with air and sea power rather than invading them. Some naval historians have attempted to give credit to the Navy, and use the term to describe the Pacific Ocean Area's campaigns in the western Pacific to capture islands such as the Marinas for airbases. However, the term was originally used for MacArthur's strategy of bypassing Japanese facilities such as Wewak and leaving the Japanese forces to "wither and die on the vine," to use the words of General George Kenney. Instead of advancing steadily northward and capturing each Japanese position, Allied troops instead moved around locations that weren't considered important to MacArthur's plans and landing further north. For example, Wewak was bypassed in the spring of 1944 and no effort was made to capture it until that November.

By bypassing Japanese strongholds such as Wewak, MacArthur was able to continue moving the Allied lines further and further north, and closer to the Philippines. The largest Japanese airfield in New Guinea was located at Wewak, but Kenny had identified suitable terrain for new airfields further north which eliminated the need to take needless casualties to capture it. The Allies had gained air and sea

Anything, Anywhere, Anytime

superiority in the Southwest Pacific so supplies could be delivered by sea. However, troop carrier operations remained an important part of Allied strategy.

Australian troops continued pressing the remaining Japanese in New Guinea while Allied air and sea power severed Japanese lines of supply. The Allied successes in New Guinea and the Solomons caused the Japanese to begin retreating northward away from Australia although strong forces remained in isolated pockets such as Wewak. Kenney convinced MacArthur to bypass the Japanese stronghold at Rabaul and isolate the defenders with air and sea power. There was still much to accomplish in the Southwest Pacific as the Allies moved their line further and further northward toward the Philippines. As he had done in his earlier campaigns in New Guinea, MacArthur continued to rely heavily on the advice of his chief airman and to depend on the abilities of the troop carrier squadrons to deliver troops into combat and keep them supplied.

Douglas Aircraft was turning out thousands of brand new C-47s and C-53s in its factories in Long Beach, Santa Monica and Oklahoma City. More than 5,000 were built in Oklahoma City alone but only a fraction were going to the Pacific. The majority were equipping the new troop carrier squadrons that were being trained in the I Troop Carrier Command but hundreds were being supplied to the British under Lend-Lease. The RAF bought more than 2,000 of the more than 10,000 produced while others went to the Soviet Union. Others were being kept in the United States for ATC's Domestic Wing. Dozens of new troop carrier squadrons were equipping and training, but the Air Staff planned to use them primarily in the European Theater where the Army intended to assign the new airborne units that were also in training. Occasionally, the Air Staff would let a squadron go to the Pacific, but MacArthur's Southwest Pacific Area of Operations was mostly getting the dregs of aircraft production and very few new units. Consequently, the 54th Troop Carrier Wing was forced to continue relying on the war-weary transports and castoff bombers with which the 21st and 22nd squadrons had begun the war. Due to the shortage of transports, heavy and medium bombers were frequently called on for transport duty.

General Kenney appreciated the contributions of his troop carrier crews, and fumed over the lack of adequate replacements for those lost in combat and those just simply worn out from the rigors of combat flying in the theater. In a dispatch to General Arnold in which he expressed the need for more troop carrier personnel, Kenney voiced his appreciation for the work of his crews and his frustration at requiring them to continue in combat past when they should have been given a rest:

"In the case of troop carrier crews, I figure that I can get five hundred hours of New Guinea operation out of them. It is asking a lot, for the figures show that between weather and Nips, a man lives longer in a P-39 then he does in a C-47 flying the troop carrier supply runs in New Guinea. These kids get a hundred hours a month, so that if I replace them at the five hundred hour mark I will need twenty per cent per month for that reason alone, instead of the seven and a half per cent per month your staff has promised me. The replacement rate per month for troop carriers should be twenty-five per cent. The Troop Carrier Group working between Australia and New Guinea is averaging over one hundred hours per month per crew. The great part of their haul is over the 750-mile overwater hop from Townsville to Moresby on schedule – which they keep regardless of weather. I don't know how much of the grind they can take but with a replacement rate of seven and one half per cent I cannot think of sending them home before fifteen hundred hours."

As a result of Kenney's pleading dispatch, Arnold authorized the assignment of additional troop carrier resources to his command.[87] However, they were far less than Fifth Air Force needed for the job it was doing. From the beginning of air transport operations in MacArthur's theater, transport units used whatever they could find that could fly and wasn't suitable for combat operations. The menagerie of cast-off combat planes, appropriated civil transports and the few C-47s and C-53s that had been on their way to the Philippines when war broke out continued to serve in the 54th Troop Carrier Wing well into 1944. The worn-out airplanes had logged thousands of hours, often without proper maintenance, by the time they were finally replaced.

Kenney was continually frustrated at the lack of support for his theater by the Air Staff in far away Washington, DC. A few weeks after Pearl Harbor, President Roosevelt and British Prime Minister Winston Churchill agreed on a policy of "Germany first" for the prosecution of the war. Britain had promised to defend Australia but Churchill was depending on the United States to provide the manpower and equipment for the task, using units that had previously been intended for the defense of the Philippines. In fact, all of the original combat units in Australia were groups that were either in the Philippines or on their way when war broke out. It wasn't until late 1942 that any units were sent to Australia that hadn't been earmarked for the Philippines. No transport units had been earmarked for Australia so the Allies had

---

[87] Although he was commander of the USAAF, General Arnold had no direct say in combat operations in that capacity. However, the USAAF was responsible for determining where the units it trained were assigned, and requests for combat groups and replacement aircraft and personnel went through him.

Anything, Anywhere, Anytime

to depend on what it could find in the theatre. Gradually, the assortment of aircraft was supplemented and eventually replaced by new C-53s and C-47s delivered from the US, but new transports were slow in coming. It wasn't until October 1942, when the 6th and 33rd Troop Carrier Squadrons departed for a classified destination, that any new troop carrier squadrons were sent to the Southwest Pacific. They were joined a few months later by the four squadrons of the 317th Troop Carrier Group but the six new squadrons were hardly enough to meet the needs of the theater. Even though MacArthur and Kenney were making good use of the troop carrier squadrons under their command, priority for new C-47s and troop carrier personnel was given to groups intended for duty in the European Theater. Kenney made his first trip to Washington in early March 1943, and one of his requests was for more troop carrier squadrons.

Yet, in spite of the lack of airplanes and trained crews, Fifth Air Force troop carriers were performing valuable service throughout the theater. It was largely because of the mobility provided by troop carrier squadrons that the war in the Southwest Pacific progressed much faster than the Allied planners had expected. In 1942 when President Roosevelt ordered MacArthur to leave Corregidor and proceed to Australia to take command of Allied forces, the Combined Chiefs were only expecting him to fight a holding action to prevent the Japanese from capturing Australia. It was his decision to put the line of defense in Australia, and it was General George Kenney's grasp of the use of air power, including air transport, that allowed him to move the line northward. The Air Staff and the Joint Chiefs took notice of Kenney's success and began assigning more combat units to the Southwest Pacific, including additional troop carrier squadrons and groups. Eventually, the 54th Troop Carrier Wing commanded four troop carrier groups along with a combat cargo group. Troop carrier strength in the Southwest Pacific was far less than in the ETO but, in many respects, Fifth Air Force troop carriers were more effective.

By early 1944, the air force in the Southwest Pacific was made up of two numbered Air Forces, Fifth and Thirteenth. Thirteenth Air Force had initially been established to service the island campaigns in the South Pacific but, as the war moved further north and west, the South and Southwest Pacific commands merged under General MacArthur's command. The two air forces were merged into the new Far East Air Forces, with General Kenney as commander. Air transport strength had increased substantially, with the 54th Troop Carrier Wing now controlling four groups, the 317th, 374th, 375th and 433rd. Thirteenth Air Force also included the 403rd, with its 13th, 63rd, 64th, 65th and 66th squadrons. In the fall of 1944, Fifth Air Force received the 2nd Combat Cargo Group and its four squadrons, some of which flew Curtiss C-46s. Previously, C-46s had been assigned exclusively to the Air Transport

Sam McGowan

Command. Fifth Air Force also received the 3rd Air Commando Group in late 1944. The air commando group included a troop carrier squadron.

Combat cargo groups were authorized in the spring of 1944. They were basically the same as a troop carrier group, except that their flight crews weren't trained for large-scale airborne operations as their peers in troop carrier units were. They were also scaled down somewhat in terms of support personnel since they were intended to operate from airfields in forward areas. It is unclear just why they were formed but it is likely that they were established as a new type of unit to get around the Congressional limits on numbers of troop carrier groups and squadrons. Three combat cargo groups became operational during the war, two of which served in the CBI while the 3rd CCG was in the Southwest Pacific. Troop carrier transports were a regular sight in all areas of the war but in the Southwest Pacific they continued to figure prominently in Allied strategy. General MacArthur had come to rely on air transportation to move his forces forward in his quest to return to the Philippines, as he had promised he would do when he left. "I shall return" had become MacArthur's motto and Bataan was his byword. In fact, when he was finally given a C-54 for his personal transportation, he named it "Bataan." MacArthur would return to the Philippines, and it was to a large extent due to the 54th Troop Carrier Wing's squadrons that he was able to make good on his promise.

C-47 flying low over Army camp

Rabaul, a city in northeastern New Britain, had been the major Japanese base in the region until late 1943, when the Japanese moved their defensive line further north. Built around Simpson Harbor, a natural harbor that offered anchorage for large ships, Rabaul was both

Anything, Anywhere, Anytime

a logistical and advanced base for Japanese forces operating in New Guinea and the Solomons and was the major target for Fifth Air Force bombers throughout 1942 and 1943. Original Allied plans had been for an amphibious landing to capture the city and the natural harbor around which the complex was built, but as the Allies defeated the Japanese in New Guinea and the Solomons, MacArthur changed his mind. Instead of capturing it, he decided to bypass the complex in view of the fact that its usefulness to the Japanese had been effectively neutralized by the FEAF, Marine Corps squadrons in the Solomons and Navy carrier aircraft. In early 1944, Rabaul was assigned to the Air Solomons Command and Fifth Air Force devoted its attentions elsewhere. The Japanese decided to abandon their attempts to reinforce and supply the garrison and left the defenders more or less on their own. Southwest Pacific forces had captured most of New Britain, leaving Rabaul as an isolated stronghold in the middle of Allied territory.

Yet even though Rabaul was bypassed, the complex remained under constant air attack, which created a need for air rescue. To provide safe havens for Allied aircrews coming off of Rabaul in shot-up airplanes and gather intelligence, Australian commandos patrolled in the vicinity of the Japanese stronghold. The long-range patrols were supplied by the 54th Troop Carrier Wing's special airdrop unit, which had been equipped with B-17s that had been replaced in the combat squadrons by B-24s. Still carrying some of their armament, the B-17s were better suited for operations in close proximity to Rabaul than the unarmed C-47s. Drop zones were picked by Australian intelligence officers based on information they received by radio from the long-range patrols. The B-17s flew unescorted due to the necessity of maintaining a low profile.

Although part of the 54th TCW, the special unit was under the operational control of the 308th Bombardment Wing, a command organization which had been set up specifically for special missions that were beyond the scope of conventional combat operations. Commanded by Col. David W. Hutchinson, the mission of the 308th was to plan and conduct missions such as the command of shore parties that went in along with ground troops on amphibious operations to set up airstrips. Once the beachhead was secure enough for aircraft operations, Hutchinson commanded air combat operations from airfields that had just been captured or constructed. Hutchinson's 308th wing served as the FEAF combat element in forward areas until combat wings moved up. The wing had no assigned groups of its own but groups from other wings were attached to it during operations from forward areas. The 3rd Air Commando Group was assigned or attached to the 308th when it arrived in the Southwest Pacific, as was the group's 318th Troop Carrier Squadron.

After the capture of Lae, the Allies' next objective was the invasion of Cape Gloucester on New Britain, an operation that was heavily dependent on air transport for reinforcement and resupply. Initial plans called for an airborne operation by the 503rd Parachute Infantry Regiment but the drop was cancelled and the paratroopers landed from the sea. In preparation for the Cape Gloucester operation, the Allies launched an amphibious attack on Arawe on the opposite side of the island. When resupply by sea failed after enemy fire sank twelve out of fourteen boats, the Allies turned to aerial resupply. Instead of being delivered by transports, the bundles were dropped by B-25s and a single B-17. The delivery of supplies to forward areas by bombers wasn't uncommon for two reasons. First, there was a shortage of transports. Second, B-24s and B-25s carried guns and could defend themselves against air attack. They could also strafe Japanese ground positions during and after the drop.

The landing on Cape Gloucester took place in late December 1943. On January 3, work was begun on the airfield. By the end of the month, a pierced-steel planking runway 4,200 feet long had been laid.[88] A C-45 was the first airplane to land. The next day the first C-47 landed, beginning a steady stream of transports arriving with badly needed supplies. As was his pattern, Kenney made maximum use of his troop carriers to bring in the materials needed to establish forward bases for his fighters and bombers. In many – if not most – instances, FEAF troop carrier planes landed and offloaded their precious cargo even while fighting was still going on within gunshot range of the airfield. Troop carrier crews continued to airdrop supplies to the advancing ground forces as they moved inland away from coastal bases.

After the capture of Cape Gloucester, MacArthur sent his troops to Los Negros in the Admiralties. The invasion took place in late February 1944, with the seizure of a Japanese airfield as the first objective. As soon as the airfield was captured, the airstrip was prepared for C-47 landings. On March 2, crews from the 317th Troop Carrier Group dropped supplies to the construction team. The mission included B-25s from the 38th Bomb Group. A single B-17 was also part of the operation. The 317th Troop Carrier Group, which had only recently returned to combat operations after several months of logistical flying in Australia, was still flying some of the decrepit transports and bombers with which the 21st and 22nd squadrons had begun the war two years before. Some of the older transports and war-

---

[88] Pierced steel planking, commonly called PSP, was officially called Marston or Marsden Matting. It consisted of sections of steel planking with large holes drilled into it to reduce weight. The planks were linked together and laid down on graded ground to produce runways and parking areas on forward airfields.

weary bombers were assigned to other groups as well. Two B-17s from the 375th Troop Carrier Group dropped medical supplies, ammunition and barbed wire.

The objective for the 1st Cavalry Division was Momote Airfield on Maus Island. As they moved inland, heavy fighting broke out and depleted the cavalrymen's ammunition supply. An emergency resupply was mounted using the armed B-17s of the 54th Wing special airdrop section. The B-17 crews dropped their loads in the center of the airfield then came back around to strafe the Japanese positions on the other side of the field so recovery teams could retrieve the bundles.

On March 2, a B-17 crew from the 433rd group's 69th TCS encountered Japanese fighters as they approached the island on a drop mission and a running gun battle took place. The pilot, Flight Officer Ralph G. Deardoff, turned for the harbor and the protection of the guns of several destroyers that were lying just offshore. His gunners shot down one of the fighters, the first credited to a troop carrier crew. After the remaining fighters left, Deardoff returned to the airfield and spent fifty-five minutes dropping supplies. By March 8, the airfield was secure enough for transports to begin landing. On March 13, thirty-three C-47s from the 317th TCG brought in almost 218,000 pounds of supplies. March 27 saw 54th Troop Carrier Wing crews fly 615 sorties carrying over 2.7 million pounds of cargo.

After the Admiralties came Hollandia, a region in Dutch New Guinea that seemed suitable for an airfield and anchorage for ships. On April 22, 1944, Allied troops landed in Hollandia and began advancing toward several airfields. Again, air transport played a major role in the overall operation. As soon as the airstrips were in friendly hands, 54th Troop Carrier Wing C-47s began landing with reinforcements and supplies for the infantry, then bringing up support personnel and equipment for the fighter squadrons that arrived as soon as the fields were serviceable. As the troops moved inland, they often advanced beyond their lines of supply and required aerial resupply.

The importance of aerial delivery and the lack of transports often led to the diversion of combat aircraft to the transport role. On April 26, B-25s from the 17th Reconnaissance Squadron dropped rations and ammunition to the 21st Infantry at Dazia. The following day, twenty-three B-24s and forty-three B-25s dropped rations for the engineers working on the airdrome at Hollandia. By April 28, the field had become operational and the first C-47 landed the next day. On May 4, the 41st Troop Carrier Squadron transferred to Hollandia and went to work flying supplies to the rapidly advancing ground forces as they moved into the interior.

Aerial delivery of supplies was very important on the New Guinea coast because the jungles were so dense and most open terrain was covered by swamps, which ruled out most ground resupply. In the case of Hollandia, the resupply of the engineers working on the airfield from the air allowed the surface supply effort to be devoted to the ground forces engaged in capturing the region. As soon as the airfield was readied for aircraft, C-47s began arriving with supplies and taking out casualties on their return to their bases.

With Hollandia in Allied hands, General MacArthur continued his conquest of the Japanese forces still remaining in New Guinea. His strategy was centered on the use of air transport to move his lines further and further north, establishing air bases for the FEAF bomber and fighter groups as quickly as ground could be taken. As soon as an airfield was captured or built, troop carriers brought in ground personnel and supplies for combat air groups. Air transport was crucial to the entire concept – first to support the advancing ground forces with resupply and reinforcement, then flying supplies to the engineers, and finally bringing in the support personnel and supplies for the arriving combat squadrons. Casualty evacuation continued to be a major troop carrier role as C-47s and C-60s that had been reconfigured to carry stretchers flew wounded and sick American and Australian troops to rear area hospitals.

Loading casualties

By 1943, air evacuation of casualties had become a major troop carrier mission. Initially, casualties were simply loaded onto the

Anything, Anywhere, Anytime

airplane in piecemeal fashion, in litters if they were available or simply loaded onto the floor if they were not. As it became apparent that using airplanes to move patients to rear area hospitals greatly reduced deaths from wounds and sickness, the Army Air Forces authorized the development of equipment to carry litters and began training medical personnel to tend to patients. Yet even though the first medical personnel completed the school at Bowman Field, Kentucky in early 1943, it was almost year before the first ones arrived in the Southwest Pacific. As with everything else about the war, the European Theater had priority and the first medical personnel went to North Africa. Yet even though there were no trained medical personnel to keep watch over them, troop carrier crews were picking up patients at forward airfields and returning them to hospitals in rear areas.

The first medical crews assigned to the Southwest Pacific arrived in Australia in late 1943; they were soon put to work on flights coming out of forward areas. On March 25, 1944, two flight nurses, Lieutenants Josephine Wright and Frances Armin, landed at Los Negros in the Admiralties on an air evacuation flight. They were the first nurses to penetrate so deeply into contested territory. Oddly enough, medical crews were assigned to flight operations in the Alaska Area, where there were few combat casualties, several months before any went to the Southwest Pacific where the air evacuation mission had actually started in mid-1942. With the assignment of trained medical personnel to the 54th Troop Carrier Wing, patients could receive medical care while in flight. In addition to battlefield air evacuation, the 54th Troop Carrier Wing set up medical evacuation flights to hospitals in Australia.

The 54th continued to operate regular logistical flights from New Guinea to Australia. Other flights operated around Australia. When the war moved further north, additional routes were added between the new airfields in northern New Guinea and Port Moresby, then on to Australia. Logistical operations were originally the responsibility of the 374th TCW but when the 317th arrived, it assumed the mission. Over the course of the war, groups and squadrons rotated back to Australia for a rest during which crews operated logistical routes into the combat zones in New Guinea then further north as the war moved northward into the Philippines. Return flights often operated as air evacs and transported patients to hospitals in Australia.

By the spring of 1944, troop carriers had been operating in the Southwest Pacific for more than two years. When MacArthur arrived in Darwin, the situation in Australia was in doubt. Senior Australian officers had decided to establish a defensive line about midway down the Continent but MacArthur changed the line to Papua New Guinea. In January 1943, the Allies defeated the Japanese at Buna, thanks in no small measure to Fifth Air Force troop carriers then moved north to capture Lae later in the year. The airfield at Nadzab, which was captured by airborne troops, was turned into a major airfield that served heavy bombers, light and medium bombers, fighters and troop carriers. Fifth Air Force heavy bombers were striking at Rabaul as well as northward along the New Guinea coast. MacArthur was moving ever closer to his promised return to his beloved Philippines.

Fifth Air Force strategy was to capture land along the New Guinea coast and then use it to establish bases for its heavy bombers, which by early 1944 were all B-24s. The older B-17s had become obsolete and since B-24 production was reaching phenomenal levels, the Air Staff decided to replace them with the longer-range Liberators. As they were replaced, the B-17s were converted to transports. Some were plushed up for VIP transports. Kenny convinced MacArthur to bypass Japanese strong points and leave them to be cut off from sea supply and neutralized by airpower. US troops were doing the same thing in the Solomon Islands. The original plan to capture Rabaul had been changed. Instead of waging a costly campaign to capture it, the Japanese stronghold would be bypassed and isolated with air and sea power.

After Hollandia, MacArthur's forces invaded Biak Island and penetrated deeper into New Britain. Troop carriers supplied advanced patrols by airdrop. By this time, aerial delivery had been refined to a science as new bundles had been developed and a system of colored parachutes to identify the contents had come into wide use. Red was used for ammunition, blue for water and green for fuel while other colors were used for other commodities.(Alternatt, 1945) At Biak, an emergency aerial resupply brought in shoes to replace those that had been quickly worn out by the island's coral surface.

In late June 1944, the Allies invaded the New Guinean island of Noemfoor. Inadequate intelligence made the Allies uncertain of enemy strength on the island, so just in case there were more Japanese than expected, the 503rd Parachute Infantry was held in reserve in Hollandia, as close as they could possibly be to any potential trouble spots. The invasion went off without a hitch and the Allied troops progressed beyond all expectations on D-Day. After the invasion, the task force commander, Brig. Gen. Edwin D. Patrick, received false reports which led him to believe that as many as 3,500 to 4,500 Japanese were on the island. Patrick called for an airborne reinforcement, to begin on July 3. As it turned out, they weren't needed. Elements of the 503rd loaded aboard 317th TCG C-47s on the morning of July 3 and departed for the drop zone, the airstrip at Kamari, in the first airborne operation in the theater since Nadzab. When they arrived, the pilots found the runway obscured by smoke that had been laid down by A-20s and B-25s to hide the descending paratroopers from the Japanese. The smoke made the drop difficult

Anything, Anywhere, Anytime

because the pilots couldn't see the runway and weren't able to determine the proper release point. Most of the troops drifted past the airstrip and landed among construction debris and parked vehicles. Almost ten percent of the force was injured in the jump. The next day, the 317th dropped the troops properly and nearly every paratrooper landed on the drop zone. The vehicles had been moved further from the runway and were not a problem. However, since the previous day the engineers had been working on the airstrip and the dirt runway had been packed to a consistency roughly that of concrete. Numerous injuries led to a cancellation of the drop planned for the next day. The remaining paratroopers were instead flown to nearby Biak and brought to Noemfoor by boat.

Paratroops landing at Noemfoor

The landing on Noemfoor and nearby Sansapor brought the long New Guinea campaign to an end. It had been a long campaign. The former Air Transport Command began operations supporting Australian troops on the massive island in mid-1942 and troop carriers had been playing a major role in Allied strategy since that time. With most of the island in Allied hands, MacArthur was free to carry out his vow to return to the Philippines.

General MacArthur's next objective was to fulfil the vow he had made to the Filipino people when he left the Philippines – at the order of President Roosevelt – more than two years before in March 1942. While MacArthur was deadset on returning to the Philippines, the Navy had other ideas; its senior admirals felt the islands should be bypassed in favor of a landing on Formosa (present-day Taiwan.) A great controversy ensued between the Army, in this case General Douglas MacArthur, and the Navy, led by the Chief of Naval Operations, Admiral Ernest J. King. Both men possessed strong personalities and both were convinced that his plan was the only way to win the war. But MacArthur held a trump card – the Philippines were an American possession and the Filipino people were, at least in principle if not in citizenship, Americans. Furthermore, thousands of Americans, both military and civilian, were in prison and internment camps in the Philippines as well. MacArthur felt that their liberation should take precedence over an invasion of a Japanese island (Formosa had become a Japanese possession at the turn of the century.) In the end, President Roosevelt agreed with MacArthur.

The Navy's plan seems illogical when considering Formosa's location and the military situation in the Western Pacific. Formosa lies north of the Philippines and southwest of Japan itself. The Ryuku Islands, which include Okinawa, are to the east and China is to the west. If Allied troops had attempted a landing on Formosa, they would have been caught between three Japanese strongholds and their supply lines would have been threatened. The nearest Allied bases would have been in the Marianas more than 1,400 nautical miles away. There were no Allied airbases within B-24 range and the B-29 force in the Marianas wouldn't become operational until November. Furthermore, the island was out of range of troop carrier aircraft.

The plan Roosevelt approved was to use Southwest Pacific Area forces to liberate the Philippines then use them as a base for military operations further to the north against the Ryukus and, eventually, the Japanese homeland. Nimitz' Central Pacific forces would move northward along the Pacific islands and invade the Marinas. A factor in the decision to capture the Marinas, which had been both Japanese and American before the war, was that the Allies would be liberating an American territory. Most of the islands had belonged to Japan but Guam was American. However, the primary reason for capturing the Marianas was to establish bases for the new Boeing B-29s. Twentieth Air Force's XX Bomber Command had begun operations against Japan from bases in China, but the situation was a logistical nightmare. All supplies had to be flown to the advanced bases in China from India. In

Anything, Anywhere, Anytime

the Marianas, supplies could be delivered right to the proposed airfields by ship.

There was another reason to liberate the Philippines before attempting to capture Japanese possession such as Taiwan; although there were Filipinos who saw the Japanese as liberators, large numbers saw them as enemies. A large resistance movement had developed in the islands as former Filipino soldiers and American officers and enlisted men who had gone into the hills became organized. MacArthur's headquarters was in close contact with the guerrilla officers, and an effort was made to supply them. MacArthur initially saw the guerrillas as a source of intelligence and discouraged military action since the Japanese were better armed and equipped. In anticipation of the invasion, the guerrillas were authorized to undertake small-scale operations and sabotage.

It is unclear if troop carriers played a role in the resupply of the guerrillas in the Philippines prior to the planned invasion. Initially after their fall, the Philippines were too far from Allied territory for the airplanes of the day to make the round-trip from Australia. From 1942 to mid-1944, supplies were delivered primarily by submarine. The capture of Noemfoor put the Allies within C-47 range of the southern islands and it's possible that missions were flown in support of guerrillas on Mindanao and other southern islands.

In preparation for the invasion, Far East Air Forces was beefed up with new squadrons and airplanes. Along with more fighters and bombers, the reinforcements included additional transports and replacements for those "kids" who had been doing so well since early 1942. One C-47 was reputed to be the tenth of the type purchased by the Army Air Corps; by early 1944 it had flown more than 2,000 missions. To reinforce the troop carrier squadrons, the War Department promised to replace the older C-47s with new C-46s. The larger C-46s afforded more cargo carrying capacity but they were more difficult to maintain. They were also more susceptible to damage from ground fire as will be noted in the chapter on operations in the ETO. (The first C-46s arrived with the 2nd Combat Cargo Group, but the group didn't arrive in the theater until November 1944, several weeks after the Leyte landings. It was based on Biak and flew mostly logistical missions around the theater.) Additional air transport support would be provided by Air Transport Command C-47s, which would be operating in the rear areas of the theater, thus relieving the troop carrier squadrons of logistics duties and releasing them for combat operations. This was within the ATC mission statement, which restricted the command's airplanes from operations in hostile areas. Since the war had moved north, New Guinea was no longer hostile except for isolated pockets such as Wewak. ATC transports had begun direct deliveries to Far East Air Forces bases in New Guinea as well as to Australia, where major maintenance and depot facilities remained. ATC's Ferrying Division continued delivering new aircraft from the United States. RAAF transports were providing support for Australian forces.

The original plan called for invasions of both Leyte in the central Philippines and Mindanao, the southernmost island, a plan that would have severely strained the resources of FEAF's troop carriers. After intelligence reports indicated that Japanese strength in the southern Philippines was light, MacArthur's planners decided to bypass Mindanao for a landing further north on Leyte and consequently cancelled many of the planned airborne operations. No airborne operations were planned in conjunction with the Leyte invasion. The Allies landed on Leyte on October 20, 1944; within four days, air force ground personnel had landed by sea and had constructed runways in preparation for the arrival of the first transports and combat aircraft. They were members of a special battalion commanded by Lt. Col. Paul I. "Pappy" Gunn. Troop Carrier Command flights began landing at Tacloban as soon as the strip was able to receive them. The first troop carriers to land were eighteen C-47s that came in on October 31. The first to land was a 375th TCG C-47 flown by the group commander, Col. Joel Pitts. Their loads consisted of personnel and equipment for a fighter squadron that was being brought in from further south. A team of air cargo specialists from the 21st Service Group was part of the initial move. Their role was to supervise the offloading of the transports and the distribution of their cargo.

The landings at Tacloban ended the World War II career of the now-legendary P.I. "Pappy" Gunn, who had been promoted to lieutenant colonel. In preparation for the invasion, General Kenney gave Gunn command of a special battalion of Air Corps personnel who were to function as a commando force. The airmen, who were mostly aircraft maintenance personnel, would land with the invading force and occupy Tacoloban airfield as an advance force and set it up for the arrival of Army fighters and light bombers. Gunn put the troops through a course of combat training, including hand-to-hand combat. Just when he actually went ashore himself is unclear. General Kenney wrote that Gunn proposed that he be landed by submarine in advance of the invasion to organize Filipinos to work on the airfield and unload supplies. Kenney implied that he disapproved the request but one thing is clear, when US troops came ashore at Tacloban, Pappy Gunn was waiting for them with a large group of Filipinos.

Gunn's combat days ended when he was struck in the arm by a piece of burning white phosphorus from a Japanese bomb during an attack on the airfield at Tacloban. The burning metal burrowed into his arm, causing intense pain and destroying nerves. General Kenney was with him during the attack. He was carried to a field hospital then

Anything, Anywhere, Anytime

loaded onto a C-47 to be evacuated to a rear area hospital. His injury was so severe that he was flown to Brisbane and hospitalized there.

C-47 during supply drop

Gunn may have been out of the war, but during the time he was at Tacloban, he continued adding to his legacy. Shortly after the invasion, Japanese ships attacked Allied ships and sank a Navy escort carrier. The carrier's planes were out on a mission and had nowhere to go except to the strip at Tacloban, where only a few hundred feet of pierced steel planking had yet been laid. Night had fallen and the runway wasn't lit. Gunn took charge. He took two flashlights and tied them to aluminium frying pans to use as reflectors, then waved each fighter in turn in for a landing.[89] Gunn also prevented the Navy from using the matting to stack supplies as they were offloaded from LSTs. Apparently, the Navy beachmaster failed to understand that there was a reason Army engineers were building a runway just off the beach.(Kenney G. C.)

As quickly as they could be brought in, Army fighter squadrons began arriving to reinforce Navy and Marine fighters which had flown

---

[89] The Navy omits this story from their history of the episode because senior naval officers had decided to blackball Gunn for not returning to his former service. The Navy Chief of Personnel had requested that he transfer back to the Navy after knowledge of his contribution to the Battle of the Bismarck Sea reached senior naval officers. Gunn declined the offer and elected to remain in the Army. The Navy punished him by removing him from its retired roles and depriving him of thousands of dollars in retired pay after the war.

in from carriers and were the first to use the strip. Leyte is an island, but it's a fairly large one. The terrain is also very hostile in places; the US Army history of the campaign says that US forces encountered more difficulty from the island's swamps than they did from the Japanese. Much of the island is mountainous, with ridges climbing to over 4,400 feet. Consequently, once the troops moved away from the beaches, supply became an issue. An eight-plane detachment of C-47s from the 317th Troop Carrier Group moved to Tacloban to provide support for the ground troops but airfield congestion prevented the assignment of a larger force.

Still, the 317th crews airdropped more than 300 tons of supplies to front line units, while losing two airplanes and three crewmembers to ground fire in the process. The 317th TCG detachment proved invaluable in the resupply of the troops operating in forward areas where ground resupply was difficult, if not impossible. Hindsight revealed that if more transports had been available, their contribution to the Leyte campaign would have been significant.

During the Leyte Campaign, the men of the 40th Troop Carrier Squadron found themselves as the target of a Japanese paratroop attack. Early on the morning of December 7, Japanese transports dropped troops near the airfield at Barauen where the 40th was in the process of setting up camp. The Japanese paratroops surrounded the camp and attacked. Thirteen troop carrier personnel were killed and four wounded during the battle, which ended when US infantry entered the fray and broke up the Japanese attack. The enemy paratroops were all killed or captured.

A common misconception among World War II historians is that the bloody battle to capture the island of Peleliu was needless because it was not used as a base for the attack on Leyte. They claim it had no strategic value (probably because they don't understand the role played by air transport in the Southwest Pacific.) In reality, Peleliu and the neighboring island of Anguar served as enroute refueling and crew rest stops for troop carrier and, once the island had been secured, Air Transport Command transports and their crews coming up from rear area bases in New Guinea and Australia. Escorting fighters accompanied the transports on their final leg from the two islands to Tacloban.

Airdropping of cargo to advancing patrols continued to be a major troop carrier mission. The 317th group had moved to Tacloban for combat operations and was responsible for the resupply missions. (54th TCW Historians) The missions were very hazardous, as evidenced by the two C-47s that were shot down. To deliver their supplies, pilots had to bring their airplanes in at altitudes as low as 200-400 feet over Japanese troops to take advantage of the element of

Anything, Anywhere, Anytime

surprise. Although some supplies were delivered by parachute, the bulk of the loads were free-dropped in specially packed containers.

Free-dropping was not only less expensive than using parachutes, it was also more accurate. Parachuted loads are susceptible to the wind, and even though airdrop altitudes in World War II were usually in the 400-700 foot range, a bundle could drift for some distance. Free drop bundles were less affected by the wind and tended to fall along the airplane's trajectory at the time of the drop. Although some items such as medical supplies were too fragile to be dropped without a parachute, others – including small arms ammunition and rations – could be packed into containers and dropped free. Special packing materials allowed more fragile items to be free-dropped as well.

Colored Quartermasters loading cargo[90]

In the Southwest Pacific, the 11th Cargo Resupply Squadron was responsible for rigging and accompanying the loads as kickers. The squadron was developed from the Provisional Quartermaster Supply Company, a Quartermaster company that was set up in Australia in early 1942.(Aerial Delivery and Rigger History) In the CBI, rigging was performed by the 518th Quartermaster Battalion. At least two companies, the 3841st & 3340th Quartermaster Truck Companies, were made up of colored troops. Oddly, responsibility for cargo rigging originally was given to Quartermaster laundry companies. Although fabric bags lined with spun Fiberglas were developed for packing

---

[90] The US armed forces remained segregated throughout World War II and Negro soldiers were assigned to units designated as "colored." One particular organization that used colored troops were the Quartermasters, who used colored troops in air cargo companies as laborers and drivers.

Sam McGowan

supplies for airdrop, wicker baskets were often used. In the CBI, cargo was packed in rice husks and wrapped with burlap.(Quartermaster Journal, 1944)

After Leyte, the Allies invaded Mindoro to establish a base for the upcoming landing at Lingayen Gulf. Mindoro was not only much closer to Luzon than Leyte, its soil was better suited to the construction of airfields and there was far less rainfall. The 503rd Parachute Infantry staged out of Leyte for the landings. Instead of arriving by air, the men of the 503rd landed from the sea to secure land around San Jose for the construction of an airfield for FEAF fighters in preparation for the invasion of Luzon. The invading forces met little opposition and captured the airfield at San Jose less than twenty-four hours after the landings. US and Australian engineers went to work and, within four hours, a 375th TCG transport came in. Within two days, transports were coming in regularly, with some coming from as far away as Biak, an island just north of New Guinea over 1,300 miles away.

Curtis C-46s replaced C-47s in troop carrier squadrons late in the war

In December, the 2nd Combat Cargo Group began operations using C-46s, which were as big as a B-17 and carried a much larger payload than the C-47. Plans were made to replace C-47s in the troop carrier groups with C-46s when they reached the point where they needed overhaul. Although it was a twin-engine airplane, the C-46 was a much larger airplane than the C-47 and carried a considerably larger payload – 15,000 pounds opposed to the C-47's 6,000 pounds. However, the C-46 was ill suited for operations in areas of heavy ground fire. The fuel system was poorly designed and the airplane was

Anything, Anywhere, Anytime

subject to catch fire if hit by tracers. The C-46 was a military derivative of the Curtis CW-20, which the company began developing as a pressurized airliner in the 1930s. Airline interest was less than anticipated but the Army liked the prototype's design and its potential as a military cargo transport. The new transport didn't begin entering service until the spring of 1942, and its first operational use on the India-China Ferry revealed major design problems. Dozens caught fire or exploded inflight while others simply went missing. Most of the problems were eventually rectified but its operating costs remained high.

Initially, the 2nd CCG transports were used for behind-the-lines logistical operations between rear area bases in Australia and New Guinea. Once their crews had become acclimated to the theater, they began operations into airfields in the Philippines and were sometimes used to drop supplies to troops in the field. By 1945, rear area logistical air transport in the Southwest Pacific was being assumed by units of the Air Transport Command, which had been established in 1942 to serve the War Department needs for non-combat air transport. Although the ATC is most often associated with four-engine transports such as the C-87 and C-54, it also operated large numbers of C-46s and C-47s, particularly on domestic routes in the US. The war in Europe was coming to its conclusion and ATC was seeking to expand its operations in the Southwest Pacific. The war was moving northward away from Australia and New Guinea so the ATC transports were able to release the 54th Troop Carrier Wing's transports for combat duty.

MacArthur had returned to the Philippines as he had promised, but there were still large numbers of Japanese troops in the islands. The next stop was Luzon, the main island in the Philippines. Manila, the Philippine capital city, is on Luzon. MacArthur had declared Manila to be an open city in late December 1941 and Japanese troops had moved in. Some distance north of Manila, Clark Field was the primary air base in the islands before the war. The island of Corregidor lies off the southern tip of the Bataan Peninsula. The invasion force landed on Luzon at Lingayen Gulf sixty miles north of Clark, near the same place that Japanese troops had landed in December 1941. A week after the invasion, troop carriers began landing at the Lingayen airfield with personnel from the fighter squadrons that were moving in to support the ground troops as they advanced into the interior of the island.

By January 23, Allied troops had advanced to within ten miles of Clark Field. Two days later US troops captured Clark and engineers immediately began preparing it for fighter and troop carrier use. Clark would serve as the base of operations for future troop carrier and airborne operations on Luzon and throughout the Philippines. On January 31, MacArthur launched a second front with another landing at Nasugba, a town about forty miles south of Manila. Prior to the invasion, C-47s dropped dummy paratroopers in another province some miles from the actual invasion beach as a diversion. Such diversionary practices were becoming common in both the Asian and European Theaters. At the time, Allied troops had yet to enter the city. The Nasugba landings were by the 11th Airborne Division's 187th and 188th Glider Regiments. No gliders were involved in the operation, however. In fact, gliders were never used in the Southwest Pacific.

The Nasugba invasion included an airborne operation with part of the 11th division jumping near Tagaytay, a town south of Manila. The drop went awry when one of the airplanes accidentally dropped a cargo bundle from an external rack before the formation reached the drop zone. Most of the troops of the 511th Parachute Infantry saw the parachute and, thinking they were over the drop zone, jumped early. They landed about six miles from where they should have been, but fortunately met little opposition and were able to link up with the men of the 188th Glider Regiment, which had arrived by sea.

A few days after the Nasugba drop, a platoon from the 11th Division jumped from nine 403rd Troop Carrier Group C-47s onto the perimeter of the Los Banos prison camp. The 403rd was a Thirteenth Air Force outfit assigned to XIII Air Service Command. It had recently moved to its new base at Clark Field. The paratroops were part of a daring mission to free more than 2,000 American and European male civilians who had been interned there since the beginning of the war. They had originally been interned at Santo Thomas University but the Japanese decided to segregate the single male prisoners from the women and families and moved them to the new location. The paratroops' mission was to attack the guard towers and clear the way for the main force, which arrived by boat and Amtrack after crossing Laguna de Bay.

In late January, intelligence reported that the Japanese had stopped feeding the civilians who had been interned at Santo Thomas University in Manila, so MacArthur called in Maj. Gen. Vernon Mudge, C.O. of the 1st Cavalry Division, and told him to drive for Manila as fast as he could move and rescue the people in the internment camp. Col. Dave Hutchinson of the 308th Bombardment Wing went with him. Hutchinson had a special mission to perform – to find Pappy Gunn's family. He was fulfilling a promise and Kenney had made to Gunn after he was wounded at Tacloban. Elements of the 1st Cav' reached the university on Sunday, February 2 and found the internees ready and waiting to be freed. Late the evening before, a pilot had dropped a message attached to a pair of goggles that said "Roll out the barrel. Santy Claus is coming Sunday or Monday." The Japanese commander and sixty-three of his men had taken 276 hostages and were holding the education building. He sent word to the Americans that unless he

Anything, Anywhere, Anytime

and his men were allowed safe passage to join their countrymen, he could not guarantee the safety of the hostages. Mudge agreed to allow the Japanese to pass through his lines.(Kenney G. C.) The internees had been freed, but they were still not safe. The Japanese had decided to fight for the city and the camp was frequently hit by Japanese artillery. The internees were being fed and were receiving medical treatment but weren't allowed to leave the camp.

On February 7 General MacArthur personally visited the camp and had Mrs. Clara Gunn and her four teenage children brought to him. He then placed them on an airplane for the flight to Australia to join their husband and father.(Gunn) During the flight, the family gradually became aware of their husband and father's notoriety because they were treated like dignitaries at each stop along the way. When they reached Brisbane, they were reunited with the man who had become famous as Pappy Gunn. The other Santo Thomas internees were not so fortunate. Repatriation continued for several months and it wasn't until September that the last internees departed Manila on ships.

Paratroopers descending on Corregidor

At 0830 on February 16, 1945, fifty-one C-47s from the 317th Troop Carrier Group appeared over the famous island fortress of Corregidor. It took an hour for all fifty-one airplanes to discharge their loads of sixteen men each on the tiny drop zone. Each airplane had to make three passes over the island but all of the men jumped, a total of more than 2,000 troops. A few paratroopers drifted over the cliffs and onto the beaches below but most landed where they were supposed to.

Fighting on the island was sometimes fierce and often tedious but within a week and a half, Corregidor was once again in Allied hands.

The Philippines campaign saw some rather unusual uses of air transport. Airfield congestion on Leyte in the early days of the campaign resulted in lack of air transport; only eight C-47s were based there to support the ground forces. Because of the lack of C-47s, the 11th Airborne Division Commander, Major Gen. J.M. Swing, used some of his division's L-5s and L-4s and an air rescue plane to drop supplies to his men in the mountains west of Bauren. Swing claimed to have supplied his division for a month, and learned some lessons about air transport that "(General Henry H.) Arnold doesn't know." In April 1945, the 317th Troop Carrier Group dropped barrels of napalm on Japanese positions on Carabao Island.[91] As the Luzon campaign continued, the troop carriers flew cargo to Allied ground units – often airdropping supplies to troops in the field just as they had been doing since 1942. In June 1945, the 317th, augmented by a few 433rd transports towing gliders, dropped 994 troops from the 511th regiment onto an abandoned Japanese airfield at Camalaniugan. Three days later the paratroopers linked up with infantrymen from the 37th division and ended the battle for the Philippines. The next step was the invasion of Japan.

While General MacArthur's forces were capturing New Guinea and the Philippines, Allied forces in the CBI were working toward the goal of running the Japanese out of Burma and, ultimately, from China as well. Just as air transport was crucial to the New Guinea campaign, it was essential for combat operations in the CBI. Additional air transport capability was sent to China in mid-1944 when the 1st Combat Cargo Group arrived at Sylhet, India, where they joined the 3rd CCG which had arrived earlier in the year. In November, a third combat cargo group, the 4th CCG, arrived to join the others as air transport strength in the region was further increased. The three combat cargo groups provided a huge boost to air transport capability in the region. With the additional air transport, the Allies were able to mount a major offensive in Burma.

In the summer of 1944, operations in Burma were in full swing. Merrill's Marauders had taken the airfield at Myitkyina and the nearby town was under siege. The Burma campaign ran into trouble when General Stilwell's Chinese troops panicked and failed to take the town after the Marauders captured the airfield. The Japanese dug in and a siege sat in that lasted from May to August. When the town did not fall,

---

[91] Napalm is very easy to make – all that is needed are detergents to mix with gasoline to cause it gel.

Anything, Anywhere, Anytime

General Stilwell feared that air resupply would not meet his men's daily needs. Not only were the transports limited by the size of the facilities to twenty-five flights a day, there were indications that the annual monsoon, with its low clouds and heavy rains, might be early. Fortunately, the indications proved false and monsoon was late that year; even when it arrived, the troop carrier crews kept flying. The air transport crews, who included the air commando troop carrier squadron and combat cargo groups, continued to land with more than enough supplies to meet the needs of all the Allied troops in the vicinity of Myitkyina. The air transport operation into Myitkyina proved to be the deciding factor in the battle for Burma.

Peasants watching supply drop

The capture of the airfield at Myitkyina had a positive effect on the India-China Ferry. Previously, ATC transports had to follow a circuitous route over the Himalayas then west to Chungking to avoid Japanese fighters. The loss of the airfield eliminated their air patrols over northern Burma and allowed the ATC transports to take a more direct route. The more southerly route allowed the use of the Douglas C-54, which had previously been unsuitable for operations over the mountains due to their limited high altitude performance. Supplies could also be delivered to Myitkyina then loaded on barges for further shipment up the Irrawaddy River into the Chinese interior. With Myitkyina in Allied hands, the Ledo Road was opened up, which allowed the delivery of supplies by truck. In February 1945, the first convoy reached Kunming.

C-47 dropping supplies in Burma

The Japanese offensive in the spring of 1944 was aimed at capturing the region around Imphal and Kohima, two cities about 60 miles apart some 40-50 miles from the Burmese border. Had the Japanese succeeded, the ATC India-China Ferry would have been over because its bases would have been in Japanese hands. It didn't, in no small measure due to Eastern Air Command Troop Carrier Command, a multinational air force. By this time, troop carriers in the CBI had become expert at cargo dropping and those skills were put to good use supplying Allied troops engaged in combat in defense of the two installations. When the Japanese laid the town of Kohima under siege, the defenders were resupplied by air. TCC transports dropped to Allied troops defending Imphal. There were airfields around Imphal; TCC used them to bring in reinforcements and supplies. When the Japanese began their attack, EAC Troop Carrier Command was equipped with only 76 transports. The ATC force in India was much larger at the time but USAAF policy had placed them off-limits to the combat commanders. Lord Mountbatten managed to obtain one squadron of ATC C-46s until additional transports arrived from the US. In response to the invasion, the Air Staff decided to beef up EAC Troop Carrier Command. There were no units in the United States to deploy to India so the 64th Troop Carrier Group, a veteran unit that had been fighting in the Middle East and Mediterranean since November 1942, was ordered to deploy to India on TDY to beef up troop carrier strength. A British squadron, 216 Transport Squadron, was also ordered to India for a temporary assignment. The activation of the 3rd Combat Cargo Group in June led to an additional 100 transports. By December, after the 1st and 4th Combat Cargo Groups arrived, Eastern Air Command commanded 364 US transports and 94 British. When the 3rd Combat Cargo Group activated in June 1944, it was assigned to a new air task force along with the just formed 1st Air Commando Group. The air commando group formed after Wingate's Special Force was withdrawn from Burma with the assets of the former 5318th Provisional Group. When the task force was formed, it had no defined mission. Two months later in September the British 177 Transport Group was added to the task force, which was designated as the Combat Cargo Task Force with the specific mission of conducting cargo operations in forward areas. Brig. Gen. Frederick Evans, the former commander of I Troop Carrier Command in the U.S., was placed in command. The CCTF was eventually expanded with the addition of the 2nd Air Commando Group and two British transport wings.

C-47s over Burma with P-40 escort

By the time Merrill's Marauders captured Myitkyina, Stilwell's Chinese troops had built several airstrips in the Hukawng and Mogaung Valleys to handle fighters and transports. Immediately after Merrill's Marauders captured Myitkyina, eight P-40s were assigned to the airfield; the small force was soon increased to twelve. The fighters would take off, make a strafing run over the Japanese positions them come back and land. Japanese machinegun positions were a little over half a mile away, and every airplane that landed and took off was brought under fire. The fighters and the Chinese and American troops engaged in the attack on the city were reinforced and supplied entirely by air. Additional fighters moved into the airstrips that had just been built.

Although the bulk of the air power in the CBI was American, the ground forces were British Commonwealth – including Canadians, Indians and Burmese – and Chinese. Stilwell's forces were entirely Chinese, although they were commanded by American officers. The only American ground combat troops were the remnants of Merrill's Marauders, which had been reorganized as the MARS Brigade and reinforced with additional regiments from the U.S. Like Merrill's troops, the men of the MARS Brigade, or Task Force, operated exclusively in Burma. All ground and air forces in the region depended on the EAC Troop Carrier Command and the Combat Cargo Task Force for resupply. Even after the Ledo Road was opened from Ledo to Myitkyina, most supplies were transported by air.

Myitkyina finally fell to Stilwell's Chinese troops on August 3, 1944. Stilwell had been expected to continue the advance to the south but he decided to establish a defensive line twenty miles south of Myitkyina, to the consternation of the American air officers and Chaing Ki Shek. Vinegar Joe felt that his troops were in need of rest. He remained in a defensive posture until mid-October when he was recalled to the United States. Immediately after Stilwell left, the Allies returned to the offensive in Burma and began one of the most spectacular campaigns of the war; a campaign that depended heavily on air transportation. General Evans' Combat Cargo Task Force hauled staggering amounts of men and equipment on a scale that eclipsed the efforts of the Air Transport Command India/China Wing, which by that time was under the command of Maj. Gen. William H. Tunner. Evans' command exceeded 50,000 tons of supplies each month beginning in February and continuing until May when Burma fell to the Allies. In addition, Tenth Air Force troop carriers, which never numbered more than 120 airplanes, were hauling in excess of 20,000 tons each month during the same period. In March 1945, troop carrier and combat cargo transports – including those assigned to the 1st and 2nd Air Commando Groups – transported 96.000 tons into Burma. Air Transport Command's India/China Wing never even came close to that kind of tonnage.

Not only were Tenth Air Force's air transport groups responsible for transporting men, equipment and supplies into Burma, they were also delivering supplies for Brig. Gen. Claire Chennault's Fourteenth Air Force in China and providing air transport for Chinese troops. One squadron of the 443rd Troop Carrier Group was assigned to duty inside China. The 2nd TCS initially operated in China but returned to India in

Anything, Anywhere, Anytime

mid-1943. The 27th TCS transferred to China in May 1944 and remained there for the duration of the war. While the other squadrons brought supplies in from India, the 27th provided air transport for Chinese ground forces and logistical support for Fourteenth Air Force's fighter and bomber squadrons. About 40% of the tonnage carried by Tenth Air Force's air transport units went to China. The battle for Burma hinged on air transport. Until the Ledo Road was opened up, practically every item of supply coming into the country came in the cargo compartment of an American or British transport. Even after the road opened, supplies were delivered to units in the field by air. While the Air Transport Command effort in the region has been widely publicized, little has been said or written about the role of the troop carrier and combat cargo squadrons in the theater. Yet, the American and British troop carrier and combat cargo squadrons were carrying as much and often more cargo across the Hump into Burma as ATC was carrying to China. During the month of March 1945, almost 100,000 tons was airlifted into Burma by the troop carriers. During the same time frame, the ATC Hump operation transported only half as much – and this was during the time after Brig. Gen. William Tunner had assumed command of the ATC effort and was "achieving maximum efficiency" from his men. (Craven & Cate, 1956) Furthermore, by this point in the war, ATC was using primarily four-engine transports and taking a more direct route, thanks to the efforts of the theater troop carriers.

Along with resupply, evacuation of wounded from Burma and the transport of reinforcements were daily responsibilities of the troop carrier squadrons. Airborne operations in Burma were frequent as well, although the troops were British – usually British Empire troops – and not American.[92] Often the paratroops were Ghurkhas and the operations were usually on a small scale. The final campaign to take Rangoon was an airborne operation involving 800 Ghurkhas and their Canadian jumpmasters. They jumped into drop zones twenty miles from the city then marched overland to Rangoon while being supplied from the air. They arrived in Rangoon to discover that the Japanese had abandoned the town. Thus ended the Burma Campaign.

By May 1945 most of Burma was in Allied hands. British paratroops were preparing to jump into Rangoon on May 2 when the Pathfinder planes spotted signs made by Allied POWs that read "Japs gone!" Rangoon was occupied without opposition. The focus of the war

---

[92] With the single exception of Merrill's Marauders, no US ground combat troops were assigned to the CBI. US participation in the region was confined to air operations while ground forces were primarily British, many of whom were colonial troops.

in the China-Burma-India Area turned toward defeating the Japanese in China. Getting supplies, particularly aviation gasoline, into China was a major logistical problem. The 443rd Troop Carrier Group and the 2nd and 4th Combat Cargo Groups were placed under the operational control of the Air Transport Command's India/China Wing and assigned to routine logistical flying across Burma into China. It was an anticlimactic end for their wartime role. With Burma in Allied hands, the effort in the CBI was now focused solely on China, where the Japanese still held control of a third of the country, including all of the seaports and the major roads and railroads. Japan still maintained a powerful military force in China, and the Chinese had achieved little success against them.

Transport taking off from airstrip in Burma

The situation in China was compounded by the political situation, where Chaing's Nationalists were opposed by the communists under Mao se Tung. Officially, the two groups had declared a truce but the communists were already in the process of renewing their war against the Nationalists. Even as their forces in Burma were being defeated, the Japanese launched attacks that turned General Stilwell's campaign

Anything, Anywhere, Anytime

into disaster. The Japanese captured large chunks of Chinese-held territory and the outcome of the war in the country was in doubt. The Chinese Nationalist generals were reluctant to engage the Japanese and the communists were taking sanctuary primarily in the mountains in the north where there were few Japanese. Chaing felt his primary goal should be to preserve his army to fight the communists after the Allies had defeated Japan. Future events would ultimately prove his thinking correct, although he would lose that war.

The combination of Japanese success and his failure to deal effectively with the Chinese led to Stilwell's replacement. Stilwell held Chaing in disdain but seemed to admire the communist leader Mao Tse Tung. As early as 1942, certain officers in the CBI had come to believe that Stilwell was sympathetic to communism. Col. Meriam Cooper advised General Marshall of Stillwell's leftist leanings and was practically banished for making the revelation. Chaing was disgusted with him and told President Roosevelt he didn't want him. Consequently, Stilwell was recalled and replaced by Lt. Gen. Albert C. Wedemeyer. Stilwell returned to the United States but was later sent to Okinawa after Lt. General Simon Bolivar Buckner was killed. Stilwell's relief was met with celebration by many of the airmen in the CBI. Claire Chennault, in particular, had frequently butted heads with him. Stilwell was opposed to Chennault's plans to mount a limited air campaign in China, and believed that the country would have to be secured before air forces could operate.[93] Stillwell was also critical of the British and Chinese. Basically, he was critical of everyone but himself.

Shortly after arriving in China, Wedemeyer and Chiang informed Washington that a large part of the Chinese troops then in Burma were needed at home. Although Burma is often thought of as a primarily British theater, large numbers of Chinese troops were engaged in combat operations even though much of China was occupied by Japanese troops. Chaing and Wedemeyer felt that the situation was a recipe for disaster and pressed to have Chinese troops brought back to defend their homeland. Operation *GRUBWORM* was set up to transport the Chinese troops back to China. In a month's time from December 1944, to January 1945, Troop Carrier Command flew two Chinese divisions, along with other support and combat functions, including some Americans, from Burmese bases to China. To supplement the troop carrier forces, two squadrons from the air commando groups were transferred to Troop Carrier Command for the move. Another contingent from the Air Transport Command assisted in the

---

[93] As it turned out, China never was completely secured before the end of the war but Chennault's Fourteenth Air Force had helped ruin Japan's hopes for the Asian mainland.

Sam McGowan

operation.[94] After their arrival in China, the Chinese troops formed a nucleus for a large force Wedemeyer planned to train to retake the offensive in China. But the war ended before the offensive could begin.

Although the CBI was a major theater of World War II, in reality China itself was not a major part of Allied plans after the summer of 1942. The only bright spot in China was General Claire Chennault's Fourteenth Air Force who, nearly by themselves, kept the Japanese from completely overrunning the country. The Air Transport Command Hump operation was maintained throughout the war and while the flow of supplies kept China in the war, the overall contribution to the Allied victory is debatable. On the other hand, there is no question but that troop carrier operations resulted in the defeat of the Japanese in Burma. After the Japanese abandoned Burma, Gen. Tunner, the ATC commander in India, convinced Gen. George Stratemeyer, who had assumed command of US air operations in the theater, to place the troop carrier and combat cargo squadrons under his operational control. Furthermore, he also gained operational control over Tenth Air Force's heavy bomber groups. The move met with resentment on the part of the combat aircrews who felt they were being slighted, especially when Tunner decreed that they had to complete a week long "checkout" with ATC instructors.

One of the lessons of World War II was that the mobility afforded by air transport is a key factor in winning battles in rugged terrain. General Kenney's meager troop carrier resources enabled the Allies to establish bases far in advance of ground supply lines, and thus drive the Japanese out of New Guinea much sooner than anyone had anticipated. It was largely due to the mobility provided by troop carrier squadrons that General MacArthur was able to turn what had been a holding action to protect Australia into a major offensive that ultimately shortened the war. American and British troop carrier crews played a major role in the liberation of Burma, where a campaign was carried out almost entirely by forces dependent upon air transport for their transportation and resupply.

Elsewhere in the Asian Campaign the troop carrier contribution was negligible in terms of combat operations, although troop carriers were heavily involved in logistical operations. The Navy campaign across the mid-Pacific required little air transport support; the small islands were easily supplied by sealift. What air transport the Navy needed, it could supply with its own air transport squadrons. Okinawa, the largest of the islands, was only sixty miles long and twelve miles

---

[94] Because of the ATC participation, historians have often attributed the operation to the Air Transport Command when, in fact, ATC participation was supplemental.

Anything, Anywhere, Anytime

wide, thus allowing supplies to come in on all sides from the sea. It was on the larger landmasses in the Southwest Pacific and on the Asian continent that air transport proved essential to the developing Allied strategy.

Fortunately, the detonation of the Atomic bomb over Hiroshima and another at Nagasaki provided an excuse for the Japanese to surrender and brought an end to the Pacific War without the massive invasion that was scheduled to take place on November 1, 1945. Had the war not ended, air transport would have played a major role in the battle for the Japanese home islands. However, US intelligence sources deduced that Japan had been defeated by mid-July and that an armed invasion would probably be unnecessary. In anticipation of a Japanese surrender, General MacArthur's staff began converting their invasion plan into a plan for a peaceful occupation of the country. Contrary to popular belief, MacArthur resisted pressure from the War Department to include airborne operations in plans for the invasion and the 11th Airborne Division was to be held in reserve along with the 1st Cavalry Division. As it became apparent that an invasion would be unnecessary, his staff began organizing a massive air transport operation to move the 11th Airborne and 1st Cavalry Divisions to Japan by air. The Air Transport Command made a play to gain control of the operation but Far East Air Forces resisted their efforts and while ATC transports were used in the movement, they were there to supplement FEAF troop carrier groups.

The Japanese government agreed to accept the surrender terms made in the proclamation President Truman put out right after an Allied summit meeting in Potsdam under one condition, and it was a major one. President Franklin Roosevelt had started proclaiming that the Allies would only accept unconditional surrender from the Axis nations after the Casablanca Conference in January 1943. Most Americans have come to believe that Japan surrendered unconditionally due to the detonation of the atomic bomb on Hiroshima but in fact their surrender offer was conditional; the Japanese Diet would only surrender to the Allies and allow the country to be occupied peacefully if Emperor Hirohito was allowed to remain on his throne.

There was a delay of almost a month after Japan sent a message to Washington with their surrender offer before the official surrender was signed. During the interim, the Allies were making plans to occupy the defeated country. On August 28 the first Allied troops arrived in Japan. They came in from Okinawa on Far East Air Force Troop Carrier Command aircraft. Five days later on September 2, Japanese officials signed the surrender documents on the deck of the battleship *USS Missouri*.

Sam McGowan

Even though the war was over, the job was not over in the Pacific for the troop carriers. As the war moved further and further northward toward Japan before the surrender, the troop carrier groups moved north to new bases. Prior to and after the surrender, FEAF troop carriers were kept busy moving occupational troops into Japan. General MacArthur and his staff, including General Kenney, flew into Tokyo aboard MacArthur's personal C-54 for the surrender ceremony. When Allied forces occupied Japan, two troop carrier squadrons moved into the country to provide air transportation for the occupational forces. Several squadrons traded in their C-47s for faster and larger four-engine C-54s. In China, troop carrier squadrons became involved in humanitarian missions delivering food and medical supplies to refugee camps. Troop carrier squadrons remained active in China until the US withdrew its military personnel from the embattled country when the Chinese Civil War increased in intensity in 1948.

American troop carrier squadrons would maintain a presence in the Far East that continues to this day. The troop carrier units that were formed and fought in the Pacific would go on to become the nucleus of the modern airlifters who continue the tradition set by their predecessors in the Pacific. Some of the units have survived. The 374th Troop Carrier Wing remained in the Pacific and would play a major role in the Korean War. It was deactivated in the late 1950s when the Air Force reorganized its airlift components. Reactivated in 1966, the 374th would be one of three tactical airlift wings to see heavy combat in Vietnam, including the infamous siege of Khe Sanh where airlifters would repeat some of the successes of World War II. The 317th

Anything, Anywhere, Anytime

remained in the Far East for a time but moved to Europe during the Berlin Airlift and remained there until 1964. The 317th would enjoy success in Africa and in an airlift in India. Both the 374th and 317th designations have remained alive in the modern United States Air Force.

Sam McGowan

Anything, Anywhere, Anytime

Chapter Six - "North Africa and the Mediterranean"

While American troop carriers were well into the war in the Pacific by mid-1942, it wasn't until autumn of that year that they flew their first combat mission in the European Theater of Operations. The war in Europe was being fought at a much more leisurely pace than in the Pacific where Japanese threats against Australia forced Allied ground forces into combat much sooner than their commanders would have preferred. The US Army was focusing on recruiting – which meant impressment – and training. Although the Soviets were engaged in an intense ground war with the German *Wermacht* on the Russian Front, the British and American war effort in 1942 consisted primarily of air attacks on occupied Europe while the British Eighth Army fought a give and take battle in Africa with the German *Afrika Corps*. The US provided limited support to Eighth Army with transports that moved to Egypt with Major General Lewis Brereton in June and some Pan American DC-3s that were operating under contract to the Army before America entered the war as a combatant. Except for limited participation by a handful of US Army Rangers in the ill-fated Dieppe raid, the first American ground troops to see action against the Germans went into combat in North Africa. Consequently, it was in North Africa that troop carriers received their baptism of fire in the ETO.

Air transport operations actually started in North Africa and the Middle East before America entered the war, but only on a small scale.

Sam McGowan

In the summer of 1941 the United States opened up a ferry route running from Florida through the Mediterranean to Natal, Brazil then across the Atlantic to Gambia and finally to Liberia to deliver aircraft to the British. Most were transports, primarily Douglas DC-3s which the British nicknamed *Dakota*. Pan American Airways contracted not only to deliver the airplanes under the auspices of the Ferrying Command, but to also provide some air transport support for the British forces in the Middle East. By the time America officially entered the war, the Ferrying Command had established routes all the way to Cairo and even on to China by way of Africa, the Middle East and Central Asia. British forces in the Middle East were receiving a large portion of the aircraft that were being delivered under Lend-Lease. To handle the arriving aircraft and provide technical training to the British, the US established US Military North African Mission in the late summer of 1941; in June 1942, it became US Army Forces in Middle East. USAFIME was also responsible for logistical operations in support of the Soviets over routes through Iran. Supplies bound for the Soviet Union were shipped to Mediterranean ports then trucked through the Iranian desert to the Soviets.

In the first months after America officially entered the war, limited US Army air strength was sent to the Middle East in the form of a mixed group of B-17s and B-24s that operated out of bases in Palestine against Axis transportation routes to North Africa – and that was not planned. Original American and British plans were for the US to supply aircraft and equipment to the RAF Middle East Command, but no combat units. The situation changed when the Germans defeated the British at Tobruk in the spring of 1942 and forced them to retreat into Egypt. The RAF asked for American assistance. The first US combat unit to see service in the Middle East was a special project under the command of Col. Harry Halverson. HALPRO was enroute to the Far East with B-24 Liberators to begin a bombing campaign against the Japanese home islands from airfields in China. The British halted the Halverson Project bombers in the Middle East and began using them against German supply lines. They were joined a few weeks later by a squadron of B-17s that transferred from India along with a detachment of transports.

During a conference in Washington in June, the US agreed to send an air force to Egypt, starting with the heavy bombers that had been dispatched to India from Java earlier in the year. Maj. General Lewis H. Brereton, who had been overseas since the preceding autumn, was ordered to move immediately to Cairo for a temporary assignment with US Army Forces in the Middle East. He was instructed to take all of the B-17s in India and enough transports to make the move. Since no plans had been made to send American combat units to the Middle East, no transport squadrons had been earmarked for the theater.

Anything, Anywhere, Anytime

Brereton left India with a number of C-47s, including some that belonged to the 1st Ferrying Group which had just started arriving in India. There were other C-47s in India that had come over with the AQUILA project earlier in the year.

Just how many transports Brereton took with him to the Middle East doesn't seem to be recorded, although there were nine B-17s and 225 men in the party. The B-17s no doubt were the airplanes that Colonel Caleb Haynes took to India in April. The B-17s ended up remaining in the Middle East but at least some of the transports were released to return to India, possibly because of the high priority that had been given to the movement of supplies to China. Heavy bombers were more in demand in Egypt and Palestine at the time than transports. Transports would, however, play a large role in the Western Desert after the British Eighth Army defeated the Germans at El Alamein and began attacking westward into Libya.

Brereton's original assignment was to be temporary duty but after he had been there a few weeks the temporary Tenth Air Force commander, Brig. Gen. Clayton Bissell, who had gone to the region as a member of Stillwell's staff, sent an inquiry to Washington regarding his status. Brereton's orders were changed and his assignment became permanent. Immediately after he arrived in Cairo, Brereton activated the US Middle East Air Force, which became Ninth Air Force the following November. Brereton's command was made up of heavy bombers, medium bombers and fighters; his mission was to help the British Royal Air Force Middle East Command support the British Eighth Army as it defended against the German Africa Corps at El Alamein, where the British finally prevailed in October 1942.

After El Alamein, Eighth Army went on the offensive and began moving rapidly across the desert into Libya. Initially, Brereton had no troop carrier units assigned to his new command. Most of the C-47s that had brought him to Egypt belonged to the 1st Ferrying Group and they eventually went back to India, although a few remained to support the new Middle East Air Force. In November, Brereton received the 316th Troop Carrier Group and immediately put it to work moving fuel and other cargo in support of the rapidly advancing British. The group's C-47s reduced transport time from Allied depots in Egypt to the advancing armored columns from more than three days by truck to a few hours by air. The group also supported heavy bomber operations from an advance base at Gambut in the Libyan Desert by moving in tents, rations, fuel and other supplies for the bomber crews prior to a mission.

Troop carrier operations in the Western Desert were almost entirely logistical in nature, although "logistical" should be qualified since much of the 316th TCG's operations involved moving fuel, ammunition and other supplies to forward airstrips for the advancing

Eighth Army. Other operations were in support of the advance fields for the heavy bombers. At the time, the 98th and 376th Bombardment Groups were based in Palestine, but they often flew into Gambut to refuel and rest before missions against German targets in North Africa, Sicily and Italy. The field at Gambut only had one semipermanent building. Whenever IX Bomber Command scheduled a mission, the airmen brought in everything needed for the mission from Palestine. It quickly became apparent that air transportation was vital to the success of Allied plans in North Africa, where the war was starting to move as the British drove the Africa Corps toward Tunisia.

In September 1942, the 51st Troop Carrier Wing and 62nd Troop Carrier Group arrived in England, where the 60th Troop Carrier Group had arrived the previous June and the 64th just months before.[95] Col. Paul Williams was placed in command of the 51st TCW and given responsibility for organizing troop carrier operations in the European Theater, which included Africa and the Middle East. By the fall of 1942, the Allies had decided to invade French North Africa to open up a new front as a step toward the ultimate defeat of the Germans and Italians on the south side of the Mediterranean. The three groups in England began training in preparation for operations with Twelfth Air Force, a recently organized Army air force under the command of a newly promoted Major General James H. Doolittle that had been created as a command organization for US Army air operations in conjunction with the landings in French Morocco and Algeria.[96]

Operation *TORCH*, the invasion of Northwest Africa, took place in early November 1942 when American troops landed at Casablanca and elsewhere along the Northwest African coast to Algiers. Spanish Morocco was not invaded because of neutrality issues. TORCH called for the use of the 503rd Parachute Infantry[97]; the troopers were to be transported to the beachhead by C-47s from the 60th Troop Carrier Group. The 64th Troop Carrier Group was assigned to move troops of British 3 Battalion to Maison Blanche Airfield in Algeria. Maj. Gen. George Patton asked for airborne operations in his sector in French

---

[95] The 50th Troop Carrier Wing was a headquarters unit that went to England to serve as the command element for the three groups.

[96] Army plans originally were for the operation to be supported by Eighth Air Force and the original organization was a subordinate command called JUNIOR. At some point Gen. Arnold decided to set up a new air force, and gave command to Doolittle, who had been turned down by MacArthur for service in his theater.

[97] The paratroops were actually the 2nd Battalion of the 503rd Parachute Infantry, and are identified as such in most histories. The rest of the 503rd had remained at Fort Benning, GA and would deploy to the Southwest Pacific a few months later.) The battalion was reinforced and became a regiment, which was redesignated as the 509th Parachute Infantry just a few days before TORCH.

Anything, Anywhere, Anytime

Morocco but the *TORCH* commander, Lt. Gen. Dwight Eisenhower, rejected the proposal. The 62nd was assigned to support the invasion in a logistical capacity. A second troop carrier wing, the 52nd, would eventually become part of Twelfth Air Force when it arrived in North Africa with its 61st, 313th and 314th Troop Carrier Groups. (At this point in the war, Fifth Air Force didn't even have a full group. The ETO had priority and all new combat groups were going there.)

The term "strategic airlift" had yet to be coined in 1942, but the movement of the 503rd from England to Africa definitely fit the definition. The flight from the 503rd base at Cornwall to Oran in Algeria on the night of November 6-7 was long – more than twelve hours in the cramped cockpits and cargo compartments of the C-47s; airplanes that been designed for local airline service in the United States. The operation was plagued with problems. Led by 51st TCW commander Col. Paul Williams, most of the flight was at night and the formations became scattered as formation lights[98] burned out and the pilots were unable to see other airplanes in the darkness. The inexperienced crews were unable to maintain contact with their leaders as the formation encountered deteriorating weather.

The agent responsible for operating a secret homing device destroyed it because he failed to get the message that the C-47s were planning to land in Algiers instead of dropping their troops from the air. Thinking the airborne operation was still on a "war plan," the agent assumed something had gone wrong when the formation failed

---

[98] Formation lights were small lights mounted on top of the wings that could be seen by other airplanes at close range, but not from a distance.

Sam McGowan

to appear at the specified time. A last homing device, a radio aboard one of the ships in the invasion force, mistakenly broadcast on 460 kilocycles instead of the 440 kilocycles the crews had been briefed to expect. Transports ended up scattered all along the Northwest African coast. In short, the whole operation was a SNAFU of magnificent proportions, and it would get even worse.

Most of the problems with the move were navigation-related. At the time, navigators weren't assigned to troop carrier crews. At this point in the war, there was a shortage of navigators and they were going to bomber and long-range transport squadrons. The need for navigators had only been realized with the appearance of the long-range four-engine bomber and the long-range transports that followed. In the 1930s, navigators were assigned mostly to airline crews that operated flying boats. Many had learned their craft on ships. The military had no need for navigators in the 1920-30s because combat operations were expected to be conducted over land. It would be more than a year after the North Africa operations before navigators were assigned to troop carrier squadrons and, even then, they were only assigned to one crew in each flight in a squadron. Whether or not the presence of navigators would have reduced the errors is open to question.

Prior to their departure from England, the airborne force had been told that a French airfield in Oran was secure and would be available for landings. A new French government had been formed after France surrendered to Germany in 1940. The new government, called Vichy France because its headquarters were at Vichy, was officially neutral but was known for collaborating with the Germans. General Mark Clark went into North Africa from a submarine in advance of the invasion to meet with Vichy senior officers and reported that they would not fight or, if they did, they would only put up token resistance. The C-47s arrived over Oran expecting no opposition but were instead met by French fighters and antiaircraft fire. Many transports landed on a dry lakebed at Sebkra d'Oran when they realized the supposedly "secure" field they were supposed to land on wasn't.

Some transports were drawn off course by a beacon in Spanish Morocco. Most pilots discovered the error and turned toward Oran but a few landed in the neutral country. Their crews and paratroopers were interned and their airplanes confiscated by Spanish authorities. The airplane carrying the task force commander, Col. William C. Bentley, developed engine trouble and was forced to land in French territory; the crew and troops were taken prisoner. Some C-47s came under attack by French fighters. Three transports were shot down and two airmen killed along with three paratroopers. Fifteen troopers were wounded. The French fighters were attacked in turn by Spitfires

Anything, Anywhere, Anytime

and were all shot down. While most of the paratroopers were landed at Tafaroui airfield by late on the afternoon of D-Day, C-47s were initially scattered all along the North African coast. Troop carrier operations in North Africa had gotten off to a bad start! (Craven & Cate, 1956) Fortunately, while French resistance to the invasion was stronger than expected, after several days of stiff resistance their senior commanders decided to surrender and join the Allies.

The 64th Troop Carrier Group left England for Gibraltar on the afternoon of November 8 with two company groups of the British 3 Paratroop Battalion aboard. Early on the morning of November 11, thirty-four of the original thirty-nine planes arrived at Algiers, where they were greeted by Allied antiaircraft fire. Two men were wounded by the "friendly fire," a problem that would plague troop carrier crews throughout the Mediterranean campaigns. On November 12, the 64th took off from Algiers and dropped 312 British troops onto the Duzerville aerodrome some six miles southeast of Bone`, where they were to link up with commandos who had landed at dawn. That evening, the Luftwaffe bombed Bone` but the next day the C-47s returned with antiaircraft guns and gasoline.

The Paratrooper Task Force, made up of the 2nd Battalion, 503rd Paratroop Regiment and the 60th Troop Carrier Group, attacked Youks-les-Bains airfield near the Tunisian border. With little intelligence of the situation, the task force took off on the morning of November 15, first with an escort of Royal Air Force Spitfires, then an escort of Hurricanes. In spite of poor visibilities that forced the pilots to go on instruments, at 0945 the formation successfully dropped 350 troops. The French offered little resistance and negotiated a transfer of the airfield to American control. The next day, the 64th TCG carried out a similar operation with British paratroops ninety miles from Tunis. The 64th transports dropped 384 British paratroopers over Souk-el-Arba airfield.

By late November the Allies, which now included French forces, were pushing toward Tunis. On the afternoon of November 28, a flight of forty-four transports from the 62nd and 64th groups took off from Maison Blanche with 530 British paratroops from 1 Parachute Brigade. With American P-38s and British Spitfires and Hurricanes as escorts, the formation dropped their troops with no losses. The British paratroops met heavy resistance and found their objective at Oudna still heavily defended by strong German forces equipped with armor. Most were killed or captured.

While smaller airborne operations continued, the drop near Oudna turned out to be the last major airborne operation of the North African Campaign, although a few smaller ones were conducted. One such operation was one of the first "special operations" by American troops of the war. A flight of two C-47s, one flown by Major Philip

Cochran, dropped a squad of paratroopers whose objective was to blow up a key bridge. Cochran was the commander of the 58th Fighter Squadron but he went on the mission because he knew where the bridge was. The operation did not go off well. Cochran's navigation was off and the troops were dropped on the wrong side of the bridge. They followed the railroad for several miles in the wrong direction before they realized their error. They backtracked and blew the bridge but few of the party returned to the Allied lines. Cochran would later be picked to command the 5318th Provisional Air Unit in India, which later became the 1st Air Commando Group, where he became proficient in glider operations. In late 1944, he became a permanent part of the troop carrier mission when he was assigned to the staff of the First Allied Airborne Army.

Even though their services as paratroop transports were temporarily no longer needed, the troop carrier crews remained very active in the war in North Africa, particularly in the logistical role supporting advanced air bases in eastern Algeria and western Tunisia. The 316th TCG continued supporting the Eighth Army and the Western Desert Air Force as they advanced across Libya into Tunisia. Just as their peers had done in New Guinea, the Allied ground commanders quickly learned that air transport provided heretofore unprecedented mobility. Because the British were terribly short of their own transports, the Americans took up the slack for their allies.

When not engaged in direct combat operations, troop carrier crews flew logistical missions into forward airfields transporting personnel and supplies for the fighter and bomber squadrons. Often, C-47s were used to transport fuel to armored columns operating far in advance of their lines of supply, a capability General George C. Patton's Third Army would exploit later in the war. After its arrival in Egypt, the 316th Troop Carrier Group played a crucial role resupplying British Eighth Army columns as they advanced westward across Libya. Sometimes troop carrier crews would carry bombs and ammunition into airfields where supplies were dwindling and the lag time involved with surface transportation made the situation critical. One major logistical effort was the support of Allied squadrons operating from the advanced base at Thelepte in western Tunisia, an airfield that was used by IX Support Command's fighters and light bombers because it was in an arid area and wasn't affected by the rains that fell over Algeria.

The value of air transportation was also recognized by the Germans, but the Japanese failed to take more than token advantage of

Anything, Anywhere, Anytime

the mobility offered by their own transports.[99] Luftwaffe transports, mostly Junkers 52s, were the lifeline for the Africa Corps because the Royal Navy had gained control of the Mediterranean. Some Luftwaffe transport squadrons operated the giant Messerschmitt Me 323, a six-engine high wing airplane that was developed from a glider. The first models were towed into the air by bombers because their engines lacked the power to take off with a full load. The wings were made of plywood and covered with fabric. The fuselage was large enough to carry small tanks and other vehicles or 130 troops. Luftwaffe transports became crucial to the German effort in North Africa after the TORCH landings. Unfortunately, they proved highly vulnerable to air attack once the Allies established air superiority over the Mediterranean.

In early 1943, Allied air forces in North Africa reorganized following a plan put forth by Lt. Gen. Frank Andrews. An allied Mediterranean Air Command was organized with British Air Chief Marshall Arthur Tedder in command. Lt. Gen. Carl Spaatz was placed in command of Northwest African Air Forces, a multinational organization made up of American and British Royal Air Force units with several subordinate organizations, including a troop carrier command. Brigadier General Paul Williams was placed in command of the NAAF Troop Carrier Command which by July included the 51st and 52nd Troop Carrier Wings and RAF 38 Wing. The 316th Troop Carrier Group remained part of Ninth Air Force but was attached to the 52nd Wing. With airborne operations in North Africa over, the troop carrier squadrons were involved in logistical missions and training for the upcoming invasion of Sicily, which was scheduled to take place as soon as the Germans had been defeated in Tunisia.

The reorganization of air forces was part of a general reorganization of Allied forces in the Mediterranean suggested in a letter to the Combined Chiefs from Gen. Andrews, who had moved to Egypt in November 1942 to take command of US Army Forces in the Middle East. An airman, Andrews was a favorite of Army chief of staff Gen. George Marshall. In the mid-thirties, while Andrews was commander of the GHQ Air Force, he flew Marshall, who had just assumed his duties as Deputy Chief of staff, on a nine-day national inspection tour of airfields and air combat units in his personal C-32 command transport. Marshall came away from the tour impressed with the possibilities afforded by air power and by Andrews himself. His first action after he was appointed Chief of Staff was to make Andrews Director of Plans, the first time an airman had ever been

---

[99] Ironically, the Japanese transports were basically the same as the American-designed C-39s and C-47s. Japan purchased a number of Douglas transports before the war and reproduced them for their own use.

Sam McGowan

given a position where he was able to influence Army policy. Marshall considered Andrews to be the brightest general officer in the Army and it is believed he intended to make him supreme commander of Allied forces in Europe. At the Casablanca Conference in early 1943, the Combined Chiefs decided to move Andrews to London and place him in command of all US Army air and ground forces in Europe. Unfortunately, he was killed in an airplane accident in Iceland in May 1943.[100]

Before the *TORCH* landings in Northwest Africa, British Eighth Army forces had won the Battle of El Alamein and driven the Germans into Libya and westward into Tunisia. *TORCH* was under the command of Maj. Gen. Dwight D. Eisenhower, who had moved from London where he had been commander of US Army Forces in the British Isles, to Gibraltar. Allied efforts out of Algeria were thwarted by the German victory at Kasserine Pass but after regrouping, American ground forces were ready to advance into Tunisia along with their British allies and catch the Germans in a pinschers movement. The reorganization put Eighth Army under Eisenhower's overall command, along with all other Allied forces in North Africa.

German transports were heavily involved in North Africa. Several transport bases had been established in Sicily and as Allied bombers and naval vessels gained control of the Mediterranean, air transportation became a major means of reinforcing and resupplying German forces in Tunisia. In fact, the Luftwaffe transports had become the lifeline of the *Afrika Corps*. Consequently, the Allies set out to eliminate the enemy's air transport capabilities by making the Junkers 52 and Messerschmitt 323 transports priority targets. Doolittle's Northwest African Strategic Command was initially given responsibility for destroying the German transports on the ground in Sicily but after their efforts failed, Brereton's IX Fighter Command commenced its role in Operation FLAX in April 1943 to interrupt the Germans aerial lines of supply in the air.

---

[100] At the time of his death, Andrews was flying on a B-24 Liberator named "Hot Stuff" which had flown over thirty combat missions and was the first Eighth Air Force bomber scheduled to return to the United States. Although they were scheduled to stop in Prestwick for fuel, the crew elected to fly on to Reykjavik, which was reporting good weather and was forecast to remain so. Before they arrived, un-forecast bad weather developed, with low clouds, rain and snow. The crew made several approaches but flew into a mountain. Only one member of the crew, the tail gunner, survived.

Anything, Anywhere, Anytime

Junkers 52 transport

On April 18, the 57th Fighter Group hit the jackpot when group pilots spotted a large formation of more than 100 German transports over the Mediterranean as they were on their way back to their bases in Sicily after delivering troops to Tunisia. In the ensuing air battle, the 57th's P-40s shot down fifty-eight Ju 52s and damaged twenty-nine more in what they called The Palm Sunday Massacre. On April 22, a formation of P-40s escorted by Spitfires intercepted a formation of twenty-seven Me 323s and shot down twenty-one of them. Over a five-day period, Ninth Air Force and RAF Western Desert Air Force fighters wiped out the Luftwaffe's fleet of Ju 52s and giant Messerschmitt 323s and ended German hopes of reinforcing the *Afrika Corps*. Just how one-sided the battle was is illustrated by the fact that only two airplanes in a 23-plane formation of ME 323's reached safety. It was a lesson that was not lost on Allied troop carrier commanders as to the folly of attempting to use transports in hostile areas without adequate fighter escort.

Sam McGowan

MESSERSCHMITT 323
As they had in New Guinea, troop carrier aircraft turned out to be a vital means of air evacuation of casualties in North Africa. Airplanes bringing supplies to forward airfields were quickly loaded with wounded personnel and turned around as air evacuation flights for their back-haul flight to their rear area bases. The I Troop Carrier Command was responsible for training medical air evacuation transport squadrons at its medical training facility at Bowman Field, Kentucky. The first operational air evacuation squadron was sent to North Africa. Each squadron was designated with an 800 series unit number, starting with the 801st, which went to the South Pacific. The 802nd MAETS deployed to North Africa in early 1943. Each MAETS included four flights consisting of one medical officer, six flight nurses and eight enlisted medical technicians. One nurse and one technician made up a team. While there were provisions for air evacuation using light utility aircraft such as the UC-64 Norseman, in North Africa the primary transport was the C-47, which could carry 18-20 litter patients. Each MAETS made up kits consisting of medical supplies, blankets, splints, litters and portable heaters, which could be loaded onto a C-47 for transport to a forward area. In North Africa, air evacuation flights picked up patients at forward airfields in Tunisia near the fighting and flew them back to rear area hospitals in Algiers and Oran. Between January 16 and May 23, 1943, troop carrier transports evacuated 4,806 patients, of which 3,840 were in litters. Prior to that, an estimated 887 patients were carried.(WW 2 US Medical Research Center)

Anything, Anywhere, Anytime

Evacuating casualties in North Africa

Air transportation was also used in North Africa to move men and equipment over long distances from one part of the battlefield to another, although such moves were on a limited basis since most Allied ground combat units in North Africa were mechanized. An exception was the US Army's ranger battalions, a new innovation that had been established in Northern Ireland for special missions such as capturing enemy airfields and coastal guns. After their initial combat in Oran, the US 1st Ranger Battalion, commanded by Lt. Col. William O. Darby, was flown from their base at Arzew to a new combat operation in Tunisia. The move required thirty-two C-47s. Darby's Rangers left Arzew, where they had been resting and training, and landed at Youks les Bains airfield near Tebessa then moved east to join Major General Lloyd Fredendall's II Army Corps just in time for the battle of Kasserine Pass. However, such operations were few in North Africa. Instead, troop carrier squadrons were mostly involved in logistical operations.

The most significant use of troop carriers was the support of the advanced base at Thelepte, an airfield in the western edge of the Tunisian desert about twenty miles from the Kasserine Pass. In early 1943, Allied air units were sent to the airfield, which lay only a few miles inside the lines, because it was in an arid area. Winter rains had turned Twelfth Air Force's Algerian air bases into seas of mud. In some respects, occupying the forward area was risky; in fact, the field was temporarily abandoned when Axis forces counterattacked and moved toward Kasserine. Thelepte was not supported entirely by air as there were roads across Algeria that allowed supplies to be brought in by truck, but the C-47s made a valuable contribution to the support of the American, British and French squadrons that operated from the remote airfield. Transports brought in ammunition and bombs for the combat aircraft in addition to other supplies. Thelepte was also a pickup point for Allied wounded for evacuation to rear area hospitals.

Air transport was not, however, used to open up new offensives in Africa as it was in New Guinea and the CBI. Doolittle and other air and ground commanders in the European theater – with the exception of George Patton and Brereton – were generally unimaginative and failed to fully recognize the tactical value of the troop carrier airplane to ground warfare, other than support of airborne operations and they were only lukewarm to them. Ground commanders, particularly Gen. Omar Bradley and, to some extent, Eisenhower, frequently thwarted plans put forth later in the war with the blessings of Marshall and Arnold to use paratroops and troop carriers for major operations after the D-Day landings in Normandy.(Brereton, 1946)[101] On the other hand, British General Bernard Montgomery appreciated airborne operations and air transport. He had seen what air transport could do during his campaign in the Western Desert when Brereton's C-47s brought in fuel and ammunition for his advancing columns.

Troop carrier operations in Europe were based on the support of paratroop forces but in North Africa paratroops were only used during the first few weeks of the campaign. Although the Army's senior leadership, specifically General George Marshall, was enthusiastic about the use of paratroops to capture and secure airfields and other strategic positions far in advance of the line of advance, his European commanders were far less imaginative. The only Allied combat commander in the ETO who truly appreciated the advantages offered by tactical air power, including troop carrier transport, was Lt. Gen. George S. Patton but he was subordinate to Eisenhower, whose military experience prior to World War II had been as an administrative and staff officer,[102] and Bradley, whose pre-war experience had been as an academic and on the War Department staff. On the other hand, Generals George C. Marshall, the chief of the Army, and Lt. General Henry H. Arnold, the chief of the Army Air Forces, were both proponents of the use of air transport to support the ground war as was Lt. General Frank Andrews, who was the senior American

---

[101] After he became commander of the First Allied Airborne Army, Brereton and his staff conceived a number of imaginative plans, including an airborne operation deep inside German territory in the Ruhr and an airborne attack on Berlin, but they were all turned down by senior ground commanders.

[102] MacArthur, under whom Eisenhower served as an administrative officer, once said about him "he was the best clerk I ever had."

officer in the theater. Andrews outranked Eisenhower and everyone else, including Arnold at the time.[103]

Arnold and Andrews were both proponents of the use of airborne forces but Arnold was in a staff position in Washington, DC and Andrews was killed in an aircraft accident in Iceland in May 1943.[104] The only other senior officer who truly appreciated the value of airborne forces, including air transportable infantry, was Brereton who, after all, had developed the plan for paratroop forces while assigned to Billy Mitchell's staff in France in 1918. Arnold and Brereton, and probably Andrews, believed that airborne forces should be part of the Air Corps, as the German's airborne forces were. Eisenhower and his subordinates considered them merely as light infantry rather than an elite corps trained for operations deep inside enemy lines. Marshall was so enthusiastic about airborne forces that he authorized several full divisions. In North Africa, the largest US airborne force was a regiment; the 82nd Division didn't deploy overseas until April 1943 and didn't see combat until the invasion of Sicily.

After paratroop operations in North Africa ceased in early 1943, the entire 51st Troop Carrier Wing was placed in XII Air Service Command, an organization that had been established to provide logistical support to the combat commands. After having dropped paratroops, ferried airborne engineers into remote airstrips to prepare them for combat operations then stocking the same fields before the fighter squadrons moved in, the troop carrier personnel felt that the transfer was a slight. Even though the transfer took place, the 51st wing crews were not through with combat.

Although no one planned it that way, the North African air campaign turned out to be heavily dependent upon air transportation for logistical support. No one had foreseen that the air force in North Africa would become highly mobile, just as Fifth Air Force was in New Guinea, or that combat squadrons would be operating as far to the east and as close to the front lines as they ultimately did. The forward field operations came about as a matter of necessity rather than convenience or overall strategy. The airfields in Algeria turned out to

---

[103] Andrews was promoted to brigadier general when he was given command of the GHQ Air Force and Arnold served under him as a colonel. Arnold replaced Andrews, who was banished to San Antonio as a colonel because of his outspoken criticism of the Army. However, as soon as Marshall became chief of staff, he brought Andrews back to Washington and restored his rank. Andrews was the highest ranking Air Corps general and the senior American officer in the ETO at the time of his death.

[104] Just how much the death of Frank Andrews affected the conduct of the war in the ETO can only be imagined, but it's likely that he'd have made more effective use of air transport had he lived and been Supreme Commander.

be unsuitable for wet weather operations and XII Air Support Command was forced to operate out of airfields in the edge of the Tunisian desert where there was less rainfall and where the soil was less likely to turn into mud. All of the equipment and support personnel for Twelfth Air Force came ashore at either Oran or Casablanca, then had to be moved much further inland as the war moved away from the coast where the depots were located into the desert. Trucks were the primary means of moving supplies but the transient times dictated the use of air transport to move critical items such as aircraft parts, bombs and ammunition.

Loading cargo using a hoist

Similarly, Ninth Air Force squadrons moved westward out of Egypt and into Libya and then on to Tunisia with the British Eighth Army. Because the ground forces required so much material, the air elements had to depend on their own resources to have their needs met. Due to the lack of adequate surface transportation, the heavy bombers would often take off with their bomb bays carrying the last bombs on their base at Biskra. The bomber commanders depended on troop carrier and service command transports to replenish their supply of bombs and ammunition for the next mission.

Although the Americans were defeated at Kasserine Pass, the subsequent victory at El Guettar paved the way for the ultimate defeat of the German and Italian forces in Tunisia and the destruction of German General Erwin Rommel's *Afrika Corps*. By mid-May, Tunisia and all of North Africa were in friendly hands. With North Africa free of the enemy, the Allies turned their attention toward southern Europe,

Anything, Anywhere, Anytime

which lay just across the Mediterranean barely a hundred miles away. A second troop carrier wing, the 52nd, arrived in North Africa with its three groups and began training for airborne operations. The 316th Troop Carrier Group, which had been operating in support of the British Eighth Army with Ninth Air Force, transferred into the 52nd wing after it arrived.

In early June, the Allies invaded Pantelleria, an island in the middle of the Mediterranean about halfway between Tunisia and Sicily which was the objective for Operation *HUSKY*, the first Allied invasion of European soil. German and Italian forces were based on Pantelleria so they needed to be eliminated as a threat. The island was forty miles off of the Tunisian coast; it would provide an advanced base for fighter squadrons until airfields could be established on Sicily. The invasion of the Mediterranean island was completely bloodless; after several days of incessant air operations by fighter/bombers and light and medium bombers, the German commander decided to surrender rather than fight a potentially bloody and needless battle. Allied troops came ashore without opposition. The only casualty was a British soldier who was nipped in the buttocks by an irascible donkey.

Once Pantelleria came into Allied hands, the Mediterranean forces could focus all of their attention on Operation *HUSKY*, the invasion of Sicily, which would involve American and British airborne forces on a much larger scale than previously seen. Northwest Africa Air Force Troop Carrier Command, which had been established under the Northwest Africa Air Force with the 51st and 52nd wings, was given responsibility for transporting the airborne units and towing gliders then, once airfields had been secured, delivering equipment and supplies to the beachhead on Sicily and evacuating wounded. The new command was headed by a recently promoted Brigadier Gen. Paul Williams, who had spent several months out of the air transport business as commander of XII Support Command, a command responsible for providing close air support to ground units. Prior to the invasion, the troop carrier crews were given extensive training. Nevertheless, the airborne operations over Sicily turned into a disaster.

Planning for *HUSKY* called for the use of both paratroops and gliders. However, instead of using them in the manner in which Mitchell and Brereton had conceived them back in 1918, Eisenhower and his staff decided to use them to assault objectives just off of the invasion beaches. Mitchell's concept was to parachute infantry behind the German lines where they would form up and mount an attack on their rear. When the Army finally started forming paratroop battalions, their intent was to seize existing airfields or areas where landing strips could be built so they could be used to build up a base behind the lines. That was how MacArthur used his airborne forces in the Southwest Pacific but Eisenhower decided to use them as part of an amphibious operation.

The air assault of Sicily was the first large-scale paratroop and glider operation undertaken by the Allies in World War II. Two missions were scheduled for the early morning hours of July 10, 1943, which meant they were to be flown during darkness. The rationale for the night drops and early morning glider releases was that the darkness would conceal the transports from Axis gunners and the troops would land in advance of the amphibious forces and cause confusion in the enemy's rear. A formation of 226 C-47s from the 52nd Troop Carrier Wing took off with 2,781 paratroops from the 82nd Airborne Division and 891 parapacks. (Parapacks were supply containers made of nylon, cotton and Fiberglas that were mounted under the airplane's belly.) A combination of high winds and a difficult route that caused the formation to miss the first checkpoint in the darkness caused the drop planes to arrive in virtually complete darkness that hid the final checkpoints from view. Fires and smoke from an earlier bombing mission obscured the drop zones. The deadly combination led to a widely scattered drop, with paratroopers spread all over the area. Fortunately, the naval gunners had been instructed not to fire that night because of the scheduled airborne and glider operations. As it was, the troop carrier planes arrived over their checkpoint at Cape Passero in anything but an organized formation. In fact, according to a US Army article on airborne operations, they arrived from all points of the compass.

LADBROKE was a glider landing near Syracuse to seize a bridge across the canal south of the city in preparation for an advance by British Field Marshall Montgomery's Eighth Army. *HUSKY* Number 1 was a paratroop drop near Farello to capture high ground and a road junction six miles east of Gela in preparation for an advance by the American 1st Infantry Division, the Big Red One. Both missions were planned with complicated dogleg courses running east from Tunisia to Malta, then northward to Sicily. The dogleg was designed to lead the Germans to believe the formation was bound for Greece. Because of the necessity for complete radio silence, the courses were conceived partly to allow the pilots to maintain visual contact with landmarks on the islands, which was extremely difficult at night, and partly to avoid friendly naval vessels which were under orders to fire at any aircraft that came in their vicinity. The *LADBROKE* force got under way at approximately 1800 hours (6:00PM) on 9 July as 133 tow planes began taking off from their Tunisian bases. All but twenty-eight of the glider-towing transports were C-47s from the 51st wing, now returned to combat duty for after a stint of logistical flying with Services Command. The glider pilots were British but all of the gliders except eight were American-made WACOs. The eight were British-built

Anything, Anywhere, Anytime

Horsas, which were considerably larger than the WACOs and capable of carrying vehicles and artillery. Inside the gliders rode 1,600 glider troops from the British 1 Airborne Division.

After takeoff, the tow planes encountered strong winds, which blew them off course. Most of the transports and their tows drifted south of their route and missed their checkpoint on Malta. Some of the crews discovered their error and made corrections, which allowed the formation to get back on course as they approached Cape Passero, their landfall on Sicily. As they neared the cape, the formation climbed and descended to their release altitudes – 1,500 feet for the WACOs and 500 feet for the Horsas. Some crews encountered flak and their pilots swung wide to avoid it, thus getting off course. Poor visibility over the landing zones forced many of the tow planes to make multiple passes to line up properly for their releases, thus causing congestion in the skies around the release area. Many of the British glider pilots were inexperienced, with only a modicum of training. Very few were more than barely familiar with the American-built WACO gliders they were flying. Furthermore, they were making night landings even though what training they had was in daylight. Several pilots turned the wrong way after they were released and flew away from their intended landing zones.

Of 133 gliders released, only twelve landed even close to the LZ; at least 47 gliders and possibly as many as 65 came down in the sea. Many of the glider troops and their pilots drowned without ever reaching the beach. Most of the men who reached shore were scattered throughout the southeastern part of the island. Yet, in spite of the sorry state of the assault, the eight officers and 65 enlisted men who landed close to the designated landing zone managed to take and hold the canal bridge until advance elements of the Eighth Army reached it. The glider troops continued holding the bridge while British infantry and armor moved across it. *LADBROKE* was a miserable failure in terms of troops placed on target, but the mission was a success because the few men who were in the right place managed to accomplish their assigned mission, even though they were under-strength. Although the assault was in many ways a disaster, the few men who reached their objective showed what a small, well-trained force could do if they caught their enemy by surprise. However, the success had come at tremendous cost. British losses were 313 men killed, most of them due to drowning, and 174 missing, wounded or captured. It was a high cost to pay for a single objective, no matter its importance. At least part of the problem can be blamed on the mission being planned for a night operation. Finding a landing field is difficult enough during daytime, but locating a field at night is practically impossible without lights to identify it.

Sam McGowan

Husky No. 1 was the first US Army airborne operation in history. The mission could have been flown more successfully than it was. Yet, in spite of the failure of the troop carrier crews to put their troops on the drop zones, enough landed close enough to their primary objective that they were able to secure the high ground and road junction, then hold the position. Other 82nd troopers captured the town of Marina di Ragusa and soon made contact with the US 45th Division, which had just landed from the sea. The drop accomplished an even more important benefit – the paratroop drop thoroughly confused the Italians and caused them to panic and withdraw inland as much as ten miles away from the beaches. The confusion was caused to a large extent by the widely dispersed troops, who were scattered all up and down the Sicilian coast. Barely half ever reached their objectives. However, the small pockets of airborne troops led the enemy to believe there were a lot more of them than there actually were. Consequently, American and British ground troops were able to move inland more quickly than anticipated.

There can be no doubt that the widely dispersed drops were caused in large measure by the decision to drop at night. Although there was supposed to be moonlight, the pilots had a hard time seeing their island checkpoints. Navigation was made more difficult by the 45-mile an hour surface winds which also complicated the seaborne landings. However, the strong winds caused the Germans and Italians to let their guard down; they assumed that no one in their right mind would attempt airborne or amphibious operations in such conditions. The danger to the paratroops was the possibility of being dragged by an un-collapsed parachute. Strong winds on the sea caused high waves.

A third airborne mission on July 11 – *HUSKY* No. 2 – was a mission into disaster. In addition to navigating the complicated course of the previous mission, the 52nd TCG crews also faced the prospect of overflying 35 miles of a battlefield occupied by jittery ground troops, every one of whom was fearful of enemy air attack. Prior to reaching the beach, the drop formation had to fly over scores of Allied naval vessels operating just offshore. Like the soldiers on the beach, the sailors were equally fearful that the Germans would attack from the air. Plans for a safety corridor through the Allied fleet were made, but as is so often the case, "someone" failed to get the word and the ships' crews were not made aware of the approaching friendly formations. Furthermore, the Germans had retaken the Gela/Ferallo airport where the troops were supposed to land. As the formation approached Sicily, naval gunners aboard the Allied naval vessels and merchant ships opened up on the friendly planes with everything they had. When the transports came over the beaches, shore batteries opened up.

Anything, Anywhere, Anytime

Some of the fire over land was "friendly" and some was German but it really didn't matter who was firing because both sides were shooting at the Allied planes! As they approached the drop zone and saw all of the tracers arcing into the sky, some pilots felt it would be murderous to drop their troops into such a firestorm and turned away. The planes that dropped were so scattered from the intense fire that troopers were scattered all along the coast. Some transports remained under fire during their exit from over the beachhead until they were more than twenty miles out to sea. Losses from friendly fire were heavy. Twenty-three transports failed to return from the mission and those that made it back to their bases in Tunisia were badly damaged. One C-47 came back with more than 1,000 holes from flak in the wings and fuselage. Many of the holes came from "friendly fire." Seven troop carrier crewmen were killed, thirty were wounded and 53 were reported missing. (An airplane or airman was reported missing if they failed to return to their home base after a mission.) Losses among the paratroops were 81 killed, 132 wounded and sixteen missing.

Two nights later, a fourth mission with British troops encountered the same confusion and friendly fire that plagued the earlier drops. Out of 124 transports, eleven were shot down, fifty were damaged and 27 returned without dropping all of their troops. Yet, in spite of the disaster, the British troops were placed close enough to their target that they managed to seize the objective, a bridge across the Simeto River, and hold it until ground forces arrived to relieve them the next day. Once again, the value of airborne troops was demonstrated, even though only a small portion of the overall force reached their intended target.

The *HUSKY* drops were a disaster, with as many as 25 airplanes shot down by friendly fire – 42 transports were lost in all – but the paratroop and glider operations were an overall success in spite of heavy losses. General George Patton declared that the actions of the 82nd Airborne Division speeded his advance by 48 hours. Field Marshall Montgomery was even more optimistic – he believed that his advance had been expedited by as much as a week due to the airborne operations forward of his troops. Yet, even though the paratroop missions were militarily successful in that they achieved their objective of disrupting German lines of communication and causing confusion, more than sixty percent of the troops landed off of their intended drop zones. Even though airborne operations accomplished their objectives, General Dwight Eisenhower was not impressed. He felt that while small units with parachute capability had a purpose, he was opposed to the idea of airborne divisions and recommended that the divisions still in training should be turned into conventional infantry. Ike's ideas were horizontally opposed to those of Marshall, in particular. Eventually, Ike would be overruled and a large airborne army would form in England.

LOADING 75 MM CANNON ON A CG-4A

HUSKY was the first time American troop carrier crews had worked with gliders in combat. Glider warfare in World War II can only be given mixed reviews. In the earliest days of the war, the Germans were quite successful in their glider assaults but only because the opposing side was caught completely by surprise and had constructed no defences against them. The glider was a weapon that found a use only because of the lack of heavy equipment airdrop capabilities from airplanes in the 1940's. Theoretically, a glider could deliver equipment too large for airdrop onto a landing zone too short for powered aircraft or deliver troop units as large as a platoon in one airplane. In actual combat operations however, most glider assaults left most of the powerless airplanes destroyed beyond repair and the equipment they carried was often unusable. Many of the troopers

Anything, Anywhere, Anytime

arrived too injured to be useful – if they survived the landing. Still, even though glider operations were costly in terms of men and equipment, they were somewhat successful because of the element of surprise they offered. If a glider managed to land reasonably intact, and if the occupants were not too severely injured from the impact of landing, a single plane could place a sizable contingent of men into an area, and often with equipment that was not available to paratroops. It was this factor that caused the US Army to continue expanding its glider capabilities right up until the Normandy invasion. A large glider pilot training program had begun in the United States in 1942 but only a small number had been trained by mid-1943. Consequently, the pilots involved in *LADBROKE* were British. They had little experience in the American WACO gliders and none at night; British glider doctrine held that night operations were impossible.

After Sicily, glider pilots and their airplanes were assigned to the same troop carrier groups as the powered transports, thus they are a part of the history of the troop carrier/tactical airlift mission. Glider pilots were themselves somewhat of an anomaly. Though trained and rated as pilots, the training of the first group of glider pilots only qualified them to fly gliders, even though the mechanics of powered and glider flight is essentially the same. Glider pilots often called themselves "half a pilot." Originally, the Army intended to use qualified pilots in gliders but the demand for pilots was too great so enlisted soldiers were recruited with the promise that they would be promoted to staff sergeant upon graduation. When a call for men with previous flight experience went out, large numbers of soldiers who had washed out of pilot training were accepted into the program. Upon graduation, they were awarded wings with a G in the shield. By 1944, glider pilots were being commissioned as flight officers and a new policy led to dual qualification for most pilots. By 1945, many glider pilots were qualified power pilots with a minimum of 200 hours of powered flight. After the war, all troop carrier pilots were required to qualify in gliders as well as transports.

Sam McGowan

WACO CG-4A with towrope laid out and attached to tow plane

The gliders of World War II were very fragile when compared to powered aircraft. They were constructed of tubular steel, wood and aluminium with fabric skins. The cargo compartment floor was constructed of plywood. The most prevalent glider was the WACO CG-4A, which was small in comparison to the British Horsa and Hamilcar, but it was large enough to carry a Jeep or a small artillery piece. The cockpit was hinged so it could be raised to allow loading of vehicles and equipment. The CG-4A could carry thirteen troops and two pilots. In many instances, ground personnel sat in the co-pilot's seat. The United States never developed larger gliders but depended on the British for larger, cargo-carrying aircraft.

Gliders could be towed by any kind of powered aircraft, but since they were assigned to troop carrier squadrons, C-47s and C-53s usually served as tow planes. The British often used older bomber types that had been replaced in combat squadrons as glider tugs. There were methods by which gliders could be picked up from the ground by low-flying airplanes but the usual method of takeoff was for the tug to take off with the glider in tow. The towlines were laid out along the runway so that the tug would have reached flying speed by the time the slack was taken up and the glider began moving. The glider – or gliders since tugs often towed two at a time – would come off the ground and the tow plane would follow. The glider pilot was expected to maintain the proper position in relation to the tug in order

Anything, Anywhere, Anytime

to avoid causing the tug to become unstable. The tug pilot was responsible for maintaining the proper airspeed.[105]

During the flight to the landing zone, the glider pilots were at the mercy of the pilots of the tow planes, to which they were attached by a long line. If the tow plane pilot got off course, so did the glider. There were many things that could go wrong during the flight, some of which could cause a glider to come completely apart in flight and spill its occupants into the skies – and, ultimately, onto the ground or into the sea. Once on the ground, glider pilots became infantrymen, although their role was to defend the landing zone rather than to fight as conventional ground troops. US glider pilots were given infantry training comparable to that given to infantry officers but were planned to be evacuated as soon as practical while British pilots were expected to fight with the troops they brought in. There were methods for retrieving gliders by aerial pick-up (assuming the glider was still intact) but glider tactics ordinarily called for the pilots to remain with the troops they had brought in until they were relieved. Although the Allies originally intended to retrieve the gliders after an operation so they could be used again, an attitude soon developed that they were expendable.

In early 1945, some more experienced pilots were given special training and assigned to "combat control teams" to set up landing fields and control arriving aircraft, perhaps borrowing a technique that had been used in the CBI by the 1st Air Commando Group and brought to the First Allied Airborne Army by Col. Philip Cochran. Each combat control team was made up of two pilots, one of whom was experienced in powered aircraft as well as gliders, along with an enlisted communications specialist. Once they were on the ground and had set up their radio Jeep, the combat control officers issued instructions to other landing gliders and to transports bringing in reinforcements or supplies.

The advantage of gliders was that a small force could be landed on an LZ as a single unit and their equipment could be landed with them. The smaller CG-4As could deliver troops while the larger Horsa and Hamilcars brought in larger vehicles and artillery that were too large to be airdropped. In order to use gliders, there had to be a field large enough for them to land and it had to be free of obstacles such as ditches or tree lines to prevent damage to the gliders and possible loss of life. In 1942-45, they were the only means of delivering troops by air when there was no airstrip large enough for transports to land. Glider operations continued in the ETO until March 1945, when American and British airborne forces jumped into Germany in advance

---

[105] Bear in mind that most troop carrier pilots were young men, some still in their teens, with only a few hundred hours of flight time.

of Field Marshall Bernard Montgomery's crossing of the Rhine River. A plan had been developed to use airborne and gliderborne troops to capture Berlin, but it came to naught because of agreements between the Allies to halt US and British forces at the Elbe River. Had the Allies developed aircraft capable of dropping vehicles and artillery, it's doubtful that gliders would have ever been used.

The confusion of North Africa and the disasters at Sicily led to a loss of confidence in the troop carrier crews on the part of the young paratroopers. Although the crews must bear some share of the blame, the navigational errors that caused many troops to be dropped miles from their objectives were largely due to un-forecast weather conditions, particularly the high winds along the route on the first night. While experienced navigators should have been able to confirm their positions with celestial navigation, the transport crews were anything but experienced and they had no navigators. Other problems were beyond the control of the troop carrier crews. The friendly fire was due to a lack of communications between the Army and the Navy; a problem that has long plagued the US military and was prevalent as recently as the 1991 Gulf War. [106] After Sicily, troop carrier commands placed a heavy emphasis on navigational training and the importance of dropping troops where they were supposed to be. New navigational equipment that had been developed for heavy bomber operations at night and under instrument conditions was adapted for troop carrier use in airborne operations.

With North Africa and Sicily behind them, troop carriers in the ETO had had their introduction to the kind of combat that would prevail there for the rest of the war. The conditions faced in Africa and the Mediterranean differed considerably from those encountered by their counterparts in the Pacific. North Africa was essentially a war of armored forces maneuvering in wide expanses of desert, supported by large columns of supply laden trucks. Sicily was an island and supplies were delivered right to the beachhead from ships then moved inland by trucks that had been landed from the sea. Airborne operations were in close proximity to ground units with whom the paratroops were expected to quickly make contact. This was not how they had been envisioned by Billy Mitchell nor was it how Marshall and Arnold wanted them to be used. There is also the question as to why the

---

[106] Friendly fire is a lot more common in wartime than historians usually record. Aircrews at Pearl Harbor and in the Philippines were frequently shot at by their own troops. Allied ground troops in Europe had a tendency to shoot at anything that flew. In the 1991 Gulf War, US troops sometimes suffered more casualties from friendly fire than from the Iraqis.

Anything, Anywhere, Anytime

airborne and gliderborne operations were planned to be at night. American and British paratroops had some training in night drops but night time glider operations were against British doctrine while the US Army's experience with gliders was limited. No doubt the night operations were designed to reduce the danger from antiaircraft but they also led to misidentification and caused navigational problems for the crews. At this point in the troop carrier experience, navigators were not normally part of the troop carrier crew. If any navigators at all were assigned, they were only to a handful of crews.

Not only were airborne forces used in a different manner than their advocates believed they should be used, the way MacArthur used them in the Southwestern Pacific, troop carrier squadrons in the Mediterranean were also misused. Their intended combat mission was not only to support airborne troops but also to provide mobility to ground forces by flying them over natural obstacles and areas occupied by hostile forces to establish a ground base from which to attack the enemy's rear and harass his lines of supply. However, in the Mediterranean, when they weren't engaged in airborne operations, they were used mostly for logistical operations bringing supplies from rear area depots to combat squadrons operating in forward areas, a mission that was vital to the conduct of the war but in which highly trained troop carriers were flying routine transport missions that could have been flown by crews with minimal transport training. Furthermore, when they were taken off of logistical operations to train for airborne missions, the logistical mission suffered. Later in the war, new transport groups were established to support the air service commands and, after the Allies had landed in Normandy, to provide logistical support to both air and ground combat forces operating on the European continent.

After Sicily fell into Allied hands, the next objective was the Italian mainland. During the planning for the invasion, Maj. Gen. Matthew Ridgeway, commander of the 82nd Airborne Division, tried in vain to find a place where his paratroopers could be used in the invasion. The most likely objective appeared to be the Volturno River, but the planned drop was cancelled when the Navy learned that sandbars at the mouth of the river ruled out the location as a beachhead. While the invasion of Italy saw no airborne participation, German counterattacks led General Mark Clark to request a drop to prevent his men from being pushed into the sea. Clark called for a parachute assault on Avellino, a German supply center near the mountains, to cut off the enemy supply routes. On the evening of September 13, 1943, the 64th Troop Carrier Group took off from Agrigento on Sicily with the troopers of the 504th Regimental Combat Team, the same unit that had encountered "friendly fire" during

HUSKY. This time, all antiaircraft guns at Salerno were instructed not to fire at all after 9:00 PM unless they were requested to do so. The first wave dropped on target using a flaming T-marker made of gasoline-soaked sand as an aiming point. Dropping from 800 feet, the pilots put all of their troops within 200 yards of the IP. The second wave was not so fortunate. They were greeted by German antiaircraft fire that filled the skies with flak. Weather conditions had worsened, reducing visibility and lowering ceilings. Consequently, the troops were scattered. The third wave dropped with more accuracy. Within fifteen hours of the urgent appeal from General Clark, 1,300 troopers were on the ground at Salerno. Two nights later, the 505th RCT jumped behind American lines to reinforce the assault force. Thanks to the airborne intervention, the invasion force was able to move forward and the beachhead was successfully established.

Once the troops were ashore and airfields were established, troop carrier transports began arriving with supplies from North Africa and England. Some were assigned to Service Command to provide a communications link between the Twelfth Air Force bases as they were established on the Italian peninsula. There was little requirement for air transport support for the ground forces because the fighting was so slow and the ground units were close to the sea, where supplies could be landed by boat. With the declining need for air transportation in the area, much of the troop carrier force in the region was withdrawn to England to train with the troops of the 82nd, which also moved to the UK, and newly-arrived 101st Airborne Divisions in preparation for the invasion of the European continent.

In October 1943, there was a reorganization of the Army Air Forces in Europe as the focus switched to the Allied invasion of France, which was scheduled for the spring of 1944. Lt. General Lewis Brereton's Ninth Air Force headquarters transferred to the UK to become a tactical air force operating light and medium bombers and fighter/bombers assigned mostly to new combat groups that were coming over from the United States. A troop carrier command was also going to be part of Ninth Air Force and the groups that transferred to England from the Mediterranean were to form its nucleus. Although Brereton was the architect of US airborne operations, to this point in the war he had played no role in them. He would be able to put his experience and ideas to good use in the invasion of France. Brig. Gen. Benjamin F. Giles was placed in temporary command of IX Troop Carrier Command until Brig. Gen. Paul Williams became available. Ninth was slated to eventually become the largest US military organization in history, with close to 200,000 men assigned. Twelfth Air Force gave up its heavy bombers and also became a tactical air force while a new air force, Fifteenth, was activated to become the heavy bomber component of the Mediterranean Air Forces. The 52nd Troop Carrier Wing and its four groups moved north to England to join the soon-to-be massive IX Troop Carrier Command that was being assembled to support *OVERLORD*, the amphibious landings on the coast of Normandy. The 51st TCW remained in the Mediterranean as part of Twelfth Air Force with the 60th and 64th groups, and continued supporting Allied operations in Southern Europe. Troop carrier operations in the theater included airdropping supplies to partisan groups in Yugoslavia, Albania and Greece. In August 1944, the 51st TCW dropped paratroops and delivered gliders during Operation DRAGOON, the invasion of Southern France.

In April 1944, the 64th Troop Carrier Group was ordered to move to India on temporary duty to support operations in Burma. For two months, the 64th operated in the CBI, flying men and equipment across the Himalayan Hump from the Imphal Valley into Burma. A 64th TCG pilot, Capt. Hal Scrugham, was credited with the destruction of a Japanese Zero which struck the tail of his C-47 and went on to crash into the ground while the transport continued to fly. In June, after two months in the CBI, the group returned to its base at Comiso in Sicily. The 64th remained in the Mediterranean for the duration of the war.

The war in the Mediterranean was far from over in the summer of 1944, but the attention of the world was turning elsewhere, toward France and the beaches of Normandy. Lessons learned in Sicily and Italy were used to develop new procedures and methods that were designed to avoid future occurrences of the problems encountered in the Mediterranean. Special "pathfinder" units were developed in both the troop carrier wings and the airborne divisions with specially trained aircrews and paratroops. The mission of the pathfinder crews was to land pathfinder paratroops in advance of large-scale airborne operations who would set up EUREKA radio beacons to guide the troop carriers to the proper drop zones which they marked with panels and/or lights to make them easier to be identified. New electronic navigational equipment, including REBECCA, a receiver designed to receive signals from EUREKA ground transponders, were installed in troop carrier C-47s. Additional training was given to troop carrier crews in navigation and low-level formation flying. Navigators were transferred into troop carrier squadrons at a ratio of one for every three crews. The new methods would be put to the test in Normandy.

Sam McGowan

Chapter Seven - "The Continent"

Insignia of First Allied Airborne Army

The invasion of France, what the world has come to know as "D-Day,"[107] remains the most ambitious military operation ever attempted. Because the landings were the first on soil that had been invaded and occupied by Germany, it also received the most attention. In part because of the American role in France during World War I, the liberation of Occupied Europe was seen by many Americans as the most important role of US troops in the entire war. The Allies' publicized goal was to establish a beachhead on the European Continent from which the Allied armies could launch a campaign to liberate France, Belgium and the Netherlands, and ultimately bring about the defeat of the German Army.

In reality, the invasion was to open up a new front that would draw German forces away from the Eastern Front where they had been battling Soviet forces since 1941. Soviet dictator Josef Stalin had been pushing Churchill and Roosevelt to open up a new front since early 1942 but Churchill resisted until the combined American and British forces had been built up to the point that they would have a

---

[107] "D-Day" was not a specific term for the invasion of Western Europe, but rather was used to identify the projected date for any military operation, including invasions. The term was used in the press for the landings at Normandy and have become part of the popular lexicon to describe that particular operation even though every amphibious operation of the war had its on D-Day.

Anything, Anywhere, Anytime

reasonable chance of avoiding defeat.[108] Over a two-year period, the US built up strength in the UK but only the air elements of the Eighth Air Force and naval elements in the Atlantic were seeing combat. US infantry divisions were trained in the US then sent to England where they continued training in preparation for an invasion that was still well into the future. In early 1944, they were joined by experienced units such as the 1st Infantry and 82nd Airborne Divisions, which had seen combat in the Mediterranean.

When US plans were first being made for an assault on the European Continent, they were actually focused on airborne operations. Generals Marshall and Arnold favored a plan that would have essentially been an airborne invasion of France. The two senior US Army officers were both enthusiastic about the use of airborne units to invade France, but they were opposed by Eisenhower, Bradley and some of the senior British officers, including Field Marshall Montgomery and Air Marshall Trafford Leigh-Mallory, who was chief of staff of the Combined Chiefs of Staff for the Supreme Allied Commander who, at the time, had yet to be appointed. Leigh-Mallory advocated that there weren't enough transports available to support such an operation while Eisenhower and Bradley were never enthusiastic about the use of airborne and air transported troops.[109]

After their initial plan for an airborne operation was opposed by the British, Marshall and Arnold came up with a newer, more specific version. The plan was drawn up by Brig. Gen. Fredrick W. Evan, the commander of I Troop Carrier Command, and Col. Bruce Bidwell of the Operations and Plans division of the Air Staff. The new plan called for three Allied airborne divisions, two American and one British, to parachute some fifty miles inside France in the vicinity of the towns of Evreux and Dreux, both of which were the sites of Luftwaffe airfields. There were four airfields in the area. Paratroops would land and secure the airfields and transports would land with infantry

---

[108] US senior commanders, particularly President Franklin Roosevelt and Gen. George Marshall, had favored an Allied landing in France in 1942. An invasion plan coded as BOLERO called for the buildup of a massive troop carrier presence in the UK. In July 1942, under pressure from British Prime Minister Winston Churchill, the Allies decided to invade North Africa instead.

[109] The American and British generals in Europe were far from the "operator" personality that performed so well in the Southwest Pacific. Rather, they were traditional in their viewpoints and had yet to recognize the value of airborne operations as they had been originally conceived by the Soviets and Germans. While Leigh-Mallory was correct in his assessment of the numbers of transports available at the time he fought to have the operation canceled, by June 6 more than 1,000 American transports alone were based in the UK while there were thousands more aircraft of other types that could have been used for resupply and transport missions into the four airfields once they had been seized by an airborne assault.

reinforcements and supplies while supported by fighter/bombers. The air-transported force would set up an airhead from which they would disrupt German lines of communications and cause general confusion to allow amphibious landings on the coast. This was exactly the kind of operation Billy Mitchell and Brereton had envisioned twenty-three years before.

When he presented the plan to Eisenhower, Marshall stated that while he didn't want to exercise undue influence, the plan had his enthusiastic support. In his letter, he told Ike that he didn't want to hear that such a plan had "never been tried before." He said that such comments "make me tired." (Warren, 1957) Eisenhower considered the plan but came up with a number of reasons to reject it. He was fearful that the airborne troops lack of mobility might allow the Germans to surround and destroy them (Eisenhower apparently had failed to realize the impact of tactical fighter/bombers) and that the weather might hamper resupply operations. He commented that the time for such operations were after the Allies were firmly established on the Continent. However, once Allied forces were on the Continent, Eisenhower never approved a plan that would have presented such an opportunity.

At the *TRIDENT* conference in Washington in May 1943, the senior Allied commanders decided that there wasn't enough time to mount a cross-Channel operation before winter set in. They set a target date for the following May then proceeded to follow through with a plan to invade "Europe's soft underbelly" in Sicily. Since a Supreme Commander had yet to be appointed, the COCSAC staff was responsible for planning.[110] Initial plans for airborne operations were to use British airborne troops to capture the town of Caen. Seven battalions of American paratroops would assault coastal guns and river crossings on the right flank of the beachhead which would be between the Vire and Orne Rivers. Requirements for troop carrier aircraft kept increasing from an initial requirement of 634 airplanes to 799 by the end of July 1943. By the spring of 1944, the requirement had increased to more than 1,000 US transports alone. Plans to increase the number of US troop carrier groups included transferring the 52nd Troop Carrier Wing and its groups to the UK from the Mediterranean to join new groups then in training in the United States.(Warren, 1957)

---

[110] The appointment of a Supreme Allied Commander was possibly delayed by the untimely death of Frank Andrews. Marshall later indicated that Andrews was his first choice for supreme commander rather than Eisenhower. Since he was an airman, Andrews' views on the use of airborne forces would most likely have been more in tune with those of Arnold and Marshall than Eisenhower's were.

Anything, Anywhere, Anytime

While the Allies were beginning to turn the tide of war against the Axis in New Guinea and North Africa, a massive military training program was underway in the United States. The United States military was developing into the most powerful force ever seen on the face of the earth. In addition to millions of infantrymen, artillerymen, tankers and paratroopers, one of the goals of the War Department was to produce a million-man air force, although that figure was never reached in terms of combat personnel. Along with fighter pilots and bomber crewmen, pilots, navigators, radio operators and crew chiefs were being trained for the new troop carrier groups that had been created and for replacements for the units already engaged in combat. Glider pilots were being trained to fly the WACO gliders that were coming off assembly lines in the United States and the Horsas that had been purchased from the British. In addition to flight crews, thousands of young men were being trained to maintain their airplanes and perform other support functions.

Horsa Glider

Original War Department plans were for the VIII Support Command to become the US tactical air force in England to support the invasion of France but by mid-1943 the plan had changed to move Ninth Air Force from the Middle East to the UK. Ninth Air Force was to be the US element of the Allied Expeditionary Air Forces, an Allied unit set up under SHAEF to command and control air operations in support of the invasion and subsequent ground war in France. The AEAF was under the command of RAF Air Chief Marshall Trafford Leigh-Mallory, who was also the deputy commander of SHAEF. Its components were the British II Tactical Air Force and Ninth Air Force. Under the original concept, the AEAF was supposed to function directly under SHAEF command as the sole Allied air force to support the invasion forces. However, military politics reduced its effectiveness as senior Allied officers, specifically General Carl Spaatz from the US side, insisted on maintaining control.

In October 1943, after leaving North Africa for his new assignment in England, Ninth Air Force commander Brereton made a visit to the United States to inspect training facilities and meet with commanders who would be coming to England with their groups to join his command. During his trip, he paid a visit to the Airborne and Troop Carrier Training headquarters at Ft. Bragg, North Carolina where he met with Maj. Gen. Joseph M. Swing, who was in charge of the training program.[111] Brereton decided that since troop carrier squadrons were not needed in England for logistical operations, their departure for Europe should be delayed to take advantage of better weather in the US for training. Since troop carrier squadrons in the UK were not engaged in combat, unlike new bomber crews and fighter pilots who had the opportunity to move into operations gradually on missions over less heavily defended targets, for most of the troop carrier crews the D-Day mission would be their baptism of fire.

Brereton also decided to make sure that all C-47s would be equipped with self-sealing fuel tanks, and that REBECCA navigational equipment would be installed at depots in the US rather than waiting until after the airplanes had arrived in England. REBECCA was the airborne component of a system used to guide airplanes to an airfield, or in the case of troop carrier aircraft, to a drop zone. It picked up signals from beacons called EUREKA that were dropped by parachute with the airborne pathfinder force to guide the main force to the drop zone. As it turned out, Brereton's request for self-sealing fuel tanks in all of his C-47s was never granted.(Brereton, 1946) For some reason, even though troop carrier squadrons were identified as combat units, USAAF headquarters was never willing to treat them as such. Consequently, dozens of airplanes were lost and countless airmen died because of the failure to equip troop carrier aircraft with self-sealing fuel tanks and armor.

In December 1943, elements of the 53rd Troop Carrier Wing left the United States for their new bases in Greenham Common, England. While the wing and its groups, the 435th, 436th, 437th and 438th, were in the process of moving overseas, the 52nd wing left Sicily for Cottesmore. A third wing, the 50th, was already in England, having arrived in October 1943 to ultimately end up at Exeter. The 50th arrived with no groups assigned but was joined by the 439th, 440th,

---

[111] General Swing would later take command of the 11th Airborne Division and take it to the Southwest Pacific.

Anything, Anywhere, Anytime

441st and 442nd when they arrived in the UK in early 1944. Except for the groups that transferred to England from the Mediterranean, none of the groups in England had seen combat.

IX Troop Carrier Command Insignia[112]

The three wings and their respective groups constituted the IX Troop Carrier Command, the troop carrier element of Ninth Air Force, which moved to England from Africa to become the American tactical air force for the invasion of Western Europe. The unit's patch incorporates the words "Airborne" and "Troop Carrier" and includes a parachute and a glider to illustrate their mission. In late winter of 1944, while Eighth Air Force B-17s and B-24s were engaged in the largest bombing campaign of the war, IX Troop Carrier Command was busy training with the paratroopers of the 82nd and 101st Airborne Divisions and their British counterparts for D-Day. The plan for *OVERLORD* included several airborne operations, both American and British. Once again, planning for the airborne operations called for the paratroops to be dropped under the cover of darkness under the belief that even though night operations were more difficult for the flight crews, the airplanes (which lacked self-sealing fuel tanks) would be concealed from antiaircraft gunners and the descending paratroopers would be less likely to be seen by defenders on the ground. For the first time, American glider troops and glider pilots would see combat in Europe; no less than six gliderborne operations were planned for the invasion. In preparation for the event, US troop carrier strength in England was built up to more than 1,200 transports and more than 1,400 gliders, including 1,100 WACOS and 300 Horsas. British transport groups provided additional transport for their forces. Still,

---

[112] The IX Troop Carrier Command insignia was authorized locally for wear in the ETO and is not considered by the Air Force to be an "official" insignia because it wasn't approved by USAAF Hq.

Sam McGowan

while troop carrier strength for the invasion was impressive, it was not enough.

In an attempt to improve accuracy, IX Troop Carrier Command managed to obtain Gee navigational sets for installation on C-47s. Gee had been developed by the British early in the war and was used for night bombing. The system allowed navigators to obtain bearings from stations in the UK and plot their position to within 2,000 feet. However, IX Troop Carrier Command assumed an accuracy of 400 feet. Some C-47s were also equipped with SCR-717 radar, a recent development that was just starting to make its appearance on troop carrier aircraft. Radar-equipped C-47s had been assigned to the Mediterranean and eleven of them moved to the UK with the 52nd Troop Carrier Wing.

The Air Corps glider training program depended heavily on the prewar civilian aviation community, particularly on the cadre of air show performers. Mike Murphy was a civilian pilot who had made a reputation on the Midwest air show circuit. Like hundreds of other experienced civilian pilots, Murphy wanted to do his bit for his country and offered his services to the Army Air Corps. While most civilian pilots were put into non-combat roles such as flying for the Air Transport Command, Murphy was put in charge of glider pilot training. Another civilian aviator, Richard DuPont, was appointed director of the glider program. By 1944, Murphy had been promoted to lieutenant colonel and sent to England where he was the ranking glider pilot in the theater. As the senior glider pilot, he was scheduled to fly the first glider to land in Normandy.

The original date for the invasion was set for June 5, 1944 but bad weather over the English Channel caused General Eisenhower to delay the mission for twenty-four hours in hopes that the weather would clear. Although there was some clearing, there were clouds over the beaches that prohibited visual bombing while low-lying coastal clouds hampered airborne operations. However, Eisenhower was fearful that conditions would not suitable again for several months and ordered the operation, called *OVERLORD*, to launch. The airborne forces would be the first to go in Operation *NEPTUNE*. Late on the evening of June 5, the first of a massive armada of troop carrier planes began lifting off from fields in England. The first flights were made up of highly trained pathfinder crews and carried specially trained paratroopers carrying EUREKA radio beacons designed to guide the drop planes to their intended drop zones. Other aircraft dropped dummy paratroopers away from the main invasion beaches to confuse the Germans. Each little paratrooper was equipped with small explosive devices that were designed to start detonating when the dummy reached the ground, to give the impression of small arms fire.

Anything, Anywhere, Anytime

General Eisenhower visiting the 101ˢᵗ Airborne before D-Day
(In his address to the troops, he referred to IX Troop Carrier
Command as "the Air Transport Command")

The pathfinder force arrived over the beaches after an uneventful flight across the English Channel, but after they made landfall they ran into problems. The lead airplane ran into a bank of low-lying coastal cloud and disappeared from the view of the pilots in the rest of the formation. The interruption completely destroyed the formational integrity that had been drilled into the heads of the pilots during training, and which were so important to airborne tactics in World War II. Some pilots elected to climb above the clouds, others tried to go below them while others tried to maintain some semblance of a formation. The disorder caused the formation to break up and the force scattered. Then, to compound the problem, German flak came up to meet the low-flying transports as they crossed the coast. Once the Germans realized that an attack was underway, they opened up on the low-flying transports with everything they had – antiaircraft guns, machineguns, rifles and pistols. A hail of fire ranging from small arms to automatic antiaircraft and single-shot antiaircraft greeted the low-flying troop carrier planes. Many were hit by ground fire and large numbers were shot down or badly damaged. Very few of the specially-trained pathfinder troops were dropped anywhere close to where they were supposed to be. Consequently, the troop carrier aircraft that followed were pretty much on their own since the beacons had not been properly placed, if they had been set up at all. (Craven & Cate, 1956)

The problem was lack of experience. Very few of the pilots had flown combat before and they were naturally apprehensive, then when things started going to hell on a handcart, they came close to panic. There's no way to approximate hostile fire in a training situation – it's impossible to fire over the heads of rookie pilots as training instructors did in the infantry schools. Young men only a few years out of high school suddenly found themselves in a situation they hadn't even been able to imagine previously.

At 0130 the planes carrying the 101st Airborne Division arrived over Normandy and began dropping their troops. In part because of the failure of the pathfinders to find their objectives, the drops around St. Mere Eglise were scattered, an occurrence that seemed to characterize World War II paratroop operations in Europe.[113] Unknown to the young paratroopers, the drop zones were not the smooth pastures they had been briefed that they would be landing on. Military intelligence had failed to detect that the "pastures" were actually swampy lowlands that the Germans had flooded in anticipation of just such an event. Many of the paratroopers drew up their legs for a parachute landing fall only to discover that they were on a water jump!

Modern revisionists, mostly troop carrier veterans and their children, have sought to "correct the record," claiming that the US airmen's performance was not as poor as reported. To make such a claim flies in the face of the official records not to mention the reality of the situation. Except for the groups that had come up from North Africa, very few of the young airmen had ever been in combat before the Normandy drops. Most of the pilots were young men barely out of their teens with a few hundred hours of flying in their logbooks at most, the majority of it in trainers, none of which had been under fire, and they were flying airplanes with only rudimentary navigational equipment and no armor to protect the crews and troops against ground fire – and no self-sealing fuel tanks. It was not a gridiron game of brawn; it was a deadly mission at very low altitude over Adolph

---

[113] In response to statements made by the late author Stephen Ambrose in his books about the 101st Airborne, a number of troop carrier veterans – or their family members – raised considerable opposition to the assertions that the troop carrier crews were not adequately trained and that the situation had deteriorated over the beaches. But the opposition ignores the fact that for the vast majority of the young troop carrier pilots, the D-Day missions were their initial exposure to combat. To say that they were scared out of their wits would be no exaggeration. As a veteran of more than 1,200 combat sorties in Vietnam, including night missions over North Vietnam in the face of heavy antiaircraft fire, this author can state with certainty that reality and imagination are two separate entities.

Anything, Anywhere, Anytime

Hitler's Fortress Europe, at night and over and through low-lying coastal clouds. It is little wonder that the drops were not on the intended drop zones.

Some drops were complicated by the jumpmasters themselves. One 314th Troop Carrier Group crew made several passes over the drop zone, with the jumpmaster refusing to jump each time, until the airplane was finally hit by ground fire. The jumpmaster finally jumped to save himself and his men followed. The crew survived the crash – landing along with a wounded paratrooper who had been left in the airplane when the rest of the stick jumped. They spent the next twenty-four hours on the ground until they were finally picked up and taken to the beach for evacuation back to England on an LST.(62nd TCS Mission Report, 1945) The 82nd Airborne Division drops were just as confused and scattered as those of the 101st. In many cases, troops from the two divisions landed on the same drop zones. Instead of integral units, the initial paratroop force on the ground in Normandy turned out to be an ad hoc force of men who assembled as best they could as individual paratroopers found each other in the dark. Very few groups even resembled a military unit, but were made up of men from different squads, platoons, companies, battalions – even different divisions!

Initially, IX Troop Carrier Command thought the drops had gone off well. Casualties had not been as great as they could have been. (Twenty-one transports were shot down and 196 were damaged. Casualties were 65 killed or missing and fifteen wounded.) However, when Brig. Gen. Elwood "Pete" Quesada, the commander of IX Tactical Air Command, returned to the UK on June 10 he reported that the drops had been widely scattered and General Omar Bradley, the US commander for the D-Day operation, was not pleased. Only ten percent of the troops were actually dropped on their intended drop zones although 55 percent were within two miles. However, some troops were as far as 25 miles from their intended destination. Less than 3,000 paratroops were anywhere close to their objectives by 0630 on the morning of D-Day. By midnight that night, the 101st only had 2,500 troops under division control and the 82nd only 2,000. This was out of a total force of over 13,000 men, of which 10,000 were supposed to be close to their intended drop zone.

After dropping their paratroops, the plan called for the transports to return to England to pick up gliders, but many transports returned to their bases too shot-up for a second mission and many failed to return at all. Several landed back in England with wounded, both crewmembers and paratroopers, aboard. The glider pilots and their passengers watched as their powered squadron mates came back to their bases one by one, with no appearance of formational integrity. They could see from the blue exhaust flames, or lack of them, that many of the transports were flying on only one engine. Some came back without having dropped their troops for various reasons. No less than twelve paratroopers came back to England because they slipped on vomit and became hopelessly entangled in the static lines of their buddies who had jumped before them![114] (Craven & Cate, 1956) As had happened in Sicily, the initial paratroop operations on D-Day were only moderately successful. Once again, the drop formations had become disorganized and scattered; and troops were dropped all over the landscape. Ground fire had taken a heavy toll among the troop carriers; a total of 21 C-47s and C-53s failed to return and many of the young paratroopers were shot as they hung in their parachutes even before their feet touched the ground.[115] The glider forces were going to encounter conditions that were just as bad – maybe even worse!

When the glider pilots landed in Normandy, they had a quick lesson in reality. They had been briefed that the "hedgerows" on and around the fields that had been picked for landing zones would be easy to break through. But the hedgerows turned out to be towering tangles of plant trunks and packed dirt over fifty feet high that had been there for centuries, and their consistency was that of concrete. Many – if not most – of the gliders were destroyed in the landings and their occupants were killed or injured by the impact.

One of the casualties was the assistant division commander of the 101st Airborne Division, Brig. Gen. Don Pratt, along with his aide, Lt. John Butler. Gen. Pratt had been scheduled to come ashore with the seaborne element of the 101st but had switched to a glider landing to boost the morale of the glider troops. The glider pilot, Lt. Col. Mike Murphy, the ranking glider pilot in the ETO, miraculously escaped injury in the crash. Yet, even though only six gliders landed intact on the right LZ, the glider missions were considered militarily successful! Although only seven gliders were reported as shot down or missing, 175 were damaged during landing out of 516 that were considered as "effective." Casualties were 463 glider troops and 57 pilots killed, wounded or missing.

---

[114] While the common image of the young paratrooper is that of rugged men who were generally fearless, in fact the reverse is true. Paratroopers went on missions generally scared to death and their tension combined with the turbulence of low altitude flight made them nearly all airsick. Once one vomited, it set off a chain reaction and every man on the airplane would throw up. Air sickness was so common among paratroopers that the 101st Airborne Division motto "Screaming Eagles" led to them being called the "Puking Buzzards" by the airmen who took them into combat and personally witnessed the evidence of their fear.

[115] Troop carrier crews on airborne operations had the most dangerous job of any American airmen. The 41 transports lost on D-Day operations were as heavy as losses taken by Eighth Air Force bomber crews.

Anything, Anywhere, Anytime

D-DAY GLIDER LANDINGS
Even though both the airborne and glider operations had been costly in equipment and loss of life, they were overall successful. True enough, the paratroopers were widely scattered, but their presence behind the beachhead caused mass confusion among the Germans and greatly increased the effectiveness of the invasion forces on Utah Beach. Other troop carrier crews brought in British paratroops and glider men in operations that met with similar success. While the paratroop operations on both the American and British beaches were carried out in the early morning hours in darkness, glider landings continued throughout the day as flights brought in units with jeeps, artillery, communications equipment and other items too large for airdrop from the C-47s.

On D-plus 1, IX Troop Carrier Command transports flew missions delivering supplies to the paratroops who had been dropped the previous morning. Although each C-47 was capable of carrying 6,000 pounds of cargo, loads were limited to 2,000 due to the amount of time required to dispense bundles. Some airplanes carried a "dropmaster," a Quartermaster who had been given a two-week course in aerial supply who flew on drop missions to provide a third man to assist with dispensing the bundles.[116] The 2nd Quartermaster Depot Supply Company was supposed to load the airplanes and provide dropmasters but not enough men had been qualified in time for D-Day and only about a third of the crews in the drop formation included one. Each load consisted of six bundles packed in British-supplied Wicker baskets, while two Fiberglas lined parachute packs were suspended beneath the airplane's belly. Although the British had developed roller conveyers for aerial delivery, the containers used by IX TCC tended to become tangled in the mechanisms. A maximum of thirty seconds was allowed for a drop to insure that all of the bundles landed within the confines of the designated drop zone. On airplanes without a dropmaster onboard, the crew chief and radio operator kicked out the bundles.(Warren, 1957)

Once the Allies had established a beachhead in Normandy, the next step was to break through the German defenses and begin an advance into the French interior. An airborne operation was planned for June 14 called *WILD OATS* to drop British paratroops in front of the British lines at Evrency in advance of an armored attack. The operation was canceled after German armored units pushed British units back onto the beaches on June 13. For several weeks, the Allied Command concentrated on building up the strength of the troops on the beaches in preparation for the planned breakout, and since supplies could come in from the sea, the troop carrier crews enjoyed a temporary lull to recuperate from the horrors of D-Day. However, the pilots and crewmen knew their rest was short-lived, and that they would be very busy once the armies started moving. However, a major reorganization changed the entire scope of troop carrier operations.

Some six weeks after the landings in Normandy, the Allies launched a second front when Allied troops landed on the Mediterranean beaches in the south of France. Operation *DRAGOON* was aimed at the area around Cannes, the region commonly known as the French Riviera. Crews from the 51st Troop Carrier Wing, supplemented by transports from IX Troop Carrier Command that had been sent on detached duty in the Mediterranean, took off from Italian

---

[116] The first known official use of the term is found in IX Troop Carrier Command records. Ground personnel, many of whom were quartermasters, started flying on cargo drop missions as "kickers" in both New Guinea and the CBI in the summer of 1942. Apparently IX TCC decided to formalize the duty and trained a number of men to fly as dropmasters on cargo missions prior to the Normandy landings.

Anything, Anywhere, Anytime

bases in 400 transports, with each either laden with paratroopers or towing a glider. While the drops were marginally successful, the crews encountered the same kind of bad luck that plagued other airborne operations. The transports carrying the pathfinder force arrived over a beach enshrouded by morning fog. Only one element managed to put their troops anywhere close to where they were supposed to be. The lead pilot recognized hilltops sticking through the fog from the sand-table model he had studied and dropped in relation to them. All of the troops dropped by his element landed within half a mile of their intended drop zone. Other elements dropped entirely by guesswork – scattering troops across vineyards, the beaches and on rooftops. One serial landed right in the middle of downtown Saint Tropez! Some of the drops were tragic – the crews dropped too early and the heavily burdened troopers drifted out over the sea and were drowned.

ITALIAN-BASED C-47S DURING DRAGOON

The first glider mission took off from Italian bases at 0500 loaded with artillery for the British paratroops.[117] As the flights approached Corsica, the pilots received word that the mission had been canceled because of the fog over the beaches. The planes towing the large Horsas turned around to return to their bases in Italy but the American-flown WACOs continued. The tow planes circled over the beaches for an hour waiting for the fog to lift. At 0930 the 33 WACOS were released; they came down with little loss. That afternoon, the 35 Horsas returned to the beaches in advance of a paratroop mission involving 41 planes. The paratroops were followed by an armada of 332 WACO gliders carrying a complete infantry battalion of the famous 442nd Regimental Combat Team, a Japanese-American unit, along with

---

[117] DRAGOON consisted of both American and British airborne troops. Although both US airborne divisions had moved to England, several independent airborne brigades and regiments were assigned to the operation from bases in Italy.

artillery and support troops. The approach of the gliders was characterized by the same confusion that seemed to accompany airborne operations in the ETO. The formation was delayed initially when the lead glider developed a vibration and the tow plane returned to Italy, followed by the rest of the formation. It was not until the glider pilot cut his airplane away to land in the ocean that the mistake was realized. Then, after returning to their course, the pilots discovered a haze layer over the beaches at 800 feet. The haze, which consisted of smoke from the bombing and artillery fire, was enough to cause the formation to drift just enough off course that they were out of the corridor through which they were supposed to fly. Naval gunners opened fire on the formation, but damage was, fortunately, slight. The glider landings were successful and once the troops were on the ground they met only minimal resistance. After the operation, the IX Troop Carrier Command airplanes and crews returned to England.

On August 1, a reorganization of Ninth Air Force and the Allied airborne divisions took place. Under a plan that had been formulated over the previous two months to consolidate IX Troop Carrier Command with the airborne units, Lt. Gen. Brereton left command of Ninth Air Force to assume command of the First Allied Airborne Army, a joint US-British organization made up of all of the airborne units in England, IX Troop Carrier Command and two RAF transport wings. As the original planner for US airborne operations in 1918, Brereton was the natural choice to command the first (and only) large airborne army in history.[118] When he learned of the plan in mid-July, Brereton was not enthusiastic. He recommended that instead of forming a new organization, the airborne divisions should simply be transferred to Ninth Air Force, a transfer that had been recommended by Arnold the previous December.

Brereton's recommendation was actually logical. The paratroop idea had originated among airmen and their stated purpose was to secure sites for airfields behind enemy lines. Airborne operations in the Southwest Pacific were planned primarily by Fifth Air Force with the intent of moving the bomb line further north. Marshall was also in favor of placing the airborne units under air force control. While Brereton and Arnold's suggestions made sense, Eisenhower did not like it because it would give the air force control of ground troops and also out of fear of offending officers of the British Army, who were also

---

[118] As noted in Chapter One, Brereton, then a major, had drawn up plans for the use of parachute troops in France while assigned to Brig. Gen. Billy Mitchell's staff in World War I.

Anything, Anywhere, Anytime

opposed to placing airborne forces under air force command.[119] The British were in favor of organizing all of the troop carrier forces into one command, a view with which Brereton had agreed when it was first suggested, but on the condition that it would be commanded by an American officer. The British had not been happy with that arrangement and the plan had been put on hold. In mid-July, the idea was brought back into play and Brereton was notified that he would be taking command of the new organization. The commander of British airborne forces, Lt. Gen. F.A.M. "Boy" Browning was appointed as his deputy commander.

The airborne army initially consisted of three American airborne infantry divisions, three British and a British air-transported division. A Polish airborne brigade was added.[120] The third American division was the 17th Airborne, which had recently arrived in the UK and was undergoing theater training. A fourth American division, the 13th Airborne, was still in training at Fort Bragg and Camp MacKall, North Carolina and would arrive in Europe in early 1945. The US XVIII Corps transferred to England and became the command organization for the American airborne divisions. That such an organization came to exist is remarkable considering Eisenhower's attitude toward airborne units. He had not been pleased with their performance in North Africa and Sicily and had advocated that existing airborne divisions be broken up and their troops reassigned to conventional infantry divisions. He was overridden by US Army Ground Forces commander Lt. Gen. Leslie McNair and General George Marshall, who, along with General Henry H. Arnold, saw the value of airborne operations. McNair had also had misgivings but returned to his previous support after maneuvers at Ft. Bragg when the 11th and 17th Airborne Divisions demonstrated their effectiveness.[121]

---

[119] Where airborne forces should be assigned was a continual problem with Allied forces. The Germans had assigned their paratroop divisions to the Luftwaffe, a logical assignment since airborne operations were originally conceived as a means of establishing landing zones for powered aircraft behind enemy lines. Both Arnold and Marshall saw airborne troops as an element of air power, but other officers such as Eisenhower and Bradley considered them to be merely infantrymen who had been trained to parachute from airplanes. The two senior US Army officers saw a much larger role for airborne forces both during the war and in the postwar military than Eisenhower and Bradley allowed.

[120] When German troops occupied most of Europe, expatriates and men from the occupied countries who escaped to England were organized into national units within the British Army and Royal Air Force. Expatriate women from occupied countries also served in various capacities, including in special service units as agents who parachuted back into their native countries.

[121] McNair was later killed in a tragic accident in Normandy when American bombs fell several hundred feet short of the established bomb line.

The troop carrier force consisted of IX Troop Carrier Command and RAF 38 Group. On August 25, IX TCC was transferred out of Ninth Air Force and placed under the direct control of the United States Strategic Air Forces in Europe, commanded by General Carl Spaatz.[122] Brereton recognized a major drawback with the reorganization. The entire IX Troop Carrier Command and its fleet of C-47s was dedicated to the support of airborne operations, as were large numbers of British transports, and they were no longer immediately available to support ground operations. He foresaw a demand for transports from ground commanders that it would be difficult to meet because IX TCC was dedicated to supporting the airborne divisions, not only on combat operations but in training in the UK. Furthermore, Spaatz was assuming control over assets that were supposed to be his.

Brereton's orders as commander of the new airborne army were to "establish bold and daring plans" to make maximum use of airborne forces. He and his staff worked constantly to develop new plans, but although Eisenhower sometimes gave at least tacit approval, the plans were ultimately disapproved by the field commanders, Bradley and Montgomery. On several occasions, operations got as far as moving the troops to the airfields and preparing to load them onto transports before an order came down canceling the operation. One such operation would have dropped troops to block German forces retreating through what came to be known as the Falaise Gap. The troops were on the airplanes and the crews were preparing for engine start when word came down that the mission had been canceled. Consequently, thousands of Germans escaped through the gap in the Allied lines. US troops would face them again the following winter in the Ardennes Forest.

Shortly before the invasion of Southern France, a C-47 lifted off from a base in England for an airfield in Normandy. Riding in back of the airplane was a man who was already a legend, and whose greatest fame lay yet before him. Lt. Gen. George S. Patton had been kept in England to confuse the Germans, in hopes that they would believe the Normandy operation was a diversion and that he would command the

---

[122] USSTAF was originally established to command US heavy bomber operations against Germany. But as with all institutions and their heads, Gen. Carl Spaatz sought increased power. When Brereton moved to the UK to organize Ninth Air Force, Spaatz pulled rank and insisted that it be under USSTAF direction and Eisenhower let it stand. When Brereton was given command of First Allied Airborne Army, the situation became even more confusing and convoluted. Brereton was an air officer in command of ground troops and was supposed to have command of IX Troop Carrier Command and the RAF transport groups as well, but Spaatz insisted on maintaining control over the US troop carrier units.

Anything, Anywhere, Anytime

"real invasion force" at another location elsewhere on the French coast. That the Allied armies were basically trapped on the beaches for several weeks added to some senior German officers' belief that the Normandy invasion was but a prelude to a larger operation elsewhere. Patton was coming to Normandy to take command of and activate the US Third Army, and to lead it to glory in a campaign that became heavily dependent upon air transport for resupply. Unlike many generals of his day, Patton had complete faith in airpower to support ground forces. While Generals Eisenhower and Bradley believed the Allies should advance steadily so that the armies could protect one another's flanks and remain tied to their ground lines of supply, Patton believed his flanks could be protected by tactical airpower while IX Troop Carrier Command could keep his armored forces supplied with fuel and ammunition as they drove deep into the heart of the enemy.

A week after he arrived in Normandy, Patton led Third Army out of the beachhead to exploit an advantage gained by the Allied breakout at Avaranches in an operation called *COBRA*. Third Army went through a gap in the German lines and mounted a spectacular driving advance that placed its tanks well beyond the trucks that constituted their line of supply. Fuel, ammunition and other supplies were flown to France to support Patton's spectacular advance. When possible, C-47s and other transports, including at least one squadron of C-109 tankers, landed on captured German airfields to deliver gasoline and ammunition, but as often as not they delivered their loads by airdrop to the fast-moving columns. Fuel was the most needed commodity delivered by the transports. Rigging crews in England prepared bundles made up of five-gallon Jerry cans of gasoline for delivery to Third Army columns.

Supporting Patton's rapidly advancing forces placed a heavy load on IX Troop Carrier Command, which was already dedicated to the newly created First Allied Airborne Army for upcoming operations.[123] Fortunately, there were two transport groups in England that were part of the service commands of Eighth and Ninth Air Force. To take up slack left by the loss of the troop carrier groups, the 302nd Transport Wing was formed to control the 27th Transport Group, which had previously been part of Eighth Air Force, and the 31st Transport Group, which was originally under Ninth.[124] While the 302nd's primary

---

[123] At least sixteen airborne operations were planned after the Normandy landings, but were canceled for various reasons. Each time an operation was planned, badly-needed transports were taken off of transport missions in support of ground forces in France and held in reserve at their English bases.

[124] The two transport groups had been formed solely to provide logistical support for combat squadrons. The 27th initially operated Martin B-26 bombers on routes around the UK.

Sam McGowan

mission was to support the air service commands, it was also given responsibility for transporting supplies to ground forces in France. To strengthen the logistical force, 100 Air Transport Command C-47s were reassigned from ATC's domestic wing to Europe. Yet even with the additional airplanes, the wing had less than 200 transports. To reinforce them, several Eighth Air Force B-24 groups were detached and reassigned to the Combined Air Transport Operations Room for transport duty. (The CATOR was a former Allied Expeditionary Air Forces agency that transferred to the First Allied Airborne Army.) Now that troops were on the ground in France, the strategic bombing mission formerly conducted by Eighth Air Force was no longer prominent and the resupply mission had higher priority. For the bomber crews, the "trucking" missions were a drastic change from the high level bombing missions they were used to. The missions required the crews to fly low and slow over parts of France that were still occupied by the Germans, some of whom were very heavily armed. For some of the veteran Liberator crewmen, the resupply missions brought back memories of the daring low-level raid the year before on the oil fields at Ploesti, Romania.[125]

FLIGHT NURSE LOADING JERRY CANS OF GASOLINE FOR PATTON'S THIRD ARMY[126]

---

[125] On August 1, 1943 five Eighth and Ninth Air Force B-24 groups attacked the oil refining complex at Ploesti, Romania at tree-top altitudes.

[126] I'm not sure about this picture; it may have been staged. It was taken by a Life Magazine photographer. Life once featured a famous photograph implying that a B-17 was flown with an all-female flight crew. In fact, the WASPS included only pilots. There were no female engineers, radio operators or navigators.

Anything, Anywhere, Anytime

Like Patton, British Field Marshall Bernard Montgomery also felt that the best way to defeat the Germans was to pour all available supplies and resources into a single advance. Quite naturally, he believed that the advance should be under his command. Montgomery tried to convince Eisenhower of the wisdom of this tactic but without success. (Patton more or less ignored Ike and Bradley and kept moving forward until the C-47s, B-24s and trucks that were his lifeline were taken away!) While Patton's Third Army was rapidly advancing through France, Montgomery was working on a "bold plan." He proposed an airborne attack in the vicinity of Arnhem in Holland to capture several bridges and seize a bridgehead across the Rhine. British tanks would cross the river and invade northern Germany after driving north out of Belgium. Under Montgomery's plan, while the paratroops were attacking the bridges, his 21st Army Group's XXX Corps would advance northward toward Arnhem then use them to cross the Rhine.

Eisenhower was under pressure from Marshall and Arnold to make more imaginative use of his airborne resources so he approved Montgomery's Operations *MARKET* and *GARDEN*, commonly knowsn as *Market/Garden* although they were actually two operations. Operation *MARKET* was the airborne phase of the dual plan, while *GARDEN* was an armored attack toward the objective, which was almost seventy miles in advance of the Allied lines. The distance itself was not so great, but the roads over which the armored columns must pass were very narrow and surrounded by marshes and water. Montgomery's plan focused solely on the bridges and failed to include any airfields, which could have been used to bring in reinforcements, equipment and supplies. *MARKET* was the responsibility of the newly created First Allied Airborne Army, which consisted of the American 82nd, 101st and 17th Airborne Divisions, along with the British Airborne Corps and the 1st Polish Parachute Brigade. Since the 17th Division was still in training, it did not take part in the operation. More than 35,000 airborne troops would take place in *MARKET*.

Planning for *MARKET* called for a daylight operation, a departure from previous airborne procedures that was ordered personally by Brereton. When he was given command of the First Allied Airborne Army, along with the order he received a note from Eisenhower directing him to improve the troop carrier navigation problems that had plagued the operations in Sicily and in *OVERLORD*. Part of the problem was that troop carrier manning only called for two navigators for every six crews in a squadron. Since troop carriers flew in three-plane elements, manning allowed for one navigator for each element, which was fine for daylight operations but when formations scattered at night as so often happened, the other two crews were left without one. Brereton also ordered an emphasis on getting troops on target, even if it meant flying into the face of ground fire or even keeping a burning airplane on course until the troops had jumped. His new policies were evident during *MARKET*.

C-47s and Gliders forming for MARKET

One of the major deficiencies with *MARKET/GARDEN* was that there simply weren't enough troop carrier aircraft and crews to go around. Ever since the *COBRA* forces broke out of the Normandy beachhead and Patton's Third Army began its rapid advance, IX Troop Carrier Command had been devoting most of its resources to keeping the ground forces supplied, flying in reinforcements and evacuating casualties. There were no airplanes available to train the paratroops in England as they were all busy flying missions to France. Eisenhower ordered that the transports supporting Patton be withdrawn to support Montgomery. Patton's ground supply resources were also taken away, in effect leaving Third Army stranded without fuel well in advance of the rest of the Allied front. Because of the shortage of transports and their value to the Allies, the *MARKET* planners were

Anything, Anywhere, Anytime

instructed to select drop zones some distance from the well-defended bridges to avoid ground fire. Air transport had become so important that the Allies could not afford to lose a single airplane. In order to increase transport capabilities, Eisenhower ordered US Strategic Air Forces Europe commander Gen. Carl Spaatz to take some of the Eighth Air Force's heavy bombers off of bombing operations and assign them to transport missions. Second Air Division, which operated B-24s, was given the mission.

On September 17, 1944, *MARKET/GARDEN* was launched. For the first time in combat in the ETO, the American and British paratroops jumped in daylight rather than at night. Unlike previous airborne operations, *MARKET* went off as planned, in spite of intense ground fire that greeted the transports as soon as they entered German-controlled territory. After several weeks of combat flying, the troop carrier pilots had become veterans. They held their course throughout the low-level flight across German territory in spite of heavy ground fire. Most of the 87 US transports shot down over Holland were lost because the pilots were concentrating on putting their troops on the drop zones. One C-47 was hit as the airplane approached the drop zone and was set on fire but the pilot held the airplane steady on course until the troopers could jump right over the DZ. The airplane crashed almost immediately afterwards; there were no parachutes from the crew. Radio operators and crew chiefs escaped from airplanes that took their pilots to a fiery death.

Thanks to the courage and dedication of the troop carrier pilots, eighty percent of the paratroopers in the 101st area of operations landed on the drop zones. The airplanes carrying the 82nd encountered heavy flak that damaged 118 airplanes and brought down ten before they dropped their troops. In spite of the heavy opposition, all troops were dropped as ordered and came down on the drop zones. For their role over Holland, instead of criticism troop carrier pilots received praise for their bravery from the paratroopers who had ridden with them into a new version of hell.

After the paratroops were on the ground, a huge armada of more than 600 gliders arrived over Arnhem with 500 vehicles and 330 pieces of artillery. More than 2,000 transports were involved in the initial paratroop and glider operations. Instead of co-pilots, an airborne soldier occupied the right seat in the American gliders, a concession to the need to get as many troops into Holland as was physically possible. The American 82nd landed near Nijmegen and the 101st near Eindhoven, while the British landed near Arnhem. More drops with reinforcements were to follow the initial assault.

Troops waiting to load for Market.

Once they were on the ground, both the American and British paratroopers quickly seized some of their objectives while the element of surprise was in their favor. But holding the bridges would be a different matter. Allied intelligence had picked up information that strong German Panzer forces had moved into the area around Arnhem, but the *MARKET* planners discounted it as false, to their eventual dismay when British paratroopers encountered much stronger opposition than expected. To complicate matters, the British ground advance became bogged down. *GARDEN* was dependent upon a single narrow road through the Dutch Lowlands to move hundreds of tanks, trucks and other vehicles. The road could not handle the load and the ground element soon came to a halt when XXX Corps found itself stuck in snarled traffic. The advance was complicated by crowds of jubilant Dutch civilians eager to greet the advancing British troops.

Anything, Anywhere, Anytime

Supply-Laden B-24s on the way to Arnhem

To maintain the airborne force so far ahead of the Allied lines, a massive aerial resupply effort was required. Since the troop carrier transports were tied up with the paratrooper and glider operations, Eighth Air Force B-24s were assigned the resupply mission. The first resupply flight was made up of 135 bombers loaded with airdrop bundles that had been rigged by the 2nd Quartermaster Company. Each B-24 carried a Ninth Air Force "dropmaster" as part of the crew. Dropmasters were a new troop carrier development that came about prior to *OVERLORD* when Quartermaster personnel were put through a two-week course to learn how to rig cargo for airdrop and dispense it from aircraft.[127] Not enough dropmasters had been trained for one to fly on each C-47 dropping cargo on D-Day but training had continued and more had become available in time for *MARKET/GARDEN*. Many of the bundles fell in the no man's land between the 82nd positions at Nijmegen and the Germans but that night the Americans went out after dark and recovered more than eighty percent of the drop. Eleven Liberators were shot down over Holland.

A reinforcement mission was flown onto the same drop zones on the second day of the operation. Once again, the transports and gliders ran a gauntlet of enemy fire as they flew over seventy miles of enemy territory. Several gliders were shot down while others were released prematurely after they became uncontrollable in the slipstream left by the transports, but most gliders reached the drop zones intact. Once they were on the ground, the glider pilots were organized into infantry units to relieve the paratroopers so they could attack the Nijmegen Bridge. Fortunately, casualties were light among the glider pilots, with only ten wounded and two killed. Glider and paratroop reinforcement missions continued over Holland for the next several days, until the slowly advancing ground forces finally reached the area. Each mission encountered ground fire so heavy that one of the British officers at Arnhem would later say that there wasn't a troop carrier pilot involved in the operation who didn't deserve the Victoria Cross.[128] (Brereton, 1946)

MARKET/GARDEN was successful in that the objectives were captured. British paratroops managed to cross the Rhine, but when they got to the other side, they encountered superior German forces and had to withdraw because they could not be relieved, although they held out for several days. Montgomery's "bold" (some say foolish) plan had managed to drive a very thin wedge some sixty miles ahead of the Allied lines, but there was no way to exploit the advantage due to the congested single road leading through the swampy lowlands to Arnhem. Much of Holland remained in German hands right up until the end of the war in Europe. *MARKET/GARDEN* was costly for IX Troop Carrier Command and the Army air forces. Sixty-eight transports,

---

[127] The IX Troop Carrier Command dropmasters are the historical forerunners of modern loadmasters. Previously, cargo had been kicked out by the crew chief (or aerial engineer) and radio operator, although ground personnel sometimes went along on cargo drop missions as "kickers." The assignment of 2nd Quartermaster personnel to dropmaster duty formalized the field, and provided the basics for what eventually evolved into the aerial port aerial delivery section.

[128] The Victoria Cross is the British equivalent to the US Medal of Honor.

Anything, Anywhere, Anytime

gliders and fighters were lost over Arnhem on D-Day alone. Resupply and reinforcement drop missions were flown every day for eight straight days. When a grass fighter strip was located near the village of Grave, plans were made to use it as an advance airfield for troop carrier aircraft. One reinforcement mission was flown into it but it was lost to troop carrier use because of demands for an RAF advanced fighter base.

B-24 Crash-Landing in Holland

In mid-December, the Germans launched fierce attacks against inexperienced American troops in the Ardennes Forest region of Belgium. The German goal was to split the Allied front and force the British into a trap, as they had done at Dunkirk in 1940. The 82nd and 101st Airborne Divisions, which had been scheduled to go to Paris for rest and recuperation after – finally – being relieved in Holland,[129]

---

[129] Although airborne doctrine called for airborne units to be relieved as soon as possible, supply and reinforcement problems for ground units in Holland led to the 82nd and 101st remaining there until mid-November. They then went to a reserve camp at Reims.

Sam McGowan

were ordered into the battle as reinforcements. Using trucks instead of airplanes for transport and scrounging ammunition from retreating units, the Screaming Eagles moved into the Belgian town of Bastogne while the 82nd occupied the town of Werbemont a few miles to the north. Brereton was notified to move the 17th Airborne, which was still in England, to Reims. He was also told that the XVIII Airborne Corps was being transferred to the control of XII Army Group.

C-47s on the way to Bastogne

Winter weather conditions caused low ceilings and fog that prevented Ninth Air Force fighters from providing close air support and ruled out aerial resupply. The bad weather also delayed the move of the 17th Airborne to the Continent. Unknown to the Americans, Bastogne was a German objective, and on December 22, 1944, the men of the 101st realized they were surrounded and completely cutoff from all means of ground resupply. Fog, snow and rain prevented troop carrier transports from flying; the Screaming Eagles were trapped. Their situation was not as desperate as has been represented by the popular media and movies; the 101st officers knew that the weather would eventually break and, when it did, the skies would be filled with supply laden parachutes and fighter/bombers would be smashing the German positions. A German party went into Bastogne under a flag of truce to offer the Americans surrender terms. With the 101st Division Commander, Maj. Gen. Maxwell Taylor, away in Washington, Brig. Gen. Anthony McAuliffe was in command. General McAuliffe replied to the Germans with a single word – "Nuts!" His next action was to call for an aerial resupply mission to keep his troops in the war. Fortunately, the weather was starting to improve.

On the morning of December 23, two teams of Airborne Pathfinders jumped into Bastogne to set up drop zones. Ninety

Anything, Anywhere, Anytime

minutes after their arrival, a formation of sixteen cargo-carrying C-47s arrived over Bastogne, the first of 241 transports that would drop over the town that day. By 4:00 PM, 1,400 bundles containing 144 tons of supplies, mostly artillery ammunition, had been delivered to the men of the 101st. Recovery of the bundles was more than 95 percent; the airborne artillerymen were soon firing shells that had been dropped in earlier in the day. The drops continued on Christmas Eve; by nightfall IX Troop Carrier Command had delivered more than 300 tons of packages to the kids on the ground at Bastogne. Fragile supplies that could not be dropped were delivered by glider. Intense enemy fire made the supply missions extremely hazardous. Eight transports were shot down over Bastogne during the first two days of drops.

Christmas Day dawned with low ceilings and snow that kept the transports on the ground at their bases in England and France. Fortunately, the men of the 101st had enough supplies from the preceding two days to last until the weather broke. The day after Christmas was clear and cold – perfect flying weather – and the airdrops and airstrikes at Bastogne resumed. By this time, the Germans were beginning to run low of supplies, especially fuel, forcing them to begin breaking off their attacks and starting a retreat. At the same time, General George Patton's Third Army was breaking through the German lines from its lead positions thirty miles from Bastogne. Late on December 27, advance elements of Patton's forces reached Bastogne. Patton's army had been augmented by the newly arrived 17th Airborne Division after it was flown into Reims from England by IX Troop Carrier Command,. The commander of the lead tank, Lt. Charles Boggess, reported that he knew they were nearing the besieged town when he saw colored parachutes dropping from C-47s ahead of his column.

The final day's resupply missions were marred by the unnecessary loss of thirteen C-47s from a formation that brought in 35 gliders. Their return route took the transports in close proximity to German forces and they fell victim to intense ground fire. With the relief of Bastogne, the Battle of the Bulge was essentially over but fighting continued in the region for several days. Bastogne had held, thanks largely to the efforts of the men of IX Troop Carrier Command, who kept the 101st supplied during the battle. At least seventeen C-47s were lost over Bastogne.(Brereton, 1946) (Craven & Cate, 1956)

C-47 after Crash-Landing at Bastogne

Supplies falling over Bastogne

The Battle of the Bulge was the final German offensive of World War II but there was still one more major obstacle to be crossed on the way to Berlin, and one more large-scale airborne operation. Field Marshall Montgomery had adapted an elaborate style now that there were plenty of resources at his disposal. For his crossing of the Rhine,

Anything, Anywhere, Anytime

Montgomery planned an operation on the scale of a major amphibious landing, complete with a massive aerial bombing and artillery barrage followed by an airborne operation before his troops hit the boats to cross the river. Transports from three American troop carrier wings joined with RAF transports to transport the American 17th Airborne Division and the British 6th to the drop zones in Germany on March 24, 1945. In terms of numbers of transports involved, the Rhine crossing was larger than the D-Day drops; 1,602 troop carrier transports and 1,326 gliders were used to lift the two divisions. The 13th Airborne Division had been planned to be part of the operation but was pulled out due to a lack of transports.

Planning for *VARSITY* included the use of troop carrier personnel who had been trained as combat controllers. Eight combat control teams made up of glider pilots, one of whom had substantial experience as a power pilot, and an enlisted communications technician were trained to land the first gliders then control further operations by radio. The combat control teams were likely an innovation developed by Col. Philip Cochran, who had joined Brereton's First Allied Airborne Army staff. Cochran had used a similar concept during Operation *THURSDAY* in Burma the previous year.(Arnold, 1944) The British had also developed advance control teams to go in and set up control towers at forward airfields.

Curtis C-46 Commando

For the first time in Europe, Curtis C-46s were used to drop paratroopers. Seventy-two of the larger transports joined the C-47s that had been the mainstay of troop carrier operations. It turned out that the C-46 was improperly designed for combat operations and twenty airplanes were shot down. The airplane fuel system was designed in such a way that when a bullet pierced a fuel tank, the fuel would run into the fuselage and pool in the belly. A single tracer bullet could turn a C-46 into a flaming inferno. Once the transports crossed the Rhine and entered German airspace, the flak came up like a huge wall. Throughout their ingress to the drop zones, during the drops and as they were returning to friendly airspace, the transports were under intense heavy fire. *VARSITY* was a costly operation, with 58 transports and fifteen B-24s shot down. Personnel losses were 116 transport crewmembers and 88 glider pilots.

Casualties were greatest among the C-46s, which caused General Matthew Ridgeway, commander of XVIII Airborne Corps, to label them as deathtraps. Ridgeway issued orders that his men would never be dropped by C-46s again. As it turned out, Ridgeway's order was moot. Within six weeks after the Rhine crossing, Germany surrendered. Airborne and troop carrier assets in Europe began returning to the United States in preparation to move to the Pacific for operations in the invasion of Japan. Fortunately for all, the B-29 firebombing missions against Japanese cities brought World War II to an end without the first American soldier setting foot on the Japanese home islands.

General Brereton and his staff planned and obtained approval for ten airborne operations after the initial D-Day drops, but only two were ever carried out. A number of unplanned airborne operations were considered. When Allied troops were engaged in the battle that came to be known as the Battle of the Falaise Pocket, Brereton placed his airborne forces on standby at the airfields to be ready to board their planes for a jump into France on a moment's notice. A similar operation was considered at the end of the war in Denmark. Brereton's most ambitious plan, *ARENA*, was for a full-scale airborne invasion of the Ruhr Valley in the vicinity of Kassel. *ARENA* called for the use of the entire First Allied Airborne Army to parachute into drop zones and arrive by glider to set up airfields onto which American and British troop carriers would fly conventional infantry from four divisions. It was exactly the kind of plan that Chief of Staff George Marshall and Army Air Forces Chief Henry H. Arnold envisioned, but while Eisenhower gave the appearance of being receptive to the idea, he expressed concern about finding the infantry divisions to carry it out.

Brereton's airborne plans were hampered throughout the European campaign by the lack of vision on the part of the Allied ground commanders, particularly General Omar Bradley and British Field Marshall Bernard Montgomery. They both considered airborne forces as mere infantry with parachute training and were not willing to use them in the kind of imaginative operations their superiors actually wanted. Even Montgomery's *MARKET* plan was a means of advancing his ground forces. Arnold, in particular, had come to see

Anything, Anywhere, Anytime

airborne forces as highly-trained troops whose mission was to seize objectives such as airfields, or terrain where they could be built, and establish airheads onto which conventional infantry, and even armor, could be delivered by troop carrier transports, a view shared by Army Chief General George Marshall. Near the end of the war, Arnold wrote Brereton a letter in which he envisioned the time when all Army ground forces would be transportable by air.(Brereton, 1946) Not a single Allied airborne operation was ever flown in Europe in the manner for which airborne forces had been conceived. It was only in the Southwest Pacific that they were properly used.

The troop carrier role in Europe was considerably different from that of the Pacific. In New Guinea the airplane was used to provide mobility to ground and air forces, and thus gave the Allies an edge that shortened the war with Japan by several months, if not years. In Europe, troop carriers were primarily involved in the support of airborne forces which were, in turn, used to support large ground armies if they were used at all. No operations were ever flown to seize airfields or other objectives in advance of the Allied lines while air combat squadrons were supplied primarily by truck. Europe saw four large-scale airborne operations in support of huge ground armies – five if the drops at Salerno are counted – while the Pacific War saw the paratroops used more as they had been intended – to seize airfields and other objectives in the enemy's rear and establish an airhead for an aerial invasion. Transport operations in Europe often involved supply of fast-moving armored columns; tanks saw limited use in the Pacific.

The creation of the First Allied Airborne Army and the subsequent assignment of IX Troop Carrier Command to it were perhaps actually detrimental to the overall war effort because of the way the senior ground commanders chose to conduct it. Since they were dedicated to support airborne operations, the IX TCC C-47s were often unavailable when they were badly needed to support advancing ground forces. Yet, at the same time, the ground commanders failed to realize that troop carrier and airborne forces could be used to advance Allied forces deep into enemy territory. The rapid mobility provided to light infantry forces in the Asiatic-Pacific Theater was nonexistent in the ETO.

Even though initial airborne operations in Europe were plagued with problems, by the time the war ended the early criticism of the troop carrier crews by the paratroopers had turned to praise. IX Troop Carrier Command had literally saved the 101st at Bastogne. Timely air evacuation of casualties saved many lives, while routine transport operations made the entire military establishment fully aware of the value of the transport airplane. After the war ended, General Eisenhower was quoted as referring to the C-47 as one of the three

Sam McGowan

most important weapons of the war. He was certainly not referring to the routine airline-type transport operations of the Air Transport Command when he made that statement.

Anything, Anywhere, Anytime

Sam McGowan

Chapter Eight - "Logistics and ATC"

C-87 Long-Range Transport Used by Air Transport Command

Military air transport began developing before World War II with a two-fold purpose, to meet the air transportation needs of the US Army Air Force Combat Command combat squadrons and, after the Army started developing a paratroop corps, to airdrop and resupply paratroops. Events in New Guinea and the CBI led to new developments as transport squadrons that became troop carrier became heavily involved in the resupply of combat troops in the field and moving intact units into battle. Air transport of ground combat forces revolutionized warfare, but there was another side to air transportation that, although it did not involve actual combat operations and its units are not considered part of the Army Air Forces lineage, was important to military operations. The large ground and air forces used in all theaters of the war called for behind-the-scenes air transportation, or air logistics.

Within a particular theater, logistical flying was a troop carrier responsibility, as evidenced by the assignment of particular groups to overwater flying between Australia and New Guinea and the Pacific islands. Initially, the primary role of the 316th Troop Carrier Group in North Africa was providing logistical support to the British Eighth Army and Ninth Force and Western Desert Air Force combat

Anything, Anywhere, Anytime

squadrons operating from forward fields. After the initial invasion in North Africa and subsequent airborne operations, troop carrier squadrons in the Mediterranean spent the majority of their time resupplying bases some distance removed from the coastal supply depots with ammunition, bombs, aircraft parts and other supplies. During lulls in combat operations, troop carrier groups were assigned to the various theater air service commands to support fighter and bomber groups. However, there was another side to logistical flying that did not directly involve troop carrier operations, which fell under the air service commands in each particular theater. Another logistical air transport organization, the Air Transport Command, reported directly to US Army Air Force headquarters.

Air service commands were established in each of the major theaters for the support of the combat air wings and groups. Each service command usually included one or more air transport groups dedicated to logistical flying, while in some theaters where transport availability was restricted, logistical support was performed by troop carrier units on assignment with the local service command. In theaters where the local service command didn't have its own air transport group, recently arrived troop carrier groups were assigned to logistical flying. Troop carrier squadrons were also assigned to logistical operations when they moved to rear areas for rest, as was the case in Australia.

VIII Service Command in England commanded the 27th Transport Group, a unit whose mission was to support the bomber groups by delivering crucial aircraft parts and other high priority items from the military depots in Northern England and Scotland to the bomber bases in East Anglia. The 27th flew a variety of airplanes, including British types, but one squadron was equipped with Martin B-26s that had been modified into transports. After the relocation of Ninth Air Force to England in the fall of 1943, IX Air Service Command had its own air transport group as well, the 31st. After the invasion of Normandy, the 302nd Transport Wing activated in England to control the 27th and 31st groups, with the 27th operating logistical routes from England to combat bases in France and elsewhere on the Continent while the 31st provided logistical support on the Continent from its base at Paris. When the 302nd Transport Wing was formed, Ninth Air Force was allowed to keep 24 C-47s and 24 C-46s which were formed into the 1st Air Transport Group and used primarily to support fighter/bomber squadrons that had moved to France from England. One hundred ATC C-47s were taken off of domestic operations in the United States and transferred to Europe to join the 302nd Wing. A squadron of C-109s was assigned to the ETO to transport gasoline to the Continent.[130]

In the summer of 1944, when First Allied Airborne Army activated and IX Troop Carrier Command was assigned to support the *MARKET/GARDEN* operation in Holland, the 302nd wing was assigned to transport cargo, mostly fuel and ammunition, to ground forces in France. Initial operations supported Patton's Third Army until those transports were also withdrawn and assigned to support British Field Marshall Montgomery's operation. The 302nd Transport Wing was responsible for most of the air evacuation of casualties from the Continent to England, and later from forward bases in France and Belgium to rear area hospitals. Air evacuation was normally a troop carrier responsibility but the 302nd assumed the duty to allow troop carriers to be used for combat cargo and troop carrier operations in support of the airborne and ground combat units. All told, 302nd transports carried almost as many patients as IX Troop Carrier Command.

Early in the war in North Africa, the logistics mission was carried out by troop carrier groups on temporary assignment to XII Service

---

[130] The C-109 was a modification of the B-24 Liberator. Tanks were installed throughout the airplane to convert it into a tanker. They were used primarily in the CBI to haul gasoline to China.

Anything, Anywhere, Anytime

Command between combat operations. In the Southwest Pacific, troop carrier squadrons flew logistical missions between Australia and Fifth Air Force advance bases at Port Moresby, either as part of their theater indoctrination or when they were taken off of combat operations for a period of rest. As the Fifth Air Force presence in New Guinea grew, one 54th Troop Carrier Wing group at a time was assigned to the logistical mission. Later in the war, the troop carrier groups were replaced by transport squadrons assigned directly to V Service Command. Still later, Air Transport Command became responsible for operating behind-the-lines logistical missions from Australia to New Guinea and on to the Philippines.

Often the combat commands provided their own air transportation. This was especially true in China, where the bomber groups assigned to General Chennault's China Air Task Force flew their own fuel, bombs, ammunition and other supplies into China from India. Chennault estimated that three Hump flights were required for every bomber for each actual mission against the Japanese. The requirement for air transport to support combat operations greatly increased the cost of bombing missions from China. A C-47 transporting aviation gasoline would consume one gallon for every two gallons it carried. The same was true for each B-25.

By late 1943, the Boeing B-29 Very Heavy Bomber was ready for combat. Originally conceived to operate against Germany from bases in the Middle East, by the time it became operational the establishment of air bases for B-24s and B-17s in Italy made the B-29s unnecessary in the ETO so they were destined instead for the Asiatic-Pacific Theater. General Arnold decided that instead of assigning the new bombers to the existing commands in the Pacific, he would place them under his own direct command and use them to mount an air offensive against Japan proper. Arnold activated Twentieth Air Force directly under USAAF with the headquarters in Washington. Because at the time the closest bases to the Japanese homeland were in China, Arnold decided to base the huge bombers in India, with advance bases in China, and XX Bomber Command was ordered overseas. Arnold was under pressure from the White House to mount attacks against Japan and, in early 1944 China was the only alternative.[131] Under Project *MATTERHORN*, the B-29s staged out of advanced bases in China, while their support facilities were located several hundred miles away in

---

[131] Since 1944 was an election year and no American bombers had appeared over Japan since April 1942 and then only briefly, President Franklin Roosevelt wanted a bombing campaign against Japan to begin as soon as possible to boost his chances for reelection to an unprecedented third term. Roosevelt was also under pressure because of the recently revealed Japanese atrocities against Allied POWs.

India. Since no land routes yet existed into China and the Japanese still controlled the China Sea, all supplies for the B-29s had to be flown in from India. A transport group equipped with C-87s was included in the *MATTERHORN* force. Twentieth Air Force planners assumed that the B-29s could be responsible for their own transportation needs, with assistance from the unit's assigned transport squadrons. A classified project known as Project X saw major participation by the Air Transport Command as the command's four-engine C-87s transported XX Bomber Command advance parties from the United States to India.

From their main support base at Kharagpur, India, the Superfortress could carry a load of cargo or fuel to the B-29 base at Hsinching, China in a flight of five to five and a half hours. Depending on ATC to deliver the same cargo would have taken several days, as it would first have to be transported by surface to the airfields in the Assam Valley then loaded onto a C-46, C-54 or C-87 for the flight to China. The B-29 groups and their intrinsic C-87s could do the job in much less time. To transport fuel, several B-29s were converted into tankers and a number of C-109s, a newly-developed tanker version of the C-87, were brought to the CBI.[132] Crews from the B-29 squadrons were assigned to fly them. An additional thirty-six C-46s were added to the ATC Hump force and the 1st Air Transport Squadron was dedicated exclusively to XX Bomber Command support.

As long as the *MATTERHORN* force was in China, the B-29s and Twentieth Air Force transports continued to transport supplies and

---

[132] While C-87s were built at the factory, C-109s were modified bombers.

Anything, Anywhere, Anytime

fuel from India to XX Bomber Command advance bases in China. Additional supplies for the B-29s came in aboard ATC transports. It was largely due to the tremendous amount of logistics involved in mounting missions from China that XX Bomber Command shifted its base of operations from the CBI to the Marianas after the islands were liberated. In the islands, supplies could be delivered by ship thus saving a phenomenal amount of time and expense. The additional workload placed on the ATC transports for B-29 support had an upside. Additional resources were added to ATC's India/China Wing. After the B-29s left the CBI, the full efforts of an increased ATC presence allowed an overall increase in deliveries to China.

There was another side to logistical flying, the support of combat units from rear area depots outside the theater and even from the United States itself. Most military cargo moved by sea but aircraft parts and other high value items required more timely transport. Logistical flying within the US and as far as Alaska and Panama originated in the years before the war but the nature of the far-flung conflict led to a new development, the use of the long-range transport to fly priority cargo and personnel from the United States to overseas terminals in rear areas distant from the battlefield. By the time the war ended in 1945, the War Department had firmly established what was essentially its own airline – the Air Transport Command. The present-day Air Mobility Command, formerly the Military Airlift Command, formally traces its history to the establishment of the Army Air Corps Ferrying Command on May 29, 1941. Since the Ferrying Command was folded into the Air Transport Command when it was created in the summer of 1942, this is technically correct but only partially so. The Ferrying Command mission was solely to deliver American-built aircraft to embarkation points where they were either loaded aboard ships or picked up by foreign and civilian contract crews for delivery to the Allies. Transportation of cargo and passengers was not part of the command's stated mission, although the command had begun some transport operations by the time the US entered the war.

President Roosevelt saw the war as a great opportunity to bring the nation out of the Great Depression, which had idled much of the American industrial complex in the 1930s. In January 1939, he advocated a massive increase in aircraft production, primarily for sale to the nations fighting the Axis. Sale of military equipment to the warring nations and the subsequent Lend-Lease Program put America back to work as the country's factories were humming again turning out military equipment and other supplies for both the rapidly rearming United States and the Allied nations. Modern military aircraft were especially needed by Britain, France, the Netherlands and the Soviet Union. American aircraft manufacturers were eager to meet their needs. Building the airplanes was one thing; getting them overseas was another. Smaller fighters, trainers, light and medium bombers and twin-engine transports could be shipped overseas by sea along with other equipment that was being purchased by the warring nations but larger bombers and transports were designed to be flown over long distances and the best way to deliver them was by air. With German U-boat wolf packs prowling the Atlantic, direct delivery was also the safest way to get the airplanes to where they were needed.

Although America was still formally neutral in the spring of 1941, President Franklin D. Roosevelt convinced Congress that the United States should act as "an arsenal of democracy" and provide the materials that could keep the nations allied against the Axis nations in the war. In March 1941, Congress passed the Lend-Lease Act, which authorized warring nations to purchase military equipment from the United States on credit. The cost was born by the American taxpayer since few of the warring nations had the means to repay their debt. Roosevelt compared the new policy to "lending your hose to your neighbor when his house is on fire." Prior to the passing of the act, foreign sales were strictly on a "cash and carry" basis and, in the case of the Soviet Union were paid in gold; afterwards, war materials were paid for by the US government and provided to the warring nations "on loan."[133]

Prior to the passage of the Lend-Lease Act, aircraft manufacturers and their customers, the warring nations, were responsible for their own deliveries. Because the United States was still officially neutral, foreign pilots were not allowed to enter the country to pick up military aircraft so they were delivered to points outside the US, particularly in Canada. Each aircraft manufacturer employed civilian ferry pilots to deliver aircraft from the factories to Montreal. There they were picked up by pilots employed by a Canadian company working under contract to the receiving governments for the flight across the Atlantic to the British Isles. Only bombers and transports could make the transoceanic flight. Fighters, trainers and light bombers were loaded onto ships and transported by sea. Passage of the Lend-Lease Act allowed deliveries from the factories but there was a problem; a shortage of pilots in the allied air forces meant that the United States was going to have to help deliver the airplanes.

In April, Air Corps Chief of Staff Major General Henry H. Arnold sent a wire back to Washington from the UK, where he had been conferring with British officers, recommending that Army Air Corps personnel make the deliveries. Benefits from his idea were twofold – it

---

[133] How Lend-Lease supplies were paid for is beyond the scope of this work, but suffice to say that payments made after the war were at a rate of roughly ten cents on the dollar. The UK made its last payment on December 31, 2006.

Anything, Anywhere, Anytime

would allow Air Corps pilots and other aircrew personnel to gain additional experience in the aircraft they were assigned to fly and would also release the more experienced civilian factory crews to make flights to England with the Atlantic Ferrying Organization. ATFERO was a British Ministry of Aircraft Production organization. On May 29, 1941, the Air Corps Ferrying Command was established. Ferrying Command was merely a headquarters organization that used pilots and other aircrew personnel from the Air Force Combat Command[134] on temporary assignments, usually of about thirty days, to pick up airplanes at the factories and deliver them to points in Canada where they would be turned over to foreign ferry crews.

There were provisions allowing overseas deliveries, but due to the hostilities in Europe, the Army Air Corps was also in the process of a rapid buildup. While the prospect of flying American airplanes to Europe would be valuable training for the Air Corps pilots and crews, there weren't enough of them to go around and the lag time required to return flight crews to the US severely interrupted training.[135] The Air Corps was rapidly expanding and new combat groups and squadrons were being formed. The new groups required cadres of experienced personnel for key positions such as group and squadron commanders, operations officers and flight leaders to train new pilots and other personnel coming out of training schools. Inexperienced pilots were assigned to ferry the aircraft types they were assigned to fly to gain experience but there were more airplanes to be delivered than there were military pilots available to fly them. The War Department decided to solve the personnel problem by establishing a special program staffed with nonmilitary contract pilots who could be trained to deliver military airplanes, particularly light aircraft and trainers, from the factories to pickup points, usually in Canada.

For overseas deliveries, the new Ferrying Command was authorized to contract with the national airlines for crews. By the time America entered the war seven months after Ferrying Command was formed, the organization had already established routes to England over the North Atlantic and also over a southern route by way of Brazil and Ascension Island, then through the Middle East and on to England. A mid-Atlantic route used the Azores for a refueling stop. The South Atlantic route was also the route to China since the Japanese controlled the western Pacific. Ferrying Command was just beginning

---

[134] Air Force Combat Command was the Army's air combat organization prior to the 1942 reorganization of Army air forces. AFCC was commanded by Brigadier General Carl Spaatz.

[135] Although Ferrying Command later used ATC transports to return ferry crews to the US, in 1941 they returned by ship.

to deliver airplanes overseas when the Japanese attacked Pearl Harbor.

Shortly after it was established, the Ferrying Command became involved in transport operations, not by mission requirement but by default. When the US began providing military equipment to its allies, it also established military missions in various parts of the world to provide training and other support functions. To support them, the War Department realized a need for air transportation. No long-range transports had yet been developed so the Army decided to convert the first B-24A Liberator bombers into transports. B-24s had just entered production and the need for long-range transports justified the conversions. The British also purchased some converted B-24s to meet their transportation needs. Ferrying Command received eleven of the four-engine bomber/transports, enough to equip a squadron. Experienced four-engine bomber crews from Air Force Combat Command were assigned on temporary duty to Ferrying Command to fly them. In July 1941, Col. Caleb Haynes made the first transatlantic flight to the UK. Routes were soon established to the Middle East and into the Soviet Union as far as Moscow. By the time America officially entered the war, Ferrying Command was operating eleven B-24 transports primarily on passenger missions providing transportation for high-ranking officers and government officials.

When America entered the war the entire country mobilized, including the airline industry, which became heavily involved in military operations although it never actually became part of the military itself. Instead, the nation's airlines worked for the War Department servicing military contracts. One of the War Department's first actions after the outbreak of war was to contract with the airlines to fly cargo and passengers, both within the United States and to overseas destinations. When the Air Service Command[136] lost its transports to the newly established Air Transport Command[137] in April 1942, it set up a Contract Air Cargo Division to handle the issuing of military contracts to the airlines to meet its air transport needs. The division was staffed by former airline personnel who came into the Army with direct commissions, usually as field grade officers. (Craven & Cate, 1956) The Ferrying Command also began issuing contracts, both for airplanes to carry military cargo and passengers and for

---

[136] The Air Service Command was created from the pre-war Air Corps Maintenance Command, under which the first air transport squadrons had been organized.

[137] This was the original Air Transport Command, which was set up in April 1942 when the Army Air Forces reorganized. Two months later it became I Troop Carrier Command when a new Air Transport Command activated with the headquarters of the former Ferrying Command.

Anything, Anywhere, Anytime

airline crews to ferry military aircraft. Some airlines, particularly Pan American, which had the most overwater experience with its fleet of Clipper flying boats, became heavily involved in military contract flying. Military contracts became a lucrative source of revenue for the national airline industry.

So many different military organizations were offering business to the airlines that the Chairman of the Civil Aeronautics Board, Mr. L. W. Pogue[138], became concerned that the industry was going to self-destruct due to the confusion. In order to centralize the issuing of contracts, Pogue proposed what would have been essentially an air version of the Merchant Marine to take over the military air transportation business, with civilian airlines operating military routes under contract to a single organization reporting directly to the White House. What Pogue wanted was a single headquarters through which the airline industry could receive military contracts and thus prevent the fragmentation of the industry as a myriad of military organizations made their own contracts. An attorney who specialized in aviation, Pogue's concern was for the future of the airline industry. His only exposure to the military had been a few months of student officer training during his first year in college. General Arnold liked Pogue's idea, at least in principle. Arnold was not in favor of a separate entity to handle all military air transportation but he did like the idea of a single agency to be responsible for issuing airline contracts. He had already established the Air Transport Command to take care of operational air transportation needs and recognized the necessity of an organization to handle contract logistical operations. He decided to set up a new organization within his Army Air Forces to handle air transportation contracts but took it a step further.

On June 20, 1942, the Army Air Forces established a new Air Transport Command from the former Ferrying Command, which became one of its two divisions. The former Ferrying Command headquarters was elevated to become headquarters for the new Air Transport Command, which was established with two divisions, Ferrying and Air Transport. In conjunction with the establishment of the new organization, the existing Air Transport Command was redesignated as I Troop Carrier Command. Both organizations were part of the recently reorganized United States Army Air Forces, but I Troop Carrier Command was established to train and develop tactics for combat air transportation units of which the new ATC was not a part. Troop carrier commands were also established in the overseas combat air forces with equal status with their fighter and bomber commands.

---

[138] Pogue was a New York attorney who was heavily involved with the airline industry. He was appointed to the CAB in 1938 and became its head in 1942.

The mission of the new Air Transport Command was:

The ferrying of all aircraft within the United States and to destinations outside of the United States as directed by the Commanding General, Army Air Forces.

The transportation by air of personnel, material, and all mail for all War Department agencies, except those served by Troop Carrier units as hereinafter set forth.

The control, operation, and maintenance of establishments and facilities on air routes outside of the United States which are, or which may be made, the responsibility of the Commanding General, Army Air Forces.

The second mission, as identified in General Orders No. 8 which established the new command as paragraph b, was clarified by the assignment to Troop Carrier units of responsibility for providing transportation for parachute troops, airborne infantry[139] and glider units; and for conducting local air transport services within the theaters of operations. Unlike the fighter, bomber and troop carrier commands whose mission was combat or direct combat support, the new Air Transport Command was established directly under the USAAF as a support command to support military operations and thus had no combat mission of its own.[140] Its primary role initially was to serve as a central agency for issuing contracts to civilian aviation corporations to fulfill military contracts, particularly those associated with the airline industry. Although it was commanded by professional military officers – Brig. Gen. Harold L. George was ATC's first commander and some other career and reserve officers were assigned – the staff was made up largely of former airline executives who had been brought into the Army as field-grade officers. Recently promoted Col. William H. Tunner, a West Point graduate and career officer who had formerly served as the administrative officer of the Ferrying Command, was placed in command of ATC's Ferrying Division but the commander of the Air Transport Division was former Braniff Airlines vice-president Col. Robert J. Smith. Smith had originally been brought into the Army to head the Air Service Command's Contract Air Cargo

---

[139] The term "airborne infantry" referred to infantry that might be transported by air.

[140] Historians and the Air Force itself have created a lot of confusion regarding the identity of the US Army Air Forces and have given the impression that it consisted of all units that eventually became the US Air Force. The order that established the USAAF gave it responsibility for all US Army air functions - except those involving combat. Basically, its mission was the procurement of equipment and training of individuals and combat groups. The Air Force, which was established in 1947, replaced the Army Air Corps, which had remained the statutory air arm of the US Army.

Anything, Anywhere, Anytime

Division,[141] which was disbanded when ATC activated. His choice illustrated the primary purpose of the new command, to issue military contracts to the airlines. American Airlines president Cyrus R. Smith became ATC chief of staff as an Army colonel. The Air Transport Command started out with a distinctly airline flavor and essentially became an airline dressed in olive drab. Nearly all of its leadership came from airline backgrounds. Some were reservists but some had never served in uniform until they were given direct commissions because of their airline experience. (Craven & Cate, 1956)

When the US entered the war, some civilian airline personnel were already operating overseas under contract to the former Ferrying Command, particularly in India and North Africa where Pan American DC-3s had been sent to meet specific theater needs. In 1942 the Douglas DC-3 was still the industry standard but larger, faster four-engine transports were under development by Boeing, Consolidated and Douglas while Curtis was working on a large twin-engine transport. ATC operated variations of the DC-3 in its infancy, but the smaller transports were quickly replaced on overseas routes, first by considerably larger twin-engine C-46s, then by four-engine DC-4s, which became the C-54 in military colors. The command also operated long-range C-87s, the transport version of the Liberator bomber, beginning in October 1942. Unlike the B-24As with which Ferrying Command began transport operations, the C-87 was developed specifically for transport use. Basically a modified B-24D, the fuselage was equipped with a reinforced floor to handle cargo and bucket seats for passengers. It could also be equipped with plush airline-type seating for scheduled passenger flights, which often carried high-ranking officers or senior government officials. A later tanker version of the versatile B-24 was designated as the C-109. They were actually B-24D bombers that had been converted into flying fuel tankers. Boeing also offered a transport version of its B-17 to the Army as the C-108 but its use was ruled out due to its smaller cabin and payload capacity.[142]

---

[141] The Army Air Service Command had established a Contract Air Cargo Division to handle airline contracts when its former transport groups were reassigned to the Troop Carrier Command when it was established on April 30, 1942. The division transferred to the new Air Transport Command.

[142] A few B-17s that were converted for executive transport use were given the C-108 designation. One was used by General Douglas MacArthur as a command airplane until he received a Douglas C-54 for that purpose.

Sam McGowan

In 1942, with the exception of a few B-24s[143] and some C-47s that had remained with the Air Service Command for logistical transport, ATC's own aircraft were all former airline aircraft that had been confiscated from the airlines by presidential order. The Ferrying Command was also operating former airline flying boats, particular Pan American Airways fleet of Clippers. On May 6, 1942, President Roosevelt directed the Secretary of War to commandeer all DC-3 type aircraft operated by domestic air carriers, except for 200 airplanes, and to refit them "for such transport services as will most effectively serve the war purposes of the United Nations." While many of the DC-3s were modified for troop carrier use, some would go the new Air Transport Command when it activated a month later.

Pan American Clipper

The new organization needed pilots and other aircrew personnel so ATC was authorized to issue contracts, not only for direct airline contract but also for airline personnel to crew military-owned transports. Another source of pilots was the civilian aviation industry, which included commercial air taxi pilots, crop dusters, flight instructors, company pilots and exhibition pilots as well as commercially rated pilots who flew for personal reasons. Beginning in January 1942, the Army began offering commissions to experienced civilian pilots as Air Service Pilots, a new rating awarded to men based on their civilian flying experience and suitability for service as

---

[143] At least three and possibly four of the B-24As were reassigned to Far East Air Force Air Transport Command in Australia in early 1942. Three were lost, including two to combat.

Anything, Anywhere, Anytime

commissioned officers or, in some cases, NCOs.[144] The service pilot rating was for limited duty in non-combat flying; including ferrying aircraft, transport operations, acceptance test flights, instructing in primary and advanced flying schools and certain other duties such as towing targets and flying airplanes used in bombardier training.[145]

Some men were commissioned directly but most were put through a process in which they were initially employed as civilian contract pilots to ferry airplanes for a period of ninety days during which they were evaluated to determine if they were suitable for commission. Those judged suitable for rating as service pilots were offered commissions, while those who weren't were offered other positions as contract instructors in primary flight schools. Some were allowed to continue ferrying aircraft under contract. Those who accepted military induction were sent to training schools where they were further evaluated and given training in high performance aircraft. A few service pilots were already commissioned officers who had not completed military flight training, but had civilian flying experience. Once they were rated, the new service pilots were assigned to Ferrying Command for ferrying duty. As ATC began developing its own air transport system, service pilots were assigned as copilots until they had enough experience to serve as first pilots.[146] Newly commissioned service pilots were sometimes assigned to fly as copilots with airline contract crews to gain experience in large aircraft. (Craven & Cate, 1956)

(There is one possible exception to the non-combat status of service pilots and I only mention it here because it is interesting. Actor James Stewart was an accomplished civilian pilot and a graduate of Princeton. He was drafted into the Army in 1940 and went into the Air Corps in early 1941. When the war broke out, he was a corporal. Because he was a college graduate, he was immediately commissioned, probably before the service pilot rating was authorized so he was probably awarded Army pilot wings. He was rated as a pilot based on

---

[144] Cowboy actor and western singing star Gene Autry enlisted in the Air Corps in the summer of 1942 as a service pilot. He was eventually commissioned as a flight officer but his initial service was as a technical sergeant, an NCO. Senator Barry Goldwater held a commission in the Army reserves and was a commercial rated pilot, but he was too old to be a combat pilot and was given a service pilot rating and assigned to Ferry Command at the supervisory level.

[145] There is a common misconception that the women who were employed by the Army as Womens Airforce Service Pilots, or WASPS, held the service pilot rating. In fact, they had no military status and were not awarded pilot ratings but were employed by the Army as civilian contractors after they had been screened and given enough training to qualify them to fly military trainers.

[146] First pilots on transports were mostly reservists who had been flying for the airlines before they were called to active duty.

his civilian flying experience after being evaluated by an Air Corps instructor. He then completed Army multiengine and instrument courses. His first assignment was flying Beechcraft bombardier trainers in New Mexico. He then went to a four-engine school but instead of being assigned to ATC, he went to a four-engine school at Gowen Field, Idaho where he instructed B-17 pilots. After he had been there for a few months and had been promoted to captain and squadron commander, a vacancy occurred for a squadron operations officer in a B-24 group that had just finished training at the field and his group commander recommended him for the job. Within a few weeks after he joined the group, something happened to his squadron commander and he was given command. He took the squadron overseas and flew a number of combat missions then transferred to another group to become the group operations officer. He then moved up to the combat wing level as a staff officer. He finished the war as a colonel.)

Although ATC recruited a sizeable number of civilian pilots for military service, it continued relying to a large extent on civilian contract pilots as well. Some were airline, but others ferried airplanes as contract pilots. Beginning in September 1942, some of these pilots were women. Actually, a few women were already ferrying airplanes when the war broke out as employees of civilian aviation concerns flying under contract to the manufacturers. One was Nancy Love, who, along with her husband, Robert Love, owned a Beechcraft dealership in Boston. Robert Love was an Army reservist; he was called to active duty before the war and assigned to a staff position with Ferrying Command. Nancy took a job with Ferrying Command herself in a non-flying capacity working in the office of Major William H. Tunner, the ATC admin officer. In 1942, she submitted a proposal to Tunner, who had been promoted to colonel, that ATC employ a number of highly qualified women to ferry airplanes. He passed it to USAAF headquarters and the proposal was accepted. She had already lined up about twenty-five women, each with over 1,000 hours flying time, and they signed contracts to ferry airplanes. The first woman recruited was Betty Gilles, and Cornelia Fort, a Nashville socialite[147], was the second. Fort was already famous because she had been working as a flight instructor in Honolulu when the war broke out and had been the first American pilot to encounter the Japanese airplanes. She came back to the US and made a movie about her experience on the first day of the war. Cornelia Fort would become the first woman pilot to die while in Army employ in March 1943 when she and an Army pilot

---

[147] Fort's father was president of a large insurance company in Nashville.

Anything, Anywhere, Anytime

collided during a ferry flight.[148] Fort was flying a fixed-gear Vultee BT-13 trainer when she died.

Love's new organization was called the Women's Auxiliary Ferrying Squadron, or WAFS, and she was the director. The WAFS was based at New Castle Army Airfield, Delaware but had detachments at airfields where there were aircraft manufacturers of training and light liaison airplanes, including one on the West Coast where Cornelia Fort was assigned. The squadron never numbered more than twenty-eight women, who had no military status. Although they wore uniforms, they were not military and they had no rank or other military status. Contrary to popular belief, they did not ferry combat aircraft but did a lot of ferrying of airplanes such as the Piper Cub and other primary trainers up to and including the BT-13.

Women's Auxiliary Ferrying Squadron Pilots

Prior to the formation of the WAFS, Arnold had made an offhand comment (to shut her up) to noted aviatrix and social climber Jacqueline Cochran, who was closely connected to the White House, that if any female aviation organization was established by the Army, she would command it.[149] Cochran had left the United States for the UK

---

[148] Recent fans of the WASPS have claimed that the accident was the male pilot's fault, but the accident report reveals that the two airplanes simply got too close to each other and collided. Both pilots were killed.

[149] Cochran's life reads like a soap opera. Born Bessie Lee Pittman, she was the daughter of an Alabama factory worker who married a sailor when she was in her early teens. When the marriage failed, she became a hairdresser and moved to New York where she worked in the salon at Saks Fifth Avenue. She met wealthy

to work for the British, who employed a few women to ferry aircraft. When Cochran learned of the WAFS, she became furious and rushed back to the US and went to Arnold's office. To pacify her, Arnold put her in charge of a Women's Flying Training Unit whose role was to train female pilots to fly military aircraft so they could be employed as ferry pilots. However, having two separate organizations of female pilots caused problems so Arnold (after being pressured by Cochran) decided to combine them into one organization called the Womens Airforce Service Pilots, with Cochran as director and Love as WASP executive with ATC.

The female contract pilots were rolled into the WASP when the organization was established. While the Women's Auxiliary Ferrying Squadron had been made up of women with considerable aviation experience, the WASPS were women with minimal experience who signed up for a program to teach them to fly military airplanes. Although some 1,800 women completed the WASP program, the maximum number of female pilots employed by ATC never exceeded 300. Half that number were transferred out of ATC when the primary ferry mission became the delivery of fighters and only the most experienced remained. Most of the rest were assigned to Training Command where they performed duties such as flight-testing training airplanes after maintenance inspections. A few were assigned as instructors in Link trainers. Not a single WASP served overseas; all of their operations were within the US and Canada. Tunner planned to allow some of the most experienced to ferry bombers to the UK and set up a flight with Love and Giles as the pilots and his personal crew making up the rest of a B-17 crew. The flight got as far as Newfoundland when it was halted and the two women were pulled off the crew and replaced by male pilots. The message came from Arnold's office but the WAFS pilots believed it was instigated by Cochran because she didn't want to be upstaged by Love and Giles.[150] Cochran was pushing Arnold to allow WASPS to be assigned to contract duty on military transports when she ran into a roadblock – the US Congress. The war had turned in the Allies favor and the pressing need for pilots had lessened. The program had been heavily glamorized and the wives and families of male contract pilots and instructors who were subject

---

financier Floyd Odlum, who was married at the time, and convinced him to set her up in the cosmetics business and buy her an airplane. She used Odlum's connections to further her own interests, including aviation. She saw herself as the successor to Amelia Earhart (who also used sex to advance herself in aviation.) Cochran was ashamed of her humble beginnings and even though she brought members of her family to her home in California, she claimed they were employees.

[150] Cochran had flown a Lockheed Hudson to Britain before the war.

to be drafted for ground combat duty raised an outcry. The entire program was canceled in December 1944 because the supply of male pilots was more than adequate to meet the Army's needs and there was no longer a need for female contract pilots. (Craven & Cate, 1956)[151]

By the end of 1942, ATC had established eight operational wings; North Atlantic, South Atlantic, Caribbean, Africa/Middle East, Alaskan, South Pacific and India/China, along with a Domestic Transportation Wing for transport operations within the United States. ATC's domestic wing continued using C-47s or some other variation of the DC-3. While the airplanes were military, most of ATC's crews were on contract from their civilian airline employers, at least for the first year or so of war. ATC's leadership was made up of airline executives who had been mobilized for the war effort and commissioned as colonels but most of the military pilots were either reservists who were too old for combat duty, many of whom had been employed by the airlines, or former civilian aviators who had taken direct commissions as Air Service Pilots. One batch of airline pilots was called up at the beginning of the war to serve as a nucleus of four-engine pilots to fly the modified B-24s.

The Air Transport Command was unique among the various military commands in that it was the only service command with overseas duties that was authorized to function outside of the responsibility of the theater commanders. ATC's headquarters was in the United States and its commander answered directly to USAAF commander General Henry H. Arnold. Each of the overseas numbered air forces had its own specified commands for both combat and service functions but ATC was an independent command reporting directly to USAAF Headquarters. It was also the only noncombat command that operated its own fleet of aircraft on operational missions, whether airline contract or assigned military.[152] All ATC missions were controlled by its Washington, DC headquarters and even its overseas wing commanders lacked control authority over them. While the

---

[151] The role of the WASPS has been greatly exaggerated to the point of mythology by feminists and politicians. They are often elevated to the same level as male combat pilots in the minds of some and are often pointed to as having flown the same combat aircraft as the men. In reality, the majority of the airplanes ferried by female pilots were single-engine trainers and light liaison aircraft. A handful of women were qualified to fly four-engine bombers and transports and about 100 were qualified to fly fighters. One woman was assigned to a demonstration crew that went around demonstrating the Boeing B-29 as a publicity stunt. Of the 38 women who were killed while employed by the Army, most died in training accidents.

[152] Training Command operated large numbers of training aircraft and was responsible for all operational training, but it had no missions other than training.

arrangement had been set up because it was considered the most efficient method of meeting military needs, it caused a myriad of problems since ATC's overseas facilities, except for enroute refueling stops such as the Azores and Ascension Island, were in combat theaters and the theater commanders were expected to provide precious resources for their support.

Douglas C-54

Shortly after the creation of the Air Transport Command, Colonel C. R. Smith, the ATC chief of staff, wrote a letter to General Arnold suggesting that ATC take over the ferry of supplies from India to China, the mission that had been set up as the India-China Ferry by Tenth Air Force. Original USAAF plans were for the mission to operate directly under Ferrying Command but Tenth Air Force commander Maj. Gen. Lewis Brereton protested that the plan was a violation of air force doctrine, to which Arnold agreed, and the ferry was assigned to his command. Colonel Smith's letter was prompted by a report a civilian by the name of Frank Sinclair sent to ATC headquarters after a visit to China. Sinclair was a former air show pilot who had gone into the military supplies industry. In his position with China Defense Supplies, Incorporated, a civilian contractor selling supplies to the Chinese government, Sinclair was concerned with the delivery of his goods to China. Under the terms of the contract, the company was not paid for the supplies until they reached China. Sinclair's company was losing money when his supplies were sitting somewhere awaiting final delivery. Sinclair severely condemned Tenth Air Force because it was having difficulties meeting the rather elaborate goals that had been set

Anything, Anywhere, Anytime

for it in Washington. This was not surprising, considering that the Japanese threatened India and there were more important concerns at hand at the moment.

Smith proposed that the 1st Ferrying Group, which had arrived in China in June 1942, be placed under ATC and that the ferry of supplies to China should be directly controlled from Washington. Untrained in military matters, Smith evidently failed to recognize the tactical situation in China – or in India for that matter, where Japanese troops were operating inside the Indian frontier. He expressed a belief that Tenth Air Force lacked "a singleness of purpose," once again not surprising since there was a war on and the main objective in 1942 was simply keeping the Japanese out of India! Moving supplies from India to China was secondary to holding back the Japanese. Had Japanese troops managed to occupy the Imphal Valley, supplying China would have become a moot issue. Partially to relieve Tenth Air Force for combat duties, and no doubt also because of pressure from the White House where both the airline industry and the American Chinese lobby wielded considerable influence, the War Department accepted Smith's suggestion and, in December 1942, General Stillwell was notified that ATC would take over the India-China Ferry, beginning on February 1. Smith's lack of objectivity is perhaps illustrated by the fact that the first ATC transports assigned to the Ferry were C-87s operated by contract crews provided by his own airline! The 1st Ferrying Group headquarters was elevated to become the India/China Wing of the Air Transport Command. For a time, the group and its squadrons functioned under the air transport designation but the group was eventually redesignated as the 1337th Air Force Air Base Unit.

Smith's optimistic assertions failed to materialize. After ATC took over the ferry, efficiency failed to improve. In fact, it actually declined and never did truly live up to expectations until the very end of the war, when combat units – including heavy bomber groups – in the region were placed under ATC operational control and assigned to transport duty on the India-China Ferry. It wasn't until August, 1943 that ATC finally met the 4,000 tons per month goal Washington had set for February. ATC began the airlift with 62 airplanes, mostly C-47s that came with the 1st Ferrying Group when it transferred to ATC from Tenth Air Force. The first aircraft to arrive from the US came with a squadron of C-87s manned by civilian contract crews from American Airlines, C.R. Smith's own company. Smith planned to replace the 1st FG's C-47s with C-46s but the larger Curtis transports were plagued with mechanical problems and deliveries were delayed for some time.

C-46 Over the Hump

Whenever military emergencies dictated, ATC planes were occasionally diverted from Hump flying to support Tenth Air Force operations against the Japanese. Although a condition of the transfer of the operation to ATC had been that Tenth Air Force would receive troop carrier squadrons, they were slow in coming and initially consisted of only two squadrons that activated in India with existing aircraft and personnel. Consequently, combat requirements sometimes led to diversions of ATC aircraft to theater needs. For example, ATC crews were called upon to assist Tenth Air Force units airdropping supplies to Chinese and British forces operating in the Naga Hills on the India-Burma border. China National Airways Corporation civilian crews were also used on occasion to drop supplies, often with Quartermaster personnel detailed to fly with them as "kickers."

While the diversions to combat operations took away from the efficiency of the India-China mission, there were other problems, some of which were caused by the civilian orientation of the ATC pilots. This was evident from the performance of the ATC crews in comparison to the Tenth Air Force troop carrier crews and the civilian crews of the China National Airways Corporation, which was also flying supplies to China. Both the troop carrier and CNAC crews were consistently outperforming the ATC units, even though their airplanes were smaller and carried smaller payloads. The CNAC crews were averaging 49 tons per month per airplane in their DC-3s while ATC was only averaging 23. ATC was flying larger C-46s by this time and even a few four-engine C-87s. Having been operating in the region since 1929, CNAC was staffed by "China Hands" who were well familiar with the routes and the conditions found in India and China. For them, the flights across the mountains to China were routine. Newly arrived troop carrier crews were also proving more efficient in their first month of operations than were the ATC crews who had been in the theater for several months, probably because they were young men who were able to adapt more easily to their situation. Unlike the ATC pilots, most of whom had come right out of civilian life, the military pilots were products of military flight training and were considerably more motivated and willing to undergo the deprivations of life in a primitive situation. (Craven & Cate, 1956)

Due to the threat of Japanese interception over Burma, the route from India's Assam Valley to Chungking, China led north across the lower reaches of the Himalayas, and then southeast to Chungking. Although the high mountains were further west in Nepal, the aircrews had to cross 15,000-foot mountain ridges that naturally came to be called "the Hump." Flying the Hump was potentially dangerous due to the extremities of the weather over the mountain ridges the air routes crossed over. Everyone who flew the Hump often encountered rain, wind, ice and snow, and this included fighter pilots, troop carrier crews and Fourteenth Air Force bomber crews as well as ATC. The airfields in China – and later in Burma – were primitive and the runways were often slick with mud. Most ATC aircraft losses were due to accident, particularly takeoff and landing accidents. While the threat of the Japanese air force was real enough, only seven (7) ATC aircraft were lost in the CBI due to enemy action during the entire war. The other seven-some-odd hundred were lost to accident and mechanical failure.

Efficiency over the Hump began to improve in late 1944 due to several factors. For one thing, by that time ATC was operating C-46s, C-54s, C-87s and C-109s exclusively; they carried larger payloads and there were more of them. The only C-47s were used for scheduled passenger flights. Thanks largely to X Troop Carrier Command, Merrill's Marauders and Chinese troops had recaptured Myitkyina, which allowed a more direct and less hazardous southern route to be established over Burma since Japanese fighters were no longer a threat. The new route also allowed the use of the Douglas C-54 on the route for the first time. Although the C-54 could carry a substantial payload, they were low-altitude aircraft and lacked the high altitude performance needed to operate over the original Hump route with a significant load. ATC strength was increased considerably with the arrival of more C-46s and C-87s to support the B-29s that operated out of advance bases in China – and which also flew transport missions bringing in fuel and supplies between missions. The B-29s carried much of their own cargo from their main bases in India to their advanced bases in the Chinese interior. A number of B-29s were converted into tankers to haul gasoline. XX Bomber Command also had a transport group equipped with C-87s and C-109s[153]. When the B-29s left China, these airplanes and their crews remained and were transferred to ATC's India/China Wing and the transports that had been dedicated to support the B-29s were released back to ATC.

By late 1944, the American military machine had swelled to tremendous proportions and plenty of transports were becoming available, along with military-trained pilots and other crewmembers to fly them as combat losses in Europe declined and the need for replacement aircrews decreased. And, in the late summer of 1944 Brigadier General William H. Tunner took command of ATC Hump operations.

If there is an individual in Air Force history who happened to be in the right place at the right time, it is Tunner. Had he been placed in charge of the ferry in 1942 or even in early 1943 when ATC took it over, it is doubtful that his career would have gone very far. For Tunner was an efficiency expert but not a general, even though he was a West Point graduate and wore the rank of one. An obscure Army Air Corps captain in 1941, Tunner was in charge of an office in Memphis, Tennessee with responsibility for developing a program to recruit and train civilian pilots to fly military aircraft in the Ferrying Command. He developed a set of standards that determined the capabilities of each pilot and the types of airplanes he (and later, after the advent of the Women's Auxiliary Ferrying Squadron, she) was allowed to fly. After the US entered the war, he was transferred to Ferrying Command headquarters and assigned as the administrative officer. Tunner soon achieved a reputation as a man who knew how to get the most out of personnel assigned to an (noncombat) operation. When the Air Transport Command activated, Tunner was promoted to colonel and put in command of its Ferrying Division.

By the time Tunner arrived in India, the war had turned solidly in the Allies' favor, which was a plus for ATC because it was able to gain additional resources and personnel that would previously have gone to combat units. The delivery rate of the India-China Ferry had increased substantially under Tunner's predecessor, Brig. Gen. Thomas O. Hardin, who expanded Hump operations to an around-the-

---

[153] The C-109 was a version of the Consolidated B-24 Liberator that was created by modifying existing B-24Ds into tankers with the installation of tanks in the fuselage. They were also designed so that fuel from the airplane's own fuel tanks could be transferred to fuel trucks or fuel farms at the destination. At least one squadron of C-109s was assigned to IX Troop Carrier Command in Europe to transport fuel to France, but most served on Hump operations from India into China. The B-17 was also considered for conversion for transport use and at least one was built as a C-108, but the Liberator proved superior and a transport version of the B-17 was never developed.

Anything, Anywhere, Anytime

clock schedule. (Hardin was a reserve officer who had served in World War I then had become an airline executive. He was called to active duty as a lieutenant colonel at the beginning of the war.) Night flying increased total tonnage being lifted into China but brought with it an increased accident rate. Additional troop carrier and combat cargo squadrons had arrived in the theater and were taking care of combat air transport needs, thus allowing the India/China Wing to devote its full attention to the India-China Ferry without interruption. Tunner arrived in India in the late summer of 1944 and found an organization that was merely in need of fine-tuning. Not having to contend with enemy opposition since his new command was in a purely logistical role, he was able to focus the full resources of the greatly swelled ATC operation toward getting supplies to China. He instituted standardized procedures for each facet of the operation, including processing and handling of cargo, maintenance procedures[154] and flight operations. He also emphasized safety, and established strict flight procedures for the crews under his command.

Under Tunner's leadership, the ATC effort increased in efficiency to the point that the command was carrying almost – but not quite – as much cargo into China as the troop carrier and combat cargo squadrons were delivering in their C-47s. In July 1945, ATC transported 71,000 tons into China, a drastic increase over the 2,000 tons the command had carried during its first month of operations in February 1943. That number, however, is misleading. One of the policies that Tunner was able to effect was that as combat operations in China declined, the troop carrier and combat cargo groups and the B-24 equipped heavy bomber groups in the theater were transferred to ATC operational control. It was only with the additional transport capability afforded by the combat air transport squadrons and heavy bombers that Tunner was able to achieve that figure. Combat operations in Burma came to an end in late May and Eastern Air Command's Troop Carrier Command transports were no longer needed to support ground combat operations. Tunner convinced Lt. Gen. George Stratemeyer, who had taken command of US air operations in the CBI, to place the troop carrier and combat cargo squadrons under ATC operational control, thus their tonnage was counted in ATC statistics. Included in the transfer were troop carrier squadrons based in China. He also convinced Stratemeyer that the amount of fuel needed to support heavy bomber operations in China was prohibitive, that missions performed by B-24s could be flown by twin-engine B-25s and single-engine fighter/bombers and that the

---

[154] Tunner called his new maintenance procedures "Production Line Maintenance," or PLM, which consisted of setting up lines akin to assembly lines and then moving the airplanes along them during routine maintenance inspections.

four engine bombers could be best utilized as transports. Since combat operations were nearing an end, Stratemeyer agreed. Combat crews transported more than 20,000 tons of the total for July, which means actual ATC tonnage hadn't increased at all.

Although the focus is usually placed on the Hump cargo operations, the India/China Wing also carried large numbers of passengers. By 1945, scheduled passenger missions were operating from Indian bases to Chungking and other fields in China. ATC air base units operated passenger terminals modeled along the lines of those used by airlines back in the States, and even had special passenger-handling equipment. Some C-46s and C-47s used for passenger flights were configured with airline-style seats and the crew included a flight traffic clerk, an enlisted man whose job was to attend to the needs of the passengers, including passing out magazines, blankets and coffee.

Outside the CBI, ATC functioned essentially as a military airline. In point of fact, it WAS an airline! Most of the command's leadership had airline backgrounds, while a large portion of the flying was performed by civilian crews still in airline employ, particularly for the first two years of the war. ATC missions originated at aerial ports of embarkation in the United States and carried cargo and personnel to various overseas destinations. As the command increased in size, the War Department instructed the theater commanders to allow ATC aircraft to deliver their loads to supply bases closer to the fighting, but not into contested areas. During major military operations when troop carriers were needed to support combat operations, ATC was ordered to temporarily assume routine logistical flying responsibilities that were usually performed by theater troop carrier squadrons.

As the war continued, passenger operations increased. After the Allies landed in Normandy in mid-1944, ATC instituted scheduled passenger operations out of New York to London and eventually to Paris. The overseas flights functioned the same as a civilian airline, even to the extent of a centralized passenger reservations service. The C-54s used on the routes were equipped with airline seats and galleys and an enlisted crewmember called a flight traffic clerk was assigned to insure passenger safety and tend to their comforts. Some of the flight traffic clerks were young women. The official history of the US Army Air Forces in World War II records that at least twenty Air WACs were assigned to aircrew duty. (Craven & Cate, 1956)

Although the India-China Ferry, now known as the Hump Airlift, is the most publicized of the World War II air logistics missions, support flying for combat units was a major contribution of transport crews of all commands throughout the world. ATC's route structure was used to transport thousands of passengers to and from overseas, while high priority cargo was delivered to overseas destinations with

Anything, Anywhere, Anytime

transit times that could be measured in days instead of weeks or even months. By 1944, Eighth Air Force combat personnel who had completed their combat tour were returning to the States on ATC transports. Previously, they had traveled by ship.

There were times when the availability of ATC transportation kept combat units in battle when they ran low of certain critical items. An emergency transport of antitank artillery fuses allowed the British Eighth Army to respond to German attacks in Egypt when their supplies began running low early in the war. An emergency mission to the Solomons delivered 15,000 pounds of hand grenades in response to an urgent message from General MacArthur's headquarters in Australia. Immediately after the daring low-level raid on the Ploesti oil fields in Romania, ATC C-87s delivered new engines to the B-24 bases around Benghazi, Libya to replace those that were shot-up and run-out on airplanes that came back with heavy battle damage from the raid. ATC passenger flights provided rapid transportation for critical military personnel whose time was precious, and for whom transportation by sea would have deprived the Allies of their services for considerable lengths of time. When Allied leaders went to their famous summit conferences, they traveled aboard US military transports operated by ATC.[155] American airmen who had completed their combat tour returned to the US on board ATC transports. ATC also provided some air evacuation of casualties but the command never lived up to expectations in the medical evacuation area.

The Air Transport Command offered a political benefit to the United States that was recognized by the War Department and the White House. The command's far-flung routes literally spanned the globe, or at least all that was not under Axis control. American military transports became ordinary sights at airfields in places where few white men had previously set foot. ATC began a tradition of showing the American flag throughout the world that has continued through the Military Air Transport Service, the Military Airlift Command and, now, the Air Mobility Command.

Air Transport Command's prodigious publicity led to considerable resentment on the part of the troop carrier crews, who were flying missions that were far more hazardous than anything ATC ever flew and sometimes took heavy losses. In the summer of 1943

---

[155] Although US President Franklin Roosevelt had a converted B-24 Liberator assigned for his personal use, he never used it but instead always traveled by ship to foreign conferences. First Lady Eleanor Roosevelt did use the B-24 on some of her well-known junkets. President Harry Truman, who followed Roosevelt, was the first US president to use a presidential aircraft.

photographer Ivan Dimitri[156] was contracted by ATC executives to document the command's worldwide mission. He departed New York in a C-87 bound ultimately for India, with stops at various bases around the world, including Benghazi, where he happened to be when Ninth and Eighth Air Force B-24s flew the famous low-level mission against the Ploesti oil refineries.[157] Dmitri's photographs are world-class, and when they appeared in LIFE magazine they were a tremendous source of publicity for Air Transport Command, but they were documenting a behind-the-lines logistical mission and the men who were facing the hazards of combat were not happy about it. Combat crews had already begun referring to the ATC initials as standing for "allergic to combat"[158] and the more publicity the command garnered, the more resentment it produced. Resentment against ATC and its successors by airmen assigned to combat squadrons continued long after the war.

The first mission of the apparatus that became the Air Transport Command was the ferrying of aircraft from the United States both domestically and to overseas bases. Routes developed by Ferry Command – and later by ATC – allowed combat crews to deliver their own airplanes overseas. Whenever a combat group or a replacement crew was sent overseas, it went to one of the ATC debarkation points where the airplanes were given a thorough inspection and the pilots and navigators were briefed on the routes and everything pertaining to them, including weather, hostile conditions, billeting, food, etc. ATC ferry pilots flew American-built airplanes overseas for delivery to Allied air forces and as replacements for those lost in combat by US Army Air Forces squadrons, but replacement combat crews made a large part of the deliveries, particularly of four-engine bombers and troop carrier aircraft.

Aircraft destined for the Soviet Union were delivered to pickup points in Alaska, where Soviet ferry pilots took delivery of the airplanes and flew them to their destinations inside the Soviet Union. Some ferry routes were over extremely hostile terrain in far-flung areas of the world. Ferry and transport crews were sometimes forced

---

[156] Ivan Dimitri was the pen name of artist Levon West, who was famous for his art work depicting national events, including Charles Lindbergh's flight across the Atlantic. He became an accomplished photographer, and used the pen name for his photography which he considered to be an art form. His book *Flight to Everywhere* is undoubtedly the best photo-essay of Army Air Forces World War II transport operations.

[157] Although TIDAL WAVE was a Ninth Air Force mission, Eighth Air Force's three B-24 groups were sent to Libya to supplement Ninth's two groups.

[158] One of Dimitri's color photographs is of an ATC C-87 named "Allergic To Combat."

Anything, Anywhere, Anytime

down in extremely difficult areas, as was the case when a C-87 crew landed their airplane on ice in the Canadian wilderness. The crew stayed with the airplane for several months while a team worked to prepare a runway in the snow from which to fly it out. A side-benefit of the ATC mission was the development of a worldwide air-sea rescue capability to locate and recover the crews of airplanes that went down either at sea or in remote parts of the world.[159]

World War II began with the transport industry still in infancy; it ended with a large military airline with truly global capabilities. The airline industry personnel who served with ATC during the war took back with them to their civilian employers a wealth of knowledge of long-range air transport operations that would have taken decades to accumulate in the civilian world. New technological developments such as advanced instrument landing procedures and navigational equipment made airline flying more reliable. Although air transportation was and still is expensive, it is a tremendous time saver. Several of the larger airlines, particularly Pan American and Trans World Airlines, established overseas routes after the war along the same routes they had flown with ATC during it.

Another benefit for the airlines was the development of new, faster and more capable four-engine transports. A ready supply of war surplus C-54s was available when the war ended and Douglas was geared up to produce new DC-4s for the airline industry. Lockheed had developed the pressurized Constellation, a fast, long-range, high altitude transport that would dominate the airline industry in the postwar years. Boeing's contribution was the Stratocruiser, a large, pressurized transport developed from the B-29. Consolidated was working on an airline transport derived from the B-24 but it was never fully developed.[160] There is no doubt but that the Air Transport Command was the most influential factor in the development of the international airline industry – ATC literally opened up the world! Yet even though ATC had played a tremendous role during the war, few in the military saw it as anything other than a military airline. Even the airline personnel who served with ATC saw the command as just a mobilization of the airline industry to support the war effort. Air Transport Command transports were usually only indirectly involved in combat operations, and when they were used to support troops in the field, it was under the control of the theater troop carrier commands.

---

[159] ATC was not the only organization with rescue capabilities. In Europe Eighth Air Force had its own rescue units, mostly equipped with boats. Fifth Air Force used PBYs to pick up crews from beaches and the sea.

[160] A single airliner was operated by American Airlines for a time while a second went to the Navy.

The ATC portion of the CBI Hump Airlift has been lauded by military historians, mostly those associated with the Military Airlift Command and its successor, Air Mobility Command, as a great achievement, although in reality it had nothing to do with the outcome of the war. The situation in China was still uncertain when Japan surrendered. ATC's other operations – with the exception of aircraft ferrying – were beneficial in that they reduced the time necessary to deliver high value items such as aircraft parts but they had no effect on how the war was fought. The vast majority of supplies sent overseas from the US went aboard merchant ships, including the cargo that was bound for China, which was delivered to seaports in India then shipped to the ATC bases by rail. They were only in ACT hands for the last 300 miles or so of their journey.

A good portion of the military supplies that reached China were not used to fight the Japanese, but were held back to continue China's civil war when the World War II hostilities ended. After 1942, China was never really a major theater of the war. Essentially, the Allied effort in China was a holding action designed to tie down large numbers of Japanese troops that might have been used elsewhere. In fact, it was probably more political than anything else and, after Japanese troops captured land that had been intended to serve as heavy bomber bases, was intended mostly to satisfy the Chinese-American lobby in the US.[161] The only bright spot in China itself was the tremendous effort put forth by Claire Chennault's China Air Task force, which became the Fourteenth Air Force later in the war. The primary Allied effort in the CBI was the effort to retake Burma from the Japanese, an effort in which ATC was a participant, although a reluctant one, when ATC transports were detached to X Troop Carrier Command control for combat operations. Air Transport Command did not exist when the war broke out and although the war ended with the command in a very prominent position, no military mission had been found for it. ATC almost did not survive the war.

---

[161] With the exception of Merrill's Marauders and the men of the MARS Brigade that followed them, no American ground combat troops served in the China-India-Burma area of operations. American participation was in the form of Tenth and Fourteenth Air Forces and the Air Transport Command India/China Wing. All ground combat troops in China were Chinese. Other US Army units in China were support, including engineers, Signals troops and Quartermasters.

Anything, Anywhere, Anytime

Sam McGowan

Chapter Nine - "Postwar"

Fairchild C-82

In 1945, as the war in Europe was winding down, Army Air Forces commander Gen. Henry H. Arnold, who had been promoted to a five-star general along with Marshall, Eisenhower and MacArthur, sent First Allied Airborne Army commander Lt. Gen. Lewis H. Brereton a letter in which he outlined his views for airborne and troop carrier forces in the postwar military. Arnold saw troop carriers as a means of delivering highly-trained airborne and glider forces to secure airfields or areas suitable for airfield construction deep in enemy territory, and then use them to fly in conventional infantry forces, a view shared by Army Chief of Staff General George Marshall. He even foresaw the use of airplanes to fly armored divisions into combat, although aircraft capable of transporting large armored vehicles were still almost a decade in the future. Arnold's plan never came to fruition, however. The tremendous power of nuclear weapons led President Harry Truman and others to conclude that ground forces were no longer necessary; the mere threat of nuclear weapons would deter future aggression. It wasn't until the Soviets detonated their own nuclear bomb in 1949 that the possibility of future large-scale conventional war was again seen as a possibility.

The detonation of the atomic bombs over Hiroshima and Nagasaki brought World War II to an end, at least in theory, [162] and

---

[162] Interrogations of Japanese officials responsible for the defense of the Homeland were classified for more than fifty years after the war in some cases, and there is evidence that while diehards in the military wanted to fight on, the Japanese civilian leaders and some military leaders knew the country had been defeated and

Anything, Anywhere, Anytime

ushered the world into the nuclear age. The new age brought with it a new conflict between the democratic West and the authoritarian communist East. Even though the Germans and Japanese had been defeated, the aftereffects of the war would still be felt for more than half a century. While the war had officially ended, peace had hardly broken out all over. In many countries, one enemy was simply replaced by another while prewar conflicts that had sunk into the mire of conflict reemerged with a new energy of their own. In war-torn China, the Nationalists and communists simply turned from fighting the Japanese to fighting each other, while a related conflict broke out in neighboring Indochina where communist guerrillas rebelled against French colonialism. Other conflicts broke out in the Balkans and elsewhere in the Mediterranean, but even though the signs were there that the world continued to be a hostile place, it took Washington – and particularly the Truman White House – some time to come to this realization.

Immediately after the Japanese surrender, Washington began demobilizing the huge military apparatus with which it had ended the war. Advances in military technology rendered weapons obsolete that had been on the cutting edge when the war broke out. This was particularly true in aviation, which had seen the ushering in of what came to be known as the Jet Age. German jet fighters entered combat in late 1944 but they weren't the only jets being developed. Both the US and British had developed their own jet fighters but they wouldn't become operational until after the war. Brand-new bombers and fighters with only a few hours of flight time were cutup for scrap, and in some cases simply pushed into holes dug by bulldozers and buried. Hundreds of airplanes were dumped into the sea and thousands were delivered to salvage yards where they were cut into scrap metal. Some were brand new airplanes that had never seen operational service. Some were sold to civilians, many of them veterans, for only a few hundred dollars. Transports, in particular, were in demand both by existing airlines and by new start-ups, some of which were started by veterans who had just returned from the war, so they avoided the scrap piles that were the fate of most combat aircraft. The Air Transport Command alone lost more than two thirds of the transports it had been operating at the end of the war. Many of ATC's C-54s transferred to troop carrier squadrons.

The troop carrier groups were spared deactivation, at least temporarily, because there was still much for them to do in the war-ravaged world. Thousands of displaced persons were scattered throughout Europe and Asia and had to be relocated, while the

---

were trying to find a way to surrender several months before the bombs were detonated.

occupational forces needed transportation and to be kept supplied. Unrest seemed to be the norm in many of the smaller countries of Eastern Europe, especially in those where there was a great deal of Soviet influence. A great ideological difference existed before the war between the Western Democracies and their eastern ally, the vast Soviet Union, which was based on the principles of Karl Marx. Although their differences had been temporarily put aside – at least on the surface – during the war, they reemerged when victory in Europe was assured and a new conflict began as the two ideologies began a struggle for dominance. The coals of the hot war were not even beginning to smolder before the Cold War began.

President Franklin D. Roosevelt died in office before the war ended and was succeeded by Vice President Harry S. Truman, a former Congressman from Missouri. Truman had only been in office for a few weeks when Roosevelt died and knew very little about war plans; he had no knowledge at all of the secret atomic weapons project. The new president was noted as a plainspoken, no-nonsense man but without the charisma of the man whose place he had taken. What the country did not know was that the new president, who had a military background with the Missouri National Guard, held professional military officers in low regard. After having risen to the rank of colonel in an artillery unit after his service in World War I, Truman considered himself to be a military expert, which was light years removed from the truth. His lack of military knowledge, combined with his disdain for the military, caused him to fail to heed the warnings of the officers in the War and Navy Departments when they advised him not to demobilize the armed services to their prewar levels.

A fiscal conservative in a party largely controlled by political progressives, Truman set out to reduce government spending as much as possible, with help from the Republican-controlled Congress. He was aided by the new Army Chief of Staff, fellow Missourian General Omar Bradley, who went along with Truman's plans to shrink the military.[163] Unfortunately, their cuts in military spending were far greater than prudence dictated. Within five years, Truman would find his country once again in a war; a war largely the result of his own doing. Eventually the country would again remobilize but in the immediate wake of the war, demobilization was the order of the day.

Along with other combat units, the troop carrier groups were significantly reduced in size and number, although the widely spread American presence around the world dictated a need for their services

---

[163] George Marshall had left the Army for a political career as Truman's Secretary of State. He became Secretary of Defense in 1950.

Anything, Anywhere, Anytime

in a peacetime role. Many groups were deactivated or relegated to reserve status but some troop carrier units remained on active duty and overseas. Most of the C-47s that had been the mainstay of the wartime troop carrier squadrons were declared surplus and sold, but some were placed in storage in the Arizona desert while others were assigned as base flight aircraft for utility duty. They were replaced in troop carrier squadrons with C-46s and C-54s that had formerly served with the Air Transport Command, and with Fairchild C-82 Packets, which had just started coming off the assembly lines when the war ended. While Fifth Air Force moved to Japan, the 374th Troop Carrier Group remained in the Philippines for a time but eventually followed its parent. The 317th TCG moved from the Philippines to Korea at the end of the war then transferred to Japan and in 1947, after equipping with C-54s, moved to Europe to take part in the Berlin Airlift. The 314th moved from Europe to the Canal Zone before returning to the United States to take up residence at Smyrna, Tennessee. Additional troop carrier resources were assigned to the reserves and National Guard, where a number of World War II heavy bomber groups were transferred as they were deactivated in the active force and reassigned to troop carrier duty.

In the immediate postwar period, the primary troop carrier bases were Bergstrom Field, Texas and Greenville Air Base, South Carolina. (Greenville became Donaldson in 1951.) Both bases were home to former Air Transport Command C-54s, which had transferred to the new Tactical Air Command, and new Fairchild C-82s, which were just coming into the inventory. Other troop carrier groups and wings were activated in the reserves.

Smyrna Army Air Field

In 1948, Smyrna Field at Smyrna, Tennessee reopened and became a troop carrier base. Gliders were still a part of the troop carrier mission and some troop carrier squadrons included gliders as well as powered transports. At Smyrna, the 2601st Troop Carrier Squadron activated to operate the Northrup C-125, a tri-motored, fixed-gear assault transport. The C-125 turned out to have design deficiencies and the 2601st dissolved. Its personnel were reassigned to other squadrons.

Troop carrier aviation had proven itself during the war as a valuable new military weapon. Particularly in the Pacific, troop carrier squadrons had provided unprecedented mobility to ground forces. In Europe, airborne forces had proven an effective means of disrupting the enemy and air transport had allowed ground combat forces to move ahead of their surface lines of supply. That airlift – although that term had yet to be coined – was to be a part of the postwar military was unquestioned[164]. What was questioned, however, was the value of a military airline such as the Air Transport Command.

Most military leaders considered the ATC to be what it was, the civilian airline industry mobilized and placed in olive drab. Even the former airline personnel who served in the AAF during the war saw no reason for ATC to continue in existence as a military organization, since its functions could be performed through contracts with the airlines. At the other extreme were those national leaders, many of whom were high-ranking military officers who had served in it during the war, who thought ATC should be expanded to become a national airline supported by the government, a thought that was anathema to believers in free enterprise. Ironically, the very man who had advocated its establishment in the first place, Mr. L.W. Pogue, led the fight to prevent ATC from developing into a single flag-carrying government-owned airline.(Miller C. E., 1988) ATC's position was complicated and its future became even more in doubt when the Air Staff proclaimed that all future aircraft development and production would be of tactical aircraft.

One of the military officers who pressed for a national airline was ATC veteran Brig. Gen. William H. Tunner, although he claimed in his memoir that he never advocated a single flag-carrying airline for the

---

[164] Although it is commonly used in articles and books about the air transportation mission in World War II, the word "airlift" did not come into use until after the Berlin air lift, when the two words were combined into one, particularly by Gen. William H. Tunner. By the 1960s, it was being used throughout the military and by aircraft manufacturers, particularly Lockheed Aircraft's Georgia Division, the manufacturer of the C-130 and developer of the C-141, which entered production in 1964, and of the gigantic C-5A that followed.

Anything, Anywhere, Anytime

country, at least not exactly. Tunner claimed that he favored a US government airline in China and later believed that if his idea had come to fruition, China would not have fallen to the communists. Yet he also stated that he believed as Pan American Airways President Juan Trippe did, that there should be a single international carrier rather than competing commercial airline companies.(Tunner, 1964) Trippe's plans fell apart when industrialist Howard Hughes revealed to a Congressional panel how Trippe had been using his influence with Maine Congressman Owen Brewster in an attempt to gain a monopoly on international travel for his airline.

Douglas C-74 Globemaster

During the war, troop carrier leaders were too busy fighting it to engage in military politics; unlike their peers in the ATC who, with a handful of exceptions, had spent the war in Washington. However, they were learning valuable lessons about military air transportation; one of which was that there was no difference between intertheater and intratheater air transportation other than distance, and even that was questionable.[165] Actually, the first air transport operation in the ETO had involved a long-range mission all the way from England to North Africa. The first US combat air transport operation ever was also a long-distance operation as Far East Air Force Air Transport

---

[165] That there was no distinction is limited solely to logistical operations. When it comes to combat operations, there's a huge difference between the two.

Command transports moved an antiaircraft battalion over 1,000 miles to defend Darwin, in Australia's Northwest Territories.

In October 1946, the commander of Third Air Force, Maj. General Paul Williams, who had commanded one of the first troop carrier groups to see combat in the ETO and had commanded IX Troop Carrier Command, expressed his view that there was no longer any validity for the existence of the Air Transport Command as an intertheater air transport force because distance should not be an issue in determining mission requirements. Williams proposed a very logical concept – that troop carrier squadrons should be responsible for ALL military air transportation operations regardless of distance – with the key word being "military." The Air Transport Command would exist more or less as Mr. Pogue had envisioned, as a quasi-military airline to move individuals and routine cargo, regardless of the distances involved, through military contracts with the airlines.

The ATC leadership seized on William's proposal but added a new twist – they proposed that ATC be responsible for ALL military airlift operations, period, including those assigned to the Troop Carrier Command! Now, bear in mind that none of these officers had been involved in combat operations during the war or, if they had, they had been in bombers at the beginning of the war. The most outspoken of these officers was Brig. Gen. William H. Tunner, who had convinced himself that he knew more about air transportation than anyone because of his experiences in India during the last months of the war. Never mind that he had command of a purely logistical operation moving cargo and passengers to China. He was not involved in combat operations at all.[166] However, Tunner's command of the India-China Ferry and his claims about increasing tonnage had given him stature and recognition in some quarters as an "air transport expert" even though he had yet to command a combat operation. In fact, Tunner's exposure to combat during the Korean War would be brief. His expertise was confined solely to logistical air transport. For that matter, until he went to India his experience was with ferrying of aircraft. Because ATC had been part of the US Army Air Forces in Washington, and because USAAF had controlled the B-29s of the Twentieth Air Force directly for a time, many ATC staff officers as well as some other USAAF personnel had become advocates of consolidation of military functions into single commands rather than assigning them to theater command. Officers who had served in the Twentieth Air Force were pressing for a strategic air command to

---

[166] One of the ironies of Tunner's career is that he didn't even become involved in air transportation until the war had turned in the Allies' favor and he had nearly unlimited resources at his command. From 1941 to August, 1944 when he was sent to India, he was involved strictly with ferrying of aircraft.

Anything, Anywhere, Anytime

control all long-range bombers. ATC officers sought the same status for all military air transports. The men who had led the Army's air forces during the war had been pressing for the creation of a separate air force since the 1920s. The war gave impetus to their ideas and Congress finally agreed.

In September 1947, the United States National Security Act established the Department of Defense, into which was folded the War Department and Navy Department. It was a concept originally suggested by Arnold in the mid-1930s. They became the Departments of the Army and Navy, respectively. DOD also included a brand new Department of the Air Force to replace the Army Air Corps[167] and most of the Army's aviation assets were transferred to the new service. The Army was allowed to keep only light liaison aircraft but the Department of the Navy retained most of its predecessor's aviation assets, including Marine Aviation and the Naval Air Transport Service. Army combat squadrons, including troop carrier, transferred to the new United States Air Force.

Although several attempts were made to consolidate all Army air transport operations into it, there was no provision for the Air Transport Command in the reorganization and its status remained in limbo for almost a year. During that year its commander, Maj. Gen. Robert Webster, and several members of his staff lobbied for the command's survival while also pressing for a military mission for it. They used General William's comments about troop deployment and began advocating Air Transport Command as the organization for deploying troops, even though no one on either the Air Staff or the Army Staff had ever advocated such a mission for it. Webster knew that ATC was seen by everyone in the military – including within the command itself – as nothing but an airline with no combat mission or capability and sought through various means to define one.

The air transportation issue was finally settled – or so it was thought – by the creation of the Military Air Transport Service on June 1, 1948. The organization was established as a logistical air transport service to serve the entire military establishment; not as a deployment vehicle for the Army. Its original name as it was authorized was to be the Armed Forces Air Transport Service but the new commander, Lt. Gen. Laurence Kuter, who had joined ATC late in the war, didn't like

---

[167] Although the Army Air Forces was established in 1941, it did not replace the Army Air Corps, which had been established by law. The USAAF was an Army organization that existed on the authority of the Army Air Corps as a training and support organization even though the former name was not used and the headquarters was not manned after December 1941 when Air Corps commander Lt. Gen. George Brett transferred to Australia to take command of all US Army personnel there.

the name and lobbied successfully to have it changed to Military Air Transport Service. The creation of MATS came about as a result of a Department of Defense effort to cut costs by combining the former War Department and Navy air transportation organizations into a single service. Although it was under the Department of the Air Force for support and administration, MATS was responsible for all DOD air transportation needs including contracting with the civilian airlines for passenger and cargo transportation and included Navy air transport assets. Transportation of troops, both ground and airborne, was assigned to the Troop Carrier Command, which was organized under the Tactical Air Command and the theater air forces. Strategic Air Command also had air transport assets to support its bomber wings, as did the Air Material Command.[168]

The issue should have been cut and dried, but ATC conjured up a cloud to obscure its mission. Prior to the activation of MATS, ATC commander Webster inserted a sentence in ATC's mission statement that the command provided *"Provision of strategic concentration, deployment and support, by air, for the Army Air Forces and the War Department."* Although no one outside of ATC had asked for such a statement, it was allowed to stand by the new Secretary of the Air Force, Stuart Symington, when the Military Air Transport Service was established in June 1948. Webster had undertaken a task to change the perception that existed within the entire military establishment, <u>INCLUDING WITHIN THE AIR TRANSPORT COMMAND ITSELF</u>, that ATC was an airline. Webster was, in no uncertain terms, attempting to elevate ATC's status to include all military air transportation, including that of the Troop Carrier Command. When MATS was created, many of its officers were unhappy with its status because it did not include all air transportation assets. One of the most vocal was Tunner, who had elevated himself to the status of expert on military air transportation of all types, in spite of his lack of combat experience.[169] Tunner had been a strong supporter of Webster's ideas and when the chance came for him to exert his position to promote MATS as THE air transportation arm of the United States, he took it. Tunner's chance

---

[168] The Material Command had been formed in 1942 to be responsible for certain aspects of logistics. In 1944 the original Material and Air Service Commands were abolished and the Air Material Command activated to assume their responsibilities. In 1961 it became the Air Force Logistics Command.

[169] During the final weeks of the war, Tunner had managed to have all air transportation in the CBI placed under his overall command, but by that point in the war air transport operations in China had become primarily the movement of gasoline and other supplies for Fourteenth Air Force combat squadrons from ATC fields to forward bases. Tunner's focus remained on delivering supplies to China.

Anything, Anywhere, Anytime

came, or at least he thought it did, within a few days after MATS was activated when the Russians blockaded Berlin.

The German capital city of Berlin was captured by the Russians during World War II, and was nearly a hundred miles within the territory the Red Army occupied by the time the war ended. Although it was located closer to Poland than to the boundary that partitioned Germany into Eastern and Western Zones, the city of Berlin itself was divided into essentially two areas, with the eastern portion governed by the Soviets while the rest was administered jointly by the United States, Great Britain and France, with each responsible for their own zone. West Berlin existed as an island of democracy within a sea of communism and the Soviets were not happy with the arrangement. Their objective was to gain complete control of the entire German capital city. In June 1948, they blockaded all land routes leading into the city and began turning away all vehicles and halting all trains coming into Berlin from the West, leaving the city cutoff from all communications with the western world – with one exception. There was still one avenue of supply to the city open – by air.

C-47s off-loading at Templehof

It is important to realize that the Soviets could have blocked the airways leading into Berlin if they had wanted to. However, in order to do so, they would have had to send armed fighters to patrol the skies between Berlin and West Germany and threaten to shoot down any Allied transport that entered East German airspace. Had they done so, the three nations that administered the Western Zone would have had to use their own fighters against the Soviet fighters. Berlin could have led to the outbreak of World War III if the Soviets had been strong in their resolve to cut the city off from all supply. That the Soviets didn't use air power to block the city completely is probably due to the fact that the Soviet Union had endured horrible warfare and casualties had been in the tens of millions. No country before or since has suffered to the extent the Soviet Union did and the Soviet leaders were not eager to expose their country to more war. Another factor was that while the United States had developed nuclear weapons and was basing B-29s capable of carrying them in the UK, the Soviets had yet to develop a nuclear capability. In short, the Soviets were bluffing in the hopes that the Allies would be unable to mount an effective air supply effort large enough to sustain the city. The situation was more of a test of the Allies will and air transport capability than it was a true threat. Yes, the Allies "showed the Russians," but they didn't show them much.

The American military commander in Europe, General Lucius Clay, wanted to test the Soviet resolve by sending ground troops against the blockades. However, his immediate superior in Washington, Gen. A.C. Wedemeyer, feared such an action would lead to war. Wedemeyer recommended the creation of an air bridge to keep the city's residents supplied with essentials instead. Shortly after it commenced, and for lack of a better word to describe the operation, the Berlin supply effort came to be known as a "lift"; it was eventually expanded into a term with "air" in front of it and the term was later shortened to a single word.[170] Apparently the new Air Force didn't want to use the word "ferry," perhaps because it was associated with the Army. The official name for the operation was *VITTLES*. At the time, the United States Air Forces in Europe had two troop carrier groups equipped with C-47s. USAFE commander Lt. Gen. Curtis LeMay began the lift with C-47s but quickly requested C-54s for his command because of their greater payloads and faster speeds. At the time, none were assigned to USAFE although C-54s had been assigned to troop carrier squadrons in the Pacific as well as within the United States. Three MATS C-54s were on duty for air transport operations in Europe but were not under USAFE control. Within two weeks after the lift began, the Air Force dispatched four troop carrier squadrons equipped with forty-eight C-54s from bases in the United States, Panama, Hawaii and Alaska to Germany. A MATS detachment with nine C-54s arrived a few days later to compliment the three MATS airplanes that were already operating in Europe to make up another squadron. The MATS

---

[170] It is difficult to determine exactly when the word "airlift" came into common usage. During the operation, the common term used was merely "the lift." General Tunner combined the words "air" and "lift", and by the 1960s "airlift" had become a common term.

airplanes were not under MATS control, however. They were assigned on temporary duty to USAFE and their status was the same as the troop carrier airplanes.(Miller R. G., 2000)

When the lift began, General Tunner lost no time in suggesting to the new MATS commander, Maj. Gen. Laurence Kuter, that MATS should "take control" of the operation. Kuter, who was more politically savvy than Tunner, advised him basically to keep his mouth shut. Tunner had been appointed deputy commander for operations of ATC in March and had continued in that position with MATS.[171] USAFE commander LeMay was acquainted with Tunner and recognized his expertise in the area of organization. It has been widely reported that LeMay requested that Tunner be assigned to his command to take control of a provisional airlift task force whose job would be to control the flow of supplies into Berlin. At least, that is the version of events that is officially associated with the Berlin Airlift. In reality, although LeMay was acquainted with Tunner in India, their association had not been that close. Their respective headquarters were hundreds of miles apart and they saw each infrequently, if at all. Tunner took command of the India/China Wing in September 1943, a few weeks before B-29 operations from Chinese bases ceased. LeMay departed India in early 1945 for a new assignment in Guam as commander of the B-29 offensive against Japan and was not a party to the massive increase in

---

[171] There are conflicting accounts of Tunner's position in the late spring and summer of 1948. His official USAF biography has him as commander of the Atlantic Wing with his headquarters at Westover AFB, Mass. A Military Airlift Command officer claimed that he was running a maintenance operation. Tunner himself said he was the MATS DCO.

tonnage that took place in the ATC India/China Division in the spring and summer of 1945 after he left.[172]

What actually happened was that Tunner, whose office as deputy commander for operations of MATS was in Washington, prowled the halls of the Pentagon looking for senior officers with whom to plead that he be put in charge of the operation. He kept one of his subordinates in the Pentagon on what was essentially permanent duty to press his case. The officer made nightly reports by telephone of his progress. Tunner was finally able to convince an undersecretary in the Department of the Army that he had known in India to make a recommendation that he be sent to Germany. Tunner also gained support from General Wedemeyer, who had been in charge of US Army operations in the CBI during the final months of the war and who was director of plans and operations on the new DOD General Staff. When he was finally put in charge of the operation, Tunner requested certain officers who had served with him in the ATC India/China Wing to be assigned to his staff.(Tunner, 1964)(Miller R. G., 2000)[173]

Tunner's assignment to *VITTLES* was not a transfer of the operation to MATS, as is often asserted, and as he evidently believed. In reality, Tunner went to USAFE on a special assignment to command a provisional task force dedicated to the movement of basic subsistence supplies to Berlin. He was subordinate to and reported directly to USAFE commander LeMay for only two months then when LeMay left for a new assignment as commander of Strategic Air Command, to his replacement, Lt. Gen. John Cannon, who took over USAFE in October. For some reason, Tunner had the idea that he still worked for MATS. He publically referred to his task force as "Military Air Transport Service Task Force Vittles" when, in reality, he and his staff were no longer part of MATS and most of the airplanes used in the operation had "Troop Carrier" written on their sides. LeMay allowed Tunner to communicate directly with MATS headquarters even though MATS was only involved in the operation in a supporting role. When Cannon took command of USAFE, he put Tunner in his place and put a stop to out-of-channels communications. Cannon

---

[172] The increase came about to a large extent because the B-29s left India and the additional air transport assets that had been sent to the CBI to support them transferred to ATC.

[173] There are differing accounts of how Tunner managed to get himself assigned to the air lift task force as commander. USAF historian Roger Miller claims that Tunner left on an inspection trip but Tunner himself claims it was Kuter who went on the trip. Some sources have put Tunner in command of an obscure maintenance depot and others have him as Deputy Commander of the MATS European wing when the lift commenced, but he had actually been brought to Washington to serve as Deputy Commander for Operations of ATC in March 1948.

recognized, correctly, that Tunner was staging a power play to gain control of the operation for MATS.

Unlike Tunner, whose career had been as an administrative officer and in logistical air transport, including ferrying of aircraft, Cannon was a true combat commander who had considerable experience with troop carrier operations under his command. He went to North Africa with Twelfth Air Force and commanded XII Support Command, a tactical organization responsible for support of ground forces. During the reorganization of air forces in the fall of 1943, he was given command of Twelfth Air Force. He commanded all air forces, including troop carriers, involved in Operation *DRAGOON*, the invasion of southern France. As a combat commander, he had seen the military politicking of the Air Transport Command staff and was one of the officers who strongly believed that they were out to garner more power. He saw Tunner as attempting to operate outside of his proper chain of command.

When he got to Wiesbaden, where the task force had its headquarters, Tunner was instructed to provide air transport to Berlin or elsewhere as he was directed by LeMay. He asked for, and was temporarily given, the right to communicate directly with MATS, the Air Material Command and the European Command without going through USAFE Headquarters, but he lost that right when LeMay was replaced a few weeks later by Cannon, who was disgusted with Tunner's power grab and insisted that since *VITTLES* was a theater operation, all communications with other headquarters should follow proper military channels and go through USAFE. LeMay had gone along with Tunner's request because, as commander of XX Bomber Command during the war, he, like Tunner, had been part of a United States Army Air Forces organization based in Washington that operated independently of and outside of theater command. He was one of the officers who believed in specified commands. Lemay was also in the final weeks of his tour as USAFE commander and his primary responsibility was to avoid a new war and to respond to it if one came. He was content to let Tunner have free rein.

Cannon had commanded Twelfth Air Force and the Mediterranean Tactical Air Forces and was thus well familiar with the myriad of problems caused by ATC's independent status during the war. There was also a problem that went far beyond merely getting supplies into Berlin: The military situation in Europe was precarious and war could break out at any moment. When and if it did, the *VITTLES* operation would be relegated to a low priority as precedent was given to combat operations. As the senior USAF officer in Europe, Cannon could not afford to have a subordinate officer running a rogue operation. In fact, it is very probable that the only thing that kept the Soviets from resorting to military action in the crisis was the threat of

US nuclear weapons. As it was, Soviet fighters harassed the transports but never took overtly hostile action.

There is a common misconception that the Berlin Airlift was a MATS operation but while Tunner and his staff came from MATS (which had only been in existence for a few weeks when they arrived at Wiesbaden), they had been reassigned temporarily to Europe and to USAFE. The operation was directly under United States Air Forces Europe and was a troop carrier operation from start to finish. The aircrews themselves were largely combat veterans; some had flown missions over Berlin in B-17s and B-24s during the war. Tunner and his staff were responsible for command and control but did not actually participate in air operations themselves. Tunner and MATS headquarters tried in vain to have the operation placed under MATS control, and did not endure themselves by doing so with senior Air Force officers who saw their actions as an attempt at gaining power.

MATS C-54 assigned to the lift

When the operation began, there were two troop carrier groups in Europe, the 60th and 61st, both equipped with C-47s. As C-54s began arriving in Germany, a provisional troop carrier group of four squadrons was set up. Eventually, all US airplanes and crews sent to Germany for the airlift were assigned to the 61st, 313th, 317th and 513th Troop Carrier Groups. This included those that came from MATS, which were assigned to USAFE on temporary duty (TDY) status. The 60th was withdrawn from the airlift in September 1948 when the 317th TCG arrived from the Far East, and its flight crews were either

Anything, Anywhere, Anytime

reassigned to the 317th or distributed among the other groups and retrained to fly the four-engine C-54s.

By the time Tunner arrived, 54 C-54s, including twelve from MATS, and 105 USAF C-47s made up the American element of the airlift task force. A British force of forty York transports[174] and fifty Dakotas (C-47s) complimented the Americans. The British were also making use of civilian contract carriers on the lift; something the US Air Force never did. However, the combined tonnage capability of the two forces was only 2,300 tons per day and the city needed 3,800 tons in summer and 4,500 tons in winter to survive. The French air force also participated in the lift but their operations were limited due to France's commitments in Indochina where it was fighting a war against communist revolutionaries. LeMay had already requested additional C-54s and nine more squadrons were on their way to Europe. Airlift strength would be further increased with the addition of 39 more troop carrier C-54s, when the 317th group moved from Japan to Germany, and 24 Navy R5Ds (C-54s).(Miller R. G., 2000)

The Berlin Airlift continued for a little more than a year, until August 1, 1949 when the Soviets finally lifted the blockade. During that time, C-54s, augmented by TAC C-82s for bulky cargo, operated an around-the-clock sustained airlift into the city. In mid-August 1948, a few days after Tunner and his staff arrived in Germany, a single Douglas C-74 was assigned to the airlift, evidently at Tunner's request as a MATS test. The large transport, at the time the largest in service, flew 24 missions into Berlin over a six-week period then was withdrawn.[175] Tunner would later claim that the test proved the value of large transport aircraft. The Boeing YC-97, a transport version of the B-29 which was under development, was also assigned briefly to the operation at the very end, but it developed nose gear problems and only made a few trips. The airlift was a peacetime operation, with a total amount of tonnage per day as the goal. Food, particularly flour, and other commodities were the primary cargo, along with coal for heating during the winter months.

There were no military objectives and the airplanes were not subject to overt hostile action, although they occasionally encountered harassing Soviet fighters. If the Soviets had elected to take hostile action, the operation would not have succeeded and the crisis would have escalated to full-scale war. No other operations were in effect to take airplanes away from the concentrated effort on moving

---

[174] The Avro York was a four-engine transport based on the airframe of the Lancaster bomber. It could carry a payload of 20,000 pounds, 2,000 pounds more than a C-54.

[175] Twenty-four missions over a six-week period is a very small number, an average of only four missions per week.

commodities into Berlin, so Tunner was able to focus full attention to the supply effort. The nuclear-equipped Strategic Air Command B-29s provided the muscle that was needed to keep the Soviets from doing anything foolish that could have led to an escalation of the tension to direct military action. Had the Soviet Union possessed a nuclear force in 1948-49, the Berlin Airlift might not have taken place and the world would probably be considerably different today.

The primary enemy of the transport crews flying into Berlin was the weather, unless one can consider the mandate to meet established goals an "enemy." The heaviest demand on the *VITTLES* force was in the winter months when low clouds, reduced visibility caused by rain, snow and fog, and ice presented major problems to the orderly flow that was needed to keep the city supplied. In many respects, the situation in Berlin was similar to that faced by the India-China Ferry crews in China, except there were no mountains to contend with and the distances were considerably less, not much over a hundred miles. General Tunner's organizational skills were put to good use; it was obvious that he was the best man for the job of running what was essentially a routine, albeit high demand, air cargo operation. The entire operation could have been performed by civilian airlines under contract.[176] Timing was of the essence to keep the flow of transports moving smoothly and Tunner knew how to establish schedules to produce the maximum results from the assets under his control. He instituted policies designed to produce maximum efficiency. For instance, shortly after he arrived in Germany he mandated a policy that if a pilot missed an approach into one of the airfields in Berlin, he would enter the flow of return traffic to the onload bases, with his load still aboard, rather than attempt another approach so as not to impede the flow of traffic.

There was a human side to the lift. The young American aircrew members were sympathetic to the plight of the citizens of West Berlin. Many of them had flown bombing missions over Germany only a few years before and they saw the bombed-out rubble every time they flew into the city. The most commonly known example of this humanness was the venture begun by a C-54 pilot, Lt. Gail Halverson. Halverson noticed the crowds of German children clustered outside the gates at Templehof Airport to watch the transports come in with the flour, coal and other staples that the city needed to survive. He began buying all the candy and chewing gum he could find, then dropping it to the

---

[176] Tunner was actually offered a position right after the war as manager of a startup airline of which USAAF commander Arnold was to be CEO. Tunner made plans to retire from the Air Force to take the position but changed his mind at the last minute, probably because of his wife's health. She was diagnosed with a brain tumor in November 1945 and was in a coma for a year and a half.

Anything, Anywhere, Anytime

children in tiny bundles. Someone in Berlin took note of the "Candy Bomber" and wrote an article that appeared in *STARS AND STRIPES*, the military newspaper for personnel stationed overseas, and made its way to the United States. Soon candy and other goodies for the children of Berlin were pouring into Wiesbaden for Halverson's personal airlift operation, which is remembered as *LITTLE VITTLES*.

German children watching arriving C-54

A major requirement of the lift was simply keeping enough airplanes in Europe and in commission to meet the daily requirements. The Air Force only owned some 400 C-54s in 1948-49 and when the lift was at its peak, 319 of those were required. (A large percentage of this number was not involved in the lift itself, but was being used to transport supplies and personnel back and forth between the US and the lift bases in Germany.) Seventy-five airplanes were always in the maintenance pipeline, which was unnecessarily long since the airplanes were being flown back to the United States for major maintenance and scheduled inspections. MATS' major contribution was ferrying those airplanes between the lift bases in Germany and depots in the United States. Eventually, the required maintenance inspections were shifted to Europe, first to Bavaria and then to England, to reduce the out-of-commission time and flying time on the airplanes.

While the Berlin Airlift is most often remembered for its political implications as the first confrontation with the Soviets in the Cold War, it is often pointed to as how an airlift should be run by supporters of the Air Mobility Command. In reality, the Berlin Airlift was not a military airlift at all, except that it was performed by a military organization. General Tunner's methodology would not have worked in a combat environment where the steady stream of transports would have been sitting ducks for fighters and antiaircraft. The air lift provided ammunition for use by Tunner and the MATS staff as they continued pressing for consolidation of all air transport assets into a single command, a command that would naturally be under their control.

While the lift was still underway, General Kuter, the MATS commander, published an article in *AERO DIGEST* in which he argued for the strengthening of MATS with the purchase of larger four-engine transports. Making hay while the sun shone, Kuter used the Berlin Airlift as an example of MATS' usefulness to the nation (even though the lift was not a MATS operation and most of the airplanes involved and their crewmembers came from troop carrier squadrons. While assigned to the lift, ALL personnel were troop carrier, either permanently or on temporary duty status.) Kuter further advocated the consolidation of all military air transport assets under MATS, with the exception of certain transports belonging to the Department of the Navy including those owned by the Marines. Somehow, the MATS commander managed to switch the role played by his command in the Berlin Airlift from support to the major effort. In 1950, he pointed to the air lift as an example of how troop carrier forces could "augment MATS" in the strategic airlift mission. In reality, the Berlin Airlift was a short-range theater airlift mission, i.e., tactical, with augmentation from MATS! After skillfully manipulating his words to switch the roles of the two air transport missions, Kuter called for a consolidation of the two.[177] The consolidation controversy would continue for decades, and still continues today as the Air Force cannot seem to reconcile a true place for the tactical – now called combat – airlift mission.

In the spring of 1950, less than a year after the end of the Berlin operation, the Air Force conducted a joint exercise with the Army in North Carolina called *SWARMER*, which was designed to test the services' capabilities to seize and maintain an airhead inside hostile territory, the concept that the Soviets had first developed and which

---

[177] Kuter's political maneuvering was strictly a power play to gain power for himself. Unlike Tunner and other senior MATs officers, Kuter's association with ATC had been after the war and had lasted for only about a year. His military background was primarily in bombers.

Anything, Anywhere, Anytime

the Luftwaffe refined to a science. Although it was an Air Force and Army operation, the exercise included Navy participation, primarily as air opposition. *SWARMER* was supposed to be a test of ideas advocated during the war by Generals Arnold and Brereton but there was a problem; none of the senior officers involved had experience in troop carrier operations or were even noted for having a particular interest in them. Although the operation was advocated as a test of troop carrier capabilities, it was actually an effort to establish the case for airlift consolidation.

Fairchild C-119 "Flying Boxcar"

The author of the plan and overall commander of the Air Force element in the exercise was General Lauris Norstad, who had served under General Henry H. Arnold on the staff of Twentieth Air Force and was a major advocate of consolidated commands. That the purpose of the exercise was slanted is evident in the appointment of General Tunner to command the airlift portion, even though he had no experience with troop carrier operations. Tunner promptly took advantage of his position by assigning MATS as large a role as he possibly could even though MATS had no aircraft capable of dropping paratroops or cargo and its C-54s and C-74s were ill suited for operations into primitive airstrips. Just what *SWARMER* actually accomplished is unclear. Perhaps the most important result was that former 82nd Airborne Division commander Lt. Gen. James Gavin pointed out the need for troop carrier aircraft, particularly C-119s.

Army Air Forces troop carriers finished the war with C-47s as their primary airplanes, with some C-46s assigned. After the war, several troop carrier squadrons reequipped with C-54s. The C-46, C-47 and C-54 – all of which were originally designed for airline use – were

Sam McGowan

not truly suited for the troop carrier role so the Army Air Forces proceeded with the development of new designs. In 1941, just before the war broke out, the Army issued a specification for an airplane designed strictly to carry military cargo and the contract was awarded to Fairchild Aircraft. Although it did not make its appearance until late in the war, the Fairchild C-82 Packet equipped some troop carrier squadrons in time for the Berlin Airlift. However, while the C-82 was an improvement over the use of airline-type aircraft for military use, it was still lacking, particularly in performance. In 1947, the Air Force instituted a program to upgrade the C-82 to a new, more powerful configuration, which became the C-119 Flying Boxcar. It also turned out to be underpowered. The Air Force had yet to consider a four-engine transport with true tactical capabilities. Neither had the service considered turbine engines, even though turboprop engines were already in use on British transports.

Chase CG-20 Glider

Unlike the C-47 and C-54, the C-119 was designed for troop carrier use. The cargo compartment could accommodate 28,000 pounds of cargo, including vehicles that could be driven up ramps into the rear of the cargo compartment. An overhead trolley system allowed airdrop of small bundles while larger containers and vehicles could be airdropped using special platforms loaded on aluminum rollers known as "skate wheels" and extracted by special parachutes. Up to 67 paratroops could jump from doors on either side of the airplane. The first deliveries were to the 314th and 316th Troop Carrier

Anything, Anywhere, Anytime

Wings at Smyrna AFB, Tennessee[178]; other Tactical Air Command squadrons equipped with the Flying Boxcar as deliveries continued through 1955. Another postwar transport design was Chase Aircraft's C-123. The original Chase design was based on the company's CG-20 glider and was designed as an assault transport that could land on rough, unimproved landing zones like a powered glider. When Chase suffered financial difficulties due to the cessation of glider production, the design was purchased by Fairchild, but the program remained on hold until the mid-fifties.

A second transport design became the center of controversy just before the outbreak of the Korean War. During the early part of World War II, the Army contracted with Douglas for the development of a large transport. What Douglas came up with was basically an oversize C-54, which is not surprising since the company used its DC-4 design as a starting point. The C-74 was possibly spawned by the inability of the US to resupply its forces in the Philippines effectively during the early months of the war. However, the rapid development of the troop carrier mission made the C-74 Globemaster already obsolete by the time of its first flight in September 1945, just before the formal end of the war.[179] The huge transport was just that, a transport, and although it could carry heavy loads, it had no military capabilities. Loading and unloading was accomplished using an elevator. It certainly was not applicable to the troop carrier role. The Army took delivery of eleven and a few saw limited use during the Berlin Airlift,[180] but the second order was canceled.

The Air Force issued a new requirement for a large troop carrier transport so Douglas redesigned the C-74 and submitted an improved version designed specifically for troop carrier use. The C-124 Globemaster II featured a fatter, taller fuselage with a second deck that could be folded down from the cargo compartment sides to carry troops or vehicles. Clamshell doors on the nose allowed vehicles to be driven on and off on self-contained ramps. An elevator well at the rear of the cargo compartment had a dual function – it could be used to load cargo and, with the elevator removed, the opening allowed cargo drops of bundles and platforms. Overhead hoists allowed loading

---

[178] Smyrna was renamed Sewart Air Force Base in March 1950.

[179] Another wartime transport design was Howard Hughes' massive H-4 Hercules, an eight-engine flying boat made entirely of wood that was designed to carry 750 troops and their equipment or a single Sherman tank. Although the war ended before it flew, Hughes vowed that the airplane would fly and made one impressive flight in 1947.

[180] A single C-74 participated in the lift for six weeks in the late summer of 1948 but their main contribution was the delivery of aircraft parts to Germany from depots in the US.

crews to position cargo. Paratroop doors on the sides allowed egress for airborne troops. Yet even though the C-124 could carry troops and equipment and was capable of airdrop, it was not a true tactical airplane.

The C-124 became an object of controversy when MATS proposed that the airplanes designated for the Tactical and Strategic Air Commands be instead assigned to it. TAC was actually not happy with the C-124 as a troop carrier but had decided to accept it as it was the only heavy-lift transport available and it did offer some troop carrier capabilities. SAC wanted transports to move its personnel and equipment when its bomber squadrons deployed overseas. MATS, on the other hand, saw the huge transport as a replacement for its C-54s. The MATS position was that the C-124s would be "better utilized" if those destined for SAC and TAC were assigned to it instead as they could be used for DOD transport functions. MATS was heavily engaged in a consolidation campaign and a successful push for control of all of the C-124s would be a step in that direction. In the end, the first deliveries of C-124s went to SAC's logistical support squadrons while subsequent deliveries were to TAC squadrons, then to squadrons in the air transport wings that made up MATS.

Douglas C-124 Globemaster II

With the creation of the United States Air Force, three combat commands were established. Strategic Air Command was an outgrowth of the B-29 mission of World War II and was charged with the long-range bombing mission, which in the nuclear age meant the delivery of atomic bombs to targets inside the Soviet Union. Having ended World War II after dropping the only two bombs it had at the time, the nuclear force was considered to be America's first line of

Anything, Anywhere, Anytime

defense. The Truman White House and many senior military officers believed that nuclear power had rendered warfare so terrible that no nation would be willing to risk it in the future as long as the US maintained a powerful nuclear force. SAC had its own air transport squadrons. Tactical Air Command was charged with responsibility for supporting US Army ground forces by gaining and maintaining air supremacy over the battlefield, providing close air support of ground forces and transporting airborne and light infantry forces and keeping them supplied. TAC included fighter/bomber wings and groups, interceptor wings and groups, reconnaissance wings and groups and troop carrier wings and groups. TAC was established by regulation as the Air Force's sole point of contact with the Army for Air Force services, including air transportation. This meant that any requests from the Army for MATS transports had to come through TAC. Air Defense Command was charged with the defense of the North American Continent and was made up of fighter wings flying interceptors. Overseas commands were established in Europe as United States Air Forces Europe; in the Pacific initially as the Far East Air Forces then as Pacific Air Forces; the Caribbean Air Command which became Southern Command and Alaska Air Command. Each of the overseas commands was tactical in nature and was a gaining command for TAC squadrons in the event of an outbreak of war. MATS, as previously described, existed as a service responsible for Defense Department airlift needs much as the Military Sea Transport Service, which replaced the Merchant Marine, existed for military surface transportation on the sea. MATS was not actually an Air Force organization but was a DOD organization supported by the Air Force. MATS also included Navy air transport squadrons staffed by Navy personnel flying airplanes that belonged to the Air Force.

In some respects, MATS' position in the Air Force was that of a bastard child. The DOD had charged the Air Force with supporting what was essentially a government airline, which meant providing and training its crews, providing support personnel, providing and maintaining its bases and maintaining its airplanes. Yet even though it was operated by Air Force personnel and its airplanes bore USAF markings, MATS belonged to the DOD. Even the Navy MATS squadrons flew airplanes with US Air Force on the side. An Industrial Fund was set up into which the various government agencies transferred funds from their own budgets in payment for MATS services. MATS used these funds to set up separate facilities on Air Force bases for its aircrews and support personnel and to pay per diem for its aircrews. The MATS staff eagerly sought missions to increase the service's military importance. The Air Force Weather and Air/Sea Rescue Services became part of MATS. MATS also managed to gain some of the Air Force's clandestine services, particularly the Air Resupply and

Sam McGowan

Communications squadrons that originally were part of SAC. The MATS public information office put out one press release after another; articles that had one purpose and that was to increase MATS' importance in the public eye. It didn't matter that MATS' role in a particular operation was minor; if there was any MATS participation at all, it became a MATS operation in the press releases. It was World War II all over again, with theater commanders providing support to MATS without having any operational control over its aircraft and personnel or receiving any benefit from having MATS aircraft passing through their areas of responsibility. MATS frequently took credit for missions that had actually been theater missions flown by troop carrier squadrons. It was like MATS was in its own little world; it was.

While MATS struggled to find a military mission, TAC's troop carrier wings had an established mission that came out of World War II. Their role was multifunctional. One mission was to transport airborne forces to drop and landing zones deep inside enemy territory, where they would seize existing airfields or land where landing strips could be constructed to serve as an airhead for additional airborne and conventional ground forces. The other was to provide logistical support to combat squadrons in combat theaters. Air transport was immune to difficult terrain, mountains and large bodies of water as the 54th Troop Carrier Wing had proven in the Southwest Pacific. Troop carrier was also responsible for providing transportation for TAC's fighter/bomber and reconnaissance squadrons by moving their support personnel and equipment in the event of a rapid deployment. It was a wartime mission that could only be performed by military aircrews in airplanes that had been designed or adapted to fill military needs. MATS claimed that role but wasn't given it and lacked the proper equipment to perform it.

The Berlin Crisis, which was met with the lift, was the first test of the United States will in the Cold War with the Soviets, but there were trouble spots in other parts of the world. A movement of displaced European Jews to Palestine led to fighting between Jewish immigrants and the British administrators of the region. Civil war raged in Greece and Yugoslavia. The United States provided military assistance to the government of Greece – including some C-47s – and limited air support to parties in some other conflicts but for the most part Washington adopted a "wait-and-see" kind of attitude. Although it was kept hidden from the eyes of the rest of the world by the repressive Soviet regime, there was fighting within the countries that made up or were controlled by the Soviet Union.

Anything, Anywhere, Anytime

Claire Chennault

The most significant of the postwar civil disturbances was in China where the opposing forces of Nationalist Generalissimo Chaing ki Shek were ultimately defeated by the communists under Mao ze Tung. The Chinese civil war had been going on since the 1920s. Even while the Japanese attempted to subdue the entire country, the opposing factions kept a wary eye on each other. They knew that as soon as Japan was defeated, they would be engaged in the larger struggle for dominance over the country. Ironically, much of the cargo and supplies that was flown into China over the Hump to fight the Japanese was actually diverted and kept in reserve for the civil war – which erupted before the ink had dried on the Japanese surrender documents. In fact, communist forces began making their bid for territory before the war ended.

Some American leaders recognized the Chinese Civil War for what it was, a struggle to impose Marxist communism on the nation as a whole, but others saw it as just another civil war with no worldwide or regional implications. The United States withheld support from the Nationalist government during the struggle, although many Americans participated in the war as mercenaries or soldiers of fortune, particularly as transport crewmembers. Airlift was a major American contribution to the Nationalist Chinese but it was without any kind of

Sam McGowan

US military involvement or sanction. For the most part, the American involvement in China was under the leadership of the same man who commanded the first American mercenaries to see action in Asia, General Claire Lee Chennault.

After being relieved of command of the Fourteenth Air Force in China in the final months of the war, Chennault returned to the United States and retirement to his home in Louisiana. He didn't stay long; a love for the Chinese people and a concern over their struggle led him to return to China.[181] Since air transportation had played such an important role in the CBI, Chennault recognized that the transport airplane could be used to establish an infrastructure in a country as large and with as many rugged areas as were found in China. After a year in the United States, Chennault returned to China to start an airline. The official name for the new airline was the China National Relief and Rehabilitation Air Transport Company but because of its length, it was usually shortened to simply "CAT."[182] CAT was founded on October 25, 1946 by Chennault and Whiting Willauer, an American politician, sometimes diplomat and businessman. Hundreds of transports were available from military surplus; the new airline purchased fifteen C-46s and four C-47s. Chennault's intent was to deliver accumulated relief supplies from the docks in the coastal cities to the Chinese interior and return with commercial cargo. However, it wasn't long before CAT found itself involved in the civil war that had resumed in China. To staff his new airline, Chennault turned to the thousands of young men who had served in the region during the war. Many of CAT's pilots came right from the ranks of the troop carrier squadrons that operated in the region during the war, and which remained to aid in China relief until the United States decided to withdraw from the chaotic country. Others were former CNAC personnel. He also recruited maintenance and cargo handling personnel, dispatchers and schedulers.

CAT crews flew supplies for the Nationalists, but they also flew other commodities to keep the Chinese government functioning. CAT airplanes carried raw materials for Chinese factories as well as money. It has long been rumored that CAT airplanes also transported opium, which was a staple for Chinese farmers, but former CAT personnel have always denied the claim. The airline began with money raised by Chennault but a two-million dollar loan from the United Nations relief

---

[181] Chennault's return to China may have been due as much to love for a young Chinese woman as for China, the country. He and his wife divorced within a year after his return to Louisiana and he left soon afterwards to return to China. He married the young woman the following year.

[182] After the communist victory in China and its subsequent purchase by the Central Intelligence Agency, the company was renamed Civil Air Transport.

Anything, Anywhere, Anytime

organization allowed it to flourish. The loan was repaid in full within a year. CAT pilots were the kind of men one envisioned from the popular comic strip "Terry and the Pirates." Essentially, they were soldiers of fortune who were in the business as much for the adventure and romance as for the money. Some were outright characters, men such as James "Earthquake McGoon" McGovern, a black-bearded pilot from New Jersey who got his name because he stood six feet tall and weighed 260 pounds; he looked like a character in Al Capp's Snuffy Smith newspaper comic series.. McGovern had fought under Chennault as a fighter pilot flying P-38s then transferred to a troop carrier squadron at Beijing when the war ended. He joined CAT after his military discharge in 1947. McGovern would have many adventures in China and his name would become legend in the Far East.

When it became obvious that the Chinese Nationalists were going to lose the civil war, Chennault decided to move CAT's assets to Hong Kong, which was under British control. In preparation for the move, Chennault and his men raised a sunken LST from the Yangtze River and loaded it with all the equipment needed for a fully equipped machine shop. As the communists closed in on the city of Shanghai where CAT was headquartered, Chennault and his men moved out. The airplanes were flown to safety while the airline's supplies and equipment moved aboard the LST. But after his arrival in Hong Kong, Chennault began experiencing problems of another kind; with China in communist hands there was no business for his airline. To make matters worse, a legal decision against Chennault in the British court gave the Red Chinese control of 76 of his airplanes. They were returned two years later, when the court reversed its earlier decision. By that time, the airplanes had deteriorated to the point of worthlessness due to lack of use and exposure to the elements.

To alleviate his financial woes, Chennault turned to a new ally, the newly created United States Central Intelligence Agency, which had been established with resources formerly with the Office of Strategic Services. Under the National Defense Act of 1947, the CIA was given responsibility for intelligence gathering and for clandestine and covert activities in places where the United States didn't want its presence known. A division called the Special Activities Division was established to conduct clandestine and covert operations. SAD is the most secret element of the United States government; it includes the nation's most highly skilled special operations forces. Since covert activities are part of the CIA's responsibilities, the Agency saw the benefits of an airline such as CAT to support its activities in the Far East, which were mostly aimed at the communists in China.

In 1949, the Agency arranged the first of several cash advances to CAT in payment for future services. The payments were a lifeline that kept the financially strapped company afloat. A new airline was organized with the money and named Civil Air Transport so the old initials would still apply. But even though the cash advances kept CAT alive, Chennault kept asking Washington for more and more monetary assistance. When the aging warrior approached the Agency in the summer of 1950, the CIA decided to offer to purchase the airline outright. Even though there were some legal questions regarding government ownership of a civilian airline, the State Department approved the plan under the condition that the CIA would divest itself of the airline as soon as practical. It would be twenty-five years before the divestiture took place. By that time, CAT had grown into a complex system of aviation proprietorships owned outright by the CIA, and the divestiture only took place under pressure from the United States Congress as it became increasingly antiwar in the immediate wake of the war in Vietnam.(Robbins, 1979)

The events in China were undoubtedly the most significant of the postwar era. The Berlin Airlift is hailed as the great crisis of the day within the modern US airlift community, but it was the communist victory in China that paved the way for America's future involvement in two wars. Both would involve the Air Force's troop carrier squadrons, and in a big way. With China and the Soviet Union, the two largest countries in the world, both under the banner of communism and both filled with an evangelical zeal to spread their form of government through the undeveloped world, it was only a matter of time before there were would be a clash between the two dominant forms of government then in existence. And the clash would come in Asia.

Anything, Anywhere, Anytime

Chapter Ten - "Korea"

The Truman Administration's postwar military cutbacks left the United States woefully unprepared for another war. While the nuclear detonations over Hiroshima and Nagasaki[183] brought the B-29s of SAC into prominence, the United States had allowed its ground forces to shrink to a fraction of their size and they were made up for the most part of soldiers who had been too young for World War II. At the same time, little thought had been given to the defense of the Far East against communist aggression. The United States had managed to keep the Soviets out of Japan by allowing them to occupy contested territory in the northern islands, Sakhalin and the Kuriles. Soviet troops invaded Manchuria during the last weeks of the war and moved into Korea but stopped at the 38th Parallel in recognition of an agreement made at Potsdam between Soviet Premier Josef Stalin and President Truman. Tiny Korea was divided into two halves, with the United States occupying the south while the Soviet Union occupied the north. Elections were held to determine the fate of the country but North Korea refused to recognize them. While the United States made little effort to build up the South Korean military and had only a small military presence there, North Korea quickly became a communist

---

[183] In order to attain maximum effect from nuclear weapons, it is necessary for them to be detonated in the atmosphere rather than on the ground. Both of the bombs used in World War II were "air bursts," detonated by barometric fuses.

dictatorship with a large, modern military that had been armed and equipped by the Soviets. On June 25, 1950, North Korean troops invaded South Korea.

When the Korean War broke out, troop carrier strength in the Far East Air Forces consisted of only one wing, the 374th at Tachikawa, an airfield on the outskirts of Tokyo.[184] The 317th TCG had transferred to Europe for the Berlin Airlift and remained. One of the wing's three squadrons, the 21st TCS, was based at Clark Field in the Philippines. All three squadrons, the 6th, 21st and 22nd, were flying four-engine C-54s. Very little thought had been given to the defense of Korea where only a small number of American advisors were based when the communist North Korean government sent troops across the 38th parallel. While the 374th operated missions into Korea in support of the small US military mission there, the "Land of the Morning Calm" was but one more stop for the wing's C-54 crews.

After the initial North Korean invasion, which drove the South Korean national forces southward in a near riot, the 374th began operating C-54 flights into Korea to evacuate American civilians, missionaries, diplomats and military advisors from the rapidly collapsing country. The first missions were into Seoul, where a MATS C-54 had been the first USAF aircraft casualty of the war,[185] then

---

[184] The difference between an Air Force group and a wing was that a wing included support functions as well as operational squadrons. As the Korean Conflict escalated, troop carrier wings were activated as the headquarters for one or more groups.

[185] The C-54 was one of the few combat losses ever suffered by MATS or its predecessor, ATC, or by its successors, MAC and AMC.

moved to Suwon after the South Korean capital was captured by North Korean troops. During the evacuation, the C-54 crews were exposed to attack by North Korean fighters. A few days after the war broke out, a 374th C-54 was strafed and burned by North Korean Yak fighters at Suwon. A crew member was wounded by a machinegun bullet, becoming the first Far East Air Forces airlift casualty of the war.(Thompson)

One of the 374th wing commander's first actions was to order the 21st from Clark to Japan. When the squadron arrived, its C-54s were taken away and turned over to the other two squadrons, along with the experienced four-engine crews. The 21st reequipped with C-47s that were pulled in from throughout the Far East; pilots with twin-engine experience were brought into the unit from desk jobs. The 21st's C-47s joined the C-54s in the evacuation effort, which included flights out of Taejon after both Suwon and Seoul had fallen to the communists. The North Korean onslaught had been so fierce that the South Koreans had retreated along almost the entire length of their country, until ROK forces held only the Pusan Peninsula on which there were three useable airstrips. Additional C-47s were pulled out of mothballs in the US and crews with World War II troop carrier experience were assigned to take them to Japan and join the 21st.

As the South Koreans retreated, President Truman ordered US troops from Japan to Korea.[186] The Eighth Army was essentially a garrison army consisting of troops who had been enjoying the easy life as occupational forces in Japan. But Eighth Army was the only military force in the region, so President Truman ordered it to Korea. The first troops to move to Korea were elements of the 24th Infantry, who were flown from Itazuke to Pusan. While the move started out in C-54s, the larger airplanes severely damaged the thin asphalt runways at the strips at Pusan, Taegu and Pohang so the 374th turned to the C-47s of the 21st TCS for the move. The larger C-54s were put to work hauling troops and cargo from Tachikawa to Ashiya on Northern Kyushu, where the loads were switched to C-47s for the hour and a half flight across the Sea of Japan to Pusan. By this time, the newly manned 21st had made so many moves around Kyushu that the men had begun calling themselves the "Kyushu Gypsies," a name that not only stuck, but soon gained semiofficial recognition. Eventually, the 21st would move to Korea as a provisional squadron and become the 6461st TCS, but its primary base during the first weeks of the war was at Brady Field, an airstrip in northern Kyushu a short distance from Ashiya and

---

[186] The war caught the Truman Administration by complete surprise and there were several days of waffling while the White House tried to decide what to do. Truman's eventual decision to send troops to South Korea was prompted to some degree by actions taken by MacArthur when news of the invasion reached Japan.

Anything, Anywhere, Anytime

the closest airfield in Japan to the Pusan Peninsula. Airdrops were frequent from the very beginning and would be a major airlift contribution to the Korean War. Since the C-54s were not suitable for airdrop, the initial airdrops were by C-47 crews. A C-47 flew into a mountain when the pilot failed to pull up after a drop and another disappeared over the Sea of Japan while enroute to Korea on a drop mission.

Flying in the first weeks of the war was very demanding for the crews, many of whom had just come out of support functions and had not flown operationally since 1945 or before. Most of the flying was over water and there were no navigational aids. A pilot would simply head out over the Sea of Japan toward Korea and, when the coastline came into sight, the crew would identify a major river near Pusan from the yellow water in the sea[187] and fly up it until they found a railroad track, then follow the railroad to Taegu. Enemy action was a constant threat. One C-54 was attacked by communist fighters but made its way back to Ashiya with damaged controls. Many airplanes picked up holes from ground fire. (Thompson A. G.)

As the importance of airlift to the effort in Korea became apparent to the US commanders in the Pentagon, steps were taken to reinforce the 374th wing. Maj. General William H. Tunner, who had commanded the recent Berlin Airlift, was sent on temporary duty to Japan from his job as Deputy Commander of MATS to set up an airlift command and control organization. Tunner arrived at Ashiya on September 10, 1950. Immediately after he arrived, Far East Air Forces organized the Combat Cargo Command (Provisional) as a command organization for all airlift assets in the Far East, which at the time consisted of the 374th TCW and its three squadrons of C-47s and C-54s. Lt. Gen. John Cannon had taught Tunner a lesson in Europe two years before; he might be DCO of MATS but he was now working for Far East Air Forces commander Gen. George Stratemeyer and General of the Army Douglas MacArthur, who was famous for not taking any nonsense from subordinates. Tunner had worked for Stratemeyer before when the latter was chief of the Air Staff and he was running the Ferrying Division of ATC. Stratemeyer was the senior air officer in the CBI when Tunner was in command of the India-China Ferry. As for MacArthur, he was the epitome of the theater commander. If Tunner made one step outside of the chain of command, it would have ended his career. There weren't going to be any more of the shenanigans he had pulled in Germany.[188]

---

[187] River water is often polluted with sand and mud and is easily distinguishable from the air.

[188] Even though Tunner made no public pronouncements about MATS and airlift consolidation, he spent a great deal of his time writing letters to officers and

Tunner was not the only experienced air transport officer who was sent to Korea. One of the first officers deployed to Korea was Colonel E. Wade Hampton, the very same Wade Hampton who had commanded the 21st Transport Squadron in Australia at the beginning of the previous war, then had commanded the 374th Group and served on the staff of the First Allied Airborne Army. He left Smyrna Air Base, Tennessee for Japan in August and was there to greet Tunner. Hampton was assigned to the new Combat Cargo Command as deputy commander. Tunner may have been the man in charge, but he had some very able assistants with the kind of experience he didn't have.

Airlift reinforcement was on the way as the 314th Troop Carrier Group from Sewart AFB, Tennessee was preparing to depart for Japan with C-119s for a temporary duty assignment. A reserve unit, the 437th Troop Carrier Wing from O'Hare Field at Chicago, had been alerted and was undergoing training with its C-46s in preparation for a move to Japan. The 437th's commander, Brig. General John "Jock" Henebry, was a well-known hero of the Southwest Pacific. He would make his mark on Korea as well, this time in the airlift role. Another C-46 unit, the 1st Provisional Group, was organized at Tachikawa with an initial cadre of personnel from the 374th TCW and equipped with C-46s that were already in the region. As had been the case with the 21st TCS C-47s, pilots to fly the C-46s were rounded up throughout the Far East. The new Combat Cargo Command had operational control of the 374th wing and the 1st Provisional Group; it would also control the 314th group when it arrived in Japan.

Tunner brought with him to Japan a staff made up of officers who had served with him in other operations, particularly the Berlin Airlift two years before. Immediately, the newly arrived staff began implementing policies to promote efficiency and, at least to some degree, safety, on what was to become known as the Korean Airlift. A transport movement control center (TMC) was set up at Ashiya and a rigid aircraft control system was implemented. Flight orders were sent down from the TMC to the wings and groups who scheduled the crews and airplanes then to the squadrons whose crews would fly the missions. The TMC scheduled flights, recorded takeoff and landing times and reasons for delay.[189] It also had the authority to divert or cancel flights by radio. A system of airways from Japan to the Pusan Perimeter airstrips was set up and each Combat Cargo Command pilot was assigned to fly at a specific altitude within the airway to reduce the risk of collision. The rigid procedures were the same Tunner had

---

the politicians back in the US advocating the transfer of troop carrier units to MATS.

[189] The TMC would become an integral part of troop carrier operations until the mid-1960s when they were replaced by Airlift Command Elements, or ALCEs.

developed for the Berlin Airlift, as it was now called, two years before. But while *VITTLES* had been a peacetime operation where hostile action was merely a threat, Korea was a real shooting war and while precise procedures might increase efficiency, there were other things to consider, such as enemy opposition. For Tunner and most of his staff, this was their first experience with a combat operation and, while they were efficiency experts, they were completely lost when it came to operations in a combat environment. Fortunately, the troop carrier wings, groups and squadrons were commanded by men who had combat experience from World War II, as did many of the pilots. Tunner's personal staff may have been lacking in combat experience, but the Combat Command was staffed by men like Wade Hampton who knew how to run a combat organization. Tunner was not one to ignore the advice of his subordinates if it suited his purpose.

Tunner was only in Japan on temporary duty and his permanent assignment with MATS led to a great deal of publicity for the service; publicity that was resented by the men who flew and maintained the Combat Cargo Command transports. Newspaper accounts ignored Tunner's TDY status with Far East Air Forces and attributed the efforts of the 374th TCW to MATS. Tunner made no effort to clarify the matter. It was a repeat of World War II in the CBI, when TIME/LIFE devoted an issue of its magazine to the Air Transport Command's India/China Wing and completely ignored the troop carrier squadrons that were carrying the lion's share of the air transport burden in the region. Personnel in the 6th Troop Carrier Squadron constructed a sign that read "6th Troop Carrier Squadron, NOT MATS!" and placed it by the flight line where it would be visible to members of the media who passed through the passenger terminal at Tachikawa. (Thompson A. G.)

Sam McGowan

In early September, the C-119s of the 314th Troop Carrier Group arrived at Ashiya from their home base at Sewart AFB, Tennessee. The 314th was sent to Japan primarily to support the 187th Regimental Combat Team, a US Army airborne unit that had just organized at Fort Campbell, Kentucky for duty in Korea and was on its way to Japan by ship. From their base at Smyrna, Tennessee, the 314th crews had worked with the 11th Airborne Division, from which the 187th was organized, on many occasions. The 314th was one of the most experienced of the Air Force's troop carrier units and the C-119 was the most capable of its transports. It and the C-82 from which it was developed were also the only ones with true tactical capabilities.[190] For the first time, Air Force transports were able to transport vehicles without time-consuming disassembly at the departure point and reassembly at their destination. While waiting for the 187th to arrive, the 314th crews were put to work on the airlift to Pusan carrying cargo too large for the C-54s, C-47s and C-46s. Its large cargo compartment made the C-119 particularly suitable for transporting vehicles. With the arrival of the 314th C-119s and the introduction of the 1st Provisional Group's C-46s, the daily tonnage moving into Korea from Japan soared.

With the arrival of reinforcements from the United States, General Douglas MacArthur, who was fighting his third war, planned to take the offensive in Korea. While Eighth Army began a breakout from the Pusan Perimeter, an amphibious landing was planned for Inchon in late September. Originally, the 187th RCT was going to jump onto Kimpo airfield in advance of the amphibious landings and secure it for transport operations, but the 187th had not yet arrived by the date set for the invasion so Kimpo was captured by US Marines, who came in from the sea. As soon as the airfield was under UN control, Combat Cargo Command transports began arriving from Japan with reinforcements. The first flights brought in a Combat Cargo Support Unit whose job was to operate the Kimpo airhead, along with flight nurses, doctors and medical personnel from the 801st Medical Air Evacuation Squadron, who set up an evacuation hospital. Fighting was still going on around the airfield; friendly artillery was firing from the north end of the airstrip. North Korean guerrillas hidden in ground cover on both ends of the airstrip took potshots at the arriving and departing transports. During the Inchon invasion, a C-54 crashed after takeoff from Ashiya with a load of troops and flight nurses aboard. More than half of the passengers and most of the crew drowned before the survivors were picked up by Japanese fishing boats. Another C-54

---

[190] Captain Ennis Thompson, publicity officer for 315th Air Division and the author of the history of the Korean Airlift, "The Greatest Airlift," makes no mention of C-82s in Korea.

Anything, Anywhere, Anytime

hit a mountain during an airlift of ammunition into Taejon with the loss of all onboard. (Thompson A. G.) The airlift into Kimpo was an around-the-clock operation with the Combat Cargo transports landing in a steady flow with supplies. Gasoline, rations and ammunition made up the bulk of the loads, but other crucial supplies were also brought in, including medical supplies, barbed wire, stoves, cots, tools and clothing. Bombs and rockets for the Fifth Air Force fighters which moved into the base were also flown in until supplies could be delivered by ship.

One particularly important mission brought in a complete pontoon bridge to span the Han River at Seoul, where all of the fixed bridges had been destroyed by the retreating South Koreans weeks before. The bridge had been delivered to the docks in Japan but had somehow been left behind by the invasion fleet. When its absence was discovered, an emergency C-119 mission was mounted to transport the bridge components to Kimpo. Troops, from allied nations as well as American, were also airlifted into Kimpo. After arriving at Pusan by boat, a British unit loaded onto Combat Cargo transports for the flight to Kimpo. When the tardy 187th finally arrived in Japan, the paratroopers were loaded right onto a train for Ashiya. They stepped off the railroad cars and onto trucks for the drive to the airbase, where they boarded C-119s and C-54s. Their next stop was Kimpo. For two days, a steady stream of transports poured into Kimpo carrying men, equipment and vehicles belonging to the airborne unit.

Combat Cargo Command C-46

Page 280

Sam McGowan

With the 187th in the theater, plans were made for an airborne operation. After initially entering the ground fighting around Seoul, the paratroopers were pulled back to Kimpo to train for future operations. At first, the men of the 187th were not told what their objective would be, but finally an airborne assault was ordered to seize key North Korean rail and communications centers at Sukchon and Sunchon. The primary objective was to take control of the area north of the North Korean capital to cut off communist troops as they retreated northward in advance of attacking South Korean and United Nations troops. A secondary objective was to intercept a train carrying POWs that was believed to be heading north from Pyongyang.

The operation was delayed for two days due to heavy rains, but on October 20, 1950 75 C-119s and forty C-47s took off from Kimpo and flew north for the drop zones at Sukchon and Sunchon. The formation flew northwest from Kimpo out over the Yellow Sea, then abruptly turned inland and headed for the drop zones. A C-54 flew alongside the formation with MacArthur and Tunner aboard; the MATS officer was observing the first combat operation he had ever witnessed. He would be awarded the Distinguished Service Cross for "his role" in the operation.[191] Over the drop zones, the C-119s dropped

---

[191] Tunner was awarded the Distinguished Service Cross for observing the airdrop. The award came about suddenly when General Douglas MacArthur was surprised by FEAF commander Lt. General George Stratemeyer with the award of the Distinguished Flying Cross at a press conference in Korea. MacArthur returned the favor by pulling out a DSC and pinning it on Tunner, who was standing on the platform with him.(Leary, 2000)

Anything, Anywhere, Anytime

paratroopers and monorail bundles of supplies; the C-47s dropped door bundles and troops. Other C-119s dropped cargo – weapons carriers, jeeps, field artillery, antitank guns and pallets of supplies. Cargo drops continued in the area for several days. The troops ran into immediate opposition from more than 6,000 communist soldiers but the well-trained paratroopers took control of the situation. More than 3,000 troops were dropped the first day and 1,000 reinforcements arrived the following day. Eighth Army infantry began pushing northward to take Pyongyang, then drive north to link up with the 187th.

The paratroopers killed more than 2,800 North Koreans and captured 3,000. They secured the area and the paratroops began fanning out. Unfortunately, the train escaped capture. It was finally located but the men of the 187th soon learned that at least 57 American POWs had been massacred by the North Koreans the day before, while the train was hidden in a tunnel. The paratroopers finally located fifteen men who had survived. The rescued POWs were transported to Pyongyang, where they were loaded aboard Combat Cargo Command transports and flown to Ashiya for medical treatment and repatriation. The Sukchon drops saw the first use of parachute recovery troops who jumped in with the paratroops. After serving as combat soldiers until the area was secure, the recovery team went to work picking up the valuable parachutes, rigging and harnesses that had been used on the drop. Airdrop supplies were limited in Japan and the recovered equipment was needed for future operations. The silk parachutes had to be guarded to protect them from Korean civilians and soldiers, who were quick to use the material for clothing and other needs.

By mid-October, UN forces were on the Yalu River, which divides North Korea from China. Combat Cargo Command transports were operating into Sinuiju, the most advanced airfield in North Korea, when Chinese troops crossed the Yalu out of China and entered the war on October 16. Two weeks later, communist MiG-15 fighters began operating over Korea, turning the Korean conflict into the first war with combat between jet aircraft.[192] Cargo drops were almost a daily occurrence for the C-46, C-47 and C-119 crews. Often the transports dropped vital loads to units that had been surrounded by communists and cutoff from other means of supply. Airlift became even more important than it already was as Combat Cargo Command supported the retreating UN forces while the Chinese drove them south.

Initially, the 374th wing C-54s and provisional group C-46s constituted the heavy airlift capability of the Combat Cargo Command but they were soon joined by the 314th Troop Carrier Group and its larger C-119s. In December, 1950, they were joined by the 61st Troop Carrier Group, a C-54 unit based in Germany which was sent to Japan to become part of the Korean Airlift. In early November 1950, the 437th Troop Carrier Wing arrived in Japan with its C-46s. Made up of reservists from Chicago, the new arrivals joined the Korean Airlift and began flying cargo into Pyongyang in support of the advancing UN forces.

General George Kenney pinning new rank on Jock Henebry's collar

The wing commander, Brig. Gen. John "Jock" Henebry, was no stranger to combat in Asia or to General Douglas MacArthur, under whom he had served from 1942 until the end of World War II flying

---

[192] German ME 262 and 363 fighters engaged Allied bombers and fighters in 1944 and 1945, but although both the British and US had jet fighters under development, none saw combat.

Anything, Anywhere, Anytime

light and medium bombers. He had risen from first lieutenant to major general in three years.[193] Along with Richard Ellis and Charles W. Howe, who also were in the 3rd Bombardment Group and commanded it at one time, Henebry was one of George Kenney's favorites and knew MacArthur personally. He had stood on the deck of the battleship *MISSOURI* during the Japanese surrender ceremony. Unlike Tunner, who was an administrator, Henebry was the real deal and had won his combat decorations, which included the DSC, the hard way – he had earned them.

After several weeks of general inactivity, the Chinese launched an attack on the ROK units in late November and cut the UN lines as the South Koreans collapsed in the face of the superior forces. The Chinese were not only experienced combat troops, there were thousands of them. The UN forces were now divided, with Eighth Army holding the west coast of the Korean Peninsula and Tenth Corps the east. Cold, arctic winds came down out of Manchuria bringing bitter cold temperatures and snow, making conditions as difficult as could be imagined. The Chinese drove through the middle, dividing the two groups. On November 28, 1950, Eighth Army began a retreat southward to the Chongchon River, where its commander, Lt. Gen. Walton Walker, hoped to set up a line of defense. But two days later, the Americans abandoned the Sinanju airstrip and headed south. To support the retreating Eighth Army, the US 1st Marine Division and USA 7th Division captured the Chosen Reservoir area in the mountains northwest of the town of Hamhung. In an attempt to help the Army, the Marines attacked the Chinese – only to discover that they were badly outnumbered. The Marines began a retreat which prompted the most historic airlift effort of the Korean War.[194]

After China entered the war and the UN forces began retreating southward, Combat Cargo Command was crucial to the retreat as the unit airlifted men and equipment out of advanced bases in North Korea and returned them to Seoul. The Chinese advance was under such momentum that even Seoul was captured for a time. Combat Cargo Command cargo support unit personnel were usually the last Americans to be evacuated. They left only after the last troops and cargo had been loaded onto division transports. A particularly poignant episode during the retreat was the airlift of 1,000 Korean orphans who were supposed to have been moved south by ship. After waiting at Inchon Harbor for a ship for several days without food or

---

[193] Henebry was on the list for promotion to temporary major general when World War II ended. He left the Army after the war and went into the reserves in Chicago as a colonel.
[194] The 1st Marine Division commander, General Oliver P. Smith later said, "Retreat hell, we weren't retreating, we were just attacking in a different direction."

shelter, the orphans were in danger of starvation and death from the cold. Prompted by Col. Dean Hess, a reserve fighter pilot and ordained minister, General Tunner authorized a squadron of twelve C-54s to go to Kimpo to pick up the children. They flew the orphans to Chejudo, where an orphanage had been set up. Unfortunately, several children died while enroute due to their malnourished and sickly condition. In late 1951 the orphanage at Chejudo was adopted by the men of the 61st Troop Carrier Group and a special C-54 flew presents and supplies to the children.

21st TCS C-47 during Chosen Reservoir evacuation

As the United Nations troops retreated, the 21st TCS's C-47s and 314th TCG C-119s became their principal source of resupply. The Chinese surrounded the Chosin Reservoir and cut off the Allied rear, but airdrops of supplies allowed the retreating troops to keep fighting. The Marines had a few R-4Ds (C-47s) in Korea, but they depended on Combat Cargo Command for most of their resupply. Flying from Ashiya, where the US Army 2348th Quartermaster Airborne Air Supply and Packing Detachment rigged the loads for airdrop then flew on missions to operate the airdrop equipment, the C-119s maintained a constant train of supplies to the hard-pressed Marines and soldiers. The 2348th was a special unit that had been made up at Ft. Campbell and transferred to Japan to support troop carrier operations.(Hospelhorn) A detachment of C-119s also operated out of Yonpo, where a Quartermaster detachment worked with Marine riggers to prepare loads for airdrops to the Marines, who were only twenty minutes flying time away. All drops were made at low altitudes, which meant the airplanes were constantly exposed to ground fire. Although many transports were hit, no crewmembers were wounded.

Anything, Anywhere, Anytime

An Army paratrooper, who was flying as a kicker, fell out of a C-119 when a load released prematurely but he managed to make his way to friendly lines after reaching the ground. Two days later, he caught a ride back to Ashiya on the same airplane from which he had fallen!

To evacuate wounded, engineers constructed a 2,300-foot airstrip at Hagaru-ri, where C-47s and USMC R-4Ds began landing. The C-47s brought in cargo from Yonpo and returned with casualties. Because of the fear of their possible capture, female flight nurses were not assigned to the missions but male enlisted medical technicians accompanied the crews.[195] At Yonpo, the wounded were placed aboard air ambulance C-54s for the flight to Ashiya. By December 6, C-47 crews had evacuated more than 4,000 casualties from Hagaru-ri. One C-47, loaded with casualties, crashed after taking off from the crude airstrip. No one was injured when the pilot put the airplane down in a snow-covered field three miles away. Marine fighters provided close air support for the crew and passengers as they made their way back to friendly forces. The wounded men and shaken crew had to ford five ice-filled creeks during their journey. Not only did the C-47 crews have to contend with enemy fire, horrendous winter weather and a primitive runway, one of their biggest hazards turned out to be falling airdrop bundles from the C-119s that were constantly dropping supplies to the retreating troops. One prematurely released load of artillery shells struck and damaged four C-47s that were waiting on the airstrip for wounded. Mechanics were flown in to repair the planes while the airlift continued.

On December 6, the Marines began moving eastward toward the village of Koto-ri, where another airstrip was being constructed to receive C-47s. Late that afternoon, the Kyushu Gypsy C-47s began landing on the new airstrip, which was even shorter and rougher than the one they had been using previously. The USAF C-47s and USMC R-4Ds were joined in the airlift by a detachment of Greek Air Force C-47s that arrived for duty in Korea at the height of the Chosin Reservoir retreat. The Marines were only at Koto-ri one day before they continued their retreat southward. At Hungnam they discovered a seemingly insurmountable problem. The Chinese had blown twenty feet of a bridge spanning an otherwise impassable gorge. The entire Marine column was held up on the narrow mountain road and there was no way around it. There seemed to be only one solution, and at the time it had never been tried, even in a training situation.

---

[195] Although it was not widely publicized, there was an incident in Korea where a field hospital was overrun and a group of nurses were captured. Allegedly, the Chinese doused them with gasoline and set them on fire, then shot them while they screamed in agony.

The Marines requested that a Bailey Treadway portable bridge be airdropped to them. When the Combat Cargo Command got the request, riggers with the 2348th QM and CCC personnel conferred. They decided that the bridge could be divided into eight sections of 4,000 pounds each and airdropped with two 100-foot parachutes on each section. The situation was critical and there was no time to experiment in Japan. The bridge was rushed to Ashiya by rail then loaded aboard eight C-119s for the flight to Yonpo. After the detachment arrived in Korea, a test drop was made of one section. When the load fell to earth without damage, the riggers knew they had the right combination of rigging and parachutes. At dawn the next morning, the C-119s took off and flew to where the column was held up. The eight C-119 crews dropped to 800 feet and followed each other in an in-trail formation to the drop zone the Marines had designated alongside the road. After the first load was dropped and the Marines reported that it had arrived in good condition, the other seven C-119 crews followed suit. Engineers moved the sections to the gorge, bolted them together and quickly spanned the obstacle. In a few hours, the Marines were once again on their way.

During the retreat, General Tunner made the cover of TIME magazine while the Combat Cargo Command role was covered inside. In the article, the MATS officer was quoted as commenting that "we can haul anything, anywhere." The comment has since been attributed to MATS and military airlift in general but Tunner had no MATS units or personnel under his command when he made it. Tunner's role in the Korean Airlift was short, as he was only in Japan on TDY status. But

Anything, Anywhere, Anytime

his contribution in terms of organization was great; at least he received the credit for it. One of his alleged suggestions was that an Air Force organization should be established in the Pacific to control airlift operations. On January 25, 1951, Combat Cargo Command became 315th Air Division (Combat Cargo) and was based at Tachikawa.[196] Tunner held temporary command for less than two weeks while a permanent staff was forming. He returned to the United States with one more feather in his cap to confirm his status as an airlift expert, along with a Distinguished Service Cross, to resume his goal of consolidation of all USAF airlift assets into one command. He didn't remain in MATS, however. He was given a new assignment as deputy commander for operations of the Air Material Command. In 1953 he became the commander of United States Air Forces Europe.

The first permanent commander of the new combat cargo division was Brigadier General John P. Henebry, a reserve officer and the former commander of the C-46 equipped 437th wing. Although he was a reserve officer, "Jock" Henebry was a highly decorated combat veteran who had spent almost all of World War II in the Southwest Pacific. Starting out as a young first B-25 pilot with the famous 3rd Attack Group[197], where he became a favorite of Far East Air Forces commander General George Kenney, he had finished the war as a major general on Kenney's staff[198]. Returning to civilian life after the war, Henebry continued his military service in the reserves. A Chicago native, he was put in command of the 437th Troop Carrier Group at Chicago's O'Hare Field and took the group to Korea. He had earned a reputation for courage and resourcefulness and was the ideal man to command the new air division. When he took command of 315th Air Division, Henebry brought with him his best friend, Col. Charles W. Howe. Howe and Henebry had flown as wingmen in the 3rd Attack Group, which Howe had risen to command when Henebry was reassigned to Kenney's staff. Howe came to Korea as commander of a light bomber wing but transferred to 315th Air Division as Inspector General before he was placed in command of the 374th TCW. Henebry and Howe had been part of a wartime trio with Richard Ellis, who would command the division during the first half of the 1960s. Howe would take his place.

---

[196] Formerly, 315th Air Division had been a very heavy bomber division equipped with B-29s.

[197] Technically, the 3rd Attack Group was the 3rd Bombardment Group, but members of the group and General Kenney preferred the prewar designation.

[198] Henebry reverted to his permanent rank of Colonel at the end of the war but was promoted to brigadier general in 1949.

Sam McGowan

Dick Ellis, Jock Henebry, Chuck Howe, Dr. John Gilmore; Ellis, Henebry and Howe would all command 315th Air Division

Henebry's deputy commander also had a history. Col. E. Wade Hampton had started out in the Air Corps as a light bomber pilot and had gone to the Philippines as General Brereton's aide. When he got there, Brereton put him on the Far East Air Force staff. When an air transport command was established in Australia, Hampton was the temporary commander. He rose to command the 374th Troop Carrier Group then went to Europe and served on the staff of the First Allied Airborne Army. No officer in the Air Force – including Tunner – had as much airlift experience and history as Hampton.

When 315th Air Division activated, some new support organizations activated along with it. Tunner's temporary staff had set up combat cargo support units to work with Army aerial port personnel in Korea; with the activation of the new division, they became permanent. The aerial port function transferred to the Air Force and the 6127th Air Terminal Group activated as the command organization for air terminal squadrons and detachments that were established throughout the Far East. The air terminal units were designed to be mobile, and able to move at a moment's notice. The 5th Communication Squadron also activated to provide communications links between 315th Air Division and the units under its command. 5th Comm. detachments were co-located with air terminal units in Korea. When the Air Force reorganized its troop carrier functions late in the war, the 6127th became the 2nd Aerial Port Group.

Anything, Anywhere, Anytime

The role of MATS in the Korean Airlift was nil, however its fleet of C-54s and C-124s were working overtime on the Pacific Airlift bringing passengers and high priority cargo to Japan. As with World War II – and, later, Vietnam – the bulk of cargo and most troops moved overseas by ship and airlift only accounted for a token amount. The Korean Airlift itself was exclusively a Combat Cargo Command show. However, in the early days of the operation, publicity put out by MATS gave the false impression that the airlift to Korea was operated by it since it was Tunner's permanent organization and his name often appeared in press releases. Combat Cargo Command flight crews and ground personnel felt slighted at the disinformation, just as their predecessors had been in the CBI when the India-China Ferry received substantial publicity while the more important role of the troop carrier squadrons was ignored. MATS operated routes to Japan from the United States but did not fly into Korea. To augment its own transports, TAC C-54s and C-124s were assigned to fly missions for MATS. Even with the additional airlift provided by TAC, MATS lacked the resources to meet the military's needs and thousands of contracts were issued to civilian carriers for overseas flights to Japan, Okinawa and the Philippines. The MATS route structure only extended as far as Japan where 315th Air Division took over for the airlift to Korean bases. MATS transported cargo and passengers to Japan and evacuated patients on the return flights. MATS had eleven C-74s in operation but for some reason they were only used on missions as far west as Hawaii. The giant C-74s flew patients from Hawaii to the United States.

Dropping Jeep on Platform from C-119

Sam McGowan

As UN forces retreated south then moved north again to retake Seoul and the rest of South Korea, 315th Air Division C-119s, C-47s and C-46s became even more heavily involved in airdrop operations than they already were. The Korean Airlift saw more delivery of cargo from the air than either World War II or Vietnam. Thousands of airdrop sorties were flown in support of UN and ROK troops. The airdrop missions were not the most pleasant thing in the world for C-119 crews. To drop cargo, the aft doors were removed, which exposed the entire cargo compartment to the sub-zero Manchurian air for the entire flight. This was especially hard on the Army Quartermasters who flew on missions as dropmasters, or "kickers." Several kickers fell out of their airplanes during drops. It could be a hazardous occupation as well as an uncomfortable one.

In February 1951, a French Foreign Legion battalion was cutoff and surrounded in a one-square mile area at Chipyong-ni. A massive resupply effort kept the French troops in the fight. Over a three-day period, C-119 crews braved heavy ground fire to drop more than 400 tons of ammunition and weapons to the surrounded French soldiers. In one instance, a flight of twenty C-119s dropped at night during a raging snowstorm. A weather reconnaissance pilot directed the planes to the drop zone, which was marked with gasoline-soaked rags, by keeping his landing lights on so the C-119 pilots would know where to look. Using the supplies that had been dropped to them, the French managed to fight their way out of the trap.

Not only did C-119 crews drop cargo, they also flew airstrikes. Troop carrier veteran Lt. Col. Bill "Bones" Blanton told in his memoir how that he was part of a mission that dropped booby-trapped containers on a communist position. Before the strike, Blanton and other crews dropped cargo at a certain set of coordinates for several days. They were then sent out to drop classified cargo, which turned out to be explosives, a short distance away at a location held by communist troops. Some transport airstrikes involved napalm.(Blanton, 1997)

In late March 1951, the 187th RCT made its final airborne assault of the Korean War at Munsan-ni. After fighting in the effort to push the Chinese and North Koreans back across the 38th Parallel, the 187th was pulled out of combat and sent to Taegu, where they set up a base. The paratroopers went into an extensive training program, including practice jumps from 315th Air Division C-119s. The troops assumed they would be jumping from C-119s and C-47s as they had at Sukchon, but C-47s were in short supply so 315th suggested that they be replaced in the airborne role by more plentiful C-46s. Practice drops were flown out of Taegu and the 187th was deemed ready for combat. The mission plan called for the troops to be flown out of Taegu while the cargo planes came from Ashiya. Vehicles belonging to the 187th had

Anything, Anywhere, Anytime

to be airlifted back to Japan to be rigged for airdrop. Originally, the airborne operation was planned to take Chunchon, but elements of the 1st Cavalry Division took the town on March 21 so a new objective was found. The 187th was directed to jump over Munsan-ni at 0900 on March 23 to seize the high ground and block enemy troop movements north of Seoul.

On the morning of March 23, eighty C-119s and 55 C-46s took off from Taegu. At 0900 the first serial of C-119s began dropping. Their drops were made according to plan, but the C-46s met with some difficulty when the lead airplane lost an engine on takeoff and had to land at another airstrip. The deputy lead took over and the formation formed behind him. However, on the way to the drop zone the lead crew mistook a check point and turned toward the south drop zone but could not find it. The C-46s dropped on the north drop zone where the C-119s had already dropped. General Henebry was observing the drop in a C-54 nearby and saw the mistake. He directed a formation of C-119s, which was bound for the south drop zone with heavy equipment, to drop on the north DZ instead. The original lead C-46 was replaced by a spare plane. The pilot, not knowing that his formation had dropped on the north drop zone, dropped his troops on the south drop zone where they found themselves alone on the ground. Again, General Henebry observed the error. He informed the 187th commander, who immediately directed a company from the 1st Battalion to fight their way through the enemy troops to link up with the men who had been dropped to the south.

Several airplanes took hits during the approach to the drop zone, but only one was badly damaged.(Leary, 2000) One C-119 left the drop zone with the engines trailing smoke. The pilot radioed that he thought his engines had been hit by ground fire and ordered his crew to bail out. Five crewmembers managed to jump, but the airplane blew up before the two pilots could get out of the cockpit. One enlisted man was carrying his pet dog on the drop – he jumped with the little animal in his arms! A C-47 equipped for psychological warfare saw the crew bail out and circled in the area, encouraging the men with loudspeaker announcements. They were finally rescued by helicopter.

Troop carrier crews in Korea – and in TAC – usually didn't include a navigator. Even when the 314th Troop Carrier Group deployed to Japan from Tennessee, only a few crews had a navigator with them. The C-119s flew in formation on an airplane that did.(Blanton, 1997) For missions into and over Korea, crews consisted of two pilots, an engineer and a radio operator. Except for C-119 crews, twin-engine airplane crews included a crew chief rather than an engineer. Aerial engineers were part of the C-54 crew. There were no loadmasters as such in the Korean War until the first C-124 made its

Sam McGowan

appearance. Army Quartmasters were responsible for rigging cargo for aerial delivery and they flew on missions as kickers.

Paratroops in C-119 on way to Drop Zone

After the spring of 1951, the Korean War became a stalemate, although there was still heavy fighting. Airdrops were almost a daily occurrence as 315th crews kept troops in the field supplied. Although a few helicopters were being used in the war, they were mostly used to evacuate casualties from the battlefield to evacuation airfields and for rescue work. The stream of flights into Korea from Japan continued on an around-the-clock basis. Special flights were set up to transport personnel assigned to Korea back to Japan for R&R. Air evacuation of casualties remained a major 315th contribution. For a time, the 21st TCS operated a psychological warfare mission dropping leaflets and making loudspeaker announcements. That mission, under Major Harry Aderholt, was transferred to fall directly under Fifth Air Force. Aderholt also conducted operations involving the dropping of agents into North Korea.

Anything, Anywhere, Anytime

C-47 with Loudspeakers

In late 1951, the Air Proving Ground sent its huge C-124 to Korea for a two-month trial in a combat environment. The huge transport proved ideal for airlifting cargo into Korea from Japan so the Air Force decided to assign enough to equip two squadrons to 315th. In the summer of 1952, C-124s arrived at Tachikawa to replace C-54s in the 374th wing and 61st Group. A subsequent reorganization included the redesignation of the 21st TCS as the 6461st Troop Carrier Squadron (Provisional) while a new 21st was formed and equipped with C-54s. The 6461st moved to Korea.

The larger and more complicated C-124 introduced loadmasters to the Korean War – and to the Air Force – for the first time. Previously, Army Quartermaster dropmasters flew on airdrop missions to check cargo rigging while enroute to the drop zone and loading and offloading on the ground was supervised by the airplane crew chief or engineer. The C-124 featured some complex cargo

Sam McGowan

handling equipment so an Air Force crewmember trained in cargo handling and identified as a "loadmaster" became a regular part of USAF cargo missions on some airplanes. Loadmasters came from the air terminal squadrons of the 6127th Air Terminal Group. Air cargo specialists were given training on the C-124's cargo handling systems and then joined the squadrons as loadmasters and were placed on flying status. (Thompson A. G.)

As the Korean War wound down to end in an uneasy truce that has lasted for decades, the officers who had commanded the Korean Airlift began looking at the lessons they had learned. While General Tunner brought organization to the Combat Cargo Command, later commanders – including General Henebry and Brig. General Chester McCarty – believed that the requirement for theater airlift to be flexible was the primary lesson learned during the conflict. Like Henebry, McCarty was a former reserve officer who came to Korea when his unit, the 403rd Troop Carrier Wing, was called up and sent to Japan.[199] In his end of tour report, McCarty said that Korea had taught that the Air Force needed a single type of transport with the capability to perform all of the missions flown by C-119s, C-54s, C-46s and C-47s.

Such an airplane was on the way; when the war first erupted, a research and development team in the Pentagon began developing a requirement for a new transport. The plan had actually come about the first weekend after the war broke out. On Sunday afternoon, a research and development team met in an office in the Pentagon to decide how to spend a special allocation that had just been voted by Congress for the Air Force to develop new weapons. One of the attendees pointed out that the aircraft most needed was a medium range transport capable of operating into short, unimproved airstrips from 1,500 miles away. The group agreed and an allocation was made to fund the project. Lockheed Aircraft was awarded the contract and the new YC-130 was under development. Although it would not enter operational service until 1956, Lockheed's C-130 Hercules would revolutionize military airlift, the troop carrier mission in particular.

Korea brought the introduction of the Air Force aerial port squadron, although it was called an air terminal squadron in 315th Air Division. When the war first broke out, US Army personnel operated the passenger and cargo terminals throughout the Far East. One of General Tunner's reported suggestions was the establishment of an Air Force air terminal system under 315th Air Division. The 6127th Air Terminal Group was organized with detachments set up all through

---

[199] McCarty elected to remain on active duty after he completed his tour as commander of 315th Air Division. He returned to Donaldson AFB, SC and command of Eighteenth Air Force.

Anything, Anywhere, Anytime

the division's area of responsibility to process passengers and cargo. Air terminal personnel supervised aircraft loading and unloading operations. Air evacuation of casualties out of the combat zone proved even more important in Korea than it had been in World War II. It also proved to be less expensive than moving casualties aboard ship. Transports returning to Japan after delivering their loads in Korea would have otherwise flown empty in many cases, so the transport of patients on return trips effected greater utilization of the airplanes' capabilities. The Army and Air Force were also finding the helicopter to be a useful means of evacuating patients right off of the battlefield and for combat search and rescue.

The Combat Cargo Command and 315th Air Division included not only USAF personnel, but also C-47 crews and maintenance personnel from other nations, particularly Greece and Thailand. Greek and Thai C-47s operated under 315th control, as did Marine R-4s and R-5s in many instances. Korea began with the United States military in the Far East in disarray, and with little real airlift capability. By the time it came to an uncertain end in 1953, airlift had proven itself as an effective means of deploying troops into a combat zone and then supporting them once they were there.

Sam McGowan

Chapter Eleven - "INDOCHINA"

CAT DC-3 in Indochina

In the late 19th century, France began colonizing the region along the South China Sea, which a French geographer called Indochina by combining the French words for India and China and coming up with Indochine. The region included the countries of Cambodia, Laos and Vietnam, part of which was also known as Cochin China. Indochina lay south of mainland China and east of Siam, or Thailand, reaching as far south as the Gulf of Siam. After France surrendered to the Germans in 1940, the Japanese occupied Indochina, but the Vichy French continued to govern the region under the control of the Japanese, who turned it into a major military region. The Japanese built several airfields and seaport facilities in Vietnam, which was bordered along its entire length on the east by the South China Sea. Its western borders were with Cambodia in the south and Laos in the north. The rugged mountain Kingdom of Laos was landlocked but Cambodia's

Anything, Anywhere, Anytime

southern reaches was on the sea, as was much of Cochin China and the entire eastern side of Vietnam.

During World War II, American bomber crews flying from bases in China bombed Japanese installations and other targets in Indochina and attacked shipping in the South China Sea. In order to create a resistance movement within the country and develop a network to rescue downed flyers, the American Office of Strategic Services sent agents into China in early 1945 with the mission of infiltrating into Indochina and making contact with guerrillas. Led by Major Archimedes Patti, the OSS team made contact before they left China with a Vietnamese expatriate who called himself Ho Chi Minh, among other names. A shady character, Ho had spent most of his life as an expatriate and had become a dedicated Marxist with the goal of driving the French out of Vietnam and establishing a Marxist state. Since the US was allied with the Soviets, the OSS, which was staffed largely by Ivy League type academics, had no qualms about supporting both Ho and Mao ze Tong, the Chinese revolutionary. Ho put OSS agents in contact with his supporters in Vietnam, although he had not himself set foot in the country since 1911.[200] Since that time, he had lived in Europe, particularly in France and the Soviet Union, before returning to China in the 1930s. He reportedly even spent a year living in New York City, where he worked as a dishwasher.

With OSS assistance and arms supplied by the United States, Ho's communist guerrillas, who called themselves the Viet Minh, secured an area in Northern Vietnam near the Chinese border. A few days later, Ho Chi Minh returned to the land of his birth and began making plans to drive the French out of Vietnam once the Japanese were defeated. Within hours after learning of the Japanese surrender, Ho declared Vietnam to be a free nation. His declaration of independence was taken nearly word for word from the one Thomas Jefferson authored in 1776. But France was not so eager to give up her colonies and, with assistance from the British, the French soon reestablished themselves in Tonkin China, the name they gave to Vietnam because the northern half of the country lay alongside the Gulf of Tonkin. Immediately, Ho Chi Minh began an organized resistance against the French with the goal of driving them from his native land. After the communist victory in China in 1949, Ho began receiving support from his brothers to the north, including large quantities of captured Japanese equipment and American equipment that had been supplied to the Nationalists during the war. By the 1950s the Viet Minh were well organized and well-

---

[200] Some accounts of his life claim that he had gone back into Vietnam as early as 1943, but there are many accounts of his life, as he had many names. Such a trip was very unlikely until he went back in 1945.

armed and had gained control of much of the interior of the country, particularly in the north.

Ho Chi Minh was an interesting and illusive character. He had been born in Indochina but like many young Indochinese, he went to Paris as a young man and found work as a waiter. He even lived in the United States for a year in 1911-1912. While in Paris, he became involved with communist organizers, and from Paris he journeyed to Moscow where he met other Asians such as the Chinese Mao ze Tong, who had also gone to Russia to study the teachings of Karl Marx. Ho went back to China in the 1930s to organize a communist resistance movement in Vietnam against the French but the war with Japan began before his movement had gone very far. He remained in China, where he prepared pamphlets for distribution within Vietnam. His main message to the followers he recruited through his pamphlets was that they would take control of their country as soon as the Japanese were driven out. Ho claimed to be a nationalist and the OSS agents who worked with him during the war believed that was his true status, or at least they said they did. But in reality he was a determined Marxist and a master-manipulator who knew all the tricks. He even modeled his "declaration of independence" after that of the United States in a ploy to gain sympathy for his movement from the Americans. He told the OSS agents he did so because of his admiration for their country, but he was actually seeking international recognition and thought this would be a way to gain it.

To combat the Viet Minh, the French turned to their Foreign Legion, a branch of the French military made up mostly of men of other nationalities. The Legion is one of the oldest military organizations in the world; it dates back to 1831 when King Philippe formed it to be a haven for the dregs of French society and give them a worthwhile purpose. From its inception, the Legion included large numbers of mercenaries of other nationalities. Consequently, Legionnaires of other than French citizenship could only serve outside of the country, which meant that they were destined for France's colonies in Africa and Asia. The end of World War II provided a ready source of recruits from countries left in disarray by the war, particularly Germany. Former German soldiers joined the Legion in droves after the war and fought with UN forces in Korea.

The Legion's role in Indochina was modeled in many ways after their experiences in Korea. The French military had been exposed to air transport during World War II and, more recently, in Korea. French officers knew that the airplane would be crucial to the campaign they planned to conduct in their Asian colony. Indochina is a rugged region, with varied terrain that includes everything from swampy lowlands and triple canopy jungle to high mountain ranges. Few roadways connected the isolated rural hamlets with the cities on the coast and there was little in the way of railroads. In short, Indochina was a region made for air transportation. Airborne operations had become part of the postwar French military and there were several paratroop battalions in the Legion. To gain an advantage over the Viet Minh, who after all were fighting a "war of liberation" in their own homeland, the French developed a strategy built around establishing a *Base Aero-Terrestre*, a combat base located in a remote area of the country featuring a heavy duty airstrip.[201] From the base, which would be established and supported entirely by airlift, French patrols would secure a given region against the communist guerrillas.(Bowers, 1986)

While the French strategy itself was sound, in Indochina it was hampered by a general lack of transportation and of air transportation in particular. The French Air Force was a relic of World War II and its squadrons were equipped with airplanes that had been surplus when the war ended. France's primary transport was the German Junkers 52, a rugged airplane designed for use in regions such as Indochina, but the Junkers had been around since the 1930s and the ones the French had were veterans of long and hard service with the wartime Luftwaffe. By 1953, when the French Indochina War came to a head, the aging Ju 52s were past being ready for the scrap pile.

France was an American ally and, like most of the country's other allies in the postwar world, was largely dependent upon the United States for its military supplies and aid. The United States government was providing funding for the French war even though some Americans thought the best route would have been to simply let nature take its course as their country had done in China. The recent experience in Korea caused the United States to be extremely wary of anything and anyone connected to Marxism and the Soviet Union, and the Viet Minh were definitely Marxist and supported by Moscow. They were also supported by Red China, which supplied them with hundreds of artillery pieces and antiaircraft guns that had been captured from the Japanese in Mongolia at the end of World War II. In November 1951, the United States provided the French air force with its first C-47s. An initial contingent of twenty of the rugged transports would eventually grow to 116 by the time the war ended in mid-1954. Although the C-47 was already an aging veteran by 1951, there was a large supply of spare parts to keep them flying and a sizable number of qualified technical personnel to provide assistance to the French. Partly because of budgetary considerations, but also due to French politics, there was a shortage of qualified C-47 pilots and crews in the

---

[201] Base Aero-Terrestre literally means an "Air-Land Base," a term widely used in the US military in the 1980s.

French Air Force. In December 1953, France had less qualified C-47 crews than it had airplanes.

To compensate for France's lack of airlift capability, the United States began contracting with Claire Chennault's old airline, Civil Air Transport, for aircraft and crews to operate in Southeast Asia. By 1952, CAT was owned outright by the Central Intelligence Agency, having been bought with funds approved by the US State Department on the grounds that CIA ownership would deprive the Chinese Communists of the airline's assets. The CAT pilots, nearly all of whom were American and veterans of World War II and even Korea, not only flew routine cargo missions into and within Indochina, they often flew their airplanes into battle zones and occasionally even dropped French paratroops. Civilians they may have been but the CAT pilots were definitely mercenary soldiers and in the employ of the United States government, although the connection was only winked at by the men of the airline.[202]

Junkers 52 Toucan

Even with CAT support, the French were still woefully lacking in airlift resources. The French government made constant requests for more American C-47s but the US Air Force believed it was impossible to provide more airplanes without also providing American crews and support personnel to fly and maintain them. The idea was suggested to provide the airplanes to France "on loan," a concept that met with few objections. In September 1952, the Pentagon directed Far East Air Forces to provide 21 C-47s to the French for a four-month period for use in Indochina. American military crews delivered the transports to Nha Trang along with a supply of spare parts. Ownership of the

---

[202] Although CIA ownership was denied at the time and for several decades afterward, the Central Intelligence Agency admitted to ownership around 2000.

Anything, Anywhere, Anytime

airplanes was retained by the United States but they bore French markings and were flown by American-trained French crews.

Several weeks after the arrival of their new airplanes, the French mechanics became overwhelmed with work. France appealed again to the United States, this time for American mechanics to assist the French air force. In December 1952 President Truman, who was nearing the end of his presidency, directed the Air Force to provide the requested mechanics. A team of about thirty USAF maintenance personnel was dispatched to Nha Trang where they remained until summer. This cadre of aircraft maintenance personnel made up the first American military airlift personnel to see extended service in Vietnam.

Just as their American counterparts had been in Korea, the French air transport force was kept extremely busy airlifting supplies and reinforcements to its remote bases in the interior of the region. French troops in Laos were entirely dependent upon aerial resupply as Viet Minh forces launched attacks against Luang Prapang and on the Plain of Jars. The heavy workload led the United States to extend the loan of the C-47s. To further boost their airlift capabilities, France asked for C-119s, with the first request coming as early as 1951 while the United States Air Force was still heavily involved in airlift activities in Korea. The French grounded their request on the assertion that the larger airplanes would be used only for airdrop and would only fly out of the major airfields near the coast.

The Truman Administration at first balked at granting the French requests for what was at the time the USAF's top-of-the-line troop carrier transport, but as the war in Indochina drug on, Washington began rethinking its Indochina policy. Truman's term in office ended and the new president, General Dwight Eisenhower, took office in January 1952 and inherited the situation in Indochina. Having been allied with the French during the war, Eisenhower was not opposed to helping them deal with the communists in Indochina. As the Korean War ground to a gradual halt, the C-119 force in Japan faced a gradually lessening demand. There were 103 C-119s in the Far East Air Forces, all assigned to the 483rd Troop Carrier Wing at Ashiya which had replaced the Air Force Reserve 437th Troop Carrier Wing as its reserve personnel returned to civilian life. When the 314th TCG returned to Tennessee and the 403rd inactivated, the 483rd TCW received the 403rd's C-119s and became responsible for the airlift burden in the Far East.

The Air Force activated the 581st Air Resupply and Communication Wing in 1951 as part of the Air Resupply and Communication Service. The ARCS was part of MATS, at least on paper, but it operated several B-29s supplied by SAC. Included in the 581st's inventory were four C-119s which were evidently actually assigned to

315th Air Division, probably to the 483rd TCW, and detached for duty with the 581st. The ARCS mission was supporting activities of the Central Intelligence Agency's Special Activities Division.[203] In 1953, the wing, which was actually an office with only a handful of personnel and aircraft, was based at Clark Field, Philippines. It would later move to Kadena AB, Okinawa where it inactivated and a new office was established under a new name. When the US decided to supply C-119s to the French, they were supplied through the office at Clark but the airplanes came from the 483rd Troop Carrier Wing at Ashiya.[204]

C-119s with French markings

In the spring of 1953, Colonel Maurice Casey, the 483rd wing commander, went to Indochina to determine how his C-119s could best be used to support the French. Colonel Casey and his team of airlift experts visited air bases throughout Vietnam, Laos and Cambodia. The team returned to Japan to report to 315th Air Division

---

[203] The Special Activities Division, or SAD, is the highest classified military organization in the US government. Staffed by veterans of military special operations units, SAD is responsible for the most secret missions authorized by the White House.

[204] Details on the ARCS and the 581st ARC Wing are sketchy due to the classified nature of the organization and its activities. The wing operated an assortment of airplanes, including B-29s, C-54s, C-118s, H-19 helicopters and HU-16s as well as C-119s. Their mission included both psychological warfare and insertion and resupply of CIA agents operating inside hostile territory. The ARCS was disbanded in the mid-1950s with the official line being that the Air Force didn't want to use its budget for non-USAF activities. In reality, the mission simply went underground and was carried out through other means, specifically 315th and 322nd Air Division troop carrier squadrons.

Anything, Anywhere, Anytime

commander Maj. General Chester McCarty that while there were several problems that would arise if American crews were used in Indochina, the French air force could provide flight crews who could be easily trained by the Americans. Col. Casey preferred that his own men fly his airplanes but he understood the touchy political issues that caused Washington to be reluctant to involve American military personnel in a combat support role in what was supposed to be France's war. By this time, Dwight Eisenhower was president and the life-long military man appreciated the implications involved.

In the spring of 1953, the commander of the United States Far East Command, General Mark Clark, requested permission to send two C-119s with Air Force crews to Indochina to deliver armored vehicles to airfields in Laos. General Clark's request came before Colonel Casey's report. When he received it, Clark changed his recommendation and instead suggested that they be used for airdrop and cargo missions between major airfields in Indochina. The American Joint Chiefs of Staff disapproved the use of USAF flight crews in Indochina so, as an alternative, Admiral Arthur Radford, commander of the United States Pacific Command, suggested using civilian crews to fly the C-119s. The Joint Chiefs liked the idea and passed it on to President Eisenhower, who approved the plan. Ike authorized what came to be a common practice – the assignment of USAF aircraft to clandestine operations with false markings (or no markings at all) and civilian crews, crews sometimes made up of foreign nationals. Such operations were designated as "covert", and fell under CIA responsibility.[205]

In April 1953, a contingent of CAT pilots flew to Clark Field, Philippines to begin checkouts in C-119s that had been flown down from Japan by the instructor crews who would be doing the training. Several French pilots were also sent to Clark to be trained in the twin-boom transports. Because of their military backgrounds and considerable transport experience, the CAT pilots had no trouble checking out in the Flying Boxcar. One of the pilots was the already legendary James "Earthquake McGoon" McGovern, an experienced CAT pilot who had been flying in Asia since the war. McGovern was not alone – most of the CAT pilots had considerable experience in Asia. At least one pilot, Wallace Buford, had recent C-119 experience in Korea. On May 4, 1953, the first of six C-119s landed at Gia Lam Airfield outside Hanoi. Eighteen USAF mechanics accompanied the 483rd Troop

---

[205] Under the National Defense Act of 1947 which reorganized the War and Navy Departments into a single Depart of Defense, The Central Intelligence Agency, which was also established under the act, was given responsibility for intelligence gathering and for covert operations, paramilitary operations which the United States government could plausibly deny.

Sam McGowan

Carrier Wing airplanes to instruct the French and civilian mechanics who were to maintain the airplanes and to be on hand to provide technical assistance. Initially, the C-119s were flown by CAT and French crews but in late June another group of French pilots who had received C-119 training with American units in Europe arrived to replace the American civilians. The CAT crews would return to the on-loan C-119 cockpits within a few months. Once the C-119s began operations in Indochina, American military leaders in the region were not too happy with the way they were employed. No significant heavy equipment drops had materialized and that was the reason the airplanes had been sent there in the first place. The French were upset that the heavy C-119s damaged the runway at Cat Bi airfield. In late July, after only a few weeks service, the C-119s and the American personnel supporting them left Indochina. By agreement, 315th Air Division kept six airplanes on a ten-hour alert to be ready to go back to Hanoi if they were needed. French crews flew to Clark for periodic refresher training to be ready in the event the C-119s were brought back to Vietnam.

After the Korean Conflict came to an uneasy end in a truce in mid-1953, Far East Air Forces could devote more attention toward helping the French in their war against the Viet Minh. With the workload for 315th Air Division reduced, some of its airplanes became available for use in Indochina if the need arose. The Air Force implemented Project *IRON AGE*, which allowed for the loan of 22 C-119s to France if and when they were needed in Indochina. Under the plan, American crews would deliver the airplanes to Vietnam then return them to Japan when they were no longer needed. American maintenance personnel would accompany the airplanes and be responsible for all repairs. In September 1953, several French and CAT pilots were trained at Clark. The CAT pilots were reported to be "exceptionally well-qualified" in the larger aircraft. This came as no surprise because nearly all of the CAT pilots had flown transports in the military. Those who hadn't had been with CNAC or one of the other Asian aviation companies. One, Wallace Buford, was a former member of the 483rd who had flown the Flying Boxcar with the 50th TCS in Korea and flew B-24s during the war. Before he joined the 50th, he had flown forward air control missions in "Mosquito" T-6s. The prospect of higher pay, adventure and the idea of remaining in the exotic Far East seemed to attract very high quality pilots to CAT.

In late 1953, the French commander, General Henri Navarre, became concerned about the Viet Minh threat against Laos. Navarre decided to establish an air-land base deep in the Indochinese interior near the valley of Dienbienphu. From the airhead, French Foreign Legionnaires could operate against communist forces across the

Anything, Anywhere, Anytime

border in Laos. Navarre also believed the presence of French troops would draw out the illusive enemy and force them into a "set-piece battle" in which his artillery and aerial firepower could destroy the communists. Had it been ten years later, Navarre's plan probably would have worked but in 1953 airlift and close air support tactics against guerrilla forces were still largely unrefined. The crucial element in Navarre's plan was resupply and there were too many obstacles in the way of the French. Dienbienphu was so far from the main supply base at Hanoi that a C-47 could only make two round-trips per day and the French air transport group was too small to maintain the kind of airlift necessary to sustain such a force. Even with the on-loan C-119s, the French lacked the resources they needed. Furthermore, Navarre was facing an enemy who was far more tenacious and resourceful then he suspected.

On the morning of November 20, 1953 two paratroop battalions jumped over Dienbienphu from sixty C-47s. The Legionnaires met little resistance. The Viet Minh forces in the valley were either overwhelmed by the airborne assault or fled; or simply melted into the nearby hills without revealing their presence. A second drop later in the day brought in reinforcements. Several airdrops each day brought in additional troops and materials to build a base and an airfield. The need for a bulldozer resulted in the dispatch of a flight of C-119s from Clark for the task. The first bulldozer met with disaster when the platform came loose from the parachutes and fell unrestrained to be demolished when it struck the ground. A second bulldozer dropped later landed safely and was put to work on the construction of the airfield. The 17,000-pound bulldozer was the largest single item to have ever been dropped in the Far East to that time. Within a week after the airborne assault, the airstrip was ready for landings. The first C-47 landed on November 25. From that day on, a daily ferry of C-47s began making the 350-mile round trip from Hanoi to Dienbienphu, with each airplane making an average of two trips a day. While the level of supplies brought in was adequate to sustain the garrison, there was no room left over for materials for fortifications. Fifteen C-119s were sent to Cat Bi on December 15 to drop heavy construction materials such as barbed wire and ammunition at Dienbienphu. C-119s were used exclusively for drops while the smaller C-47s landed with reinforcements and supplies.

Once they arrived in Vietnam, the C-119s made almost daily flights to Dienbienphu. The American military advisors in Indochina recommended that US Air Force crews fly some missions, but the requirement to keep American military personnel out of combat ruled against it. Some Americans did visit the combat base at Dienbienphu, including Colonel Casey who flew in with a maintenance team who went to the base to recover a C-119 with mechanical problems. Some

Sam McGowan

483rd flight personnel managed to sneak by the regulations prohibiting their presence on the airplanes in Indochina and flew on missions over Dienbienphu although their presence was unofficial.

The French thought that Dienbienphu could be defended against Viet Minh attack by a combination of close air support and artillery. General Navarre believed the French air force would be able to detect signs of a communist build-up and then pound the enemy forces to pieces before they were even within artillery range of the combat base. But Navarre had grossly underestimated his adversary. Under the cover of darkness and triple-canopy jungle, thousands of Viet Minh troops and porters, many of them women, struggled valiantly to move heavy artillery pieces and antiaircraft guns along narrow jungle trails – often using pure manpower. It took the communists more than three months to move their artillery from their sanctuaries along the Chinese border to the ridges overlooking Dienbienphu but they did it – and the French failed entirely to detect the movements. They had no idea the guns were there until shells began impacting on the combat base. Once they reached the hills overlooking the valley where the base was located, the Viet Minh engineers located the guns across the ridge from the valley and placed them in dug out emplacements that were practically impervious to air and artillery attack. In spite of the tremendous logistics involved, the Viet Minh soon had more artillery aimed at the French positions in Dienbienphu then the French had to defend themselves.

By early March, the base was completely surrounded but the French had not the slightest inkling that they were about to be attacked. The Viet Minh launched their attack with a tremendous artillery barrage; hundreds of shells rained down on the base. Several French batteries were destroyed before they could even be brought to bear on the Viet Minh batteries. The shells the French fired in return had little effect on the attackers due to the superior Vietnamese engineering. The Viet Minh guns had been placed so they were protected from the French guns by intervening ridges. One of the primary targets for the communist artillery was the airstrip. Every time a transport landed, it was greeted by a rain of shells falling on the runway and parking areas. The artillery attacks severely hampered the French airlift operation but the C-47s continued to land for a time while the C-119s delivered their loads by airdrop. Eventually, the shelling intensified to the point that further landings had to be curtailed. Dienbienphu was completely cutoff from the outside world. The only means of supplying the base was by airdrop, and considering the volume of the Viet Minh antiaircraft around the airfield, airdrop had become a dangerous proposition.

Anything, Anywhere, Anytime

French paratroops at Dienbienphu (French Photographer)

General Navarre's plan to use airpower and artillery to defend the base was not working. The Viet Minh had, using sheer manpower and personal resolve on the part of their soldiers, dragged heavy guns over hidden mountain trails and dug them in on the other side of the mountain where they were invisible from the air. Their artillery had the airfield zeroed in, which made landings and takeoffs at Dienbienphu practically suicidal. Antiaircraft guns filled the mountain pass leading into the valley. Each C-47 and C-119 had to fly through "The Slot" to approach the base – and run a gauntlet of fire in the process. The airdrops that were the base's only means of supply had become extremely hazardous.

Initially, French crews flew the C-119 missions over Dienbienphu but, as the situation deteriorated, CAT pilots returned to the Flying Boxcars' cockpits. In spite of the many hazards of flying over the base, the French military and American civilian crews persevered to deliver as many supplies as possible. The CAT pilots took a special interest in the Frenchmen on the ground and often included special goodies they had bought with their own money with the supplies they dropped.

Sam McGowan

When "Earthquake" McGovern heard that the colonel in charge of the base had been promoted, he went out and bought the proper insignia and attached it to a bottle of champagne and dropped it into the camp. McGovern used the flights to get rid of his unpaid bills – he ripped them up and tossed the pieces out of the window of his Dollar Nineteen as he came into "The Slot" leading into the valley!(Robbins, 1979)

Loading casualties at Dienbienphu

Every mission was greeted by flak. General Giap, the Viet Minh commander, was well aware that the fate of the men in the camp hinged on the success of the airlift crews. Giap would remember the lessons of Dienbienphu fourteen years later at Khe Sanh. His troops were instructed to make every effort to shoot the big birds down as they were on their approaches or to at least make the skies so hazardous that the drops would go wild. But the American C-119 crews were no strangers to danger; for some, this was their third – and in some cases, even fourth – war. For CAT pilots, getting shot at had become a way of life. On one of the drops, CAT chief pilot Paul Holden was hit in the arm when his transport penetrated a wall of flak over the valley. Holden ripped off his shirt and applied a tourniquet to his half-severed arm while the co-pilot, Wallace Buford, flew the airplane back to Cat Bi. When they landed, McGovern inspected the flak-riddled cockpit and remarked to Buford that "somebody must have been carrying a magnet." A week later, McGovern's airplane was hit as he was pulling up after a drop. The C-119 pitched off onto one wing in the beginnings of a spin. As he was adding rudder to bring the huge transport out of the spin before it hit the ground, McGovern commented over his radio that, "I seem to be having a little trouble

Anything, Anywhere, Anytime

holding this thing." On the way back to Cat Bi he commented, "Now I know what it's like to ride a kangaroo." When he landed, Buford came up and asked, "Did you borrow my magnet?"

Supplies descending at Dienbienphu

Buford posed for a photograph by the C-119 he and Holden were flying that day. The hole where the shell penetrated the airplane is visible right above his head. He is standing with his hands clasped behind his back. According to family members, he struck the pose so his mother wouldn't see the bandages on his arms from his own wounds.(Walker)[206] One of the CAT pilots overheard McGovern admonishing a young Chinese boy not to cut school, but to study and make something of himself. "You don't want to grow up and be like me, pushing a freight plane around the jungle and getting shot at." The next day McGovern was crewed with Wallace Buford. As they walked to their airplane, McGovern kidded Buford, "Now we'll know who's got that magnet!" McGovern was scheduled to go on leave the next day with pilot Steve Kusak. They had made plans to go to Saigon for some R&R. On their previous leave, they had seen a British war movie in which the hero greeted each difficult situation with the comment "a piece of cake." The phrase had become part of McGovern's vocabulary.

Kusak was leading the formation. As he was pulling up, he looked back and saw the parachutes from McGovern's load opening higher than normal. McGovern reported that he had been hit, so Kusak slowed to drop back beside the other airplane to inspect the damage. He saw that the left wing leading edge was gone and the left engine was throwing oil. As he watched, another shell hit the right boom. The crippled Flying Boxcar lurched and dropped off on a wing. Kusak told

---

[206] This photograph is available on the Internet.

his friends to bail-out, but McGovern came back that he was going to try to nurse the crippled transport home. He had been shot down over China before and walked several hundred miles to freedom. He didn't want to have to go through that again. Kusak watched the shadow of the C-119 grow progressively larger. He knew that if the crew didn't bail out soon, the airplane would be too low. He asked McGovern if he thought he could make it to Hanoi.

"A piece of cake," came the reply.

They continued southeastward toward Hanoi for seventy-five miles, on a course that took them over the edge of eastern Laos. According to a Life magazine article at the time, McGovern was trying to crash-land in a river valley. The crippled airplane dropped lower and lower. McGovern made one last radio transmission – "Looks like this is it, son." The left wingtip hit the side of a hill and the airplane began a cartwheel. It exploded as it hit the ground not far from the river. A French officer who was flying with him and survived the crash said he was trying to land at an abandoned airfield near the village of Ban Sot and crashed a mile and a half short of the strip, The bearded giant went down with Buford and three crewmembers on his forty-fifth mission over the valley of Dienbienphu.[207] Some of those in the back survived the crash but McGovern and Buford died. . The man was dead but the legend of Earthquake McGoon would live on. The next day the outpost fell. In spite of the intense ground fire over the valley, McGovern and Buford's airplane was the only C-119 lost over Dienbienphu.

Dienbienphu fell because of the French failure to properly prepare for the eventuality of a strong enemy presence around the combat base, not because of any failure on the part of the airlifters. The French and CAT crews continued dropping supplies to the base right up until the day the camp surrendered. In spite of intense flak, the transport crews persevered, but the resupply was hampered when the Viet Minh effectively closed the airstrip with their incessant shelling. As long as the strip was open, the Frenchmen at the combat base had a chance. Landing airplanes could deliver their supplies intact and without worry that they would perhaps fall into enemy hands. Returning transports could take out casualties, while reinforcements could be brought in along with the supplies. When the landings were halted, the French troops realized they were cut off from the rest of the world and surrounded by a determined enemy. The morale of the French and colonial troops trapped in the combat base plummeted with each passing day. The Viet Minh shelling served

---

[207] The Viet Minh buried McGovern's remains, which were discovered and returned to the United States in the 1990s. He and Buford are now recognized by the CIA as employees. Buford's remains have yet to be discovered.

Anything, Anywhere, Anytime

its purpose of disrupting the flow of supplies and reinforcements by making the airstrip too hazardous for landings. When the French turned to airdrop, antiaircraft fire made the drops only marginally accurate. A good portion of the supplies that were intended for the Frenchmen was recovered and used by the Viet Minh.

The real French failure at Dienbienphu was on the part of their artillery. Even though General Navarre planned to use artillery to defend the base, he had not reckoned on the caliber and range of the guns that were provided to the Viet Minh by the Chinese. Nor had he reckoned on the engineering skills of the Viet Minh artillerymen, who were able to locate their guns in such a way that French shells and airstrikes could not harm them. While the guns could have perhaps been destroyed by heavy bombers, the French had none. Rumors of a massive strike on the guns by American B-29s failed to materialize, as did rumors that the US was going to drop an atomic bomb in the hills overlooking the base. The alleged B-29 attack was evidently canceled at the last minute out of White House fear of involving the United States more deeply in a situation that the world considered to be France's problem.(Fall)[208]

More than 8,000 French and colonial soldiers surrendered to the Viet Minh at Dienbienphu, yet only about half that number survived captivity. Many became weakened during the march away from the camp and were left beside the road to die by their captors, not so much as an act of cruelty but because the Viet Minh had few doctors and no facilities to tend to them. Among the survivors of the battle was a single woman, a French flight nurse whose name was Genevieve de Galard. Mme. Galard was aboard the last C-47 to land at Dienbienphu and was stranded along with the rest of the crew when the airplane was set afire by artillery fire. The nurse attended the wounded men of the base right up until the last and helped to lift their spirits as the end drew near. She became famous as "The Angel of Dienbienphu." When the Viet Minh marched their captives away from the base, they left Mme. Galard behind along with the most seriously wounded men so they could be evacuated by French transports.(Fall) Mme. Galard was later evacuated to Hanoi, then flown to the United States in a USAF transport. She was given a parade in New York. She was decorated by both the French and the United States. (Fall)

The fall of Dienbienphu, which was referred to by Bernard Fall as *Hell in a Very Small Place*, dashed French hopes for victory in Indochina. French and Viet Minh representatives met in Geneva and

---

[208] The gift of hindsight reveals that the canceling of the B-29 strikes and other US military involvement was a mistake. France left Indochina and the Indochina War became an American war.

signed the Accords that ended the war. Neither the Vietnamese government nor the United States signed them. Under the terms of the Accords, Vietnam was divided into two halves, with Ho Chi Minh's Viet Minh in charge of the north while the non-communist Vietnamese government, which was already in existence under the French, controlled the southern half. Free elections were supposed to decide the future of the country but elections were never held. A similar plan had been set forth to end the Korean Conflict. In Korea the elections were held, but the North Koreans refused to participate. The agreement for elections in Vietnam was between the Viet Minh and the French, with support by the Soviet Union, and without Vietnamese government or American agreement.

American troop carrier squadrons participated in the French withdrawal. Between sixteen and eighteen C-119s remained in Indochina after the fall of Dienbienphu, although their operating base shifted south to the seaport city of Tourane, which a later generation of Americans would come to know as Da Nang. In July 1954, the C-119 force was cut to eight airplanes at Tourane with four in American markings to stand by to evacuate USAF personnel from Indochina if the need arose. On September 7, the last of the C-119s was withdrawn from Vietnam after having been there for nine months. During their stay, the French and CAT crews parachuted 14,800 tons of cargo to French forces. Three C-119s were lost to accident and enemy action but no American military personnel were acknowledged to have been lost in Indochina.

In the early summer of 1954, 315th Air Division C-124s from the 374th Troop Carrier Wing were used to evacuate 500 wounded Frenchmen from Saigon to Japan. Medical crews from the 6481st Air Evacuation Group, also part of 315th, accompanied the missions to tend to the injured men. When the C-124s arrived in Japan, their patients were transferred to TAC and MATS transports for the second phase of their journey home to Europe. (It wasn't the first time C-124s flew French troops. In April 1952, TAC C-124s from the 62nd Troop Carrier Wing flew French troops from Paris' Orly Airport to Indochina.) In July and August, 315th C-124s flew 106 tons of tents to Vietnam for use as shelters for refugees.

For a time, it appeared that USAF transports might become involved in the evacuation of Vietnamese refugees from what was to become North Vietnam but the mission was given to civilian aviation companies. Although more than 200,000 Vietnamese were flown out of the country, they made the trip in civilian airlines – including CAT. Another civilian company involved in the airlift of Vietnamese was a charter company from the Philippines owned by a retired USAF officer, Colonel Paul I. Gunn, also known as Pappy Gunn and the same Captain Paul I Gunn who pioneered US air transport operations in the

Anything, Anywhere, Anytime

Southwest Pacific in early 1942. After the war and extensive surgery in the United States, Pappy Gunn had returned to the Philippines and his airline. When the new government of the Philippines nationalized the airline, Gunn started an air taxi company and became heavily involved in US clandestine operations.[209] Some 483rd Troop Carrier Wing missions into Tourane from Gia Lam transported American diplomats.

American military transports left the skies of Indochina with the French in 1954. They would be back within less than a decade however, and in a big way. As for the mercenary pilots of CAT, many would remain in Asia. By 1954, CAT was the largest and most profitable airline in Asia. The mercenary effort in Indochina was but one sideline of the company's efforts in the region. CAT operated scheduled service throughout the Far East Air Forces region from Japan to Okinawa, the Philippines and Taiwan, to Hong Kong and into Saigon and throughout South Vietnam and its Southeast Asian neighbors. In addition to normal airline service flying commercial passengers and cargo, CAT provided contract services for US government agencies. While much of the government-funded airlift was for the military units in the region, the airline also supported secret Central Intelligence Agency operations in Asia.

Throughout the 1950s, 1960s and 1970s CAT remained active in Asia, although its role became more associated with scheduled airline service. A CAT spin-off named Air America would become the primary covert operations airline asset in the region. Much of Air America's assets came directly from CAT, including airplanes as well as pilots. The value of CAT and Air America to the CIA led to the creation of Southern Air Transport for operations in the Caribbean and points south although SAT airplanes would become a familiar sight in Asia as well. Air America would serve several presidential administrations, both Democrats and Republicans, for two decades. The "civilian" nature of the airline provided a good cover for covert US government operations where the use of Air Force aircraft would have been too obvious, as had been the case in Indochina. As for Indochina itself, the region was divided into three countries, Laos, Cambodia and Vietnam,

---

[209] The role of Pappy Gunn in covert operations after World War II is not generally known but the author is well acquainted with his youngest son, who returned to the Philippines as a teenager to live with his dad, who taught him to fly. Gunn returned to Philippines Airlines then, when it was nationalized, he formed his own air taxi company and became involved in government contract work flying US-supplied cargo to places where the US government didn't want its presence known. One such operation was the delivery of US supplies to Indonesian guerrillas who were combating the Dutch in the late 1940s. A second operation supported Indonesian rebels against the Sukarano government. After Pappy Gunn was killed in an aircraft accident in 1957, his sons took over operation of the company. In 1960, they went to Laos under contract to the Laotian government.

with Vietnam being split in half as Korea had been almost a decade before, effectively making a fourth. The Viet Minh victory brought no peace to the region but rather a very uneasy unrest as other Southeast Asia nations watched the region with a wary eye.[210] In both Cambodia and Laos, rival factions struggled for dominance of their respective countries while the situation in Vietnam became very much like that of Korea.

Even while the French were withdrawing from Indochina, the United States was making plans to finance and train a 234,000-man Vietnamese National Army. An Air Force officer, Colonel Edward Lansdale, who had formerly served with the OSS in World War II, was sent to Vietnam as chief US military advisor. Lansdale had successfully advised the Philippines government in an effort to defeat communist rebels there in what is commonly known as the Huk Rebellion. Included in the new Vietnamese military was an air transport group equipped with US-supplied C-47s. Airborne forces were part of the Vietnamese army, or ARVN. By the end of the decade, new fighting would erupt in the region that had been French Indochina. This time, the enemy that the successors of the Viet Minh would seek to drive from Vietnam was the United States.

---

[210] By definition, Southeast Asia is the southeastern portion of the Asian continent along with the offshore islands including the Philippines, Taiwan, Indonesia and New Guinea. On the Asian continent, Thailand, Burma, India, the Malayan Peninsula and parts of China are included in the region.

Anything, Anywhere, Anytime

Sam McGowan

Chapter Twelve - "A NEW FACE"

If the United States Air Force learned anything from the Korean War, it was that the service must be as prepared to fight conventional wars at a moment's notice as it was to launch a massive nuclear response to Soviet aggression. The two main deficiencies of US preparedness when the North Koreans crossed the 38th parallel was a lack of rapidly mobile air and ground units trained to go into battle with little notice, and the resources, particularly air transportation, to get them there. Postwar planning had developed around the nuclear-carrying B-29s of SAC, but when the United States suddenly found itself in a real shooting war in Asia, the star of the Tactical Air Command was suddenly on the rise.

Tactical Air Command, TAC for short, had been created immediately after World War II following the model of the IX and XIX Tactical Air Commands which saw such spectacular service in Europe. TAC's mission was to support theater forces, and its backbone was the fighter/bomber, a single-place fighter designed to attack ground targets with guns, bombs, napalm and rockets as well as to engage in air-to-air combat to secure the skies over the battlefield. It was a command heavy with fighter/bombers, but it was also the parent unit for all troop carrier groups in the US, just as Ninth Air Force had been in Western Europe.

In the 1950's, new technology was leading toward the development of low-yield nuclear weapons, small nuclear bombs that would give TAC's fighter squadrons a nuclear capability. Battlefield reconnaissance was provided by TAC's photoreconnaissance squadrons. Supporting the Army also meant providing airlift for its airborne and light infantry divisions while TAC's own combat squadrons required air transportation as well. The Marine Corps had a similar force, although on a much smaller scale. Tactical Air Command

Anything, Anywhere, Anytime

was established on March 21, 1946 with its headquarters at Langley Air Base, Virginia, a historic base and one of the most important of the Army Air Corps bases. The Air Corps Tactical School was established at Langley in 1920; most of the leaders of the new United States Air Force had attended the school. Those who hadn't attended at Langley attended its successor, the Army Air Forces School of Applied Tactics at Orlando, Florida. The school later moved to Maxwell Field, Alabama where it became the Air University. From 1946 to 1992, when it was replaced by the Air Combat Command, Langley was TAC.

In 1953 as the Korean War was drawing to a close, the Air Force reorganized its troop carrier forces. Cargo and passenger handling functions that had previously been Army responsibility transferred to the Air Force and were assigned to new aerial port squadrons that were set up as part of Eighteenth Air Force, a unit that was organized under Tactical Air Command in March 1951 at Donaldson AFB, SC to control troop carrier operations. Donaldson had formerly been known as Greenville Air Base. In the Far East, the 6127th Air Terminal Group became the 2nd Aerial Port Group with the 6th and 7th Aerial Port Squadrons. The 5th Aerial Port Squadron was established in Europe to support troop carrier forces assigned to USAFE. Included within the aerial port squadrons were airfreight and passenger service sections that had been formed during the Korean Conflict. Additional sections included aerial delivery and combat control sections; functions that had previously been carried out by Army personnel.

Aerial delivery included airdrop specialists called dropmasters who took the place of the Army Quartermasters who had previously flown as "kickers" on C-119s, C-46s and C-47s. The dropmaster role had developed during World War II but had remained with Army

Sam McGowan

airborne Quartermaster units when the Air Force became a separate service. After 1953, dropmasters were part of the Air Force. Their role was to inspect cargo that had been rigged for airdrop by Army or Marine Corps riggers and to install and operate aerial delivery equipment. Dropmasters were given the same Air Force specialty code as the loadmasters who became part of the C-124 crew in 1950 and had similar, if not identical, duties. TAC dropmaster/loadmasters didn't normally fly on cargo missions and paratroop drops, however. Their role was to inspect cargo that had been rigged by Army Quartermasters and to install and operate the aerial delivery equipment installed on C-119s. TAC's C-124s carried loadmasters on cargo flights but C-119s didn't.

374th Troop Carrier Wing C-124 in Japan

Aerial port passenger service and airfreight sections were responsible for manifesting passengers and cargo and loading baggage and cargo onto the airplanes. They were the lineal descendants of the World War II traffic specialists who first saw service in the Southwest Pacific with the Allied Directorate of Air Transport. Because their role was tactical, they could expect to operate at forward airfields during

Anything, Anywhere, Anytime

combat operations. Airfreight personnel were trained in load planning and other functions involved with air transportation. At the rear area airfields where missions originated, airfreight was responsible for receiving the cargo and processing it then loading it. At the forward airfields, airfreight personnel unloaded the airplanes and distributed the cargo to the proper recipient. The airfreight field was the input for the new aircraft loadmaster field, which was a shredout of the air transportation field, as was airfreight and passenger service.

Combat controllers were descended from the Army pathfinder platoons that had been developed during World War II to jump in to set up and mark drop zones in advance of airborne operations and the combat control teams that were established late in the war to control glider and transport operations in forward areas. There was a difference, however. World War II combat controllers were all qualified troop carrier pilots, but the new combat controllers were enlisted men who had been given some air traffic control training. They were assigned to sections commanded by company grade officers with an air transportation officer AFSC. Their role was identical to that of the World War II pathfinders – they were even still referred to by many troop carrier personnel as pathfinders as late as 1964 – which was to jump in ahead of a main airborne assault force and set up radio beacons and mark drop zones with panels and lights. They might also go in to the potential drop zone by helicopter, ground vehicle or from the sea.

While the new aerial port squadrons were important and their duties put them in close proximity to combat operations, they were not combat units per se, but were support units whose role was to support troop carrier operations. Without the troop carrier squadrons, the aerial port units might as well have spent their time in base beautification projects while maintenance painted their airplanes yellow and turned them into expensive power carts. Aerial port and maintenance were important, but only in relationship to their support of the aircrews who flew the planes.

TAC's airlift in the immediate post-Korean War era was provided by its troop carrier squadrons, which operated C-119s and C-82s for tactical operations and C-124s for long-distance, heavy-lift requirements. The World War II vintage C-47s and C-46s were being phased out as were the C-54s. Aging C-54s in Europe were being replaced with C-119s; the 483rd TCW in Japan had been flying them since the Korean War. The C-119 and C-124 were reciprocating engine aircraft and both required relatively long, hard-surfaced runways to take off with a heavy load. To truly perform their mission as Generals Arnold, Marshall and Brereton had envisioned, troop carrier squadrons needed airplanes with true tactical capabilities. Such an

Sam McGowan

airplane was on the way. TAC had a new airlifter under development when the events in Korea and Indochina came to a close; an airplane that could land just about anywhere, deliver cargo and troops by parachute and could use runways far shorter than those required by any other airplane its size. It had a ramp that allowed easy loading of vehicles ranging in size from Jeeps to light tanks. It could carry paratroops, troops or patients in litter straps and stanchions that were part of its equipment. Lockheed Aircraft Corporation, the company responsible for the P-38, the P-80, Constellation and the U-2 reconnaissance aircraft, was in the process of developing the C-130 Hercules.

The C-130 was a direct result of the war in Korea. According to noted aviation author Martin Caidin, a special meeting was held at USAF Headquarters in the Pentagon on the Sunday after North Korean troops invaded South Korea to discuss how to spend a new appropriation for research and development. One of the participants, an unnamed colonel, remarked that the Air Force needed a rugged troop carrier transport capable of carrying a load of troops over a 1,500-mile distance and landing on an unimproved runway. Such an airplane had to be able to carry vehicles as well as cargo and to deliver them by airdrop if necessary. The participants discussed how much of the appropriation to allocate to the transport project and an amount was determined and written down. That was in June 1950. Over the next few months, a specification was developed and issued for bids. Lockheed won the contract to build it.

YC-130 first flight (Lockheed)

Anything, Anywhere, Anytime

Ironically, some of Lockheed's own engineers were not enthusiastic about the design their employer was working on. The company had a reputation for building sleek, fast airplanes – and the new YC-130 promised to be anything but sleek! It was also a propeller-driven airplane, at a time when everyone was going to jets, although the propellers were linked through gear boxes to jet engines so, at least technically, it was a jet. The C-130 was a jet-prop airplane, a new concept that essentially began with its design.[211] By using a turbine engine to turn a propeller, the turboprop was and still is the most efficient of all aircraft engines in terms of power and fuel consumption. Its only drawback is that the propellers create drag, which limits them to speeds well below the speed of sound. Yet, while the C-130's speed was limited by its aerodynamics, the four Allison engine's pulled the airplane through the air at speeds far beyond that of any other large propeller-driven airplane. Furthermore, the powerful engines and the high aspect ratio wing gave it tremendous load-carrying ability. Its typical payload would be established at 30,000 pounds, which was five times that of a C-47. The C-130's range was greater than the 1,500 miles that had first been suggested, and it could be extended with the installation of portable Benson tanks in the cargo compartment. Climb performance was spectacular and the maximum altitude was over 43,000 feet, although normal operating altitudes were in the 25,000 feet vicinity. The cabin was pressurized, which allowed passengers to be carried without supplemental oxygen.

The Air Force had asked for a simple, rugged airplane that could take-off and land on short, unimproved runways for assignment to TAC as a troop carrier transport. TAC asked for no frills, but for utility in the new design. That airlift must be flexible was one lesson the Air Force had learned in Korea and the Hercules had been designed with just that in mind. It might not look like much in the eyes of men who were famous for designing fighters but it had been designed to have capabilities that would make it integral to military aviation well into the Twenty-First Century. The complaints by the Lockheed "Skunk Works" engineers were silenced forever on August 23, 1954 when the YC-130 took to the skies for the first time. When pilot Leo Sullivan lifted the silver airplane off of Burbank's runway after a take-off roll of only 855 feet, a gasp of amazement went up from the crowd of company employees and VIPs who had assembled for the occasion. Even though the airplane's first takeoff was nothing short of amazing, the assembled crowd had no idea they were witnessing the birth of an

---

[211] The Air Force had also put out a specification for a larger, non-tactical turboprop airplane, but not until 1952. That specification resulted in the Douglas C-133. Although experiments had been made with turboprop engine aircraft as early as 1945, the C-130 was the first successful design.

institution. Except for the U-2, all of Lockheed's 1950's designs have gone by the wayside but the company is still building C-130s. (The C-130 was designed in the early 1950s; it is STILL the primary tactical transport not only in the US Air Force but also in many other Air Forces around the world.)

Before the new airplane could go into production, it had to be put through a rigid flight test program by Lockheed engineering test pilots. The prototype was delivered to the Air Force Flight Test Facility at Edwards Air Force Base, in the Mojave Desert near Lancaster, California. Lockheed decided to produce the new transport at its Marietta, Georgia facility, where the company had been refurbishing Boeing B-47s. The facility, known as Air Force Plant Number 6, had originally been operated by Bell Aircraft, who built B-29s at the plant under license from Boeing. The plant was about to become idle again when the refurbishment contract was completed, so it was the ideal place to produce the new transport. There was an experienced labor force at the facility and they would have no trouble transitioning from refurbishment to production. Once the initial testing at Edwards was completed, test flying transitioned to the Marietta facility. Production was starting on the new transport, but it would be almost two years from the first flight before the first airplane was turned over to the Air Force.

During those two years, Lockheed and Air Force test pilots and engineers went over the YC-130 with a fine-tooth comb as they looked for problems that needed to be corrected before the airplane entered operational service. They developed performance data to allow flight crews to operate the airplane into the shortest runways, and developed procedures for off-runway operations on surfaces as soft as sand. Airdrop testing was conducted with both personnel and heavy equipment. The new C-130 had several distinct advantages over its predecessors, not the least of which was that the hydraulically operated cargo ramp and door eliminated the need to operate with the rear of the cargo compartment exposed to the elements. Airdrop platforms that had been developed for the C-119 could be dropped from the new transport, but instead of a maximum of two platforms, the C-130 could drop three on a single pass. One early problem was the recognition that the electric propellers that had originally been planned for it proved inadequate. They were replaced by hydraulically operated propellers which turned out to be more reliable. A new radar with a larger antenna was added to the production models. The larger antenna required a larger compartment, or radome, which gave the production C-130s the bulbous, porpoise-nose appearance that is now associated with the type.

If the Lockheed employees were impressed, they were no more so than the Air Force pilots who were the first to fly the new transport

Anything, Anywhere, Anytime

operationally when it entered service with the 463rd Troop Carrier Wing at Ardmore AFB, Oklahoma in December 1956.[212] Most of them had been flying C-119s and some had flown C-47s or C-46s. The C-130 was so much more powerful and maneuverable than the C-119 that the pilots felt they had moved out of transports and into fighters. The rest of the Air Force learned just how maneuverable the airplane was when crews from the 774th Troop Carrier Squadron came up with an almost-aerobatic routine and got permission to demonstrate their new airplane at military airfields all over the world. Calling themselves *Hercules and the Four Horsemen*, the four crews, commanded by Captains Gene Chaney, Jim Akin, David Moore and William Hatfield, demonstrated the airplane to the men of the 314th Troop Carrier Wing at Sewart AFB, Tennessee just before the Tennessee wing began its own conversion from C-119s into the jet age. The *Horsemen* applied for aerial demonstration team status but were turned down by the Air Force because the service could not spare the airplanes from the troop carrier mission for which they had been purchased.

The new C-130 was not only maneuverable, it was also powerful. In fact, instead of being underpowered as every other transport had been, it was actually overpowered. During the test phase, a Lockheed test crew took off from an airport in Florida and immediately shut down both outboard engines then flew the airplane all the way across the country to Edwards AFB, California – at low altitude! It was also

---

[212] This is the date of the first deliveries to an operational squadron. In reality, the Air Force had been taking deliveries for almost a year before this date. The first ones were used for testing and others were used for training. At least one airplane had been delivered to the Air Force Systems Command for conversion for the electronics intelligence mission.

versatile. Although other transports could operate from grass runways, the C-130A could operate off sand and mud. Granted, the new design had its share of problems. The original propellers were Curtis-Wright electric props and they proved to be less reliable than desired. Lockheed switched to Aero Products hydraulic props. The cargo compartment lacked adequate heating, and it could get cold back there on long flights. The cargo compartment was also noisy due to the close proximity of the prop tips to the fuselage and their supersonic sound. Still, the problems were minor when considered in the context of the airplane's tremendous performance and capabilities. It truly was a revolutionary airplane, and it would revolutionize the troop carrier mission.

It has been more than sixty years since the YC-130 made its first flight, and since that time the Hercules has achieved a reputation paralleled by no other airplane. Unfortunately, many C-130 enthusiasts champion the airplane because of the many offshoot missions to which it has been assigned, missions ranging from electronics intelligence gathering to the much vaunted AC-130 gunship but it is not the various hardware and systems that have been hung on it that has made the C-130 a truly great airplane. It is great because it has done such an effective job of filling the requirements under which it was designed that the only suitable replacement for it is another model incorporating the latest technological advances. If not a single C-130 had ever been modified and turned into an ELINT airplane, a search and rescue vehicle, a refueler, a special operations craft or a gunship, it would still be a fantastic airplane simply because of its troop carrier, tactical airlift, combat airlift, or whatever you want to call it, abilities. It's a transport, but it's more than a transport – it's a transport that can land on short, unimproved landing strips, carry a substantial payload and survive in the combat environment. Only one other design has ever come close to approximating its capabilities and that design, the Douglas DC-3, was long since obsolete by the time the first C-130 was delivered to TAC in December 1956.[213]

Air Force plans called for six C-130 squadrons in the United States and six overseas, three squadrons each in Europe and the Far East. The 463rd Troop Carrier Wing at Ardmore AFB, Oklahoma was chosen to be the first wing to equip with the new transport. The 314th TCW at Sewart AFB, Tennessee would be second. Both wings were flying C-119s before the conversion although the 463rd had previously included a squadron of C-123s. As it turned out, barely two years after the first C-130s were delivered to the 463rd at Ardmore, the base was

---

[213] The DC-3 has been greatly romanticized by the aviation media and enthusiasts but World War II troop carrier commanders already considered it obsolete for a number of reasons by 1945.

Anything, Anywhere, Anytime

in the process of closing and the wing and its squadrons were moving to Sewart. From 1958 to 1960, all of TAC's C-130s were based at Sewart. Even before the first C-130 was delivered at Ardmore, the Air Force was already in the process of modifying enough for a squadron for electronics intelligence work in Europe and Lockheed was making plans to sell C-130s to other countries. A new emphasis on rapid deployment of ground and air forces was developing in the wake of the war in Indochina and the Air Force saw a need for more C-130s. Lockheed and the Air Force started looking at ways to improve the Hercules.

A few months after the first flight of the YC-130, TAC began taking deliveries of Fairchild Aircraft's C-123 Provider. Originally designed by Chase Aircraft as a powered version of its CG-20 glider during World War II, the design was shelved when the war ended but was revived during the Korean War and developed by Fairchild Aircraft, who had bought Chase's assets including its designs, when the company declared bankruptcy. The C-123 was a rugged airplane with excellent short field capabilities but the final version was underpowered. Surprisingly, the first version, the C-123A, was powered by four jet engines but the cost was higher than the Air Force wanted to pay. TAC settled on the C-123B, which featured a pair of Pratt and Whitney R-2800 Double Wasp reciprocating radial engines, which turned out to be insufficient for an airplane that size. Had Fairchild equipped the design with the new turbo-propeller power plants, the C-123B would have been an excellent airplane but there were thousands of surplus R-2800 engines left over from World War II and using them reduced the purchase cost. The C-123 was the last aircraft design to use the R-2800 engine and the last tactical airplane produced for the Air Force that used reciprocating engines.[214] During the Vietnam War, the C-123 fleet would be upgraded with the addition of a jet engine under each wing to boost takeoff and landing performance, but the version TAC and USAFE flew in the fifties and early sixties was very much underpowered.

TAC and the Army saw the C-123 as a replacement for gliders. Even though they hadn't been used since World War II except for training, troop carrier pilots were required to be qualified on them until the early 1950s. In fact, the C-123 was based on Chase's CG-20 glider. Essentially, in tactical operations the C-123 was originally intended to be used like a glider. The pilot would fly it into an unimproved landing zone with a load of troops or cargo then, when the area had been secured, engineers would construct an airstrip from

---

[214] The Dehaviland Caribou was not produced for the Air Force. All Caribous were purchased by the Army. They transferred to the Air Force in 1966.

which it could be flown out. Because it was intended for operations in hostile areas, the nacelle tanks behind the engines were designed to be dropped prior to the assault to reduce the possibility of fire. Pylon tanks under the end of the wings would provide fuel for the approach and landing. C-123s were crucial to TAC and Army airborne tactics in the 1950s. Paratroops would jump in and secure a landing area on which C-123s could land. Engineers would then construct a strip long enough for C-130s.

C-123B

TAC's other transports were the C-119, which was a fixture of troop carrier operations in the Korean War and, until 1958, the Douglas C-124. The C-124 was the result of an Air Force requirement issued in the late 1940s for a large troop carrier airplane. Douglas modified its existing C-74 design and the Air Force bought it even though TAC wasn't happy with the design. Although it could carry a substantial payload, the C-124 was underpowered and slow. It was unpressurized and the heating system was inadequate. The C-124 became controversial when the MATS staff insisted that all of the new airplanes should be assigned to it rather than to SAC and TAC as the Air Staff had planned. Finally, in 1957 while General Tunner was deputy commander for plans on the Air Staff, the Air Force decided to transfer all C-124s to MATS.

TAC also had a troop-carrying helicopter capability, with five squadrons activated by 1955. TAC's helicopter squadrons flew the Sikorski H-19 until they were replaced by the Piasecki H-21, a twin rotor design that was known as the *Flying Banana* because of its curved, elongated shape. But the Army was not impressed with TAC's plans for helicopters because the service had its own ideas for them

Anything, Anywhere, Anytime

and their development. It saw a future in the air and it saw it in the form of Army helicopters flown by Army crews assigned to Army aviation companies. In fact, the Army actually wanted its own troop carrier force but since that mission had been given to the Air Force, Army aviation leaders decided to go through the back door and develop a troop carrying helicopter capability. When the Army rejected TAC's helicopter plans, the squadrons were disbanded and the aircraft were distributed throughout the Air Force for special airlift duties. TAC would resurrect its helicopter capabilities during the Vietnam War when the troop carrier and helicopter control situation came to a head.(Tolson, 1972)(Bowers, 1986)

Piasecki H-21 Shawnee

The Air Force went through a period of intense criticism in the 1950s as it made plans to introduce intercontinental-range ballistic missiles to SAC's nuclear deterrent force. Some elements within the military had the idea that nuclear missiles, based both on land and on submarines beneath the sea, would deter aggression by America's enemies and make the world a safer place. The Air Force started making plans to give the C-123s to the reserves before deliveries had even started. At the same time, the Army was seeking to drastically expand its aviation forces. The Air Force was told that if it didn't get on the ball and find a tactical mission for itself, it would become a force made up of "silo-sitters in the seventies."(Tolson, 1972)[215] Yet even as SAC began focusing on ICBMs and making plans to retire many of its heavy bombers, the star of Tactical Air Command was beginning its ascendancy. There were military officers and politicians who weren't

---

[215] Ironically, in the 2010s the Air Force is again in danger of the same thing, although now instead of ICBM missiles, the new golly, gee-whiz weapons are remotely piloted vehicles operated from bunkers thousands of miles removed from the battlefield.

convinced that nuclear weapons would deter conflict. The most likely threat was a Soviet invasion of Western Europe from East Germany. Fighter/bombers armed with either conventional or low-yield nuclear weapons could be used against them. Fighter/bombers were TAC's specialty. Conventional ground forces would oppose the Soviet invasion, and they would need to be transported and supplied. There was also the threat of what strategists referred to as "low intensity conflict" in less developed regions of the world.

As the C-123 and C-130 entered service with TAC, the command's C-124s were transferred to MATS and the C-119s went to the Air Force Reserve. The transfer of the C-124s was part of a compromise that had been worked out in response to constant political pressure from MATS for consolidation of all airlift resources. Lt. General William H. Tunner had become the deputy commander for plans on the Air Force staff and he was using his position to advance MATS' role and responsibilities. He also used his position to gain control of a new turboprop transport that was being developed for the Air Material Command, the Douglas C-133. It wasn't long before reserve units began receiving C-123s as well, with units in Memphis, Tennessee and Birmingham, Alabama converting to the Provider by the late 1950s. Not long after the 463rd Troop Carrier Wing completed its conversion to the C-130, its base at Ardmore, Oklahoma closed and the unit moved to Sewart to join the 314th. With the two wings both at Sewart, the Tennessee base and Pope AFB, NC, where the C-123 equipped 464th Troop Carrier Wing was based, constituted TAC's active duty troop carrier bases until 1960, when the 64th Troop Carrier Wing activated at Dyess AFB, Texas.

The Korean and Indochina Wars had demonstrated that the threat of conflict in diverse parts of the world was very real. Some US politicians and military leaders believed that such conflicts should be met with strong US military forces to prevent them from spreading into neighboring countries and escalating to regional war. The Eisenhower Administration developed the concept of dispatching heavily armed tactical fighters supported by US Army airborne and light infantry forces to the vicinity of such conflicts as soon as they emerged to act as a deterrent to prevent a widening war. Such forces would be deployed entirely by air, and TAC's troop carrier wings were seen as the means of deployment. The new concept was identified as a Composite Airstrike Force.

A CASF would consist of at least one TAC fighter squadron and a battalion of US Army airborne or light infantry troops and their equipment along with a contingent of reconnaissance aircraft. Additional fighter squadrons or other air and ground forces could be added, depending on the nature and location of the conflict. Not only

Anything, Anywhere, Anytime

were US-based units marked for possible deployment, troops in Europe and the Far East were subject to be deployed. Three squadrons of C-130s were assigned to both theaters, beginning in 1958. C-130 squadrons would deploy air and ground forces from bases within their region to the region of conflict and they would be joined by a CASF from the US supported by TAC troop carrier squadrons.

TAC's fighter/bomber forces had become much more powerful than their World War II and Korean War predecessors. New generation "century series" fighters were being developed, starting with North American's F-100 and continuing through Lockheed's F-104 and Republic F-105.[216] The F-100 and F-105 were both designed as fighter/bombers and although the F-104 was originally designed as an interceptor, it could carry bombs, rockets and small nuclear weapons. CASFs were not equipped with nuclear weapons, however. Their primary purpose was to be prepared to enter a conflict if necessary, but not to escalate it. TAC had received its own aerial tankers – KB-50s – to refuel its forces as they were being deployed overseas. TAC also had tactical reconnaissance squadrons equipped with fighters that had been reconfigured with cameras.

TAC had adopted the Transportation Movement Control concept that had been used in the Korean War. TMCs were set up at troop carrier bases as a coordinating center for requests from the Army with the troop carrier squadron that was to perform them. Transportation Movement Detachments, or TMDs, were set up at airfields where troop carrier aircraft might operate. With the development of the CASF, TAC also adopted the Consolidated Airlift Support Unit, or CALSU. CALSUs were set up at Air Force bases frequented by TAC troop carrier crews and at airfields through which aircraft assigned to a CASF operated.

The CALSU was the coordinating point for all of the services aircrews might need, whether it was communications, maintenance or aerial port functions. At Pope, where crews from other TAC bases came for airdrop training, the CALSU coordinated all of the functions needed to keep the TDY aircraft in the air. When a CASF deployed, CALSU teams were sent out in advance of the deploying troop carrier force. There were instances during short-notice deployments when the CALSU was actually the cockpit of the airplane operated by the Standardizations/Evaluation crew that was part of the deployment. Whenever their role at one airfield was complete, they continued to their deployment base.

---

[216] McDonnell's F-101 started out as fighter/bomber but became prevalent as a photo-reconnaissance aircraft. The Convair F-102 was an air defense fighter, as was the F-106 that followed. There was no F-103 in operational service.

CALSU at Pope (Don Hessenflow)

A major aspect of the post-Korea troop carrier mission was the almost constant political activity by the Military Air Transport Service to take it over. Although he was no longer in MATS, Maj. General William H. Tunner was the architect of the effort although the various MATS commanders and members of the MATS staff were also active. Shortly after he returned to the US from Japan in early 1951, Tunner was transferred from MATS to the Air Material Command where he became the deputy commander. Air Material Command had its own transports so Tunner began a campaign to have them transferred to MATS. His next assignment was in Europe as USAFE commander. USAFE had several troop carrier wings assigned; Tunner activated 322nd Air Division to control them. In his end of tour report, he asserted that MATS could handle airlift in Europe and that the command's troop carrier units should be removed from USAFE control and placed under the air transport service.[217] From Europe, he went to Washington to the Air Staff where he was director of plans, arguably the most important position in the Air Force since the office of plans was responsible for establishing doctrine.

Tunner's goal was the ultimate consolidation of all military air transport in one organization – MATS. His position was that air transport, which he had begun referring to as "airlift," was a weapon in itself. While in a sense he was correct, Tunner never understood the

---

[217] When his plan was adopted, instead of MATS "handling" airlift in Europe, the existing 322nd Air Division simply transferred to MATS but its assigned squadrons transferred to the US and airlift was performed by TAC troop carrier squadrons on TDY to France, then later, England.

distinct nature of the troop carrier mission, not even during his brief tenure as commander of the Combat Cargo Command in Japan during the Korean War. In his memoir, his focus is on the movement of cargo in large aircraft over long distances. He separates himself from "combat pilots" without acknowledging that the sole purpose of air transport is to support combat squadrons and combat operations. (Tunner, 1964)

Throughout the 1950s, Tunner and other MATS leaders convinced certain members of Congress to hold hearings before which they pled their case and before which other Air Force officers were forced to give their reasons for why airlift consolidation was a bad idea. MATS found an ally in South Carolina Congressman L. Mendel Rivers, who was an influential member of the powerful House Armed Services Committee. Charleston Air Force Base, a MATS base, was in his district. The chairman of the committee, Carl Vinson, was also a strong supporter because his district uncluded Marietta, where Lockheed's Georgia Division was located. Georgia Senator Richard Russell, the chairman of the Senate Armed Services Committee, was sympathetic to MATS. There was a MATS base at Savannah and Lockheed-Georgia, Lockheed's military transport division, had been established in Marietta.

In the early 50s, the primary opponent of the MATS consolidation proponents was the TAC commander, Lt. General John K. Cannon, the same General Cannon who put Tunner in his place during the Berlin Airlift. Cannon retired in 1954 but other able TAC officers took up the challenge including Colonel William W. Momyer, an officer with a long career in tactical operations who was on the TAC staff. Momyer commanded a fighter group engaged in support of ground forces in North Africa then returned to the United States to a position on the staff of the School of Applied Tactics. Few officers were as well-versed on tactical operations as he was. Momyer remained a proponent of a separate tactical airlift force until his retirement in 1974. During the Vietnam War, Momyer saw the benefits of tactical airlift, a term that came into use in 1967, as commander of Seventh Air Force. No other senior Air Force officer has presided over the kind of combat operations that Momyer did. While other senior officers succumbed to lobbying by MATS officers and their successors, Momyer insisted that the tactical mission was completely different from the logistical mission and that the tactical mission required aircrews with different training and a different philosophy. He believed that consolidating the two missions would be a huge mistake.

MATS' position was that air transportation was all the same, and that there should be a single manager to control all Air Force transport assets. TAC's position, which was based on four years of combat experience in World War II and three more in Korea, was that troop carriers were combat personnel (the Army Air Staff had identified them as such in 1942) whose mission was to operate into hostile areas and they needed to maintain a high degree of proficiency and motivation beyond that necessary for routine transport operations. The loss of more than 500 IX Troop Carrier Command crewmembers in less than a year of combat operations while ATC lost less than a dozen during the entire war graphically illustrated the difference. The point was well taken and both Congress and the Air Staff ruled against the airlift consolidation advocates. Although they failed in their goal of consolidation, at least temporarily, the MATS officers and their supporters nevertheless made gains in that direction, particularly the acquisition of all of the Air Force's C-124s.

It is difficult to reconcile the assertions of Tunner and other airlift consolidation advocates when considering their status in World War II and Korea. As a logistical air transport agency, ATC was barred from combat operations and none of its senior officers, many of whom had airline backgrounds, ever participated in them. The only operation remotely connected to combat was the India-China Ferry, and even there ATC crews operated well out of the threat areas. Granted, ATC suffered high losses on the ferry but they were due to accident. ATC only lost seven transports to enemy action in the entire war and they were all on flights over the Hump.[218] MATs lost one C-54 on the ground in Korea on the opening day of the war but after that its operations were only to Japan. Tunner himself is only known to have flown one mission that would be considered a combat mission in his entire career and, in that instance, he was observing an airborne operation with General Douglas MacArthur in MacArthur's command transport. Granted, he commanded the Combat Cargo Command during the most difficult weeks of the Korean War but just how much he and his immediate staff actually contributed is open to question. He was working for two officers, Generals George Stratemeyer and MacArthur, who were at the top of the list when it came to experience commanding air units, including troop carriers, in combat and the units under him were commanded by men with extensive combat experience. His deputy was Col. E. Wade Hampton, whose combat air transport experience went back to the very beginning of World War II.

In many respects, the battle over airlift consolidation was between the Air Force's combat officers and those who had no combat experience or, if they had, it was limited, as Tunner's was. In his memoir, Tunner frequently refers to combat pilots, which is an indication that he felt inferior because of his own limited experience in

---

[218] There was a short period when Japanese fighters operated close enough to the supply routes to threaten it, but their base was quickly neutralized after a flurry of losses, not only to ATC but also to troop carriers and Tenth Air Force bombers.

Anything, Anywhere, Anytime

combat operations. Those who proposed consolidation were mostly men who had served in staff positions in the Air Transport Command during World War II. They had some support from officers such as General Lauris Norstad, whose background was with Twentieth Air Force, on which Tunner and other airlift consolidation advocates based their position that airlift was a "strategic asset" that should be controlled by a single headquarters rather than "operated piecemeal" by a number of headquarters. Tunner and others in favor of consolidation strongly believed that placing troop carrier airlift under theater commanders was inefficient utilization of "valuable assets."

MATS had played a limited role during the Korean War and even then a substantial portion of its missions were flown by the commercial airlines under military contract. The MATS fleet was supplemented by TAC C-54s and C-124s on the Pacific Airlift to Japan. Within the military, MATS was perceived as an airline and was not considered to have any form of combat mission. Since MATS functioned essentially as an airline, the service could be expected to meet its needs for new aircraft by buying "off-the-shelf" commercial transports. MATS had purchased DC-6s, designating them as C-118s, and the Lockheed Super Constellation which became the C-121. But while these airplanes were excellent transport aircraft, they had no military capabilities.

MATS crews, who flew in Class A uniforms and looked like airline crews when carrying passengers, even included female flight attendants. MATS was operating scheduled service throughout the world transporting passengers and military cargo for the US government just as the Air Transport Command had done during World War II. The service had its own system of terminals at various locations in Europe, the Pacific and elsewhere; terminals staffed by MATS personnel. MATS set up its own billeting facilities on airfields that belonged to the overseas commands and had its own support squadrons to service its transports. MATS support squadrons included fleet service personnel who cleaned MATS transports and provided amenities such as meals, coffee, water and blankets for passengers. There was no doubt in the minds of those who flew on them, and thus in the public mind, that MATS really WAS a military airline!

In fact, their perception was entirely correct; MATS had evolved from the Air Transport Command, which had basically been the US airline industry wearing olive drab uniforms and paint. MATS also had a large and active public information office at its headquarters at Scott AFB, Illinois whose job was to publicize MATS. Often, MATS PIOs claimed credit for troop carrier operations. What MATS did not have was a fleet of modern aircraft. At the end of World War II, the Air Staff had established a policy that government funds would not be used to develop non-tactical aircraft, which meant that the military would

Sam McGowan

have to depend on the airline industry to develop logistical transports. The rest of the Air Force had entered the Jet Age but MATS was still flying airplanes that had been designed in the 1940s. When the Korean Conflict ended, there were no new transports under development for MATS use.

WAF flight attendant checks off names on manifest

The only new non-tactical transport under development was the C-133 and it wasn't originally intended for MATS. It had been proposed and sold to Congress as a special purpose transport designed to transport SAC's new ICBMs, which was an Air Material Command function. Douglas was awarded a contract to meet an Air Force requirement for a logistics carrier support system, meaning it was to be designed to provide logistical support to Strategic Air Command's nuclear force, which was in the process of developing an intercontinental missile capability. SAC wanted a transport capable of transporting its new fleet of missiles and MATS would take any transport it could get. There can be little doubt that the C-133s went to MATS due to Tunner's efforts and influence. Tunner, who was vice-commander of the Air Material Command when the C-133 was purchased, was opposed to the concept of intrinsic air transport in Air Force commands. SAC's plans to equip with large land-based missiles created the need for a transport large enough to transport missiles, a

Anything, Anywhere, Anytime

mission that should have been assigned to Air Material Command's logistic support squadrons. Instead of supporting the command to which he was assigned in a leadership position, Tunner advocated for the C-133's assignment to MATS and that is where they went.

Interestingly, MATS had no domestic mission and hadn't since shortly after World War II. During the political wrangling after the war, the transportation industry convinced Congress that it could meet the military's domestic transportation needs through military contracts. Although military transports could carry military passengers, but not on scheduled flights, they were forbidden from transporting non-tactical cargo. A system was set up known throughout the military as Log-Air, for logistical air transportation, that used civilian aircraft operating under contract to the Air Force to transport aircraft parts and other high-value items between military bases. Cargo bound for overseas had to be processed through an aerial port but military aircraft could not be used to get it there. Instead, cargo bound for overseas was transported by commercial rail and truck from Air Material Command depots to MATS aerial ports where it could be loaded on military transports for shipment overseas. For that matter, TAC transports weren't allowed to transport non-tactical cargo and passengers within the confines of the Continental US either, except military personnel traveling as space available passengers.[219] The single exception to the domestic transportation rule was transportation of patients. MATS was allowed to operate scheduled medical flights between military hospitals.

As TAC's troop carrier squadrons received C-130s and the C-124s transferred to MATS, TAC gave the air transport service responsibility for providing some airlift to assist in the deployment of CASFs overseas. Under the terms of the agreement allowing the transfer of TAC's C-124s to MATS, the troop carrier squadrons were to retain their troop carrier identity, with the crews maintaining proficiency in aerial delivery; in the event of war, they were to return to TAC. C-124s and C-133s were to carry outsize cargo too large for C-130 lift. Support functions for combat squadrons included large items such as fuel trucks and large generators that had been designed to provide electrical power in forward areas. Such items were too large to fit into a C-130 and needed C-124 lift, which had previously been provided by TAC's own squadrons. Although most Army vehicles would fit in the cargo compartment of a C-130, there were some that needed a larger transport – if they could be airlifted by air at all. To move such items, TAC could request outsize cargo airlift from MATS. MATS could also be

---

[219] The ability to travel when space was available was considered a benefit for active duty military personnel.

called on to supplement TAC's troop carriers. MATS other transports were tasked to transport personnel and other cargo to supplement TAC's troop carrier squadrons, which at the time was limited to six squadrons in the United States. In 1958, the 322nd Air Division in Europe was just starting to equip with C-130s; PACAF's 315th would start receiving airplanes a few months later.

The new mission provided MATS leaders ammunition to press the Department of Defense and ultimately, Congress, for improvements in the MATS fleet. At the same time, Tunner and other MATS-oriented officers had an agenda – the upgrading of MATS to full command level and the assumption of all military air transport duties. Even though few MATS staff officers had actual combat airlift experience – with the exception of Tunner's brief stint in the Korean Airlift – they considered themselves to be experts in military airlift. Along with the transfer of the C-124s, MATS was given status as the "Single Manager for Airlift" but its responsibilities were only for logistical airlift and did not include deployment, troop transport, or tactical operations. MATS involvement in those operations came through and had to be requested by TAC.[220] MATS had achieved a part of what they wanted but the service was still without a defined military mission.

MATS' role in the deployment of a CASF was to transport fighter squadron support and Army personnel and equipment that TAC's troop carriers couldn't handle; and to carry outsize cargo such as generators, large fuel trucks and other equipment. MATS C-124s and C-133s also provided airlift of larger Army vehicles and tanks. Whether or not MATS was involved in a deployment was dictated by how many personnel were involved and what kind of equipment they had. For example, if C-130s were available, there was no reason to involve MATS in the deployment of airborne forces. MATS' passenger airplanes were sometimes used to move troops, although their primary role was routine air transport of government passengers moving back and forth between overseas assignments.

The transfer of the TAC C-124s to MATS opened the door for the assumption of more military airlift roles, especially the logistical support mission of the Strategic Air Command's transport squadrons, which were equipped with C-124s. AMC had three squadrons, at Hill AFB, Utah, Kelly AFB, Texas and Robins AFB, Georgia. MATS' position, as had been argued since the end of World War II by its leaders, was that all military air transport should be consolidated into a single command and the assets controlled by a single command center that

---

[220] The increase in MATS' responsibilities all came about during the period when Tunner was serving as Deputy Chief of Staff for Operations on the Air Staff. He assumed command of MATS the following year.

Anything, Anywhere, Anytime

would disperse airlift aircraft to "where they were most needed." In their quest for consolidation, MATS would become a highly politicized military service whose leaders would not hesitate to use members of Congress, particularly those with MATS bases in their districts such as South Carolina Congressman Rivers, to press their case. MATS lobbied Congressional leaders, particularly Senate Armed Services Committee chairman Richard Russell of Georgia, for funding for the development of new transports that the Air Force itself did not want and for a specified command for airlift, another idea that was exclusively MATS.

In 1958, Tunner was given command of MATS, which had gained new power and had been designated as "single manager for airlift." He commanded MATS until May 31, 1960, when he retired. During his tenure as MATS commander, he devoted most of his efforts toward bringing his command into the Jet Age. Although aircraft manufacturers were starting to develop new jet transports for the airline industry, the Air Force had not made plans to develop jet transports of its own. In fact, it was not allowed to do so. Air Force policy was that aircraft development was limited to airplanes with true tactical capabilities. Except for C-133s, of which MATS only had a handful when Tunner took command, the service was equipped with reciprocating C-118s, C-121s and C-124s. Tunner made it his personal mission to argue for new transports for MATS. His primary opponent was the President of the United States, who was also the former General of the Army who had commanded ALL Allied troops fighting in the European Theater during World War II and knew far more about war and the military than Tunner.

Tunner and the MATS staff developed a master plan that called for the replacement of its fleet of reciprocating transports with turbine-powered aircraft. MATS sought the development of a "workhorse" jet transport to service the service's system. Tunner wanted a "swing-tail" turboprop transport to supplement the C-133s. He was willing to accept enough C-130Bs to equip several MATS squadrons that were currently flying C-118s and C-121s, including some Navy squadrons. Another option was a transport version of Boeing's new 707 transport. The Air Force had ordered a modified version as the KC-135 to replace SAC's aging KC-97 and KB-50 tankers. Tunner was willing to accept enough of a transport version to equip squadrons on each coast. Nowhere in Tunner's plan did he address the issue of tactical air transportation. He only saw MATS as a strategic organization responsible for the movement of cargo and passengers between the United States and overseas.

When it came to deployment of troops, Tunner's focus was on the movement of troops overseas from the US. He didn't seem to realize that deployment is only the first aspect of military airlift. Except for the C-130s, which he saw as a stopgap measure until a new jet transport could be developed, he wanted large aircraft with transoceanic capabilities. His main arguments were the Air Transport Command role in the India-China Ferry, which he had started calling the Hump Airlift, and the Berlin Airlift, both of which were purely logistical in nature. He would refer to himself as "a troop carrier commander" based on his five months in Japan in 1950-51 in his consolidation arguments. His master plan, however, was focused solely on long-range air transportation operations.

Eisenhower saw the MATS plan to develop its own transports as an unnecessary use of taxpayer funds since none of the proposed transports were suitable for combat applications, unlike the C-130 and KC-135. MATS was not a combat organization and had no wartime duties other than providing logistical support to combat forces. As a Republican, the president believed in making wise use of taxpayer funds and was opposed to what he came to call the "military-industrial complex," an association of senior military officers and the defense industry. (Allegedly, Eisenhower originally referred to the association as the "military-industrial-Congressional complex" but when he referred to it in his farewell address to the nation, he left out the word "Congressional." It is very likely that Eisenhower's comments were prompted by Tunner's association with members of Congress and the aircraft manufacturers.)

When the Eisenhower White House disapproved Tunner's MATS master plan, he decided to retire and turn his efforts toward politics. Although he whitewashed his political role in his memoir, he became an advisor to the presidential campaigns of Senator John F. Kennedy and certain Democrats in Congress, including Senators Richard Russell of Georgia and Henry Jackson of Washington, both of whom were tied to the defense industry, and Congressman L. Mendel Rivers, who had made sure that his district had become a veritable arsenal. River's district was home to several military installations, including a major MATS base.

In his first State of the Union Address on January 30, 1961, the new president said "*I have directed prompt action to increase our airlift capacity. Obtaining additional airlift mobility, and obtaining it now, will better assure the ability of our conventional forces to respond, with discrimination and speed, to any problem at any spot on the globe at any moment's notice. In particular it will enable us to meet any deliberate effort to avoid or divert our forces by starting limited wars in widely scattered parts of the globe.*" Tunner would continue to advise the Kennedy and Johnson White Houses on airlift-related matters. Although he failed to accomplish most of his goals while in uniform, he was able to accomplish them after he retired through political influence. Kennedy's first act as president was to reinstate the MATS master plan Tunner had drawn up, and that his predecessor had rejected, and to request an appropriation to fund the development of a new jet transport for MATS.

While Tunner's influence was directed toward MATS, TAC's troop carrier force benefited. In addition to funding the C-141, Congress also appropriated funds for additional C-130s for TAC. After all, Lockheed's plant was in Georgia, the home state of the chairman of the Senate Armed Forces Committee and just a few miles from the district of the chairman of the House Armed Forces Committee. An additional C-130 wing, the 64th TCW, had activated at Dyess in 1960 when the new B-models started replacing the As at Sewart, but the increased emphasis on rapid deployment led to the authorization of an additional wing and the conversion of the 464th TCW at Pope, although the conversion was placed on hold due to events in Southeast Asia. The 314th at Sewart would be equipped with the longer range C-130E and its B-models would go to the new wing, which replaced an inactivating SAC B-47 wing at Forbes AFB, Kansas.

MATS wasn't the only service grabbing for a piece of the airlift pie in the 1950s and early 60s. Many of the US Army's new leaders, who had been young officers in World War II, remembered the mobility Army air forces troop carrier squadrons had provided their units and they wanted it back. When the Air Force was established as a separate service in 1947, the Army lost all of its airlift assets, except for small liaison aircraft and a few C-47s it was allowed to keep for logistical purposes. In order to use Air Force transports, Army units had to request them through Tactical Air Command. When the Army disapproved the Air Force's plans for troop carrying helicopter squadrons, the decision was politically motivated. It wanted its own air force, and it saw the helicopter as the means of attaining it. Troop carrying helicopters had been developed during the Korean War with the Air Force, Army and Marine Corps all involved but the Army wanted to have its own. At the same time, the Army began looking for its own fixed-wing transport. The Army purchased several civilian light transports, particularly the Beechcraft Travel Air and later the Queen Air, but the service wanted something larger with true troop carrying capabilities. In the late 1950s, the Army contracted with DeHavilland Aircraft of Canada for the purchase of the company's twin-engine Caribou transport, which had been developed for military sales as a battlefield transport. The Caribou was designated by the Army as the CV-2.

Although very slow even by 1950s standards and only capable of carrying an 8,000-pound payload, the Caribou featured short field landing and takeoff capabilities and could operate from unimproved runways that were barely more than clearings in the forest. After all, the airplane was developed by a company that had a history of

Sam McGowan

designing airplanes for bush work in the Canadian wilderness. It had decided to develop a bush plane for military use and presented the concept to the US Army. The Caribou's main deficiencies were lack of range and payload in comparison to other transports, but the airplane was suited for the kind of operations the Army had in mind, or thought they did at the time, which was to deliver troops and cargo to forward areas.

DeHavilland CV-2 Caribou

In 1959, Congress appropriated funds for the Army to order 173 of the DeHavilland transports with deliveries to start in 1961.The Air Force opposed the move on the grounds that the Army was endeavoring to establish a mission that rightly belonged to the Air Force. The Air Staff pointed out that while the Caribou had excellent short-field capabilities, they were no better than those of the C-123 with similar payloads. The Air Force position was that there wasn't a need for such a transport and that it could meet the Army's transport needs. In 1965, events in South Vietnam would confirm the Air Force's argument but by that time the Army had 159 of them in operation. Army aviators saw the Caribou as a vehicle to support the new airmobile forces it planned to develop. Although the new aviation companies would operate mostly helicopters, Caribous would support them by delivering fuel, ammunition and other supplies to forward areas. Events in Southeast Asia would soon prove that while the Caribou was suited for certain types of operations requiring minimum amounts of cargo or a few troops, it was incapable of meeting the Army's air transportation needs in a combat situation.

Anything, Anywhere, Anytime

As far as the Air Force was concerned, its leaders felt the Army did not need the CV-2, or a transport of any kind. After all, airlift and airdrop were Air Force responsibilities that had been established by the law of the land. Both the C-130 and the C-123 were fully capable of meeting the Army's transportation needs as the Air Force saw them. Both airplanes were capable of landing on airstrips much shorter than those required by most civilian twin-engine light planes, and both were airdrop capable. In fact, a C-123 could carry the same load as a Caribou into a similar length landing strip. If the Army needed transport into an existing airstrip that was shorter than the C-123 needed, all they had to do was cut down a few more trees and lengthen it. Furthermore, the CV-2 was severely limited in terms of vehicle carrying capabilities, which were very important in the modern military force. The Caribou's cargo compartment was large enough to carry Jeeps and trailers but was too small to handle a 2 1/2 ton truck. On the other hand, the C-123 and C-130 could transport the equipment needed by a light infantry battalion. The Caribou was airdrop capable but the size of the bundles and platforms was limited. CV-2s could deliver small bundles into confined areas such as Special Forces camps but it took four of them to deliver the load of a single C-130. Ultimately, the Army would go ahead with its purchase of the Caribou but the airplane's service with it would be limited. It turned out that the air mobility proponents underestimated the needs of helicopter-borne forces in combat and overestimated the CV-2 capabilities. At the height of the Vietnam War, all but a handful of the Army's Caribous transferred to the Air Force.

The Caribou was at the center of a controversy over Army and Air Force responsibilities. The Army had also purchased another fixed-wing airplane, the Grumman OV-1 Mohawk, which it planned to use for battlefield reconnaissance. The OV-1 was equipped with infrared sensors and cameras. The Air Force opposed the purchase of the airplane because reconnaissance was an Air Force mission. Furthermore, the Army had put guns on the airplane, which was another source of controversy. The Army also intended to use the Mohawks on resupply missions, using hard points under the wing to attach airdrop bundles. Airdrop was also an Air Force mission.

With the advent of the C-119, the Air Force attained new airdrop capabilities, some of which carried over to the C-123. The C-130 afforded additional heavy drop capabilities, with 25,000 pounds established as the maximum weight for a single airdrop platform; enough to deliver a bulldozer or even a light tank. The future envisioned by Generals Arnold, Brereton and Marshall in 1945 had become reality. Arnold and Marshall did not live to see it but Brereton did. Heavy equipment drops were the primary method of aerial delivery in TAC in the 1950s and early 1960s while containers weighing up to 2,200 pounds were used to deliver items such as rations, ammunition, fuel and water. A single C-130 could deliver up to eighteen of the Army's standard A-22 containers on a single pass. Depending on the platform's size, a C-130 could drop one, two or up to three in rapid succession. Extraction parachutes that had been developed to extract platforms from the C-119 could also be used on the C-130 and C-123. The new Hercules and C-123 could also drop the platforms that had been developed for use on the Flying Boxcar.

TAC C-130B dropping heavy equipment (Frank Gawell collection)
TAC and the Army experimented with new aerial delivery methods with the C-130 then adapted some of them to the C-123. The Ground Proximity Extraction System, or GPES, allowed pinpoint delivery of platforms as the airplane barely skimmed the ground. A hook suspended beneath the airplane's belly snared a steel cable stretched across an open space to extract the load. The GPES method remained in use in TAC until the mid-sixties when it was replaced by LAPES, the low altitude parachute extraction system, which used a parachute to extract the load. LAPES was less accurate, but was less involved because no ground equipment was required. Any generally level clearing long enough for a C-130 to drop down and make a drop was suitable for a drop zone. GPES would be resurrected in Vietnam at the height of the siege of Khe Sanh after several LAPES malfunctions.

A highly accurate airdrop method was developed by 315th Air Division. Two officers in the 815th TCS came up with the method. The Parachute Low Altitude Delivery System, commonly known as PLADS, was designed to deliver a single container from low altitude with

Anything, Anywhere, Anytime

unprecedented accuracy. PLADS used an electric squib to cut a reefing line that prevented the extraction parachute from opening when it was flipped off the top of the load by the loadmasters a few seconds from the drop zone. The squib was connected to the green light and fired when it was activated. The force of the parachute broke a piece of nylon webbing that held the bundle on the airplane ramp and the bundle swung free of the airplane. A properly trained crew could place bundles within twenty-five feet of the designated impact point ninety percent of the time.

The highflying C-130 also allowed airdrops from very high altitudes. With the emergence of the Special Forces within the Army's airborne forces, high altitude, low-opening parachute methods known as HALO became a means of inserting special operations teams behind enemy lines without detection. Soon after the 314th Troop Carrier Wing at Sewart received C-130s, the wing was tasked with developing a method of dropping supplies from 25,000 feet. A crew commanded by Major Bill Blanton went to Edwards Air Force Base to fly test missions using methods he and his navigator had developed themselves. They determined that the best method was to use a radio beacon on the ground to identify the drop zone and to drop as soon as the needle swung. The accuracy requirements were liberal, with the stipulation being that all of the bundles would fall within a one square mile area. The test drops were successful, but high altitude airdrop capabilities would have to wait until more accurate methods could be developed.(Blanton, 1997)

Shortly after the delivery of the first C-130s, the Air Force issued a requirement for a new cargo handling system designated as the 463L System. The contract was issued to AAR Cadillac Manufacturing to develop the system, which would be designed around the C-130 as a complete cargo handling system utilizing aluminum pallets to assemble crates and boxes and secure them with nets for easier loading. The aircraft component of the system was developed by Brooks and Perkins and included a portable system of rails and rollers to install in the C-130 cargo compartment. Although the system was initially designed for the handling of palletized cargo in logistical operations, in the early 1960s the Air Force conducted tests at El Centro, California of an airdrop system that used the 463L dual rails instead of skate wheels, which had been carried over from the C-119. The tests proved the system could be used for airdrop and by the mid-sixties drops using dual rails had become standard.

TAC and the Army worked together to develop new methods of using airlift to insert troops into combat. The primary method was a variation of the original airborne methods of World War II, which was to use paratroops to capture and secure an enemy airfield for troop carrier transports to bring in reinforcements. The tactic developed in

Sam McGowan

the 1950s – which had actually been conceived during World War II – called for paratroops to jump in and secure an area, into which airborne engineers would jump. Their heavy construction equipment would be parachuted in behind them. They would construct an assault landing strip and C-123s would begin bringing in reinforcements as soon as it was serviceable while they continued lengthening the strip to accommodate C-130s.

Prior to the initial assault, an Air Force combat control team would arrive to inspect the area to insure the soil was sufficient for runway construction. The combat control team would arrive either by parachute, on foot, by vehicle or from the sea, depending on the location of the site. Combat controllers were trained in HALO techniques so they could parachute into a drop zone at night, undetected. They would then set up the drop zone for the arriving assault force, along with radio beacons to guide the transports. Combat controllers, who were the heirs to the legacy of the Airborne Pathfinders and troop carrier combat control teams of World War II, were assigned to aerial port squadrons.[221] Since their role was to go in

---

[221] After the advent of GPS and more accurate airdrop methods, the Air Force decided that combat controllers were no longer necessary. To keep the field alive, the Air Force Special Operations Command decided to expand the role of the controllers and combine them with the tactical air control mission and they were assigned to new "special tactics" squadrons. Although the mission had changed to tactical air control, they kept the combat control name.

Anything, Anywhere, Anytime

prior to the assault force, combat controller team personnel were given limited combat training, enough to defend themselves until they could be relieved.

TAC aerial port squadrons were divided into airfreight, aerial delivery, mobility, passenger service and combat control sections and, since they were part of TAC, were ready to be deployed anywhere with little notice. The airfreight section was responsible for receiving and processing cargo for air shipment then loading it on the airplane. Airfreight was also responsible for unloading at the receiving end. Aerial delivery was a special section concerned with the delivery of cargo by parachute, and included cargo and parachute riggers as well as loadmasters, who were often called dropmasters because they were especially trained for airdrop. They were responsible for inspecting loads that had been rigged by Army Quartermasters. Mobility teams were set up to move into the forward airfields to offload cargo from the arriving airplanes and break it down for further delivery by ground vehicles or, after the Army began developing aviation capabilities, by helicopter. Passenger Service processed passengers while the Combat Control Section maintained teams for duty in the field. The arrangement of the aerial port squadrons was similar in MATS, although TAC units were more oriented toward operations in forward areas.

TAC also included a number of aerial evacuation squadrons made up of medical personnel whose role was to deploy to a trouble spot where they would set up an evacuation hospital and manage the evacuation of casualties. AME squadrons included doctors, flight nurses and enlisted medical technicians, most of whom were on flying status. All TAC C-130s were equipped with litter stanchions and straps as part of the airplane's extra equipment. A medical team working with a crew loadmaster or scanner could reconfigure the airplane to carry a full load of litter patients in less than half an hour. Tactical air evac squadrons were responsible for moving patients from forward area airstrips to rear area hospitals.

TAC and – after MATS got TAC's C-124s – MATS crews trained with the Army's airborne forces on a regular basis. Every week, TAC and/or MATS transports flew to Pope AFB, North Carolina and Campbell AAF, Kentucky to drop troops from the 82nd and 101st Airborne Divisions. Air National Guard and Air Force Reserve C-119 units also spent time at the two bases dropping troops and their equipment; Reserve C-119s also supported the US Army jump school at Ft. Benning, Georgia. The airborne training missions served a dual purpose as they provided a means of training both the aircrews and the paratroopers. Frequent TDY was a fact of troop carrier life. In the States, TAC personnel were frequently sent TDY for training and for maneuvers with the Army.

Sam McGowan

As the squadrons became proficient in the new C-130, TDY meant duty overseas as well. TAC C-130 squadrons began regular overseas rotations to Europe and Asia as soon as the squadrons were declared "Combat Ready." By law, military air transport squadrons, whether they were troop carrier or MATS, were prohibited from transporting logistical cargo in the United States, with the exception of nuclear cargo. As previously noted, except for tactical cargo, all air transportation in the US was provided by civilian air carriers operating under contract to the Air Material Command, which became the Air Force Logistics Command in 1961. However, troop carrier units were responsible for logistical operations in both Europe and the Pacific where 322nd and 315th Air Divisions operated scheduled flights. The two overseas divisions were also involved in training. US Army Europe included airborne units and the 173rd Airborne was based on Okinawa. Troop carriers dropped troops on training drops and participated in exercises in addition to flying operational missions, some of which were classified. The United States was engaged in classified operations against the communists in Asia and Europe and troop carriers provided airlift support. 315th Air Division supported *HIGH GEAR*, a project involving the movement of nuclear weapons to forward areas from a Pacific base in the event of a nuclear strike.

Initially, TAC C-130 squadrons were sent on temporary duty to both Ashiya, Japan and Evreux, France to support the 315th and 322nd Air Divisions until they received their own C-130s. Overseas TDY continued even after C-130s were based overseas, with TAC squadrons supplementing the permanently assigned units. Overseas TDY was typically for ninety days, with airplanes and crews rotating on a weekly basis. Although troop carrier missions in the United States were mostly tactical in nature and for training, overseas missions were operational and mostly involved logistical transportation. Some overseas missions involved training of locally based airborne units. During their TDY, TAC personnel were under the operational control of the theater airlift division. Some overseas TDY was in support of military training exercises, which started out with the deployment of US-based troops to an overseas location from which they conducted training operations, often with overseas forces. Some training exercises were with NATO forces in Europe or SEATO forces in Asia.

Troop carrier units overseas began replacing their C-119s and C-123s with C-130s in 1958. The 317th Troop Carrier Wing at Evreux, France was the first overseas unit to receive them. Pilots and other flight and maintenance personnel from the two wings at Sewart and Ardmore received orders to France to serve as the nucleus of the new squadrons. The 317th's airplanes were not the first Hercules in Europe; C-130 squadrons from TAC rotated to France to take up the slack while the men of the 317th transitioned into the Hercules. A second USAFE

Anything, Anywhere, Anytime

unit, the 475th Troop Carrier Wing, operated C-123s but it was inactivated and its personnel transferred into the 317th. A few months after the consolidation of the two wings and equipping with C-130s, 317th headquarters inactivated and the wing's assigned squadrons were placed directly under 322nd Air Division. The wing remained inactive until 1963.

After the wing inactivated, the three troop carrier squadrons, the 39th, 40th and 41st, reported directly to the division, as did the maintenance squadrons, which retained their 317th identity. During the period when the squadrons were under 322nd, they were often the focus of the world's attention as they participated in airlift operations in Africa and Asia. They were sometimes supplemented by TAC rotational squadrons. The wing reactivated in 1963 to command the division's three permanently assigned squadrons while the division controlled the TAC squadrons on rotation to Evreux.

In the Pacific the 483rd Troop Carrier Wing at Ashiya AB, Japan traded its C-119s for C-130s. The 21st TCS had been at Tachikawa Air Base outside Tokyo, but the squadron transferred to Naha AB, Okinawa and equipped with the new jet-prop transports. The 21st provided airplanes for covert operations flown by civilian crews employed by Claire Chennault's former airline, Civil Air Transport, which now belonged to the Central Intelligence Agency. The arrangement would continue with the C-130s. The Air Force deactivated its Air Resupply and Communications Service in the mid-1950s but the mission itself became a troop carrier responsibility. At the time, the principle target for covert operations was Tibet but by 1961, Laos had also become a target for CIA-sponsored covert military operations. Not long after the conversion, the 483rd wing inactivated

Page 348

Sam McGowan

and one of its squadrons, the 817th, moved south to Naha to join the 21st while the second, the 815th, moved to Tachikawa Air Base outside Tokyo. All three squadrons reported directly to 315th Air Division headquarter at Tachikawa. Yet, even though 315th had its own C-130s, TAC squadrons rotated to bases in the Pacific to supplement the permanently assigned troop carrier squadrons.

The covert operations story is interesting. Such operations had actually begun immediately after World War II when the US provided Air Force airplanes to the French for use in Indochina and had continued as the hot war became cold. It is not too much of a stretch to say that they started when the White House authorized former Air Corps Captain Claire Chennault to recruit Army, Navy and Marine fighter pilots and maintenance personnel to work for CAMCO, an American-owned maintenance company in China that served as a cover for the operation. 315th Air Division supported an office at Clark Field in the Philippines that was responsible for providing C-119s that came down from Japan for clandestine airlift operations in Asia. It was this office that coordinated the assignment of the Japan-based C-119s to the French during the French Indochina War and conducted training for the French military and American civilian crews.

The Clark office had originally been part of the Air Resupply and Communications Service, an Air Force organization that was officially assigned to MATS, at least on paper. The ARCS was set up to conduct psychological warfare against nations unfriendly to the United States and drop supplies to insurgents. The service had three wings, one at Mountain Home AFB, Idaho, one at Wheelus AFB, Libya and one at Clark. The Clark wing, the 581st Air Resupply and Communications Wing, commanded the 581st Air Resupply Group at Kadena AB, Okinawa, which operated black B-29s on leaflet and agent resupply missions over China and North Korea. The ARCS disbanded in 1953 and its mission was picked up by 315th and 322nd Air Divisions. A cover story was put out that the unit disbanded due to funding issues and the Air Force discontinued the mission. It merely went underground.

A special unit was set up at Kadena with the innocuous designation of the 1095th Operational Evaluation and Training Group but it was really a front for the CIA and was responsible for providing airlift and other support for covert operations. Although the office was staffed by Air Force personnel, they were on special assignment to the CIA. The 1095th was the successor to the 581st Resupply Group that had once been based at Kadena with black B-29s. The B-29s had been phased out and the new group equipped with C-54s and C-118s but they lacked the performance for the kind of operations necessary in parts of Asia. (The CIA also operated at least one old B-17 that had been part of the OSS during the war. It was flown by European pilots who had been recruited by the CIA for covert operations.(Robbins,

Anything, Anywhere, Anytime

1979)(Kenneth Conboy and Jim Morrison, 2002)) The office depended on 315th Air Division for additional support. While the rest of the 374th TCW flew four-engine C-124s, the 21st TCS operated C-47s and C-54s. When the wing inactivated in 1958, the 21st was assigned to clandestine operations and the C-47s and C-54s were joined by C-119s that came down from Ashiya.(Kenneth Conboy and Jim Morrison, 2002)

As soon as the Air Force started receiving C-130s, the CIA saw them as an ideal vehicle to support its operations in Tibet, where the Agency was supporting insurgents, and the 21st TCS was earmarked to receive them. Tibet activities originally involved the old B-17 and USAF-supplied C-54s and C-118s, but their lack of range and performance led the CIA's Special Activities Division to look for a more capable aircraft type and turned to the new C-130A. Tibetan recruits were first sent to a Pacific island for training. They were then sent to Colorado for airborne and mountain training at Camp Hale, a training camp in the Rockies north of Leadville. The entire operation was classified at the highest levels, not to keep the Chinese from finding out about it, but to keep it from the eyes of the American public and the media.

A young lieutenant aircraft commander, Billie B. Mills, and his crew were sent TDY to Peterson Field, Colorado from Sewart for what they thought was to be a mission to carry Air Force Academy cadets on familiarization rides. Although Mills had spent several years in the Air Force as an enlisted radio operator – he had flown in the Berlin Airlift – and had flown C-119s and C-130s as a copilot at Ardmore, he had just been checked out as an aircraft commander. Apparently, the TMC at Sewart wasn't aware that the mission was anything other than for orientation of the Academy cadets either, since a brand new aircraft commander was given the mission instead of one of the more experienced ACs. Mills and his crew were expecting to spend a few days in Colorado Springs then go back to Sewart. Instead, when they arrived, they were met by men in suits who told them the airplane belonged to them and the crew was to do their bidding. Mills called Sewart and talked to the wing commander, who told him to "do what they tell you, but don't let them kill you."(Mills, 2005)

Lt. Mills and his crew were soon making airdrops in the Rockies, at night, into drop zones marked by signal fires. The personnel they were dropping were Asians, who arrived at the airplane in busses with the windows covered up so no one could see what was inside. They were actually Tibetans who had been spirited out of Tibet and taken to Saipan then to Colorado Springs and on to Camp Hale, an Army camp north of the town of Leadville where the Army conducted mountain training in World War II. Mills and his crew dropped the Tibetans onto drop zones in the mountains around the camp. The CIA men were so impressed with Mills and his crew that they had them temporarily transferred to Japan to train the CAT pilots who would fly USAF C-130s on clandestine missions over Tibet.[222] (Kenneth Conboy and Jim Morrison, 2002) The USAF/CIA/CAT relationship would continue until the 1970s, although by that time CAT had gone bankrupt and the C-130 mission had transferred to Air America. Billie Mills would remain in the Air Force and become a fixture in the C-130 troop carrier mission and the tactical airlift mission that followed it.

Camp Hale, Colorado (Author)

After Mills and his crew trained the CAT crews, an arrangement was made for the 21st TCS to supply the airplanes for CIA use and maintain them. The 21st was in the process of transferring from Tachikawa to Naha and equipping with C-130As. A squadron crew would fly the airplane to Kadena, which lay only twelve miles to the north, and turn it over to the CIA office. Maintenance personnel would begin stripping the Air Force markings off the airplane and replacing the airplane identification placard with a new one with bogus numbers. A bogus number was put on the tail. When the airplane was ready, the CAT crew would fly the airplane to Takhli, Thailand where the CIA had a secret base and the Air Force crew would accompany them as instructors. Once they arrived at Takhli, some of the crew

---

[222] The account of Billie Mills' involvement is chronicled in Conboy and Morrison's book about the operation in Tibet, but the author got the story straight from the horse's mouth. Mills went on to make his mark in the troop carrier and tactical airlift world and retired as a colonel.

Anything, Anywhere, Anytime

would be released to travel to Bangkok to wait until it was time to take the airplane back to Kadena while supervisory personnel remained at Takhli to work with the CIA. Air Force maintenance personnel remained at Takhli to maintain the airplane. Some maintenance personnel flew on missions as cargo kickers. Missions over Tibet continued until at least sometime in 1965.

TAC wings were subject to be deployed at any time, and practice alerts were frequent. To maintain combat ready status, TAC crews were constantly training, which for troop carrier crews meant a steady diet of five-hour local training missions, either at their home base or at Pope or Campbell Army Airfield. The typical troop carrier C-130 crew was made up of three officers, two pilots and a navigator, who were usually men in their twenties to early thirties, an enlisted flight mechanic who had spent at least four years on the flight line as a mechanic before assuming flight status and an enlisted scanner, who was probably a first-term junior airman, who worked on the flight line when not flying. TAC C-123 crews usually consisted of two pilots and a flight mechanic; navigators flew on airdrop missions and overseas deployments. TAC operating procedures called for loadmasters to fly on cargo drops but not on paratroop drops or flights carrying rolling stock or cargo. Loadmasters were assigned to aerial port squadrons and attached to the flying squadrons for flying, but they weren't assigned to crews. Flight mechanics were trained to compute weight and balance and load planning was conducted by terminal personnel. Cargo was loaded by airfreight while Army troops loaded and tied down their vehicles under the supervision of aerial port mobility personnel as their predecessors had done in World War II and Korea.

The history and role of the flight mechanic and loadmaster has become somewhat convoluted over the decades due to changes in the Air Force specialty system. Although there was no requirement for an aerial engineer or flight mechanic on any of the tactical transports, TAC wanted an experienced mechanic to be a member of the crew primarily so they could perform maintenance when the airplane was away from home station. In order to better utilize them, TAC had Lockheed install a seat between the pilots on the C-130 for the flight mechanic to sit and assist the pilots with monitoring of the aircraft systems in flight. There was no seat in the cockpit for C-123 flight mechanics. Originally, each airplane's ground crew chief doubled as a flight mechanic and flew on his airplane as a member of the flight crew whenever it was scheduled to fly. Another member of the ground crew flew as the scanner on C-130s. The arrangement caused problems because the men weren't afforded an opportunity to obtain proper rest between flights. By the early sixties, flight mechanics were no longer assigned to ground crews and maintenance was supervised by a ground crew chief, who was not a flight crewmember even though he might be on flight status because he accompanied the airplane when it was sent on TDY. In 1967, the title was changed to flight engineer and the former flight mechanics were given a new flight engineer Air Force specialty code.

The duties of the loadmaster were to supervise loading and offloading of cargo and to install and operate airdrop equipment in flight. The loadmaster position had originated with the C-124 but spread into other aircraft types when radio operators were phased out. Loadmasters were trained to compute weight and balance and to maintain forms and manifests used in cargo operations. Initially, they had no in-flight duties except on missions involving cargo drops but they gradually assumed additional responsibility in troop carrier squadrons. Loadmasters were originally assigned to aerial port squadrons and attached to troop carrier squadrons for flying but by 1964 loadmasters were assigned to the squadrons and had been given scanner duties and had become permanent crewmembers.

The purpose of all of the constant training for TAC crews was to maintain preparedness and proficiency, to insure that the United States would be able to respond and respond quickly to any threat as it came, and that the aircrews were proficient in the operations they would be called on to perform in combat. For troop carriers, this meant proficiency in airdrop and assault landing techniques. After several years of maintaining a strong nuclear deterrent, the United States was developing an interest in maintaining the peace by responding to small "brushfire" wars as they occurred. There were a number of potential trouble spots all over the globe as many nations were emerging out from under the cloak of European colonialism. As the Fifties turned into the Sixties, new threats were emerging at diverse points throughout the world.

Anything, Anywhere, Anytime

Sam McGowan

Chapter Thirteen - "PUT TO THE TEST"

Loading bridge for earthquake relief in Tunisia

The mission of the US military is to protect the United States against foreign enemies, but the Constitution does not specifically forbid the use of Federal troops to quell domestic disturbances and enforce Federal law. The Army has been used in America for domestic purposes occasionally over the years since George Washington sent troops to Western Pennsylvania to put down the Whiskey Rebellion, and in 1958 President Eisenhower ordered elements of the 101st Airborne Division to Little Rock, Arkansas to maintain order as United States marshals enforced a Supreme Court order integrating the Little Rock school system. The very distasteful mission saw the first operational use of TAC's upgraded troop carrier forces. For the Sewart-based crews, the mission was simple; it involved a short flight to Ft. Campbell to pick up troops and vehicles then another longer leg across West Tennessee and eastern Arkansas to Little Rock. The mission could have been just another training flight. It was not the last time USAF airlift aircraft would be used to send troops to quell domestic disturbances.

While the late 1950s were the beginning of a time of great change within the United States, they were very turbulent in other parts of the world as well. Having yet to meet defeat, the communists were busy throughout the world in their attempt to spread their Marxist doctrine. Political unrest seemed to be the norm in many parts of the world, including parts of the Americas. In May 1958, TAC was called on to airlift the 101st Airborne Division Ready Force to Puerto Rico in response to an international crisis in South America. While on a goodwill mission, Vice President Richard Nixon's motor cavalcade came under attack by a rock-throwing mob of anti-American demonstrators in Caracas, Venezuela. A flight of TAC C-130s was dispatched from Sewart to Ft. Campbell to pick up paratroopers then on to Ramey AFB, Puerto Rico. At Ramey, which was 600 miles from Caracas, the force would be in position for airlift to South America in

Anything, Anywhere, Anytime

the event they were needed to protect the Vice President. While enroute to Ramey, the C-130 formation encountered heavy turbulence that tossed the airplanes around and caused some minor injury among the troops. Fortunately, the violence in Venezuela subsided and the troops returned to Fort Campbell in the same C-130s that brought them down.(Dabney, 1979)

A more serious crisis erupted a few weeks later, this time in the Middle East, and the United States responded by dispatching its first Composite Airstrike Force (CASF) overseas. In mid-July 1958, dissidents assassinated the president of Iraq and political unrest spread throughout the region. Fearful of similar violence in their country, the government of Lebanon asked the United States to intervene. President Eisenhower responded by sending a CASF to Turkey and ordering troops from the 24th Infantry Division in Europe to Lebanon. Within hours, TAC C-130s and MATS C-124s were on their way across the Atlantic with ground personnel and support equipment for TAC fighter and reconnaissance aircraft that were on their way to the region.

While the TAC force was underway, C-119s and C-130s from USAFE's 322nd Air Division were enroute to Turkey and Lebanon with US Army troops from Germany. A Marine amphibious force had been dispatched to the area by sea. The airlifted force arrived in Turkey long before the Marines arrived offshore at Beirut, but were held back so the Marines could be the first to land, according to veterans of the move.(McGowan, 1988)[223] For nearly two weeks, TAC and USAFE transports, with some assistance by MATS C-124s, continued the airlift of troops and cargo to Turkey, where the CASF would be in place for a quick response in the event of an outbreak of violence in the region.

The situation in the Middle East had barely subsided when a new crisis broke out on the other side of the world in the Formosa Straits. Evidently taking advantage of the distraction on the opposite side of the Asian continent, the Chinese Communists increased the intensity of their previously infrequent shelling of Quemoy and Matsu, two small islands lying just off Mainland China which were occupied by Chinese Nationalists. In anticipation of a possible invasion of the islands, the United States dispatched a second CASF overseas, this time across the Pacific. With most of TAC's C-130s still in Europe and the Middle East, MATS transports were called in to airlift the ground echelons of the fighter squadrons. Pacific Air Forces ordered 315th Air Division to begin moving troops to Formosa, or Taiwan.

---

[223] The late Dan Reider, a personal friend of the authors, was a loadmaster in the 5th Aerial Port Squadron at Evreux at the time and described his experiences in detail in a letter to the author in the 1980s. Excerpts were published in The C-130 Hercules, Tactical Airlift Missions, 1956-1975, later published as Trash Haulers.

Sam McGowan

C-130A at Naha, Okinawa during Formosa Crisis (Unknown)

While the TAC CASF was enroute to Formosa and the Philippines, 315th Air Division was busy moving troops from Japan and Okinawa to the island. At the time, a TAC C-130 squadron was deployed to Ashiya where the 483rd TCW was in the process of converting to the C-130A. The TAC airplanes were brought back to the United States from the Middle East, then sent right back out again on missions westbound. The two nearly simultaneous crisis situations on either side of the globe demonstrated the value of highly mobile military quick-reaction teams.[224] They provided solid evidence of the value of airlift and the need for more of it but they also demonstrated that the C-130As lacked the range for rapid mid-Pacific deployments, which prompted TAC to add fighter drop tanks to their wingtips.[225] As they were on the P-80s for which they had been designed, the tanks could be dropped prior to entering hostile airspace so the airplane would be more maneuverable.

A new mission developed for the 314th's 61st Troop Carrier Squadron when the Air Force began building the Defense Early Warning – or DEW – line of radar stations across the top of the world. The Air Force initially equipped several C-47s and C-123s with skis to support the operation, but the difficulties of operating reciprocating engines in the severe Arctic cold caused insurmountable problems. Petroleum engine oil becomes as thick as molasses while the engines become cold-soaked and require extensive preheat to get them

---

[224] In his memoir, *Over the Hump*, MATS commander Gen. William H. Tunner pointed with pride to the Lebanon and Taiwan crises as MATS operations. He made no mention of the much larger role played by TAC and PACAF troop carriers or that MATS was supporting TAC.(Tunner, 1964)

[225] In order to make the long trans-Pacific flights, C-130As required the temporary installation of Benson tanks in the cargo compartment, which reduced payload capacity.

Anything, Anywhere, Anytime

started; that is, if the spark plugs don't frost. The turboprop engines of the C-130 were nearly immune to the effects of cold weather. Turbine engines require only fuel, a good battery and an ignition source. They use synthetic turbine oil, which is much thinner and more thermally stable than the petroleum oil used in reciprocating engines. Because the C-130A was equipped with a Gas Turbine Compressor, all the battery was required for was to provide power to start it, then the GTC-powered Air Turbine Motor could provide electrical power while the GTC itself supplied compressed air for the engine starters. The Air Force realized that the C-130 was the ideal candidate for Arctic operations and contracted with Lockheed for a ski-equipped version. In 1959, the 61st TCS received twelve C-130Ds. Although they were technically a new model because of the modification, they were the same C-130A transports in use with the other troop carrier squadrons but modified with the addition of a set of hydraulically operated skis mounted over the landing gear. As a footnote, the skis on the C-130D are the largest ever mounted on an airplane.

With their ski-equipped C-130Ds, the 61st began deploying to Sondestrom AB, Greenland for duty flying onto the Greenland Ice Cap. Pilots who flew in Greenland describe the missions as the most demanding flying of their career. With no outside navigational aids and few landmarks on the ice, navigation had to be precise. Arctic storms often caused whiteouts, which made landing nearly impossible. When not landing on snow and ice, the 61st crews flew into remote gravel strips in the middle of nowhere – literally! Temperatures were usually well below freezing and often as much as twenty below zero on the Fahrenheit scale. It was in just such conditions that turbine engines proved so superior to reciprocating engines. The C-123 was the last airplane purchased for the Air Force with reciprocating engines.

The success of the ski-equipped C-130s in the Arctic led the Navy to request TAC to lend a hand with their mission at the other end of the world, in Antarctica. Operation *DEEP FREEZE*, the Navy's research mission on the frozen continent, was almost exclusively dependent on air resupply to support its most remote stations. Since its inception, Navy C-47 crews had been responsible for the mission, but they were plagued by the same problems the Air Force C-47s encountered in the Arctic so the Navy asked the Air Force for help. To support *DEEP FREEZE*, the 61st set up operations at Christ Church, New Zealand. From Christ Church, the ski birds flew south to McMurdo Sound, the Navy's main Antarctic base, and from there to the remote bases in the interior of the inhospitable continent. For the TAC crews, flying in the Antarctic was in some ways even more demanding than the DEW Line flights. A flight south to McMurdo from Christ Church meant more than 2,000 miles of flying over water with temperatures well below freezing, where a ditching in the ocean would have meant almost certain death. Navigation had to be precise or an airplane and its crew and passengers would all be lost. The Navy was so impressed with the C-130's performance that it purchased its own C-130Fs, a ski-equipped version of the B-model, which was just entering production. When the 314th equipped with C-130B-models, the ski-equipped Ds transferred to Dyess. The mission transferred to Elmendorf AFB, Alaska in 1964.

In late 1959, the C-130B entered service with TAC. As they received the new B-models, the 463rd and 314th A-models went overseas and to the newly activated 64th TCW at Dyess. In the Pacific, the 483rd inactivated and one squadron moved south to Okinawa and the other went to Tachikawa where 315th Air Division was headquartered. Tachikawa, known as "Tachi" in the Air Force, was also home to the 6th and 22nd Troop Carrier Squadrons, which were equipped with C-124s for heavy-lift operations in the Western Pacific under 315th Air Division operational control. Although the two squadrons had transferred to MATS and were officially assigned to a MATS transport wing that had activated at Tachikawa, their mission did not change. The new wing's mission was to provide outsize cargo capability to 315th Air Division and its C-124s were under the division's control. In Europe, 322nd Air Division's three C-130 squadrons and TAC rotational squadrons provided airlift for the United States Air Forces Europe. Outsize cargo capability was provided by US-based C-124s operating through Chateauroux, France where MATS had an air transport wing. The MATS wing had no airplanes assigned, but controlled transports from the United States.

The transfer of the TAC C-124s to MATS has caused considerable confusion among troop carrier and MATS veterans, particularly those whose military service started afterwards. Although the Eighteenth Air Force inactivated and its C-124 squadrons transferred to MATS, they

Anything, Anywhere, Anytime

retained their troop carrier identity and mission; the transfer was approved by the Air Staff under the condition that they would transfer back to TAC in the event of war. The 62nd and 63rd Troop Carrier Wings retained their troop carrier identity and mission until January 1966, when Military Airlift Command activated and the former MATS units were given "military airlift" designations.

C-130B on dirt strip (Gawell Collection)

In the summer of 1960, 322nd Air Division was ordered to mount another airlift of magnanimous proportions. Belgium had recently granted independence to its African colony in the Congo region and fighting broke out almost immediately between rival factions within the country. At the urging of the United States and Belgium, the United Nations dispatched a peacekeeping force to Africa. While the troops came from other nations, the United States was required to provide airlift. When 322nd got orders to begin the airlift, the division command post immediately began dispatching C-130s from its assigned squadrons and TAC rotational squadrons on duty in France to points as diverse as Ireland, Morocco and Ceylon to pick up troops.

To assist 322nd, the Pentagon directed MATS to provide additional transports for the mission. Assigned to a MATS wing at Chateauroux, France while in the theater, the MATS transports were placed under the operational control of 322nd Air Division for airlift duties from Europe to the Congo. Operation *SAFARI* was quickly expanded as air routes were developed into the Congo from points in France, Sweden, Norway, Libya, Mali, Morocco and Ceylon. MATS public relations officers were quick to seize the opportunity to publicize the MATS role, which was called *NEW TAPE*, and the MATS

PIO-issued news releases were designed to imply that the entire operation was a MATS mission. It was a PR tactic that was encouraged by the MATS staff. General Tunner had just retired after serving as MATS commander, but his influence remained. Even today, articles about the operation, which was identified as Operation *SAFARI* with the MATS portion as *NEW TAPE*, imply that the airlift was solely a MATS operation.

Offloading supplies in Leopoldville

For more than two years, the Congo Airlift continued as USAFE, TAC and MATS transports continued operating into Africa in support of the UN mission. While the MATS transports operated primarily into the Congo from elsewhere, 322nd's C-130s also operated within the former Belgian colony delivering troops and cargo into remote airfields where there were no facilities. Ostensibly, the Congo Airlift was a noncombat operation but some airplanes were occasionally hit by small arms fire. The most dramatic publicized incident of the airlift occurred when members of a MATS C-124 crew from Charleston, South Carolina were dragged from their airplane at Stanleyville by a hostile mob and severely beaten. Only the intervention of a Congolese nurse, who prevailed upon the crowd to let the men go, prevented

Anything, Anywhere, Anytime

disaster.

Flying in Africa was real "bush flying," which required the USAFE crews to operate virtually independently and without supervision, the kind of environment where troop carrier crews thrived. Conversely, MATS personnel were accustomed to extensive support facilities and stringent operational controls, features that did not exist in Africa. Veterans who served with 322nd Air Division remember the MATS crews as frequently complaining about their loads and lack of "proper facilities." There were occasions when MATS crews refused to offload their airplanes at points where there were no aerial port facilities. They took their cargo to airfields where there were facilities even if they were hundreds of miles from the cargo's destination. The cargo would then be offloaded from a C-124 then loaded onto a USAFE or TAC C-130 and delivered to where it was supposed to be.(Hoisington, 1988)

Operations in Africa continued to add to the legacy of the troop carrier squadrons as the 322nd crews demonstrated their resourcefulness in the remote operations. While the crews demonstrated their capabilities by using unorthodox methods to offload their cargo at remote airstrips, 317th Consolidated Aircraft Maintenance Squadron and 317th Field Maintenance Squadron personnel had to make do as well.[226] When one C-130 lost an engine at a remote African airstrip, a maintenance team arrived to discover there was no engine stand available to remove the old engine and hang the new one. The crew taxied the airplane to position the affected engine between two trees, which the maintenance crew used to jury-rig an A-frame and change the engine. (Caidin, The Long Arm of America, 1963)

While 322nd was engaged in a highly publicized airlift in Africa, its counterpart in the Pacific was operating an airlift into another remote Third World nation. In the mountainous kingdom of Laos, communist Pathet Lao forces supported by North Vietnam and the Soviet Union mounted an insurgency against the Royal Laotian government. In March 1958, 315th Air Division C-130s airdropped construction equipment – including two bulldozers – to Lao government forces. The C-130s returned to Japan but several C-119s remained at Bangkok for missions into Laos then eventually shifted to the Laotian capital at Vientiane. Over the next two years, 315th transports continued flying missions into Laos and often flew airdrop missions inside the country.

Although little has been written on the subject, there is reason to believe that 315th aircraft flew missions in support of Chinese troops

---

[226] Although the 317th Headquarters inactivated, the wing's squadrons remained active but reported directly to the commander of 322nd Air Division.

Sam McGowan

operating in the vicinity of the Burma-Chinese border. When Chaing ki Shek's Nationalists were driven out of China, a large number crossed the border into Burma, where American CIA agents began training a secret army in the mountainous region of eastern Burma near the Thai border and close to Laos. The secret Chinese army was supplied by airlift, airlift primarily provided by CAT and Air America. For ten years, from 1951 to 1961, the CIA-sponsored Army raised havoc with Chinese forces in China's Yunnan Province and Burma until a combined Chinese-Burmese operation finally ran them out of Burma. The Kuomintang troops moved into the area around Chaing Mai, Thailand and the CIA set up a new base there. It's been alleged that USAF C-130s flew clandestine missions in support of these troops.(Robbins, 1979)

Another Asian region where 315th crews, and possibly some from the 322nd as well, flew clandestine missions was the high mountainous kingdom of Tibet. After their victory over the Nationalists, Chinese troops moved into Tibet, a kingdom that was part of China but politically and culturally distinct from the rest of the country. For centuries, Tibet managed to maintain its independence from the rest of China, in part because the region bordered India and partly because of its remote location in the high Himalaya. When the Chinese Communists decided to bring Tibet under their rule and occupied the region in 1950, many Tibetans rebelled and began an insurgency against the Chinese-sponsored government. The full extent of the American effort in Tibet is not fully known because it was conducted primarily as a clandestine operation run by the CIA and details of the operation have only recently been revealed. Airdrop missions to insurgents in Tibet occurred with regularity through the 1950s and into the 1960s.(Kenneth Conboy and Jim Morrison, 2002)

Once again, CAT and Air America crews flew most of the missions in company transports but the advent of the C-130 provided new capabilities not available with Air America's B-17, C-46s and C-54s. Men who served in the Okinawa-based C-130 squadrons in the late 1950s and early 1960s were bound by oath not to reveal their participation in classified activities and most refuse to this day to talk about what they did over there, except in very general terms, and many have gone to their graves without ever discussing what they did. It is known that classified missions were a regular part of C-130 activities in the Pacific from the beginning of the airplane's use there. Some crewmembers have revealed that they flew low-level, night airdrops in undisclosed locations after taking off from airfields in South Vietnam and Thailand.(McGowan, 1988)

US Air Force direct involvement in the insurgency operations in Tibet commenced with the assignment of a single C-130 from Sewart AFB, Tennessee to Peterson Field, Colorado in 1958 to drop Tibetan

Anything, Anywhere, Anytime

guerrilla recruits into secret drop zones in the mountains at Camp Hale, Colorado. The Tibetans had been flown to Colorado from a CIA base on a Pacific island (Kwajalein), where they had been sent for training. To conceal the US role in the insurgency effort, the CIA came up with a plan under which the Air Force would provide C-130s and civilian contract crews would fly them on missions over Tibet. The pilots, who were trained by Lt. Billie Mills and his crew from Sewart, were employed by Civil Air Transport and based in Japan at Tachikawa. They were all veteran transport pilots, some of whom dated back to the China National Airways Corporation days. Most were combat veterans of service in World War II and Korea.

The airplanes used in the operation came from the 21st Troop Carrier Squadron, which transferred from Tachikawa to Naha AB, Okinawa just prior to receiving C-130s. Operations over Tibet were conducted from what was then a secret CIA base at Takhli, Thailand, a town a little over a hundred miles northeast of Bangkok. (Trest, 2000) Air Force crews flew the airplanes the short distance from Naha to Kadena, where the CIA maintained an office staffed with Air Force personnel whose role was to coordinate CIA operations with 315th Air Division. Prior to gaining access to the C-130s, the office, which was officially organized as an Air Force test squadron, used its own WW II vintage C-54s and C-118. The CIA also used an old B-17 for some missions.(Kenneth Conboy and Jim Morrison, 2002)

While the role of troop carrier squadrons in Burma and Tibet is sketchy at best, their role in Laos has been chronicled in the public domain. In 1961, President John F. Kennedy took office and immediately made clear his support of overt and clandestine operations in support of the Royalist forces in Laos. Shortly after the president took office, the CIA-sponsored Bay of Pigs Invasion turned into disaster. It was perhaps because of this failure that Kennedy became somewhat overzealous in his efforts to thwart communist takeovers of other Third World countries. Kennedy enthusiastically authorized the continuation of CIA activities in Laos, including the airlift of supplies to Royalist forces. While Air America was heavily involved in air transport in Laos with its C-47s, C-46s and C-123s (which had come from the Air Force), President Kennedy authorized the use of 315th C-130s there as well when the need arose.

Kennedy did something else. The president, who was attracted to the idea of clandestine warfare, authorized a covert C-130 mission whereby the Air Force would provide "on loan" four C-130s for CIA missions into Laos. A special flight, made up of highly qualified instructor personnel, was set up within the 21st TCS at Naha and designated as "E-Flight." A contingent of maintenance personnel was transferred to the flight to maintain the airplanes when they were on missions.[227] The entire operation was classified, but no more so than certain other Naha activities. Beginning in late 1961, E-Flight became responsible for ferrying it's specifically funded C-130s to Takhli Airfield in Thailand, where the airplanes were turned over to the CIA for flights into and over Laos with contract crews from Air America at the controls.(Bowers, 1986)[228]

Another development in Laos was the establishment of an unconventional warfare mission under the direction of Major Harry C. Aderholt, the commander of the CIA liaison detachment on Okinawa. "Heinie" Aderholt, who had been a member of the 21st TCS during the Korean War, directed the establishment of a number of airfields and airstrips in Laos for use by transports of sizes ranging from the C-130 down to the tiny U-10 Heliocourier single engine utility airplane.[229] The airstrips, some of which were little more than jungle clearings, were designated as "Lima Sites." Aderholt was also responsible for the C-130 operation. He once told the author that he was the "customer" for E Flight's services but the unit had no direct connection to him.[230] President Kennedy authorized the CIA to recruit and train an army of 200,000 Meo, or Hmong, tribesmen from the mountains of northern Laos to fight the Pathet Lao and North Vietnamese who were rapidly taking over the eastern half of the country. Airlift, in the form of clandestine operations by both military and pseudo-military or paramilitary resources, would be required to keep the Meo supplied.

The war in Laos "ended" in 1962 when a new set of Geneva Accords called for the withdrawal of "all foreign troops" from the tiny mountain country. Both the United States and the Soviet Union officially withdrew their advisors and ceased overt military operations, but the North Vietnamese did not. Several thousand North Vietnamese troops remained in Laos, where they established infiltration routes to move supplies and personnel south to support

---

[227] The rest of the C-130s at Naha were assigned to the 51st Fighter Interceptor Wing under USAF policy at the time of assigning all aircraft on a base to the host unit. C-130 maintenance personnel were assigned to the fighter wing's maintenance squadrons. Men assigned to the E Flight mission transferred out of the 51st FIW to the 21st Troop Carrier Squadron.

[228] In his account of US airlift activities in Southeast Asia, Col. Bowers does not acknowledge the connection between E Flight and the already existing arrangement between 315th Air Division and the CIA for the Tibetan operation, which was still largely classified at the time of his writing.

[229] In the Mel Gibson movie "Air America," a Pilatus P-6 *Porter* is featured and represented as a Heliocourier. The Air Force did purchase a number of Porters and gave them the designation U-23, and some were used in Laos but the U-10 was the primary STOL airplane used by Air America and the Air Force.

[230] Gen. Aderholt also told the author that there was a similar operation in Europe, one that has never received the publicity E Flight has.

Anything, Anywhere, Anytime

their own efforts in adjacent South Vietnam.(Bowers, 1986) The United States began what at first were covert operations to oppose them.

Brig. Gen. Harry C. "Heinie" Aderholt

With the Laotian Civil War having ended and the country having declared itself as a "neutral" nation, US activities in Laos were conducted deep underground and were not publically acknowledged at any level. US military personnel were not allowed in the country, so the CIA Air America operation became even more important than it had been. President Kennedy had already authorized the mechanism that would allow the CIA to deliver supplies to a secret air base in Central Laos at a place called Long Teing, where the Agency had established a headquarters for Laotian Lt. Col. Vang Pao, who was from the Hmong tribe. Vang Pao recruited his own army from the Hmong people, an army supported completely by the US Central Intelligence Agency. The E Flight C-130s were used to ferry supplies into Long Teing and from there smaller Air America transports and helicopters redistributed the cargo. As the "secret war" intensified, the C-130s were used for other things, particularly airdropping supplies to Meo units in the field. While the pilots and flight mechanics were CAT employees, the "kickers", some of them at least, were employed by

Intermountain Airways, a US company that provided smoke jumpers for the US Forest Service.[231] In early April 1964, a USAF special warfare unit equipped with four modified T-28 trainers began operating out of Udorn, Thailand as Project WATER PUMP. Flare support of the WATER PUMP T-28s and Navy and Air Force fighters that started flying missions over Laos a few weeks later became a Naha C-130 mission.[232]

The late 1950s and early 1960s were an exciting time for personnel in Air Force troop carrier squadrons, but their constant on-the-go life caused severe strain on the personal lives of the married men, who were often separated from their families for several months out of the year. It was said that all a troop carrier crewmember had to do to learn where he would be going next was read the morning newspaper or watch the 6 O'clock News. The United States had come to rely heavily on airlift, particularly C-130s, to further its aims throughout the world. By the early 1960s, the C-130 had become "an instrument of national policy," in the words of author and former Air Force intelligence specialist Martin Caidin. (Caidin, The Long Arm of America, 1963)

It was not just international political and military events that resulted in troop carrier deployments. Natural disaster and simple goodwill efforts often called for troop carrier participation. Earthquakes in the Mediterranean brought disaster relief in the form of C-130s loaded with tents and medical supplies, while famine in Africa necessitated the airlift of food for the hungry. International good-will missions sent TAC, PACAF, USAFE and MATS crews to undeveloped regions parts of the world with construction equipment to build roads and airstrips. While most overseas flying was operational, whenever a troop carrier crew returned to their home base, they soon found themselves on the training schedule. Official policy was for crewmembers to have one hour off for every 72 hours they were gone from home base, but that was only up to a maximum of 72 hours. Unless a crewmember took leave, he was back on duty 72 from the time he finished up his crew day on his return from TDY.

TAC's worldwide mission required that crewmembers be "combat ready" at all times, which for troop carrier crews meant maintaining proficiency in airdrop and short field landing skills. Daily training flights were scheduled at troop carrier bases. For TAC C-123 crews, missions were primarily of a training nature since the smaller

---

[231] Intermountain, like Air America, was a CIA front company.
[232] Crews from the 815th in Japan also participated in the missions, but due to Japanese constitutional issues, they were sent TDY to Naha for duty with the 6315th Operations Group and sent on missions from there.

Anything, Anywhere, Anytime

airplane lacked the range for overwater airlift. Many C-123s were assigned to Air Force Reserve squadrons after only a few years service when their active duty squadrons equipped with C-130s. Those squadrons were called up during the Cuban Missile Crisis in 1962, and some of the personnel remained on active duty along with their airplanes. They transferred to Pope to form a new squadron. By 1961, only one active duty wing was still equipped with C-123s, the 464th Troop Carrier Wing (Assault) at Pope AFB, North Carolina, although a single squadron remained at Sewart AFB, Tennessee. Most of the events of the 1950s and early 1960s were largely precautionary and generally peaceful, but it was only a matter of time before TAC and PACAF troop carrier squadrons would find themselves in "harm's way", in the words of Admiral John Paul Jones. To their surprise, C-123 crews would soon find themselves in a combat zone.

Sam McGowan

Chapter Fourteen - "Farmers, Cowboys, Mule Skinners and the Dirty Thirty"

MULE TRAIN C-123 in Vietnam

Throughout the 1950s and very early 1960s, USAF troop carrier crews came perilously close to war many times but never actually engaged in combat. Perhaps the closest was when a squadron of TAC transports was loaded with supplies for the beleaguered Cuban freedom fighters who landed at the Bay of Pigs in early 1961. Ever afterwards, there were bitter feelings among many TAC troop carriers toward President Kenney for his decision to cancel the airdrops that would have allowed the Cuban volunteers on the beach to continue as an effective fighting force.[233] The young president was determined to maintain the appearance of an operation planned and carried out entirely by Cuban refugees without US support. Had USAF transports been used to drop supplies or US fighters had provided close air support for the invaders, the US government role would have lost its covert status and the "plausible deniability" that went with it. It was a decision Kennedy agonized over for the rest of his short life, a decision that influenced his later focus on counterinsurgency efforts elsewhere. Within a year after the failure at the Bay of Pigs, the president ordered the Air Force to begin operations in support of South Vietnamese forces in Southeast Asia, thus paving the way for the huge military effort that was to come over the succeeding decade and a half.

Kennedy supporters often claim that it was Eisenhower, not

---

[233] One of the primary reasons the Bay of Pigs operation failed was because a supply ship loaded with ammunition was sunk by a rocket-firing Cuban air force fighter.

Anything, Anywhere, Anytime

Kennedy, who began US involvement in South Vietnam. However, while the Eisenhower Administration sent military advisors to South Vietnam, they were only there to assist the South Vietnamese military in training – and South Vietnam was but one of dozens of countries that had US military advisors. It is true that Americans were killed in South Vietnam before Kennedy became president, but they were not engaged in combat activities when they were killed by insurgents. Kennedy dispatched 400 of his new Special Forces advisors to South Vietnam in May 1961, thus beginning America's role in the conflict between South Vietnam and North Vietnam-supported communist insurgents. Their first commander, Col. Ben King, had been an air commando in World War II and he decided to call his new unit "air commandos."

Among the first USAF personnel to go to Vietnam was a small detachment of transport crewmen who claimed descendancy from the World War II air commandos who flew in Burma almost twenty years before. Ironically, the airlifters of Project *FARM GATE* were flying the same airplane the World War II air commandoes had used, the venerable and versatile Douglas C-47. Even while TAC was upgrading its airlift capability with the turboprop C-130, the command was also in the process of developing a counterinsurgency capability along the lines of the advisory program of the US Army's Special Forces. The purpose of the new force was to advise foreign air forces so it was made up of experienced officers and enlisted men, all of whom were capable of providing instruction to their foreign counterparts. Because foreign military services mostly operated surplus World War airplanes, the Air Force counterinsurgency forces were equipped with piston-powered attack and transport aircraft similar to those in use by the military services of most of the Third World nations.

The C-47 and A-26 attack bomber that were the backbone of the force were World War II veterans and had seen service in Korea. Only the T-28, a trainer that had been converted to the attack role, was a postwar product. The flight line at Hurlburt Field, Florida where the air commandos were headquartered, looked liked the set for a World War II movie. Although they were actually of 1960's vintage, the USAF air commandos claimed the heritage of the 1st, 2nd and 3rd Air Commando Groups of World War II even though their missions were not even similar. The original air commandos had been activated in India and Florida in early 1944 and operated in the CBI in support of Allied forces in Burma with a third group active in the Southwest Pacific. Conceived to support a British special force in Burma, after the operation was over, the original air commando units were rolled into the theater air forces then were inactivated when the war ended. Their successors two decades later inherited nothing but the name.

While the World War II air commando's were established to

support gliderborne operations in enemy-held territory, the 1960s air commandos were trained to be advisors to Third World military forces and conduct counterinsurgency operations. They came about as a direct result of President Kennedy's fascination with clandestine warfare and his desire to respond to Soviet Premier Nikita Khrushchev's threat to "bury" the free nations of the world. On February 1, 1961, just a few days after his inauguration, the president directed his Secretary of Defense, Robert McNamara, to study ways to combat insurgencies in the Third World and to develop an American counterinsurgency force of its own. McNamara, who had come to government from his position as the head of Ford Motor Company[234], passed the matter to the Joint Chiefs of Staff with the admonition that the development of a US counterinsurgency force was critical for the defense of the Free World.

"Counterinsurgency," commonly referred to as COIN, became the buzz word in early 1960s military circles and was applied to all US military efforts to aid foreign governments in Third World countries, many of which saw little, if any, participation by the Hurlburt Field-based 1st Air Commando Wing. Kennedy and McNamara were attracted to the idea of counterinsurgency forces because they were cheap and held promise for clandestine activities conducted away from the prying eyes of the press since they would involve military personnel of the affected nation and US personnel could claim to be there strictly in an advisory role. Special forces are typically made up of volunteers, military professionals who can be trusted to keep mum about their activities.[235] Because such forces would be working with Third World governments whose militaries were equipped with World War II surplus equipment, no expensive military equipment was required and no money had to be appropriated by Congress for new purchases. The airplanes most useful in such operations had been bought by the American taxpayer two decades before, which kept budgetary costs to a minimum. Operational costs were mainly

---

[234] McNamara was often disparaged by some in the military because he was a civilian, but he actually had a military background. In World War II he had served with the Army Air Forces as an analyst and had risen to the rank of lieutenant colonel. His military assignment was evaluation of the effectiveness of B-29 operations against Japan.

[235] In a note of irony, the Army term "special forces" was so similar to the existing term "special services" that they were often confused, much to the chagrin of the military "special operators". Special services in the US military is a term dating back to World War II that was applied to units whose mission was to entertain the troops and operate service clubs. In the British military, "special services" were highly-trained units formed to carry out missions beyond the scope of normal combat operations. The most famous British unit is the Special Air Service or SAS.

personnel-related. Counterinsurgency operations, since they were conducted in remote parts of the world, lacked the political risk of overt military intervention. Since appropriations were minimal, no Congressional oversight was required.

The Air Force had developed an unconventional warfare force after World War II in the form of air resupply and communications wings equipped with a variety of aircraft, but particularly with B-29s. Their role was to insert and resupply US-recruited agents operating in communist-controlled territory in both Europe and Asia. After the Korean War, these units were reduced and were finally deactivated in 1957 and the classified mission passed to conventional troop carrier squadrons. Both 315th and 322nd Air Divisions were involved in such operations, but the focus in the 1960s was on Asia. In response to the president's directives, the Air Force looked at the examples of British efforts in Malaysia and the French wars in Indochina and Algeria. The British concluded that air transport was the most important contribution of the Royal Air Force in Malaysia. Consequently, the Air Force determined that airlift would be a major part of the service's new counterinsurgency role.

On April 14, 1961, the Air Force activated the 4400th Combat Crew Training Squadron at Hurlburt, Auxiliary Field # 9 of the huge Eglin Air Force Base complex at Ft. Walton Beach, Florida. The squadron formed the nucleus of what would later become the 1st Air Commando Wing. Code-named *JUNGLE JIM*, the mission of the 4400th CCTS was to train aircrews and ground personnel for flight operations against insurgents in a friendly country in either an overt or covert role. Personnel for the program were drawn from volunteers from the Air Force at large who answered the call for rugged duty with a special unit. Men assigned to the unit's airlift section were trained to operate and maintain the C-46 and C-47 since they were the airplanes most likely to be used by Third World nations. The squadron also included armed T-28s and A-26s. When the 1st Air Commando Wing activated, the C-47s were assigned to the 319th Troop Carrier Squadron, a new unit that activated at Hurlburt with the designation of the squadron that served with the original 1st Air Commando Group in India. Throughout the summer of 1961, *JUNGLE JIM* personnel endured a tough regimen designed to turn them into self-reliant, highly versatile airmen who were equally proficient performing technical and aircrew duties or engaging in limited combat on the ground.[236] Each man was also expected to be able to provide instructions to their foreign counterparts. Training in foreign languages, particularly Spanish and

---

[236] Modern military personnel like to refer to themselves as "warriors" but such a term was not commonly used until long after Vietnam, and anyone in the Air Force who used it would have been considered pretentious.

Sam McGowan

French, was part of the curriculum, along with hand-to-hand combat and the use of infantry weapons. *JUNGLE JIM* personnel were expected to be able to take care of themselves in adverse situations. Each man also completed paratrooper training, although there really was no airborne role for the Air Force personnel except for members of the troop carrier section combat control team. Flight training emphasized operations into hostile territory to supply friendly forces operating in remote areas.

When Army Special Forces adopted jaunty green berets for their special headgear, their Air Force counterparts adopted the Australian-style bush hat but it was only authorized for wear with the fatigue uniform. The new air commandos – the 4400th CCTS was redesignated as the 1st Air Commando Wing in 1963 – also wore their heavily starched fatigue pants bloused over their boots, although this was not uncommon throughout the Air Force in the 1960s, particularly in Tactical Air Command. In fact, beginning in 1963, all TAC personnel were required to maintain one set of fatigues to be worn with bloused boots and blue scarves when engaged in mobility operations with Army personnel.

Speaker mounted in SC-47 door

In October 1961, President Kennedy ordered the deployment of an Air Force advisory team to South Vietnam. Project *FARM GATE* was dispatched to South Vietnam to train local military personnel in counterinsurgency tactics but it wouldn't be long before the unit's aircrews were flying operational missions themselves. Included among the project's sixteen airplanes were four modified SC-47s, the "S" designation indicating that they had been modified for "special"

Anything, Anywhere, Anytime

purposes. The four airplanes flew from Florida to South Vietnam where they arrived at Bien Hoa Air Base in early November. As soon as they arrived, the SC-47s went to work dropping flares and propaganda leaflets, broadcasting propaganda messages on their internal speakers and flying air transport missions.

FARM GATE was the first of a number of deployments that steadily increased the USAF role in Southeast Asia. Within a month, *FARM GATE* was joined by a flight of six C-123s equipped with spray equipment that deployed from Clark Field in the Philippines as Project *RANCH HAND*.[237] The *RANCH HAND* mission was to spray defoliants along key roadways and railways to eradicate possible ambush spots. It wasn't long after that before a contingent of American pilots arrived for duty flying with the Vietnamese. Within two months after the arrival of the *FARM GATE* C-47s, conventional USAF troop carrier units were flying missions in Vietnam in C-123s.

While the *FARM GATE* crews went to Vietnam to train the South Vietnamese military, their role quickly expanded to include flight operations. The airlift element was assigned to support the South Vietnamese military by providing airlift, aerial resupply, airdrop of Vietnamese paratroops, intelligence gathering, psychological warfare and "other missions as required." A major airlift responsibility was the resupply of some two dozen remote bases along the Cambodian and Laotian borders. To maintain their advisory status, a requirement was established that a South Vietnamese air force (VNAF) crewmember had to be aboard each flight. While the stated purpose was for "receiving combat or combat support training," the real reason the South Vietnamese were aboard was to camouflage the operational nature of the mission. The American markings on the planes were replaced with South Vietnamese air force identification to further camouflage their identity and purpose. Although the insurgents were poorly armed in 1962, the air commando flight crews were occasionally exposed to ground fire. In early February 1962, a SC-47 crashed near Bao Loc and burned. The eight Americans and one Vietnamese aboard were all killed. No reason for the crash was ever determined, but hostile fire was suspected as a possible cause.[238] When it crashed, the airplane was flying at low altitude through a valley in clear weather.

---

[237] The RANCH HAND crews had evidently come from the 464th TCW at Pope – details are sketchy as to just where they came from. Reportedly, TAC began modifying the airplanes in November 1961 and deployed them to Clark, and from there to Tan Son Nhut.

[238] If there was no readily apparent cause for a crash in Vietnam, it was attributed to hostile fire.

Sam McGowan

The *RANCH HAND* C-123s began operations in early 1962. They flew nearly daily missions throughout South Vietnam dispensing liquid defoliants designed to rid the country's road systems of the natural camouflage provided by the dense forests of the country. The spray missions involved flying at very low altitudes over hostile territory in an environment that invited small arms fire. One airplane was hit so many times that the crews gave it the nickname *Patches* because of the numerous sheet metal repairs to the aluminum skin. The spray missions continued for most of the war, as the crews flew missions that were considered invaluable by the troops on the ground at the time, although they have since become controversial as the debate over the use of herbicides, particularly one identified as Agent Orange, continues.[239] A *RANCH HAND* airplane was the first casualty of the war when a crew flew into the ground while on a spray mission only days before the SC-47 was (possibly) shot down.[240]

---

[239] Although Agent Orange is the agent commonly associated with RANCH HAND, several different agents were actually used. The 55-gallon defoliants were identified with colored bands painted around the middle, with each color identifying the manufacturer. At some point, some Army personnel saw some of the barrels with the orange bands and when the Vietnam Veterans Against the War movement began associating certain medical maladies with defoliants, they identified Agent Orange, which was manufactured by Dow Chemical, as the chemical.

[240] As the war continued and more and more aircraft were lost, the Air Force adopted an unofficial policy of attributing unexplained aircraft losses to "possible ground fire." Since the war, as crash sites have been excavated, many of the reported combat losses have been found to have been due to other causes, particularly flying into the ground, what is now commonly known in aviation as Controlled Flight Into Terrain, or CFIT.

Anything, Anywhere, Anytime

In April 1962, the Air Force sent thirty USAF pilots to Vietnam to fly missions with the South Vietnamese air force. The Vietnamese 1st Air Transport Group included two squadrons of C-47s, but experienced pilots were in short supply in the VNAF attack squadrons and some of the more experienced transport pilots, including the flamboyant Lt. Col. Nguyen Cao Ky, transferred to the attack squadrons, which had been equipped with Douglas A-1s. The American pilots arrived to replace the Vietnamese pilots. The "Dirty Thirty," as the men soon began referring to themselves, were to fly as copilots on Vietnamese crews. At first, the Americans were resentful of their role as copilots and dubious of the qualifications of the VNAF pilots, but a few weeks of flying led to an appreciation of the skills of the Vietnamese, many of whom had years of experience flying in their native land.

Vietnamese Air Force C-47s in formation

For the "Dirty Thirty," the exchange resulted in an exposure to a different culture, including different attitudes toward flying safety. The Americans had been fed a steady diet of flying safety while the Vietnamese adopted an attitude more along the lines of *Laize Faire*. American pilots were trained to fly instruments when possible, but the Vietnamese preferred to remain visual at all times, which often meant dropping down to low altitudes to avoid flying through clouds. Even though the Vietnamese procedures were unorthodox to the Americans, they worked. Still, the Vietnamese practice of putting a cardboard panel in the windshield to block the sun tended to unnerve the Americans!(Bowers, 1986) Two groups of pilots flew with the South Vietnamese before the program was discontinued.

Sam McGowan

While the *FARM GATE* force was advisory and The Dirty Thirty were augmentees, the men of Project *MULE TRAIN* were conventional TAC troop carrier crews. *MULE TRAIN* was made up of crews and support personnel from the 464th Troop Carrier Wing at Pope AFB, North Carolina, the only TAC wing still flying C-123s, although there was still one C-123 squadron, the 345th TCS, at Sewart at the time. The C-123 had been selected for assignment to Vietnam after a panel in Saigon chaired by British counterinsurgency expert Robert Thompson placed a lack of sufficient air transport at the top of a list of Vietnamese deficiencies.

The Army wanted to send its CV-2 Caribous to Vietnam to test their new airmobile ideas and pressed hard for the assignment, but the C-123 was selected because of its excellent short field landing capabilities and superior payload capacity. Undaunted, the Army managed to introduce the Caribou to Southeast Asia by coming in through the back door and stationing some in Thailand "for test purposes." In truth, the C-123 was the wiser choice. Although the Caribou was an excellent airplane for short field work, they lacked adequate payload capabilities and were unsuited for the kind of operation necessary in South Vietnam. Furthermore, although the Caribou had better short field performance when both airplanes were loaded to maximum gross weight, a C-123 could carry the same load into the same length field. At max gross weight, the C-123's payload was three times that of a Caribou. The C-123's reversible propellers made it better suited to operations on wet runways.

TAC notified the 464th to prepare a squadron for extended TDY in the Pacific and the 346th Troop Carrier Squadron was chosen for the move. Loadmasters transferred into the squadron from the 3rd Aerial

Anything, Anywhere, Anytime

Port Squadron. The *MULE TRAIN* mission left Pope in early December 1961 for the flight to Clark Field. Each airplane was equipped with Benson tanks for the long overwater flight from California to the Philippines. After two weeks at Clark for theater orientation, the first C-123s moved on to Tan Son Nhut Airfield outside Saigon where they arrived on January 2, 1962 less than two months after the *FARM GATE* transports. The following day, they flew the first conventional airlift mission of the Vietnam War.[241] Unlike the *FARM GATE* C-47 crews, the C-123 crews were not in Vietnam as advisors; their mission was to provide airlift for the Vietnamese military and no South Vietnamese personnel accompanied the missions. Their primary mission was tactical airlift support for the Vietnamese, with logistical airlift a secondary responsibility, but it wasn't long before the logistical mission had become the larger of the two.

In the late summer of 1962, four U-10 Heliocourier light single-engine transports arrived in South Vietnam. The U-10s were able to land on very short airstrips and were ideal for carrying emergency supplies into Special Forces camps, especially when the landing strips were too short for C-47s and C-123s. The tiny airplanes were well suited for a number of special tasks. Emergency medical evacuation became a U-10 responsibility and Air Force U-10s sometimes evacuated casualties after US Army helicopter crews had refused the mission. In one instance, a U-10 pilot landed at a camp at night, during a battle, to bring out a captured Viet Cong officer for immediate interrogation.

Support of remote camps was an important airlift responsibility from the beginning of the war. Initially, the role was a C-47 responsibility but it was eventually assumed by the C-123 force, then later in the war by US Air Force Caribous. The camps were located in very remote areas, often in mountainous regions where obstacles made flying even more hazardous than it already was. Flying in Vietnam was made even more difficult by the low ceilings and reduced visibilities that prevailed in the northern third of the country during the winter and early spring months when easterly winds brought moisture in from the South China Sea and created an upslope condition. Supplies were airdropped to camps where no runway existed, or when the combat situation ruled out landings. A single C-47 could airdrop up to a dozen 200-pound bundles on a single pass. The larger C-123 could drop heavier bundles or platforms when they were needed. Because the drop zones were usually minuscule, multiple passes were frequently required, which meant an increased exposure

---

[241] This statement perhaps should be qualified since 315th Air Division had been operating in South Vietnam since the French Indochina War, although most of its missions were logistical.

Sam McGowan

to ground fire. At that point in the war, ground fire consisted exclusively of small arms. There was often high terrain around the drop zones, which compounded the problem. Pilots frequently had to fly dangerously close to ridges that were higher than they were while making their drops in the mountainous regions of the country.

To compensate for poor weather and other conditions, the crews learned to improvise. One C-47 crew found the Special Forces camp where they were supposed to drop their load obscured by fog. For more than two hours, the airplane circled over the general vicinity of the camp as the crew looked in vain for a familiar landmark. Nor were they able to make contact with the camp. Finally, a flare shot up out of the clouds beneath them. The crew marked the position and circled back toward the smoke. As the C-47 passed over the trail of smoke, the pilot told his crew to kick out their bundles. They learned the next day that every bundle had been recovered, and one had landed exactly on target!

MULE TRAIN veteran Bobby Gassiott, who went over from Pope as a Stan/Eval navigator on the first plane to leave, described the "chicken airdrop method." His crew was on an airdrop mission to drop supplies, including livestock, to a remote camp and found it obscured under a low overcast. They were in radio contact with the Special Forces people on the ground. Somebody got the idea of tossing out a live chicken when the airplane was over the spot where they

Anything, Anywhere, Anytime

calculated the camp was located.[242] The Special Forces people watched to see if the chicken came out of the overcast over the camp. It did, so the crew came back around and dropped their load, which fell right onto the drop zone!

Livestock were frequently part of the loads the C-123s carried, since they were the lifeline for the remote camps. Chickens, ducks, pigs and cattle were frequent cargoes. Livestock were even loaded onto airdrop pallets in crates, as in the case of the incident in which Bobby Gassiott was involved. Livestock were often carried on passenger missions since Vietnamese troops were often accompanied by their family, who carried everything they owned with them.

Paratroop operations were part of the training for both the *FARM GATE* C-47 and *MULE TRAIN* C-123 crews and were one of their assigned Vietnam missions. One of the reasons the C-123s were sent to Vietnam was to provide greater mobility to ARVN airborne units, and to set up quick reaction forces to respond quickly to Viet Cong attacks. The first C-123 drop mission took place in March 1962, shortly after the airplanes began operations in Vietnam. Heavy Viet Cong attacks against the outpost at Bo Tuc led to the dispatch of a quick reaction force of Vietnamese paratroops. Three USAF C-123s dropped 198 Vietnamese troops and their American advisors in two lifts. The drops were unopposed, but the paratroopers failed to make contact with the enemy. In June, a combined American-South Vietnamese airlift dropped troops onto drop zones thirty-five miles northwest of Saigon. Again, the paratroopers failed to make contact.

Eventually, paratroop operations were abandoned due to their lack of success. The preferred means of inserting troops was by heliborne assault. But the helicopter operations were just as unsuccessful. The problem in Vietnam was that the enemy preferred to fight when and where he chose, not at the whim of the South Vietnamese government, and later, American, forces.(Bowers, 1986)[243]

Night flare missions were also an airlift responsibility. To aid the defenders of installations that came under night attack, flareships were kept on nightly alert ready for dispatch to any point in South Vietnam where they might be needed. Sometimes the flareships were diverted to other missions, as happened on the night of July 20, 1963 when Captain Warren Tomsett's crew was asked to land at Loc Ninh to evacuate wounded troops. At the time, the crew was on a flare mission

---

[242] Although chickens can fly, they can only fly for short distances. The crew assumed the chicken would land pretty close to the point from which it was dropped, considering allowances for aircraft speed and wind drift.

[243] Veteran *FARM GATE* C-47 and C-130 pilot Curtiss Messex, who is now deceased, once told the author in an Email that he participated in a drop of a contingent of USAF combat controllers to block a group of VC.

Sam McGowan

over the Mekong Delta south of Saigon. Captain Tomsett landed at Loc Ninh, an airfield that was designated as a "daylight only" strip, then took off again with a load of wounded onboard. During the takeoff roll, the instrument lights all failed. The copilot and flight mechanic quickly directed the beams of their flashlights on the instrument panel while the pilot continued the takeoff. Captain Tomsett and his crew were awarded the MacKay Trophy for the most meritorious flight of the year by an Air Force aircraft for 1963. The prestigious trophy would be won by airlifters again the following year, but for an operation in Africa.

C-123s dropping ARVN paratroops

Logistical flying quickly became a very important part of airlift operations in Vietnam. The rugged country was severely lacking in roadways and railways and those that existed were often the scene of ambushes. Airlift was the only safe means of transporting cargo and passengers between the major bases. Immediately after the C-123s arrival in South Vietnam, the 315th Air Division TMC in Saigon established a route structure linking eleven Vietnamese airfields – Da Nang, Tan Son Nhut, Nha Trang, Bien Hoa, Pleiku, Ban Me Thout, Hue,

Anything, Anywhere, Anytime

Da Lat, Soc Trang, Qui Nhon and Vung Tau. Every mission either landed or took off from one of these airfields. Missions originating from these fields delivered troops and cargo to several remote airfields in the country's interior.(Bowers, 1986)

By the summer of 1962, the *MULE TRAIN* C-123s had proven so useful that a second squadron was ordered to Vietnam from Pope. This time it was the 777th TCS that deployed to South Vietnam on Project *SAWBUCK II*.[244] Some of the crews included navigators from the 345th TCS at Sewart, who went TDY to Pope for the mission. To reduce crowding at Tan Son Nhut, and also to reduce flying time to the northern third of the country, Pacific Air Forces[245] decided to base the second squadron at Da Nang, on the northern coast some fifty miles south of the Demilitarized Zone. Twelve C-123s arrived at Da Nang in mid-June while four others were sent to Bangkok, Thailand to begin an airlift operation there. The Bangkok mission was soon assumed by a company of US Army CV-2s that arrived at Korat, Thailand after a circuitous route by way of Africa and the Middle East.

The assignment of the Army transports to Southeast Asia was the continuation of a major interservice rivalry that had developed between the Air Force and the Army. In the early sixties, the Army which had become somewhat disorganized in the 1950s after the Korean War, began trying to establish a mission for itself and was

---

[244] The original SAWBUCK deployment was not Vietnam related and involved only a single C-123.
[245] Far East Air Forces was redesignated as Pacific Air Forces in 1957 and the headquarters transferred from Japan to Hickam AFB, Hawaii.

looking at various options. In mid-1962, an Army panel known as the "Howze Board," because it was chaired by General Hamilton Howze, recommended the service develop an "airmobile" capability, an endeavor that would result in the development of essentially a new tactical air force within the Army. The board recommended that a number of Army divisions would become "airmobile' by the assignment of aviation companies and battalions to provide rapid transport for light infantry units. Although the primary vehicles would be helicopters, each division would also include a company or two of fixed-wing transports so the Army purchased the De Havilland Caribou, which was designated as the CV-2. The Army tried to introduce the CV-2 to Vietnam instead of the C-123, and when that effort failed, the Army Chief of Staff got permission to deploy a company to Thailand "for evaluation." (Tolson, 1972)(Bowers, 1986)

US Army Caribou in Thailand

In December 1962, with Southeast Asia becoming a testing ground for new military concepts, the Army got permission to move the Caribous on to South Vietnam. They began operations out of an airfield at Vung Tau, a coastal city about forty miles from Saigon where the Army established an aviation facility. The CV-2 was ideal for limited airlift use in Vietnam, including resupply of small camps, but its lack of range and payload made it unsuitable for major airlift operations. A C-123 could carry more than twice the payload of a CV-2 over three times the distance, while with the same payload it could land almost as short as the Caribou. Yet even though they were lacking in capability, the Caribous possessed certain advantages that made them suited for operations into forward areas. In addition to their

Anything, Anywhere, Anytime

short field landing capabilities, they had excellent maneuverability, which allowed them to operate under conditions where the survivability of the Army's larger helicopters would have been in doubt. They also were simply designed and constructed airplanes; bullets would pass right through them without doing significant damage.

The Vietnamese air force transport squadrons were also a valuable asset, even though they eventually became secondary to the American units as the US role in Vietnam increased. For two years, American augmentee pilots flew with VNAF C-47 squadrons, until the program was discontinued in 1964. An attempt was made to give the VNAF some C-123s and Vietnamese pilots were sent to Pope to learn to fly them. However, for some reason the Vietnamese, who tended to be small in stature and of slight build, had difficulty mastering the airplanes and the project was cancelled.

Ranch Hand Crews wearing Bush Hats

Mule Train and *Sawbuck II* were temporary duty tours but instead of rotating airplanes as well as personnel, the crews and support personnel flew back and forth on MATS passenger flights. The original *Mule Train* crews were gone for 120 days. They were replaced at the end of March 1961. Crews and support personnel continued on rotational duty in 1963.

The original nature of the US Air Force mission to South Vietnam was advisory and counterinsurgency and it quickly was identified as "air commando" when the 1st Air Commando Wing was established at Hurlburt Field, Florida. All personnel assigned on a permanent basis in South Vietnam were identified as air commandos, whether they truly were or not. After the first *FARM GATE* personnel arrived in South Vietnam, some of them began wearing Australian-style bush hats that were in vogue with some of the South Vietnamese military units at the time and when they returned to Florida, they wanted to continue

Page 384

wearing the hats there. Many also bought leather gun belts with loops for .38 caliber pistol cartridges and started wearing them instead of their standard issue gun belts – and they wore them everywhere! Naturally, the idea quickly caught on and spread through Air Force personnel in South Vietnam. Everyone wore them, even clerks in offices in Saigon and medics, cooks, aerial port personnel and motor pool drivers. The hat eventually spread to Thailand, where new air bases were soon established.

The hats were merely decoration but as US troop strength in Southeast Asia increased, the Air Force began designating more units as "air commando," eventually including the 315th Troop Carrier Group which activated at Saigon on December 8, 1962 to replace a provisional troop carrier group that had been set up to control C-123 and C-130 operations. The new group was established under 315th Air Division as the controlling agency for the C-123s, which were on temporary duty from TAC and included provisions for Transport Movement Control detachments in its manning document. The TMCs also controlled 315th AD C-130s operating in South Vietnam. The new group was a conventional troop carrier unit but because C-123 training had moved to Hurlburt Field, it was given an air commando designation as were its squadrons when the C-123 mission in South Vietnam became permanent.

In early 1963, the TAC C-123 crews were replaced by permanently assigned personnel drawn from the Air Force at large, who went to Vietnam on a one-year assignment. Many came from aircraft types other than transports while some were former MATS personnel. Prior to departing for their one-year tour, they went initially to Pope for C-123 training but the training program had

Anything, Anywhere, Anytime

moved to Hurlburt Field by mid-1964. A third C-123 squadron was sent over from Pope as a permanent transfer. The Pope squadron became the 311th Air Commando Squadron and was based at Da Nang. Two other squadrons, the 309th and 310th, were permanently assigned to Tan Son Nhut to replace the two TAC rotational squadrons. The three C-123 squadrons were assigned to the 315th Troop Carrier Group, which was headquartered at Tan Son Nhut. A fourth squadron, the 19th ACS, activated at Tan Son Nhut in October 1964. As the C-123 mission became a permanent PACAF responsibility, the 464th wing at Pope began a transition into C-130s and began equipping with the newest version of the Hercules, the C-130E, and the C-123 training mission moved to Hurlburt Field on the vast Air Force complex of Eglin AFB, Florida.

While the C-123 was becoming the workhorse of the Southeast Asia airlift system in the early sixties, 315th Air Division's C-130s and C-124s were no strangers to South Vietnam and neighboring Thailand. Since the Army's Special Forces were under a headquarters on Okinawa, scheduled C-130 flights rotated personnel between Vietnam and Okinawa and brought in Special Forces cargo. Japan-based C-124s operating under 315th Air Division control supported the C-130s by bringing in items too large for the C-130 cargo compartment. In early 1962, when the first USAF personnel were arriving in South Vietnam, C-130s and C-124s were bringing in heavy equipment and personnel to set up a tactical air control system. The four-engine transports landed at Da Nang, Tan Son Nhut, Nha Trang, Pleiku and Bien Hoa. Over a two-week period, 74 C-130 and C-124 missions landed in South Vietnam.

Prior to 1965, C-130s generally operated into South Vietnam and Thailand on an "in and out" basis, although a quasi-rotational operation was set up at Tan Son Nhut as a "Southeast Asia Trainer" operation for in-country missions when needed. Missions coming in from Okinawa and the Philippines were scheduled for multiple in-country stops to move cargo within the country. When they were needed, C-130 crews were sent to Vietnam to airdrop cargo items such as bulldozers that were too large for C-123 delivery. Consideration was given to sending a detachment of C-130s to South Vietnam on TDY status as early as 1962, but a PACAF study determined that there weren't enough C-130-capable airfields at the time and their heavier weights would do damage to existing fields. Frequent special lifts brought in military cargo and personnel from Okinawa, Japan and the Philippines. MATS was also active in airlift missions to Southeast Asia from the United States. MATS flights brought in high value cargo,[246] with the transports making their deliveries to Tan Son Nhut and Da Nang. They sometimes took out aircraft parts, particularly helicopter rotor blades, that needed to go to repair depots in the US for servicing. MATS C-135s were used to airlift personnel to and from the combat zone, but the increasing American presence in Southeast Asia dictated the issuing of contracts to civilian airlines for passenger and cargo lift.

C-130 at An Khe 1965 (Don Horton)

To handle the cargo and personnel arriving in Vietnam and requiring further airlift to up-country destinations, 315th Air Division established the 8th Aerial Port Squadron at Tan Son Nhut to replace the temporary duty personnel from other squadrons elsewhere in PACAF who had been handling the task. Another aerial port squadron, the 6th APS, was activated in Thailand. Aerial port detachments were established throughout Vietnam and mobility personnel from the squadron were sent on assignments wherever their services were needed. To manage the aerial port squadrons in Vietnam, the 2nd Aerial Port Group moved to Saigon. The 2nd Aerial Port Group had been based in Japan since right after the Korean War when it replaced the 6127th Air Terminal Group. The 6th Aerial Port in Thailand reported to 315th Air Division, as did the 7th APS on Okinawa.

---

[246] "High value cargo" is cargo that is considered to be too expensive or time sensitive to be moved by surface shipment and include, among other things, aircraft parts. Much of the cargo moved to South Vietnam by MATS included US Army helicopters and parts and parts for USAF aircraft.

Anything, Anywhere, Anytime

The years from November 1961 to April 1965 are considered to be "the Advisory Years" when considering the stages of American involvement in Southeast Asia. Most of the Americans who served there during that time look upon their service with some degree of fondness. South Vietnam in the early sixties was still an exotic replica of the French Colonial Period, and the war was, for the most part, in the countryside and not in the cities. Many Americans had their dependents with them in Saigon; C-130 crewmembers based on Okinawa sometimes took their wives on leave to the exotic city. Shopping in Saigon's shops was excellent; servicemen found bargains in the form of carved ivory, jade and other precious stones and other goodies. Few had any idea that the country that looked so peaceful from the air was about to turn into a raging wildfire from which the United States would walk away with its head hung in defeat.

Sam McGowan

Chapter Fifteen - "The Troubled Sixties"

The 1960s are most remembered for Vietnam, but there were other serious international crisis situations elsewhere in the world at the time, situations that all involved some degree of hostility and US military force, including – especially – troop carrier. Africa, India, Southeast Asia, the Caribbean and Latin America were all seething cauldrons of turmoil and American airlift crews were often sent to assist a government in distress.

Evreux-Fauville Air Base, France (Author)

Throughout the early sixties, the 322nd Air Division in Europe was involved with the airlift in the Congo, and in late 1962 it found itself supporting another airlift on the eastern reaches of its sphere of responsibility at the same time. While the Congo was still in turmoil and the United States was becoming increasingly involved in Southeast Asia, President Kennedy ordered United States Air Forces Europe to begin an airlift in India as well. Although India is on the Asian continent, the demarcation line dividing USAFE and PACAF ran through Calcutta, which put most of India inside USAFE's area of responsibility. India's Assam Valley lies in the shadow of the Himalayas just south of the country's northeast border with Tibet. The valley, from which the Air Transport Command mounted its airlift of supplies to China during World War II, was also claimed by Tibet, and thus by China. Traditionally a theocracy governed by a religious leader, like most other Asian nations Tibet is ethnically Chinese. The mountain kingdom was occupied by the Chinese Communists in the 1950s; in late 1962 the Chinese moved troops into the Assam Valley in an attempt to wrestle it from Indian control. In an eastward turn in the

Anything, Anywhere, Anytime

early sixties, India began purchasing military equipment from the Soviet Union, including a fleet of Antanov AN-12 turboprop transports for its air force. To combat the Chinese invaders, the Indian air force began airlifting troops into the high, mountain valley – and immediately ran into problems.

While the AN-12 was a good airplane in many ways, it was not designed for the kind of high altitude operations encountered in the lower reaches of the Himalayas. With only two engines, the AN-12 was underpowered and its lack of performance soon began to show. Several of the Russian-built transports were involved in accidents when the IAF tried to operate them into airfields in the higher elevations. The high altitudes got the better of the AN-12s and almost wiped out the entire Indian fleet within two weeks. With the situation becoming desperate, India turned to the United States for help, an action that was somewhat out of character as the Indian government had taken a political stance that was essentially anti-Western. President Kennedy responded to the request by ordering the Air Force to supplement the Indian Air Force with additional airlift capability. Twelve C-130As from the 317th Troop Carrier Wing were dispatched from their base at Evreux, France to New Delhi.[247]

Immediately after their arrival in India, the USAFE C-130s were put to work airlifting 5,000 Indian troops into the Assam Valley. After the initial airlift went off without mishap, India asked the C-130 crews to mount a second airlift into Leh, an airfield on the opposite side of the country in Ladakh Province in the country's northwestern reaches on the opposite side of the Himalayas. Leh Airfield lay at the 10,500 foot level, with mountains as high as 25,000 feet not far away. Getting to Leh meant flying over and through the legendary Himalayas, the highest mountains in the world. Flying in the Himalayas is undoubtedly some of the most demanding in the world, with high mountain peaks, turbulent mountain wave winds and rapidly changing weather conditions all presenting hazards to air navigation, as some of the older crewmembers knew from their own World War II experiences. Some C-130 missions in India involved landings on airstrips as high as 14,000 feet above sea level, in valleys in close proximity to mountains as high as 25,000 feet. The conditions had not changed since World War II, but the airplanes had. The C-130 was light years ahead of the World War II C-46s and C-87s in performance and payload, while the crews were considerably more experienced as well.

For nine months, the 317th airplanes and crews operated in India in an operation that tested their skills and courage nearly every day.

---

[247] The demarcation line between PACAF and USAFE areas of responsibility ran through Calcutta. The US Pacific Command boundary has since shifted westward to the border between India and Pakistan.

Many missions required the C-130 pilots to maneuver their loaded airplanes through narrow valleys between high peaks to land at remote mountain airstrips at elevations previously thought impossible for an airplane of such size. While some operations were into the Assam Valley where the World War II India-China Ferry bases were located, the most dangerous flights were into areas hundreds of miles west of the Hump routes into the highest terrain in the world. Once again, troop carrier crews and support personnel demonstrated that same sense of mission and a willingness to try whatever worked that had prevailed in troop carrier operations since their commencement in New Guinea in 1942. When a C-130 damaged a nose gear on landing at Leh, a maintenance team used parts from an AN-12 and a wrecked C-119 to jury-rig the airplane so it could be flown to New Delhi for repairs. In 1963, the conflict known as the Sino-Indian War began winding down and the 322nd AD C-130s returned to France.

The 322nd Air Division was commanded by Colonel Charles W. Howe, a veteran airlifter whose World War II service had included service as a B-25 strafer pilot and command of an A-20 attack squadron in the Fifth Air Force under General George Kenney. After commanding the 3rd Bombardment Wing in Korea, Howe moved into airlift with 315th Air Division as Inspector General then took command of the 374th Troop Carrier Wing. Prior to assuming command of the 322nd, Howe commanded the 314th Troop Carrier Wing and 839th Air Division at Sewart AFB, Tennessee. According to some sources, in spite of the success of his men in India, Howe was fired as commander of 322nd when the division transferred from USAFE to MATS in 1964. (He may have been replaced because MATS wanted a MATS officer in charge.) There is no doubt but that Colonel Howe's attitude of "get the job done" was in direct contradiction with the "safety first" attitude that prevailed in MATS. Howe returned to the United States to become Director of Air Police but was only in that position for a year. His extensive airlift experience and expertise led to his return to operations when he took command of 315th Air Division in 1965 just as the division's role in Southeast Asia was expanding. He replaced one of his best friends, Brig. Gen. Richard Ellis, who had served with him in A-20s and B-25s during WW II.[248]

In March 1963, while the India and Congo Airlifts were underway, Howe decided to reactivate the 317th Troop Carrier Wing. The 317th had inactivated in September 1958 a few months after it equipped

---

[248] Col. Lester Ferriss, Jr. served as temporary commander for four weeks while Howe was enroute to Japan. Ferriss had spent most of his career in MATS and in 1970 would write a paper for the Air University Review advocating MAC as a single airlift organization. At the time he was chief of staff for MAC's Twenty Second Air Force.

Anything, Anywhere, Anytime

with C-130s. The wing's squadrons had remained active but the headquarters was folded into 322nd Air Division and the squadrons reported directly to the division. The division's many activities led Howe to reactivate the wing to command the C-130 squadrons and its support functions. Additional C-130 strength in 322nd Air Division came in the form of TAC rotational squadrons.

Ghurkas Loading on C-130 in India

In April 1964, 322nd Air Division transferred from USAFE to MATS. The transfer was the result of recommendations made by General Tunner in the mid-1950s when he commanded the division. Tunner was well along on his battle for airlift consolidation and while he was USAFE commander, he felt that having an airlift division assigned was a waste of resources. Ironically, it was Tunner who activated 322nd in the first place! After he took command of MATS, he continued to argue for the transfer of 322nd to his service. Apparently, he pressed his case to the Kennedy and Johnson White Houses after he retired. Johnson was concerned about the cost of keeping US troops and their families in Europe and someone, most likely Tunner, convinced him that many units could be brought back to the US and returned by airlift in the event of war. Air Force units could be replaced by TAC rotational squadrons. Using TDY personnel reduced the flow of US gold to European coiffers because they didn't have their families with them.

Along with the transfer of the division, USAFE lost its C-130 squadrons. In June the 317th Troop Carrier Wing and its three squadrons transferred from Evreux-Fauville AB, France to a new home at Lockbourne AFB, Ohio outside Columbus. The 317th hadn't been based in the US since late 1942 before it left for the Southwest Pacific.

Sam McGowan

The wing joined Ninth Air Force, which was also the parent unit for three other C-130 wings. The 18th TCS, which was the only squadron of C-130As left in the US, moved to Lockbourne from Sewart to join the wing. No sooner did the 317th arrive at Lockbourne before it started a rotation right back to its old home at Evreux. Young officers and enlisted men resumed the relationships they had with the shop girls in the town. Although the 317th transferred to the US, the 5th Aerial Port Squadron which supported it remained at Evreux and transferred to MATS. There were still C-130 squadrons at Evreux, two of them, but they now were TAC rotational squadrons. In addition to the squadron of C-130As from Lockbourne, there was a squadron of C-130Es from the 464th TCW at Pope.

In June 1964, the Congo Airlift also came to an end when the United Nations withdrew its peacekeeping force from Africa. The UN forces had barely left before a new crisis erupted. First, the Katanga Province seceded from the rest of the country, which prompted a major crisis in the region. Then new troubles arose when a group of Marxist-led tribesmen rebelled against the Congolese government. Calling themselves Simba, or "Lion," the rebels began battling government forces. Mostly uneducated tribesmen, the Simbas were led by a few educated men who had adopted Marxist teachings and were seeking to establish communist rule in the region. The Congolese military had been trained by Belgium but while it possessed some modern equipment, it lacked the resources to defeat the rebels without assistance. To beef-up their own forces, the Congolese government hired Irish soldier of fortune Mike Hoare to recruit an army of mercenary soldiers to assist in the battle with the rebels. Hoare, a former British commando and veteran of the Chindit operation in Burma under Orde Wingate[249] in 1944, recruited an army made up primarily of white South Africans. Because they were African, many of the mercenaries were as concerned about the chaotic situation in the newly developing country on their native continent as they were interested in the money.

Not only did the Leopoldville government need additional manpower, the country also needed outside military assistance. The Congolese asked the United States to come to their aid, not only by providing supplies and financial assistance but also military advisors and other support – including airlift. In response to the Congolese request, President Lyndon Johnson dispatched a small Military Assistance Advisory Group to Leopoldville. In addition to advisors, the

---

[249] Some internet sources claim that Hoare was an armor officer in the British Army in North Africa, but in his own biography, he said that he served in the CBI. News magazine articles published in 1964 state that he served under Wingate.

Anything, Anywhere, Anytime

president also ordered a task force from the United States Strike Command to the region. Designated as Joint Task Force *LEO*, the task force included three TAC C-130s from Pope's 464th Troop Carrier Wing; a fourth C-130 rigged with special communications equipment and code-named *TALKING BIRD*; a few US Army helicopters; Strike Command communications personnel and a platoon of 82nd Airborne Division paratroopers to provide security for the airplanes and crews at the forward fields on which they landed. Additional military support was provided by the CIA in the form of a mercenary air force made-up of former Cuban refugee pilots who had been trained for the Bay of Pigs invasion, and who were now flying armed T-28 trainers and A-26 attack bombers. There was also a small detachment of air commandos from Hurlburt Field who operated a C-46 and were somehow involved with some CIA-sponsored Cuban mercenaries.

The *LEO* C-130s came from Pope and many of the crewmembers and maintenance men were veterans of the C-123 mission in South Vietnam. The 464th wing had since converted to the new C-130E. The former C-123 crews had transitioned with ease into the C-130 while the same spirit of "press-on and get the job done" typical of troop carrier crewmembers continued to prevail. Each crew flew two missions a day out of Leopoldville Airport into primitive airfields close to the fighting. Missions delivered fuel and ammunition to the government forces and transported Congolese soldiers and mercenaries to new areas of operations.[250] With the support from the United States and the military enhancement afforded by the mercenaries, the Congolese began retaking rebel-held territory. By August, the military situation had turned very much in favor of the government. In frustration, the Simbas began taking whites living in regions under their control as hostages and holding them for use as possible bargaining chips for future demands. The largest group of hostages was held in the city of Stanleyville in the north central region of the country; another large group was held at Paulis, still further north and east.

At Stanleyville, the Simbas besieged the US Consulate and took the remaining Americans hostage along with other whites in areas under their control. At the same time, the Simba rebels undertook a reign of terror over the black inhabitants of the city. Atrocity after atrocity occurred in Stanleyville, including the public execution by torture of city officials at a shrine to the memory of former president Patrice Lumumba. The mayor of Stanleyville was brutally murdered by Simba leaders, who cut open his chest, then reached in and pulled out

---

[250] Officially, the *LEO* C-130s did not transport mercenaries, and their transport was by Belgian C-47s. However, C-47s could not carry vehicles and other items of cargo used by the mobile mercenary force.

the heart and liver of the dying man – and began eating it in front of the crowd!(Reed, 1966) (Dabney, 1979) For 111 days, the Simbas controlled Stanleyville while the entire world watched in trepidation. No end appeared in sight to the chaos and no solution could be found to free the hostages, who were being held captive in a Stanleyville hotel. Threat after threat came from the Simbas, with most directed at the Americans. An American medical missionary, Dr. Paul Carlson, was "identified" by the Simbas as a US Army major spying for the CIA, and was threatened with execution unless their demands were met.[251] Central to their demands was the withdrawal of the American forces from the Congo, including the white mercenaries whom the Simbas took to be Americans. (TIME, 1964)

Within the Pentagon, the Joint Chiefs of Staff considered several possible plans to rescue the hostages, while elsewhere in the military other officers worked on other plans with the same goal in mind. There was one certainty – Stanleyville was hundreds of miles from the nearest ocean so any rescue effort was going to have to take place without the highly publicized United States Marines! The Marines were neither trained for such a long-range mission nor did they possess the resources to carry it out.[252] The Strike Command plan called for a major military operation involving a massive airborne assault by the 82nd Airborne Division, combined with bombing missions against rebel positions. It would have been a massive military intervention in a Third World country that would undoubtedly have provoked an adverse reaction in the world press, and severe criticism by many world leaders. The Special Air Warfare Center at Eglin had also come up with a plan to use a small force of Cuban refugees to effect a rescue. Their plan was for the Cubans to float down the Congo River in rafts and attack the city – but they failed to realize that there is a large waterfall just below the city! Fortunately, that plan never came to fruition.

In Europe, other plans were being considered as American military officers worked with officers from the Belgian military. The international team came up with a rescue plan that called for a small-scale operation, using Belgian paratroopers to capture the airport at Stanleyville then rush into town to free the hostages. Since Stanleyville had once been a Belgian city, the Belgian military was well familiar

---

[251] Dr. Carlson's relationship with the US government is unknown. He was a missionary from the Covenant Church, and missionaries – along with oil company personnel, journalists and others – quite often were recruited to work with CIA operatives in the countries where they resided. He was not, however, a US Army major.

[252] As part of the Navy, the mission of the Marine Corps was to secure beachheads and conduct shipside boarding operations at sea.

with its layout and Belgian troops were the logical force to provide the muscle for a rescue. The American contribution would be a squadron of C-130s to airlift the rescue force to Africa and deliver them for the rescue mission. This was the plan, designated by the Belgians as *DRAGON ROUGE,* and by the US as *RED DRAGON,* that was finally accepted by the US State Department and the White House, as well as by the Belgian government in Brussels.(Glasgow, 1965)

Africa fell within the area of operational responsibility of the United States Air Forces Europe and USAFE was responsible for providing the airlift. In 1964, 322nd Air Division, which had transferred to MATS only a few months before, controlled two TAC C-130 rotational squadrons at Evreux. The 317th TCW had transferred back to the United States to Lockbourne AFB, Ohio and was providing a squadron of C-130As while the 464th from Pope had a squadron of sixteen C-130Es on rotation there. MATS also had some C-130Es, but they were based in the United States and the crews lacked the experience and training for such a mission. The distances involved dictated the use of the longer-range C-130Es, so the momentous mission was assigned to the Pope squadron.

In mid-November, 322nd began recalling the Pope crews back to Evreux from missions throughout Europe. When the crews arrived at their base, they were told only that the squadron was on stand-by for an important mission and they were to go to their quarters to begin crew rest. On the afternoon of November 17, the crews were told to report to the squadron briefing room. At 1800, the first crew took-off with orders only to climb to 2,000 feet, then open a manila envelope that had been given to each navigator just prior to take-off. The instructions told the crews to pick up a flight plan to Kline Brogel, a Belgian military air base outside Brussels. When they arrived at Kline Brogel, each crew loaded personnel and equipment from the crack *Commando 100* paratrooper regiment commanded by Colonel Charles Laurent. The unit had been trained under the British model, and the men wore the traditional British red beret to show that they were airborne troops. After loading, the airplanes departed at intervals for their first refueling stop at Moron, a SAC *"REFLEX"* base on the Spanish Mediterranean.[253] At Moron, only the navigators left the airplane; the rest of the crew and their secret passengers remained inside their airplanes while air police security personnel maintained a strict guard. Only refueling personnel were allowed close to the airplanes; they were told absolutely nothing about the contents of the airplanes or

---

[253] In the 1950s and into the 1960s SAC maintained overseas bases that were designed to receive SAC nuclear bombers in the event of war. SAC conducted frequent exercises, called *REFLEX,* that saw B-47 and tanker crews deploy on a moment's notice for temporary duty overseas.

where they were going. From Moron, the C-130s continued south to Ascension Island, a British possession off the coast of Africa. When the strike force arrived at Ascension, they discovered that rations and cots that were supposed to have been delivered by MATS C-124s had yet to arrive. The MATS C-124s left Rhine-Main, Germany six hours before the TAC C-130s left Kline Brogel, but did not arrive at Ascension until SIXTEEN HOURS after the C-130s!(Glasgow, 1965)[254]

Belgian Paracommandos enroute to Africa

For three days, the rescue force remained at Ascension. On Saturday evening of the weekend before Thanksgiving, the C-130 crews and the Belgian officers were alerted that they were to proceed to African soil. At daybreak the next morning, the fifteen airplanes arrived at Kamina, an American-built airfield in Katanga Province that lay some three hours flying time south of Stanleyville. There were no facilities and only a few hangars at the spartan base that had been built to recover SAC bombers after strikes in the Soviet Union. The crews slept in the airplanes, while the Belgians pitched their bedrolls in a

---

[254] The whereabouts of the C-124s during those sixteen hours is unknown, but considering the amount of lag time before their arrival at Ascension, it appears that the crews took crew rest somewhere even though they were supporting a high priority mission that had been ordered by the White House.

Anything, Anywhere, Anytime

hangar. They rested Sunday and Monday then were told late on Monday evening that the mission would be mounted at dawn the following day.

At 0245 on Tuesday morning, November 23, 1964, the first five airplanes launched from Kamina. They were followed by the seven other C-130s of the twelve-plane mission. Chalks One through Five were each configured for paratroop drop; 320 troops would jump from them.[255] Chalk Six carried a "special cargo" consisting of some armored Jeep-like vehicles that the Belgians planned to use to rush downtown. Its cargo also included some brooms to drop to the Belgians to use to sweep the runway if needed. Chalks Seven through Eleven carried more troops and rolling stock – trucks and special little three-wheeled all-terrain vehicles the Belgian troops used on the battlefield. Chalk Twelve was configured as a hospital ship, and included medical evacuation personnel and an Air Force doctor as part of the crew. There was also a maintenance ship and at least one spare airplane at Kamina.

At the very moment the African sun peeked over the rim of the earth, a B-26[256] flown by a Cuban pilot made a strafing pass down the runway of the Sabenas Airlines airfield on the outskirts of Stanleyville. Seconds behind the B-26, Captain Warren "Huey" Long and his Stan/Eval crew appeared over the airfield in Chalk One. Colonel Burgess Gradwell, a 322nd staff officer who had accompanied the mission as the division's mission commander[257], was an additional crew member on Long's airplane. The four other C-130s of the assault force were right behind. Colonel Charles Laurent led his men out of the lead C-130 and the dawn skies over the airport filled with parachutes.

---

[255] During World War II airborne troops were identified by putting the identification number of the airplane from which they would be jumping on their helmet in chalk. Ever after, airplanes, troops and cargo loads on tactical missions were identified by "chalk numbers."

[256] The Cuban-flown airplanes were Douglas Invaders that had originally been designated as A-26s, but after World War II they were redesignated as B-26s. In 1965 the A for "attack" prefix was again adopted and the former B-26s became A-26s once more. These particular airplanes had been appropriated by the CIA for the ill-fated Bay of Pigs Invasion in 1961.

[257] The command arrangement was somewhat convoluted. Although the airplanes belonged to Tactical Air Command, they were on temporary duty in France with 322nd Air Division, which had recently transferred from USAFE to MATS. Yet even though 322nd was now part of MATS, its purpose was to provide airlift within USAFE's area of responsibility. The Congo mission, however, came under US Strike Command and once the rescue force entered African air space, operational control transferred to Strike, and thus back to TAC. Gradwell was a MATS officer and although he was the designated mission commander, he actually had no control over the rescue mission itself but was along on the mission as an observer.

Captain Long banked to come around for a second pass to drop cargo bundles and allow the Belgian jumpmasters to follow their troops and the other four airplanes followed.

The TAC crews had been briefed to expect small arms, but no large caliber antiaircraft fire. At this hour of the morning the Simbas would still be asleep and, as far as anyone knew, they had no antiaircraft guns. But the Simbas did have a few .50-caliber machineguns and the rebels were alerted by the noise of the B-26s and the low-flying C-130s. As the drop formation came over the drop zone for a second pass, tracers came up to meet them. All five airplanes took hits, although none were serious until Chalk One was hit again while orbiting over the airfield after the drop so Gradwell could observe the unfolding events. The heavy rounds knocked out part of the hydraulic system. Chalk One departed the area for Leopoldville, following the other four drop planes which were already on their way.

Exactly forty-five minutes after he jumped, Colonel Laurent radioed that his commandos had cleared the runway and C-130 landings could commence. Immediately, Chalks Seven through Eleven departed their holding pattern near the city to land and discharge the troops and vehicles of the rescue team. Each of the airplanes encountered ground fire and took hits. After discharging their troops, the five C-130s took off again for Leopoldville to join the rest of the force for refueling. Chalk Twelve, the hospital plane, landed behind the rescue force and prepared to receive the hostages as soon as they arrived from Stanleyville. As it turned out, the medical team would have a very busy day.

Shortly after take-off from Kamina, a life raft deployed from the

Anything, Anywhere, Anytime

wing of Chalk Six. Pilot Capt. Mack Secord[258] returned for the spare airplane, which caused his crew to be late reaching Stanleyville. The previous evening, Secord had bumped his head on the top of the crew entrance door in the darkness when he went to the airplane to try to get some rest and he had "one hell of a headache." His crew arrived over Stanleyville just as the last airplane was taking off. Fortunately, the Simbas hadn't littered the runway with broken glass and other debris and the brooms that had been brought along for that eventuality weren't needed. They had parked vehicles on the runway but the Belgian commandos drove them off. They were told to land and remain on the ground with Chalk Twelve to airlift the hostages to Leopoldville. The two C-130s waited on the ground at Stanleyville for more than two hours, with their engines running the entire time.(Dabney, 1979)(Secord, 1986)

As soon as the rescue force landed, they organized and began making haste toward downtown Stanleyville, where the hostages were being held in the Victoria Hotel. Unknown to the rescuers, the Simba leaders had evidently decided to turn the hostages over to the rescue force when they saw the parachutes spilling from the C-130s over the airport. They roused the prisoners from their rooms and assembled them in the street, than began moving toward the airport. Even if the intentions of the rebel leaders were good, their men were very upset that the hated Americans had dared to attempt a rescue. The Simbas, who were mostly primitive rural tribesmen, were hopped up after a night of drinking home-brew and smoking hemp, and were very hostile. One of the rebels fired a burst from his automatic weapon at his commander and the others followed suit. After shooting down their own officers, the Simbas turned their weapons on the hostages. Picking women and children as their targets, they fired a volley into the terrified group. Some hostages – including Dr. Carlson – attempted to flee, and were shot down. The rebels stopped firing and were preparing to turn over the bodies and finish off the wounded when a Belgian in a Red Beret rounded a corner. Knowing the jig was up, the Simbas broke and ran, leaving thirty dead and dying whites and scores of injured behind them.

The sight of the dead and wounded whites severely angered the young Belgians, but they maintained their military discipline. The same cannot be said for the mercenaries, most of whom were white Africans. The airdrop had been timed to coincide with the arrival of

---

[258] Mack Secord is often confused with the notorious general with the same last name who was involved with US clandestine activities in Central America during the Reagan Administration. Mack Secord retired from the USAF as a lieutenant colonel. The airplane he and his crew flew into Stanleyville that day is now on display at the Robins Aviation Museum in Warner Robins, Georgia.

the mercenary column and when the undisciplined mercs' realized what had happened, they were incensed. It was open season on Simbas for the rest of the day in Stanleyville, and every one that was found paid with his life for the carnage he and his comrades had inflicted on their hostages. (TIME, 1964)

As soon as they could get the crowd moving, the Belgians directed them toward the airport. The most seriously wounded were loaded onto trucks while the rest moved by foot. As they made their way through the city streets, they were joined by other whites and non-African people of color who had been hiding throughout the city for weeks[259]. The first group to reach the airport was those in the vehicles. Seeing Secords' airplane sitting with the engines running, the frightened former hostages evidently believed it was about to takeoff, so they rushed to climb aboard. The two loadmasters were overwhelmed by the hostages, many of whom were seriously injured. Finally, they were able to convince the worst of the wounded to move to the hospital ship, where a doctor waited to tend their wounds. Then Secord began taxiing toward the runway.

As they passed a large patch of elephant grass, two Simbas ran out with submachine guns. One fired a burst straight up into the wing while the other attempted to force the paratroop door. The crew was unaware of the Simbas; the entire episode was witnessed by the crew

---

[259] Stanleyville had a large population of Indians, Chinese and Jewish merchants.

Anything, Anywhere, Anytime

of Chalk Twelve.[260] As Secord pulled onto the runway, Captain B.J. Nunnally shouted a warning over the radio that his airplane's wing had been shot up, but Secord ignored him until they were in the air. Their airplane was streaming fuel from the integral fuel tank and the hydraulics on the right side had been shot out. In spite of the damage, they landed safely at Leopoldville. Secord, whose pain was so great that he had to be lifted out of his seat, was taken immediately to the hospital where he was diagnosed as having a brain concussion from when he had bumped his head on the airplane crew entrance door the night before.(Dabney, 1979)(Secord, 1986)

With the hostages now in friendly hands, an airlift began to move them out of Stanleyville to safety in Leopoldville. The other C-130s returned to Stanleyville, along with the airplanes of the *LEO* force, to pick up more people. For the rest of the day, the C-130s shuttled back and forth with whites and other people from the city, particularly Indians and other non-African people of color. The airlift was joined by Belgian military and commercial transports that were in the area. Several times during the day, the airlift had to be halted when groups of Simbas attacked the airfield. The last C-130 of the day landed just as a mortar barrage struck the field. That evening, a Belgian airman was killed by a sniper while working on a stranded DC-4. (Strobaugh D. , 1964)

On Thanksgiving Day, the rescue force flew another mission to free the hostages held in Paulis, a town northeast of Stanleyville. The C-130 crews arrived to find the airfield enshrouded in fog and mist, but the commandos jumped even though they couldn't see the ground. When the fog began to lift, the C-130s began landing, but their props stirred up a dust cloud that joined with the remaining fog to again obscure the runway. One pilot was unable to see the ground and hit so hard that his engines flamed out, but the airplane was still flyable. Operation *DRAGON NOIR* was a success, just as *DRAGON ROUGE* had been two days before. Once again the Belgians found that the hostages had been tortured and some had been killed. One American missionary had been beaten to death. (TIME, 1964)(Dabney, 1979)

After the Paulis mission, the rescue force withdrew to Kamina to await further instructions. There were still hundreds of whites in areas under rebel control and their fate was uncertain. While the news of the rescue was greeted with praise in the West, the Third World media raised a terrible outcry. Many African papers criticized the United States and Belgium for intervening on their continent. (TIME, 1964) Yielding to the criticism, President Johnson ordered the rescue force to

---

[260] Secord told the author that he and his crew either didn't hear, or didn't want to hear, the message and weren't aware of what had happened until they had become airborne.

leave Africa even though there were still many whites in danger in the Congo. Scores of women and girls would be raped and many whites would be tortured and killed before the rebellion was finally put down the following August. For their role in the mission, the TAC C-130 crews were awarded the 1964 MacKay Trophy for the most meritorious flight of the year, the second time in a row that the award went to airlifters. Each aircrew member was also awarded the Air Medal, while Captain Mack Secord was decorated with the Distinguished Flying Cross.

While Africa and Asia were major trouble spots, the Western Hemisphere was not immune to trouble. With a communist government sitting in Cuba only ninety miles from Miami, the entire Caribbean was subject to insurgency and rebellion. In the spring of 1965, rebels attempted to overthrow the government of the Dominican Republic, a small country that shares the island of Hispaniola with Haiti. Chaos seemed to be reigning in the city of Santa Domingo and President Johnson dispatched the USS *BOXER*, a Marine helicopter assault ship, to the area. On the evening of April 28, Marines from *BOXER* were ordered ashore to protect American Embassy personnel. Meanwhile, the United States was preparing for a larger intervention; TAC and MATS C-130s were on their way to Pope to airlift the 82nd Airborne Division Ready Force to secure San Isidro Airport at the city of Santo Domingo in preparation for an airlift of a larger force of paratroopers to secure the city. The planned operation was called *POWER PACK*.

Late on the following evening, 140 C-130s, representing all of TAC's troop carrier wings and MATS' C-130 squadrons, departed Pope for a massive airdrop with the airfield as the drop zone. After the formation was underway, word came from San Isidro that the airfield was still in friendly hands so the mission was changed from an airdrop to an air-landing operation. There were also political considerations as

Anything, Anywhere, Anytime

the Johnson Administration became concerned about how news photographs of American parachutes filling the skies over a neighboring country would appear in the eyes of the rest of the world.[261]

The change led to pure chaos since no plan had been made for a landing operation. When they got on the ground, the lead C-130 crew set up an ad hoc command post, a CALSU. The mission commander, Col. William Welch, the 464th TCW wing commander, was on the airplane, which was flown by the Stan/Eval crew commanded by Captain Carl Wyrick. The navigator, Captain Bobby Gassiott, rounded up a crew of Army personnel to break down the airdrop platforms so the vehicles could be driven off the airplanes. Although there was no problem for the troop carrying airplanes, all of the airdrop platforms had to be de-rigged and enough of the cardboard honeycomb beneath the vehicles had to be removed to allow the wheels to touch the platform. Prior to landing at San Isidro, some C-130s diverted into Ramey AFB, Puerto Rico and Homestead AFB, Florida to de-rig the airdrop loads. The vehicles were loaded back onto the airplanes and flown to San Isidro.

C-130s at San Isidro, April 1965 (Author)

The Dominican Airlift continued for several weeks as more and more paratroopers and Marines were moved to the island. From Pope, the flight to San Isidro involved an eight-hour roundtrip that soon became routine. Occasionally, airplanes landing in the D.R. were hit by ground fire but none were seriously damaged. A few Marines and

---

[261] The assault was actually planned to be a night operation and photographs would have been unlikely.

Page 404

Sam McGowan

paratroopers were hit by sniper fire. There was one airlift casualty when an airfreight technician from Lockbourne AFB, Ohio was crushed by a pallet when it fell from the tines of a forklift. He suffered serious injury but survived. Although the flights carrying 82nd personnel and equipment originated at Pope, other flights originated from other bases in the southeastern United States. Marine Corps and Navy transports – including the Navy's C-130s that had been modified with skis – operated out of the Marine fields at Jacksonville and Cherry Point, NC. Some MATS aircraft picked up loads at Pope while others went direct to San Isidro from Charleston AFB, SC and Hunter AFB, Georgia.

The India, Congo and Dominican Airlifts were the milestones of the American troop carrier missions of the 1960s outside of Vietnam. But there were other missions of international importance during the period. In late summer of 1965, crews from the 779th Troop Carrier Squadron, who were on deployment at tiny Mactan Island in the Philippines from Pope, were sent to Dacca, East Pakistan (now Bangladesh) to evacuate American Embassy personnel and their dependents when unrest broke out in that country. Periodically, the Soviets threatened to close the air routes into Berlin and, when they did, the United States responded by mounting a sustained C-130 mission into the city just to test the Russian resolve. Fortunately, even though they sometimes sent MiGs up to harass the C-130 crews, the Soviets were always bluffing.

There were also clandestine missions in Europe and Africa, just as there were in Asia. The 7th Air Commando Squadron, a special unit operating out of Sembach, Germany flew a variety of airplanes on missions that have yet to be fully revealed to the American public. Another unit at Sembach had a few C-97s. Where they went and what they did was classified[262], but there is good reason to believe that one of their missions was running guns to Africa. Some missions may have also dropped guns and ammunition to insurgents in communist countries in Europe.

In August 1965, the LEO mission in the Congo came to an end. The region settled down to an uneasy peace and the Congo became Zaire. (It has since changed names several times and is now called The Democratic Republic of Congo.) In the late 1960s, another rebellion

---

[262] Throughout the fifties and sixties and into the seventies the United States conducted a number of operations that were highly classified, not to protect those involved but rather to prevent the people of the United States from knowing what their government was doing without their knowledge. Such missions were most often conducted covertly by the Central Intelligence Agency using assets from the military services, each of which had classified units whose mission was to support CIA-sponsored covert operations run by its Special Activities Division.

Anything, Anywhere, Anytime

took place in Zaire, and once again the United States sent a detachment of C-130s to help the government. The airplanes were again from Pope, and some of the same crewmembers who had flown there in 1964 and 65 returned. This time, they found that the mercenaries were on the other side! Airlifts into and within Africa were almost a regular occurrence throughout the 1960s and 1970s.

There were also some American special operations in Central and South America in the sixties and early seventies, although they received little public notice. A TAC rotational squadron of C-130s at Howard AFB, Canal Zone supported military operations of the Southern Command. Crews flew missions throughout Latin America, often supporting US Army Special Forces operations. The most notable mission in the region resulted in the interception and death of Argentine revolutionary Ernesto "Che" Guevara, who had served as Fidel Castro's right hand man during the Cuban Revolution and who was active in other insurgencies in South America.

C-141 (Lockheed)

The changes in airlift that began in the late 1950s continued through the sixties. In 1965, MATS began taking deliveries of the "workhorse" Lockheed C-141 Starlifter transport that Congress had authorized as a result of the efforts by Congressman L. Mendel Rivers and MATS commander General Bill Tunner and his successors, Generals Joe Kelly and Howell Estes. The Eisenhower Administration refused to authorize the development of the airplane because they felt it was unnecessary and Tunner, who retired in 1960, actively campaigned for John F. Kennedy, who made airlift a campaign issue. Kennedy rewarded Tunner by ordering the development of the new airplane as his first official act.[263] Although the Air Staff had adopted a policy of only purchasing tactical aircraft, MATS got around the requirement by having Lockheed design the airplane so it could be used for airdrop of personnel and cargo. It was also supposed to be able to land on unimproved runways but in tests the airplane failed to live up to expectations in that area. It kept blowing tires when landing on dirt. Lockheed also designed the airplane to meet Federal Aviation Agency's certification requirements for transport aircraft.[264]

Along with the purchase of the new C-141, MATS also achieved its long-time goal of attaining specified command status when the service became the Military Airlift Command on January 1, 1966. The new status brought with it MAC's designation as "single manager" for airlift. Once again, MAC had no role in troop carrier operations other than providing outsize cargo capability and supplemental airlift to TAC and PACAF when needed. In reflection of MAC's new military role, the old air transport wing designations were replaced with the designations of World War II troop carrier groups.[265] In most cases, the squadrons retained their previous numerical designations, but their identity was simply changed from air transport to military airlift. The former TAC C-124 squadrons that had retained the troop carrier designation were also redesignated as military airlift. As the fanjet[266] C-141 came into service, the C-135s that had been MATS' jet airlifters were converted to tankers and transferred to SAC refueling squadrons. The young female flight attendants lost flying status as MAC tried to shed MATS' airline image. In the early sixties, MATS C-124 squadrons were directed to attain tactical proficiency along with the service's C-130 squadrons. As C-141s entered the inventory, the squadrons that operated them assumed a tactical role, at least on paper. The C-141 afforded heavy and paratroop drop capabilities as well as the troop carrier and air ambulance features of the C-130. As C-141s came into the inventory, MATS C-124s transferred to the reserves.

---

[263] Just how Kennedy was able to "order" that the airplane be developed is unclear, since budgets for aircraft development are in the Congressional domain, not that of the Executive Branch of government.

[264] Although the FAA certified the airplane as the Lockheed 300, the company could find no customers for it and only one civil version was ever built.

[265] The redesignating of the MATS air transport units was somewhat ironic. With the creation of MAC, all of the former air transport wings, which were descended from non-combat units, now bore the designations of World War II and Korean War troop carrier units. Yet at the same time, two of the most prominent TAC troop carrier wings, the 463rd and 464th, bore the designations and carried the lineage of former heavy bomber groups.

[266] The fanjet engine, which incorporates a large "fan" as part of the engine compressor to move air on the outside of the engine core was a new innovation and the C-141 was one of the first airplanes to use them.

Anything, Anywhere, Anytime

TAC's troop carrier wings were not included in the new Military Airlift Command but there were changes. As SAC began phasing out its B-47s and was reduced in size, many SAC flight and maintenance personnel transferred to TAC and MAC airlift units. At Forbes AFB, Kansas, a SAC wing was replaced by a TAC C-130 wing, the 313th Troop Carrier Wing, and the bomber pilots and navigators became airlifters; flight mechanics and loadmasters came from other sources, although some had been B-47 maintenance men. The 313th had been inactivated after the Korean War and the designation was brought back to active service. The 464th at Pope completed conversion to the C-130E while the 314th at Sewart also equipped with the E-model. Along with the 516th TCW at Dyess AFB, Texas, they made three wings of C-130Es in TAC. Sewart's B-models went to Forbes to the new 313th. The 463rd moved to Langley AFB, Virginia where it replaced a TAC KB-50 tanker wing; the reorganization gave SAC responsibility for all aerial refueling and the KB-50s were phased out. TAC's remaining C-123s transferred to the air commando wing at Hurlburt Field, Florida.

TAC's 464th Troop Carrier Wing's 779th Troop Carrier Squadron was selected to assume a new Special Forces support mission with a modified version of the C-130E designated as the C-130E-(I). It was equipped for night low-level penetration missions by the addition of terrain-following radar and to make aerial pickups of personnel using the Fulton Personnel Recovery System. The Fulton Recovery System was not a new system in the mid-1960s. It had actually been developed during the Korean War by an inventor by the name of Robert Fulton. After experimenting with weather balloons, Fulton determined that the idea was feasible and presented it to the CIA. The CIA had already developed its own system; they felt that Fulton's system was more applicable to the military and referred him to the Navy. Fulton continued experimenting with his Skyhook at El Centro, California using a Navy P2V and by 1958 had developed a workable system. In 1961, the Navy decided to use the system to retrieve a piece of Soviet equipment from the Arctic icecap and caught the CIA's attention. They installed the equipment on their B-17 and the pickup was made about 600 miles out from Thule, Greenland.

The Air Force installed the equipment on a C-130A and conducted test pickups at Dyess AFB, Texas. It decided to adapt the system for rescue and recovery work and ordered a new version of the C-130 with more powerful engines and the Fulton System installed that had been designated as the HC-130H. The HC-130Hs were assigned to the newly redesignated Air Force Rescue and Recovery Service, formerly Air Rescue Service, which was part of MATS. ARRS had a dual mission; rescue and the recovery of packages dropped from satellites. The Army also installed the system on a Caribou that operated out of

Sam McGowan

Simmons Army Air Field on Ft. Bragg for tests with Special Forces, but the mission was given to the Air Force.

In 1964, TAC placed an order for enough modified C-130Es equipped with the system to equip a squadron and picked the 779th Troop Carrier Squadron at Pope to deploy it, beginning in the summer of 1965. The modified C-130E-(I)s were not designed for rescue, but for clandestine operations deep inside hostile territory to insert, resupply and recover agents, and to resupply guerrillas engaged in conflict against countries unfriendly to the United States. Within a few weeks after the men of the 779th (including the author) were briefed on the new mission, the entire squadron departed for Mactan, a tiny island in the Philippines, for one last TDY so squadron crews could gain more combat experience before transitioning into the new airplanes and new mission.

Anything, Anywhere, Anytime

C-130E(I) after modification and paint

While later events made it appear that the military buildup of the early to mid 1960s was in response to events in Southeast Asia, in reality it was the result of changes in military thinking that had taken place in the late fifties and early sixties, when the military philosophy changed from preparing for all-out nuclear war to fighting small scale *conventional wars in countries threatened by Marxism, and the subsequent response by the Kennedy-Johnson Administrations. The relationship to the emerging conflict in South Vietnam and its neighboring countries was merely coincidental. The new concept was to be able to quickly respond to "brushfire wars" that might break out anywhere in the globe before they could spread into the surrounding region and blaze into full scale war. Nevertheless, although there was plenty of trouble elsewhere in the world, it was the rapidly escalating war in South Vietnam that would become the dominant event of the times.

Sam McGowan

Chapter Sixteen - "The Cold War Turns Hot"

Prior to 1965, the Vietnam War was still a war of military advisors in green berets and cowboy hats and airplanes that had been designed, if not used, during World War II. A few "punitive" airstrikes and other military operations had been carried out against North Vietnam but there were no US combat troops on the ground in the South. All of that began to change when President Lyndon Johnson decided to try to force North Vietnam to abandon its plans for a military takeover of the South by escalating "punishment" bombing and thus forcing the North Vietnamese to reconsider their plans to overthrow the South Vietnamese government. Throughout 1963 and into 1964, the primary American role in Vietnam was helping the South Vietnamese combat the Viet Cong insurgents by providing military advice and providing some logistical support. The twin-engine C-123 and, to a lesser extent, the C-47 were crucial elements in the advisory phase of the war. The American transports supplied remote camps and provided rapid mobility for South Vietnamese ground forces. They also, along with C-130s operating in South Vietnam for short periods, operated a rear area logistical system between the port cities of Saigon, Da Nang and Qui Nhon and about a dozen inland airfields. Johnson's *ROLLING THUNDER* bombing campaign, on the other hand, was the prelude to the escalation of the war and the ultimate introduction of American ground combat troops. With an increased US military presence in Southeast Asia, there was also a massive increase in USAF airlift resources, particularly 315th Air Division's C-130s.

Just as the French had used airlift to establish and maintain remote bases in the Vietnamese interior, the Americans and South

Anything, Anywhere, Anytime

Vietnamese used C-123s and C-47s to move troops into the A Shau Valley and other isolated areas to search for and block communist infiltration routes. When Viet Cong forces attacked remote camps, the transports airlifted reinforcements into nearby airfields to meet the attack. While the airplanes were both American and Vietnamese, the troops were exclusively South Vietnamese government forces accompanied by US military advisors, including Air Force liaison officers whose role was to coordinate between the Vietnamese commanders and Second Air Division in Saigon. Resupply of remote camps was of the highest priority during the advisory years. In early 1963, a detachment was set up at Nha Trang with three C-123s and two C-47s for exclusive duty in support of US Army Special Forces, who maintained a system of camps and "strategic hamlets" around the wartorn country. While the C-123s were most often scheduled for landings to take advantage of their larger payloads and short field landing capabilities, the detachment usually scheduled the two C-47s for airdrops. Whether it involved landing or dropping, supplying the camps was a very risky mission that called for superior airmanship and courage on the part of the crews. The runways were short, the camps were often located in rugged terrain and there was always the threat of ground fire from any enemy troops who happened to be in the area. Innovation was often the order of the day for airlifters on missions to the camps. Low clouds and poor visibilities usually prevailed in the mountainous regions of the country; the clouds not only sometimes obscured the nearby hills but also covered the camps with a shroud of fog, making them difficult to spot from the air.

The escalation of the American role in Vietnam began in August 1964, when North Vietnamese torpedo boats attacked the destroyer *MADDOX* as it was operating just offshore in conjunction with South Vietnamese commando operations. *MADDOX* was on an electronics intelligence-gathering mission to monitor North Vietnamese radio transmissions. A second perceived attack two nights later, which may or may not have actually occurred, led to the first American and South Vietnamese bombing attack on targets in North Vietnam.[267] To beef-up American airpower in the Pacific in response to the incident, President Johnson ordered the deployment of several TAC fighter squadrons to bases in and near Southeast Asia. Along with the fighters, two TAC troop carrier squadrons were also deployed to the Far East, where they began airlift operations under control of 315th Air Division. The TAC rotational squadrons supplemented the division's four assigned squadrons of C-130As.

---

[267] The attack on MADDOX definitely occurred but the second "attack" may have been a false alarm. Later analysis concluded that the US Navy radar operators mistook returns bouncing off waves for North Vietnamese PT-type boats.

While the attacks on North Vietnam were announced to the world, a "secret" interdiction campaign was begun against the communist supply routes leading out of North Vietnam into neighboring Laos, then south through the mountains and into South Vietnam. Operation *BARREL ROLL* included nightly missions by C-130s from the 6315th Operations Group at Naha, Okinawa acting as flareships to provide light for strike aircraft bombing targets in Laos. *BARREL ROLL* increased the level of American military activities in the region and established a need for additional airlift.

Exactly when 315th AD C-130s started flare missions over Laos is unclear. Some enlisted veterans of the 21st TCS' E Flight who flew as flare kickers insist that it started in November 1964 but there are other indications that it began much sooner before the E Flight personnel became involved. The history of the 374th Tactical Airlift Wing and its predecessor, the 6315th Operations Group, relate that the first missions consisted of merely tossing the flares out of the paratroop doors, the same metho used by C-47 and AC-47 loadmasters in South Vietnam. The author has a letter from the late Lt. Col. Bill Cooke, a Naha navigator and personal friend, in which he states that he was on the first mission and that it was flown in April 1964. This date coincides with the beginning of US air operations over Laos in support of the *WATER PUMP* T-28s. *YANKEE TEAM* operations by Air Force and Navy fighters and reconnaissance aircraft began a few weeks later, in May. While the mission was assigned to the 6315th Ops Group, crews from the 815th TCS at Tachikawa also participated. The squadron couldn't participate directly because of US-Japanese treaty stipulations but its personnel could be sent TDY to Naha and then on to Vietnam from there. The flare mission operated out of Da Nang until the spring of 1966 when it moved to Ubon, Thailand.

The first American ground combat personnel to see duty in Vietnam arrived at Da Nang in February 1965. Fifty-two C-130 flights airlifted the men and equipment of a United States Marine Corps Hawk antiaircraft missile battalion from Okinawa to Vietnam in response to a Presidential directive.[268] Other airlifts supported the movement of PACAF fighter squadrons from bases in Japan, on Okinawa[269] and in the Philippines to operating locations in South Vietnam and Thailand. In March, two battalions of the 3rd Marine Division moved to South

---

[268] The Marines were not "ground combat" personnel in the sense that they were infantry. Their role was actually antiaircraft defense. Incidentally, no communist air attacks on South Vietnamese bases ever occurred. The first actual ground combat personnel arrived a month later.

[269] After World War II Okinawa was a United States military trustee, governed by a US military governor. It did not revert to Japanese control until the 1970s.

Anything, Anywhere, Anytime

Vietnam. One battalion was airlifted by 315th Air Division transports while the other moved by sea. MATS C-124s based at Tachikawa airlifted outsize cargo; although 315th's C-124s had transferred to MATS in 1958, they operated exclusively under 315th operational control. With the assignment of additional US military personnel to Southeast Asia, the demand on 315th Air Division's airlift forces increased considerably. There were already two TAC rotational squadrons assigned to 315th; within a few months, their numbers would increase to five.

In early April, the White House ordered the commencement of *ROLLING THUNDER*, a graduated bombing campaign of North Vietnam that was supposed to escalate in response to Viet Cong and North Vietnamese aggression against South Vietnam. The *ROLLING THUNDER* campaign placed new demands on PACAF so additional fighter, reconnaissance and two additional TAC troop carrier squadrons were ordered overseas for rotational duty in the Pacific. The two C-130 squadrons, one each from Pope and Dyess, joined the squadrons from Sewart and Langley that began rotations to the Philippines and Okinawa the previous August. The Pope squadron went to Kadena, Okinawa and the Dyess squadron to Naha. The Langley squadron moved to Clark. A second Pope squadron would deploy to Mactan, a tiny island in the Philippines, in late summer.[270] When the 779th TCS from Pope arrived at Mactan, it brought 315th Air Division C-130 strength to nine squadrons. The division also commanded the 315th Troop Carrier Group[271] in Vietnam and the 6485th Operations Squadron at Tachikawa. The 315th TCW flew C-123s while the 6485th operated C-118s on air evacuation missions. Three aerial port squadrons, the 6th in Thailand, 7th in the Pacific and 8th in South Vietnam, were also under 315th.

While the C-123 force continued supporting South Vietnamese combat operations, 315th Air Division C-130s and C-124s were put to work transporting troops and supplies into Vietnam and Thailand from Japan, Okinawa and the Philippines. Scheduled missions moved cargo and passengers between the out of country bases, where the PACAF and TAC rotational fighter wings were based, and their rotational units in Southeast Asia. Additional missions brought in

---

[270] Each deployment was given a code name with a number and *BUCK. ONE BUCK* was the original deployment in response to the Gulf of Tokin incident. The April 1965, deployment was *TWO BUCK*. The deployment of the 779th TCS from Pope to Mactan Island was *SIXTEEN BUCK*. Other deployments in between were given various BUCK designations. The deployments ranged from squadrons down to individual airplanes.

[271] The 315th Group was redesignated as "air commando" in March 1965. It was later elevated to wing status.

Sam McGowan

specific items as they were requested. When the supply of bombs in Thailand and Vietnam ran low, the transports replenished the stocks from supplies elsewhere in the Pacific until more could arrive aboard ship from the United States.

As the United States escalated its air war against North Vietnam, the Viet Cong stepped up the tempo of their attacks against government installations. The Military Assistance Command Vietnam, commonly referred to as MACV, depended on airlift to move troops into battle to reinforce those who were under attack. Three separate attacks in May 1965 were met with airlifted reinforcements who were flown into the airfields of Phouc Vinh, Dong Xoai and Quang Ngai. The attacks prompted Washington to alert the US Army's 173rd Airborne Brigade for a move to Vietnam and the 6315th Operations Group at Naha was ordered to provide the necessary airlift. With assistance from the other 315th Air Division and TDY TAC squadrons, including 6th and 22nd Military Airlift Squadron C-124s, the group moved the advance elements of the 173rd to Bien Hoa and Vung Tau.

463rd TCW C-130B at forward field in Vietnam (note that TAC patch has been removed. This photo was taken soon after the wing moved to the Philippines, as evidenced by the outline of the recently removed TAC patch.)

The 173rd paratroopers and the 3rd Marines went to Vietnam to provide security for American air bases, a mission that called for limited combat operations into areas under Viet Cong control to deny them the use of the bases they had established in the countryside. With

Anything, Anywhere, Anytime

the capabilities of the C-123-equipped 315th Troop Carrier Group already strained, PACAF decided to introduce C-130s into combat airlift operations in Vietnam in addition to the intratheater and logistical missions they were already flying. A few missions had been flown inside Vietnam earlier in the year, while the 6315th Operations Group maintained a detachment at Da Nang for flareship work and also kept a few airplanes at Tan Son Nhut as "Southeast Asia trainers", but airlift operations had generally been temporary. On June 4, 1965, 315th set up a C-130 operating location at Tan Son Nhut with four airplanes for in-country operations on an "indefinite" basis. The airplanes and crews were from a TAC rotational squadron.[272]

The Air Force had actually considered introducing the C-130 to the war in South Vietnam as far back as 1962 but 2nd Air Division, the Air Force controlling agency in the country at the time, felt that there were really wasn't a need. Late that year, PACAF established a policy allowing the 315th Troop Carrier Group to request deviation of scheduled C-130 flights operating into the country for brief in-country operations, subject to 315th AD approval. Flights from Okinawa or the Philippines were normally scheduled to make at least one stop in-country on their return flight with cargo coming out of Tan Son Nhut or Da Nang. Flights could be diverted on sudden notice for emergencies, which were often medical evacuation flights.

In the summer of 1964, Military Assistance Command, Vietnam (MACV) requested four C-130s to supplement the 315th Troop Carrier Group until a fourth C-123 squadron became operational. In early August 1964, the Joint Chiefs directed PACAF to send eight C-130s to Vietnam on four-to-six month TDY. 315th Air Division was opposed to permanently assigning C-130s to Vietnam but favored sending them in for short TDYs ranging from a few days to two weeks. MACV and 315th suggested using offshore-based airplanes for multiple in-country stops instead, and their proposal was adopted. Some crews were kept in-country for short periods of about four days. These were the missions Naha and Tachikawa crews referred to as "Southeast Asia Trainer" flights. The 815th TCS at Tachikawa was in a unique situation. Japanese constitutional issues prohibited US units based in Japan from engaging in military conflict in which the nation was not involved. Consequently, 815th crews couldn't go straight to South Vietnam from Japan for combat operations. Neither could 815th TCS and 7th Aerial port personnel go to Da Nang for the flare mission. To get around the restriction, 815th and 7th APS personnel based at Tachikawa were first sent to Naha on TDY to the 6315th Operations Group then went on further TDY from there.

In September 1965, C-130s dropped Vietnamese paratroopers

---

[272] They were evidently from the 314th TCW rotation at Clark.

onto a drop zone just north of Lai Khe. The fifteen-plane formation was made up of C-130s from each of the 315th Air Division units, including the TAC rotational squadrons. Although the drop itself went well in spite of an initial delay at Tan Son Nhut and poor weather over the drop zone, the paratroopers made only "light contact" with the enemy. A B-52 strike preceded the airdrop and the DZ was then prepped by airstrikes, which possibly alerted the enemy that an operation was about to begin. MACV speculated that the airstrikes may have given the communists forewarning and caused them to go underground or melt into the jungle.

C-130s taxiing out at Tan Son Nhut for paratroop drop

The 173rd Airborne's transfer to Vietnam was the first of many transfers of US Army combat units who would soon see combat in Vietnam. The war was going badly for South Vietnam in the summer of 1965 as strong enemy attacks continued throughout the Central Highlands region.[273] In September, the Army's new airborne cavalry unit, the 1st Air Cavalry Division, arrived by ship. The cavalry division had been established only a few weeks before at Ft. Benning, Georgia when the 11th Air Assault Division, a former airborne division that had been converted to a new role with the assignment of helicopters and

---

[273] In fact, the war had been going badly for the South Vietnamese for more than two years. The Battle of Ap Bac in January 1963 was a communist victory. The Pentagon Papers later revealed that many senior US officials, civilians as well as military, had realized that the South Vietnamese could not win the war without US assistance.

Anything, Anywhere, Anytime

light transports, was combined with the 2nd Infantry Division and given the designation of the 1st Cavalry Division, which was stationed in Korea. The 2nd ID designation went to Korea to replace that of the original 1st Cav'. The swap was designed to recognize the mission of the new airmobile unit as "roving cavalry," but using helicopters instead of horses or armored vehicles. Army plans were for the cavalry division to be self-supporting, including providing its own airlift using Caribous and helicopters. It was an optimistic plan that failed to live up to the realities of combat operations.

In October, a few weeks after the division arrived at its base at An Khe, General William C. Westmoreland, who had assumed the role of MACV commander, committed the cavalry to battle in the Ia Drang Valley in the Central Highlands near Pleiku. Communist forces had attacked a Special Forces camp at Plei Mei and the cavalrymen were sent in to bring relief. The resulting battle, the first between US Army and North Vietnamese troops, cut the camp off from all outside resupply other than by air. Air Force C-123s and Army Caribous flew drop missions delivering ammunition and rations, with the 310th Air Commando Squadron at Nha Trang bearing the Air Force burden. Heavy enemy fire made the drops extremely hazardous, with more than forty hits reported by C-123 crews. The resupply effort continued at night as C-123s made drops under flare light. The drop missions were escorted by USAF fighters, which sprayed the nearby ridges with cannon fire and rockets, and dropped bombs and napalm to reduce enemy fire.

When they realized they could not capture the advanced camp, the enemy appeared to begin retreating – or perhaps they were setting a trap. In a blocking move, Westmoreland ordered elements of the 1st Cavalry Division into the Ia Drang Valley north of the camp, a move that set off the first major battle between American and North Vietnamese troops of the war. The Army had created the cavalry division to test the recommendation of the Howze Board, which had recommended the development of an independent air mobility force that would be responsible for its own support. However, the resupply demands of combat proved too much for the unit helicopters and Caribous, so the division called on the Air Force for help. Fuel for helicopters was the most critical need, especially at Pleiku where the battle had depleted available supplies.

The superiority of the C-130 over both the Caribou and the C-123 was clearly demonstrated during the Ia Drang Valley battle. One C-130 could carry fifteen 500-gallon rubber fuel bladders while a Caribou could carry only two and the C-123 only four. A single C-130 could do the work of an entire fleet of Caribous and almost four times that of a C-123, a point not lost on the senior staff members at MACV. C-130s delivered fuel into both Pleiku and the Catecka Tea Plantation, an airstrip several miles closer to the scene of battle. The closer proximity of the Plantation led to it becoming the principle helicopter refueling point. General Harry Kinnard, the 1st Cavalry Division commander, would later report that the C-130 airlift into the Plantation was "...a Godsend." Without it, the entire operation would have ground to a halt as the helicopters ran out of fuel and were unable to deliver supplies to the embattled troopers. The resupply of the 1st Cavalry's aviation brigades set a precedent for future operations in the war, and demonstrated the need for an increased C-130 presence in the theater. From that time on, the C-130 was the prime mover in the in-country tactical airlift mission and the smaller C-123s were relegated to second place.[274] Furthermore, the Army began backing off on its plans for the Caribous and began thinking of how to use them as pawns in the chess game it was playing with the Air Force over helicopter development.

Immediately after the Ia Drang battle, the Pentagon directed the Air Force to transfer eight C-130 squadrons from TAC wings in the US to the Pacific to join the four already there. The eight squadrons consisted of all three models of the Hercules; three squadrons of Es, four of Bs and one of As involved in the transfer. They would join the four C-130A squadrons already in the Pacific. With twelve C-130 squadrons, four C-123 squadrons, a squadron of C-118s and a squadron of C-124s, 315th Air Division controlled nearly as many transports as MATS! None of the C-130 squadrons were to be based in Southeast Asia proper but would instead be based outside of the country where maintenance could perform scheduled inspections and extensive maintenance that required hangars, shops and other facilities. The squadrons would send individual crews and airplanes to operating locations in South Vietnam and Thailand for periods of sixteen days for airlift duty along with just enough maintenance personnel to perform routine maintenance and engine changes. Airplanes and ground crews rotated in country for nine days at a time. If an airplane needed major maintenance, it was flown back to its home base and another C-130 went in to take its place. The transfers took place beginning in December, with the last squadron moving to Clark from Forbes AFB, Kansas shortly after the first of the year.

It was also during this period that the Air Force started camouflaging its tactical aircraft, including troop carrier transports. The first C-130s were painted in the US but most of the airplanes that transferred overseas were still unpainted because the transfer came about suddenly. Contracts were awarded to civilian aviation concerns in Japan, the Philippines and Taiwan to paint airplanes. Airplanes that were scheduled for IRAN inspection in the US received a coat of green,

---

[274] From late 1965 on, the C-123s were used primarily for operations into airstrips that were too short for safe C-130 operations.

Anything, Anywhere, Anytime

tan and gray paint upon completion of the inspection. One book on Vietnam claims that the first airplane to be camouflaged in Southeast Asia was a C-130 and that it was in December 1964, but this is unlikely unless it was a local operation for a special mission.[275] Lt. Col. Bill Cooke related in a letter to the author that the C-130s used on the first flare mission were spraypainted black, however the dates don't coincide. By February 1966 when the author arrived on Okinawa, a program was underway to camouflage all C-130s assigned to PACAF but at the time most were still unpainted. Contracts were let with civilian concerns for the paint, with the As going to Gifu, Japan while the Bs in the Philippines were painted in Manila and the Es that ended up on Taiwan were painted in Taipei. C-123s and other tactical aircraft were sent out of South Vietnam for paint and major maintenance.

TAC C-130E at Dong Ha (Author)

With the increased use of C-130s in South Vietnam, 315th Air Division adopted a scheduling policy under which C-123s were scheduled into fields too short for C-130 operations, with a minimum length of 1,800 feet. The C-123 could actually takeoff and land in 1,000 feet, but it needed an additional 800 feet to clear a fifty-foot obstacle. Originally, 315th Air Division had established a minimum C-130 runway requirement as computed takeoff distance plus 1,000 feet, which came out to a minimum of 3,500 feet. TAC, however, had determined during field tests in the US that C-130s could operate safely off of a 2,000-foot dirt runway. TAC pilots returning from rotational duty in the Pacific reported that the C-130s were being

---

[275] For that matter, there were no C-130s based in Southeast Asia. While the Philippines are in SEA, no C-130s had been permanently based there in December 1965.

Page 420

underutilized, to which 2nd Air Division agreed. The 2nd Air Division commander, Lt. Gen. Joe Moore, advised 315th Air Division and the Air Force that it would lose the airlift mission to the Army unless the policy was changed.

By this time Col. Charles W. Howe had assumed command of 315th Air Division, replacing his friend General Dick Ellis (Col. Lester Ferris, Jr. held interim command for a brief time.) Col. Howe was an experienced troop carrier commander whose experience dated back to 1951. He had been involved with the C-130 program almost from the get-go as commander of the 314th TCW and 839th Air Division at Sewart and 322nd Air Division in Europe. He was also a believer in doing what it takes to get the job done, including taking a calculated risk if necessary, as he and his squadron mates had done in the Southwest Pacific when he was flying A-20s and B-25 strafers. Howe was the third veteran of the 3rd Bombardment Group to command 315th; the first division commander, Brig. Gen. John Henebry was the first and Dick Ellis was the second.[276] In November, Howe changed division policy to allow C-130 operations into all fields that met minimum takeoff and landing requirements.

C-123 offloading troops
The new directive allowed operations into 2,000-foot strips –

---

[276] General William G. Moore, who took command of 834th Air Division when it activated in October 1966, was also a 3rd Bombardment Group alumnus; he commanded the unit in Korea. In the early 60s, he commanded the 314th TCW and 839th Air Divisions at Sewart. The 3rd Bombardment Group was well represented in the troop carrier mission.

Anything, Anywhere, Anytime

only 200 feet more than the minimum for a C-123 – but a 500-foot safety margin was eventually added, which made the minimum field for C-130s 2,500 feet. Although combat ready TAC pilots all met this requirement, 315th AD pilots who had come from other commands had not all been given assault field training so the division came up with a designation for pilots who were "short stop" qualified. Pilots who were not short stop qualified were assigned to logistical and passenger missions or to special operations missions (i.e., the C-130 flare mission), which operated off of hard surface runways until they had gained enough experience in the airplane to be able to handle it on the shortest runways.

After the Ia Drang battle, the Army accepted its dependency on the Air Force for airlift to support even its airmobile division. Within a year, the Army would surrender its fleet of Caribous to the Air Force in return for all rights to future helicopter development, with certain exceptions.[277] For the remainder of US involvement in South Vietnam, combat operations saw the Army and the Air Force working together as a team with Air Force transports hauling men, equipment and cargo "as far forward as possible" to a point where Army and Marine Corps helicopters would pick up the cargo for distribution to the troops in the field. Fuel would remain a major commodity along with ammunition. The Army Caribous were still used for operations into very short runways, or "landing zones," that had been established at fire bases and Special Forces camps. However, the chiefs of staff of the Air Force and Army were already engaged in discussions that soon led to the transfer of the Caribous to the Air Force.

Where did MATS/MAC fit into this equation, one might ask. The answer would be; it didn't. Although at least one author has written that the C-7s, C-123s and C-130s were part of Military Airlift Command, there was no relationship whatsoever other than 315th AD's control over the Tachikawa-based C-124s. MATS, and after January 1, 1966, MAC, aircraft only landed at three or four airports in South Vietnam and initially only went into Bangkok in Thailand. In 1967, MAC C-141s started stopping at Udorn. The closest MAC airplanes came to the war was at Tan Son Nhut, Da Nang, Bien Hoa and Cam Ranh Bay. There were certain exceptions – as previously mentioned, the 6th and 22nd Troop Carrier Squadrons at Tachikawa remained under 315th Air Division operational control and were tactically oriented. The 6th transferred to Hawaii when MATS became

---

[277] The Air Force retained the rights to develop helicopters for search and rescue and for special operations missions, as well as long-range helicopter operations. The Army's helicopters were short-range, capable of operations of only about a 50-mile radius.

Sam McGowan

MAC but the 22nd Military Airlift Squadron continued working for 315th until the spring of 1969 when both units inactivated. MATS aircraft landed at Pleiku during Operation *BLUE LIGHT* but the operation was a test of MATS capabilities. MATS, which was replaced by MAC during the operation, requested permission to move part of the 25th Infantry Division from Hawaii to Vietnam. There was only one other such move during the war. In the winter of 1968, MAC transports moved elements of the 101st Airborne Division from Fort Campbell to Vietnam.

C-141 at Da Nang, 1967 (Author)

The use of helicopters in Vietnam is most often associated with the Army and Marine Corps, but the Air Force operated transport helicopters almost from the beginning of the US ground combat role. In October 1965, the Air Force established a helicopter squadron at Tan Son Nhut for airlift work. Air Force helicopters had been involved in South Vietnam from the beginning in the air rescue and firefighting role, but the mission of the 20th Helicopter Squadron was different. Equipped with large Sikorski CH-3 helicopters, the squadron's mission was to haul cargo to Air Force communications and tactical air control system sites, to augment the search and rescue mission and to participate in counterinsurgency operations. Initially, helicopters were controlled by the local base flight units, but in early 1966 they were placed under the 14th Air Commando Wing when it activated at Nha Trang. Even though the helicopters were used in the airlift role, they operated outside of the fixed-wing airlift system. Air Force helicopters would play a major role in special operations missions, particularly out-of-country missions into Laos and even North Vietnam.

Anything, Anywhere, Anytime

TAC CH-3 during stateside exercise

With the increasing role for American ground combat troops in South Vietnam, the role of the Air Force transports increased as well. Each ground operation depended on fixed-wing airlift to bring in fuel for helicopters and ammunition for artillery to the nearest forward airfield. When no airstrip existed, the transports delivered their loads by airdrop. An operation by the 173rd Airborne Brigade into the "Iron Triangle" region northwest of Saigon[278] was supported by Caribou and C-123 airdrops. One five-plane emergency resupply mission on October 10, 1965 was greeted by intense enemy fire as the C-123s approached the drop zone. The aileron control cables on the lead airplane were shot away while another airplane was hit by ground fire that severely wounded the navigator. The three remaining C-123s had to make seven passes each through intense fire to deliver their loads.(Bowers, 1986)

In late November, the 173rd moved into a communist stronghold around the village of Vo Dat to interrupt the rice harvest. Initial plans called for Australian troops to land by helicopter to secure the airfield, while two battalions of the 173rd parachuted into the opposite side of the valley. When the brigade commander learned that the enemy had possibly learned of the plan, he elected to land the troops at the airfield and the airborne operation was called off. The operation got

---

[278] The region was called the Iron Triangle because it was a major communist stronghold.

underway when forty UH-1D Iroquois helicopters landed the initial wave. As soon as the field was secured and the runway cleared of mines, a stream of C-130s began arriving from Bien Hoa with troops and vehicles. Fifty sorties, 35 by C-130s and fifteen by Army Caribous, brought in four batteries of artillery along with the battalion and brigade command posts. Two days later, an overland route into Vo Dat was opened from Bien Hoa, which decreased dependence on air resupply. Three weeks later when the operation ended, the troops were airlifted back to their base at Bien Hoa.

With more and more American air and ground units arriving in Southeast Asia almost weekly, new bases were constructed to accommodate them. In early December 1965, a new base at Cam Ranh Bay began receiving C-130s laden with construction materials. Located on the South China Sea at Vietnam's largest natural harbor, Cam Ranh Bay was ideally suited for a major American supply base. Plans were made for a C-130 operating location there, and rumors flew that a wing would be permanently assigned to Cam Ranh Bay. As things turned out, Cam Ranh became a major C-130 base but the airplanes and crews were there on rotation from bases elsewhere in the Pacific, and were never permanently assigned.

There were several reasons that C-130s were never permanently assigned to South Vietnam. One was that by basing them out of country, they could participate in the logistical mission of moving cargo and personnel into the country from Okinawa and the Philippines. Another was that with them based at one of the existing PACAF bases, construction of support facilities for major maintenance and inspections would not be required. A large support force could be maintained elsewhere in the Pacific to contribute personnel on a temporary basis to perform daily maintenance chores. When ceilings were placed on the number of troops that could be assigned to South Vietnam, out-of-country basing allowed a much larger force of both airplanes and personnel to support the mission than would have been possible with permanently assigned units. It also allowed a more experienced airlift force since tours at the out-of-country bases ranged from fourteen months to three years instead of the standard one-year tour for men based in country. Married officers and NCOs in Japan, Okinawa and at Clark were allowed to bring their families to their permanent duty station, which was a morale factor.

In late 1965, eight TAC C-130 squadrons transferred to PACAF as the Air Force geared up for long-term involvement in Southeast Asia. The entire 463rd wing moved its C-130Bs from Langley AFB, Virginia to new bases at Clark and Mactan in the Philippines, while a squadron from each of the other TAC wings also transferred. The three C-130E squadrons, one each from Pope, Dyess and Sewart, were assigned to the 314th, which moved overseas from Sewart. A new wing activated at Sewart as the 64th Troop Carrier Wing with the two remaining squadrons. A third squadron activated to bring the wing to full strength. A fourth B-model squadron from Forbes AFB, Kansas joined the 463rd at Clark while the 317th wing at Lockbourne AFB, Ohio contributed its veteran 41st TCS to the 6315th Operations Group at Naha. The arrival of the 41st increased the number of squadrons flying the older – some were already carrying the "O" for obsolete on their tail – C-130As to five. In mid-1966, the 6315th was replaced by the 374th Troop Carrier Wing when the original World War II and Korean War airlift unit reactivated at Naha. The reactivation was mostly an upgrading of the headquarters and the transfer of maintenance personnel from the 51st Fighter Interceptor Wing into the new unit. Airplanes and flight line maintenance personnel were reassigned to the four squadrons while the 374th Field Maintenance Squadron activated for the specialized maintenance sections. The 314th wing was based at Ching Chaun Kang AB, Taiwan with three squadrons. The 463rd was headquartered at Mactan along with two squadrons; two were at Clark.

The first year of heavy American involvement was costly for 315th Air Division. In April, a C-130A from the 815th TCS at Tachikawa was lost to accident at Korat, Thailand in bad weather. In July, two flare mission C-130As were destroyed by an enemy attack on the flight line at Da Nang; a C-130B was damaged. A third C-130A received major damage in the attack but was repaired on site and returned to service a year later. Accident claimed two more C-130As, in August when a crew from the 35th flew into the water while landing at Qui Nhon and in December when an 817th crew crashed on takeoff at Chu Lai. On December 20, the enemy reportedly shot down their first C-130, an E-model from the 345th squadron which had just transferred to Naha from Dyess, as it was landing at Tuy Hoa.[279] A second, a B-model from the 463rd wing, was lost while landing at Pleiku a few weeks later and was believed to have been shot down. Three days later another B-

---

[279] There is some question as to whether this airplane was shot down or was lost to accident. The weather at Tuy Hoa at the time was not good, and the loss was generally believed to have been an accident although the investigating board attributed it to enemy action. In an odd twist, the tail number of this airplane, along with that of a MATS C-130 lost a few months later, was mysteriously resurrected many years later and given to a C-130E that had been stricken from the Air Force inventory in mid-1965 and assigned to "another government agency." Apparently not realizing that Vietnam aircraft losses would eventually be declassified, some idiot came up with the bright idea of assigning the tail numbers of airplanes previously written off to the two airplanes when they returned to the Air Force inventory.

model crashed while landing at An Khe. Two others were lost in March, both to accident, an A-model at Tuy Hoa and a B-model at Pleiku.

As the New Year got underway, the American ground combat units increased their role in the war. A number of operations with names like *MARAUDER* and *SILVER CITY* depended on C-123 lift to bring in supplies from Saigon and Bien Hoa. Operation *DENVER* involved the movement of the 173rd fifty miles north of its base at Bien Hoa to Song Be. The move was made by 129 C-130 flights over a four-day period. An air bridge of C-130 flights kept the brigade supplied the entire time they were in the field. Two weeks later the 173rd returned to Bien Hoa, once again by C-130s, after sweeping the area in search of enemy base camps.

While both the 173rd and the 1st Cavalry Division were airborne units and accustomed to airlift to support their operations, several conventional infantry units soon arrived in Vietnam as well. The 1st Infantry Division, commonly known as "The Big Red One," arrived by ship in October 1965. A few weeks later, the 25th Division arrived from Hawaii. Although most of the division moved by ship, elements of the 25th were airlifted to Pleiku by Military Air Transport Service transports in Operation *BLUE LIGHT*, a move that was more of a test of MATS capabilities than a true military necessity.[280] The new units quickly took advantage of the capabilities of airlift. In late February, the 1st Infantry began Operation *MASTIFF* with a C-123 lift of its 2nd Brigade from Bien Hoa to Bau Tieng, an airstrip too short for C-130 use. The C-123s flew eighty-two missions delivering ammunition and POL. For the first time in the war, USAF helicopters assisted the Army. Several CH-3 flights flew artillery pieces into firebases and supplied units in the field.

On April 24, a formation of four C-130s landed at Tay Ninh at thirty-second intervals to discharge 400 1st Division troops to kick off Operation *BIRMINGHAM*, the largest American operation of the war up to that time.[281] Nine C-130s shuttled into Tay Ninh from Lai Khe, Phu Loi and Phouc Vinh, for a total of 56 sorties in one day. One airplane

---

[280] At the time of the operation, MATS had not been elevated to become MAC. The change took place on January 1, 1966.

[281] The normal passenger load for a C-130 was 92 passengers or 74 ground troops in seats, but by 1966 315th had authorized "combat loading" of 100 combat troops by simply seating them on the floor on top of aluminum 463L cargo pallets and, at least theoretically, putting a 5,000 pound tiedown strap across their legs for restraint. In practice, although they were stretched across the pallets, the tiedown straps were rarely used. Fortunately, no C-130s were lost while carrying a load of combat-loaded passengers. Scheduled passenger runs were rigged with seats and seatbelts.

Anything, Anywhere, Anytime

was hit by ground fire and two men were wounded. For six days, a shuttle of C-130s, supplemented by an occasional C-123, airlifted an average of 424 tons per day into Tay Ninh City. Roads were opened on May 1 but the airlift continued. BIRMINGHAM followed a similar operation that kicked off a few weeks earlier when C-130s deployed an infantry brigade into the Central Highlands between Pleiku and Ban Me Thout. An around-the-clock C-130 airlift into Ban Me Thout brought in 300 tons per day in support of an operation designed to rid the area between Ban Me Thout and Tuy Hoa of Viet Cong. As the fighting moved northward, the airlift shifted into Boun Bleck and Cheo Rio. Other operations in the Highlands involved the airlift of the 1st Brigade of the 101st Airborne into Kontum in December in response to North Vietnamese activities in the area. In early 1967, the 1st Brigade of the Fourth Infantry Division also moved into the Highlands when they were airlifted into Plei Djereng, an airfield west of Pleiku that had just been opened to C-130s.

In March 1966, the communists overran the Special Forces camp at A Shau. Low mountain clouds often obscured the peaks of the ridges surrounding the valley in the early spring, and the communists took advantage of the weather. Clouds obscured the area but an A-1E Skyraider pilot, Major Bernard Fisher, managed to find a hole through which he spiraled down into the valley. No less than 210 airplanes, mostly fighters and C-123s, took advantage of Fisher's hole to drop into the valley for airstrikes and supply drops. Fisher won the Medal of Honor when he landed to rescue a fellow pilot who had crash-landed his stricken A-1E on the airstrip outside the camp. In spite of the heroic efforts of the A-1 pilots and C-123 crews, the camp was overrun; the A Shau Valley would remain under communist control for more than two years.

By the summer of 1966, four C-130 operating locations had been established in Vietnam, with a fifth at Bangkok to support US forces, mostly Air Force fighter squadrons, in Thailand. Aircrews and airplanes went to one of the operating locations for a period of sixteen days, one to go in, fourteen in country, then one to return to home base. Surface lines of communication supplied the upcountry bases in Thailand but there was a need for airlift to move aircraft parts and passengers. The "Bangkok Shuttle" had started first with C-123s from South Vietnam. It was operated by Army Caribous for a short time then, when the Army got permission to move the Caribous to Vietnam, it was returned to the Air Force and operated with C-123s. In September 1965, due to the massive buildup of Air Force fighter squadrons at the up-country bases and an increasing demand for cargo and passenger transportation, TAC C-130Es on temporary duty to Mactan replaced the C-123s. When the 463rd transferred to Mactan, it assumed responsibility for the Thailand operation for a few months. In the spring of 1966, the Bangkok Shuttle was assigned to the 6315th Operations Group in order to get better utilization from the group's C-130As because they required considerably more man-hours per flight hour and because of the C-130B's suitability for the short-field work which was becoming common in South Vietnam.

C-130A at Bangkok's Don Muang Airport

By August, C-130s were hauling more cargo than all of the Air Force C-123s and C-47s, Army Caribous and Vietnamese C-47s combined – and this did not include cargo carried in Thailand. Originally, in country operations were supported by the former TAC B and E-model squadrons while the original PACAF A-model units retained responsibility for overwater airlift into Vietnam from Okinawa, along with their special operations missions. In May 1966, an A-model operating location was established at Cam Ranh Bay. A-model crews from Naha also took over the Bangkok Shuttle mission in Thailand, replacing B-model crews who had assumed the operation as they replaced the TAC rotational squadron at Mactan. As facilities expanded at Cam Ranh, the E-models, which had been flying out of Nha Trang and Vung Tau, eventually moved to Cam Ranh as well, while the B-models remained based out of Tan Son Nhut.[282] All of the C-130 operating locations were manned by crews and airplanes on TDY status from their permanent bases in Okinawa, Japan, the Philippines

---

[282] The E-model operation moved first to Cam Ranh, then moved to Nha Trang where it became a "permanent" operation until the spring of 1967 when it moved to Cam Ranh. Previously, the C-130Es operated out of Nha Trang, but picked up many of their loads at Cam Ranh, particularly after the West Ramp opened in late 1966.

and Taiwan.

On April 1, 1966, 2nd Air Division was upgraded to a full air force and became Seventh Air Force. Lt. Gen. Joe Moore, who had commanded the division since 1964, retained command until July when he was replaced by Lt. General William W. Momyer. Although his background was in fighters, Momyer had long been affiliated with the troop carrier mission during his tenure in various capacities at TAC Headquarters where he had been Director of Plans.[283] Momyer appeared before a number of Congressional committees representing TAC during the controversy over airlift consolidation and he played a large role in the development of the C-130 as a project officer.

General William W. Momyer

Immediately after he arrived in Saigon, Momyer expressed his desire for the assignment of a full C-130 wing to South Vietnam and the establishment of "clear lines of control" over all airlift functions.

---

[283] Momyer was one of the most experienced officers in the Air Force in terms of tactical airpower. Before the US entered World War II, he served as an observer with the British in North Africa. He commanded the 33rd Fighter Group in North Africa then returned to the US and joined the staff at the School of Applied Tactics. He served in various capacities in Tactical Air Command and was well versed in the role of troop carrier aviation.

Sam McGowan

Although the Air Force decided to continue basing C-130s out of country for practical reasons, it agreed to establish a new air division under Seventh Air Force to provide command and control of airlift in Vietnam. The 834th Air Division had previously been a fighter unit based in Louisiana that lost all of its F-100s to Southeast Asia. It moved to Saigon along with a cadre of personnel with airlift backgrounds, most of whom came from TAC C-130 wings.

834th AD commander General William G. Moore

Brig. Gen. William G. Moore, an experienced C-130 pilot who had previously commanded the 314th Troop Carrier Wing and 839th Air Division at Sewart, took command of the new division when it activated on October 15. Like 315th commander Col. Charles W. Howe, Gen. Moore was a 3rd Bombardment Wing alumnus; he commanded the wing in Korea.[284] He had also followed Howe in the 314th TCW and 839th AD at Sewart. The two senior officers maintained a working relationship as Howe's division provided a major portion of Moore's airlift assets.

---

[284] For some reason, Col. Howe was never promoted to star rank even though he held commands that were normally held by one and even two star generals. Obviously, he had made somebody mad at some point in his career. When he retired, he was the senior colonel in the Air Force.

Anything, Anywhere, Anytime

315th AD commander Col. Charles W. Howe

The new division controlled the 315th Air Commando Group and its C-123 squadrons, and had operational control over the C-130s of 315th Air Division while they were operating within South Vietnam. Detachments were set up at Tan Son Nhut and Cam Ranh, through which operational control was provided for the C-130s at each location, and in the case of Cam Ranh, those operating out of Nha Trang as well. A third detachment was set up at Tuy Hoa in 1967.

Another new Air Force airlift unit came into being in South Vietnam when the 483rd Troop Carrier Wing activated at Cam Ranh Bay simultaneously with the activation of 834th Air Division. Air Force pilots and maintenance personnel had been replacing Army personnel in aviation companies for several weeks prior to the wing's activation. The 483rd commanded six squadrons of C-7A Caribous, the former Army CV-2s, which came under Air Force control as a result of an agreement between the Chiefs of Staff of the Air Force and Army. The combination of lack of Caribou capabilities and the Air Force initiative with helicopters led the Army to relinquish its claim to fixed-wing airlift resources in return for the Air Force's agreement to allow the Army to develop its own heavy-lift helicopter units and give up claims to helicopter troop-carrying operations, except for those involving long-range special operations. The six Caribou squadrons were dispersed between Cam Ranh, Phu Cat and Vung Tau, with operating locations at other installations to allow Army commanders some degree of flexibility. The Caribous were assigned to 834th Air Division but under the agreement under which they were transferred between the two services, the Air Force allowed the Army to maintain operational control over some of them at the division level.

Caribou at Pleiku (Author)

During the first two years of the war, MACV operated under the "Enclave" strategy, a concept developed by Secretary of Defense Robert McNamara. The Enclave Strategy was based on securing "enclaves" around major US bases, usually airfields, most of which were located at or near the coast. US combat troops, Australians and South Koreans were responsible for securing their assigned areas and ridding them of Viet Cong forces while South Vietnamese troops operated in the interior. The one exception was the 1st Cavalry Division which MACV considered to be a roving brigade. In I Corps, the military sector in the extreme north of the country, Marines moved into key positions at Dong Ha and Quang Tri from which they conducted operations along the Demilitarized Zone that separated the two Vietnams. The two cities are both in Quang Tri Province, which spanned the narrow northern region of South Vietnam. The US constructed an airfield at Khe Sanh, in the extreme northwestern corner of the province, in 1962 and a Special Forces camp was set up there, along with a Civilian Irregular Defense Group camp. The camp was used for long-range operations across the border into Laos, and was supported by C-123s operating out of Da Nang. Other CIDG camps had been set up at other points along the border to the south. The Central Highlands city of Pleiku was crucial to the defense of the interior of the country. A large military airfield was located there and several C-130 flights were scheduled in each day. Another inland complex was at An Khe where the 1st Cavalry Division had set up its

Anything, Anywhere, Anytime

headquarters.

Once the coastal areas had been secured, MACV launched a new phase of the war that came to be known as "search and destroy." The US media misrepresented the term, implying that it meant to destroy everything. In reality, it meant to search out specific communist units and destroy them in the field. MACV commander Gen. Westmoreland was hoping for a major "set piece battle" in which artillery and air power could be brought to bear on a large communist force, particularly one from the Peoples' Army of Vietnam or PAVN, commonly known to Americans as the NVA. Such a battle never took place. The search and destroy strategy of moving troops around the country relieved heavily on airlift to move the troops and keep them supplied in the field.

In February 1967, MACV launched Operation *JUNCTION CITY*, the most ambitious military operation yet seen in Vietnam and the first – and only one – to see the use of American paratroopers in a large-scale airborne operation. The goal of the operation was to establish a firm Allied presence in the area of South Vietnam along the Cambodian Border in what was known as War Zone C, a region northwest of Saigon that was heavily infested with Viet Cong. The 2nd Battalion of the 173rd Airborne Brigade jumped onto a drop zone at Katum, a village only a mile inside South Vietnam. The name would strike fear in the heart of airlifters in coming years.[285] The airborne assault was coordinated with a massive heliborne operation into the area as 250 helicopters brought in eight battalions of American and South Vietnamese troops. The airborne portion of *JUNCTION CITY* was made up of 26 C-130s from all three C-130 wings, and included all three models. The first sixteen airplanes carried troops while the ten following were rigged for airdrop of containers and heavy equipment. During the approach to the drop zone, the formation encountered no enemy fire and the drops were normal with no malfunctions. After the drop, the troop carrying planes returned to Tan Son Nhut and Cam Ranh for assignment to other missions while the cargo drop planes went to Bien Hoa to reload for a second drop.

Once they were on the ground and organized, the troopers moved out to secure the area and begin construction of an airstrip. Airborne engineers used equipment that had been airdropped to them to begin work on a 2,900-foot airstrip near the village of Katum. First, they cleared the area of trees then they rolled and packed the landing strip they carved out of the jungle. A layer of laterite, a red clay similar to

---

[285] Katum was the scene of the most C-130 losses of any single location, including An Loc in 1972. In addition to airplanes physically shot down at Katum, several were hit there and made crash or emergency landings elsewhere.

Sam McGowan

that found in Alabama, Georgia and Tennessee that predominates in the area, was spread on top of the graded and tightly packed soil as the final step. A week after the drop, C-130s were landing on the new Katum airstrip. Another airfield was constructed a few miles south at Prek Lok while engineers worked to improve the existing airstrips at Tay Ninh, Trai Bi and Soui Da. The second phase of the operation established another assault landing strip at Tonle Cham. The two airfields, Tonle Cham and Katum, along with nearby Bu Dop, would become the most respected (in many respects – feared) airfields in South Vietnam.

C-130A dropping containers during Junction City

JUNCTION CITY was the beginning of a new era for C-130 crews as they began almost daily cargo drops, a routine that had previously been performed by C-123s, except for an occasional C-130 drop of cargo too large for C-123 delivery. The most common method used was container delivery, referred to as CDS, which involved the gravity drop of from twelve to eighteen A-22 containers made of cotton and nylon webbing, each of which was capable of holding up to 2,200 pounds of cargo, hence the name. A single G-12 parachute was used to lower the container to the ground. CDS was a new name for an old system dating back to before the Korean War. The difference was that the "new" method used the dual rail cargo handling system instead of the old skate wheels conveyer system that had been a holdover from C-119s. The containers were the same but a piece of plywood was attached to the bottom so they would roll on the dual rail roller conveyors. While heavy equipment drops involved extraction parachutes, the container method used an extraction parachute to cut a web gate that held the load in the airplane. A later method developed at the Tactical Airlift Center at Pope used the airplane's electric static line retriever winches to cut the gates instead of a parachute.

A train of containers after a CDS drop

Before CDS became common in Vietnam, C-130 crews approached the drop zone at normal paratroop drop altitude of around 700-800 feet, but a new technique was developed for combat operations. The drop plane approached the drop zone at low altitude then, as the restraint gate was cut, the pilot would pull the nose up sharply and began a climb, which caused the bundles to begin moving out of the airplane. The containers would spill out in a train and the parachutes would blossom open just before the first containers reached the ground. The approach procedure was varied when there was a strong enemy presence around the drop zone – the pilot would approach the area at an altitude above the effective range of automatic weapons and then spiral down to drop altitude from overhead. C-130 drops were on an occasional basis in 1966-67 but C-7s and C-123s made frequent airdrops, usually to remote camps including times when the camps were under siege. When *JUNCTION CITY* wound down,

Sam McGowan

the 196th Infantry Brigade remained in the area as a "roving brigade." As the unit moved through the region, it was resupplied for the most part by C-130 airdrop. When possible, C-7s landed on short landing strips to deliver cargo such as medical supplies that was too fragile or valuable to be dropped by parachute.

Airfreight technician loading pallet with 10 K parachute (Gawell Collection)

In any discussion of troop carrier/tactical airlift operations, it is important to include the role of the aerial port squadrons. The 8th APS was established at Tan Son Nhut in 1962 to process cargo and provide other aerial port functions. The squadron set up detachments throughout South Vietnam while 6th Aerial Port operated terminals in Thailand. When the US role in Southeast Asia escalated, the 2nd Aerial Port Group transferred to Tan Son Nhut to become the parent unit for the aerial port squadrons. New squadrons were set up; the 14th at Cam Ranh Bay and the 15th at Da Nang. Each squadron included airfreight and passenger service sections. The 14th APS included an aerial delivery section and the 8th included a combat control section. All three squadrons maintained detachments at certain key airfields within their area of responsibility. Not only did the aerial ports provide airfreight and passenger services at their bases, they also maintained detachments at forward airfields where airlift operations were frequent; mobility teams deployed to fields where large-scale airlift operations were scheduled.

The role of the combat control teams was somewhat different than it had been in TAC and PACAF before the war. They were still responsible for setting up drop zones and controlling airdrops, but

Anything, Anywhere, Anytime

their role was largely to provide communications between forward airfields and the airlift command center in Saigon and its elements in addition to providing airfield information to arriving flight crews. Combat control teams used the call sign "Tail Pipe" and the name was soon applied to combat control teams in general. Normally, combat control teams consisting of two enlisted men with a communications Jeep accompanied an airlift mission commander from 834th Air Division on operations at forward airfields.[286] There are indications that some combat controllers did not understand the role of the airlift mission commander.

Combat controller with radio Jeep

Airlift mission commanders were qualified C-130 pilots and navigators from the out-of-country C-130 wings who were sent on TDY to Saigon. Whenever an airlift operation was scheduled at a forward field, an airlift mission commander was sent to the field to control the operation. They decided when conditions allowed continued landings. The combat control team's role was to provide radio communications with the pilots and with the 834th AD command center and airlift command elements. Combat control veterans sometimes refer to the mission commanders as "safety officers," a term applied to officers assigned to drop zones in TAC, but their role in

---

[286] Airlift mission commanders were not the same as the drop zone safety officers that went out onto DZs in the US. Their role was to command operations, and the combat controllers served as their communications link with 834th Air Division and the cockpits of the airplanes involved in operations at the airfields where they had been sent.

Sam McGowan

South Vietnam was actually command and control. As the name implies, they were in command of airlift operations at the airfield or drop zone where they were assigned.

Combat controllers watching CDS bundles

Airlift command element, usually called ALCE, was a new name for an old component of the airlift mission, the transportation control detachment or TMD. ALCEs were detachments of the airlift command center in Saigon, which had formerly been the Transportation Movement Center, or TMC. Why they were renamed is anyone's guess. MATS had long had airlift command posts, or ACPs. The redesignation probably had something to do with the trend in the Air Force to start looking at the troop carrier mission as just another aspect of the Air Force air transportation mission. Regardless of what they were called, the ALCC and its ALCEs were command and control communications centers whose role was to provide a link between 834th Air Division and the aircrews. They were staffed by officers on a year-long non-flying assignment who matched the daily scheduled missions with airlift requests. Missions were scheduled at the ALCC in Saigon and passed on to the crews by the ALCEs at the onload bases. The airlift mission commander was the final link in the communications chain.

Anything, Anywhere, Anytime

He was a field grade officer, a major or lieutenant colonel, who was assigned to 834th Air Division for an extended period, usually ninety days, to go out into the field to oversee airlift operations at forward airfields. Airlift mission commanders oversaw all airlift operations at whatever airstrip to which he was assigned. He was accompanied by a combat control team usually made up of two enlisted combat controllers to provide a communications link between him and arriving aircraft. All 834th Air Division personnel on the airfield – combat controllers, airfreight personnel – answered to the airlift mission commander.

C-123B at remote airfield

In July 1967, the deputy chief of staff of the Air Force, General Bruce K. Holloway, sent out a letter advising that effective August 1, 1967 the troop carrier designation would be done away with permanently and the existing troop carrier units would become tactical airlift. The letter stated that the reason for the change was because it more adequately described the mission, which was no longer the transport of troops. The mission had been called troop carrier for a quarter century but somebody suddenly decided it was an outdated term.[287] General Holloway had previously served in Strike Command and was familiar with troop carrier operations. The chief of staff was General John P. McConnell, who had served in the CBI during World War II and had had a varied career since. In reality, nothing

---

[287] Veteran airlifter Myles "Mike" Rohrlick claims that the name change came as the result of a memo he wrote to the TAC commander when he was assigned to TAC headquarters after a tour at Tachikawa. He says that since fighter units had been redesignated as "tactical," troop carrier units should be as well.

changed except the name. Tactical airlifters were still responsible for transporting airborne and ground troops and delivering supplies to forward areas, both by airdrop and landing. The name change was really nothing but another example of the Air Force constantly reinventing itself.

By mid-1967, American ground troops had been in Vietnam for almost two years, yet there appeared to be no end to the war in sight. While the enemy at the beginning of the period had primarily been guerrillas from the south, by 1967 large numbers of North Vietnamese regular troops had infiltrated into South Vietnam. Two years of operations had seen several rotations of C-123 crews and the C-130 squadrons were receiving replacements lacking in troop carrier experience. Many of the men filling the cockpits of the transports were from backgrounds other than airlift, particularly bomber pilots whose previous flight experience had been in SAC bombers and tankers.[288] Others came from desk jobs where they only flew enough to log their required four hours a month for flight pay. For the new arrivals, flying in Vietnam was completely foreign to what they had experienced in other commands. While day to day operations into short, unimproved runways was far from boring, the transition period as the new arrivals gained experience was a time when they were especially susceptible to accident as operations into forward airfields were on the increase. There was another problem with the C-123 squadrons – their airplanes were underpowered.

The C-123s in Vietnam were B-models; they had been ordered by the Air Force with two Pratt & Whitney R-2800 engines, of which the Air Force had a supply left over from World War II. With the reciprocating engines, the C-123s were underpowered. To compensate for their lack of performance, the Air Force experimented with the addition of two small jet engines to boost their takeoff performance. The first conversion used a small jet engine mounted on each wingtip. After it became apparent that the C-123s needed additional power, a program was begun to convert the fleet into C-123Ks with the addition of a General Electric J-85 engine mounted in a pod under each wing. C-123Ks started appearing in Southeast Asia in late 1966.

As the aircrews gained experience and learned lessons, so did the command and control personnel in the ALCC at Tan Son Nhut, many of whom had come to Southeast Asia from assignments in other than

---

[288] For some reason, pilots from MAC rarely were assigned to the offshore C-130 squadrons. Instead, they usually went to assignments in South Vietnam in C-123s or AC-47 or EC-47 units. Later in the war, some MAC C-141 pilots were assigned to C-130 squadrons but except for men who had been in MATS/MAC C-130 squadrons that transferred to TAC, such assignments were rare in the 1965-70 time period.

Anything, Anywhere, Anytime

airlift. One lesson was especially expensive; the cost was two C-130Es destroyed and a third badly damaged. Previously, two C-130s had been lost in a rocket attack at Da Nang in July 1967 but Da Nang was a major base, although it came under mortar and rocket attack so often that it came to be known as "Rocket Alley." In fact, the only C-130s lost on the ground to enemy action at this point in the war had been at Da Nang. There had been no attacks on C-130s at forward airfields except for an occasional rocket or mortar salvo at Dong Ha or one of the other fields along the DMZ. It was evidently a false sense of security that led 834th Air Division to schedule as many as five airplanes at a time into Dak To even though a fierce battle was going on in the hills nearby. With helicopters and C-130s constantly going in and out of the airfield, it was the congestion in the sky around the field that led the acting 834th commander, Brig. Gen. Hugh Wild,[289] to declare to his bosses at Seventh Air Force that they must be prepared to accept the loss of an airplane if operations were to continue into Dak To. However, it was not a rash of accidents that suddenly changed the dynamics of the airlift mission in Southeast Asia.

Mortar rounds struck the airfield on November 12, but in spite of the warning shots fired by the enemy, 834th scheduled four C-130s into the airfield shortly after daybreak on November 15. Three had landed and shut down engines. A fourth was on the runway when a rain of mortar rounds began impacting on the airfield. The pilot of the fourth C-130 turned his airplane around on the runway and took off again, but the other three crews abandoned their airplanes and headed for shelter – they had no other choice. The communist gunners had the range and the parking ramp, where the aircraft had been parked for unloading, was their target. About ten rounds hit the ramp where the C-130s were parked; two airplanes were set on fire and the third received severe shrapnel damage and began leaking fuel. The attack continued for half an hour, during which time the main ammunition dump was hit and erupted in a series of explosions.

About twenty-five minutes after the attack began, Staff Sergeant Joe Mack, a flight engineer from the 776th Tactical Airlift Squadron, suggested to his pilot, Capt. Joseph K. Glenn, that they should go out and move their airplane away from the burning wrecks before it was also set on fire and destroyed. Glenn hesitated at first, but finally agreed they should do something. The two airmen ran out of the bunker in which they had taken shelter and across the ramp to their airplane. After a quick check of the airplane, they started two engines

---

[289] General Wild was a former MATS and MAC officer who had gone to Vietnam from command of a MAC wing at McCord AFB, WA to serve as deputy commander of 834th AD. He was temporary commander of 834th Air Division for only two weeks in November 1968 until General Moore's replacement arrived.

Sam McGowan

and backed it away from the burning wrecks. For their efforts to save their airplane, Glenn and Mack were awarded the Silver Star. Five hours later Glenn and his crew flew the airplane back to Cam Ranh in spite of a shattered windshield and numerous shrapnel holes. For the flight, the five crewmembers were awarded the Distinguished Flying Cross. The Vietnam War had taken a drastic new turn for airlifters – and the road ahead was very rough.

C-130 burning at Dak To

Anything, Anywhere, Anytime

Sam McGowan

Chapter Seventeen - "MORTAR MAGNETS"

C-130B at Khe Sanh[290]

In late November 1967, about the time of the Battle of Dak To, intelligence sources in Vietnam detected a buildup around the Marine combat base at Khe Sanh, a remote camp in the extreme northwestern corner of South Vietnam. Although there had been an airfield at Khe Sanh since early in the war, the Marines had only been there since July 1966. Ever since they set up their combat base, Khe Sanh had been a hot spot. Airdrops of building materials were common. In October 1967 a C-130 from the 314th Tactical Airlift Wing crashed at Khe Sanh while making a drop and everyone on board died except for the pilot, who somehow managed to escape from the burning wreckage.[291] Command of 834th Air Division was held by Maj. General Burl W. McLaughlin, who had a history in troop carrier and C-130s. He commanded the 64th Troop Carrier Wing at Dyess then took over the 516th TCW that replaced it. Prior to his assignment to Saigon, he commanded 322nd Air Division in Europe.

---

[290] Although the smoke in the background in this famous prize-winning photograph is often represented as smoke from air attacks, Marines who were at Khe say it is actually from burning garbage. There is a ravine just north of the runway and this is where details disposed of garbage. The photo was taken by 315th AD information specialist A1C M.L. Ray when he was at Khe Sanh in October 1967 before the seige. It was awarded a prize by PACAF in early 1968. Because of the timing, many C-130 veterans think it was taken during the siege.

[291] At the time of the crash, the crew was in the process of dropping platforms of sandbags, evidently using a non-standard method of delivery. Just what caused the crash is uncertain, but the airplane evidently contacted the ground during the approach for the drop.

Anything, Anywhere, Anytime

North Vietnamese General Giap has since denied that his objective was to take Khe Sanh, and has asserted that the attack on the base was a diversion for his real plans; the promotion of a general uprising in the rest of the country. In either case, Giap failed to accomplish his objective, although the events of early 1968 constituted a major political victory for the communists, thanks largely to the American media. If Giap was hoping that the attack on Khe Sanh would draw troops away from the cities, he was sadly mistaken because no large reinforcing force rushed to the scene of the battle. Instead, MACV commander General Westmoreland decided to rely on airpower to hold the North Vietnamese at bay, and airlift to keep the defenders who were already there supplied until the camp could be relieved when the weather improved in the spring.

By the beginning of 1968, the American and South Vietnamese leadership was beginning to believe that the North Vietnamese intended to make Khe Sanh the "Dienbienphu of the Second Indochina War." The situations were somewhat similar but hardly identical. Both bases were located in remote areas and the garrisons were largely dependent on air transportation for resupply, but the similarities ended there. The primary difference was that Dienbienphu had been more than 150 miles from the primary French base at Hanoi while Khe Sanh was less than half that distance from Da Nang and only 22 nautical miles from the US Marine Corps base at Dong Ha, which was open to ground supply. Dong Ha was capable of handling C-130s; they landed there several times a day. Supplies could be flown into Dong Ha on C-130s where the pallets would be broken down and the cargo placed in slings for helicopter lift to the outposts around Khe Sanh. This left the airfield open for deliveries to supply the base itself and negated the need for helicopter operations from the combat base. The French had no helicopters and their transports had been slow and lacking payload capability when compared to the C-130s that made up the bulk of 834th Air Division's airlift strength. The Marines at Dong Ha had heavy-lift helicopters within easy range of Khe Sanh while 834th had enough transports that the resupply of the base was only one more mission, albeit a hazardous one, rather than a massive effort as had been the situation during the Dienbienphu battle. Not only that, while the French air force had been small, MACV had a powerful air force upon which to call to support the fire base with everything from airlift to massive B-52 strikes.

The battle got underway in mid-January, when shelling of the base intensified. On January 19, more than 200 artillery rounds struck the base. Communist shells blew up the main ammunition dump two days later. Suddenly, the situation became critical. Since debris on the runway from exploding ammunition effectively shortened the runway length below that required for the larger C-130s, six C-123s were sent to Khe Sanh with an emergency resupply of ammunition. The Providers arrived as darkness began to fall and landed using light from artillery flares to find the runway. Enemy shells continued falling on the base while they were on the ground but all six delivered their loads and departed safely. On the following day, C-123 missions continued. Marine helicopter missions brought in additional cargo and 500 reinforcements from nearby Dong Ha. C-130 landings resumed the following morning after the runway was of debris. Only two transports at a time were allowed on the ground to avoid the potential for another Dak To. A steady stream of transports and helicopters continued into the combat base until darkness brought a halt to operations for the day. Over the next eight days, USAF transports brought in an average of 250 tons per day with C-130s doing the bulk of the work. The C-130's larger payloads dictated their use for the airlift; C-123 and C-7 landings were restricted to an average of two flights per day at that point in the siege to reduce congestion in the vicinity of the base. By the end of January, C-7 flights had ceased altogether, since their lack of payload capacity offset their superior short field landing capabilities. Only eight C-7s landed at Khe Sanh during the entire period of the siege.(Bowers, 1986) (McLaughlin, 1968)[292]

    Just getting into Khe Sanh made for a dicey operation, but it was little different than airfields troop carrier crews had landed on in the past – except for the presence of large numbers of enemy troops in the hills around the base. The runway was located on top of a knoll in the middle of a valley surrounded by 1,500-foot peaks. Landings were like landing on an aircraft carrier. Shifting winds sometimes caused significant wind shear just as an airplane approached the runway threshold.[293] To make matters worse, the communists timed their attack to coincide with the Cochin winds of the annual monsoon, which brought in moisture from the South China Sea and backed it up against the mountains, thus causing almost daily low ceilings, fog and rain. The C-130 crews were reminded that one of their own had been lost only a few months before when it crashed while dropping a load of sandbags in adverse weather conditions. The wreckage of the airplane lay just off the runway and was clearly visible to all of the crews that landed there. Khe Sanh was not a fun place, and things were about to get

---

[292] Some Caribou veterans have challenged this number, but it is taken from 834th Air Division records as recorded by the Khe Sanh ALCE.

[293] "Wind shear" occurs when the wind direction suddenly shifts at differing altitudes. For example, an airplane flying into a headwind may suddenly encounter a tailwind as it descends for landing. The sudden wind shift will cause a rapid loss of airspeed, which can cause an airplane to stall.

Anything, Anywhere, Anytime

worse.

The North Vietnamese were well aware that the transports were the lifeline of the troops at Khe Sanh just as the C-119s and C-47s had been for the French more than a decade before. Interrupting the flow of supplies to the base was their number one priority, just as it had been with their predecessors at Dienbienphu. As the siege continued, the North Vietnamese brought in more and more antiaircraft guns and heavy machineguns and set them up in the hills overlooking the combat base. Small PAVN units set up crew-served automatic weapons along the approach and departure routes to the runways. Personnel on the ground at Khe Sanh realized another transport was on its way in when they heard the guns open up. Fortunately for the C-130 crews, the North Vietnamese air force never dispatched any of its MiGs that far south, so they only had to contend with ground fire. On January 25, a USAF C-130 was shot-up while on approach but the crew managed a safe landing. It was but the first of many transports that would receive battle damage ranging from minor to severe during the resupply of the combat base.

Once the transports were on the ground, they had to contend with the constant threat of artillery. Khe Sanh is in the very northwest corner of what was then South Vietnam and only a few miles from the demarcation line that divided the two countries. Laos, which the North Vietnamese had turned into their private playground, is only a few miles to the west. North Vietnamese artillery positions had been set up on the other side of the demilitarized zone, commonly known as the DMZ, and some guns had a range of as much as twenty miles. North Vietnam had received a supply of 122-MM rockets from communist Europe and while they weren't that accurate, they could do considerable damage to a C-130 if a rocket crew got lucky.

Within a few days after they began the siege of Khe Sanh, the communists launched their infamous Tet Offensive of 1968. The attacks started on the night of January 30 when the Viet Cong attacked most of the major population centers in South Vietnam. Airfields were primary targets – Nha Trang, Kontum, Ban Me Thout, Pleiku and Da Nang all came under enemy mortar and rocket fire. Some airfields, including Tan Son Nhut and An Khe, were targets for infantry attack. Viet Cong commandos occupied the radio and police stations at Qui Nhon; the civilian airport at Ban Me Thout fell into Viet Cong hands for a time, but the military field remained under friendly control. The 834th Air Division C-130, C-123 and C-7 force was crucial to the response as the transports airlifted reinforcements to areas under attack.

The following evening, the communists carried the attack further. Strong Viet Cong forces struck at targets within the city limits of Saigon as well as Tan Son Nhut and Bien Hoa air bases. The American

Sam McGowan

Embassy in Saigon was attacked and a team of Viet Cong managed to get onto the Embassy Grounds, but they never penetrated the Embassy itself. Although the media at the time and several writers since have implied that the attacks came without warning, US military forces in and around Saigon had been alerted to expect them. On the eve of Tet, the C-130 crewmembers from the 463rd Wing, who were quartered at the Merlin Hotel in Saigon's Cholon District, were moved from the hotel to quarters on Tan Son Nhut Air Base in anticipation of enemy activity in the city. Nevertheless, six officers from the offshore C-130 wings, who were in country on special assignments as airlift mission commanders, somehow were not notified. They were asleep in their rooms in the hotel when the attacks came. Communist soldiers occupied the hotel's lower floors for a time, but fortunately never ventured up the stairs to the upper floors where the officers were hiding.

C-130A landing out of the mist at Khe Sanh

Many C-130 crews, especially, were caught in the Tet attacks. Under 834th Air Division operational policy, C-123s flew mostly daylight operations but the C-130 mission operated around the clock. One 29th Tactical Airlift Squadron crew was preparing to take-off at Tan Son Nhut when the attacks came. Major Frank Blodgett took off and remained over the airport for several hours. The attacks had caused the tower operators to evacuate their posts so Major Blodgett and his crew became temporary air traffic controllers. They pointed

Anything, Anywhere, Anytime

out other aircraft to helicopter gunship and attack pilots who came in to strike the communist positions. When his fuel supply began to dwindle, Blodgett landed at Vung Tau, then took off again after refueling with a load of Vietnamese marines and their American advisors and brought them to Tan Son Nhut. Blodgett's crew went back to Vung Tau to pick up a second load of marines, but when they landed back at Saigon, the airplane's brakes caught fire and put them out of action. The crew retired to sandbagged bunkers behind C-130 Operations where they spent the rest of the day; a day in which communist attackers came within 100 yards of their position.

A C-130A crew was on the ground at An Khe when enemy forces hit the airfield. Communist troops ran by their airplane and sprayed the cargo compartment with AK-47 fire. The airplane was only partially loaded and the crew, fortunately, were all in front of the cargo pallets and were not harmed by the flying bullets. The tracers started a fire in the cargo but the crew put it out. They reportedly even urinated on the flames![294] A C-130B was also on the ground at the same time. Attacking communist sappers threw a satchel charge under the nose landing gear bay and the explosion blew some of the skin off of the airplane, but the crew escaped without injury.[295]

---

[294] One of the crewmembers has said this is not true. However, a rumor was spread that they did. It's unlikely that they would have needed to since C-130s were equipped with several fire extinguishers in the cockpit and cargo compartment.
[295] An article appeared in the 315th Air Division newspaper, The Airlifter, about the attack on An Khe. While the C-130A crew's experiences were covered in detail, the article barely mentioned the B-model even though it suffered considerable damage. The C-130B crew, including flight engineer Craig Clifton, a personal friend of the author, were not happy about it.

But even though the Tet attacks were politically successful as they attracted the attention of the US media, militarily they were a disaster for the South Vietnamese communists, who lost many of their best-trained men in the attacks in the cities. The attacks were met by counterattacks that were even fiercer than those by the communists, and very few Viet Cong escaped with their lives. After Tet '68 and the destruction of the Viet Cong units, the communist effort in South Vietnam depended primarily upon the North Vietnamese Army.

The attacks also led to an increase in American personnel in Southeast Asia, including more airlift. Tactical Air Command C-130 squadrons rushed to the Pacific to augment the PACAF units. Many of the TAC crewmembers were recently returned from airlift duties in Southeast Asia; their experience greatly increased 315th Air Division's capabilities at a time when its resources were becoming strained. The Tet attacks were evidently timed to coincide with an event off the coast of North Korea, when a US intelligence-gathering ship was captured and the crew held prisoner.[296] In response to the Pueblo Crisis, TAC sent two C-130 squadrons to Japan to support troops in Korea, but they were quickly integrated into operations in Vietnam. The in-country C-130 force increased from 72 airplanes on February 10 to 88 the following day, the equivalent of a reinforced squadron. By February 28, the in-country C-130 force had further increased to 96 airplanes, or six squadrons although there were no C-130 squadrons as such in Southeast Asia. A new C-130 operating location had started operating out of Tuy Hoa the previous October while revetments were under construction at Cam Ranh. The detachment, called 315th Air Division Task Force A, remained at Tuy Hoa to accommodate the additional airplanes. The Tuy Hoa location remained open until February 1969. The utilization rate ran high, with 91 C-130 missions per day being scheduled from February 28-April 11 when Khe Sanh was relieved. (McLaughlin, 1968)

The Tet attacks came just as the siege of Khe Sanh was beginning and as the North Vietnamese were increasing their presence around the camp. On February 5, a C-130E commanded by Lt. Col. Howard M. Dallman took a number of hits from heavy machineguns during landing. Fire broke out in the cargo compartment as wooden ammunition boxes smoldered then erupted in flames. The loadmaster, SSgt Wade Green, fought the fire with a hand-held fire extinguisher while Dallman backed the airplane as far as possible from the cargo ramp. When the fire was out, they taxied to the ramp. By this time,

---

[296] The USS Pueblo was boarded on January 23, 1968, only a week before the commencement of the Tet Offensive.

Anything, Anywhere, Anytime

enemy fire had flattened a tire. Using a jury-rigged jack that the aerial port came up with, the flight engineer, SSgt Charles Brault, changed the tire. Before they could take off, incoming fire knocked out an engine. The co-pilot, Capt. Roland Behnke, managed to start the engine while Dallman was in the aerial port shack trying to make contact with the airlift command center in Saigon.[297] The crew got the airplane off the ground and to safety at Da Nang. Dallman was awarded the Air Force Cross while his crew received lesser decorations.[298]

Khe Sanh 1966

Artillery and mortar fire was a major problem for crews landing at Khe Sanh. The North Vietnamese were determined to interrupt the airlift, and the presence of a transport on the ground was a signal for an increase in the already fierce bombardment of the camp. There were mortars within 3,000 yards of the runway, while the heavier artillery and rocket positions were located in the mountains to the west. Some were across the DMZ in North Vietnam and others were in Laos, where they were closer to the communist supply lines. To suppress the enemy fire, USAF and USMC airstrikes against the enemy gun positions were coordinated with transport arrival times. Marine artillery units returned the incoming fire. Aircrews did everything they

---

[297] This information is from a letter from copilot Behnke to the author.
[298] The award of the Air Force Cross to Dallman is an illustration of the inequity of the military awards and decorations system. It wasn't Dallman who put out the fire, it was his loadmaster, Wade Green. Charlie Brault, the engineer, changed the tire. The copilot, Roland Behnke, and Brault managed to get the engines started while Dallman was inside on the telephone, yet the Air Force Cross was awarded to him as the aircraft commander and ranking member of the crew even though it was his crew that actually saved the airplane.

Sam McGowan

could to minimize their time on the ground, including and particularly "speed offloading." During speed offloading operations, the loadmaster would lower the cargo ramp until it nearly touched the ground. The navigator would come down from the cockpit and unlock the cargo pallets and the pilot would let the airplane roll forward while the pallets rolled off the end of the ramp. As soon as the last pallet cleared the ramp, the loadmaster would start closing the ramp and door while the pilot taxied onto the runway and began his takeoff roll. Aerial port personnel would come out with forklifts and scoop up the pallets and move them to the cargo area, where they would be broken down so the load could be distributed to the proper recipients. Using this method – which was also referred to as "combat offloading" – ground times could be held to a minimum, often no more than five minutes from landing to takeoff. It normally took the communist gunners a little longer than that to line up their guns. The smaller C-123s were able to stop short of the cargo ramp, but the larger and heavier C-130s required landing distances that were just barely too long for them to make the turnoff. They usually had to turn around on the runway and taxi back to it.

C-130B taxiing past rocket damage while combat off-loading at Khe Sanh

On February 11, another C-130E was hit by mortar fire immediately after landing. Two passengers were killed and the loadmaster was seriously wounded. The other crewmembers came down from the cockpit to fight the fire, with assistance from members of the USAF detachment on the ground. They got it out, but the airplane was not fit for flight – all four tires were shot out, the engines were riddled with shrapnel and the hydraulic systems were shot up. A

Anything, Anywhere, Anytime

maintenance team flew in from Da Nang and went to work with the assistance of the flight crew. One mechanic worked on the tail under the cover of darkness using a flashlight. On the second day, another mortar round hit the airplane but by the following day the airplane had been repaired to the point that it could be flown out. Captain Edwin Jenks and his crew flew the airplane to Da Nang where repairmen added up 242 bullet holes before they stopped counting. Jenks and his crew were recommended for Silver Stars.(Bowers, 1986)

C-130B after combat offloading ammunition at Khe Sanh

The day before Jenks' airplane was hit, the most serious incident on the airfield at Khe Sanh took place when a Marine KC-130 was hit several times while on approach with a load of fuel bladders. Fire broke out in the cargo compartment as the airplane touched down and, as the airplane came to a halt, it became engulfed in flames. A combat cameraman recorded the entire event on film. Chief Warrant Officer Henry Wildfang, the pilot, managed to escape through a side window along with the co-pilot and navigator. Four passengers perished in the flames; the loadmaster and flight mechanic died later. Film footage of the burning airplane was shown repeatedly on the 6 0' clock News in the United States for several days after the airplane was shot down.

The loss of the Marine transport and near-loss of Jenks' C-130E led General Momyer to suspend all USAF C-130 landings at Khe Sanh and order a turn to airdrop. The combination of shelling and ground fire made the destruction of a transport on the ground at the combat base inevitable, and Momyer felt that C-130s were a "valuable national resource" of which the nation could ill-afford to lose a single one. On February 12, Seventh Air Force suspended C-130 landings. The smaller (and obsolete) C-123s were still allowed to land when conditions allowed, but C-130 deliveries would be exclusively by airdrop. Since they didn't belong to the Air Force, the Marine Corps KC-130s were not affected by the order. They continued to land occasionally, but were usually thwarted by incoming fire, as were the C-123s.

As the siege developed, alternate methods of delivering supplies to the combat base were considered. Night landings would have been less susceptible to ground fire but the Marine combat base commander ruled them out. Frequent low clouds and mist also presented a problem. During the preceding year, Tactical Air Command had developed an airdrop technique using ground controlled approach radar to position the transport for a drop, but the method was still considered unproven and its accuracy questionable.[299] Two 834th officers, Majors Myles Rohrlick and Henry Van Gieson, who were both experienced C-130 pilots with long service in PACAF and TAC, ran a few test missions at Khe Sanh early in the siege with the Marine GCA and determined that the method would suffice should the need arise.

On February 13, C-130 airdrops began at Khe Sanh. When

---

[299] Ground controlled approach radar, GCA for short, was developed right after World War II and first used during the Berlin Airlift. The GCA radar provides both position and altitude information to the ground operator, who uses it to "talk" the pilot in and position them over the runway for a landing. In this case the Marine GCA operators used their radar to position the C-130s and C-123s for an airdrop.

Anything, Anywhere, Anytime

possible, pilots flew visual approaches but when the weather went bad, as it often was at Khe Sanh, they turned to the GCA method. The Marine GCA operator gave the pilot headings to fly to position the airplane over the end of the runway. The navigator plotted a course from there to the drop zone and used his stopwatch and the airplane's onboard Doppler computer to determine the release point. The first few missions were flown under the overcast, but the crews reported that they could have dropped in the clouds. Once the method had been proven, missions in all kinds of weather were commenced. The low clouds and poor visibilities offered one special advantage – they concealed the approaching transports from the eyes of the enemy! GCA-controlled drops continued throughout the siege, except for a temporary interruption when shelling knocked out the GCA equipment. With GCA, airdrops continued during weather conditions too bad for C-123 landings.

Even though airdrop became the principle method of resupply at Khe Sanh, some items were too fragile to be dropped. At the same time, the morale of the Marines dictated that landings should continue; as long as airplanes were landing, they knew they were not cut off from the rest of the world. An average of three C-123s landed at Khe Sanh each day, with heavy incoming greeting each arrival. They brought in medical supplies and troops, and took out casualties and men who were due to rotate home or go on emergency leave on their return flights. In late February, the prohibition against C-130 landings was temporarily lifted. Fifteen C-130s landed during a four-day period before the prohibition was reinstated. Not affected by General Momyer's order, the Marine C-130s still landed when possible, although their landings were few and far between. A few Caribous also made landings.(Bowers, 1986)(McLaughlin, 1968)

In early March, three C-123s were lost at Khe Sanh. The first crashed on take-off on March 1 after an engine failed after it was struck by mortar fragments. The crew escaped without injury, but mortar fire destroyed the airplane. Less than a week later, a C-123 was shot down several miles east of the base, with the loss of all 49 persons aboard. The pilot aborted a landing approach to avoid a Vietnamese light plane and the C-123 was hit by ground fire as he maneuvered at low altitude for another landing attempt. That same afternoon, another C-123 was hit by artillery fire while on the ground. Although the damage was not that great, it was destroyed by shelling before it could be repaired. The losses led to restrictions on C-123 landings – they landed only when absolutely necessary with cargo such as fragile medical supplies that could not be airdropped. Sometimes the shelling was so frequent that C-123 landings were prohibited. For a time, the only means of delivery was airdrop and helicopter resupply.[300]

Most drop missions at Khe Sanh involved CDS, the container delivery method. Some items were too large for the CDS bundles and were delivered by LAPES, the low-altitude parachute delivery method that used an extraction parachute to pull a pallet out of the airplane as it skimmed the ground. While CDS bundles could only hold 2,200 pounds, a LAPES platform could hold 30,000. The small drop zone ruled out the use of conventional heavy equipment drops. LAPES drops were hindered by a lack of rigging equipment; after each drop, the equipment and special sleds had to be recovered and returned to Cam Ranh Bay so it could be used to rig another load. There was also some loss of control with LAPES platforms. Two LAPES loads broke away from their parachutes and went wild, and in each case killed Marines on the ground. To insure pinpoint accuracy, 834th Air Division commander Maj. Gen. McLaughlin elected to resurrect the GPES method, with which he was familiar from his service in TAC in the early sixties.

GPES, the ground-proximity extraction method, was developed in TAC in the late fifties for use with both C-130s and C-123s but was discontinued after the development of LAPES, which required no equipment on the ground. GPES required the installation of a pair of winches, buried in barrels, with a steel cable suspended between them. The low-flying C-130 or C-123 would skim the ground and snare the cable with a hook, the winches would let out cable to absorb shock and the platform would be pulled from the airplane. Although GPES had been discontinued, the equipment, which consisted of the winches and cables that were placed across the drop zone and the hooks that were attached to the airplane, were in storage at TAC bases in the States. The equipment was flown to Vietnam from Sewart AFB, Tennessee. Sets were delivered to the 374th Tactical Airlift Wing at Naha and crews began GPES training on the island of Ie Shima (the island where WW II columnist Ernie Pyle was killed by a Japanese sniper.) While the crews were training, an Air Force combat control team installed the equipment at Khe Sanh, with the assistance of Marines and Navy Seabees. The first GPES mission was flawless, and the load came to a stop so smoothly that the combat control team found that only two eggs had been broken in a crate that had been put aboard for them.[301](Strobaugh D., 1968) The second drop pulled the

---

[300] Since they were not bound by fixed approach paths, the Marine helicopters were able to approach the field from different angles and avoid the areas where the communists had positioned their antiaircraft guns.

[301] This information was recorded in a diary kept by USAF Maj. Donald Strobaugh, who spent several months with the 8th Aerial Port Combat Control

Anything, Anywhere, Anytime

winches out of the ground and they had to be reinstalled. There were some problems with GPES as crews occasionally missed the cable, but the general consensus was that GPES was superior to LAPES for the conditions at Khe Sanh. It also offered a number of advantages, one of which was that it used standard modular airdrop platforms instead of specially made sleds. As it turned out, only eleven GPES missions were flown because 1st Cavalry Division troops linked up with the Khe Sanh defenders and ground routes into the camp were reopened.(McLaughlin, 1968)

C-130B performing LAPES drop at Khe Sanh

General Giap, the North Vietnamese commander, had hoped to repeat his earlier success at Dienbienphu at Khe Sanh. (In his memoirs Giap denied that he intended to capture the base, but his denial is suspect since his casualties in the vicinity of the camp were heavy.) He believed that the characteristically bad weather of the season and his own antiaircraft would be able to halt the resupply effort, and the Marines would be forced to surrender as the French had. But Giap had

---

Team before he had to return to the States due to the illness and death of his wife. It's also mentioned in Bowers' TACTICAL AIRLIFT.

Sam McGowan

not reckoned on the superior abilities of the C-130s and C-123s over the C-47s and C-119s that had been available to the French. In spite of ground fire and sometimes intense artillery fire from points up to twenty miles distant, the North Vietnamese were never able to stem the flow of supplies into Khe Sanh.

Naha-based C-130A dropping by GPES at Khe Sanh. The tail-code indicates that the airplane was from the 817th TAS but that doesn't mean the crew was. No effort was made to keep squadron airplanes and crews together in Vietnam.

In early January, in response to heavy enemy pressure in northern I Corps, the US Army's 1st Cavalry Division moved north from its base at An Khe to Camp Evans, a base about midway between Quang Tri and the Imperial City of Hue in Quang Tri Province. Intense communist attacks during Tet were especially heavy in the vicinity of Hue and Camp Evans was surrounded by NVA troops. The runway was still under construction so 834th Air Division mounted a four-day airdrop effort in early February, right in the midst of the Tet attacks. An Air Force combat control team parachuted into Evans from the first airplane over the DZ to control the remaining drops.

The 26 missions flown over Camp Evans were just as difficult and dangerous as those over Khe Sanh. Low ceilings forced the drop planes to approach the drop zone at low altitudes where they were especially susceptible to ground fire, and it was described by crews that encountered it as "severe." In order to stay visual, C-130 pilots approached the combat base with the huge tails of their airplanes barely skimming the bases of the clouds! They often dropped from altitudes well below the prescribed drop altitudes of 500-600 feet. One crew flew five missions and took hits on three. On one mission, they lost an engine; on another they lost all the fuel from three tanks after they were holed by enemy fire. By the third day of the drops, the weather was beginning to improve to the point that crews could drop from more conventional altitudes. Even though hostile fire was as intense as before, no more C-130s were hit. Within a week after the beginning of the drops the first C-7s landed; they were followed a few days later by C-123s. The 1st Cavalry Division commander praised the C-130 crews for the "tremendous job" they did during the airdrops to his men. With their supply base open, the cavalry division was ready to rescue the Marines and Operation *PEGASUS* commenced.[302](Bowers, 1986)

In early March, the enemy effort around Khe Sanh seemed to be declining, as evidenced by the lessening intensity of the shelling. Marine patrols reported that the enemy forces seemed to be withdrawing into the mountains of Laos. Although they had rained shells on the combat base, the PAVN troops had also been subject to a waterfall of ordnance dropped by Air Force, Navy and Marine aircraft, including B-52s. Seventh Air Force had ordered Operation *NIAGARA* at the beginning of the siege and it had taken its effect on the communists. Airdrops by both C-130s and C-123s continued. General Westmoreland based his decision not to evacuate the camp in January on the assumption that the Marines could hold until poor winter weather gave way to better conditions. *PEGASUS* was planned to include a 1st Cavalry attack westward from Camp Evans along Highway 9 while Marines attacked from Dong Ha. On March 20, construction got underway for a new airstrip, LZ Stud, at Ca Lu to serve as a delivery point for C-7s and C-123s during the attack. Within a week, C-7s were landing on the tiny airstrip. By early April, the relief effort was well underway. C-130 landings resumed on April 9. Two days later, Highway 9 was reopened and trucks began arriving at the base.

The airlift effort at Khe Sanh was monumental. A total of 1,128 missions brought in 24,860,000 pounds of cargo; 306 patients were brought out of the base by USAF transports. Although the C-123s had the difficult burden of landing after Seventh Air Force halted C-130 landings, more than ninety percent of the total tonnage delivered by fixed-wing transports came in aboard C-130s. C-130 landings totaled 273 compared to 179 by C-123s, while C-130s made 563 airdrops and

---

[302] The first cavalryman to make contact with the Marines is a personal friend and former coworker of the author, Jerry Nesbitt. Jerry served two tours in South Vietnam. Books on Khe Sanh report that first soldier to greet the Marines was "a wise-cracking young sergeant." Jerry told the author that what he said to the Marine officer was, "Yeah, you (effing) Marines! Always getting in trouble and then the Cav' has to come and bail you out!"

the C-123s 105. Caribous made eight landings and no airdrops.(Bowers, 1986)(McLaughlin, 1968) The C-123s suffered the worst losses with three airplanes destroyed at and in the vicinity of the base. CWO Wildfang's airplane was the only KC-130 lost at Khe Sanh (and the only USMC C-130 lost in Vietnam while on a transport mission. Another was lost during a refueling mission when it collided with a fighter.) No Air Force C-130s were lost during the siege, but one crashed while landing at Khe Sanh shortly after the base was relieved. Another had crashed at the base the previous October, several months before it came under siege. Both losses were due to accident.

While Khe Sanh dominated the events of the winter of 1968, other airlift efforts were mounted to supply and reinforce garrisons that were cutoff to ground resupply due to the communist attacks. For several days immediately after Tet, it seemed that every major town in South Vietnam was under attack. Dak To was cut off, except by air resupply, and an emergency C-130 lift was mounted. In early February, C-123s airdropped supplies to Kontum. The battle to retake portions of the city of Hue required an increased airlift effort into nearby Phu Bia. Troops were moved all over the country to respond to communist attacks. As they were defeated one by one, MACV resumed its efforts to secure the country.

With the relief of Khe Sanh, the Americans and South Vietnamese were able to turn their attention toward defeating the large numbers of North Vietnamese who remained in South Vietnam. The 1st Cavalry Division mounted Operation *DELAWARE* into the A Shau Valley, a large valley along the Laotian border that the communists had been using as a sanctuary and supply route since 1966 when the Special Forces camp at A Shau was overrun. Plans were developed to invade the valley as early as mid-1967, but the events of early 1968 led to a temporary delay. *DELAWARE* called for a major aerial assault into A Loi airfield in the valley and the old airfield at A Shau itself. Until the two airfields could be restored to operational conditions, the cavalry units would be dependent on C-130 airdrops for all resupply.

The attack began on April 19, 1968, only eight days after the relief of Khe Sanh, when elements of the 1st Cavalry attacked south from the direction of Khe Sanh, but it was not until April 25 that the airfield at A Loi came under Allied control. Early the following morning, an Air Force airlift mission control team landed after an attempt the previous afternoon was thwarted due to bad weather. The Army was reluctant to use their CH-47s to move the combat controller's equipment since every available helicopter was needed to transport ammunition into the valley. Payload restrictions forced the CCT to leave the equipment that would have allowed blind drops behind at Da Nang.(Strobaugh D., 1968)

Anything, Anywhere, Anytime

Weather conditions in the A Shau Valley were terrible on the morning of April 26 when twelve C-130s loaded for drops at Bien Hoa and Cam Ranh Bay. All three 315th AD C-130 wings were represented, with four A-models, four B-models and four E-models assigned to the missions. When the first drop plane arrived over the valley at 0830, the crew found a solid undercast beneath them with cloud tops at 8,000 feet. Beneath the clouds were mountains as high as 6,800 feet on either side of the valley; the cloud bases extended all the way down to 500 feet above the ground. Each C-130 would have to descend through several thousand feet of solid cloud into a valley with 4,000-foot ridgelines nearby, ridgelines controlled by the enemy. Just getting into the valley required every measure of pilot and navigational skill in the cockpits. A fighter squadron from Da Nang was supposed to fly missions into the valley to provide fire suppression for the C-130s, but they canceled their missions because of the weather. The transports would have to fly into the valley unescorted.(Bowers, 1986)

The first crew began their descent from a TACAN[303] fix and cautiously descended through the clouds into the mountain valley. While the pilot flew headings based on Doppler readouts, the navigator used his radar to establish the airplane's position relative to the nearby ridges. They broke out of the clouds at about 500 feet above the ground. The drop zone appeared out of the mist when they were about two miles out. At the release point, the pilot pulled the airplane into the nose-high attitude required for CDS and the airplane disappeared into the clouds. The combat control team watched in awe as the bundles came spilling out of the clouds!(Strobaugh D. , 1968)

Though the first airplane encountered no ground fire, its approach alerted the PAVN troops, who had retreated into the hills when the 1st Cavalry arrived in the valley. The second crew heard exploding shells and felt shrapnel peppering the sides of their airplane. Ground fire also greeted the third and fourth crews but the fourth crew was not aware they had been shot at until they landed and found ten bullet holes in their airplane! All twelve airplanes had dropped by noon and some were on their way back with a second load. By mid-afternoon, more than 270 tons of supplies, mostly ammunition, had been dropped. Seven C-130s had been hit by ground fire. A C-130B flown by Lt. Col. William Coleman of the 29th Tactical Airlift Squadron had taken heavy damage from multiple hits. His loadmaster, Tom Stalvey, says that over 150 holes were counted in the airplane.

At about 3 PM, a C-130B flown by Major Lilburn F. Stowe, also of

---

[303] The Tactical Air Navigation system was developed in the 1950s. TACAN transmitters broadcast signals that equipment in the airplanes converted to azimuth and distance from the station. Aircrews were able to determine their position by plotting the information on the navigator's map.

the 29th Tactical Airlift Squadron, approached the drop zone for their second mission of the day.[304] Observers on the ground noted that the airplane broke out of the clouds further out than had the others. They watched as 37-MM and .51-caliber fire began striking the airplane. Radio transmissions from the stricken C-130 ceased. The crew tried unsuccessfully to jettison their load as the airplane passed over the drop zone. Smoke was streaming from the cargo compartment and an engine while large holes could be seen in the wings. After passing over the field, the pilot made a turn and came back to attempt a landing, but the airplane struck trees and exploded, killing all of the six-man crew and two USAF combat photographers who were aboard. Army personnel who witnessed the crash have since reported that the pilot could have landed but he spotted recovery personnel working in the field and pulled up to avoid hitting them and struck the trees.[305] The combat control commander, Major Don Strobaugh, ignored "orders" from an Army lieutenant to stay away from the burning airplane and ran alongside the wreckage searching for survivors, but found none. Major Strobaugh was awarded the Airman's Medal for his actions.[306]

After the loss of Major Stowe's airplane and crew, drop missions were halted for the remainder of the day. They resumed the next morning, with the first airplane coming over the DZ at 0900. The same dismal weather prevailed in the A Shau Valley and the promised fighter escorts were again conspicuous by their absence. But luck was with the airlifters that day and again on the following day. Seventeen drops were completed on the second day and fifteen more on the third. By the end of the third day, the weather was starting to improve but only slightly. Antiaircraft fire greeted nearly every one of the drop planes but poor visibility and low clouds shielded the C-130s from the enemy gunners until they were almost over the drop zone. The fighters that were supposed to provide fire suppression again refused to fly into the valley because of the weather. US Army helicopter gunship operations were also hampered.

By the fourth day, the weather was beginning to lift. As Captain Ross Kramer and his TAC crew from Langley AFB, Virginia approached

---

[304] It was actually a mixed crew. While the navigator and enlisted men were from the 29th, the two pilots were from other squadrons. The crew's regular pilots had both been medically grounded due to illness.

[305] This information came from 1st Cav' veterans who witnessed the crash in an Email to the author. There are photographs of the stricken airplane on a web page devoted to the 1st Cavalry Division.

[306] Major Stowe's wife and children were living in Oklahoma at the time of his death. After his death notice was published in the local paper, the family began receiving hate mail from members of the antiwar crowd, mail that asserted that he had it coming. His wife also died not long afterward and the children, all teenagers, were orphaned.

Anything, Anywhere, Anytime

A Loi, they could see the tops of the ridges through broken clouds. They could also see the F-4s that were supposed to be escorting them; the fighters were high above them, well out of harm's way and making no effort to provide fire suppression for the transports as they were supposed to do. With the veil of clouds lifted, the NVA gunners could see the C-130. When they were six miles from the drop zone, the crew encountered tracers; Kramer took evasive action but continued toward the drop zone. When they were five miles out, they were hit by several 37-MM shells; at four miles .51-caliber bullets began hitting the airplane and at three miles a shell exploded beneath the cockpit. At two miles out, an engine was shot-out and shut down then a second engine began losing oil pressure and had to be shut down as well. Only then did Kramer decide it was time to jettison the load and think about getting the airplane to safety. South Vietnamese troops later recovered the bundles. Kramer and his crew managed to restart one of the engines; it was enough to allow them to begin an upwards spiral over the airfield until they were high enough to clear the ridges and head for Da Nang. When they landed, the crew discovered that seven feet of horizontal stabilizer was shot completely away. The airplane was so badly damaged that it could not be flown without extensive repair. It remained at Da Nang for several months while a team worked to return it to service.

After the near-loss of Kramer's airplane, General Momyer ordered the fighter pilots to get down into the valley with the transports. It is reported that the Seventh Air Force commander, who had a reputation for being an aggressive fighter pilot during World War II, made a trip to Da Nang to give the F-4 crews a personal chewing out. From that time on, fighters were in the valley escorting each transport and no more losses occurred.[307]

The C-130 drop missions at A Loi were the most demanding missions of the period of heavy American involvement in South Vietnam, with one exception, which didn't involve airdrop. Only the 1972 supply effort at An Loc would require as much personal courage on the part of the crews. Compared to Khe Sanh, the A Loi drops were far more dangerous and required the utmost in skill, especially on the part of the navigators. No outside guidance was available to guide the crews during their descent. They were responsible for providing their own clearance from the nearby mountains using the airplane radar. Drop crews reported frequent ground fire and four airplanes received major battle damage; one was lost to enemy fire. US Army Major General John J. Tolson, commander of the 1st Cavalry Division, witnessed the drops. In a letter to 834th Air Division, Tolson praised

---

[307] The account of Momyer's visit was related to the author by Ross Kramer. It can also be found in other sources.

Sam McGowan

the C-130 crews as he referred to their missions as "one of the most magnificent displays of courage and airmanship that I have ever seen."(Bowers, 1986)

Anything, Anywhere, Anytime

Sam McGowan

Chapter Eighteen - "KHAM DUC"

Kham Duc during rescue of stranded airlift mission control team

If there is a single day that stands out in the history of tactical airlift in Southeast Asia, it would be Sunday, May 12, 1968. For on that day, which was Mothers Day in the United States, United States Air Force tactical airlifters demonstrated for once and for all that they were willing to go into the face of Hell itself to carry out their mission, regardless of how dangerous it might be. By the end of the day, a dozen airlift crews had conquered their fears as they put their very lives on the line to save others. Some had lost their lives in the process. At the end of the day, the only Medal of Honor ever given to an airlifter had been won. In truth, there should have been several more.

Kham Duc was one of many isolated outposts that dotted the landscape of South Vietnam; particularly in the remote, rugged areas along the Annamite Mountains that separate coastal Vietnam from the rest of Indochina. Located in an isolated mountainous area south of Khe Sanh and the A Shau Valley, the camp was located ten miles from the Laotian border. Originally, it had been the location of a hunting camp used by the former president of South Vietnam, President Diem. When US Special Forces advisors went to South Vietnam, they picked it as a base for operations against the communist infiltration routes coming out of Laos. A Vietnamese Civilian Irregular Defense Group (CIDG) unit was based at Kham Duc to conduct training for operations

Anything, Anywhere, Anytime

in remote areas. A South Vietnamese strike force was responsible for reconnaissance of the infiltration routes that passed through the area and conducting offensive actions against North Vietnamese troops. Except for the dependents of the troops in the camp, there were few civilian inhabitants of the area which was remote even for Vietnam's highlands. A small detachment of US Army Special Forces officers and NCOs served as advisors to the South Vietnamese. Like all such camps, Kham Duc had an airstrip to allow fixed-wing transports to bring in supplies and, should the need arise, reinforcements. The camp's isolated location made airlift crucial. In many ways, Kham Duc was like Khe Sanh except that most of the defenders were South Vietnamese instead of United States Marines.

C-123 flight mechanic doing walk around at Kham Duc 1967

In early April, after the siege of Khe Sanh began to wane and the attacking NVA forces slipped back into the mountains, MACV intelligence concluded that Kham Duc might be their next target. Like Khe Sanh, it was a remote camp located in a border region not far from

Page 468

Sam McGowan

the North Vietnamese infiltration routes and supply lines. While Khe Sanh had been the base camp for a large US Marine force, Kham Duc was primarily a South Vietnamese camp defended by CIDG troops rather than South Vietnamese Army troops. The CIDG had been set up early in the war and was the US Army Special Force's personal baby. Special Forces teams recruited and trained local civilians and provided them with uniforms and equipment.

Made up primarily of local tribesmen such as the Montagnards, the mountain people, few of the CIDG personnel felt any particular loyalty to the South Vietnamese government. The Montagnards of South Vietnam were made up of several tribes from the Central Highlands and were primitive in comparison to the educated coastal Vietnamese. The group had been organized by US advisors in 1961, shortly after the US began operations in South Vietnam, out of fear that the "mountain people" of the Central Highlands would be recruited to the communist cause because of their hatred and distrust of the lowland Vietnamese and, particularly, the South Vietnamese government. (US Army Historians, 1973)

C-130E(I) at Kham Duc (70th Engineers, Co A)
500-gallon fuel bladders on pallets in foreground

Kham Duc was not a new facility. It had been a frequent destination for C-123s since the *MULE TRAIN* days and C-130s had been frequent visitors since their introduction to the war. Because of its location, it was a jumping off point for special operations into Laos, which lay just twelve miles to the west, as evidenced by the above photograph of a special operations C-130E-(I) at the camp. The camp's strategic location made it an attractive target for the North Vietnamese.

Anything, Anywhere, Anytime

Kham Duc (70th Engineers, Co A)

C-130A at Kham Duc (70th Engineers, Co A)

Large concentrations of communist troops were known to be in the area of the camp and MACV intelligence concluded that they were going to mount an attack. General Westmoreland initially decided to defend it and ordered the I Corps commander to reinforce the camp. Engineers were brought in to upgrade the runway for sustained C-130 use so the camp could be reinforced and supplied. In early May, a captured NVA soldier revealed during interrogation that his unit had been sent to overrun the camp at Kham Duc. In response to this bit of intelligence information, MACV sent a battalion of US Army troops from the 23rd Infantry, popularly known as the Americal Division,[308] to reinforce the camp's defenders, most of whom were Vietnamese.

On May 10, more than 600 troops and supporting artillery from the division's 196th Infantry were airlifted into the camp from their base at Chu Lai aboard C-130s in a "tactical emergency," the highest level of priority in the airlift system in Vietnam. The arrival of the additional US troops brought the total number of people in the camp to 1,760, as reported on the afternoon of May 10; 272 of the number were civilian dependents of the CIDG troops in the camp. A C-124 from the 22nd Military Airlift Squadron, a MAC unit controlled by 315th Air Division and used by 834th AD for outsize cargo capability, brought in large items, including two bulldozers for a company of the Army's 70th Engineers who were sent to Kham Duc to beef up the runway for expected heavy C-130 use. The airlift of the C-124s to the camp was the closest MAC transports ever got to combat in Southeast Asia, and in this case they were operating under 834th Air Division operational control. MACV's intentions at this point were to hold the camp. Events of the following day led senior commanders to change their plans.

C-124 at Kham Duc (70th Engineers, Co A)

When the emergency airlift to Kham Duc was ordered, the 834th Air Division command post, known to airlifters by its call sign *HILDA*, dispatched a tactical airlift control team to the camp.[309] The team was under the command of Major Jack Gallagher, a C-130 pilot from the 773rd Tactical Airlift Squadron at Clark. He was one of a number of

---

[308] The AMERICAL Division got its name from having been organized in New Caledonia in the South Pacific during World War II.

[309] The three-man team at Kham Duc is often referred to erroneously as a combat control team.

Anything, Anywhere, Anytime

pilots and navigators who were constantly on temporary duty with 834th Air Division to serve as mission commanders during sustained operations at the many forward airfields that dotted the countryside. As the airlift mission commander, Gallagher was responsible for the safety of the airlift personnel who operated into and upon the site, including his team as well as the crews that were scheduled into the airfield. An experienced pilot whose career dated back to World War II, Gallagher was exceptionally well qualified for the mission. Two enlisted combat controllers, TSgt. Morton Freedman and Sgt. James Lundie, accompanied Gallagher. Their job was to provide information to the arriving transports such as altimeter settings, wind information, weather conditions, reports of enemy hostility levels and other pertinent information, and to arrange communications with the airlift command center in Saigon and the ALCE in Da Nang. If airdrops were scheduled, they would set up the drop zone. There were also evidently aerial port personnel with Gallagher. Army records show that there were ten USAF personnel at Kham Duc on May 11. Gallagher was a veteran USAF pilot whose career had begun in B-17s during World War II. He flew B-29s in Korea then continued through several years in Strategic Air Command B-47s before he was assigned to C-130s. The extent of Freedman and Lundie's combat experience is unknown other than that Lundie, who was a young first-term airman, had been at Khe Sanh but they were members of an elite group of men who had been given rudimentary training in ground combat tactics. Freedman's previous assignment was as the advisor to the skydiving team at the Air Force Academy. Combat control teams were the descendants of the World War II airborne pathfinders and the IX Troop Carrier Command combat control teams.[310] Lundie and perhaps both of them had spent time on the ground at Khe Sanh during the siege only a few weeks before. But none of the three men had ever been in the kind of situation they were about to find themselves in at Kham Duc. For that matter, neither had anyone else.

The team had just landed at the camp when a mortar round struck their jeep trailer. They lost some of their radios, along with some small arms and other equipment they needed for their task. The two combat controllers determined to do the best they could with

---

[310] IX Troop Carrier Command set up special "combat control teams" in early 1945 to go in on the first wave of gliders to set up communications with arriving transports. Unlike the combat control teams that were developed in TAC in the 1950s, the WW II combat control teams were made up of pilots who had both power and glider experience and a single radio technician to take care of their radios.

what was left.[311] Mortar shells continued to rain onto the camp for some time. During a lull, Lundie tried to retrieve some equipment from the damaged trailer and broke his hand. A Special Forces medic advised that he should be evacuated but for some reason Lundie refused. He thought his presence was needed although there were other combat controllers in Saigon who could have been flown up to relieve him within a matter of hours.[312]

A stack of C-130s was soon orbiting near the camp awaiting their turn to land, and the two combat controllers did the best they could to keep the pilots informed with the limited communications resources they still had. While the airlifters were arriving with reinforcements, communist forces attacked Ngoc Tavak, an old French position three miles southwest of the main camp at Kham Duc itself. The small force of US Marines, Special Forces troops, CIDG soldiers and three Australian advisors fought bravely, but it appears that some of the CIDG turned and joined the communists in the attack. Such treachery was not uncommon.[313] Two out of a flight of four Marine CH-46s were shot down as they attempted to bring in reinforcements that had been sent to their aid. The loss of the helicopters led to the decision to abandon the camp. The defenders disengaged from combat and slipped through the North Vietnamese positions to make their way to positions where they could be picked up by helicopter and brought to Kham Duc. Fortunately, most made it.

---

[311] There are a lot of questions regarding the combat controllers' actions. They were assigned to the 8th Aerial Port Squadron combat control team at Tan Son Nhut and could have asked for additional equipment to be flown in from Saigon. One of the C-130 operating locations was at Tan Son Nhut and it would have been a simple matter to load another Jeep onto an airplane and fly it to the camp. Lundie injured himself and could have been replaced but he refused to be evacuated from the camp.

[312] In reality, combat control teams were supplemental to the airlift mission rather than crucial to it. While their presence allowed aircrews to receive weather and other information, such information was beneficial but not essential. Combat control teams were only used for some operations, but not all. In 1972, when USAF C-130s dropped cargo to the defenders of the besieged camp at Kham Duc, no combat control team was present. The original intent of combat control teams was to mark drop zones for airborne operations. When ground personnel were already present on the ground, they could designate and mark the drop zone themselves.

[313] Throughout the Vietnam War, it was difficult for Americans to determine where their South Vietnamese "allies" loyalty actually lay. It was not uncommon for loadmasters to discover booby-trapped hand grenades on their airplanes after hauling Vietnamese troops. At least two C-130s were lost to "suspected sabotage". At the end of the war South Vietnamese troops switched sides in considerable numbers and several highly-placed South Vietnamese officers and civilian officials revealed that they had been part of the COSVN all along.

Anything, Anywhere, Anytime

The battle continued through the day on May 11 but C-130s continued arriving with ammunition and other supplies. Airstrikes hammered the nearby forests where the North Vietnamese were setting up in preparation for their attack. Late in the day, the US commander in I Corps, USMC Lt. Gen. Robert Cushman, recommended that the camp should be evacuated. General Westmoreland pondered the situation well into the evening hours. He decided that the camp lacked the defensive potential of Khe Sanh and was likely to be overrun. The political consequences in the United States of losing a large number of American troops in an attack by superior North Vietnamese forces weighed heavily on his mind.(Westmoreland, 1976) Sometime before midnight, the MACV commander ordered an evacuation of the camp, with the actual timing of the withdrawal to be at the discretion of the commander of the US Army 23rd Infantry Division, Maj. Gen. Samuel Koster, who had operational control of the region in which the camp was located. Contingency plans had been drawn up for a withdrawal over a three-day period, but unfolding events would compress the actual evacuation into a few hours.

C-130A at Kham Duc (70th Engineers, Co A)

Even though the decision to evacuate had been made, an air of confusion seemed to prevail within the military headquarters in Saigon and Chu Lai. While some units at Kham Duc got the word that they were to evacuate, others didn't. The same was true with the Air Force. The first instructions given to 834th Air Division were to mount an emergency resupply; several C-123 and C-130 missions were ordered for airdrops of ammunition to the camp and cargo missions were scheduled for the next day as previously planned. At 0800 on May 12, Seventh Air Force notified the 834th AD Airlift Command Center at Tan Son Nhut to standby to begin extracting people from the camp.

In spite of the impending evacuation order, the command center proceeded with the resupply missions that had previously been scheduled for the camp. Initially, a helicopter evacuation was planned, but that plan fell apart when the first helicopter to arrive was shot down and crashed on the runway. A second CH-47 pilot broke off his approach when his wingman was shot down and left the area. He proceeded to a nearby landing zone to await further instructions. Army engineers worked feverishly to repair a bulldozer that had been put out of commission in preparation for the evacuation. When they got it running, a driver took it out to push the wreckage from the runway. At about the same time the engineers were trying to clear the runway, an Air Force A-1E was shot down just outside the camp. A trio of Army helicopters, two gunships and a conventional UH-1, were in the vicinity and saw the pilot bail out of his stricken airplane. They followed him to the ground as he descended in his parachute. While the gunships laid down a covering fire, the Huey pilot landed nearby. A member of the crew got out of the helicopter and ran to the downed pilot, then drug him in his harness and threw him bodily into his ship!(Gropman, 1979)

Lt. Col. Cole's airplane landing or attempting takeoff with flat tire. (70th Engineers Co A)

After about an hour, the runway was clear and a C-130 landed. The pilot Lt. Col. Daryl Cole of the 21st Tactical Airlift Squadron,

Anything, Anywhere, Anytime

evidently was not aware that the camp was being evacuated.[314] He landed with a load of maintenance equipment – six tires and a jack – and his airplane was immediately mobbed by frightened Vietnamese civilians, who scrambled into the cargo compartment before the loadmaster could get the pallets off. His airplane had been hit several times while landing and fuel was leaking from several holes in the wings. The veteran pilot attempted a takeoff with the Vietnamese on board but a mortar round impacted by the airplane just as it started to roll and a piece of shrapnel flattened a tire. The combination of too much weight and a flat tire would not allow the airplane to get up enough speed to become airborne. Cole taxied back to the cargo ramp and shut down engines. The Vietnamese ran out of the airplane as quickly as they had run aboard and took shelter in a ditch.

Cole was advised during a telephone conversation with HILDA that no further fixed-wing landings would be made that day and to advise Gallagher. About the same time, a message was sent to the Army personnel on the ground that they were to prepare to exfiltrate from the camp. Some authors have written that the message was sent in error. It was not an error; due to the heavy enemy opposition around the camp, the Americal Division commander had decided that an airlift evacuation would be suicidal.

Burning wreckage of CH-47 (70th Engineers, Co A)

When Army personnel offered Cole's crew weapons and ammunition and asked them if they wanted to go out with them, Cole's copilot, Maj. Farrar, suggested that they try to remove the tire.

---

[314] Lt. Col. Cole had originally been assigned to the 35th TCS while the author was in the same squadron a year earlier but had evidently changed squadrons.

Although there were spare tires and a jack in the cargo he had just brought in, Cole's flight engineer lacked the proper tools to remove the old one. The crew worked feverishly for more than an hour using a blowtorch and a bayonet to remove the remains of the shredded tire from the rim. Major Gallagher and other USAF personnel at the camp, which included the two combat controllers and an Air Force liaison officer from Chu Lia, helped Cole's crew as they worked. While they were working on the tire, a C-123 commanded by Major Ray D. Shelton landed and took out a load of troops. When the tire was removed, with no hope of being brought out by air, Gallagher directed the other three airmen – the two combat controllers on his team and the Air Force liaison officer with the 196th Infantry – to get on board the airplane. There may have been additional Air Force personnel onboard. In his mission report, Cole said they brought out ten passengers. Writing years after the fact, co-pilot Farrar only remembered the four. Exactly what role Cole played in the decision is unknown and he has been deceased for many years but comments made by members of his crew indicate that he supported Gallagher. As the ranking Air Force officer at the field, he may have made the decision to get them out.

Cole's airplane as he swerved off the runway (70th Engineers Co A)

While Gallagher has been criticized for his decision – the two combat controllers later said they wanted to stay although it is not

Anything, Anywhere, Anytime

clear why – the situation was changing rapidly. The evacuation plan called for the Air Force personnel to be the fifth group to go out. However, the message Gallagher had received through Cole indicated that the plan had gone by the wayside and that the camp's defenders were going to abandon the camp and attempt to make their way through the attacking communists on the ground. By that time, some of the Army engineers had already been evacuated on Shelton's C-123 and a few helicopter flights that had managed to get into the camp. USAF personnel were supposed to follow the US Army infantrymen and the Vietnamese civilians, as well as a handful of Psy/Ops people who were at the camp. The infantrymen were in the process of being evacuated whenever a helicopter was able to take advantage of the airstrikes and get in. Because of the damaged tire, Cole was going to be severely limited in the number of people he could carry in his damaged airplane. Gallagher felt that considering the situation, it was either now or never.

Cole took off from Kham Duc empty except for his crew and the four (or ten) USAF personnel from the camp.[315] He nursed the damaged airplane back to the C-130 operating base at Cam Ranh Bay. For the flight, he was awarded the 1968 MacKay Trophy for the most meritorious flight of the year by a USAF aircraft. As for Gallagher, while he felt his decision to evacuate was a good one, somebody in the 834th AD chain of command was not pleased.[316] (Maj. Gen. Burl MacLaughlin, the 834th AD commander, took responsibility for sending the four men back in to the camp.) Major Farrar reported that when he notified *HILDA* that they had taken off successfully from Kham Duc and brought all of the Air Force personnel with them, he was advised that the airlift mission control team should have stayed. Farrar and Cole protested but *HILDA* wasn't interested. Gallagher was ordered to get right back on the next C-130 bound for Kham Duc with the two combat controllers and go back to the camp. Evidently, *HILDA* was not aware of the true situation at the camp; neither was anyone really interested in hearing what Gallagher had to say. Somebody at 834th Air Division unwittingly set up a disaster, although the courage of a handful of

---

[315] Another question arises as to whether or not they really were the only Air Force personnel at the camp. The mission reports mention a Tactical Air Control Party bunker adjacent to the Special Forces bunker. Tactical Air Control parties are typically Air Force personnel. There may have also been some aerial port personnel. The report also shows that ten USAF personnel were in the camp on May 11. It does not relate when and how the other six airmen left the camp.

[316] The author is personally acquainted with Major Gallagher and has discussed the events with him, although not in deep probing detail. Lt. Col. Cole's loadmaster made a comment on an Internet web site that someone higher up wanted the combat controllers to go back so they would be the last out. The combat control team motto is "First in, last out."

Sam McGowan

airmen saved the day.[317]

At the time that Cole flew out of the camp, a reign of confusion prevailed throughout the military chain of command. Someone rescinded the earlier order for the camp's defenders to fight their way out on the ground and reinstated the fixed-wing evacuation plan, at least for US personnel. A new evacuation plan was put out in which the Americans would be pulled out by air and the Vietnamese would be left to fend for themselves. The Special Forces commander at the camp protested the plan and it was evidently modified to bring the Vietnamese civilians out by air along with the Americans. However, none of the Vietnamese troops were evacuated. Instead, they made their way to pickup points some distance away and were picked up by helicopter.

Lt. Col. Daryl Cole (R) receiving 1968 MacKay Trophy

Cole's airplane was the last to depart the camp for several hours as senior commanders considered whether or not to attempt an air evacuation. An increasing toll at Kham Duc in terms of lost and damaged aircraft caused MACV to put a halt to further attempts to evacuate by C-130 – which reinforces that the message that no further airplanes would be landing was not sent in error. Communist gunners were positioned in the hills on the approach to the runway and an Air Force FAC who was shot down over the camp believed they made landings too hazardous to attempt. Plans were reportedly made for an emergency airdrop resupply, which would have made the presence of the combat controllers desirable, but not essential, if such a decision was actually made. (The combat controller name is a misnomer.

---

[317] There have been reports that the actual decision to send the airlift control team back into the camp was made by the airlift command element commander at Da Nang. The 834th AD commander, Maj. Gen. Burl McLaughlin, was aboard a C-130 on the way to Kham Duc at the time the order was given.

Anything, Anywhere, Anytime

Combat controllers designate and mark a drop zone but the navigator actually provides the pilot the course information to get to the release point and give the signal to release the load.) A C-130 may have made a drop while Cole's airplane was still on the ground at the camp although the actuality of such an event is unclear.[318]

In preparation for the evacuation, which had been placed on hold, a fleet of C-130s and C-123s had assembled in the skies in the vicinity of the camp and were maintaining stations not far away. The 834th Air Division commander was aboard a C-130, a B-model from the 463rd Tactical Airlift Wing flown by Major Robert Archer,[319] which had taken off from Tan Son Nhut. After Cole's crew departed, no more airplanes or helicopters got into the camp for almost four hours.

Republic F-105

At one point a large PAVN force was massing just off of the end of the runway in preparation for an assault. A FAC saw them and authorized an air strike by a flight of two F-105s that had been diverted from a planned airstrike in North Vietnam. Coincidentally, the lead pilot, Captain Wayne Warner, was a former C-130 pilot who had previously served with the 21st TCS at Naha. Warner and his wingman each dropped their load of eight 750-pound bombs, a total of sixteen, on the massed troops. Warner received a message a few days later from an officer in the Americal Division thanking him and his wingman for the strike. Their bombs destroyed the large communist force and literally saved the camp. Warner was awarded the Silver Star for the strike.(Warner, 2012)

---

[318] The Americal Division report records that a drop was made, but it doesn't say when.

[319] This information comes from 463rd TAW veterans who knew Maj. Archer.

Sam McGowan

The situation at Kham Duc had become dismal. The camp had been nearly surrounded and hundreds of PAVN troops armed with automatic weapons had taken up stations off of the end of the runways and machinegun positions had been set up on the hills overlooking the runway. Some were American positions that had been overrun. A barrage of automatic weapons fire greeted each helicopter crew that attempted to get into the camp. By mid-afternoon, only two airplanes and a handful of helicopters had been able to make it in and out. Not more than 150 people had been evacuated so far. Meanwhile, communist troops had overrun the outlying outposts around the airfield and killed or taken the 196th Infantry troops manning them prisoner, except for a few who managed to escape and were attempting to make their back into the camp. Finally, realizing that the situation at Kham Duc had become desperate, MACV ordered 834th Air Division to evacuate the camp. Although there were C-123s in the queue of airplanes that had gathered nearby, because of their larger payload capacity, the C-130s were given the job. The C-123s, some of which had been circling for hours and were running low on fuel, were shuffled aside.

As soon as the order was given for the C-130s to begin landing, Major Bernard Bucher and his 774th TAS crew swung out of their position as the first airplane in the orbit and approached the camp. No one knows what was going through the crew's minds, but they no doubt faced the task they had been called on to perform with trepidation. The transport crews had been orbiting in the vicinity of the camp for some time and had been monitoring the radio transmissions and observing the situation below them. They knew that several airplanes and helicopters had been shot down and that ground fire was intense. The actions of the C-130 crews over the next thirty minutes were some of the most heroic ever performed by US airmen in any war! They were literally risking their lives to evacuate the camp's defenders. They went in anyway.

Witnesses on the ground saw the airplane take numerous hits during the approach, but Bucher landed safely and taxied to the loading ramp. There, Special Forces soldiers supervised the loading of most of the Vietnamese dependents onto the airplane. One of the Special Forces officers, Captain George Orr, also boarded the C-130, although his presence was not confirmed until decades later when his remains were found and identified by DNA analysis. As Bucher was taking off, the airplane took more hits. Right after the airplane lifted off and left the area of the runway, it flew into the fire from two large caliber machineguns positioned on ridges overlooking the camp just off the northwest end of the runway. The guns are believed to have been American guns that had been captured when US outlying positions manned by 196th Infantry personnel were overrun by PAVN

Anything, Anywhere, Anytime

forces earlier in the day.(Gropman, 1979)[320] The transport shuddered, then fell into a ravine where it exploded and burned. Though no one could get to the airplane to check for survivors due to the strong enemy presence around the crash site, the fire was so fierce that those who witnessed the crash believed no one could have survived.

C-130B starting takeoff roll – this may be Maj. Bucher's airplane (70th Engineers, Co A)

Capt. Herbert J. Spier, an O-2 pilot, was over Kham Duc when Bucher's airplane was shot down and witnessed the crash. Spier also saw where the tracers came from and within thirty seconds of the crash he had a fighter drop a load of cluster bombs on the position.[321] Spier kept watch on the position for the rest of the day and saw no further firing from it. By this time, four aircraft had been shot down over and around the camp and more than 200 people had been killed, but less than 150 had been evacuated from the camp.

As Bucher was taking off, Lt. Col. William Boyd, Jr. from the 50th Tactical Airlift Squadron at CCK, was beginning his approach. Bucher had talked to the A-1E pilot who had been rescued earlier – the man told him "Stay out of Kham Duc, it belongs to Charlie!" He and his crew saw Bucher's airplane go down in a ball of flames and no doubt felt considerable anxiety at the thought of going into the same situation. His loadmaster, a young airman named Sam Kerro, was watching the scene below from the cargo compartment. He took photographs of the

---

[320] There is really no way to confirm or disprove this belief. PAVN infantry units often carried their own .51-caliber machineguns.

[321] Cluster bombs, commonly known as CBUs, were bombs filled with clusters of tiny fragments that were developed for use against personnel. Considered inhumane by some, they were not originally used in South Vietnam but were confined to Laos and North Vietnam where they were used against antiaircraft crews. By 1968 restrictions against their use had been lifted and they had come into use in South Vietnam against enemy troop concentrations.

Sam McGowan

camp and of the burning wreckage of the ill-fated C-130.[322] The flames and billowing black smoke from the burning airplane were ample evidence of the hostility into which they were about to fly. They could see enemy soldiers on the ground taking aim with their AK-47s and firing away; they felt round after round strike their airplane. Just as the airplane was about to touch down, a shell struck the ground right in front of it; Boyd pulled up then started back around for another attempt even though he knew that the enemy gunners were primed and their chances were even less for a second attempt than they had been for the first.

Bucher's crash site (Sam Kerro)

Miraculously, Boyd made it. The wheels touched down and Boyd slowed to taxi to the pickup area. People came rushing out from ditches alongside the runway and ran toward them. At the loading area they loaded as many people as they could onto the airplane and then Kerro closed the door. Boyd decided to takeoff in the opposite direction from that taken by the C-130B that had been shot down only moments before. The airplane took several hits as they taxied and during the takeoff roll, but it came off the ground and began climbing until they reached a safe altitude. Boyd took the shot-up airplane to Chu Lai. After they landed, Boyd's copilot, Major Reed, took a can of spray paint and wrote "The Lucky Duc" on the side of the airplane. Boyd's engineer, SSgt Harlan "Gene" Johnson, made repairs to the fuel system and they took the airplane on to Cam Ranh. Lt. Col. Boyd was awarded the Air Force Cross. Another Air Force Cross went, posthumously, to Bucher.

---

[322] See http://sammcgowan.com/khamduc.html

Anything, Anywhere, Anytime

Troops in ditch waiting for evacuation (70th Engineers Co A)

Boyd's copilot writing LUCKY DUC on side of airplane (Sam Kerro)
As Boyd's airplane was taking off, a third C-130, the fourth to land at Kham Duc that day, was on approach. Lt. Col. John R Delmore and his 21st TAS crew also had to go around, in their case to miss Boyd's airplane, and come around for a second attempt. They were not as lucky as their predecessors had been. When their C-130A was about 400 feet off the ground, it began taking hits. The impacting bullets sounded like sledgehammers striking the airplane's metal skin to the crew. Smoke began to curl up through the cockpit floor while six-inch holes opened up on the side of the cockpit. Bullets came through the floor and went out through the ceiling over the crew's heads. At one point, the airplane was forced over on its side but the two pilots

managed to right it. Finally, the throttle linkage for all four-engines was shot-away. Delmore reached up and feathered ALL FOUR engines and turned the C-130 into a glider!

In spite of the damage and loss of all power, the airplane made the runway. Fortunately, the landing gear had already been extended before the hydraulics failed with the loss of the engines. But there was little directional control and no brakes. Somehow, Delmore managed to steer the airplane off the runway; it crashed into the wreckage of the CH-47 that had been shot down earlier in the day. In spite of all of the fire they had encountered, none of the crew was injured seriously. They evacuated the airplane through the opening that had been left when the flight engineer, TSgt John McCall, jettisoned the crew entrance door just before they touched down. The airplane did not burn. Alone and armed only with their .38 revolvers, the crew took shelter and prepared to meet their fate. Fortunately, ground troops were able to get to them. Within twenty minutes, they were aboard a helicopter and on their way to safety.

According to the 196th Infantry account, further landings were put on hold while the FACs working over the camp directed airstrikes against the airfield perimeter and the gun positions in the hills. Some napalm strikes were so close that the defenders waiting for evacuation could feel the heat of the fires. The weight of thousands of pounds of ordnance and napalm severely reduced the communist's numbers and will to fight. Mortars and rockets continued to impact on the field, but the rate of fire was lessening.

Another A-model crew was orbiting over the camp when Delmore's airplane crash-landed and veered off the runway. Lt. Col. Franklin Montgomery of the 41st TAS spiraled down from directly over the airfield and landed "in a hail of tracers." His crew took on a full load of passengers while "more than fifty" mortar shells and rockets impacted around the taxiing airplane. The loadmaster was mobbed by the horde of Vietnamese; he was knocked down and trampled, then knocked down again by a mortar blast. With more than 150 Vietnamese soldiers, a few Americans and some CIDG aboard, Montgomery took off. By this time the constant ground strikes had suppressed the communist fire to the point that not a single bullet struck Montgomery's airplane during the entire time they were over and on the ground at Kham Duc.

Throughout the events at the camp, an Air Force C-130 had been orbiting over the battlefield. It was an airborne command post, or A, B, Triple-C in Air Force jargon. The ABCCC C-130s carried a large module in the rear that contained several communications stations where Air Force officers manned stations to provide command and control of strike aircraft and coordinate operations. The urgency of the situation

Anything, Anywhere, Anytime

at the camp led the senior controller to call for a *GRAND SLAM*, a code word calling for a maximum effort by strike aircraft. Essentially, every strike aircraft in Southeast Asia was directed to Kham Duc to lay down covering airstrikes for the evacuation. Some, such as the flight led by Captain Wayne Warner, had been on their way to North Vietnam when they got the call. Hundreds of tons of high explosives, napalm, cluster bombs and other ordnance was brought to bear on the attacking North Vietnamese. Under the onslaught from above, the intensity of the ground fire decreased substantially.

The weather was practically clear at Kham Duc and there were plenty of fighters in the area, along with at least two forward air controllers and the airborne combat command post orbiting overhead to control them. Fighters flew within a hundred feet of the wingtips of the C-130s to drop napalm and CBU's on the enemy positions. In their haste to shoot down the transports, the communist soldiers revealed their positions and became easy targets for the fighters. Hundreds of communist troops were killed and wounded by the exploding bomblets and flaming napalm. With the enemy's attention diverted by the arriving and departing C-130s, Army and Marine helicopters were able to get into the camp and pick up troops, mostly Americans from the Americal Division.

Right after Montgomery took off, another C-130, possibly a B-model flown by Major Billie B. Mills, a Stan/Eval pilot at Clark, landed and took off again with 130 people onboard. Mills is the same C-130 pilot who, as a young lieutenant, worked with CIA agents to develop procedures for dropping friendly agents into the mountains of Tibet. Here is Col. Mills account in his own words:

I knew Major Bucher and the crew who were from our squadron. I arrived at Kham Duc and the airborne mission commander, (The Commanding General, 834th Air Division), who was on scene in a C-130) assigned me as "number 6 in the holding pattern. Later he directed my crew as the next aircraft to land to pick up the remaining personnel on the ground. When I arrived in the stack I could see some smoke from the mountainous river bed where Major Bucher had crashed.

I was in the 774th TAS, that is, I was attached to the 774th, and happened to be the last C-130 who landed at KHAM DUC that day. I was assigned to 13 AF, as Chief C-130 Stan Eval and as such I flew at least 2 weeks each month in Viet Nam, with my Stan/Eval crewmembers one week, taking any mission as a regular crew and one to two weeks flying with other C-130B/E aircrews from 463 TAW or 314 TAW, including aiding in TAC Rotation Aircrews Theater orientation (as if most of the rotators had not already spent a significant amount in Theater and I

Sam McGowan

knew a great number of them).[323]

My crew that day were 774th line crews, (I have a copy of those flight orders-but like most all old flyers I can't find them just now but I will - I remember that Lt. Pat MacNanee was the cp and Capt. Bryan Peach was my nav. - my problem is I need the orders to identify the FE and LM - I sincerely apologize for not having their names at the moment - all did good work that day.)

We were to take out the last remaining troops - about 115 men who were the final rear perimeter guard. That group included an infantry company/detachment, about a dozen US Marines, and a few Special Forces troops.

My crew had watched the C-130 that had gotten shot up and crashed on the runway landing but managed to get his C-130 off the runway before it quit skidding, so the runway was open enough for us to land and take off. An earlier C-130 had managed to struggle off even though it had received extensive fire. So we reworked the performance data and began our approach from the east and were advised to takeoff to the east since the heavy guns were near the west end of the runway.

When I contacted the Ground Commander's CP, I was asked to land as short as possible since the ground troops were located at the approach end of the runway and they were the only people left on the ground at Kham Duc. We landed in about 1,000 feet, stopped and turned the airplane around to be ready to take off when the troops boarded. Looking down the runway, we saw about 100 troops, full field packs, weapons, and running as hard as they could to our position. I asked the CP if they wanted us to pick them up and that we would wait on them since we were the last opportunity to leave. They said they were ok and for me to go as quickly as the troops boarded (later at a Kham Duc reunion, the senior army at the CP said they were in a chopper at that time).

I sent my 2 LM's out to get in front of the airplane and insure that no soldier ran under the props since the anxiety was running very high and the troops had been at their final defense post for at least a day. I asked Capt. Peach to take charge of the troop loading and to make sure they went to the front of the cargo compartment since there were many soldiers heavily loaded and tired. Capt Peach and the LM did a super job in expediting loading. I had told Peach that I wanted him to watch out back since I was going to back down the runway so I had enough takeoff

---

[323] Col. Mills wrote this account around 2009 and may be confused on his assignment at the time. In 1968 the 463rd and all of the other C-130 wings were assigned to 315th Air Division. When the division deactivated a year later, the 463rd transferred to Thirteenth Air Force. He may have still been in 463rd Stan/Eval.

Anything, Anywhere, Anytime

runway. He had the ramp up level and was watching for the extensive debris strung along the runway, the damaged or crashed aircraft, helicopters and vehicles on the runway.[324]

When we had backed about 1,200 to 1,400 feet down the runway I asked Peach to have the LM close the ramp just as I stopped, started up the power to max, ramp closed, brakes released and we were fortunate to get off the ground without a single hole in the airplane from enemy fire or that debris. We landed about 25 minutes later at CHU LIA AB where busses met the troops. The troops were generous to us with their words of appreciation. We then got on board, took off, and headed back to KHAM DUC. On reporting in as we approached the area, we were advised that all troops had been evacuated successfully and for me to return directly to TSN and report to 834th CC. The General met me at the airplane and said "Good Job, Thanks," and told his aide that I was awarded the "Silver Star" and to take care of the paperwork. I asked to have all my crewmembers awarded the same Silver Star. I never heard any more about it for about 2 years when I received that award in a ceremony at 13th AF HQ. I SEARCHED BACK, WENT TO SEE THE 463rd WING COMMANDER TO SEEK HIS ASSISTANCE TO GET THE CREW RECOGNIZED BUT ALL I EVER GOT WAS NO HELP. I HAVE ALWAYS WONDERED HOW ONE GUY CAN GET THE MOON AND THE OTHERS GET ANOTHER DAY'S SERVICE COMPLETED.[325]

Another airplane got in and out again with ninety people, possibly before Mills. Neither of the two airplanes took any hits.[326] It was obvious that the enemy's strength was being severely reduced by the constant airstrikes on their positions. Major James Wallace landed his C-130E; it was, according to some reports, the eighth C-130 to land that day.[327] The 196th report states that only six C-130s and two C-123s landed at the camp during the evacuation and two of the C-130s were shot down. News of the loss of two C-130s had reached Saigon but evidently Seventh Air Force had not received word that the enemy fire was lessening and the airplanes were getting in and out without

---

[324] In his account Col. Mills had the words "because of my hours under enemy fire" which evidently meant that he had told the loadmaster to keep an eye out for debris because of his experience in forward field operations.

[325] Col. Mills has since determined that one of his loadmasters was Tom Stalvey, from the 29th TAS. Tom received no decoration and no recognition for his role in the historic and heroic mission.

[326] Col. Mills stated that his was the last airplane to land at the camp and evacuate troops, but other sources indicate there were two more. One other definitely landed to reinsert the airlift mission control team.

[327] There are conflicting reports of the sequence of landings and even the names of the aircraft commanders. Some reports name a pilot who evidently didn't land and leave out Mills, who did. The 315th AD newspaper The Airlifter featured Mills in an article about the evacuation.

Sam McGowan

damage. General Momyer was in the process of telling *HILDA* to discontinue C-130 flights into the camp to avoid further losses while Wallace (or more likely, Mills) was on approach. Fortunately, he landed before he received the order. He and his crew brought out the last load of defenders with the exception of the members of the Army Special Forces detachment. They were setting off charges at the time; a few minutes later, they were extracted from the camp by helicopter.[328]

By this time, all of the American defenders of the camp who were inside the perimeter had been evacuated. There were other Americans and Vietnamese still in the vicinity however, particularly members of the Americal Division who had been manning the outposts that had been overrun earlier in the morning, and who had been unable to get into the camp. One American, Private Julius Long from the 196th Infantry, became a prisoner of the North Vietnamese and was held until 1973. No one knew he was a POW until he was released.[329] Other Americans, also from the Americal, were trying to get into the camp to be evacuated but began moving away from it when they realized that everyone else had gone and they had been abandoned. One group arrived at the camp just as the last aircraft took off (it is uncertain if they saw the last C-130 or Joe Jackson's C-123) and one man became so demoralized that he took off running and firing his weapon wildly. He was never seen again. One group was picked up by helicopter from a nearby ridge two days later. Most of the Vietnamese exfiltrated from the camp and were picked up by helicopters over the next few days.[330] All told, only about five hundred of the camp's defenders and civilian camp followers were evacuated by air that day.

But even though the camp had been evacuated – with the exception of the men who had not made their way inside the perimeter and the South Vietnamese who had begun exfiltrating through the depleted enemy forces to helicopter pickup points – a potential disaster was in the making. When they got to Cam Ranh, Major Gallagher was ordered back to the camp. He and the two combat controllers were put on a C-130 flown by a Tactical Air Command crew

---

[328] There is some discrepancy in this assertion. Col. Mills states that the senior Army officer told him later that he was already in a helicopter when he and his crew landed. When Army personnel returned to the camp in 1970 to search the area for MIA remains, they found the camp essentially intact so it is doubtful that any charges were set. The author went to Kham Duc on a C-130 bladder bird in 1970 and spent about half an hour. I took one picture, which shows all of the buildings still standing.

[329] Communist reports indicate that other Americans were taken prisoner, but their fate is unknown.

[330] The Special Forces report relates that when they were ordered to leave the Vietnamese, they refused.

Anything, Anywhere, Anytime

commanded by Major Jay Van Cleef. However, instead of going straight to the camp, Van Cleef was first sent to Da Nang, apparently to load for an airdrop. After they got there, they were told to proceed to the camp. By the time they reached the vicinity of the camp, the evacuation was in its final minutes. He was approaching the camp as Wallace (probably Mills) departed. Somehow, Van Cleef was not informed that the last load of people had been brought out. He landed on the runway by the now-deserted camp and taxied to a stop. When he did, Gallagher and the two controllers ran off the airplane's ramp and into the camp, which they quickly found to be deserted. After the men got off the airplane, Van Cleef waited for several minutes while North Vietnamese mortar crews walked their rounds toward his airplane. As the rounds began impacting dangerously close, and when no one appeared to board the airplane, Van Cleef taxied out and took off again.

As soon as they were off the ground, the crew heard someone say that the evacuation was now complete and it was okay for the fighters to start putting their ordnance into the camp itself. Van Cleef immediately interrupted and informed all who could hear that the camp had NOT been evacuated but that he had just left the three men that 834th Air Division had ordered back into the camp. An airborne controller in the C-130 command post in orbit nearby, Captain Robert Gatewood, reported that the sudden silence on the radios as everyone realized the seriousness of the situation was so heavy it could literally be felt!(Gropman, 1979)

On the ground, Gallagher, Freedman and Lundie thought their time had come. The three men, who were only lightly armed with M-16s and pistols, ran frantically to the camp command post and discovered that it was deserted. They checked each unit command post in turn but found no one there. Then they ran to the same ditch where they had taken shelter that morning before they boarded Cole's airplane for the flight to temporary safety. They knew their only hope lay in "someone" coming in to rescue them. Yet, at the same time, they felt that no one in their right mind would attempt a landing on a runway at a camp that had been abandoned to the enemy – and by this time they realized this was the true nature of the situation. The airlift control team had been ordered back into the camp but no one had bothered to provide them with any equipment.[331] Freedman carried an

---

[331] Just who ordered Gallagher and the two combat controllers back into the camp has not been publically revealed, although General MacLauglin took responsibility, nor has the exact reason why. Some airlifters who were there at the time attribute the decision to the commander of the Da Nang ALCE. One reason given for them being sent back was that airdrops were planned and the team needed to be on the ground to control them. Another is that they were needed to control the flow of traffic, but although combat control teams were qualified to act as air traffic

Sam McGowan

emergency UHF radio but it would not work. They had been left on the ground in an extremely hostile situation and had no means of communicating with the aircraft that were still in the area. But even while they were beginning to give up hope, a rescue attempt was being organized.

When the order to evacuate the camp was given, several C-123s that had been in the holding patterns over the camp were shifted aside as the larger C-130s were put on the line to save the defenders at Kham Duc. Seven C-130 crews had by this time already confronted their moment with destiny and had either been shot down or had made pickups and, except for Van Cleef, had left the area with evacuees. The FAC pilots made several low, high-speed passes down the runway but were unable to spot the three airmen. Captain Gatewood, who had been coordinating the flights into and around the camp, asked the first C-123 crew in the orbit to attempt a landing in the hopes that the three men would come out of their hiding place if an airplane was actually on the ground. There were North Vietnamese on the field, but they were only on one end of the runway, which was over a mile long. One team reportedly had set up a light machinegun under the wing of Delmore's abandoned airplane. While a landing was not impossible, everyone knew it would be dangerous.

Lt. Col. Alfred Jeanotte did not hesitate – he pointed the nose of his C-123 toward the runway and pulled back the throttles. The thought was going through the minds of the crew that while they were surely planning to land in a hornet's nest, they were the only hope for their three American airlifter comrades. Jeanotte's C-123 touched down in a hail of enemy fire; bullets were striking the ground all around it as the pilot taxied slowly down the runway. His crew had no idea where the three men were hiding – or even if they were still alive – and when they did not appear, he pushed the throttles forward to takeoff.

The stranded team saw the C-123 land. Hesitant to expose themselves, they were waiting in the shelter of the ditch until it reached their position. But they were some distance down the runway and by the time the airplane was adjacent to where they waited, Jeanotte had started his takeoff roll and it was moving too fast to stop. They jumped up and ran out onto the runway, with each man waving his arms frantically. But as the C-123 lifted off, they ran back to the ditch, their hopes dashed. They thought the C-123 crew had failed to spot them but as the airplane banked, the flight engineer saw them

---

controllers, in Vietnam their role was advisory. It's doubtful whether their presence at the camp would have made any difference in the course of events as they unfolded. Another reason given is that they went back to search the camp to make sure everyone had gotten out, but this assertion does not fit the evacuation order.

Anything, Anywhere, Anytime

scrambling back into the ditch. Jeanotte and his crew had been circling over the camp for some time before they made their daring rescue attempt. Their fuel supply was getting very low and there was not enough for a second attempt. But the crew had seen the men and now everyone knew that they were still alive and where they were.

Another C-123, *BOOKIE* 771, was the next airplane in the stack. The crew, made up of Lt. Col. Joe M. Jackson and Major Jesse Campbell as pilots and TSgt. Edward Trejo and SSgt. Mansford Grubbs as flight engineer and loadmaster, had departed Da Nang earlier that day for a routine cargo flight. It was also a proficiency check flight for Jackson, who was detachment commander of the Da Nang unit, which was part of the 315th Air Commando Wing at Phan Rang.[332] While Campbell was a highly experienced C-123 pilot and a flight examiner, Jackson was an older officer who had been pulled back into the cockpit from a desk job for a combat tour. Vietnam was his first experience in transports; previously he had flown fighters and U-2s. He had started out as a B-25 crew chief before going to cadets and becoming a B-24 pilot during World War II. In the 1950s, he joined the U-2 program but his most recent service before he went to Vietnam was as a staff officer. He was one of a number of field grade officers who had been pulled back into the cockpit for duty in Southeast Asia in transport type airplanes. As the situation at the camp deteriorated, the crew was diverted from their assigned mission and sent to the vicinity of Kham Duc to stand by in case they were needed.

After the three men were spotted, Jeanotte passed along their location to the airborne command post, which passed it to the second C-123 crew. Jackson was flying the left seat, while Campbell was in the right seat acting as copilot even though he was an instructor pilot and Standardizations/Evaluations flight examiner (check pilot). They came over the runway and made a high approach from directly above the end of the runway, a maneuver that was common for operations into airfields where the threat of ground fire was strong. When the airplane was on the ground, Grubbs opened a rear door and stood by to pull the three men into the airplane. Trejo stood beside him to assist. Jackson slowed to a fast taxi. As the C-123 approached their position, the three stranded airmen jumped out of the ditch and ran toward the open door. Lundie and Freeman threw a few shots from their M-16s in the direction of NVA troops who were advancing toward them from the

---

[332] Earlier in the war the 311th Air Commando Squadron had been based at Da Nang, but it had transferred to Phan Rang when the 315th Wing moved there. The 315th was redesignated as "special operations" in 1968 but became "tactical airlift" in January, 1970. Regardless of its designation, the 315th Wing and its squadrons were tactical airlift and part of 834th Air Division. They were "air commando" in name only.

opposite end of the runway.

Joe M. Jackson

As Grubbs and Trejo were pulling the men into the airplane, the two pilots saw a 122-MM rocket hurtling toward them. It struck the ground in front of the airplane and spun around a few times but did not explode. Jackson taxied around the smoking rocket and pushed the throttles forward for a successful takeoff. His C-123 did not receive a single hit! Jackson would become the first (and only) airlifter ever to be awarded the Medal of Honor[333] while Campbell was decorated with the Air Force Cross.[334] Grubbs and Trejo, who had exposed themselves to pull the three men into the airplane, received the next level of

---

[333] A loadmaster, Sgt. John Levitow, received the only Medal of Honor awarded to an Air Force enlisted man during the Vietnam War but he was assigned to AC-47 gunships and was out of airlift at the time of his action. Since the war, pararescueman A1C William Pitzenbarger, who had been awarded the Air Force Cross, was also awarded the Medal of Honor, posthumously. Another recent posthumous award went to a former senior master sergeant who had been discharged from the Air Force and employed by Lockheed as a civilian to work on a classified project.

[334] Boyd, Campbell and Jeanotte were all awarded the Air Force Cross while Bucher was awarded the medal posthumously. At least three of the other C-130 pilots – Cole, Delmore and Montgomery – were put in for the Air Force Cross but received Silver Stars instead. Some of the enlisted men involved in the mission were awarded the Distinguished Flying Cross; some got nothing.

Anything, Anywhere, Anytime

decoration, the Silver Star.[335]

The events of May 12, 1968 were undoubtedly the most hectic of the war for those who were involved and probably of the entire Vietnam War, at least during the period of American involvement. During the course of the day, at least eight C-130 crews and a trio of C-123 crews overcame their personal fears and demonstrated exemplary courage as they literally laid their lives on the line to save others. For one C-130 crew, the attempt cost them their lives.

For conspicuous gallantry and intrepidity in action at the risk of his life above and beyond the call of duty. Lt. Col. Jackson distinguished himself as pilot of a C-123 aircraft. Lt. Col. Jackson volunteered to attempt the rescue of a 3-man USAF Combat Control Team from the special forces camp at Kham Duc. Hostile forces had overrun the forward outpost and established gun positions on the airstrip. They were raking the camp with small arms, mortars, light and heavy automatic weapons, and recoilless rifle fire. The camp was engulfed in flames and ammunition dumps were continuously exploding and littering the runway with debris. In addition, 8 aircraft had been destroyed by the intense enemy fire and 1 aircraft remained on the runway reducing its usable length to only 2,200 feet. To further complicate the landing, the weather was deteriorating rapidly, thereby permitting only 1 air strike prior to his landing. Although fully aware of the extreme danger and likely failure of such an attempt. Lt. Col. Jackson elected to land his aircraft and attempt to rescue. Displaying superb airmanship and extraordinary heroism, he landed his aircraft near the point where the combat control team was reported to be hiding. While on the ground, his aircraft was the target of intense hostile fire. A rocket landed in front of the nose of the aircraft but failed to explode. Once the combat control team was aboard, Lt. Col. Jackson succeeded in getting airborne despite the hostile fire directed across the runway in front of his aircraft. Lt. Col. Jackson's profound concern for his fellowmen, at the risk of his life above and beyond the call of duty are in keeping with the highest traditions of the U.S. Air Force and reflect great credit upon himself, and the Armed Forces of his country.

---

[335] Jackson's recommendation for the Medal of Honor reportedly came from his squadron commander. Other airplanes were over the camp. One took a photograph of Jackson's airplane on the ground. The author once met a retired USAF pilot who was over the camp in an A-37 during the rescue. Another officer observed the rescue and commented in his mission report that the C-123 troop deserved the Air Force Cross. Jackson has since said that General Westmoreland told him that it was he who made the recommendation for the award. (He probably endorsed it.) Campbell was awarded the Air Force Cross – the citation is identical to Jackson's.

Sam McGowan

The President of the United States of America, authorized by Title 10, Section 8742, United States Code, takes pleasure in presenting the Air Force Cross to Major Jesse W. Campbell, United States Air Force, for extraordinary heroism in military operations against an opposing armed force as a C-123 aircraft pilot of the 311th Air Commando Squadron, 315th Special Operations Wing, DaNang Air Base, Vietnam, in action at Kham Duc, Republic of Vietnam on 12 May 1968. On that date, Major Campbell volunteered to attempt the rescue of a three-man U.S. Air Force Combat Control Team from the Special Forces Camp at Kham Duc. Hostile forces had overrun the forward outpost and established gun positions on the airstrip. They were raking the camp with small arms, mortars, light and heavy automatic weapons, and recoilless rifle fire. The camp was engulfed in flames and ammunition dumps were continuously exploding and littering the runway with debris. In addition, eight aircraft had been destroyed by the intense enemy fire and one aircraft remained on the runway reducing its useable length to only 2200 feet. To further complicate a landing, the weather was deteriorating rapidly. Although fully aware of the extreme danger and likely failure of such an attempt, Major Campbell set up the approach from approximately 7300 feet above the airfield. Through a superior display of pilot expertise, he side slipped the C-123 aircraft steeply to an altitude of 500 feet above the ground. The landing roll was terminated near the point where the Combat Control Team was reported to be hiding. While on the ground, the aircraft was the target of intense hostile fire. A rocket landed in front of the nose of the aircraft but failed to explode. Once the Combat Control Team was aboard, the C-123 succeeded in getting airborne despite the hostile fire directed across the runway in front of the aircraft. Through his extraordinary heroism, superb airmanship, and aggressiveness in the face of hostile forces, Major Campbell reflected the highest credit upon himself and the United States Air Force.

Anything, Anywhere, Anytime

Chapter Nineteen - "THE NEVER-ENDING WAR"

C-130A at Khe Sanh (Sandy Alderson)[336]

Officially, the 1968 Tet Offensive ended with the evacuation of the camp at Kham Duc. But the war continued, although the intensity eventually dropped back to the levels of just before the communists launched their fierce attacks during the Chinese New Year. Even though the Tet Offensive was over, some of the heaviest fighting of the Vietnam War was yet to come. The heaviest American casualties of the war occurred from 1967-70, with 1968-1969 being the worst years. There were enemy attempts to overrun camps such as the attack on Duc Lap, but there were also numerous conflicts with large numbers of well-armed NVA forces. An American brigade was airlifted into Dak To. The camps at Dak Pek and Dak Seang were supplied by airdrop for several weeks in June. In August another airlift was begun into Katum, the airfield that had been constructed during Operation *JUNCTION CITY* more than a year before.

Thousands of communists remained in South Vietnam; a particularly strong concentration was along the Cambodian Border in the region known as "The Parrot's Beak" because of its shape. No major battles had decimated the communist forces in that area as they had done in the I Corps battles and they were in close proximity to Cambodia, which they used as a sanctuary and supply depot. The communist headquarters, the mythical COSVN, was believed to be just

---

[336] Sandy Alderson is the current manager of the New York Mets. His father was an Air Force pilot and he was a USMC officer at Khe Sanh.

Anything, Anywhere, Anytime

across the border in Cambodia where it had moved after *JUNCTION CITY*.[337] Even though Air Force, Navy and Marine fighters were conducting a massive interdiction campaign against the Ho Chi Minh Trail, a campaign that now included AC-130 gunships, North Vietnamese trucks were getting through with supplies and arms that were stockpiled in Cambodia.

Cargo ramp at Qui Nhon

Bu Dop cargo area (Author)

The battle of Kham Duc was the highlight of the Tet Offensive and of the entire Vietnam War for the C-130s and C-123s. The C-7 crews were not involved in the evacuation although some had landed there the day before. They only played a limited role at Khe Sanh, but they

---

[337] The COSVN was mythical, there was some question that it even existed.

Page 498

continued to perform their day-to-day duties in a war that had reached the apex of its intensity. The communists made other attempts to overrun remote camps and C-7s were used to keep their defenders supplied. After Kham Duc, the communists backed away from the population centers and retreated back into the heavily-wooded hills along the Laotian border and into Laos itself, as well as into "neutral" Cambodia where the Khmer Rouge were in opposition to the government. Their hopes for a general uprising among the South Vietnamese population had been dashed, as had General Giap's plan for a major defeat of American forces. Over most of Vietnam, they turned back to their strategy of attacking isolated camps in hopes of winning a psychological victory by gaining headlines in the world's press. While the C-130s and C-123s had had their finest hour, the C-7 crews were about to have theirs.

C-123 at Da Nang 1967 (Author)

Duc Lap was a border camp west of Ban Me Thout, with a garrison much like the one at Kham Duc – several half-strength CIDG companies and their American Special Forces advisors. While the camp itself was surrounded by three rings of barbed wire, the airstrip lay outside the camp perimeter and was unprotected. The communists attacked Duc Lap after American and South Vietnamese troop movements into the area caused them to break off a planned attack on Ban Me Thout. The small camp with its under-strength garrison seemed like a much easier target. Shortly after midnight on August 23, 1968, the communists launched their attack with a coordinated effort involving artillery, sapper charges and conventional infantry. More than 4,000 troops from the North Vietnamese 1st Division circled the camp. The defenders beat off the initial attacks and the North

Anything, Anywhere, Anytime

Vietnamese took the camp under siege. The 5th Special Forces Group asked for an emergency air resupply. The first supplies were flown into the camp by helicopter, along with Vietnamese reinforcements. Other reinforcements were airlifted into Ban Me Thout by C-123s and C-130s in preparation for an operation to relieve the camp. Meanwhile, the C-7 crews of the 457th and 458th Tactical Airlift Squadrons made plans to begin airdrops.

Loading Caribou at Pleiku, note cow to right of forklift (Author)

Originally purchased by the Army to serve as a battlefield transport, the De Havilland Caribou was a rugged airplane, at least in the sense that its construction was simple and it did not depend on complex hydraulics as did the much larger C-130. Its top speed was only about 180 knots and the published payload was only 8,000 pounds. Originally designed to serve as a bush plane in Canada, the C-7 was able to land on unimproved landing strips and its minimum takeoff and landing distance was only 1,200 feet. Yet even though it was slow, it was very maneuverable, which allowed the pilots who flew it to take violent evasive action to avoid ground fire.

When the Army operated them, Caribous flew with a crew of two pilots and the airplane's crew chief. When the Air Force took them over in 1966, crew chiefs initially flew with their airplane but the third crewmember eventually became a flight engineer whose duties were actually more like that of a loadmaster. The initial Caribou crew chiefs and engineers were drawn from the ranks of men with experience on twin-engine reciprocating airplanes such as the C-47, C-46 and T-29 but there weren't enough of them to go around. There was already a demand for crew chiefs/engineers on airplanes such as the AC-47 and EC-47. The Air Force then turned to the ranks of lower ranking flight

Page 500

engineers who had previous mechanical experience on reciprocating aircraft.

Oddly enough, many Caribou flight engineers were men whose previous assignment had been on four-engine jet transports with Military Airlift Command who were chosen because of previous experience on large reciprocating aircraft such as the C-124, although they really had no engineer duties since the Caribou didn't have a flight engineer's panel. Caribou flight engineers were trained to rig cargo for airdrops and operate the aerial delivery equipment. In essence,, they were loadmasters. They were sometimes assisted by Army riggers, who flew with the crews as kickers just as their predecessors had done in Korea. Since there were no Caribou units in the United States from which to draw, the leadership in the Air Force squadrons came from TAC C-130 wings. Pilots were drawn from the Air Force at large and included men who had flown B-47s and B-52s as well as C-133s and C-141s. Copilots were young lieutenants fresh out of undergraduate pilot training. Initially, Caribou pilots and flight mechanics were trained at Sewart in the 4449th Crew Training Squadron but by 1969 the training program had relocated to Dyess where the 18th Tactical Airlift Training Squadron activated for Caribou training. Sewart was in the process of closing.

The first airdrops at Duc Lap were made by Captain David Rogers and his crew on August 24. Captain Rogers was on his last day of flying in Vietnam when his crew got the assignment for the mission. Although scheduled to begin out-processing the next day for his return to the United States, Captain Rogers pressed on as his C-7 encountered heavy tracer fire. He flew a series of evasive turns then leveled the airplane at 300 feet only fifteen seconds from the drop zone. All but one bundle landed within the camp compound. Rogers' crew returned to Ban Me Thout where they discovered that although their plane had been hit, the damage was minor. They reloaded and took off again for Duc Lap. The ground fire was as intense the second time as it had been on the previous mission but they made a successful drop. A third mission by another crew delivered another load, making a total of six tons of ammunition and fuses dropped during the day. Two helicopter missions were the only other deliveries to the camp that day. That evening, a third C-7 crew was called out while on alert duty at their home base of Cam Ranh Bay. Major George Finck's crew picked up their load at Nha Trang and took off with a pair of Army riggers aboard to help the engineer over the drop zone. Finck took-off in darkness and headed for Duc Lap, which was easy to find due to the light of illumination flares over the besieged camp. With their lights out and exhausts dampened, Finck's crew made two passes over the compound to dispense their load onto the tiny drop zone. They were told that the drops were successful, but the 5th Special Forces Group later reported

Anything, Anywhere, Anytime

that the bundles landed outside the compound.

Major Hunter F. Hackney and his 458th TAS crew made two trips to Duc Lap the following day before they were able to deliver their load. As they approached the first time, the crew learned that fighting was too intense to allow the loads to be recovered, so they landed at nearby Ban Me Thout. Hoping that the fighting had subsided and that enemy gunners had been driven under cover by the frequent airstrikes, Hackney and his crew took off again in mid-afternoon. They were about two miles out when they encountered heavy ground fire. Hundreds of AK-47 rounds struck the Caribou, but Hackney continued toward the drop zone and made an accurate drop. He made a second pass from a different direction and again encountered heavy fire, but the second drop was also successful. When they landed at Ban Me Thout, Hackney's crew discovered extensive battle damage – the airplane was too damaged to fly again without repairs. They switched to another airplane and the flight engineer rigged the loads so that all four bundles could be released on a single pass. As they approached the camp, the airplane took numerous hits, but they managed to make their way home. Two other C-7 missions brought in additional supplies for a total of more than eight tons – including water, rations, munitions and medical supplies. Majors Hackney and Finck were both awarded the Air Force Cross for their role at Duc Lap.(Bowers, 1986) USAF C-7 crews dropped to Duc Lap over a three-day period. Army CH-47 helicopters operating out of Ban Me Thout finally took over the heavier resupply effort after the ground fire threat around the camp lessened. After reinforcements were brought into the camp and a relief effort was begun from Ban Me Thout, the defenders at Duc Lap finally forced their attackers to withdraw. Eleven helicopters were shot down during the course of the battle but the USAF C-7 crews made their deliveries under extremely hazardous conditions without losing a single airplane.(Bowers, 1986)

As 1968 passed into history, the tempo of the war remained high, especially in the border regions where the enemy forces could operate in strength while being supplied from their sanctuaries in Cambodia and Laos. In late February, the camp at Ben Het came under attack. Located in an isolated region on the Laotian border south of Kham Duc, Ben Het was similarly dependent on airlift for resupply. On February 24, 1969, a pair of C-7s made airdrops to the camp, then that evening they were followed by the first C-130 night drop of the war. Major Curtis Messex and his 21st TAS crew made the drop under the light of flares.[338] In mid-May, the communists managed to cut the road

---

[338] Curt Messex was an experienced troop carrier pilot who had previously served with the air commando wing at Hurlburt. He had flown C-47s in South

between Dak To and Ben Het in preparation for an operation they had code-named *LITTLE DIENBIENPHU*. With the road cut, airlift became even more important to the defense of Ben Het. On June 1, all landings at the camp ceased because of heavy shelling. Two days later, C-7 crews began dropping supplies. Each morning and afternoon, one or two C-7s made resupply drops to the Special Forces team and South Vietnamese in the camp. As the resupply effort continued, more and more flights reported encountering steadily increasing ground fire. On June 13, two out of the four C-7s over the camp were hit and three crewmen were wounded. Then the enemy overran the airstrip thus ruling it out for further use as a drop zone. With the runway no longer available, the C-7 crews were forced to drop their bundles right into the camp itself.

The diminutive size of the new drop zone made the C-7 the only suitable airplane for the resupply mission. The Caribou's slower speeds and smaller size made it more maneuverable, while the simplicity of the airframe and lack of sophisticated hydraulics allowed it to take a considerable number of hits without suffering substantial damage as long as the control cables were not severed or an engine shot out.[339] For more than a month, the Ben Het resupply continued with the C-7 crews and the Special Forces riggers who sometimes flew with them as the sole participants. Airstrikes in conjunction with the drops helped suppress enemy fire. Initially, the C-7s operated over Ben Het as single-ships but when the volume of fire increased to the extent that the 483rd commander threatened to discontinue the drops, new tactics were worked out. Up to six C-7s would approach the drop zone at fifteen-second intervals while fighters bombed and strafed the enemy positions surrounding the camp. Heavy air and artillery missions preceded the airdrops and, while the Caribous were over the camp, propeller-driven A-1E Skyraiders continued strafing alongside the slow-moving transports. With the new tactics, enemy opposition to the airdrops began to decline. In early July, Ben Het was finally relieved when South Vietnamese troops succeeded in clearing the road leading to the camp from Dak To.

In the spring of 1969, crews from the 463rd Tactical Airlift Wing

---

Vietnam in the early sixties. He was considered by many to be one of the best pilots in the Air Force. After retiring from the Air Force, he authored a number of magazine articles and had a couple of audio books published. He died of cancer in the early 2000's.

[339] Caribous, like World War II B-17s, are often referred to as "rugged" airplanes when, in fact, they were just the opposite. Unlike C-130s, Caribous were simple airplanes without the sophisticated hydraulics that could be knocked out by hostile fire.

Anything, Anywhere, Anytime

assumed a new mission, the delivery of huge 10,000-pound M-121 bombs to create instant helicopter landing zones. The Army had expressed a desire to use bombs to create clearings for LZs early in the war and experiments had been carried out with various types of bombs but none had proven successful. There was a supply of 10,000-pound bombs that had been built to be dropped by the huge ten-engine Convair B-36 bomber in the 1950s in storage at Kirtland AFB, New Mexico. After initial tests using CH-54 helicopters in South Vietnam, more tests were conducted in October 1968 using C-130s. The tests were successful and since C-130s offered a less expensive and more versatile means of delivering the bombs, the mission was given to the 463rd with 834th Air Division acting as the intermediary for mission scheduling. Another series of drops was carried out in December 1968, probably to qualify additional crews.

M-121 bomb (Author)

The 463rd had been operating out of Tan Son Nhut since 1965 but its operating location was changed to Cam Ranh Bay since that was where the huge bombs would be delivered by ship. Air Force riggers from the 14th Aerial Port Squadron rigged the weapons, which consisted of mounting them in wooden cradles and securing them with cotton and nylon webbing then attaching rigging for the extraction parachute and a stabilization parachute. Regular drops commenced in

March 1969 and continued until the end of the war although they became less frequent when US troops began withdrawing in 1970. Two bombs were loaded on the airplane for the mission. If a second bomb was needed for the target, it was dropped at the same location. If a second bomb wasn't needed, it was dropped on an alternate target.

Instant LZ made by M-121 (Author)

Four bomb-qualified crews were maintained in each of the 463rd's four squadrons and at least two crews were on rotation at Cam Ranh at all times. Bomb crews were assigned to the regular airlift mission and flew cargo and passenger missions if no bomb drops were scheduled. Since bomb crews were the most highly qualified in each squadron and since a bomb mission only used a few hours of the crew duty day, after the bombs had been dropped, the crews were assigned to the most demanding airlift missions of the day, which usually meant shuttling into the forward airfields along the Cambodian Border.

Sometime in late 1967 or 1968, 834th Air Division came up with a new innovation, the C-123 and C-130 "bladder bird." Previously, fuel had been transported in 500-gallon bladders that the crews commonly referred to as "elephant turds" because of their appearance. The new bladders were actually portable fuel bladders designed to store fuel at forward airfields but smaller 3,000-gallon bladders could be strapped to a modular airdrop platform and loaded onto a C-123 or C-130. C-123s could carry a single bladder but C-130s could carry two hooked in tandem. A gasoline-powered pump was chained to an aluminum cargo pallet and secured to the airplane ramp. Fuel specialists from the POL sections of the supply squadrons at the tactical airlift bases were placed on flying status and flew with the crews to operate the equipment. Bladder missions accounted for a sizeable portion of

Anything, Anywhere, Anytime

tactical airlift operations during the final years of US involvement in the war. Several bladder missions were scheduled each day.

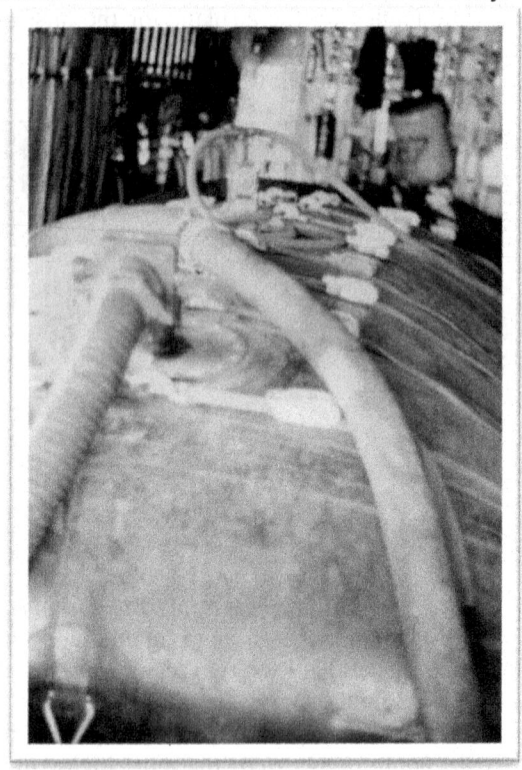

Filled bladders on C-130 (Stan Davis)[340]

Bladder flights were used primarily to transport jet fuel to forward airfields, where it was offloaded into portable fuel farms that had been set up to refuel Army and Marine helicopters. The drawback to the use of bladder birds was that it took approximately thirty minutes to pump 6,000-gallons of fuel off of a C-130, during which time the airplane was exposed to artillery attack. The pilots normally left the engines running and procedures called for the fuel specialist to shut down the pump and disconnect the hoses so the airplane could depart immediately in the event of an attack. Loadmaster duties were light since the bladders were left on the airplanes for several days at a time. In the event of a fire, the loadmaster would jettison the pallets. Bladder missions operated into forward airfields where the Army and Marines had set up advanced bases that couldn't be supplied by truck.

---

[340] The bladder bird concept evidently was conceived in late 1967. The author's last shuttle from Naha was in July and the missions hadn't started yet. By early 1969 when I reported to Clark, bladder missions were routine.

Fuel continued to be delivered to the unsecure fields along the Cambodian border in 55-gallon drums secured to pallets so the airplane could be easily offloaded in less than five minutes.

C-130B offloading fuel at Kham Duc 1970 (J. Gary Fenderbosch)

As the war moved further south to the area northwest of Saigon, the airfields at Bu Dop, Quan Loi, Tonle Cham and Katum became the "hot spots." No sieges of the airfields took place as had occurred at Khe Sanh and Kham Duc but each airfield was within artillery range of communist gun and rocket positions across the border in Cambodia. Katum was only a mile from the border. In the spring of 1969, the NVA moved a "quad-fifty," a .51-caliber machinegun with four barrels mounted on a truck into the forests near Katum.[341] The gun managed to shoot down a C-130B from the 463rd and damage others, one heavily (also from the 463rd) before it was finally located and destroyed by US Army helicopter gunships. Two other C-130s were shot down and several others suffered damage raging from minor to major while landing and taking off from Katum in 1968-69.

While ground fire was far more of a threat then it was before Tet '68 – thanks to the larger calibers and more sophisticated nature of some of the guns – artillery fire was the primary worry for C-130 and C-123 crews landing at the forward airfields. Several of the fields in the vicinity of the Parrots Beak were within range of NVA positions across

---

[341] There is some question as to whether or not this gun was a truck-mounted Quad-Fifty or a single-barrel conventional machinegun. The author was flying with the 463rd TAW at the time. We were told in our intelligence briefings that it was a truck-mounted gun and that it was eventually knocked out by a helicopter gunship. However, a Special Forces medic who was at Katum claims it was a conventional machinegun and that a patrol from the camp finally managed to knock it out.

Anything, Anywhere, Anytime

the border in Cambodia; positions from which the communists had been waging war for years. Every transport that landed at any of the airfields in the region was subject to artillery attack while on the ground as well as ground fire during approaches and takeoffs. As often as not, the shells and rockets were fired from positions in Cambodia. Miraculously, few transports were destroyed by artillery fire, primarily because the crews were able to get in and out of the airstrips before the communist gunners could zero their guns. Only ten C-130s were lost to ground attack during the entire war and half of those were at Da Nang. Only one was lost in the Parrot's Beak area, a C-130E that was left at Tonlecham with an engine problem and was destroyed by artillery before it could be repaired and flown out.

Quan Loi 1970 (Author)

After Tet, airlift crews were subject to enemy attack even at "secure'" Cam Ranh Bay. When the base was built, the Viet Cong were equipped only with mortars that lacked the range to hit Cam Ranh from outside the base's heavily guarded and wide perimeters. But that changed with the advent of the 122-MM rocket and Cam Ranh became a favorite target for communist harassing attacks. The rocket attacks were infrequent, very inaccurate and rarely did any damage but they came in without warning and the threat of an attack kept the rear-echelon personnel at the base on edge. The North Vietnamese also trained daring squads of explosive-laden sappers to penetrate the American bases and attack major targets – particularly airbase flight lines.

Just how the communist ground attack teams came to be called sappers is unclear. The term was originally applied to engineers who built bridges and constructed fortifications in the nineteenth century and was in common use among British forces by World War I.

Sam McGowan

Somehow, highly-trained communist commando teams came to be referred to as "sappers" by US forces. The Vietnamese commando attacks were initially directed at airfields and were usually in conjunction with mortar attacks to drive the defenders into bunkers. One of the most successful attacks was aimed at the cargo ramp at Da Nang in July 1965 when two flare mission C-130s were destroyed. One sapper mission against Cam Ranh was aimed at "Herky Hill", the complex on the west side of the base where the C-130 crews and support personnel lived, and the C-130 flight line. Fortunately, alert air police security teams spotted the intruders and killed them with machinegun fire. The Army replacement depot and evacuation hospital was not so lucky. An attack aimed at the complex killed and wounded several Americans, including a young US Army nurse who was one of the handful of American women to lose their lives in Southeast Asia.[342]

In April 1970, a year after the airdrop effort at Ben Het, the Special Forces camp at Dak Seang came under attack. Located only a few miles north of Ben Het, Dak Seang had been the object of attacks on several occasions and C-7 crews had often been called upon for airdrops to the camp's garrison. Allied intelligence sources in February and March had indicated that enemy activity in the area was again on the increase. In spite of the warnings, large numbers of North Vietnamese troops managed to move through the forests without detection and occupy dug-in positions around the camp. During their buildup, the enemy forces positioned several crew-served weapons along likely approach paths for resupply transports. The surprise was complete – only twelve hours before the first attack, C-7s had been

---

[342] Inexplicably, the loss of the nurse at Cam Ranh does not appear in published lists of American women killed in Vietnam. Only one nurse is shown as having been killed in action, and her death is reported as having been at Chu Lai. The Chu Lai casualty occurred during the same timeframe as the one at Cam Ranh and it is possible that the location was misreported. The author was at Cam Ranh the night of the attack and carried the body of the deceased young woman to the Army mortuary at Tan Son Nhut the following morning. Nurse Sharon Lane was reported to have been killed at Chu Lia, which was serviced by the military mortuary at Da Nang and her body would not have passed through Cam Ranh Bay but would have gone to Da Nang, which was only fifty miles away. My crew didn't arrive at Cam Ranh until the afternoon of the day on which Lt. Lane was killed in the wee hours of the morning and didn't fly our first mission until the following morning – a bomb drop. Human remains rarely, if ever, were shipped through Cam Ranh as there was no mortuary there and no place to store them while awaiting shipment. The body of the nurse the author transported was brought to the flight line and stored in a refrigerated container until the next morning when we transported it to Tan Son Nhut. Former graves registration personnel have advised the author that the death records are stored in a Conex container in Hawaii and have never truly been catalogued.

Anything, Anywhere, Anytime

taking off from the camp with ammunition that was needed at another camp.

Late on the morning of April 1, 1970 the garrison at Dak Seang requested airdrops. However, the Special Forces command centers at Pleiku and Nha Trang decided to wait and use the crew and airplane that was scheduled for a practice drop mission the following day. But the situation at the camp began to deteriorate and a resupply mission of crucial items was desperately needed. Two C-7s were diverted from other missions and sent to Pleiku to load for airdrops over Dak Seang. Three sorties were flown that afternoon to deliver loads of flak vests, helmets, water and medical supplies. The drop planes encountered only light opposition during their approach but picked-up more fire as they pulled away after the drop. The next morning the drops resumed. After the first C-7 crew reported ground fire during their exit from the drop zone, the second departed in a different direction. They were hit as they left the area of the camp and crashed five miles away, with no survivors among the three-man crew. After the loss, *HILDA* suspended further drops but the situation became critical before nightfall. Later in the day, MACV declared an immediate need for thirty tons of supplies to be delivered to Dak Seang. All available C-7s with drop-qualified crews were diverted to Pleiku. Within an hour, eighteen Caribous were on their way to the air base in the Central Highlands.

Eleven C-7 crews dropped at Dak Seang that afternoon and early evening. The crews used tactics learned during the similar supply effort to Ben Het the previous year. In order to avoid ground fire, they made descending approaches at twenty-second intervals over the drop zone. Forward air controllers coordinated preparatory airstrikes in advance of the drops while A-1s escorted the transports. In spite of the fire suppression, all eleven airplanes drew ground fire and three took hits. The same tactics permitted thirty-one drops over the next two days, with fourteen airplanes taking hits. One airplane was forced to land at Dak To after being shot-up so badly over the drop zone that the crew felt they were unable to make it back to Pleiku. Most of the hits occurred during the final seconds of the approach for the drop and in close proximity to the camp itself. The buildings at Dak Seang had nearly all been leveled by this time, so the C-7 crews used the entire camp as a drop zone!

To describe aircraft losses at Dak Seang as "heavy" would have to draw the question "as compared to what?" They were heavy for airlift operations in Vietnam but nothing to compare with World War II losses. During the first two days of drops, only one airplane was shot down, although several transports received battle damage. On April 4, the third day of drops, a second C-7 was shot down when it encountered heavy fire. The Caribou crashed two miles from the camp. Two days later a third C-7 was shot down. Three airplane losses in less than a week were pretty heavy for a mission that lost only twenty airplanes during the entire Vietnam War, especially since they were all lost over the same camp. That more Caribous were not lost can only be attributed to their maneuverability and simple construction, which resulted in only minimal battle damage to most airplanes. More complex airplanes wouldn't have survived in such an environment.

Every airplane over Dak Seang encountered some ground fire and most took hits. Many loads were dropped outside the camp where they were not retrievable. On April 6, the 483rd wing changed tactics as they switched from multiple-plane formations back to single-ships. That morning, three airplanes made drops while escorted by jet fighters and prop-driven A-1s. One C-7 was shot down, the third lost in the resupply. A three-ship formation later in the day met with dismal results as the first airplane was hit just before the drop and jettisoned its load, the second missed because the load hung in the airplane and the third was told to abort because the escorting fighters were low on fuel. With the situation at Dak Seang very grave, the Air Force began considering other methods. Night C-130 drops were considered but were ruled out because of the danger presented by the falling 2,200-pound bundles to the camp's defenders.[343] Night C-7 drops seemed to be the answer but C-130 LAPES missions were also considered. Finally, AC-119 gunships starting illuminating the drop zone with their searchlights and the C-7s were able to drop at night with reasonable accuracy. Other missions were flown by C-123 crews to nearby Dak Pek where the loads were airdropped; the cargo was then loaded onto helicopters and transported to the camp. This system eventually ended the need for C-7 deliveries directly to the camp. For the Caribou crews, the Dak Seang drops were the most intense and heroic missions of the entire Vietnam War.

After more than a year of enduring constant communist attacks on American and South Vietnamese bases along the Cambodian border by troops operating from across the border, President Richard Nixon decided he had had enough. During the first week of May 1970, American and ARVN troops crossed the Cambodian border. The border crossing was kicked off by a *COMMANDO VAULT* mission to clear LZ's for the initial assault. The surprise attacks forced the North Vietnamese to abandon their sanctuaries and supply bases and flee back up the Ho Chi Minh Trail deep into Laos. It would be two years before they would launch another significant attack in South Vietnam. Every airlifter flying missions in Vietnam (except one) applauded the move; no one could understand why so many American students rose

---

[343] The containers used by the Caribou crews were much smaller than the standard A-22 container.

Anything, Anywhere, Anytime

up in protest of a move that would save hundreds – if not thousands – of American lives. The single exception was a pilot with the 50th TAS at CCK, Charlie Clements, who eventually resigned his commission in protest of the war. Clements would resurface years later after becoming a doctor and going to Central America to aid communist insurgents in El Salvador.(People Magazine)

Troops awaiting airlift during Cambodia Incursion

With the success of the invasion of Cambodia, the Vietnam War sank to a low ebb that allowed troop withdrawals to accelerate. President Nixon had actually ordered a downsizing of the US presence in South Vietnam shortly after he took office in January 1969. However, the intensity of combat prevented large-scale withdrawals until late in the year. When Nixon took office, there were 480,000 US troops in South Vietnam with countless others at offshore C-130 bases. By the time of the invasion of Cambodia, the numbers had been reduced by some 200,000 men. Marine strength in I Corps had been substantially reduced in reflection of the communist shift to the Cambodian Parrots Beak region. By 1971, troop levels had been reduced to 171,000 men.

But even as the American presence was reduced, search and destroy missions continued. In the summer of 1970, a multi-brigade operation returned to Kham Duc. Their mission, at least in part, was to search for the remains of Americans who were missing in action from the evacuation of the camp. To their surprise, they found the camp very much as it had been when the last defenders were brought out more than two years before. Some items of ordnance and construction equipment were salvageable, including the combat controllers' Jeep. The communists had evidently never occupied the camp after the evacuation and if US airstrikes were directed against it after the evacuation, they were ineffective. After repairs to the runway, C-123 landings began on July 17. When repairs had added an additional 1,000 feet, C-130s joined the airlift into the camp.[344] That the enemy was still in the vicinity was signaled by frequent artillery fire that sometimes brought airlift operations to a halt. The force remained at the camp for a month and then it was evacuated once again. During the withdrawal, a Chinook was lost to enemy fire. It went down with thirty-one people aboard.

Kham Duc, 1970 (Author)

The war in Vietnam began with 315th Air Division in Japan as the responsible agent for airlift activities in the Pacific but in April 1969 the division was inactivated and the three C-130 wings were reassigned to the respective numbered Air Forces in whose territory they were based. While the 374th on Okinawa, along with the 815th Tactical Airlift Squadron at Tachikawa, shifted to Fifth Air Force, the 314th at CCK and the 463rd at Clark became part of Thirteenth. The 815th transferred into the 374th. The C-130 wings were still responsible for support of 834th Air Division but there was no longer a PACAF airlift organization outside of Vietnam. As the war wound down, the need for C-130s decreased because Military Airlift Command had assumed most of the overwater flying in the Western Pacific. MAC was retiring its C-124s since the massive Lockheed C-5 would soon be coming into service. The 22nd MAS at Tachikawa inactivated, but four former MAC C-124s transferred to Clark and were

---

[344] The author flew into Kham Duc on a bladder bird mission carrying fuel for the Army helicopters that had moved in to operate out of the base. We were escorted by a Marine OV-10 turboprop advanced forward air controller aircraft. Since we were carrying fuel in a large bladder, we were on the ground for at least half an hour while the fuel was pumped out of the bladders on the airplane into portable bladders on the ground. I wish now I had looked around more. At the time, I wasn't fully aware of the details of the events that had occurred there two years before.

Anything, Anywhere, Anytime

assigned to the 463rd Tactical Airlift Wing for outsize cargo duty. The huge transports were assigned to the 20th Operations Squadron, which also operated C-118s for medical evacuation missions. The 20th had formerly been the 6485th Operations Squadron. It was redesignated when the unit moved to Clark in September 1968. Four C-124s were also assigned to the 17th Tactical Airlift Squadron at Elmendorf AFB, Alaska for outsize cargo duty in Alaska Air Command's area of responsibility. On May 31, 1971, the 374th inactivated and its C-130As returned to the United States and were assigned to the Air Force Reserves and Air Guard to replace C-119s, C-124s and C-97s. Eventually, some C-130As would go to the Vietnamese Air Force. The unit designation for the 374th transferred to CCK while that wing's 314th designation went to Little Rock where the C-130s from Sewart had moved when the Tennessee base closed. The 21st TAS designation also moved to CCK; it was given to the 346th TAS, the newest squadron on Taiwan.[345]

C-123s (Skip Tannery)

Although tactical activity in South Vietnam was obviously on the decline, airlift remained an important American role in the country and would remain so until the final withdrawal. "Bladder bird"

---

[345] There are indications that PACAF originally intended to transfer all of the 374th squadron designations to CCK along with the wing. Apparently, the plan was opposed by some officers at CCK and, except for the 346th, the squadrons retained the designations of the units which had transferred to PACAF from TAC in the winter of 1965-66. Why the Air Force didn't close CCK and move the wing's assets to Naha has never been revealed. Instead, the USAF pulled out of Naha and kept CCK open, but it closed within two years.

missions carrying fuel for helicopters remained at high levels well into 1971. Airdrop missions by C-130 crews all but ceased, and would not resume until the spring of 1972. The C-7 force assumed responsibility for most of the emergency supply drops in view of the decreasing size of the units in the field. C-123s flew 31 drop missions in support of the Dak Seang relief in April 1970 but the level of C-123 and C-130 drop missions declined to an average of ten missions per month.

Cargo ramp at Phan Rang (Kent Hoffman)

The tempo of the war picked up again in January 1971 when South Vietnamese troops crossed the border out of extreme northwestern South Vietnam into Laos. Prior to the operation, the airfield at Khe Sanh was reopened as a supply base to support the South Vietnamese troops. According to the press, *LAM SON 719* turned into a major disaster when the South Vietnamese encountered very heavy concentrations of PAVN troops at Tchepone, a city in Laos that had long been in North Vietnamese hands and was one of the most heavily defended communist bases in Southeast Asia. Yet, in spite of heavy helicopter losses on the first day of the operation, the South Vietnamese captured the city. Even though they had succeeded in cutting the Ho Chi Minh Trail, the South Vietnamese elected to withdraw from Laos rather than continue the possibility of heavy combat. Airlift support was mostly in the form of C-130 lift into Khe Sanh where cargo was picked up by helicopter for delivery into Laos. No airdrop missions were flown in Laos with the exception of several *COMMANDO VAULT* C-130 bombing missions flown by the 463rd wing.

One unique aspect of the period was that, for the first time in the war, Military Airlift Command C-141 Starlifters were used on in-country missions to take up slack made by the demands on the C-130s

Anything, Anywhere, Anytime

by flying cargo and passengers between the major aerial ports in South Vietnam. The MAC crews were not assigned to South Vietnam on TDY as the C-130 crews were but remained at Cam Ranh Bay for a few days at a time to fly in-country missions during the course of a normal MAC mission rather than immediately starting the return to their home base after dropping their load as was normal MAC practice.

After *LAM SON 719*, the United States continued its drawdown of forces. By this time, nearly all of the American ground combat units had been withdrawn. US Army aviation units and Air Force squadrons also became the targets of reductions. In August 1971, Secretary of Defense Melvin Laird directed the Air Force to close the airlift bases in South Vietnam and to base all airlift resources out of the country. The Caribous and C-123s were given to the Vietnamese. A single squadron of C-7s and C-123s operated out of Tan Nhut as the 310th Tactical Airlift Squadron for about a year while the South Vietnamese Air Force was transitioning into them. On December 1, 1971 834th Air Division inactivated and all C-130s operating in South Vietnam were controlled directly by the 374th wing which was based at CCK but maintained an operating location at Tan Son Nhut for in-country operations. A new Directorate of Airlift was set up directly under Seventh Air Force, initially with personnel who had been with 834th. The 463rd at Clark had also been inactivated but a single squadron of C-130Bs, the 774th, remained, although it was also awaiting impending inactivation.[346] The

---

[346] The 774th inactivated in June, 1972 and the designation went to Dyess along with that of the 463rd Wing.

Page 516

Sam McGowan

463rd's C-130Bs returned to the US and, like the A-models, were reassigned to reserve units. The 463rd Wing inactivated on December 31, 1971. The designation went to Dyess AFB, Texas on June 1 to replace the 516th designation, which was retired. The war had lowered in intensity to a guerrilla insurgency and the airlift mission which was now performed almost entirely by C-130s, had become routine; so routine that only part of the crews maintained tactical proficiency. In the spring of 1972, "routine" suddenly turned into anything but.

In early April 1972, three North Vietnamese divisions came out of Cambodia and attacked South Vietnamese positions in Binh Long Province northwest of Saigon. Loc Ninh was seized and the provincial capital, An Loc, came under siege by strong communist forces. The PAVN forces surrounding An Loc were equipped with a proliferation of heavy antiaircraft weapons, the first time such antiaircraft had been seen in South Vietnam in such large numbers. The 1968 bombing halt had allowed North Vietnam to build up their antiaircraft defenses in the north to the point that they were able to afford the luxury of sending 37-millimeter guns south with their troops. In spite of the massive interdiction effort by USAF fighters and AC-130 gunships based in Thailand, the North Vietnamese had been able to move motorized infantry supported by tanks down the Ho Chi Minh Trail for an attack that was aimed at the South Vietnamese capitol in Saigon. Other communist forces attacking out of Laos struck South Vietnamese positions in the Central Highlands around Kontum, while NVA units poured across the Demilitarized Zone to attack the northern provinces of South Vietnam in the vicinity of Quang Tri.

The siege of An Loc turned out to be arguably the most difficult

Anything, Anywhere, Anytime

period of the war for American airlifters, which now consisted of only four squadrons at CCK and one at Clark that was in the process of inactivation. While the dramatic events at Kham Duc had lasted for only a few hours and only involved a few crews, the airdrop effort at An Loc would last for several weeks and cost the lives of several C-130 crewmembers – including two crews – as well as two VNAF C-123 crews. There was one major difference, however. While the high intensity airdrop operations of 1968 had been supporting US Army and Marine Corps units, the An Loc drops were supporting South Vietnamese.

When the city first came under siege, MACV attempted a helicopter resupply but the heavy concentration of antiaircraft guns and automatic weapons made resupply using fragile helicopters impossible. Next, MACV turned to the Vietnamese Air Force's C-123s but that effort failed as well. The Vietnamese crews encountered heavy antiaircraft fire and were forced to drop from high altitudes to avoid heavy losses. But the Vietnamese lacked the high-altitude rigging equipment necessary for drops above 1,000 feet and the loads drifted with the wind and very little – if any – of the cargo was recovered by friendly forces. The VNAF crews attempted low-altitude drops but lost two C-123s to ground fire. With no other alternative, MACV placed the burden of resupply of the beleaguered garrison on the shoulders of the 374th wing C-130 crews.

At this point in the war, the PACAF C-130 force had become essentially a logistical force. Only a portion of the crews in the 374th Tactical Airlift Wing at CCK were even tactically qualified and few had real combat experience. After the Cambodian Incursion in May 1970, the airlift mission had become largely logistical with the only drop missions being an occasional *COMMANDO VAULT* operation. Enemy opposition had become practically nonexistent. Only one C-130 had been lost in South Vietnam since June 1969, a B-model that was hit by rockets at Da Nang in February 1971. The general proficiency of the crews had declined considerably and except for a handful of officers who had returned to the Pacific after long stateside assignments, few of the pilots had seen actual combat. A number of flight engineers and loadmasters had served previous tours in C-130 or C-123 squadrons but the majority of the crewmembers were generally inexperienced in combat operations. In an address to the Airlift/Tanker Association, the late Brig. Gen. Ed Brya, who had served as a captain at Naha then had spent several years in SAC in B-52s before returning to PACAF to become the wing Stan/Eval pilot for the 374th Wing, outlined the situation. General Brya pointed out that most of the veteran C-130 pilots who had served in Southeast Asia earlier in the war had either gone to other assignments outside of airlift, left the service or retired by the time all hell broke loose at An Loc. Consequently, the burden of resupplying An Loc fell to a handful of experienced tactical airlift pilots.

On the afternoon of April 15, a three-ship formation of C-130Es approached An Loc. The first crew over the drop zone managed to drop their load successfully in spite of several hits. The second crew aborted the drop after a piece of rigging fouled the load of A-22 containers so they would not move out of the airplane.[347] The third crew, commanded by Captain William R. Caldwell, failed to find the drop zone on their first attempt and had to come around for a second pass. When they were thirty seconds out, their C-130 flew into an antiaircraft barrage. The flight engineer, TSgt Jon Sanders, was killed instantly when a burst of .51-caliber machinegun fire struck the cockpit and the copilot and navigator were both wounded by fragments of flying debris. Fire broke out in the cargo compartment. The senior loadmaster, SSgt Charlie Shaub, battled the blaze with a fire extinguisher that was so hot that the metal severely burned his hands. When the airplane entered the landing pattern at Tan Son Nhut, the landing gear would not come down. Shaub supervised the other loadmaster, Sgt Dave McAleece, as he used the emergency gear extension to crank down the landing gear. Captain Caldwell and SSgt Shaub were both awarded the Air Force Cross. Sergeant Shaub also received the William H. Pitzenbarger Award – named for a pararescue technician who had been killed earlier in the war – from the Air Force Sergeant's Association. SSgt Shaub was nominated for the Medal of Honor for his role in saving the airplane. According to some CCK veterans, the aircraft commander refused to make the recommendation on the grounds that Shaub was just doing his job. The navigator, 1st Lt. Rick Lentz, made the recommendation after he was visited in the hospital at Tan Son Nhut, where he was recovering from wounds, by a senior lieutenant colonel from his squadron. At some point in the process, the award was downgraded to the Air Force Cross. Even so, Shaub's Air Force Cross is the highest decoration ever awarded to an Air Force enlisted man for an airlift mission.[348]

Over the next several days, the 374th crews attempted several drops to An Loc but with little success. On April 18, Captain Don B. "Doc" Jensen and his crew were shot down when enemy fire set their right wing on fire. Jensen turned toward Tan Son Nhut and kept the burning airplane in the air for approximately fifteen minutes until pieces of the right wing started coming off. Fearing the fire would burn

---

[347] Charlie Armistead in Email to author. Charlie was the loadmaster. Due to a lack of proper rigging equipment, the loadmasters had to scrounge equipment, some of which was non-standard, in order to rig the CDS gates for the drops.

[348] Loadmaster John Levitow was awarded the Medal of Honor but he was out of airlift at the time of his action.

Anything, Anywhere, Anytime

through the wing and knowing the airplane was too low for the crew to bail out, Jensen managed to crash-land in a swamp near Lia Khe. A flight of US Army helicopters witnessed the crash. While helicopter gunships fired on enemy troops who were in the vicinity and kept them at bay, other helicopters landed by the wreckage and rescued the crew within minutes of the crash.

Dave McAleece and Charles Shaub

Miraculously, all seven crewmembers, one of whom was a Vietnamese loadmaster, survived the crash-landing. SSgt. Ralph Bemis, one of the loadmasters, was critically injured when he was tossed around in the cargo compartment and hit by flying debris. He was thrown into the forward bulkhead and trapped. The navigator and the other loadmaster worked for half an hour in the burning airplane trying to free him. He spent almost six months in the hospital recovering from his injuries. Sgt. Charlie Armistead, the other loadmaster, who had been one of the loadmasters on the second airplane in the formation on the first day of drops, was wounded by ground fire and suffered additional injuries in the crash-landing. Both loadmasters were hospitalized for several months. Bemis was a veteran loadmaster who had served in the 29th TAS at Clark on a previous tour in 1968-69. During his earlier tour, he was on seventeen different airplanes that were hit by ground fire! Both loadmasters and the navigator, Major Robert Kirkpatrick, were awarded the Silver Star for the mission.

Attempts at supplying the base using conventional low-altitude methods proved impossible without the prospect of very heavy losses.

Sam McGowan

In an attempt to supply the base with less risk, the 374th turned to the ground-directed aerial delivery system known as GRADS that had been developed using the same techniques as those used to direct the *COMMANDO VAULT* bombing missions. But the lack of reliable high-altitude, low-opening cargo parachute opening devices caused the Americans to encounter the same problems as had the VNAF C-123s. After high-altitude drops failed, the 374th returned to night drops on the night of April 23-24. During the first two nights, the C-130 crews enjoyed the element of surprise and managed to get their loads inside the compound. They were supported by AC-130 gunships orbiting over the city and laying down covering fire as they made their approach to the drop zone. That many of the AC-130 crewmembers were former airlifters gave them an appreciation for the plight of their comrades, and a familiarity with the tactics involved. Still, the enemy continued to fill the sky with flak and, on the third night of drops the fourth airplane over An Loc was shot down when it encountered a "virtual wall of fire." Another C-130, the third to be lost over An Loc, went down on the night of May 3-4 although the loss wasn't certain to have been due to ground fire. Three C-130s and two crews had been lost in less than two weeks.

The third loss led to the decision to halt all low-level airdrop attempts. Two airlift experts, Major Myles Rhorlick and TSgt. John Limbach, were sent to Tan Son Nhut to work on the problem. Both were Vietnam veterans, Rhorlick from a tour with 834th AD and Limbach from an earlier tour as a loadmaster on C-123s.[349] They discovered that the Army riggers were improperly rigging the reefing lines that restrained the parachute skirts and the parachutes were opening too high. The problem was rectified but the supply of electrical squibs used to cut the reefing lines was limited so the issue was still not completely resolved.[350]

The problem at An Loc was finally solved when someone remembered the old high velocity drop techniques that were sometimes used in World War II. Several experimental missions were flown at altitudes above 10,000 feet with loads rigged under slotted extraction parachutes designed only to stabilize - but not retard the descent velocity of – the load. The method not only proved satisfactory but was actually superior to other methods because of increased accuracy. Because the bundles fell at terminal velocity instead of floating down leisurely, drift was minimized so the drops were more accurate than if conventional parachutes were used. The high-velocity airdrops required no sophisticated opening equipment while the

---

[349] Rohrlick had served an earlier tour with the 815th TCS at Tachikawa.
[350] The Air Force CHECO report on the Battle of An Loc explains the problem in great detail.

Anything, Anywhere, Anytime

padding used was sufficient to allow even ammunition and fuel to be airdropped. Finally, the problem of supplying An Loc was solved and once again airlift foiled the communist's aims. The method came about at the right time, too because at about the same time the first report of an SA-7 shoulder-launched missile firing in South Vietnam was reported. Although the SA-7 "Strela" missiles were limited in altitude and ineffective against fast-moving targets, they could be deadly against a C-130 making a conventional low-altitude airdrop. The high-velocity airdrop method allowed accurate drops from above 10,000 feet, an altitude well above the effective range of both the Strela missiles and most automatic antiaircraft fire.

Another major airlift operation in the wake of the 1972 attacks was the resupply of Kontum where the airfield was under almost constant attack. One C-130 bladder bird remained on the ground at Kontum for more than four days. Lt. Col. Reed Mulkey, a maintenance officer in the 374th Field Maintenance Squadron, was preparing to take off when a rocket exploded right in front of the nose of his airplane. A repair team flew in and worked with the flight crew to repair the damage. Finally, even though further attacks caused additional damage to the airplane, Mulkey and his crew managed to fly the airplane to Pleiku. The intensity of enemy shelling led to night landings at Kontum as the attacks increased both in number and intensity. Finally the NVA captured the airfield, at which time the C-130 crews turned to airdrop. Fortunately, the experiences of the airlifters at An Loc had led to the development of the high-velocity method so the Kontum drops were not plagued by the problems of the previous weeks. By early June, the city had been reclaimed by friendly forces and on the night of June 8-9 landings resumed.

The 1972 Spring Offensive prompted the return of TAC C-130 squadrons to the Pacific, including a squadron from Little Rock equipped with airplanes featuring the AWADS all-weather aerial delivery system that allowed blind airdrops without radar guidance from the ground. The squadron was commanded by Lt. Col. Billie B. Mills, who had won a Silver Star at Kham Duc in 1968 and who, as a young lieutenant, had pioneered the C-130 covert operations mission. As the war began to wind down once again, the AWADS C-130 crews made a number of airdrops to RVN forces throughout the country. Frequent airdrop missions were also flown in support of friendly forces in Laos and Cambodia. After the arrival of the TAC crews, they assumed the bulk of the airdrop mission because their AWADS systems allowed accurate drops without the maneuvering required to position for a radar-guided release using GRADS.

The return of the TAC troops also brought the 317th Tactical Airlift Wing into the war for the first time. Prior to 1971, the 317th had

Sam McGowan

been equipped with C-130As and although it's 41st TCS went to Naha, the wing itself never participated in the war but was providing airplanes and crews for airlift operations in Europe. The reduction in the C-130 force included the inactivation of the wing at Lockbourne. However, instead of retiring the 317th designation, the Air Force decided to retire the 464th designation at Pope. The 317th transferred to Pope on paper to replace it. The airplanes and personnel that deployed from Pope belonged to the 317th and its assigned squadrons.

Finally, in early 1973 the American role in the Vietnam War came to an official end, but PACAF C-130s would continue flying in Southeast Asia until the final fall of Saigon in 1975. Undoubtedly, the most satisfying missions of the war for the participants were the missions into Hanoi in preparation for the return of the American POW's. Without orders to do so and through an entirely spontaneous effort, the first Americans to greet the returning POW's were members of two C-130 crews who had brought the negotiating team into Hanoi the morning of the day of the release.

Operation *HOMECOMING*, the plan for the return of the POWs, called for them to be airlifted out of North Vietnam to the Philippines by MAC C-141s. There really was no reason for C-141s to be used for the pickups in Hanoi and their use was purely political. After the US reduced its presence in South Vietnam and the war itself became less of an issue, the plight of the POWs came to the forefront due to efforts on the part of the families and POW-MIA activists. The POWs were all ambulatory, although some had difficultly walking; PACAF aeromedical evacuation medics and nurses could have accompanied the C-130s to provide any care that might be needed. Due to lack of

Anything, Anywhere, Anytime

tactical experience on the part of the MAC crews, PACAF combat controllers had to fly into Hanoi on C-130s in advance of the C-141s to set up beacons to guide the MAC transports to the Gia Lam airport. Procedures had been set up to fly the released POWs to Clark for medical examination and debriefing before they continued their journey back to the United States.

C-130 crewmember escorting just-released former POW

Over about a two-week period in advance of the release, 374th wing C-130 crews made several flights into Hanoi and were the first Americans to land in North Vietnam with peaceful intentions since shortly after the French withdrawal almost two decades before. On the day of the release, two C-130 crews arrived with members of the negotiating team and a combat control team carrying portable navigational equipment to guide the C-141 crews to the airport. For the release itself, the C-130 crews had no duties; they were standing by as spectators when the first prisoners arrived at the airfield. Both crews were made up of combat veterans; only a few days before Captain George Elwood and his crew had been involved in the last confrontation between American airlifters and the communists. They had been caught on the ground with mechanical problems at Dalat in the middle of a firefight between South Vietnamese and communist troops. The crew managed to get their airplane started and flew it to safety, while earning recommendations for the Silver Star in the process.

The most seriously injured men were released first. As the first prisoner was released, Elwood's loadmaster, SSgt. Ronald Zgoda, realized that the man was injured and had a long walk across the parking ramp to the waiting C-141. The MAC crews had been given strict orders to remain aboard their airplanes, although why is not clear since a number of USAF personnel were on the airport – although none were from MAC. Zgoda stepped forward on his own initiative and took the man's arm, then led him toward the waiting airplane. Each of the other C-130 crewmembers followed the young loadmaster's lead and fell into line to escort each succeeding prisoner. It was an extremely emotional moment for the airlifters, a moment some participants recall today as the most emotional of their lives. When the POWs reached Clark, they were adamant that they appreciated having been met by combat veterans like themselves instead of a special reception team made up of dignitaries or some other group of noncombatants (such as MAC crewmembers.) As a result of their praise for the conduct of the airlifters, the C-130 crews on subsequent releases were instructed to escort the returning POWS to the waiting C-141s.(Bowers, 1986)[351]

While the most notable POW releases took place in Hanoi, some prisoners were released in South Vietnam. There, American C-130 crews flew communist POW's to release points in areas under communist control where they were exchanged for South Vietnamese and American prisoners. The Vietnam experience of one C-130 pilot, Major Bernard Clark, dated all the way back to the *MULE TRAIN* C-123 mission. Major Clark flew into Loc Ninh with 75 communist prisoners. After he landed, a truck came out with 27 Americans, who departed for Saigon later in the day aboard six US Army helicopters. After the Americans departed, Clark left with approximately eighty South Vietnamese who had just been released. A second C-130 landed right after he departed with another load of communist prisoners who were exchanged for captured South Vietnamese. The repatriation flights continued in South Vietnam for two months. A number of releases in North Vietnam were scheduled through the end of March, with each release following the same pattern. Two C-130s landed at Hanoi in advance of the MAC transports in order to set up equipment to guide them in and arrange for the prisoner release. With the return of the POWs, the American role in Vietnam was officially over. Still, airlifters would continue to play their part in the region.

Shortly after the return of the POWs, the last American military

---

[351] The author first learned of the role played by the C-130 crews in a personal letter from Col. Robert Penny, who was the navigator on George Ellwood's crew. The emotions of the former POWs were conferred to Thirteenth Air Force Commander Gen. William G. Moore, who had served as 834th Air Division's first commander after it became an airlift unit, and are reported by Bowers.

Anything, Anywhere, Anytime

personnel were withdrawn from South Vietnam. In fact, the last American ground combat personnel were withdrawn six months before the prisoner releases began. In anticipation of the withdrawal, enough C-130As to equip two squadrons were given to the South Vietnamese Air Force. They were drawn from those assigned to Air Guard and Reserve squadrons in the US. A contingent of USAF personnel accompanied the transports to provide instruction to the Vietnamese who would fly and maintain them. The American advisory role ended on January 28, two weeks before the prisoner release. MACV deactivated on March 29, 1973. A new office opened at Nakhonphanom, Thailand that was supposed to be responsible for planning and controlling operations in the event the war resumed. Officially at least, the American role in the war had ended.

Airlifters could look back with pride on their performance in the twelve years they had operated under combat conditions. While the vast majority of airlift flying in Vietnam was routine, it fit the classic description of aviation as "hours and hours of pure boredom, punctuated by seconds of stark terror." Actually, Vietnam flying was rarely boring, except perhaps during the two years between the Cambodian incursion and the communist invasion in 1972 when airlift operations were pretty much routine except for the activity during the Lam Son 719 operation into Laos. During the period from 1961-1973, a total of 122 transports were lost in the war. Forty of the total were lost to ground fire while seventeen were destroyed on the ground by artillery or sapper attack. The remaining sixty-five were lost to "operational" causes, most often accidents caused by the difficult operating conditions at the forward airfields.

The breakdown by aircraft type is as follows:

Type	Accidents	Ground fire	Ground Attack	Total
C-130	21	19	12	52[352]
C-123	32	14	4	50
C-7	12	7	1	20
CH-3	3	13	1	17
CH-53	0	2	0	2
UH-1	6	13	0	19

---

[352] C-130 losses do not include two Aerospace Rescue and Recovery HC-130s that were destroyed on the ground at Tuy Hoa or six AC-130 losses. Nor do they include three C-130s shot down over Laos and North Vietnam while on special operations missions and another C-130 that was lost to accident over North Vietnam or an E Flight C-130 operated by Air America. There were also two US Marine Corps KC-130s lost, one to accident and one to enemy action at Khe Sanh. One C-130 crashed at CCK after a flight from Cam Ranh Bay.

Sam McGowan

During 1975:
C-130   0   0   1   1
CH-53   1   3   0   4

Out of Country Losses:
C-130   1[353]   3   4[354]
C-123   3   3

A total of 229 transport crewman were killed or came up missing during missions in South Vietnam and Thailand while forty others were lost in non-airlift missions over North Vietnam and Laos. Of the total airlift losses, 103 were C-130 crewmen, 95 were C-123 and 31 were C-7. Some thirty crewmembers lost their lives in non-rescue helicopter operations. Other losses occurred among support personnel, mainly aerial port airfreight technicians and maintenance troops.(Bowers, 1986) While these losses are shocking, they fail in comparison to troop carrier losses in World War II.

The men who flew in Vietnam, as undoubtedly did those in World War II and Korea, look back upon the period as the greatest adventure of their lives. Griping about the decisions made by the command and control centers was commonplace but there was a feeling of accomplishment when a crew successfully completed a combat emergency mission where they knew that their efforts had perhaps saved the lives of fellow servicemen. Off-duty socializing in the clubs, barracks and off-base bars between men of different backgrounds and races is fondly remembered by all veterans. Undoubtedly, the saddest moments were when crewmembers lost a buddy, or when they picked-up the familiar olive drab body bags containing the remains of a young man (and occasional young woman, either a nurse or Red Cross worker) who had lost their lives.

Transport crewmen remember Vietnam from a perspective experienced by no one else. Airlifters, C-130 crews especially, operated the length and breadth of South Vietnam as well as over most of nearby Thailand and some crews flew special operations missions

---

[353] A C-130A was lost in Thailand in 1965. A second was lost in Laos but it had been baled to the CIA and was operated by a civilian crew when it flew into a mountain.

[354] Two airlift C-130s were lost on the flare mission over Laos. A TAC C-130E was lost in the attack on the Than Hoa Bridge. A special operations C-130E-(I) was lost on a mission over North Vietnam and at least one C-130 was lost in Laos while being flown by an Air America crew. The actual number of out-of-country C-130 losses was at least five, not three.

Anything, Anywhere, Anytime

over Laos and even North Vietnam. Some operated into Cambodia and Laos, particularly after 1970. They learned to appreciate the region's lush green-forested mountains and the deep blue of the South China Sea ringed by pure white beaches where the ocean met the jungle and rice fields. But they also remember the vacant expressions on the faces of the young men they picked up at the remote airfields; young men dressed in fatigues that had been bleached almost white in the sun; men whose bodies reeked from days and weeks without a shower; young men who seemed far older than their years.

Sam McGowan

Chapter Twenty - "THE MILITARY AIRLIFT COMMAND"

While the troop carrier squadrons of TAC and the overseas commands were busily engaged in fighting the war in Vietnam, the Military Air Transport Service was developing into the Military Airlift Command. Years of politicking by MATS leaders finally came to fruition when Congress, led by House Armed Services Committee Chairman L. Mendel Rivers of South Carolina, authorized the creation of Military Airlift Command effective January 1, 1966. Rivers had only assumed the committee chairmanship on January 1 of the previous year, but lost no time in pushing to have MATS upgraded. He first raised the possibility of creating a specified command from MATS at a hearing conducted by his Congressional committee on airlift.

The upgrade from service to specified command status came about to a large degree because of the new US emphasis on the rapid deployment of ground and air forces to overseas trouble spots that began in the late 1950s. Senator John F. Kenney made airlift a major campaign point in his 1960 presidential campaign; after he was elected, he started making good on his campaign promise to upgrade MATS. By the time the war in Vietnam came to an end, the role of airlift in the United States military had changed dramatically. The 315th Air Division, which had formerly been responsible for all airlift operations in the Western Pacific, had ceased to exist and much of the theater airlift it had been responsible for had been assumed by MAC C-141s and C-5s. Vietnam had firmly established the role of airlift in military operations, but MAC would reap the benefits of the accomplishments of the troop carriers and their tactical airlift successors.

After the Department of Defense was established in 1947, the old Army Air Transport Command became the Military Air Transport Service, but its leaders had a hard time establishing a military role for themselves and their organization. Some former ATC officers who were in uniform while on military leave from positions in the airline industry during the war believed that the logistical air transport mission could be performed by the nation's airlines operating under contract to the military, a view shared by most combat commanders. Many within the military saw the ATC as a paramilitary airline with no real military mission. But ATC leaders seized on the idea of transporting combat troops and cargo over long distances, something they had never done, and began advocating themselves as America's long-range airlift arm for the deployment of troops overseas.

In 1948, the new MATS, which had only come into being two weeks before it started, was in its heyday as the service's four-engine transports assumed a role in the Berlin Airlift.[355] In the minds of some people, the airlift WAS a MATS operation, although in reality the MATS transports were under the control of the United States Air Forces Europe and were assigned to one of five troop carrier groups. An airlift taskforce made up of officers from MATS was set up in Wiesbaden, Germany but they were assigned on temporary duty to USAFE, and were not MATS. During the Korean conflict, MATS transports and civilian contract carriers flew high priority cargo and troops to Japan, then returned home usually either empty or with casualties while Far East Air Forces transports operated the Korean Airlift. They would do the same thing during the Vietnam War.

After the Korean War came to an indefinite end, MATS returned to its role of providing air transportation for various Department of Defense agencies. MATS was operated by the Department of the Air Force but its function was as a military airline whose mission was to support the DOD and its various agencies. MATS included US Navy aircraft and crews who had formerly been part of NATS, the Navy's Naval Air Transport Service. To justify its existence in the face of frequent criticism from the airline industry, MATS classified its overseas missions, which carried both cargo and passengers, as "training missions" whose purpose were to keep the service's crews prepared for their wartime mission of worldwide airlift, and to keep the overseas route structure operational. In the 1950s, MATS even

---

[355] MATS aircraft and personnel assigned to the airlift were not there as an entity, but were on temporary duty with USAFE to augment the troop carrier groups that operated the airlift. General Tunner and his staff transferred to USAFE from MATS for the duration of the operation. See Chapter Eight.

went so far as to begin charging the user for its services. MATS established an "Industrial Fund" through which it paid the costs of its operations, including billeting and meals for its crews. MATS "customers," who were other services and other government agencies, transferred funds to MATS from their own accounts as payment for transporting their cargo and passengers. In effect, MATS functioned as a government airline.(Ulanoff, 1964)

Douglas C-118

In nearly every respect, MATS WAS an airline, with a strong influence left over from the civilian airline legacy of World War II. The Industrial Fund system even required payment from the user for MATS' services. Following the example of Lt. General William H. Tunner, who served as MATS commander in the late 1950s until his retirement in 1960, MATS stressed safety over operational necessity, a philosophy that stood in stark contrast to the "let's get the job done" attitude that prevailed within the troop carrier community. Several MATS squadrons operated C-118s and C-121s, the military versions of the DC-7 and Constellation airliners that served in the national airlines at the time. Air transport squadrons flying those airplanes included flight attendants, many of whom were young Women in the Air Force, or WAFs, who gave further credence to the service's "military airline" image. MATS crewmembers on passenger flights flew in Class A uniforms rather than flying coveralls, which lent even more of an airline atmosphere to their operations. Flight attendants were also assigned to MATS C-135 crews when they entered service in the early

Anything, Anywhere, Anytime

sixties.

MATS crews were even treated like airline personnel. MATS support squadrons with Fleet Service and other intrinsic functions were set up as tenant units at overseas bases to service MATS airplanes – and no one else. MATS units functioned within their own world and their exclusiveness caused great consternation among the rest of the Air Force, particularly the troop carrier crews who often had to fend for themselves when they were transient at an air base with a MATS support squadron. Special quarters were set up on overseas bases exclusively for MATS flight crews and, if they happened to be full, the crews were sent to downtown hotels. MATS established certain standards for quarters and meals on the bases their crews frequented and if they were not met, there crews were authorized to go out "on the local economy" and draw full per diem, perks that were not available to other military personnel, including troop carrier crews who sometimes had to sleep in their airplane and eat whatever they could scrounge. Troop carrier crews, particularly, resented the special treatment given to MATS aircrews. A popular song among C-119 crews in TAC was *"I'd Rather Have a Sister in a Whorehouse Than a Brother in MATS."* The song was sung around the piano in officers clubs, especially when there was a MATS crew in the room.

Lockheed C-121 Constellation

While most MATS crewmembers were content with their easy duty, the MATS leadership was anxious to rid the service of its airline image and promote a more military role for it. General Tunner, who became MATS commander in 1958 after returning from Europe where he commanded United States Air Forces Europe,[356] preached a doctrine stressing airlift as a weapon in the same manner that the Strategic Air Command's nuclear bombers were. Never mind that SAC's star had reached its apex and was starting to sink on the horizon while TAC's was on the ascent. Tunner believed that the system of allocating "precious airlift resources" to the specified commands was a waste of men and aircraft. Tunner, who had managed the Berlin Airlift under USAFE commanders Generals Curtis Lemay and John K. Cannon, envisioned a single airlift command that would be responsible for all airlift, theater as well as long-range, or "strategic" to use a term that was coined during World War II to describe the heavy bomber mission in the European theater, which Tunner appropriated.

Naturally, Tunner believed that this command should evolve from his own service, and that men from MATS – whom he considered "airlift experts" – should be in charge. It was not a view shared by Cannon, who returned from Europe to take charge of TAC, and who felt that Tunner's efforts was nothing but a power grab. Cannon was one of the "combat pilots" that Tunner often railed against; he had seen the value of troop carrier squadrons in North Africa and the Mediterranean while Tunner was running ATC's Ferrying Division from an office in Baltimore. The two had butted heads during the Berlin Airlift and would continue to be at odds with each other until Cannon retired, often offering counter-testimony before Congressional hearings on airlift (that Tunner was responsible for.)

Nor was Tunner's view shared by the men, such as General Paul Williams, who ran troop carrier operations in the Mediterranean and Normandy. His views ran counter to those of Generals John Henebry, who took over 315th Air Division when Tunner returned to the US from Japan in early 1951, and Henebry's successor, General Chester McCarty, who had served in ATC during the war. Neither was it shared by the President of the United States, former General of the Army Dwight D. Eisenhower, who had commanded ALL Allied forces in the European Theater, including American and British airborne forces. In fact, Eisenhower disapproved Tunner's ideas, which caused the latter to decide to retire and support Senator John F. Kennedy for president. The only people who agreed with Tunner were his personal supporters and certain Democratic politicians such as Congressmen Carl Vinson and L. Mendel Rivers and Senator Richard Russell, who had aircraft factories and/or MATS bases in their districts. When

---

[356] Even while he was commander of USAFE, Tunner maintained his focus on MATS and used his position to gain more power and authority for it. He recommended that USAFE's 322nd Air Division, which was designated as a "combat cargo" operation, should be transferred to MATS. The transfer finally took place in early 1964.

Anything, Anywhere, Anytime

Tunner retired in 1960, his successors, Generals Joe Kelly and Howell M. Estes, picked up the banner and continued to press for consolidation of all airlift into a single military airlift command. Kelly came to MATS after commanding the Air Proving Ground. Before that, he was the Congressional liaison officer at USAF Headquarters. He commanded a Martin B-26 group in Europe during World War II. Like Tunner, Estes had spent most of his Air Force career in staff positions. His World War II service was all in stateside assignments, much of it in Training Command. After the war, he was assigned to SAC and flew a few missions in B-29s over Korea.

While Tunner's expertise in the field of military airlift is open to question – except for five months during the Korean War when he commanded Far East Air Force's Combat Cargo Command, all of his airlift experience was in ATC and MATS logistical operations – his credentials as a politician are beyond dispute. Tunner caught the ear of South Carolina Congressman L. Mendel Rivers, within whose district Charleston Air Force Base lay, and House Armed Services Committee Chairman Carl Vinson, whose district included Marietta, Georgia where Lockheed had established its transport division. Charleston had started out as a TAC base with C-119s but transferred to MATS, which already had an air transport group based there, in 1955. The C-119 wing inactivated and Charleston became primarily responsible for operating passenger missions to Europe and the Near East using C-54s and Lockheed C-121s. The epitome of the "pork barrel politician," Rivers had been in Congress since 1941 and had served on the House Armed Services Committee for most of that time, and had lobbied for as much military as he could get in his district. Because Charleston Air Force Base was in his district, Rivers had himself appointed head of a committee on airlift within the House Armed Services Committee and turned a willing ear toward Tunner and the MATS staff.

Georgia Congressman Carl Vinson's Congressional service dated to 1914, when he was elected to Congress at age thirty and served for over half a century. He became chairman of the House Armed Services Committee when the War and Navy Departments merged and maintained that position except for years when Republicans took control of the House. Vinson appointed Rivers to chair a Congressional committee on airlift, and when he retired in 1965, Rivers took his place as Chairman. Vinson was responsible for most of the airlift programs of the 1960s, including the development of both the C-141 and C-5A, both of which were developed and produced at the Lockheed factory at Marietta. Another Tunner ally was Georgia Senator Richard Russell, who had achieved a reputation by the 1960s as the most knowledgeable politician in the country on national defense. He was chairman of the Senate Armed Services Committee then became chairman of the House Appropriations Committee. Like

Rivers and Vinson, Russell was in favor of any legislation that brought military business to his state, which was home to Lockheed's Georgia division. They were all Democrats.

To provide ammunition for his battles before Congress and with the rest of the Air Force, Tunner organized a series of joint training exercises with US Army units. His goal was to demonstrate to Congress that his service was ill equipped to perform its military role (which had been given to it as a result of extensive lobbying on his part) of providing mobility to US-based ground combat units. Operation *BIG SLAM/PUERTO PINE* involved the airlift of 20,000 US Army troops from their US bases to Puerto Rico and back again. TAC troop carrier squadrons had equipped with C-130s by this time and were fully capable of the move but only MATS units took part, for Tunner's goal was for the operation to fail – he was out to prove a point. He felt that if MATS was unable to complete the requirements of the exercise, Congress would be forced to respond by appropriating funds to develop a new jet transport to replace the C-118s, C-121s and C-124s that were the mainstay of MATS in the fifties.

Boeing C-135

Having found allies in Senator Russell and Congressmen Rivers and Vinson, Tunner began pressing Congress and the Air Force for funds to develop a new "workhorse" transport that eventually came to fruition as the C-141 after Senator Kennedy became president. He also wanted a large military transport with "swing-tail" loading and offloading but this airplane was never developed. Tunner offered to accept as an interim measure the replacement of C-118s and C-121s with a long-range version of the C-130B, which became the E-model. In the end, Congress diverted most of the C-130Es to TAC but MATS got enough to begin upgrading its fleet. MATS was already receiving the Douglas C-133 Cargomaster, a large four-engine turboprop transport that had been developed primarily to transport SAC's ICBM missiles to bases near their silos and had originally been intended for the Air Material Command. Tunner, who had served as deputy commander of the Air Material Command, managed to convince the Air Staff that the

Anything, Anywhere, Anytime

new transports should be assigned to MATS instead, under the premise that they could be used on channel traffic cargo missions when they were not being used for logistical support of SAC's bomber and missile wings. The C-133 turned out to be plagued with problems and several were lost to seemingly unexplainable accidents, but they served as an outsize cargo carrier with MATS until 1971.[357] MATS got its first jet transports in the form of C-135s, a militarized version of Boeing's 707 airliner. Congress had already purchased a tanker version, the KC-135, for SAC's refueling squadrons. The KC-135s carried cargo in their upper deck and transported cargo on overseas deployments. Unlike the 707, the C-135 had no windows for passengers.

When the Vietnam War broke out, MATS was equipped primarily with propeller-driven C-124s, C-130Es, C-133s and C-135s. The older C-118s and C-121s had been phased out in MATS, although there were still some C-118s in service with other commands and Air Defense Command was using EC-121s for radar early warning picket planes. The C-141 was under development, but it would be 1965 before it would enter operational service with MATS squadrons. As the US assumed a larger role in Southeast Asia, MATS began flying more and more missions into the region. The C-124s, C-130s and C-133s were used mainly for cargo missions while the C-135s were used to transport both cargo and passengers. MATS C-130s doubled their role by providing additional airlift capability to TAC, and were sometimes used to deploy US military unit personnel to Southeast Asia. Several MATS C-130s, including some flown by Navy crews, joined their TAC counterparts in the Dominican Airlift. All three of the propeller-driven planes required a lengthy amount of time to deliver their loads to Saigon and return – 95 hours of flying time alone and numerous stops was required for a round trip by a C-124 flying from the East Coast. The C-130 and C-133 required considerably less time, but were still slow by the standards of the Jet Age. In spite of their slow speeds, MATS transports were soon a familiar sight at airfields in South Vietnam and neighboring Thailand. (However, until early 1966, two squadrons of MATS C-124s were actually under the operational control of PACAF's 315th Air Division. From 1966-1969 315th controlled one squadron and it was those C-124s that were seen at the forward airfields.) Generally, MATS flights operating into South

---

[357] A number of explanations for the loss of the C-133s has been given, with the most popular being that the performance charts in the Aircraft Flight Manual were wrong and crews were trying to operate at too high of an altitude at higher gross weights, which led to high speed stalls. One crashed off the coast of Okinawa after taking off from Kadena and was believed to have been lost due to buildups of algae in the fuel tanks.

Sam McGowan

Vietnam went to Tan Son Nhut or Da Nang while their destination in Thailand was usually Bangkok.[358] Other destinations at Bien Hoa and Cam Ranh were later added. Udorn in Thailand also became a MAC stop later in the war.

As the war increased in tempo and military requirements, MATS contracted with the airlines for flights to the region. All military passengers bound for overseas destinations were soon traveling aboard MATS contract flights. MATS contract flights, civilian airline flights contracted by MATS, also accounted for a large portion of the cargo that was transported to the region by air. Even though dozens of MATS aircraft – including contract – were in the air at any given time, as much as ninety percent of all cargo bound for Southeast Asia was transported by sea. When US ground combat units deployed to South Vietnam from the United States, they went by sea. In the early days of the conflict, MATS C-135s airlifted US Army and USMC personnel to South Vietnam from their bases in the United States. Some of the first casualties of the war occurred in June 1965 when a MATS C-135 flew into a ridge right after takeoff from El Toro MCAS, California with a load of Vietnam-bound Marines aboard. This was the first of only a handful of MATS/MAC airplanes that would be lost during the Southeast Asia hostilities.[359]

MATS flying, even to Southeast Asia, was little different than normal peacetime operations. Except for when they were operating for TAC on troop deployments, MATS flights originated out of aerial ports in the United States and were bound primarily for Tan Son Nhut or Da Nang until the airfield at Cam Ranh Bay opened up. Although the US Army and Marine units that deployed to Southeast Asia from the US went by ship, advance personnel were airlifted by MATS. Normally,

---

[358] In late 1967 or early 1968, MAC C-141s began stopping at Udorn while on their way to Bangkok. On September 1, 1968, TSgt. Paul Yonkie, a flight engineer from the 76th Military Airlift Squadron at Charleston, was struck by fragments from a grenade thrown by communist commandos at Udorn and became MAC's only airlift combat casualty of the war. He died in the hospital at Clark. A building built to house the three flying squadrons at Charleston was named after him. As far as is known, not a single building, street, airplane or any structure has ever been named for any of the 249 tactical airlift crewmembers who were killed in Vietnam.

[359] During the course of the war, MATS/MAC lost two C-141s, two C-130s and one C-5. One of the C-130 losses was attributed to possible sabotage but considering that it had taken off from Cam Ranh Bay, sabotage is unlikely. It more likely was hit by naval artillery firing from offshore. The other C-130 loss was due to a pilot landing short at Quang Tri when MAC got permission to try direct deliveries to forward fields. One C-141 was lost when it collided with a Marine fighter at Da Nang and the other was lost due to a mechanical malfunction right after takeoff from Cam Ranh. The C-5 was lost in 1975 due to a mechanical problem caused by supervisory error at the highest level in MAC.

Anything, Anywhere, Anytime

cargo and passengers bound for Southeast Asia would have passed through Travis AFB, California but as the intensity of the war increased, aerial ports on the East Coast, particularly at Dover, Delaware, began shipping cargo directly to the combat zone. Passengers bound for the Pacific continued embarking through Travis although a new embarkation point was opened at McChord AFB, Washington as the number of troops moving overseas increased.

MATS C-130E

MATS C-124

The principal MATS bases were Travis AFB, California, McChord AFB, Washington and Norton AFB, California on the West Coast and Dover AFB, DE, McGuire AFB, NJ and Charleston AFB, SC on the east coast. Kelly AFB, Texas also became an aerial port later in the war as it was a major shipping point for aircraft parts and other USAF materials destined for Vietnam and Thailand. Kelly, however, was operated by the Air Force Logistics Command and was never a MATS or MAC base, although a C-124 squadron that had formerly belonged to AFLC's predecessor, the Air Material Command, was based there. Cargo from other AFLC bases such as Hill AFB, Utah and Robins AFB, Georgia was trucked to Travis and Dover or shipped by rail, then processed for shipment overseas. Passengers were processed at Travis and McChord, which had originally been the aerial port for Alaska but also became responsible for troops bound for Southeast Asia and Japan when Travis became saturated.

Ironically, cargo bound for overseas could only be processed through designated aerial ports. The Air Force Logistics Command operated large facilities at Warner-Robins, Georgia, San Antonio, Texas and Ogden, Utah as well as at its headquarters in Dayton, Ohio. Each facility was responsible for supporting several weapons systems by purchasing and maintaining aircraft and parts and for distributing parts to the bases were they were used, both domestically and overseas. AFLC operated its own air transport system called LOGAIR, which contracted with civilian operators to provide aircraft and crews to transport its cargo to US bases.

Military regulations forbade military transports, whether troop carrier or MATS, from transporting AFLC cargo (except for nuclear weapons and materials) or from transporting passengers within the Continental United States. The only exceptions were transport of unit cargo and troops; military personnel could travel on military aircraft on a "space available" status but civilian dependents were forbidden on domestic operations by law. MATS squadrons that had previously belonged to Air Force Logistics Command were allowed to transport nuclear components outside of the MATS system. The regulation was pure protectionism politics, and had been instituted as a result of airline and other transportation companies lobbying of Congress. One justification for forbidding the transport of military cargo within the US was that military contracts supported the Civil Air Reserve Fleet, an organization of civilian airlines that were contractually obligated to provide transportation to the military when called on to do so.

In 1967-68 the author was assigned to the 58th Military Airlift Squadron at Robins AFB, Georgia, which was home to a large Air Force depot that supported several weapons systems, including the C-130 family as well as the C-123 and B-57. Robins generated a lot of cargo for shipment to Southeast Asia but our squadron never carried a single box out of our home base. We would depart Robins empty for Dover, where we often picked up loads of wooden crates marked as having originated at Robins and headed west on the first leg of their journey

Anything, Anywhere, Anytime

to Southeast Asia. Each crate had been shipped by truck or rail from Warner-Robins to Dover, where it was processed for shipment overseas on MAC transports. The warehouses were just down the ramp from our squadron ramp.

While Vietnam was the major focal point of the early 1960s, MATS was heavily involved in events in other parts of the world as well. When the United Nations ordered a peacekeeping force to the Congo in 1960, the United States was asked to contribute airlift. The 322nd Air Division in Europe was given the task of airlifting men and equipment from throughout Europe and parts of Asia to Africa. MATS was assigned to help with the mission by providing transports and crews to supplement 322nd Air Division's C-130s. MATS' 1602nd Air Transport Wing at Chateauroux, France was responsible for controlling MATS transports operating in the European theater. The 1602nd coordinated with 322nd Air Division and controlled MATS aircraft involved in the airlift. A MATS C-124 crew from Charleston was involved in a major incident in the Congo when they were attacked by a mob at Stanleyville. Only the intervention of a Congolese nurse prevented the men from being beaten to death. A number of articles have been written about the Congo airlifts which give the impression that MATS was responsible for them but such was not the case; MATS functioned solely in a supporting role for United States Air Forces Europe, whose 322nd Air Division (Combat Cargo) was responsible for the airlift.[360] MATS C-124s delivered fuel trucks, tents and rations to Ascension Island and Kamina for the *DRAGON ROUGE* assault force in November 1964. MATS C-130s were part of the Dominican Airlift, including the initial airborne assault, which departed Pope for an airborne invasion of the island. MATS C-124s delivered outsize cargo to Santo Domingo Airfield.

MATS' 322nd Air Division supplied the squadron of C-130Es that were used in the *DRAGON ROUGE* mission but they were not MATS airplanes. A few months previously, 322nd AD had transferred from USAFE to MATS, but its muscle was two TAC rotational squadrons. When the United States European Command and Belgian rescue plan was approved, the TAC squadron from the 464th Troop Carrier Wing at Pope AFB, North Carolina was chosen for the mission. 322nd assigned Col. Burgess Gradwell, the commander of the division's detachment at Evreux (322nd moved to Chateauroux when it transferred to MATS) to accompany the mission as mission commander. However, all of the other officers in leadership positions were TAC personnel, as were the crews. MATS itself had no role in the mission other than some C-124s

---

[360] In his memoir, former MATS commander Tunner praised MATS for its role in the airlift but did not even mention the troop carrier role.

and an Air Weather Service WC-130 were assigned in a supporting role. One C-124 airlifted fuel trucks to Ascension Island while others took tents, rations and other supplies for the rescue force. However, even though the C-124s were supposed to depart for Ascension three hours before the C-130s left Kline Brogel, Belgium, they did not arrive until SIXTEEN HOURS after the C-130s arrived! Obviously, the crews refused to take the mission, even though it was of the highest priority, and went into crew rest.

After the semi-successful rescue, MATS headquarters lost no time in announcing the news to the world. Headlines reading MATS RESCUES HOSTAGES appeared in US newspapers even though MATS had no role in the actual rescue other than that Col. Gradwell was flying on the lead airplane as an observer. He wasn't even mission commander at that time. As soon as the rescue force entered Congo airspace, command and control of the mission transferred to Strike Command, a unified service command located at McDill AFB, Florida supported by TAC. The mission was under the command of Col. Clayton M. Issacson, the commander of Joint Task Force LEO, the Strike Command mission responsible for operations in the Congo. Col. Issacson, who was later promoted to brigadier general, observed the mission from a TALKING BIRD[361] C-130E assigned to the LEO force.

MATS C-130 crews were given the same tactical training as their counterparts in TAC with the exception of "exotic" airdrop training, but their involvement in the logistical mission that MATS was primarily responsible for resulted in decreased tactical proficiency for individual crewmembers.[362] Although there were a few operational airdrop missions, most MATS crewmembers flew just enough airdrop missions to remain current. MATS C-130 crews on temporary duty with the Chateauroux wing sometimes flew airdrop missions in USAFE's area of operations. One MATS mission involved the aerial delivery of building supplies to construction crews working on a secret airfield at Peshawar, Pakistan, near the famous Khyber Pass leading into Afghanistan. MATS C-124 crews in troop carrier squadrons that had formerly been in TAC were also trained in airdrop procedures. The C-124 was not designed for airdrop but cargo pallets and containers could be dropped through the elevator well, and there were

---

[361] TALKING BIRD was the code name for transports that had been modified for long-range communications and command. In the 1950s and early 1960s, C-97s were used for the role but in the 1960s the mission transferred to TAC troop carrier C-130 squadrons. TALKING BIRD airplanes accompanied Strike Command missions on worldwide deployments.

[362] While TAC troop carrier squadrons and most overseas units operated with integral crews, MATS crewmembers were assigned to sections and only assigned to crews for the duration of a mission, a practice that came from the airlines.

Anything, Anywhere, Anytime

troop doors for paratrooper exit. Until the late 1950s, about half of the Air Force's C-124s were assigned to TAC troop carrier squadrons. As the C-130 became the primary tactical airlifter, the TAC C-124 squadrons transferred to MATS, but they retained their identity as troop carrier squadrons, as opposed to the air transport squadrons that were formerly part of MATS, and which had no tactical mission. In the early 1960s, tactical training was ordered for all MATS C-130 and C-124 air transport squadrons.

C-141s lined up at Norton AFB, California

In late 1964, MATS began receiving new jet Lockheed C-141 Starlifters and by April 1965 they were operational. The C-141, the airplane General Tunner had dubbed the "workhorse airlifter," was essentially a jet transport with some tactical capabilities. Immediately after World War II, the Air Staff established a policy that all new aircraft developed for the air force would be designed to fill a tactical mission so the C-141 was designed with tactical capabilities.[363] In many respects it was a C-130 with jet engines and swept wings and had, in fact, originally been referred to by Lockheed as "the Super Hercules" because of its higher speed and increased payload capacity. Its Pratt and Whitney TF-33 P-7 engines produced 21,000 pound of thrust per engine, which allowed much higher gross weights than the Allison turboprops on the C-130. The operational payload was roughly twice the C-130's. Its rear-opening cargo ramp and petal doors allowed airdrop of platforms that had previously only been deliverable

---

[363] The C-133 was evidently exempted from the policy because it was developed specifically to transport SAC missiles.

Sam McGowan

by C-130 and before that, by C-119. Except for length, its cargo compartment dimensions were the same as the C-130.

Although the C-141 was faster and could carry twice as much as it's older sister, it was not a true tactical transport. The jet transport was supposed to be able to land on dirt but proved deficient in testing. It was also lacking in short field takeoff and landing performance. Consequently, C-141s were limited to established airfields with long, hard-surface runways.

The C-141A could transport ten cargo pallets while the C-130 could carry five fully loaded ones and a smaller one on the aft ramp.[364] One difference between the C-130 and the C-141 was that Lockheed had included an integral cargo handling system in the cargo compartment consisting of rails and rollers that could be flipped upside down to become part of the floor. The C-141 was considerably faster than anything then in use with MATS except for the C-135 and had considerably longer range. A C-124 might take a week to transport a load from the East Coast to Saigon, but a C-141 could carry a much bigger load over the same route in just three days, with only two enroute stops. East Coast C-141s could also make the trip to Saigon with just two stops by going through Elmendorf AFB, Alaska, and could have the cargo on the ground in Vietnam in less than three days after the initial takeoff from Dover by using the crew stage method.

To keep the airplanes moving, MATS depended on a "crew stage" system much like that of the stagecoaches of the Old West. MATS crews were prepositioned at certain bases along routes used by the service's airplanes. When a crew arrived at an enroute base, they would surrender their airplane to a new crew who were fresh from crew rest. Depending on whether or not offloading and reloading of cargo were involved, ground times were no more than an hour, assuming there were no mechanical problems to deal with. Inbound crews notified the Airlift Command Post, or ACP, of their mechanical condition and if the airplane was sound; the outbound crew would be alerted and would meet the airplane when it landed. The inbound crew would offload their bags and the outbound crew would then load theirs onto the airplane. Maintenance personnel from the MATS support squadron would service and refuel the airplane while the two crews were swapping places.

Missions bound for Southeast Asia were filled to capacity with cargo so there usually was no on or offloading at enroute stops. The new crew would take the airplane on to the next stop while the inbound crew would enter crew rest and wait for their turn to come up in the stage 12 hours later. Using the stage system, MATS could

---

[364] Existing C-141s were "stretched" and redesignated as C-141Bs between 1977 and 1983.

Anything, Anywhere, Anytime

drastically reduce the total time needed to deliver a load of cargo to Southeast Asia or elsewhere in the world, although the policy greatly increased personnel requirements and costs, even though it increased aircraft utilization. Stage bases were set up at Elmendorf AFB, Alaska, Yokota AB, Japan, Hickam AFB, Hawaii, Kadena AB, Okinawa and Clark AB, Philippines. For a time, MATS C-124s and C-130s staged through Mactan, a tiny island in the southern Philippines adjacent to Cebu that also served as a base for two 315th AD C-130 squadrons.

Other stage bases were set up in Europe, at Rhine Main, at Frankfurt, Germany, Torrejon, outside Madrid in Spain and Incirlik, near Adana, Turkey. Except for brief periods in 1971 and 1972, MATS/MAC crews did not remain overnight in Vietnam, although there was a stage base set up in Bangkok, Thailand. The stage method increased flight crew manning in MATS squadrons, as additional crews were always in various stages of crew rest throughout the MATS system. Unlike TAC troop carrier squadrons where fifteen crews were normally assigned per squadron, MATS squadrons had so many crewmembers that people might be in the same unit for years and never meet! Due to the size of the MATS squadrons, there were far more slots for supervisory personnel for both officers and enlisted men, which created a higher rank structure.

On January 1, 1966, MATS ceased to exist when the Military Airlift Command activated as an Air Force major command. The new MAC included all of the Air Force's transport aircraft – with two major exceptions. TAC retained its C-130 equipped troop carrier squadrons and its remaining C-123s, which had all transferred to the air commando units at Hurlburt Field, Florida and England AFB, Louisiana. Troop carrier units in the overseas commands, particularly PACAF and Alaska Air Command, remained under those commands. USAFE's C-130s had transferred back to the US in 1964 and were replaced by TAC squadrons on temporary duty to 322nd Air Division which was part of MAC.[365] By the end of 1967, the troop carrier designation had been replaced by tactical airlift.[366] MAC received the logistical support squadrons, which had been flying C-124s in support

---

[365] Having TAC squadrons in a MAC organization didn't work out too well so the 513th Troop Carrier Wing activated in France to control the TDY TAC Squadrons. Although 513th was a USAFE unit, it was under 322nd Air Division operational control.

[366] The redesignation came in the form of a letter from USAF Vice-Chief of Staff General Bruce Holloway that stipulated that the change "more accurately reflected the former troop carrier mission, which was no longer carrying troops." Just who was behind the redesignation is unclear although it seems to have been a response to a memo written by troop carrier veteran Myles Rhorlick.

Sam McGowan

of SAC. By 1968, the Navy air transport units, which had long been part of MATS, were transferred out of the program or deactivated.

While MAC had a new name and new airplanes, it was essentially still the old MATS operating at faster speeds. The same attitudes found in MATS prevailed in MAC. Safety was still given preference over mission responsibilities and MAC crews still got upset if they found quarters on a military base or food at the flight line cafeteria to not be up to their expectations. The MAC commander, Lt. Gen. Howell Estes, and his staff came out of MATS and they still operated the same way they had for more than a decade and a half. Many of the crewmembers flying the new C-141s came out of C-124 squadrons and they saw the Starlifter as just a faster version of Old Shaky. MAC continued to operate C-130s from Charleston, McGuire and Travis for a time, but in 1968 the last C-130s in MAC went to TAC as MAC received its full complement of C-141s. The Navy had C-130 squadrons at Lakehurst NAS, New Jersey and Moffett NAS, California but lost them when MAC's C-130s went to TAC. The Navy was allowed to keep some of its C-130s for logistical purposes while some of the MAC airplanes went to the Aerospace Rescue and Recovery Service and were converted for aerial refueling of helicopters.

Only one MAC airlift squadron had a combat mission after 1965. The 22nd Military Airlift Squadron, which was based at Tachikawa AB, Japan, was under the operational control of 315th Air Division. Its sister squadron, the former 6th TCS, transferred to Hickam. The 22nd was the descendant of the old 22nd Troop Carrier Squadron, which began life in Australia in early 1942 and fought with General George Kenney's Fifth Air Force. The 22nd equipped with C-124s during the Korean War and remained under PACAF until 1958 when all C-124s transferred to MATS. From its base at Tachikawa, where it was officially assigned to the 1503rd Air Transport Wing – later downgraded to a group – which had been activated when the 374th Troop Carrier Wing inactivated, the 22nd flew outsize cargo missions for 315th Air Division throughout its area of responsibility, including into and within Southeast Asia. When MATS became MAC, the 1503rd Air Transport Group became the 65th Military Airlift Group. Tachikawa's huge C-124s were a common sight throughout the Pacific and were sometimes seen at the forward airfields in South Vietnam as they delivered large items of military cargo such as generators, fuel trucks and heavy construction equipment that were too large to fit into a C-130.[367] Their crews were no strangers to forward field operations. A 22nd C-124 carried bulldozers into Kham Duc two days before the

---

[367] The author has heard accounts that a C-133 operated into Song Be on one occasion, but finds this doubtful.

Anything, Anywhere, Anytime

camp was evacuated. In early 1969, MAC transferred its last C-124s to the reserves and 22nd inactivated.[368] Four C-124s transferred to PACAF for outsize cargo operations and were based at Clark with the 463rd Tactical Airlift Wing; four others went to the 17th TAS at Elmendorf.

22nd MAS C-124 at Kham Duc (70th Engineers Co A)

With the advent of the C-141, MAC began developing a major long-range air evacuation mission. Air evacuation had been a MATS mission since World War II, but the slower speeds of the C-118s and C-121s formerly used in the mission often meant that the most seriously injured men had to be treated on hospital ships or at overseas bases. The C-141 allowed rapid transit of patients from Southeast Asia to hospitals in the Philippines and Japan, then on to the United States if necessary. Air evac became a major MAC mission beginning in 1965 when the first American ground combat troops arrived for duty in Southeast Asia, and continued through the end of the war. MAC air evacuation missions operated between Cam Ranh, Da Nang and Saigon in South Vietnam and Clark and Yokota. Missions bound for the East Coast operated through Yokota and Elmendorf while missions bound for the West Coast went through Clark and Hickam. A mission from

---

[368] The 22nd reactivated at Travis in 1972 as a C-5 squadron.

Sam McGowan

Clark to Yokota connected patients coming from Clark with the route to the East Coast. By staging air and medical crews, MAC C-141 air evac missions could depart Yokota and arrive at Andrews AFB, MD in a little over 24 hours. West coast missions arrived at Travis AFB, California. MAC also operated a domestic air evac system using C-118s and Douglas C-9s based at Scott AFB, IL. The Scott wing, the 375th Military Airlift Wing, was responsible for moving patients to hospitals nearer to their homes. Some air evac crews were reservists.

MAC air evac nurse and technicians transferring patients to ambulance

MAC's transport fleet was also used to bring home the remains of the young men who lost their lives in the combat zone. Surely, there were no MAC flights that were as sad as those when the cargo compartment contained anywhere from one to a hundred of the silver aluminum shipping containers the military used for the transportation of human remains. The human remains were shipped out of the mortuaries in Da Nang and Saigon, and arrived in the United States at either Travis or Dover where the Air Force operated mortuaries serving military units based overseas. The two mortuaries in Vietnam were originally operated by the Air Force but transferred to the Army when the US role escalated. No ceremony was attached to the missions and the coffins were treated and handled as cargo, with certain considerations, particularly that they were loaded headfirst and the

Anything, Anywhere, Anytime

only thing that could be stacked on top of them was another aluminum shipping container. No American flags were placed on them.[369] Occasionally, GI escorts accompanied remains, but usually the escorts, who were members of special units based with the Stateside mortuaries, whose sole military duty was to escort remains, joined them at the mortuaries and accompanied the bodies to the casualties' hometowns. The escorts usually only knew the men whose remains they were escorting by the paperwork that accompanied the containers. The nearest military base provided honor guards.[370]

Though MAC transports were heavily involved in the Vietnam War, it is difficult to say how essential their contribution really was. There were only a few instances when MAC transports were used to move intact combat units to the combat zone and the first of those, Operation *BLUE LIGHT*, was actually a training mission. MAC C-141s (actually MATS since the command change took place while the mission was underway), C-124s and C-133s airlifted a brigade of the 25th Infantry Division from Hawaii to Pleiku but the bulk of the unit moved by sea. While there might have been some military benefit from the move, *BLUE LIGHT* was instituted to test MAC's troop movement capabilities. The division had been alerted to move to South Vietnam and MATS asked for permission to move an element by air.

The second major MAC move was Operation *EAGLE THRUST*, which took place in late 1967 when the command moved elements of the 101st Airborne Division from their base at Ft. Campbell, Kentucky to Bien Hoa. Most troop movements to Vietnam took place either by ship or through the normal MAC system using civilian contract airliners although advance parties were sometimes moved in MATS transports. The *EAGLE THRUST* missions operated through the MAC stage system along with normal channel traffic, although additional loadmasters were sent out to supplement crew loadmasters – primarily to serve lunches. The operation was not the initial move of the division to Vietnam – some 101st units had been in South Vietnam since 1965.

MAC's airlift fleet proved useful when the United States responded to the Tet attacks of 1968. Just before the communists launched their offensive in South Vietnam, North Korea seized the intelligence-gathering ship USS *Pueblo*. In response to the events in Korea, the United States rushed reinforcements to the region. MAC's

---

[369] There are photographs of aluminum coffins with Amerian flags on them but they were taken early in the war before US casualties began mounting.
[370] While public perception is that men buried in national cemeteries are war dead, most are actually veterans who requested to be buried there. Men killed in combat as often as not were buried in their hometown cemetery.

fleet moved men and equipment from bases in the United States to Korean airfields. While the Korean reinforcement was underway, MAC was directed to move additional troops to South Vietnam in response to the communist Tet Offensive. A brigade from the US Army's 82nd Airborne Division and a regiment of Marines from the 5th Marine Division constituted the move. More than 6,000 troops and 3,500 tons of equipment were involved. MAC would again prove useful in the spring of 1972 when its fleet of C-141s and C-5s transported personnel from TAC fighter squadrons back to Southeast Asia and SAC personnel to Guam.

Troops of the 101st Airborne boarding C-141 at Fort Campbell for flight to Vietnam

MAC transports operated primarily on cargo missions – passengers traveled on civilian airliners contracted by MAC – and the cargo was largely "high value" items, particularly aircraft parts and even whole helicopters. Helicopter blades were a frequent cargo. With the advent of the gigantic Lockheed C-5A, MAC was able to transport three of the Army's CH-47 Chinook helicopters at a time from the Army depot at Harrisburg, Pennsylvania to Cam Ranh. MAC not only contracted with airline companies to transport passengers, it also contracted for cargo services as well. Yet even though MAC transports and MAC contract civilian transports were always in the air enroute to and from the combat zone and at least one was usually on the ground offloading at Cam Ranh, Da Nang and Saigon, MAC only carried a very

Anything, Anywhere, Anytime

small percentage of the total tonnage of cargo that was shipped to Southeast Asia over the course of the war. The majority, more than ninety percent, traveled by ship.

It wasn't just active duty MAC squadrons that were engaged in air transport operations from the United States to Southeast Asia. As the war in Vietnam intensified, MATS and then MAC used its reserve and Air National Guard squadrons to assist in the airlift effort. Most of MAC's reserve units were equipped with C-124s that they received as C-141s became the mainstay of the active duty squadrons, but some still flew the Boeing C-97. MAC also received airlift assistance from Tactical Air Command C-130 squadrons, who used the MAC missions to provide logistical training to their crews. Because the efforts of the MAC C-141 squadrons were concentrated largely on Southeast Asia missions, MAC requested that Tactical Air Command provide C-130s and crews for cargo missions to Europe under Project *RARE DATE*.

In 1968, MAC's last C-130s transferred to TAC, to new squadrons that replaced TAC squadrons that had moved overseas in late 1965 and early 1966. The move had been planned since the early sixties when MATS first took delivery of C-130Es and was the result of MAC's reception of the last of the C-141s for which the Air Force had contracted. While many MAC C-130s transferred to TAC without crews, their crews remained in MAC to transition into the C-141, an entire squadron from McGuire transferred to Dyess. Many of its personnel had previously transferred from Charleston to McGuire. In early 1969, many of the former MAC personnel transferred to CCK with the 346th TAS. MAC had already given up its fleet of C-135s. The C-135 and the C-130E had been a stopgap measure to allow MATS to upgrade the service's capabilities while the C-141 was under development. While MAC's C-130s went to TAC, its C-135s transferred to SAC and were converted to KC-135 tankers.

MAC's plans called for an all-jet airlift fleet, and another new airlifter was under development when the command was created in 1965. The C-5 was the product of an aircraft development program the Air Force put out as the CX-X Project, commonly called the CX. The program was instituted in the early 1960s and was no doubt one of Tunner's ideas. Although he had retired from the Air Force, he was heavily involved in politics. The project was sold to Congress under the proposition that a large transport capable of delivering tanks and other large military vehicles to overseas destinations would allow the return of thousands of US troops to the United States. The United States was transferring millions of dollars in gold and silver to Europe each year to redeem US dollars that were spent by US troops. Theoretically, units in Europe could be transferred to the US and then redeployed on short notice using airlift to move men and some

Sam McGowan

equipment. Some equipment such as large tanks and armored personnel carriers were placed in ready storage at European bases.

C-5A at loading dock

The Lockheed C-5A Galaxy first flew in 1968 and deliveries began to MAC's 3rd Military Airlift Squadron at Charleston in June 1970. For the first time since its creation, the Air Force purchased a major "weapon system" without putting the airplane through an intense, extensive test program. MAC had convinced the Air Force to conduct operational testing in active service with operational transport squadrons. The 3rd MAS was selected to conduct the tests and a Joint Task Force made up of MAC personnel from Charleston, Dover and Travis was set up to conduct the tests and work with Lockheed to correct problems as they arose. Ordinarily, airplanes were tested by test crews in programs that kept them out of sight of the rest of the Air Force and problems were corrected before operational airplanes entered production. In the case of the C-5, the tests were conducted before the public eye and problems that would not have been known outside of the test programs in the past became public knowledge within the Air Force, and in some cases in the public media as well. Although the initial C-5 force was plagued with problems due to growing pains, the Galaxy was an amazing airplane that would dramatically increase MAC's airlift capabilities. A single C-5 could carry 36 pallets of cargo, an amount equal to the bulk capabilities of 3.6 C-141s and almost an entire squadron of C-130s. With a 200,000 pound payload, a single C-5 could carry almost as much tonnage as three C-141s. With such capabilities, the C-5 would decrease MAC's ton-mile costs dramatically.

The "Lead the Force" airplane made its first trip to Cam Ranh Bay

Anything, Anywhere, Anytime

in early August 1970. From then until the end of the war, MAC scheduled C-5 missions into South Vietnam. Cam Ranh and Rhine Main, Germany were the two destinations intially used by the huge transports. Initially, C-5s operated only into Cam Ranh but when the US left the huge base, they were scheduled into Tan Son Nhut. On one occasion, three C-5s went into Da Nang.

Both the C-141 and C-5 featured some tactical capabilities but their runway requirements ruled them out as tactical transports. Dirt field testing of the C-141 failed to demonstrate that it was capable of using anything other than paved runways; the C-5 could land on dirt but the airplane was so large that using them on unimproved forward airstrips was unfeasible. Both airplanes were designed to drop cargo and troops but problems with the C-5 wing eventually led to a hold on the airplane's tactical training program until Congress authorized funding for a fix and the repairs could be made. There were other problems with the C-5 program as well. While the airplane was under development, an air transportable loading dock was also developed for use with the C-5. The dock was designed so that the airplane could pull up to it and offload its cargo and then load an outbound load using a train of pallets. But the dock turned out to be difficult to use and even though at least three were set up – including one at Cam Ranh Bay – their use was discontinued in favor of conventional loading methods.[371]

A major C-5 mission was the transport of US Army helicopters from the depot at Harrisburg, Pennsylvania to Cam Ranh Bay. Until the C-5 entered service, the Army sent most of its fleet of CH-47s to Harrisburg for major repair by ship and rail, and they were then returned the same way. A few went by C-133 but they could only handle one at a time and there were only 50 C-133s in MAC's inventory. A single C-5 could transport three helicopters at one time and reduce transient times from weeks to days. Other items of outsize cargo that previously required surface transportation were also shipped to Vietnam aboard C-5s. However, by the time the huge transport entered service, the United States was engaged in

---

[371] The author was a C-5 loadmaster from September 1970 to July 1975 and frequently used the loading docks at Charleston, Dover and Cam Ranh. Although there were some issues with using the docks, the main problem was that the older MAC loadmasters who had come out of C-141s and C-124s before that simply did not like using them. The problems with the docks were compounded by the unreliability of the aircraft kneeling system, but that situation was rectified when the pneumatic kneeling motors were replaced by a hydraulic system. Had the loadmasters been more enthusiastic about using them, the docks would most likely have remained in service.

withdrawal from the war in South Vietnam and the new capabilities were of less value to the war than they would have been in 1965 when US strength in Southeast Asia was being built up.

Lockheed C-5A Galaxy

The C-5 proved its value as a military transport in the spring of 1972, when the huge transports were put to work moving men and equipment back to the combat zone in response to the strong Eastertide enemy attacks. By 1972, the American presence in Southeast Asia had been greatly reduced, and the intensity of the attacks required a beefing up of the air resources in the region. C-5s and C-141s were used to airlift support personnel and equipment for TAC and SAC combat units that were returning to bases in or within range of Southeast Asia. No US ground units were returning to the war but some heavy armored equipment was rushed to the Vietnamese. A major C-5 contribution was the airlift of six large tanks from Japan to Da Nang for use by the South Vietnamese to meet North Vietnamese armor that had poured into the country and was operating in the region of Dong Ha, some fifty miles northwest of the destination airport. MAC publicists hailed the movement of the tanks as a combat operation but, in reality, they were delivered to an airfield over fifty miles from their final destination.

The 1972 Spring Offensive also saw the first use of the C-141 and MAC crews in South Vietnam in the semi-tactical role, although their contribution was limited. A few C-141 missions had been flown in South Vietnam the previous spring transporting backlog cargo when the reduced force of PACAF C-130s were busy supporting the South Vietnamese Lam Son 719 cross-border operation into Laos. But the urgency of the situation in 1972, combined with the severe reductions

Anything, Anywhere, Anytime

that had been made in PACAF's C-130 force, dictated the use of MAC transports to move reinforcements and cargo into the Central Highlands region where some of the enemy attacks were particularly fierce. Several C-141 missions were flown into Pleiku; on the return flights the MAC transports carried Vietnamese refugees who had been driven from their homes by the communist invasion. There were rumors throughout MAC that MAC Headquarters tried to convince PACAF to use C-141s for an airdrop so the command could take credit for having made a combat airdrop.[372]

Offloading C-5 at Tan Son Nhut

The American role in South Vietnam came to an end in the winter of early 1973 with the signing of an agreement worked out between the US and North Vietnamese negotiators meeting in Paris. One of the conditions of the agreement was the release of all prisoners held by each side. MAC lobbied for and was given responsibility for returning the released POWs in North Vietnam to Clark, and ultimately to the United States. But while MAC C-141s flew the prisoners home, they had a lot of help from PACAF's C-130 fleet. For two weeks prior to the first release, C-130s operated in and out of Hanoi's Gia Lam Airport. On the day of the first release – and for each subsequent release – C-130s carried an Air Force combat control team and portable navigation

---

[372] If such an airdrop had been allowed, it is likely that MAC would have lost at least one C-141 and probably more to the very heavy antiaircraft fire that greeted C-130 crews at An Loc and Kontum, the two places where airdrops were most used during the offensive.

Sam McGowan

equipment into Hanoi to guide the MAC transports to the airport. Even though C-141s were equipped with sophisticated navigational equipment and MAC crews included a navigator, the command didn't trust them to be able to find Gia Lam airport on their own!

As it turned out, the first Americans to greet the returning POWs were members of the PACAF C-130 crews who were at the airport and who had no assigned duties during the actual release. While the MAC crews had strict instructions not to leave their airplanes, C-130 crewmembers were available and had no orders to avoid contact with the released men. Seeing that many of the prisoners were injured, they took matters into their own hands. Once the prisoners reached the waiting C-141s, they were helped into passenger seats and airlifted to Clark, where they were repatriated. After debriefings and medical examinations, those not requiring extensive medical treatment were flown to the US. Once they reached the United States, the POWs were transported to hospitals near their homes by MAC Aeromedical Service C-9 Nightingale transports.

Even after the last of the POWs returned home and the American presence in Southeast Asia was reduced to an advisory role, MAC transports continued to operate into South Vietnam, but on a much smaller scale than before. Appropriations for the South Vietnamese government were having a harder and harder time passing in Congress but America was still sending support to its ally. Dwindling support had doomed the country, however, and as it became more and more apparent that South Vietnam's days were numbered in the spring of 1975, MAC transports began bringing refugees out of the country on their return flights.

In October 1973, MAC faced its most severe test of its history when it was called on to mount an emergency resupply to Israel during the Yom Kipper War. The Israeli Self Defense Forces met the combined Egyptian/Syrian attacks, but the resulting battles severely depleted the country's ammunition supplies. Israel turned to the United States for help, but at first the resupply proved politically difficult. Even though President Richard Nixon agreed without hesitation to send supplies to Israel, getting them there was a problem. Initially, the White House did not want to involve the American military in the effort. Israel itself lacked the resources to transport the volumes of cargo needed. An offer to the American airlines to bid for contracts for the missions was met without a single bid! None of the airlines wanted to touch it, regardless of how much money they would have made. Some Israeli civilian transports picked up ammunition in the US, but there were too few of them to meet their homeland's needs.

Finally, with no other option, President Nixon gave MAC the order to begin an airlift but there were still problems. Normally, MAC flights

Anything, Anywhere, Anytime

bound for Israel flew by way of Torrejon AB, Spain or through bases in Germany. Both of those countries informed the United States that their bases were not to be used to resupply Israel. This was also true of England and Italy as well as Turkey. All of Europe refused to come to Israel's aid because they feared that the oil-producing Arab countries would cut off their supply of oil. Eventually, the United States convinced Portugal to allow the use of Lajes, a base in the Azores, which are a Portuguese possession. Portugal had its own oil supplies in Angola at the time and was thus immune to Arab threats.

But even with Lajes as a refueling stop, the airlift – the first ever for the Military Airlift Command – was not a picnic. The flight from the United States to Lajes was routine but from there the crews faced a very long mission that transited areas in close proximity to countries whose feelings toward the United States were doubtful. The first crews into Lod Airport were told before leaving Lajes that there was a possibility they would be intercepted by Arab fighters and attacked.[373] They were also informed that the Israeli Air Force had promised to protect them. As it turned out, the Arabs failed to make good on their threats, perhaps because the United States had told the Soviet Union, whose transports were conducting their own airlift into Damascus and

---

[373] The author was on one of the first C-5s to depart Lajes for Lod and was incensed when the aircraft commander briefed the crew that the Arabs had threatened to shoot us down and we were not equipped with parachutes even though USAF regulations stipulated that aircraft entering an area where there was a threat of hostile fire were to carry them. But MAC had not thought to put parachutes on the airplanes and there weren't any available at Lajes. Had Egypt and Syria made good on their threats to intercept and shoot down US transports coming to Israel's aid, we would have been doomed, with no possibility of escape.

Cairo in support of Egypt and Syria, that Soviet airplanes would be subject to attack if any American transports were fired on.

Operation *NICKEL GRASS*, as the airlift was termed, turned out to be a blessing for the C-5. Previously, the massive airplane had endured frequent criticism in the press for its many problems and production cost overruns. But the criticism turned to praise as the entire world saw what American airlift forces, particularly the C-5s, could do. By this time, most of the problems that had plagued the first C-5s had been rectified and the fleet reliability for those in the airlift was as good as or better than the C-141s. The lesson was not lost on the Soviets, who began developing large military transports of their own. The Soviet designs, one of which is the largest aircraft ever built, are very similar to the C-5. The success of the airlift led Congress to fund repairs to the C-5 wings and also convinced MAC Headquarters to resume plans for routine aerial refueling of C-5s. It also led to the stretching of the fuselage of the C-141 fleet and the installation of aerial refueling equipment on them as well. Operation *NICKEL GRASS* was the first airlift in US history that didn't see extensive troop carrier/tactical airlift participation. A handful of C-130 missions were flown into Israel delivering equipment to airfields that were not suitable for C-141s.

The American evacuation of Vietnam was marred by the tragic (and needless) loss of a C-5 that crashed after taking off from Saigon's Tan Son Nhut Airport in early April 1975. Prior to their departure from their home base at Travis, the crew had reported problems with their aft pressure door. The MAC airlift command post obtained a waiver from MAC headquarters to fly the airplane even though it had known problems that had been rectified by an unorthodox procedure.[374] On the return flight, the C-5 was carrying several hundred Ameriasian children and their – mostly female – American escorts. As the airplane was climbing out after taking off from Saigon, the aft pressure door let go and came out of the airplane and when it did, it caused major damage to the aft fuselage and flight controls. Some of the crew and passengers in the cargo compartment were sucked out. With only

---

[374] The ill-fated C-5 had developed a problem with the hydraulic locks that held the door in place after picking up a load of artillery pieces in Georgia. Rather than waiting for the proper part to be delivered from Lockheed, MAC Headquarters authorized the local maintenance facility at Travis to take a lock from another C-5 that was grounded there. After the lock was replaced, the airplane flew to Clark and on to Saigon without opening the rear doors. It turned out that the two locks had been produced at different times and were similar, but not identical and the replacement lock failed when the doors were operated at Tan Son Nhut. As the airplane was climbing out, the pressure door came unlocked and since the airplane was pressurized, it flew out of the rear of the airplane.

minimal control, the crew attempted a crash-landing back at Tan Son Nhut, but without success. The airplane impacted the ground some distance short of the runway, then came apart. Most of the children and their escorts were killed by the impact and resulting fire but some members of the crew and some passengers survived and managed to escape. Even though the tragedy was an accident, the pilot and copilot were awarded the Air Force Cross, which ordinarily is only given for heroism in combat, by MAC Headquarters.[375]

As the Vietnam War drew to a close, the Air Force took a look at the lessons it had learned from it. One area that was closely scrutinized was airlift. Although the focus had been on fighting the war, some MAC officers continued the campaign for airlift consolidation. In September 1970, the Air University's Air Power Journal published an article from Col. Lester Ferriss, Jr., the chief of staff for MAC's 22nd Air Force, arguing for airlift consolidation on an essentially financial basis. Ferriss was a longtime MATS officer who had spent his entire career in the command, except for a staff assignment in Japan with 315th Air Division. He had briefly commanded 315th during the interim between Gen. Richard Ellis and Col. Charles Howe. Ferriss based his article on the basis of the duplication in various commands of airlift resources. It was a definite case of shooting while the ducks are flying. Throughout the war, MAC and PACAF maintained separate aerial port facilities in the Pacific, although in Vietnam PACAF aerial ports handled MAC transports. In fact, MAC received large quantities of aerial port equipment and had rows and rows of 40K-loaders parked at its bases while the airlift bases in Southeast Asia scrimped to come up with enough equipment to service C-130s and C-123s and support the MAC fleet at the same time. Due to duplication of aerial port resources, an Air Force evaluation team recommended the consolidation of all airlift assets into MAC.

Gen. William Momyer, the TAC commander, and his staff opposed the move on the basis that tactical airlift called for a different attitude on the part of the crews and more emphasis on tactical training than advocated by MAC. Having commanded Seventh Air Force in Vietnam during the most intense years of the war and presiding over some of the most dramatic airlift operations of the war, Momyer was far more familiar with the tactical airlift mission than any of the officers who

---

[375] The author asked Ray Snedegar who was on the airplane as an additional crew member, how MAC was able to award the two pilots a high combat decoration and he said he had no idea. Originally, the surviving crewmembers were told they would be given an Air Medal, but since some of them already had several, they said that wasn't appropriate. Most of the crew was awarded the Airman's Medal, an award for heroism in a non-combat situation.

were pushing for the change. In spite of Momyer's protest, the change nevertheless took place starting on December 1, 1974 when TAC's tactical airlift units transferred to MAC control.[376] The TAC C-130 wings in the States were the first to transfer to MAC, thus some of the C-130s that operated into Saigon during the last days of the war bore MAC markings.

RC-130A

While MAC was THE airlift command, it also served as an umbrella command for other services – specifically the Aerospace Rescue and Recovery Service and the Air Weather Service. Although neither of these services was involved directly in airlift, they operated special versions of airlift aircraft, particularly the HC-130H, which was used primarily as an airborne rescue command post and a helicopter refueler. The HC-130H and its variations were equipped with the Fulton personnel recovery system. ARRS also equipped some of MAC's airlift C-130Es to refuel helicopters but did equip them with the Fulton system. The ARRS also operated different models of helicopters for rescue and recovery work. Hundreds of aircrew members were rescued as a result of the efforts of SAR forces made up of ARRS HC-130s and HH-3 or HH-53 helicopters. ARRS also recovered satellites and packages dropped from satellites and were heavily involved in the growing space program.

MAC's Air Weather Service was responsible for weather services all over the globe, including within Southeast Asia. The Air Weather

---

[376] A featured point in former Seventh Air Force commander General William Momyer's end-of-tour report was the need to keep tactical airlifters out of MAC. Momyer commanded Seventh Air Force at the height of the war during the Khe Sanh resupply and the evacuation of Kham Duc.

Anything, Anywhere, Anytime

Service had equipped many of its squadrons with modified C-130Bs, which were given a W prefix to show that they were equipped for weather operations. Each WC-130 was equipped with racks for dropsondes, and an enlisted weather observer was included as part of the crew. He was responsible for monitoring readings from the dropsondes and passing the information along to weather forecast stations. AWS also operated a classified program called *POPEYE* which used a modified C-130A to seed clouds over sections of Southeast Asia in an attempt to produce thunderstorms and cause flooding of rivers and trails in the mountains of Laos.

Another MATS mission which passed to MAC was the aerial charting mission, which used modified RC-130As equipped with an array of cameras to photograph uncharted areas of the world. The photographs were then used by cartographers to produce charts and maps for military use.

While the war in Vietnam began with MATS, it ended after the old air transport service had not only become a full command, but had moved out of the propeller driven transport all together and had equipped with two long-range jet transports that been developed specifically for military use. MAC came of age during the Vietnam War.

Sam McGowan

Chapter Twenty One - "Special Applications and Operations"

C-130 flareships at Ubon, Thailand (Author)

Transporting personnel and equipment is the primary mission of airlift and this was as true during the Vietnam War as in any other. But there were other missions that came into being in Southeast Asia that involved airlift aircraft in other roles. Some of these roles were offshoots of the tactical airlift mission itself and involved transportation of men and equipment, while others were more along the lines of tactical strike missions. Some involved special units whose mission was to support Special Forces operating deep inside enemy territory and some were in support of conventional missions. Some were classified at the time and details have yet to be fully revealed – and may never be.

Air evacuation of casualties became a major airlift mission during World War II and continued to be important in Korea. Vietnam was no exception. Flight nurses and medical technicians joined C-47 crews to tend to casualties in both World War II and Korea. Thousands of lives were saved due to the rapid transport afforded by the use of airplanes instead of ground ambulances. As a result, air evacuation of casualties became a part of military doctrine. During the 1950s, role agreements between the Army and the Air Force confirmed that the Air Force was responsible for evacuating patients to points outside the combat zone and from airheads to rear areas during airborne operations while Army helicopters would be used within the confines of the battlefield itself.

As it turned out, most battlefield evacuation in Vietnam was conducted by helicopter but there was a fixed-wing air evacuation mission as well. Beginning in late 1962, a C-123 air evacuation route was set up between Nha Trang and Tan Son Nhut where it connected with a C-130 flight to Clark. The C-130 air evac route also served Thailand. Medical crews from the 9th Aeromedical Evacuation Squadron at Tachikawa Air Base, Japan tended the patients. The 9th AES maintained detachments at several locations, particularly Tan Son Nhut and Don Muang Airfield at Bangkok.

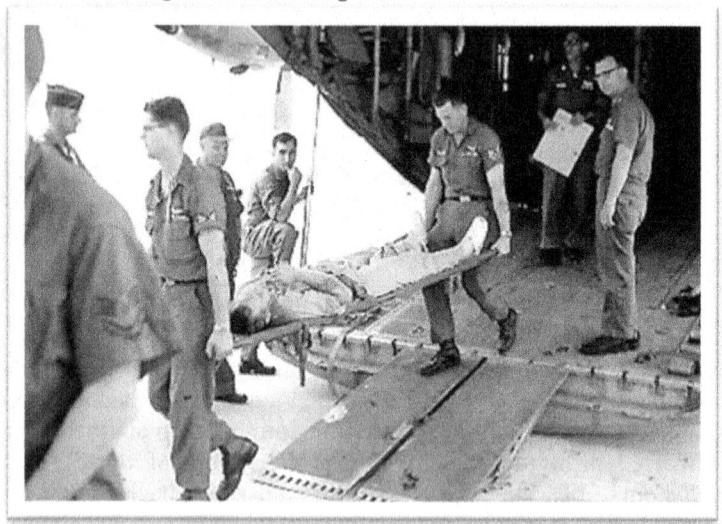

Offloading patients from C-130

At first battle casualties accounted for less than forty percent of the total, but the tempo picked up as the war escalated. A policy was established under which patients who required more than a thirty-day hospital stay were airlifted out of Vietnam to military hospitals in either Japan or the Philippines. The most seriously wounded were transported from there to the United States aboard MAC transports, which usually were C-141s after 1965. In 1966, scheduled C-141 air evacuation flights began picking patients up in Vietnam, which eliminated the need for C-130 air evac flights to the Philippines. Fixed-wing transports were still used for emergency and routine air evac missions within Vietnam and nearby Thailand.

Additional patient airlift was provided by the 6485th Operations Squadron, a 315th Air Division unit which flew C-118s from its base at Tachikawa, and which maintained four airplanes and crews on rotation to Cam Ranh Bay. In early 1968, the squadron transferred to the Philippines to join the 463rd Tactical Airlift Wing and was redesignated as the 20th Operations Squadron. Beginning in early

Sam McGowan

1969, the 20th also operated four C-124s for outsize cargo airlift after the 22nd MAS at Tachikawa deactivated. The squadron's C-118s began in-country air evac work in January 1968. Squadron crews spent three days at a time flying out of Cam Ranh Bay, servicing fourteen airfields in South Vietnam before returning to Clark. In 1972, the C-118s were replaced by C-9 Nightingales, which began in-country operations on March 15. The 903rd Aeromedical Evacuation Squadron provided the medical personnel for the air evac mission within Vietnam. Based at Tan Son Nhut, the 903rd operated detachments at several bases throughout South Vietnam. Each detachment was made up of two male flight nurses and as many as ten technicians[377]. The air evacuation mission was an important aspect of airlift operations in Southeast Asia. Because of rapid aeromedical evacuation, the death rate among wounded was reduced from four and a half percent in World War II to one percent in Vietnam.(Berger, 1977)(Bowers, 1986)

Air evacuation has long been associated with airlift, but as events in Southeast Asia began to develop, airlifters soon found themselves flying missions that were more along the lines of those flown by bomber crews during World War II. Such missions, which were classified by the Air Force as special operations because they were outside of the airlift mission, included dropping flares and leaflets and even attack missions against suspected Viet Cong targets. Troop carrier C-47s dropped bombs on Japanese positions in 1945 and from time to time transports were used in the offensive role in other conflicts, but during the Vietnam War, C-130 crews perfected the art of dropping bombs and were responsible for the delivery of the most powerful weapons used in the war.

The most visible of the special operations missions undertaken by airlift crews were the flare missions flown in support of friendly installations in South Vietnam. Prior to early 1966, nightly flare missions operated throughout the country on an on-call basis to provide flare light to illuminate the battlefield as Allied troops fought communist attackers. On occasion, flareships dropped flares to illuminate targets for airstrikes. When the *FARM GATE* SC-47 force deployed to Vietnam, their mission included psychological warfare and flare support for ground forces as well as conventional airlift operations. Each evening, SC-47 crews were placed on standby to be ready to provide flare illumination for friendly forces who came into contact with the enemy during hours of darkness. As the war continued and enemy attacks became more frequent, the flareship role

---

[377] Male medical personnel were used exclusively in Vietnam until late in the war when female flight nurses began flying in-country missions in C-118s and C-9s.

Anything, Anywhere, Anytime

was assumed by the 315th TCG's C-123s. Each night, a C-123 flareship maintained an airborne alert while two others were on ready ground alert in anticipation of enemy attacks. Non-aircrew enlisted men accompanied the crews to kick flares. They were mostly from the 8th Aerial Port Squadron.(The Airlifter, 1966) Because they could carry more flares, C-123s were able to remain on target longer than C-47s. By mid-1964, C-123s were doing the bulk of the flare work. Flare missions remained a C-123 responsibility until the arrival of AC-47 gunships in 1965. South Vietnam C-123 flare missions came to an end in mid-1966. At about the same time, the 606th Air Commando Squadron at Nakhonphanom AB, Thailand began flare operations over Laos to supplement the C-130s that had been flying out-of-country flare missions since 1964.

While the C-47 and C-123 flare mission were common knowledge from the beginning of the war because they were visible, C-130s were also engaged in flare work but of a different nature. On April 3, 1965, a C-130A from the 6315th Operation Group took off from Da Nang then joined a pair of USAF B-57 Canberra attack bombers and a USMC EF-10 electronic countermeasures airplane known as "Willy the Whale." The formation headed west to Laos to search for communist vehicles moving south along the Ho Chi Minh Trail. Their mission was the kick-off for Operation STEEL TIGER, the Allied interdiction mission against communist supply lines. Officially, this was the first use of C-130s in the attack role during the Vietnam War, but flare missions actually commenced over Laos in late 1964 with Operation *BARREL ROLL* and possibly even earlier, possibly as early as April of that year.[378] While the flare missions flown by C-123 and C-47 crews in South Vietnam were to defend against communist attack on friendly installations, the C-130s operated offensively as one-third of a hunter/killer team whose mission was to locate and destroy enemy targets. While most troop carrier missions were combat support, the C-130 flare mission in Laos and North Vietnam was combat.

After late 1966, increasing antiaircraft in southern Northern Vietnam restricted the C-130 flareships to the skies over Laos but during the first two years of operations they were active over North Vietnam as well. Prior to the restriction, missions over North Vietnam operated using the call sign *LAMPLIGHTER* while those over Laos flew

---

[378] The beginning of C-130 flare missions in Southeast Asia has not been publically recorded. There is no doubt that C-130s from the 6315th Operations Group were flying missions over Laos as early as November 1964, but it is likely that missions actually started as early as April of that year. Flare missions may have also been flown by Naha-based C-130s in support of operations in Laos as early as 1963 and possibly even during the Laotian Civil War, which ended in a truce in 1962.

as *BLIND BAT*. During the first year of operations, the flareships worked in a formation with strike aircraft, usually a pair of B-57s. The flareship would navigate to the target area then drop flares while the three planes searched the ground for signs of enemy trucks. The EF-10 would stand off and be prepared to jam North Vietnamese radar.

In early 1966, the tactics and the base changed when the operation moved from Da Nang to Ubon, Thailand and became associated with the 8th Tactical Fighter Wing, with the airplanes and crews coming down from Okinawa on temporary duty status for periods that varied from forty-five to 179 days.[379] The move to Thailand was not actually a transfer, per se, but rather the termination of the mission out of South Vietnam and the commencement of a new one from Ubon where the flare mission was conducted under the auspices of the 8th TAC Fighter Wing.[380] The mission was officially designated the 8th TAC Fighter Wing ABCCC (FAC/Flare). There was also a change in tactics. After the move, the flareships began working with F-4s as well as B-57s and other strike aircraft, and flew as single-ship forward air controllers. How effective the flareships were is difficult to determine, but they evidently were a cause of concern for the North Vietnamese. On July 1, 1965, a Viet Cong mortar and sapper attack was aimed at the ramp at Da Nang where the flare ships were parked. Two flare ship C-130As were destroyed in the attack; another was badly damaged, along with an airlift C-130B parked nearby. Both damaged airplanes were returned to service. There were also ground attacks aimed at the flare mission quarters at Ubon.

While the mission operated from Da Nang, the flight crews were supplemented by maintenance men flying as kickers. Maintenance men who were assigned to the classified E Flight section in the 21st Troop Carrier Squadron claim that they were the only kickers but this may not be entirely true. When the mission was at Da Nang, only two or three airplanes and crews were involved at a time but after the move to Ubon, the size of the mission increased to at least eight airplanes and crews, which would have involved at least two dozen kickers. In early 1966, USAF Headquarters ordered the removal of the maintenance men from the flare mission due to the increasing danger of operations over North Vietnam and directed that loadmaster

---

[379] Personnel from the 815th TCS at Tachikawa also participated, but because of Japanese constitutional issues, they went TDY to Okinawa first then from there to Southeast Asia.

[380] In some respects, the employment of the C-130s at Da Nang and the change to Ubon is a matter of semantics, but there was actually a funding change. The funding for the Da Nang operation was shifted to the new C-130A operating location that opened up at Cam Ranh Bay in May 1966.

Anything, Anywhere, Anytime

manning in the Naha C-130 squadrons be increased.[381] Additional loadmasters arrived in February 1966 and the kickers were taken off of the mission a few weeks later. From then on, flareship crews included three additional loadmasters, with the number reduced to two when the chutes used to dispense the flares were modified with the addition of levers to hold the flares in place. Previously, one of the loadmasters sat on the cargo door and held the flares in place with his feet.

Loadmaster/Flare kicker

During the early days of the mission, the loadmaster simply threw the flares out of the open paratroop doors as their peers in SC

---

[381] Several Naha maintenance veterans claim that they flew missions as "extra kickers" but the author find this very doubtful. At one point, a shortage of loadmasters developed at Naha and loadmasters from other 315th AD wings were sent to Ubon to supplement the Naha and Tachikawa crews. A few maintenance men were sent to a basic loadmaster course and awarded loadmaster AFSCs, then sent to Ubon to fly on flare crews but the assertion that crew chiefs flew on their airplanes on flare missions or that other maintenance personnel were suddenly drafted because another loadmaster was suddenly needed is likely to be a figment of someone's imagination.

and AC-47s were doing. The need to drop strings of flares led to the development of launchers that were placed between the raised cargo ramp and the partially open cargo door. The flare launchers were locally manufactured in the sheet metal shop at the 6315th Ops Group home base at Naha. At one point, a paratroop door-mounted launcher was tested but it didn't work out. On one of the test missions, a flare hung up in the rack and went off. It would have burned through the side of the airplane but one of the loadmasters kicked the launcher out of the door with his feet. As the war progressed, a more sophisticated automated system was developed using compressed air, but it proved unsuitable for operational use and was never adapted.

By the time the mission came to an end in 1970, some flareships became test beds and were equipped with sophisticated detection devices such as the BLACK CROW ignition detector system and a fairly powerful Night Observation Device. When the mission began, however, it was dependent primarily on the sharp eyes of the two pilots and navigator. Their only equipment at the time was a pair of binoculars designed for night use, although some crews received STARLITE scopes when they became available. Sometime in 1968, improved versions of the STARLITE scopes known as Night Observation Devices were installed on the flare mission C-130s and a second navigator was added to the crew. Mounted in a paratroop door, the NOD was manned by one of the navigators who sat on a bicycle-like device.(Hansen, 1982) During the last months of the mission, some crews carried laser designator devices that were used to test the capabilities of laser-guided bombs.

In early 1966, the C-130s were joined over the Trail by C-123s of the 606th Air Commando Squadron from Nakhonphanom, Thailand who used the call sign *CANDLESTICK*. While the C-130s and their crews were drawn from conventional troop carrier squadrons and were assigned to the mission on temporary duty, the C-123s operated almost exclusively in the flareship role. Basically, the two missions were identical, with the exception that the C-123s were confined to Laos while the C-130s operated over North Vietnam as well until sometime in late 1966 or early 1967 when missions "up north" were halted due to increasing antiaircraft defenses in the southern half of the country where the flareships operated.

Flare missions were sometimes productive but they were often frustrating. Even though the American press was reporting that US fighter pilots were throwing bombs all over Southeast Asia with reckless abandon, in reality the flareship and strike crews were adhering to a strict set of rules of engagement that worked in the enemy's favor. Crews would spot truck convoys, only to watch them pull into safe havens such as artificially constructed "villages" while they were waiting for clearance to run a strike against them.

Anything, Anywhere, Anytime

Operations over Laos were complicated by the rules of engagement, which were based on preserving Laotian neutrality. All targets in Laos had to be approved through the local province chief through radio communications with the US Embassy in Vientiane. An ABCCC C-130 maintained station over Laos at all times to coordinate communications but the approval process took time, even under the best of circumstances. The frustration was further compounded when the flareship crews watched the fighter pilots miss their targets, often by wide margins. But the frustration was made up for when everything went right and the targets the crews found were hit squarely by fighter pilots who knew what they were doing.

The C-130 flareship role came to an end on June 15, 1970. By that time, the fixed-wing gunship program was well along in development and the first AC-130s were operating out of Ubon, where they had been for more than a year. Not only did the highly modified AC-130s carry flares and special detection devices, they also packed the wallop necessary to destroy the targets they found without having to rely on fighters to deliver the ordnance. Funding for flare missions was transferred to a project that used modified B-57Gs in the FAC/strike role and the C-130 crews returned to airlift. Some of the airplanes stayed at Ubon and went to the gunship squadron for training and observation missions. Although the mission was continually hazardous as crews worked in proximity to North Vietnamese antiaircraft positions, casualties were surprisingly light. In more than five years of operations, only two C-130s were lost to enemy fire, both over Laos, while two others were lost to ground attack at Da Nang. One C-130 crew even managed to tangle with a pair of North Vietnamese fighters and escape.

Perhaps the most important role played by the flareships was one they were not even aware of. After US Navy pilot Lt. Dieter Dengler was rescued after escaping from a Pathet Lao POW camp, he revealed that the motivating factor in his and the other prisoner's decision to escape was the nightly C-130 flare mission that operated in the vicinity of their camp. He and his fellow prisoners hatched up a plan to overpower their guards and take control of the camp, then signal the C-130 when it came over that night. They managed to secure the guard's weapons and killed most of them, but instead of staying in the camp as originally planned, they decided to take their chances in the jungle. Dengler and USAF Lt. Duane Martin paired off after the successful escape.

Sam McGowan

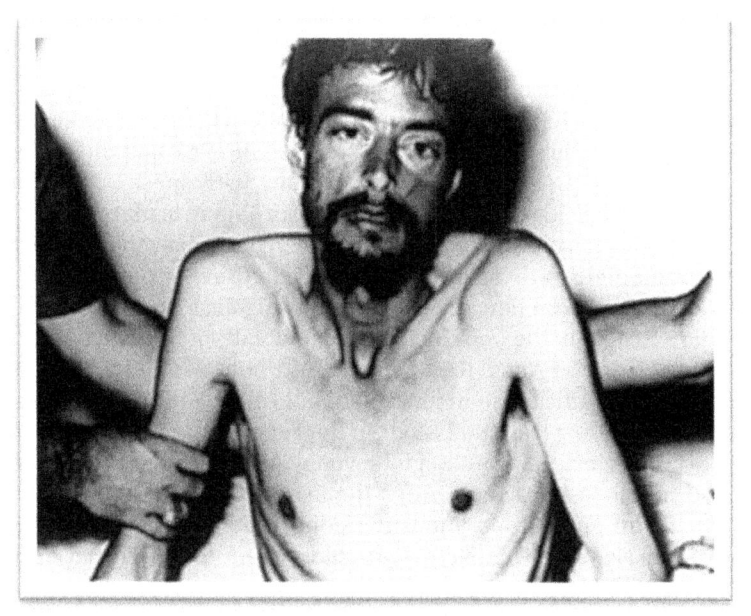

Dieter Dengler

By the time of their escape, the rainy season was beginning and they were initially thwarted in their efforts to signal a flareship. Finally, there was a break in the weather and one night they managed to get a fire going when they heard the flareship approaching. They waved burning torches in the air and the C-130 circled back and dropped a couple of flares. They believed they had been spotted and expected a rescue helicopter at first light, but it was raining and no rescue team appeared. The following day they were attempting to steal food from a nearby village when they encountered a local farmer who killed Martin with a machete. Greatly demoralized, Dengler decided to make one last attempt at signaling a C-130.

That night when he heard the C-130 approaching, he started setting the entire abandoned village where he had been hiding on fire. The C-130 crew spotted the fires and dropped flares but no rescue team arrived, much to Dengler's dismay. The crew reported the fires during their debriefing but, for some reason, military intelligence and rescue failed to act on it. Dengler retrieved the parachute from one of the flares and carried it around with him. Finally, almost two weeks after his fires were spotted, he managed to attract the attention of an Air Force A-1 pilot who was passing over by waving the parachute. Even then, Rescue was hesitant but the A-1 pilot, who was a lieutenant colonel and squadron commander, used his rank and position to influence them to investigate. Dengler was picked up and returned to Da Nang. He was eventually returned to his ship where he received a

Anything, Anywhere, Anytime

Hollywood-style welcome from his shipmates.(Dengler, 1997)[382]

Leaflet drops were another mission undertaken by airlift crews. The *FARM GATE* SC-47s were initially used in the psyops role dropping leaflets, but their efforts were suspended in 1962 and did not resume until several C-47s arrived at Nha Trang with special equipment for the role. The C-47s and other types dropped leaflets over enemy-infested areas of South Vietnam, but there was a psychological warfare mission aimed at North Vietnam as well. Crews from the 35th Troop Carrier Squadron flew their first mission against North Vietnam in July 1965. Though the missions originated out of Okinawa, the crews staged from Da Nang, then later out of Ubon. While the 1965 starting date is the "official" commencement of Project *FACT SHEET*, 35th crews had been flying leaflet missions in the Pacific since at least late 1963 as part of Project JILLI, although they may have used base flight C-47s for the missions for a time. After the arrival of modified C-130s in the Pacific for special operations missions in 1966, some leaflet missions were assigned to their crews to allow them to gain experience over North Vietnam.

The leaflet missions were very strenuous for the loadmasters. Each box had to be manhandled into and out of the airplane and, at seventy pounds a box, this required a lot of exertion on the part of the cargo compartment crew. Even though the airplanes were equipped with roller conveyers, the weight of the boxes would cause the rollers to sink into the cardboard on the bottom of the boxes, making them difficult to move. A medical technician from the flight surgeon's office at Naha and a training technician from the physiological training flight at Kadena were added to the crew to keep an eye on the loadmasters to insure that they did not succumb to the effects of altitude sickness. Medical problems did occur, especially prior to 1967 when the Air Force finally realized that exertion at high altitudes made loadmasters more prone to the effects of altitude then were pilots and other crewmembers whose duties involved little physical activity. Some loadmasters were hospitalized with the Bends, a disease caused by the formation of gas bubbles during decompression, after departing Naha immediately after loading their airplane for a target that was much

---

[382] The 35th TCS crew consisted of Captains Robert Bartunek and Steve Taylor, Lieutenant Richard Herman, SSgt. Bill Rambin and Airmen First Class Sam McGowan, Sam McCracken, Mike Cavanaugh and Willy Donovan. Although Bartunek was called in by intelligence after Dengler was rescued, none of the rest of us were told that there was a connection. Years later, Bartunek, who flew A-1s later in the war, and Dengler came into contact through their membership in the Skyraider Association. It was only then that Dengler learned that his fires had been reported to Intelligence.

Sam McGowan

nearer to Okinawa then was North Vietnam – North Korea. Prior to the problems with the leaflet mission loadmasters, it was believed that the Bends would only result during unpressurized flight at very high altitudes, but medical research conducted by the 35th TCS' flight surgeon determined that the condition could occur at much lower altitudes in persons who were fatigued.

C-130A loadmasters preparing to eject leaflets

Leaflet drops were flown at high altitudes where the winds would catch the tiny pieces of paper and disperse them across a wide area. Two navigators were used to compute the proper release points. By 1968, crews from the 35th had dropped more than eight million of the tiny pieces of paper over North Vietnam. North Vietnam was not the only target for leaflets. Missions were flown against North Korea as well. The Korean missions – which were code-named *JILLI* – departed Naha when the winds were out of the east so the leaflets could be dispensed offshore over the Sea of Japan. The official US Army history of the *JILLI* project relates that the mission commenced in late 1963 when the Army's 7th Psychological Warfare Group and the 35th Troop Carrier Squadron began working together to develop a leaflet capability.

The history also relates that leaflets were dropped from C-47s until 1965. The use of C-47s for a mission that had been assigned to a C-130 squadron is inexplicable – unless the older airplanes were used after the rumored loss of a C-130 on a *JILLI* mission to North Korean fighters on August 6, 1963. Some lists of US military aircraft lost to North Korean fighters show a mysterious airplane lost on that date with a crew of six that is identified only as an "LT." Some internet sites identify it as an Army airplane while others identify it as Air Force.

Anything, Anywhere, Anytime

Some former Naha personnel have reported that an airplane was lost but that the loss was covered up. An Air Force accident report of the loss of a Naha-based C-130 to a "defueling fire" later in the same month is bizarre. According to the report, the airplane was destroyed to the point that it had to be written off by a fire that had been completely extinguished within five minutes after it started. (Investigators, 1963)

C-130A at treetop level inbound to drop powder on Commando Lava mission (John Butterfield)

One of the most bizarre missions of the Vietnam War was that flown by crews from the 41st Troop Carrier Squadron as Project *COMMANDO LAVA* in mid-1967. Military scientists had reasoned that since Laos is primarily underlain by limestone, and since limestone is known to be subject to erosion from rainwater laden with acidic chemicals produced by decaying vegetation, perhaps manmade chemicals might be used to hasten the process and create landslides in the mountain passes through which ran the roadways of the Ho Chi Minh Trail. Test drops were flown at Eglin, then in July 1967, crews from the 41st began dropping the chemicals, which in essence were simple laundry detergents manufactured by Calgon. To dispense the agents, the C-130As approached their targets at very low levels and dropped from only 200 feet above the tops of the ridges.

On the first mission, two of the four C-130s took hits from ground fire but none were damaged seriously. On the second mission the following day, the third airplane in the formation took heavy ground

Sam McGowan

fire as the crew was coming off the target after the drop.[383] Captain John Butterfield managed to land his stricken C-130 at Chu Lia after crossing Vietnam in an airplane with two engines shot out and a fire in the right wing. Butterfield was awarded the Silver Star for the mission, while his crew all received the Distinguished Flying Cross. Mission tactics changed after the ordeal suffered by Butterfield and his crew. Seventh Air Force commander General William Momyer was so upset at the near loss of the airplane that he was heard to say that, "There is not a mission in Vietnam worth the loss of a C-130 and crew." Acting under the assumption that the four-ship formations alerted enemy gunners who concentrated their fire on the trailing airplanes, subsequent missions were flown single-ship. The change in tactics worked; no more C-130s received major battle damage during the remainder of the drops. But even though the drops themselves were successful, there was no evidence that any landslides ever took place as a result. (Another explanation for the use of the detergents was that they were supposed to enhance the creation of mud holes and make the roads impassable.)

Bags of detergent prior to drop (Gary Peters)

Detergents were not the only seemingly innocent materials dropped over Laos by airlift crews. In 1969, C-130Bs from the 463rd dropped 1,200 tons of "gravel," small antipersonnel mines designed to

---

[383] There is some dispute as to whether Butterfield's airplane was hit on the second or third mission. In a letter to the author, Butterfield related that it was on the second mission. Another pilot who was also involved in the missions says that a second mission was flown with only light ground fire and that Butterfield's airplane was hit on a third mission.

Anything, Anywhere, Anytime

look like rocks, during Project *COMMANDO SCARF*. A three-plane C-130 mission deployed to Udorn, Thailand from the 463rd Tactical Airlift Wing at Clark to deliver the remaining stocks of gravel after drops using F-4s proved very costly in monetary terms. In just over a month, the three transports flew 100 missions and dropped the remainder of the gravel. The crews referred to the missions as "Dempster Dumpster" after Thirteenth Air Force vice-commander Maj. Gen. Kenneth Dempster, who was in charge of the project. A later mission using the same techniques involved the dispensing of small "noisemakers," tiny explosive devices that would be set off by a passing truck. The sound would be picked up by listening devices that had been sown by helicopter along segments of the Ho Chi Minh Trail and broadcast to a monitoring station at Nakhonphanom, where the technicians would pinpoint the location and call in airstrikes. (At least that is how it was supposed to work! There were reports that the technicians who monitored the devices picked up sounds of North Vietnamese soldiers urinating on the listening devices, which were designed to appear as small trees!)

Strike missions by transports had been attempted in World War II, sometimes out of desperation and sometimes as an experiment. In Vietnam, they became almost routine – and in one case they were. One of the less-routine missions involved the dispensing of contaminated fuel in 55-gallon drums and setting it afire in the hopes that the flames would start forest fires and burn out the Viet Cong sanctuaries. In March 1965, a 24-plane formation of C-123s attacked the Boi Loi woods, commonly known as the Hobo Woods, northwest of Saigon. As soon as the barrels were dropped, fighters dropped napalm to ignite the fuel. On subsequent missions, the pallets were modified with incendiary grenades attached to each pallet so that they would be set off on impact and ignite the fuel in the barrels. Similar missions were flown periodically by C-123s and C-130s as part of Project INFERNO/*BANISH BEACH* until they were finally halted in the late summer of 1968. The original name of the project was *INFERNO* but it was changed to *BANISH BEACH* in 1968. A variety of targets were selected, including suspected enemy base camps, supply dumps and rocket launch sites. They were also used against tunnel complexes, under the theory that the flames would suck the oxygen out of the tunnels and cause the occupants to suffocate. While the strikes were successful when they were aimed at particular targets, the forest-burning missions did not seem to work. Vietnam is a humid country and the fires produced rising heat which combined with the humidity to create tropical thunderstorms with drenching rains which put out

the fires![384]
Transports were also used to drop mysterious containers that are identified in the USAF history of the tactical airlift mission in Southeast Asia as tear gas. The author has seen photographs of gray containers rigged for airdrop in the cargo compartment of a C-130B from the 463rd Wing. The crew who flew the mission wasn't told what was in the containers, but they didn't believe it was tear gas because of the protective equipment they were issued. There are rumors that various types of gases and chemicals were dropped in Southeast Asia but the Geneva Accords, to which the United States is a correspondent, prohibited the use of gas after World War I. (USAF Historians, 1975)

One of the most daring missions of the Vietnam War was flown by two C-130 crews from the Sewart AFB, Tennessee-based 64th Troop Carrier Wing shortly after it was activated to replace the 314th TCW when it deployed to the Far East. Development of the project actually began before the 314th departed for the Pacific but it took nearly a year for the system to be developed to the point that it could be deployed for operational use. Project *CAROLINA MOON* involved the delivery of specially made, magnetically-activated aerial mines against no less a target than the infamous Than Hoa Bridge, the most difficult target in all of North Vietnam. Located less than a hundred miles south of Hanoi, the bridge spanned a gorge across the Song Ma River and its destruction would severely impede the flow of troops and supplies southward toward South Vietnam. Airstrike after airstrike was flown against the seemingly indestructible target, but when the fighters departed and the smoke had cleared, the huge bridge was still standing.

Experiments with the mass focusing of the force from explosives resulted in the development of large aerial mines that sent their explosive force upward in a single direction rather than outward in all directions. The weapons were described by one veteran who worked with the project as looking "like hot tubs." Such weapons were hoped to be effective against well-constructed targets such as the bridge at Than Hoa. The problem was that the new weapons were huge; they were much too large for delivery by fighters. The only aircraft in the inventory able to deliver the unconventional weapons was the C-130. While Air Force planners felt that a direct attack on the bridge by

---

[384] The official reason for the termination of the project is that it was cost-prohibitive. However, an officer from the 463rd Tactical Airlift Wing told wing personnel that he went to the Pentagon to brief the Joint Chiefs on the use of transports in the attack role and one of the chiefs said the project was inhumane. "We're not there to win the war. We're there to contain it," was the alleged comment.

Anything, Anywhere, Anytime

transports would almost certainly be suicidal, there was a possibility of success by using an upstream delivery method. They were dropped using slotted extraction parachutes to stabilize them so they would go into the water in the proper attitude. Magnetically-activated fuses were developed and fitted to the weapons, which were modified so they could be dropped into the river and allowed to float beneath the bridge. The fuses would activate as they were influenced by the magnetic field of the bridge's steel structure. The project was approved and crews were selected to go to Florida and train for the mission.

In May 1966, the two crews left Sewart for Da Nang. By the end of the month, they were in place. On the night of May 30, Major Richard Remers and his crew flew the first mission. After flying up the coast at wavetop heights, Remers turned the C-130 inland for the drop upstream from the bridge itself, which spanned a gorge the Vietnamese knew as *The Dragon's Jaw*. In spite of heavy ground fire, the crew dropped their five weapons and returned safely to Da Nang. Reconnaissance photographs taken early the next morning revealed that the bridge was still standing, but there was no sign of the weapons anywhere in the river. Five more weapons were at Da Nang in the other airplane. A second mission was scheduled for that evening by Major Thomas Case and his crew. They departed Da Nang for the target a little over an hour after midnight. They were never heard from again. A *LAMPLIGHTER* C-130 flareship crew operating south of the target reported the flash of a large explosion in the direction of Than Hoa.[385] An F-4 assigned to a diversion mission nearby was also lost that evening. Later interrogation of a captured North Vietnamese sailor revealed that the weapons dropped by Major Remers had detonated, but damage to the bridge was repairable. It was not until the spring of 1972, when bombing of North Vietnam resumed after the halt in 1968, that the Thanh Hoa Bridge was finally knocked off its pilings by new generation high explosive weapons.(USAF Historians, 1975)

A C-123 mission operating over Laos possessed a stinger. Project *BLACK SPOT* involved the use of a pair of modified C-123s equipped with sensors and a CBU bomblet dispensing unit mounted in the airplane's cargo compartment to attack trucks on the trails and boats on the rivers. *BLACK SPOT* began operating over Laos from the project's initial base at Phan Rang, where all C-123 operations had been consolidated under the 315th Tactical Airlift Wing. Before the

---

[385] The author was the loadmaster on that crew. The aircraft commander, Lt. Col. Robert Bartunek, USAF (Ret.), recalls that the officers had been briefed that a secret mission would be flown in that area before we took off.

Page 576

Sam McGowan

operation came to a temporary halt in May 1969, the two airplanes had relocated to Ubon, Thailand. After refurbishment the two C-123s, made distinctive by their special black and green camouflage patterns and snout-like nose, returned to Ubon and continued operations until June 1970.

BLACK SPOT C-123

Two M-121 bombs ready to go (Author)

Though most excursions by airlift crews into the strike realm met with dubious results, there was one mission that not only proved successful, it became critical to tactics in the war after 1968. Project *COMMANDO VAULT* came about almost by accident as far as C-130

Anything, Anywhere, Anytime

participation is concerned. A fortuitous discussion between two colonels from Air Force Systems Command, one Army and one Air Force, and a 29th TAS C-130 crew led to the assignment of the mission to the 463rd Tactical Airlift Wing. *COMMANDO VAULT* involved the delivery of M-121 10,000-pound bombs that had been originally built for the B-36 bomber to create "instant" helicopter landing pads. The bombs had never been used and had been kept in storage in New Mexico since the early 1950s. The two colonels were in Vietnam to evaluate the use of US Army CH-54 Sky Crane helicopters to drop the bombs. During the course of their conversation with the C-130 crew with whom they were riding as passengers, they asked the aircraft commander, Major Robert Archer, what he thought of the potential of the C-130 as a bomber. They revealed that the C-130 had been considered as a delivery platform for the huge weapons because their operating costs were considerably lower than helicopters; they could reach any target in Southeast Asia and could carry two weapons at once. As a result of the meeting, Maj. Archer became project officer for the mission and it was given to the 463rd.(Anderson, 1969)

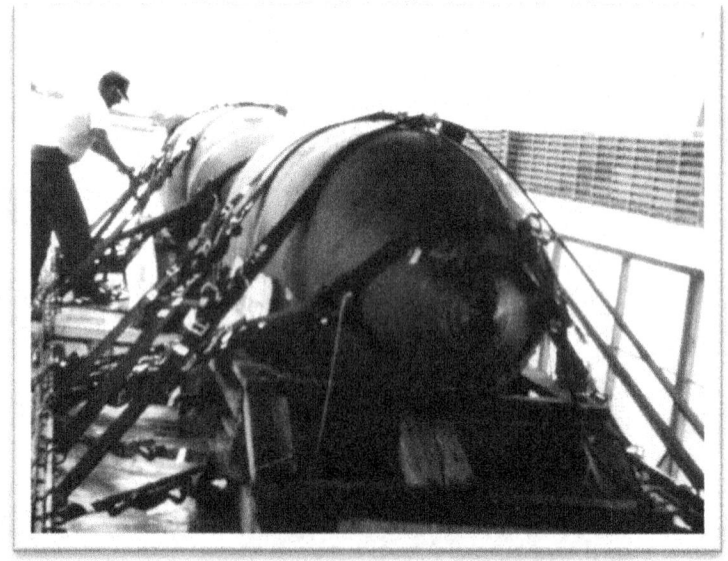

M-121 bombs prior to loading (Author)

After a series of test drops in Vietnam in October 1968, operational missions were set to begin in March 1969.[386] Another

---

[386] There are reports from some C-130 veterans that some of the huge bombs were dropped in Vietnam by C-130s as early as the siege of Khe Sanh in early 1968, but there is no verification of such drops in any official sources. The Army began using the bombs at least by the summer of 1968 to clear helicopter landing pads but they were dropped by CH-54 Sky Crane helicopters. However, test drops

series of ten bombs were dropped in December. Crews in each of the four squadrons of the 463rd at Clark were selected and trained in bomb-delivery techniques that had been developed at Kirtland AFB, New Mexico. It quickly became apparent that not only were the versatile C-130s suitable for the task of dropping the huge bombs, the technique using ground radar to position the airplanes for the drops resulted in unprecedented accuracy. During the 1969-1970 time period, the average circular error was 58 meters, with more than sixty percent falling within fifty meters of the desired impact point.(Porter, 1970) Even the worst drops were within 250 meters. Soon C-130 crews were dropping the bombs right on top of mountain peaks and blasting nearly level landing zones suitable for helicopter landings. Sometime in late 1969 or 1970, a letter was posted on the bulletin board at Det. 2, 834th Air Division congratulating the division for having the lowest average circular error of all aircraft dropping bombs in Southeast Asia using the Skyspot radar bombing method.

Not all C-130 crews were qualified to drop bombs. Each squadron picked its most qualified crews and gave them special training to work with the MSQ-77 radar sites in Vietnam and to operate the extraction system. The bomb drops were basically the same as heavy equipment drops with certain modifications. The 15-foot extraction parachute was deployed a few seconds before the drop and the loadmaster released the load using the emergency release handle for the dual rails. It was said that the *COMMANDO VAULT* loadmasters were the only enlisted men to release an aerial weapon since early in World War II when many bombardiers were enlisted.

There was a limited supply of 10,000-pound bombs and even before regular drops commenced, the Army pressed the Air Force to create a replacement with more power. The M-121 10,000-pound bomb was replaced by 15,000-pound BLU-82 devices made of a slurry explosive mixture derived from aluminum. Because the bombs looked like propane tanks with a nose cone, some people got the idea that propane was somehow used in the mixture. It was not – the explosive was known as GSX. By October 1, 1970, 323 bombs of both types had been delivered; 107 were BLU-82s.

Not only were the huge bombs used to clear landing zones, they were sometimes dropped on known or suspected troop concentrations as well.[387] The invasion of Cambodia in the spring of 1972 was initiated by the detonation of a pair of BLU-82s that created a sterile landing zone for the initial assault. Lam Son 719 in Laos also

---

had been made using 3,000 pound bombs, although it is not clear what type of aircraft was used to deliver them. (Porter, 1970)

[387] After the author's first drop, the FAC gave a bomb damage assessment (BDA) of an estimated 100 KIA.

Anything, Anywhere, Anytime

involved several bomb drops by crews from the 463rd. Some drops were made in Laos from high altitude. When the 463rd was inactivated in late 1971, the mission passed to the 374th wing at CCK. Bomb missions by C-130s continued until the end of the war, although the frequency decreased after mid-1970. During the final weeks of the war, the US provided a number of rigged BLU-82s to the South Vietnamese Air Force, who dropped them from their C-130As. One detonation near the town of Xuan Loc reportedly killed some 1,000 North Vietnamese troops.

M-121 exploding on top of ridge (Author)

Other non-airlift missions included daylight reconnaissance missions over Laos and the airborne command and control center mission supporting strike missions against North Vietnam and Laos. After experimental missions by *BLIND BAT* flare crews, C-130As from the 374th were assigned to fly daytime patrols over the Ho Chi Minh Trail to search for trucks and other signs of infiltration. Although they were not flown by assigned airlift crews after 1966, the airborne combat command and control missions out of Udorn were an important contribution to the out-of-country air war. The ABCCC mission was begun by C-130E crews TDY to Da Nang from CCK, but it eventually became a permanent assignment after the mission moved to Udorn, Thailand when the 7th Airborne Command and Control Squadron was established with permanent airplanes and crews. The unit operated three daily missions using the call signs *HILLSBORO* for daylight missions and *MOONBEAM* and *ALLEYCAT* at night.

The AC-130 gunship mission developed separately from airlift, as did the AC-47 and AC-119 missions, but they all used transport crewmen, particularly pilots and engineers, whose duties had included assignments with troop carrier squadrons in the past. Another non-

Sam McGowan

airlift mission was search and rescue, which fell under the Military Airlift Command's Aerospace Rescue and Recovery Service. The ARRS used three models of C-130s as search and rescue airplanes, helicopter tankers and flying command posts in a mission that had started using C-47s and B-17s equipped with Boston Whalers rigged for airdrop during World War II.

While many of the special applications and special operations involved non-airlift activities, some were well within the airlift realm. The 817th squadron at Naha included crews who were trained for high-altitude, low-opening tactics known as HALO to deliver US Army Special Operations personnel and USAF combat controllers from high altitude. While HALO training was widespread throughout the tactical airlift community both in the United States and overseas, whether or not they were used operationally is not generally known. Such activities fall under the category of classified and covert operations and only limited information has yet been revealed about the extent and nature of such activities during the period of US involvement in Southeast Asia.

There is one covert activity that has been publicized. It really wasn't a special operation since the missions were conventional airlift; however, they were classified and operated outside of the airlift system. During the French Indochina War, the US used civilian contract pilots to fly airlift missions for the French in Indochina. The use of civilian contract crews, or military personnel who had been "sheep-dipped" and placed in special status[388], continued throughout the 1950s and right on through Vietnam. Shortly after the C-130 entered operational service, the CIA recognized that they were ideal for support of its Special Activities Division, the organization responsible for covert operations. The 21st Troop Carrier Squadron, which had been providing C-47s, C-54s and C-119s for covert missions, moved from Tachikawa AB, Japan to Naha AB, Okinawa and equipped with them. The 21st immediately began providing C-130s for use on CIA missions over Tibet. The airplanes were stripped of all markings and flown by civilians employed by CAT.

In 1961, President Kennedy authorized the establishment of a special unit on Okinawa whose task was to provide military C-130s for use by the CIA-owned airline, Air America which had picked up most

---

[388] "Sheep-dipping" is a term used to describe the use of military personnel for sensitive assignments where their official records indicate that they are doing something else. In some cases, officers and enlisted men are separated from the military and employed by civilian concerns, but their records are kept in a special file so they can return to the military upon completion of the assignment.

Anything, Anywhere, Anytime

of CAT's operations, to deliver cargo to forces in Laos that the United States had decided to support. Crewmembers were drawn from within the 21st TCS at Naha and assigned to a special section within the squadron known as E Flight, and given responsibility for delivering the airplanes to the CIA base at Takhli, Thailand and training the civilian crews who flew them on missions. E Flight crews also flew missions in support of CIA intelligence-gathering missions. When the 374th wing at Naha inactivated and the designation moved to CCK, the 21st designation transferred to CCK and the E Flight mission went with it. The C-130As that had been in use on the mission were replaced by Es.

Within Southeast Asia, airlift crews were frequently assigned to special operations tasks. In the early years of the war the 310th Air Commando Squadron was based at Nha Trang for the sole purpose of supporting Special Forces operations. Its C-123s airlifted Special Forces teams throughout the region, sometimes delivering them by airdrop, and keeping teams in the field supplied. When the Air Force took over the Caribou fleet from the Army, Special Forces support became a major responsibility for the 483rd Tactical Airlift Wing, the controlling organization for the C-7 fleet. Most of the missions were conventional airlift but some were classified as special operations because they were supporting cross-border operations into Laos.

While many special operations missions could be flown by conventional airlifters in unmodified airplanes, a few required men with special training and airplanes equipped with special electronics equipment to jam enemy radar for operations into hostile airspace. In mid-1964, six specially equipped C-123s arrived at Nha Trang as Project *DUCK HOOK*, the first true special operations unit to see duty in Vietnam. *DUCK HOOK* included foreign personnel, particularly Chinese, as well as Americans. The Asian crews allowed the luxury of deniability because they could pass for Vietnamese in the event an airplane was lost in hostile territory. The project's mission was to drop and resupply teams of agents operating inside Laos and North Vietnam. The specially painted C-123s also flew occasional leaflet missions over North Vietnam, although leaflet drops were primarily a C-130 responsibility.

A year after the arrival of *DUCK HOOK* in South Vietnam, TAC established a special operations C-130 mission when the 779th Troop Carrier Squadron at Pope began equipping with modified C-130E-(I) airplanes. The modified airplanes were essentially C-130Es, but were made distinctive from the rest of the C-130E fleet by their beetle-like nose, which featured the extensions for the Fulton Recovery System; a method of retrieving personnel from the ground using helium-filled balloons to loft a nylon pickup line. Developed in the 1950s, the Fulton System had been installed on a number of aircraft used by the CIA in the past and had been added to HC-130Hs that the Air Force purchased for the rescue role. The special operations airplanes were the same as the conventional C-130Es assigned to Pope's squadrons, with certain modifications. Known generically as Skyhooks, the modified C-130s were further modified with the addition of terrain-following radar. Electronic countermeasures equipment and an airborne radio operator station were added later.

Before the mission deployed overseas, the airplanes were painted in a distinctive camouflaged pattern using black, green and gray radar-absorbing paint. As the project developed, new airdrop methods for high altitude and high speed cargo delivery became part of the training. Although it is commonly believed that the airplanes were developed due to US involvement in Southeast Asia, the new mission was actually conceived to support CIA-sponsored covert operations in communist countries worldwide. By mid-1966, the Pope crews had been trained, and a detachment deployed to Ching Chuan Kang AB, Taiwan as *COMBAT SPEAR*. The deployment itself was code-named *STRAY GOOSE* and is the name preferred by mission veterans. The *COMBAT SPEAR* airplanes were initially assigned to the 314th wing at CCK and operated out of Nha Trang on TDY as Detachment 1, 314th Tactical Airlift Wing. A second team deployed to Europe and became the 7th Special Operations Squadron. In 1968, as the Air Force reorganized its "special" units, the CCK team moved permanently to South Vietnam, where they became the 15th Special Operations Squadron under the 14th Special Operations Wing. The *COMBAT SPEAR* force was trained and equipped for work over North Vietnam at night, but in reality most missions were conventional supply flights in support of Studies and Observations Group (SOG) units operating just across the border from South Vietnam inside Laos. Crews delivered personnel and supplies into airfields located near the Laotian border such as Ban Me Thout. A few missions were flown into North Vietnamese airspace but they were so infrequent that the crews were assigned leaflet missions just to maintain proficiency.

Two *COMBAT SPEAR* airplanes were lost in Vietnam, one to a mortar attack on Nha Trang in 1967 and the other during a mission a year later. The airplane was on a mission over North Vietnam that involved two operations; after dropping leaflets at high altitude, the crew descended to low altitude for a supply drop. No further word was received from the crew after a radio transmission sent out to signal that the leaflet drop had been completed. The airplane crashed on a ridge just across the border in Laos with the loss of all aboard. Rumors abounded as to what the crew had been doing at the time of their loss. The author was told of one rumor that evidently spread through the Army special operations units that at the time the airplane was lost, it was in the process of making a pickup of a Special Forces team and

Anything, Anywhere, Anytime

was hit by a SAM missile. A SOF major was supposed to have just been picked up when the airplane was hit. Never mind that no live pickups were ever made in combat! Excavation of the crash site in the 1980s led to the conclusion that the loss was operational; the crew simply flew into the side of a mountain. When American troop withdrawals began, the mission left Vietnam and moved to Kadena, Okinawa. After the communist Easter Offensive in 1972, the special ops C-130s maintained a detachment in Thailand to assist the 374th Tactical Airlift Wing with all-weather airdrops.

Another project that was loosely associated with the Skyhook project was *HEAVY CHAIN*, the code word for a unit that was established at Norton AFB, California as the 1198th Operational Evaluation and Test Squadron. The squadron's activities were classified, but they involved primarily the testing of new equipment to support CIA-sponsored world-wide special operations. Two C-130Es were pulled out of the Air Force inventory and transferred to "another government agency" and assigned to the project. Personnel were drawn from the 314th Troop Carrier Wing at Sewart AFB, Tennessee. Two additional C-130s were later assigned to the squadron to operate courier missions transporting classified documents and personnel. The courier missions were classified due to the nature of the operation – it involved transporting CIA documents and personnel – but the squadron also operated some classified missions, including operations in Southeast Asia with a single airplane based at Nha Trang.

While fixed-wing special operations have received a great deal of attention from Vietnam aviation enthusiasts, it was actually the USAF helicopter squadrons that bore the brunt of the burden of special operations airlift in Laos and North Vietnam. Although the Air Force

Sam McGowan

got out of the troop carrying helicopter business in the late 1950s when the Army turned a cold shoulder to the idea of Air Force troop carrier helicopters, interest in airlift helicopters revived in the early sixties. In October 1965, a squadron of CH-3 heavy-lift helicopters began operating from Tan Son Nhut. The unit was expanded to include UH-1 helicopters. The mission of the 20th Helicopter Squadron was to resupply USAF remote communications stations and provide support for the Army and Marines when requested.

In 1968, the 20th became part of the Air Force special operations forces. Squadron detachments operated out of bases in both South Vietnam and Thailand supporting small ground teams whose mission was to locate targets for airstrikes. Air Force helicopters dropped the listening devices that were used to monitor North Vietnamese truck traffic on the Ho Chi Minh Trail in Laos. In South Vietnam, the 20th supported long-range reconnaissance teams working deep inside Viet Cong and NVA occupied regions. In 1967-68 alone, unit crewmen won six Air Force Crosses and 1st Lt. James P. Fleming was awarded the Medal of Honor for extracting a team from right under the guns of the enemy. The 21st Helicopter Squadron operated out of Nakhonphanom, Thailand. Initially, the 21st operated CH-3s but in 1970 the squadron received larger CH-53s. Like the 20th, the 21st supported specially trained ground teams made up of Laotian Meo tribesmen and Chinese Nung mercenaries who were recruited and paid by the CIA. Project *PRAIRE FIRE* operated into Laos and was supported by both the 20th and 21st. Missions began into Cambodia in 1967.

One USAF special operations supply mission involved a twist,

Anything, Anywhere, Anytime

when A-1 propeller driven fighters were used in the airlift role. Although either fixed wing transports or helicopters could have been used to support the long-range ground teams, USAF and US Army Special Forces officers felt that A-1s could drop supplies in such a way that observers on the ground would think they were flying airstrikes. A single A-1 could carry eight canisters like those used for napalm, but were instead filled with up to 500 pounds of supplies. To conceal their real mission, the A-1 crews flew strafing missions after their drops. Such techniques came in handy in the "secret war" in Laos.

Sam McGowan

Chapter Twenty Two - "SECRET WAR"

While the war in Southeast Asia is thought of as The Vietnam War, in reality it was much wider. Long before the first American ground troops arrived for combat duty in South Vietnam – and long after the last were gone – the United States was involved in a secret war in Laos, a war that eventually spread into Cambodia as well. The "secret war" was primarily an air war, at least as far as direct American military participation is concerned. But it was no secret to the men involved.

"Secret" CIA airfield at Long Tien, Laos

When France left Indochina in defeat in 1954, the region was divided into three countries; Vietnam, Cambodia and Laos. Of course, Vietnam was divided in two. Cambodia lay to the south between the Mekong River and Thailand while Laos comprised the northern two-thirds of what had been French Indochina. At the same time that the Viet Minh were working to turn the two Vietnams into a single Marxist country, similar efforts organized and orchestrated from Hanoi were taking place in the other two nations. The communist movement in Cambodia was known as the Khmer Rouge and the Laotian communists were the Pathet Lao.

By the late 1950s, the Pathet Lao movement was gaining strength; a strength that was largely due to technical, material and advisory assistance from the various communist states in both Europe and Asia. American assistance to the Lao government was modest in comparison; it was primarily a program to develop roads and airfields into a transportation infrastructure that would be valuable in the event of future military operations. USAF airlift was available, but

Anything, Anywhere, Anytime

seldom entered Laos itself. Most supplies were delivered to Thailand, then trucked into Laos. There were some exceptions, such as the use of C-130s to airdrop bulldozers and other construction equipment to road building teams inside Laos in the late 1950s. Two C-130s from the 483rd Wing at Ashiya made a total of seven drops while flying out of Bangkok. After the drops, the C-130s returned to Japan but several C-119s remained in Southeast Asia for a time. Eventually the C-119 operation was shifted inside Laos to Vientiane, the national capital.

For several weeks, the American C-119s operated in Laos delivering a variety of cargo to destinations throughout the mountainous and generally remote country. Some loads were delivered by airdrop to tiny drop zones adjacent to villages. Though the purpose of the 1958 mission – codenamed *BOOSTERSHOT* – was officially humanitarian, the real intent was to influence upcoming local elections. The effort failed to prevent communist gains in the elections but the mission did demonstrate the potential for airlift in Laos. A similar venture took place two years later when C-130s dropped two trucks and a DH-4 bulldozer into a remote area for construction work. A second drop did not go off well; the parachutes failed to open and the bulldozer was destroyed.

In the summer of 1960, the United States increased direct material assistance to the Lao royalist forces. Military and other assistance materials were shipped to Bangkok by sea and air, then were loaded on Air America C-46s and C-47s for delivery to the royalist base at Savannakhet. Overt civil war broke out the following December and the Air America transports joined the fight. Royalist paratroops jumped onto drop zones near Vientiane and began a campaign to drive the neutralists northward. Air America transports made hundreds of drops to the royalists while Soviet transports supplied both the fleeing neutralists and the communist Pathet Lao force who occupied the Plain of Jars.

Concerned over the possibility of a communist takeover of Laos, in March 1961 President John F. Kennedy, who had been in office for less than two months, authorized the use of USAF C-130s for deliveries to Vientiane should the need arise. At the same time, the president authorized the use of USAF C-130s with civilian crews to fly missions in Laos. It was not truly a monumental decision; Naha C-130s flown by civilian crews had been flying covert missions in Asia for the CIA since 1958. In April 1961, four Air America crews and four C-130s moved to Takhli from Naha, Okinawa for use by the Central Intelligence Agency.[389] Over the next few weeks, both civilian-crewed and 315th Air Division C-130s flew missions to Laos. Included among the cargo and

---

[389] The C-130s were from the 21st TCS at Naha but the crews were from the Air America office at Tachikawa, Japan.

passengers was a Thai artillery unit and its equipment which was airlifted to Seno. President Kennedy also approved expansion of a CIA program to convert 200,000 Meo tribesmen in the highlands of northeast Laos into an independent anti-communist army. Led by Lt. Col. Vang Pao, the Meo had no allegiance to either the Vientiane government or the Pathet Lao and essentially became the CIA's private army in Laos. By May 1961, the CIA had equipped an army of 5,000 Meo, who are also known as Hmong, and established a separate line of communications unrelated to the one bringing in supplies for the government forces.(Bowers, 1986)

To support the Meo, a network of short airstrips was established in northeast Laos under the supervision of USAF Major Harry C. Aderholt, who was commonly known as "Heinie." Aderholt's involvement in covert and special operations dated back to the Korean War when he ran a unit responsible for dropping agents into North Korea and supplying them. (Few of the agents survived.) In the early 1960s, Aderholt commanded the 1095th Operational Evaluation Group, a small unit based at Kadena AB, Okinawa whose role was to develop unconventional warfare tactics; he also filled an additional role as senior air advisor to the CIA on matters related to Southeast Asia. He had a close relationship to the Agency dating back to the mid-1950s when he was assigned to USAFE headquarters in Wiesbaden, Germany as an unconventional warfare planning officer. In early 1960, Aderholt went to Vientiane to organize operations using single-engine U-10 Helicouriers, small versatile aircraft capable of operating off of short, unimproved runways on the sides of mountains. Working with Vang Pao, Aderholt crisscrossed much of Laos in a U-10 surveying and arranging for improvements of old French airfields. Aderholt also established what became known as "Lima Sites," small airstrips just long enough for use by the U-10s and other short field capable airplanes to make deliveries to the Meo forces. In April 1961, Aderholt established the Air Force segment of the Military Advisory and Assistance Group (MAAG) assigned to Laos. Aderholt brought 1st Lt. Lawrence Ropka Jr. and two other officers from his Okinawa unit to Laos to take charge of contract airlift operations.(Trest, 2000)[390]

After the 1962 Geneva Accords ended the Laotian Civil War, a short-lived peace followed. The terms of the accords called for the removal of all foreign troops from Laos. Initially, the United States complied, as did China and the Soviet Union. North Vietnam, however, did not – an estimated twelve battalions of North Vietnamese troops

---

[390] There is a great deal of information available on the Internet about the aircraft involved, contracts issued, and tons of other superfluous information about the operation.

Anything, Anywhere, Anytime

remained in Laos while another 3,000 were working with Pathet Lao forces. North Vietnamese construction crews continued working uninterrupted on the system of trails and roadways that came to be known as the Ho Chi Minh Trail. The ink on the accords was still drying when new fighting broke out in the troubled country, fighting that was prompted and directed by the Hanoi government.(Prados, 2000)

U-10 Heliocourier

When fighting once again erupted, the United States began covert operations to aid the Lao government, thus beginning the secret war that continued in Laos until the mid-1970s. For most of the war, airlift, which was a major US contribution, was provided by Air America and an assortment of contract carriers with ties to the CIA. Yet while the crews were usually civilians, some airplanes were often provided by the military. In late 1961, E-Flight was set up within the 21st TCS at Naha, Okinawa to provide C-130s for CIA use with Air America crews.[391] Over the next decade and a half, E-Flight crews ferried airplanes a few miles north from Naha to Kadena where the USAF markings were removed, bogus numbers were taped to the tails and the military crewmembers were joined by civilians from an Air America office at Tachikawa AB, Japan. The "baled" C-130s were then flown to the secret CIA base on one side of the air base at Takhli, Thailand. The Air Force crews accompanied the Air America pilots and flight engineers to Takhli as instructors while USAF maintenance

---

[391] When the covert program first began in 1958, the mission was to support CIA operations in Tibet and the flight crews were employed by Civil Air Transport. When CAT began a legitimate airline operation, the C-130 mission went to Air America and the CAT pilots changed companies.

personnel called Cat Zs, because they were categorized as "not otherwise specified" due to their classified assignment, went along to take care of the airplanes while they were on the covert assignment. After the airplane arrived at Takhli, the Air Force flight crew would be flown to Bangkok where they waited in a civilian hotel until it was time to take the airplane back home. The Cat Z maintenance personnel remained at Takhli to service the airplane and otherwise assist with missions. (Trest, 2000)[392]

USAF "baled" C-130A at remote airstrip in Laos (Long Tien?)

As often as not, the civilian crewmembers were recently retired or separated Air Force personnel who had simply traded their uniforms for shorts and tee shirts and a larger paycheck. Some were "sheep-dipped" military personnel who had been officially discharged from the military but who remained on classified Air Force personnel rolls so they could be brought back into military status without going through the normal enlistment process. Several pilots and navigators who had been assigned to the Naha and Tachikawa squadrons and had gone back to TAC squadrons in the US were recruited for a tour as sheep-dipped civilians. Unlike the Air Force, Air America did not use loadmasters per se but instead continued using "kickers" who had been trained in aerial delivery methods. Many of the kickers were US Forest Service smoke jumpers who went to Asia to fly for Air America during the off-season. The company employed its own riggers. It is

---

[392] In Air Force accounting, anything not otherwise specified is listed as Category Z, and the term is used in military records as a means of identification for accounting and other purposes. In Air Force flight records, personnel who are on flight status for duties not specified such as guards or maintenance personnel whose duties do not normally require flight, are categorized as "Z" on flight logs.

probable that USAF "Cat Z" maintenance personnel from the 21st TCS may have sometimes flown as kickers.[393]

Although the C-130s landed at several fields in Laos, including Vientiane, Luang Prubang and Sam Thong, their most frequent destination was the CIA complex at Long Tieng. Located in central Laos, Long Tieng was ringed by mountains while several nearly vertical cliffs rose right off one end of the runway. All landings were to the northwest and all takeoffs were in the opposite direction. Long Tieng was the central distribution point for supplies brought in for the Meo/Hmong; cargo flown in aboard baled C-130s was distributed throughout the country by Air America transports and helicopters. Deliveries to Long Tieng not only brought in military equipment, they also included rice and other food for the Meo tribesmen who populated the region. In the early sixties, E Flight airplanes also operated in South Vietnam where the war was still primarily an advisory war and where the CIA was playing a large role.

Only rarely did USAF C-130 crews fly into Laos, but there were times when operational necessity dictated their use. In early 1970, USAF C-130s operated into Long Tieng to take up the slack while the Air America crews were involved in evacuating the Plain of Jars in the face of a major enemy offensive. A few weeks later, USAF crews again flew into Laos after one of the contract crews was killed when their C-130 crashed into a hillside near Long Tieng. Air Force C-123s (probably from the 606th Air Commando Squadron at Nakhonphanom) occasionally were used in Laos in support of the CIA-sponsored irregular army of Meo tribesmen as well, although Air America operated its own C-123s.(Bowers, 1986)

With certain exceptions, the C-130s used in Laos belonged to the Air Force and were baled to the CIA for covert missions. However, Air America had its own fleet of transports. Some were C-46s and C-47s that had belonged to CAT while others were newer types that had been purchased by the airline. Still others were military aircraft that had been transferred to the Agency for operations by Air America and an assortment of other proprietary companies.

While USAF fixed-wing transport crews were rarely used in Laos, it was there that airlift helicopters were most active. In early 1966, a detachment of CH-3Cs from the 20th Helicopter Squadron began operating from Nakhonphanom, Thailand, an airfield on the Laotian border, under the code name *PONY EXPRESS*. Their original mission was to support counterinsurgency operations against communist

---

[393] One former E Flight member told the author that during his time with the mission in the early 1960s, the pilots and navigators were CIA and the rest of the crew was USAF.

guerrillas operating in Thailand, but it was not long before missions into Laos became frequent. A high-priority mission for the helicopter crews was the resupply and maintenance of several radar and communications sites that had been established in Laos to support airstrikes against North Vietnam. *PONY EXPRESS* crews airlifted heavy construction materials and equipment to the sites, then kept the detachments that operated and maintained them supplied. Without doubt, the most difficult task for the USAF helicopter crews was support of special operations teams working deep in Laos and even in western North Vietnam. In 1966 alone, *PONY EXPRESS* flew 315 missions into North Vietnam.(Bowers, 1986)

Air America C-123

The very existence of the airlift helicopters was not well known and most of their operations were conducted in secrecy. The CH-3 and CH-53 helicopters were practically identical to the HH-3s and HH-53s operated by the Aerospace Rescue and Recovery Service (ARRS) and most who saw them assumed they were rescue "Jolly Greens" who were part of MAC and whose rescue efforts were well-publicized. Few knew that the rescue mission provided a convenient cover for Air Force special operations helicopters engaged in a secret war.

In December 1967, the 21st Helicopter Squadron arrived at Nakhonphanom in response to an increased need for heavy-lift helicopter capability to support operations in Laos. Early missions for the 21st HS involved the dispensing of electronic-intelligence listening sensors along segments of the Ho Chi Minh Trail. The sensors were designed so they could be dropped from an airplane or helicopter in flight and burrow into the ground and leave the antennae sticking out. Dispensing them was simple; they were tossed out the doors of the helicopter by the flight engineer. In late 1968, the squadron began

Anything, Anywhere, Anytime

working with Special Forces teams conducting cross-border operations into the Laotian panhandle from South Vietnam. In August 1970, the CH-3Cs were replaced by CH-53s; a considerably larger helicopter with load-carrying capabilities comparable to a C-123. USAF helicopters sometimes flew tactical missions in support of Lao and Meo ground units. As the intensity of the war in Laos picked up, USAF helicopter crews became more involved in the kind of operations typical of US Army helicopter operations in South Vietnam, but on a much smaller scale. In June 1969, a helicopter task force made up of USAF and Air America helicopters evacuated a 350-man Thai unit and several hundred Lao from Muong Soui as Pathet Lao troops were advancing on the town.[394]

In the summer of 1969, USAF and Air America helicopters supported Vang Pao's advance across the Plain of Jars[395] and almost to the North Vietnamese border. Unfortunately, the Allied gains were only temporary. In December, the North Vietnamese counterattacked and pushed the Meo back onto the Plain of Jars and precipitated the most dramatic fixed-wing effort of the war in Laos. The Laotian government decided to abandon the Plain of Jars and every available Air America plane was put to the task of flying Meo soldiers and civilians off of the plain. Meo were herded aboard C-130s, C-123s and C-47s and flown to the vicinity of Vientiane. Even Long Tieng was threatened. As North Vietnamese artillery shelled Long Tieng, Air America C-123s brought in reinforcements including Thai troops dressed in unmarked uniforms. Every available Air America transport joined the airlift, as did the USAF helicopters. By the end of March 1970, the communist attack had stalled and the situation was reversed.

Over the next three years, the war in Laos ebbed and flowed. Contract-crewed Heliocouriers, Cessna U-17s and Pilatus Porters operated into the smallest strips while C-123s and Caribous operated into the longer ones. Air America-flown C-130s continued to operate into strips that were long enough to handle them and to make drops to units in the field. Helicopter troop lifts were frequent. In 1972, another offensive by Vang Pao's troops was defeated by a combination of bad

---

[394] Due to neutrality issues, the United States did not use American ground combat personnel in Laos, with the exception of a few Special Forces troops who served with SOG on cross-border operations out of South Vietnam and long-range patrols operating from border bases. US ground advisors in Laos were CIA agents while air personnel were, at least officially, civilians. Because Laos adjoins Thailand, the Thai government provided a number of its combat personnel in support of the Lao government.

[395] The Plain of Jars is a generally flat valley in Central Laos that is known for the prehistoric stone pots, or jars, that dot the landscape.

weather, the set of rules regarding the use of USAF helicopters in Laos, and communist artillery and tanks. On January 20, 1973, the last major operation in Laos involved the use of Air America and USAF helicopters to reopen the road connecting Vientiane and Luang Prabang. Seven CH-53s and two Air America CH-47s airlifted more than 1,000 Lao troops during the operation. A month later, the ceasefire in Laos brought an end to US military operations in the remote mountain country.

As war clouds poured their fiery rain onto neighboring Vietnam and Laos, Cambodia attempted to stay out of the conflict by declaring itself neutral. The government in Phnom Penh looked the other way while North Vietnam turned the eastern region of the country into a sanctuary for its forces in South Vietnam. Regardless of the official position of the Khmer government, Cambodia was very much in the war from the very beginning. Because Cambodia adjoined South Vietnam's western border south of Laos, the North Vietnamese turned much of the country into an armed camp and supply base. Even though such an act violated Cambodia's neutral status, there was very little the government could do about it so it chose to simply look the other way. Viet Cong forces in the region northwest of Saigon received their supplies through routes coming out of Cambodia. Because Cambodia was neutral, at least technically, US efforts against the supply routes were confined to Laos even though the southern terminus of the Ho Chi Minh Trail lay within the land of the Khmer. For most of the war, communist porters and truck drivers coming down the Trail were home free once they passed out of Laos and into Cambodia where they were immune from air attack.

When their 1968 Tet Offensive failed, the North Vietnamese adopted a new strategy that centered on their Cambodian sanctuaries. NVA and Viet Cong troops, who had moved out of South Vietnam, conducted cross-border operations against American and South Vietnamese units from sanctuaries in Cambodia. Such activities were strongest in the region northwest of Saigon where the Cambodian border bulged into South Vietnam, the area known as "The Parrot's Beak," which became the most contested area of South Vietnam in 1969. The communist Central Office for South Vietnam, the headquarters for communist troops operating in the southern half of South Vietnam, was believed to have moved to Cambodia (if it even existed) when Allied troops invaded War Zone C in Operation JUNCTION CITY in early 1967. Fed-up with the North Vietnamese activities in the area, President Nixon authorized American forces to begin their own cross-border operations. In early May 1970, a combined American/Vietnamese operation invaded Cambodia, a move that forced the North Vietnamese to abandon their sanctuaries and

Anything, Anywhere, Anytime

flee back up the Ho Chi Minh Trail into Laos as well as deep into the Cambodian interior. The "Cambodian Incursion" spawned widespread opposition in the United States, particularly on college campuses by students who were either ignorant of or chose to ignore the true nature of the situation, but it was generally applauded by the troops who had been enduring the cross-border attacks by North Vietnamese forces. Protesters lamented the "widening" of the war into Cambodia, which was already heavily involved in spite of the neutrality pronouncements from Phonm Penh.

With North Vietnamese troops operating deep inside Cambodia, the country was now very definitely in the war. Now that they were unable to use Cambodia to attack South Vietnam, the Hanoi government turned its attention toward building up the Cambodian communists, the Khmer Rouge, and destabilizing the Cambodian government. Even while the NVA were maintaining a low profile in South Vietnam through the remainder of 1970 and all of 1971, they were busy little beavers in Cambodia where they were chipping away at the foundations of the Khmer nation. It wasn't long before the Cambodian government realized they were in big trouble; Phnom Penh turned to the United States for military assistance.

By the summer of 1972, the situation in Cambodia was becoming very serious as communist Khmer Rouge forces supported by North Vietnamese troops were making gains against the government. Airlift missions into Cambodia began in June 1972 when the C-130 mission at U Tapao, Thailand started regular flights into Phnom Penh. Previously, the primary supply routes into the country had been the Mekong River with boats coming upriver from Saigon, and the port of Kampong Saom on the South China Sea. But as the Nixon Administration was fulfilling its campaign promises to withdraw American troops from Vietnam, the United States felt it was necessary to shift Cambodia's lines of communication away from Vietnam. In January 1973, the Phnom Penh government declared a ceasefire in the country in concert with similar declarations made by South Vietnam and Laos. The Cambodian ceasefire was unilateral but was not reciprocated by the Khmer Rouge and North Vietnamese. New attacks blocked the surface routes leading into Phnom Penh, including the Mekong River. Suddenly, like Berlin some 26 years before, Phnom Penh was a city cut off from the rest of the world except by air. The United States responded by commencing an airlift that would exceed the Berlin Airlift, both in duration and tonnages involved. On April 7, 1973, the Secretary of Defense authorized funding for C-130 deliveries of fuel to Phnom Penh. Two days later, the Joint Chiefs directed the commander of the Pacific forces to begin delivering 6,000 gallons of jet fuel, one bladderbird load, to Phnom Penh each day. The first C-130 landed the next day, April 10; two more followed on April 11. On April 12, the airlift was expanded to include ammunition, rice and general cargo.

The Cambodian Airlift was begun by crews from the 374th Tactical Airlift Wing, which by 1973 was the only C-130 wing still assigned to Pacific Air Forces. Previously assigned to CCK, the 374th had only recently transferred to Clark Air Base, Philippines.[396] With the American role in Vietnam officially over, all C-130 airlift operations in Southeast Asia were now centered in Thailand, at the huge American base at U Tapao that had originally been built as a relief base for B-52s. Even though the American role in Vietnam was officially "over," there was still heavy fighting in the region and the Cambodian Airlift was a wartime mission. Airplanes landing at Phonm Penh were subject to ground fire, including the new SA-7 Strela missiles that had made their appearance in Cambodia only weeks before.[397]

Aircraft approaching Phnom Penh were controlled by a C-130 ABCCC airborne command post orbiting high over Cambodia. At the airfield, a USAF combat control team kept track of arriving and departing aircraft and maintained an orderly traffic flow. In order to avoid ground fire, the C-130 pilots came over the airfield at high altitude then spiraled down from directly overhead for a close-in landing pattern using techniques developed during the long experience in Vietnam. Many pilots were Vietnam veterans; some had years of experience with TAC and PACAF troop carrier/tactical airlift squadrons. To insure their position, the crews maintained ground contact at all times even if it meant flying through small breaks in the clouds. During the descent, the loadmasters stood in the open paratroop doors with flare guns, standing ready to fire flares to decoy the heat-seeking Strelas if a firing was observed. Phnom Penh was blessed with a 10,000-foot runway so short field landing techniques were not necessary. Civilian airlines still landed at Phnom Penh, including those that were part of the CIA proprietary system Congress was in the process of demolishing.[398] The airfield itself was not being

---

[396] Although it bore the same designation, the 374th that moved to Clark wasn't the same wing that served in South Vietnam at the height of the war. In May 1971, the original wing at Naha inactivated, and the 314th wing transferred, on paper, to Little Rock. The 374th reactivated at CCK the next day, replacing the 314th. No personnel or aircraft transfers were involved; it was all on paper and the transfer of the unit guidons.

[397] The SA-7 Strela was a small shoulder-fired heat-seeking antiaircraft missile that had been developed primarily for use against helicopters. It was a short-range missile that was ineffective against high-performance aircraft but was effective against slow-moving transports, particularly as they were approaching for landing or an airdrop. The SA-7 was limited in both range and altitude.

[398] In the early 1970s as Vietnam was winding down, a series of Congressional hearings were held regarding the CIA's proprietary aviation companies. As a result of the hearings, CIA involvement – which was never publically admitted - was

shelled, so crews usually shut down engines for offloading. On departure, pilots would begin an upwards spiral right after takeoff and would not leave the immediate vicinity of the airfield until the airplane had reached 10,000 feet and were out of range of SA-7s and automatic weapons fire.

Pochentong airfield at Phnom Penh was the primary destination for the C-130 crews but they sometimes landed elsewhere in Cambodia as well. Airdrops of supplies to Cambodian government forces and South Vietnamese working with them were frequent. All airdrop missions were flown by Tactical Air Command crews on temporary duty in Thailand with Project *EASTER BUNNY* which had originally been sent to Southeast Asia the previous year. The TAC airplanes were equipped with AWADS, an all-weather airdrop system that allowed high altitude drops from above the clouds without ground guidance. The airdrops kept friendly forces supplied when runway conditions or enemy shelling ruled out landings at the airfields away from Phnom Penh. Most drop missions were within a 45-mile radius of Phnom Penh itself. The 1973 *EASTER BUNNY* force was made up of four airplanes and four crews from the 317th Tactical Airlift Wing, which was the new designation for the C-130 wing at Pope.[399] A team of US Army riggers was stationed at U Tapao to prepare loads for airdrop. Additional riggers were sent to Thailand in May, 1973; after their arrival, the team was capable of rigging enough loads for six sorties per day.

Prior to August, the skies over Cambodia were congested with a variety of aircraft, including fighters and AC-130 gunships. Airstrikes were suspended in August but the airlift was allowed to continue, with the stipulation that "serious risk" to aircraft and crews was to be avoided. All land routes into Phnom Penh remained blocked, but the Mekong River was reopened to barge traffic in May shortly after the airlift began. An average of fourteen C-130s landed at Phnom Penh each day, usually to offload military cargo; rice was also a frequent commodity. In October, a special airlift of rice was mounted to

---

scaled-down. The Air Force became directly responsible for some activities that had previously been conducted through contract airline operations.

[399] Like the 374th, the 317th designation had gone around the merry-go-around. The 317th Troop Carrier Group had been the first intact group to deploy to Australia in late 1942. The unit had remained in the Far East after the war but transferred to Germany for the Berlin Airlift. In the 1950s, the group equipped first with C-119s then in 1958 became Europe's C-130 wing before it was inactivated for several years and its squadrons were controlled directly by 322nd Air Division. In 1964 the wing transferred to the United States, to Lockbourne AFB, OH. In 1971, when its C-130As were given to the reserves, the Lockbourne wing deactivated but the designation went to Pope AFB, NC to replace the 464th Tactical Airlift Wing.

Sam McGowan

alleviate a shortage that developed when Khmer Rouge troops blocked the roads leading into the city.

During the winter, the communists turned their attention to the countryside as the dry season allowed them to move around. While the change reduced pressure on the city, it increased the need for airdrops to remote locations. At one point, C-130s actually hauled rice out of Phnom Penh to U Tapao, where it was packaged for airdrop and loaded aboard *EASTER BUNNY* airplanes to be dropped to troops in the field! As the requirement for airdrops increased, the TAC C-130s were joined by the special operations airplanes of the 1st Special Operations Squadron from Kadena. The 1st SOS was the same unit that had originally deployed to CCK as *COMBAT SPEAR* on the *STRAY GOOSE* deployment, and had then moved to Nha Trang. Now the unit was at Kadena. The Kadena-based airplanes featured special airdrop equipment that allowed high altitude airdrops independently of the AWADS system.

By early 1974, the Department of Defense was becoming concerned for the safety of the military crews involved in the missions. Although the Cambodian Airlift was being carried out with public knowledge, including coverage in the media, the Nixon Administration was worried about possible repercussions in the event an airplane and crew were lost to communist fire. As a means of avoiding such repercussions, preparations were made to use civilian crews to continue the airlift using USAF C-130s. In August 1974, the Air Force contracted with a company known as Birdair to provide pilots and other crewmembers for C-130s that would be provided "on loan" from the US military. Birdair was a subsidiary of Bird & Sons, a small aviation company owned by William H. Bird, an American contractor who had been doing business with the US government in Southeast Asia for many years. Little is really known about Bird, except that he was a West Coast contractor with offices in San Francisco and Seattle who did a lot of work in Southeast Asia in the early 1960s when the US was building up its forces there. His company was large enough that it had its own aviation company, which also serviced government contracts, particularly in Laos. Sometime in the 1960s, Bird sold his aviation interest to Continental Air Services and agreed to not start any competing services for a specified period of time. Birdair was his reentry into aviation.

The contract with Birdair called for the company to provide enough personnel to crew five C-130s. To find qualified flight crews and management personnel, Birdair turned to the ranks of recently retired and separated military personnel with C-130 experience. Many were reservists assigned to reserve and guard units in the United States. The majority had Southeast Asia experience. The chief pilot, Doug Spitler, had been with the 35th Troop Carrier Squadron at Naha

Anything, Anywhere, Anytime

then had gone into the reserves after he left the active Air Force. Since most crewmembers were current in C-130s or had recent experience, the only training required for most of the men was AWADS training. Birdair began operations with an airdrop mission on September 26, 1974. Less than two weeks later on October 8, the civilian contractor replaced all USAF personnel on flights into Cambodia. All markings were removed from the airplanes involved in the missions and they were dedicated to Bird operations but a new procedure allowed for the immediate replacement of airplanes requiring extensive maintenance with airplanes from the 374th flight line. This clause was a departure from procedures used with the E Flight concept. Under E Flight, specific airplanes were reserved for CIA use and were "baled" to it during operations; meaning they were given bogus markings and were shown on paper as being sent somewhere other than where they actually were operating. The airplanes used by Birdair remained on the Air Force rolls and the crews were contracted through the company by the military. Maintenance and other support functions were provided by the Air Force.

In early 1975, the Khmer Rouge increased pressure on Phnom Penh. Road traffic into the city was completely blocked while river traffic coming upriver from Saigon was subject to attack by heavy weapons on the shore. Pochentong Airfield came under frequent rocket attack. On January 9, the Air Force increased the frequency of operations to thirteen flights a day, with ten airplanes bringing in ammunition while two arrived with fuel and another brought in general cargo. Even though C-130s were landing in spite of incoming rockets, the flow of supplies was well short of the requirements that would be needed if the river was closed.

In anticipation of another blockade of the river, several options were considered including the possible return of USAF personnel to the resupply effort. In response, DOD authorized the Air Force to contract with Birdair for additional crews and to assign more C-130s to duties with the airlift. As an interim measure, the Air Force also contracted with several civilian airlines for DC-8 flights into Phnom Penh. In late February, contract DC-8s began operating into Cambodia bringing cargoes of rice from Saigon that had been intended for river shipment. At the same time, Birdair's mission was increased to 26 flights a day. By the end of March, the airlift effort had further increased as five cargo airlines – Airlift International, World Airways, Trans International, Flying Tiger and Seaboard World – contracted for a total of seven DC-8 flights per day. In addition, five C-130 flights with military crews were scheduled into Phnom Penh each week to transport military supplies and personnel assigned to the US military mission to Cambodia.

Sam McGowan

In the spring of 1975, the North Vietnamese began their final offensive, which resulted in the ultimate fall of South Vietnam. The tempo of the war in Cambodia increased as well. In early March, artillery fire was hitting the airfield at Phnom Penh. Eight airplanes were damaged by shrapnel in March but no Americans were killed. While the communist fire hindered the resupply effort, it did not bring it to a halt. The aircrews remained in civilian status but several US military personnel worked on the ground as members of the combat control team, in aircraft maintenance and loading equipment maintenance. Throughout most of the siege, the military personnel did not remain in Cambodia overnight. They flew into Phnom Penh each morning on the first plane in then left in the evening on the last flight of the day. The urgency of the airlift effort caused the Air Force at U Tapao to consider anyone on the base as a potential worker in the airlift. Clerks, cooks, supply clerks and other administrative personnel assisted with cargo handling. More than seventy Strategic Air Command maintenance personnel with previous C-130 experience were pulled from the SAC flight line to assist the 374th maintenance section. Some aerial port personnel flew on missions to assist the Birdair loadmasters.

By early April, the situation in Cambodia was very bleak, and plans were made for an evacuation. Beginning on April 3, Birdair and Air Force C-130s began evacuating Americans and some Cambodians from the city, along with a few people of other nationalities. Nearly 1,000 people were brought out of Phnom Penh by C-130 including 52 orphaned children. The C-130s also transported aircraft engines and other equipment considered too valuable to lose back to Thailand. On April 11, the Air Force decided to discontinue landings at Phnom Penh by both the C-130s and DC-8s although airdrops continued for several days. On April 12, Air Force and Marine helicopters brought out 276 evacuees in Operation *EAGLE PULL*. The final landings were made by ARRS HH-53 crews who brought out members of the Marine ground security force. For almost a week after the final evacuation, Birdair crews continued airdropping supplies to the city. Many of the missions delivered badly needed rice that was brought from Saigon, but it took fifty C-130s to deliver the load of a single barge. While the airlift effort was sufficient to sustain Phnom Penh, it was hardly an efficient means of doing so. By this time, the communists were defeating the Cambodian forces in battle after battle and their final victory had become certain.

There was another secret war that was run during the 1960s, an effort that is cloaked even today in secrecy. While the world's attention was turned toward Southeast Asia, other insurgencies were underway elsewhere in the world. One region was Latin America, where several

Anything, Anywhere, Anytime

insurgencies were ongoing, some of which continued into the 1980s. The United States Southern Command was conducting counterinsurgency operations in several countries from its base in the Canal Zone. Airlift for COIN teams was provided by C-46s and C-47s assigned to an air commando squadron based at Howard AFB, Canal Zone, with additional airlift provided by TAC C-130s on rotational duty. Just what the US did in the region has yet to be publicized – with one exception. An American Special Forces team was credited with the ambush slaying of the legendary Latin American revolutionary, Che Guevara.

American secret airlifts were frequent in the past and they continued in the post-Vietnam era. Men who were junior officers in Vietnam-era special operations rose to star rank to play major parts in events of the 1980s. Some of these men, particularly Dick Secord and Larry Ropka, attracted the attention of the world's media for their role in the Iran/Contra operations. No doubt, there have been other "secret" wars and they will continue.

Sam McGowan

Chapter Twenty Three - "A Disastrous End and a Dismal New Beginning"

As the American role in Southeast Asia came to an end, the Department of the Air Force reorganized itself. In the early 1970s, the Air Force undertook Project *CORONA HARVEST*, an extensive study of the records of its operations in Southeast Asia. Airlift was a major focus of the study and the historical record revealed that the medium had changed drastically since 1961 when *MULE TRAIN* introduced USAF tactical airlift to South Vietnam. The biggest change was in the Military Airlift Command, which did not even exist prior to 1965. During the Vietnam-era, MAC had gone from an air transport service utilizing primarily propeller-driven aircraft to an all-jet airlift command with worldwide capabilities.

A study of the USAF airlift system for the years 1965-1968 led Air Force reviewers to recommend that the entire airlift force be consolidated on the basis that there was too much duplication between MAC and the tactical airlift forces in terms of aerial ports and support elements. The review team recommended the consolidation of the two airlift missions, strategic and tactical, into one command as a money-saving measure. The proposed consolidation was opposed, however, by the commander of Tactical Air Command, General William Momyer, who had commanded Seventh Air Force in Vietnam before taking command of TAC. General Momyer was well acquainted with the tactical airlift mission, both from his past experiences as a member of the TAC staff in the 1950s and 1960s and, more recently, as commander of all USAF units in Vietnam. In fact, General Momyer had addressed the issue of airlift consolidation in his end-of-tour report

Anything, Anywhere, Anytime

when he left Vietnam. It was Momyer's opinion, based on his observation of the role of tactical airlift at Khe Sanh, in the A Shau Valley and at Kham Duc, among other places, that the tactical mission was definitely unique in comparison to air transportation in general and that it should always remain separate from the strategic mission. Momyer considered tactical airlift to be "a highly specialized form of warfare."

In spite of the TAC commander's objections, the Air Force chief of staff, General David Jones, proceeded with the consolidation. Although Jones had served in Vietnam with Seventh Air Force, his Vietnam service was from February – August, 1969 and he had not come to appreciate the special nature of tactical airlift the way Momyer had. Most of Jones' service had been in SAC and in Europe with USAFE where airlift operations were a MAC responsibility. He had served as General Curtis Lemay's aide in the mid-1950s and was no doubt acquainted with former MATS commander Gen. Tunner. Tunner's role in the consolidation is unknown but he was in his seventies and no doubt still connected to the Pentagon. With the US role in Southeast Asia nearing its end, the Air Force was seeking ways to cut costs and consolidation of all airlift assets into one command seemed like a logical step for a peacetime military. Momyer retired before the consolidation actually started.

TAC's tactical airlift resources transferred to MAC in December 1974; the PACAF and Alaska Air Command units followed in mid-1975. But even before the change of command, other transfers and unit deactivations had taken place. Beginning in 1969, several tactical airlift squadrons were inactivated as the Vietnam War wound down. The 483rd and 315th wings deactivated and their C-7s and C-123s returned to the United States to the reserves, with most of the C-123s going to the bone yard. Some went to South Vietnam's air force but older C-130As and C-119s were seen as the best transports for the VNAF. South Vietnam also received a few Caribous. The 374th at Naha had also been deactivated, along with the 317th at Lockbourne, the 463rd at Clark and the 313th at Forbes. The A and B models from the four units transferred to the reserves, giving the Air Force Reserves and Air National Guard increased airlift capabilities for the first time as the more modern and capable C-130s replaced C-119s and C-124s.[400] The 374th, 317th and 463rd designations all remained alive as they replaced the designations of other units. As of 1975, the 374th was in the Pacific, the 314th was at Little Rock, the 317th was at Pope, the 463rd was at Dyess and the 316th was at Langley, although its days were numbered. After the transfer to MAC, the 316th inactivated and

---

[400] The 313th at Forbes had begun transitioning into new C-130Es; its airplanes and personnel went to other TAC bases, particularly Dyess.

its squadrons were divided, with one going to McChord and another transferring to Europe, from which all permanently assigned C-130s had been withdrawn a decade earlier, to operate a European Distribution System.

Two years took place between the end of the American effort in Vietnam and the transfer to MAC but during those two years the Air Force tactical airlift force remained active in Southeast Asia, although in a more subdued manner. After the 1973 ceasefire, the 374th detachment at Tan Son Nhut was withdrawn. Thereafter, airlift activities in South Vietnam were met by the *KLONG* detachment at U Tapao in Thailand. For the most part, in keeping with the US policy of Vietnamization, the South Vietnamese Air Force assumed all airlift duties within South Vietnam. Prior to the withdrawal, the US gave South Vietnam C-119s, C-123s, C-7s, and finally C-130As. Even though the Vietnamese aircrews adapted to the C-130As, their maintenance people had a hard time keeping them in an airworthy condition, just as USAF maintenance people previously had similar problems with them.[401]

American C-130s still flew into Vietnam on occasion, but they no longer took an active role in the war. One regular mission was the weekly flight between Saigon and Hanoi rotating personnel belonging to the Joint Control Commission responsible for overseeing the ceasefire in South Vietnam. Missions between Tan Son Nhut and Hanoi's Gia Lam airfield began two weeks before the release of the first POWs and continued right up until the last week of the Vietnam War in the spring of 1975. After the withdrawal, Clark-based C-130s flew into Hanoi and brought out the remains of POWs who had died in captivity, when the North Vietnamese released them. The flights originated out of Clark then went to Hanoi by way of Saigon and back again. Officers from the 374th met with the Vietnamese officers, and inspected and received the remains. Other C-130 missions flew into South Vietnam in the final weeks of the war to retrieve American equipment. On March 31, 1975, a C-130 flew into Dalat to retrieve a load of US-owned nuclear fuel that had been on-loan to South Vietnam to power a nuclear reactor.

As the situation in South Vietnam began to rapidly deteriorate in April 1975, the United States stepped up the role of its airlift forces. MAC C-141 and C-5 flights brought in military assistance supplies for South Vietnam and took out refugees on the return flights. As the

---

[401] The C-130As with which the Vietnamese Air Force was equipped had all been built in the 1950s, and many were already considered obsolete even as the US was building up forces in Southeast Asia. Not only were they old, they featured a DC electrical system with wiring nearly two decades old.

Anything, Anywhere, Anytime

northern provinces fell one by one, Air America, South Vietnamese Air Force transports and other civilian airlines took more than 10,000 refugees out of Pleiku. A similar effort brought thousands more out of Da Nang. Hysteria gripped the country as North Vietnamese forces advanced toward Saigon. An attempt to organize an American C-130 evacuation of Da Nang came to naught when enemy artillery began striking the airfield where so many C-130 flights had landed over the preceding years.

As it became apparent that South Vietnam's days were numbered, the United States began an escalating pullout of Americans and eligible Vietnamese from the embattled country. The evacuation got off to a slow start; extensive paperwork prevented many from leaving while many Americans with Vietnamese families refused to leave. In early April, MAC mounted Operation *BABY LIFT* to bring out more than 2,000 Ameriasian children whose Vietnamese mothers had abandoned. On April 4, a C-5 crashed shortly after takeoff from Saigon with more than 200 passengers aboard, all children and their American escorts, most of whom were women. The airplane went down after an aft pressure door blew out and took most of the hydraulics that operated the empennage flight controls with it. The crash caused the death of 155 persons, mostly children.

By mid-April, many of the restrictions that held back most refugees had been lifted and the flow of evacuees increased. C-130 flights were scheduled to compliment the C-141 missions that were bringing out most of the refugees. On April 21 and 22, more than 6,400 people were flown to Clark in 33 C-141 and 41 C-130 flights. Over the next three days, an average of twenty C-130s landed at Tan Son Nhut each day, although the C-141 role began to decline as MAC became concerned about conditions at the airfield. PACAF's C-130s had not yet transferred to MAC so they were not affected by MAC's reservations. The former TAC units at Pope, Little Rock, Langley and Dyess had become part of MAC but the airplanes and crews on duty in the Pacific were on temporary duty to PACAF and operated outside of MAC control.

Even while USAF and civilian flights were bringing thousands of refugees out of the country, the Joint Control Commission flights between Saigon and Hanoi continued. On April 25, two days before North Vietnamese troops entered Saigon, a 345th Tactical Airlift Squadron crew made one last flight to Hanoi to bring back delegates. The pilot, Major John Butterfield, was an old Southeast Asia hand. He had served at Naha with the 41st TAS and was now stationed at Kadena, again with the 374th wing.[402] For Butterfield, the flight across

---

[402] When CCK closed, the 374th Wing and the 21st and 776th squadrons moved to Clark while the 345th went to Kadena.

Vietnam brought back many poignant memories. As he flew north, he looked down on Cam Ranh Bay, where he had spent many a week TDY flying airlift missions. As he crossed Chu Lia, he remembered when he had landed his burning C-130A after being shot up on the second *COMMANDO LAVA* mission. While flying up the coast of North Vietnam, Butterfield remembered his many nights dodging flak while flying *LAMPLIGHTER* flare missions over the North.(Butterfield, 1985)

During the final weeks of the war, the United States provided South Vietnam with several BLU-82 15,000 bombs for use against the advancing North Vietnamese. A single BLU-82 detonation near the town of Xuan Loc killed hundreds of NVA soldiers, and temporarily slowed the communist advance. Arriving C-130s brought in the bombs already rigged for airdrop then departed for the return flight to Clark with refugees aboard. The huge bombs were shifted to VNAF C-130As; they dropped them on the advancing enemy. While the BLU-82s had a demoralizing effect on the North Vietnamese, they were too little and too late. Panic was rising throughout South Vietnam and many government soldiers were throwing away their weapons. Some were switching sides and going over to the enemy, including Vietnamese Air Force pilots who repainted their aircraft with North Vietnamese markings. If they would fly, the C-130s that the US had given to South Vietnam were flown out, usually with a cargo compartment crammed with refugees.

Tan Son Nhut was the primary pickup point for refugees but some flights landed at other points as well. On April 27, two C-130s landed at Vung Tau and brought out 250 dependents of South Vietnamese marines while the marines defended the airfield. On April 26, Birdair C-130s began bringing military equipment out of Bien Hoa. The increasing urgency as the victorious NVA moved ever closer to Saigon upped the tempo of the evacuation. More than 12,000 people were brought out of Tan Son Nhut on April 26 and 27; 46 C-130s and 28 C-141s landed in the face of increasing North Vietnamese opposition.

By April 27, North Vietnamese troops were attacking Tan Son Nhut. Impacting communist artillery made landings very risky. At nightfall, MAC put a halt to C-141 landings. The next morning, C-130s resumed the evacuation in the face of constant artillery attack. One USAF C-130 was on the ground when North Vietnamese pilots – perhaps turncoat South Vietnamese – attacked Tan Son Nhut in American-built A-37s. A C-130 was chased to the South China Sea by an A-37 but the transport was only threatened and not fired upon. The attacks severely retarded the evacuation; only eighteen of a planned 58 C-130 flights got into Tan Son Nhut and only 3,500 refugees were evacuated. During the day on April 28, the NVA managed to position their huge 130-MM artillery pieces within range of Tan Son Nhut.

Anything, Anywhere, Anytime

Shortly after midnight on April 29, the big guns opened up on the base. Three USAF C-130s were on the ground, each having just landed with a rigged BLU-82 aboard. The first rounds of impacting artillery destroyed one American C-130E and at least one VNAF C-130A that was parked nearby.[403] None of the crewmembers were seriously injured; they left Tan Son Nhut during a lull in the attack aboard one of the other C-130s.

In spite of the close proximity of the NVA troops and the shelling of Tan Son Nhut, preparations were underway for a "maximum practical" C-130 evacuation to begin on the morning of April 29. Sixty C-130 flights were scheduled to bring out as many evacuees as possible. The C-130 missions were to be escorted by carrier-based strike and electronic countermeasures aircraft. Ambassador Graham Martin was determined to bring out as many refugees as possible aboard C-130s before a final helicopter effort was mounted to bring out Embassy personnel. Ambassador Martin remained in telephone contact with the White House in Washington. In a conversation with USAF Lt. Gen. Brent Scowcroft, the ambassador made his feelings known that the evacuation should commence if at all possible. But conditions at Tan Son Nhut were rapidly deteriorating. Artillery fire was striking the base and the runways were littered with debris. A crowd of people was waiting for the evacuation to begin and they were becoming uncontrollable. People were shooting at South Vietnamese transports as they took off. American combat controllers noted fire from 57-MM antiaircraft guns and at least one SA-7 missile firing. Some orbiting C-130s waiting for the word to land began receiving airbursts at 20,000 feet.

The combination of factors led US Army Major General Homer D. Smith to advise Ambassador Martin that a C-130 evacuation was "just not in the cards." Sorrowfully, the ambassador accepted the news and ordered that the helicopter evacuation of the embassy itself should begin. The orbiting C-130s were told to go home, and the airlifters left Vietnamese skies for the last time. The final airlift operation of the Vietnam War was the helicopter evacuation of the American Embassy by USAF, USMC and Air America helicopters.

The long Vietnam War ended on April 29, 1975 when victorious North Vietnamese troops took the city of Saigon. But there was a post-script to the war that, while fixed-wing participation was minimal,

---

[403] This airplane is not counted among those lost during the war because the loss occurred after the cessation of hostilities between the US and the communists. It also has the distinction of being the last American transport destroyed by air or ground attack. All US military transport losses since then have been due to accident.

placed USAF airlift helicopters once again in the line of fire. On May 12, 1975, only two weeks after the fall of South Vietnam, Cambodian Khmer Rouge gunboats seized an American commercial vessel, the S.S. *MAYAGUEZ*, in international waters just off the south coast of Cambodia. Immediately, the United States began making plans for a rescue. Every available helicopter in the Nakhonphanom, Thailand based 21st Special Operations Squadron was sent south to U Tapao. A number of airmen from the base security detachment were sent along for possible duty with the rescue force. The rescue effort got off to a bad start when one of the CH-53s crashed during the flight; the five-man crew and eighteen security policemen were all killed. The loss gave forewarning of what was to come.

USAF Security Police – they all died when their helicopter crashed

While the CH-53s made their lumbering way southward, a battalion of Marines was inbound to U Tapao aboard C-141s. Intelligence sources estimated that about 100 troops were stationed on Koh Tang Island where the ship had been taken, and there were heavy weapons present. Somehow, the Marines, few of whom had combat experience, received faulty intelligence indicating that only about twenty Cambodian irregular troops were on the island. They were expecting an easy operation; instead they landed in a hornet's nest.

On the morning of May 15, the assault force took off from U Tapao bound for Koh Tang. Eight USAF helicopters, five CH-53s from the 21st SOS and three HH-53s from the Air Rescue Service, carried the 175-

Anything, Anywhere, Anytime

man Marine assault force. Three additional HH-53s headed for the USS *HOLT*, a US Navy destroyer that was lying in Cambodian waters in close proximity to the captured ship. The three Jolly Greens landed on *HOLT* and discharged their troops, who then boarded the *MAYAGUEZ* and found it unoccupied. Airstrikes by AC-130s and fighters had attempted to prevent all Cambodian gunboats from reaching the ship but a fishing vessel had managed to run the gauntlet of fire. The Khmer Rouge used the vessel to transport the crew to shore.

Marines running from helicopter

The main assault force was directed to land on Koh Tang and search for the crew of the captured ship. As the eight helicopters approached their landing zones, they were greeted by heavy fire. The first CH-53 touched down on the beach at about 0600; small arms, rocket and mortar fire immediately raked the landing zone. After discharging his load of Marines, the pilot managed to get airborne on only one engine, but a short distance from shore the badly damaged helicopter slipped into the sea. The second CH-53 took numerous hits during the approach and was unable to land. The pilot broke off his approach and set a course for the Thai coast. A third CH-53 lost an engine after being hit over the LZ and settled onto the beach where the occupants came under heavy fire. The fourth CH-53 burst into flames after being hit while inbound to the beach and crashed into the sea. Thirteen Marines and airmen were either killed in the crash, drowned or died when they were hit by enemy fire after escaping the wreckage. The death toll had already reached 36 and the mission was just getting underway!

Marines running to rescue helicopter

After four CH-53s had either been shot down or failed to deliver their troops, the fifth CH-53 managed to land and offload then depart the area, but not without harm. When it reached U Tapoa, the helicopter was found to be so badly damaged that it was not safe to fly. Meanwhile, the three ARRS HH-53s made repeated attempts to reach the beach and were finally successful. While the battle was taking place, word came that the ship's crew, who were not on the island, had been released. The crew was actually released about the time the first helicopter touched down on the island, where they had never been. By this time, nearly 100 Marines and airmen were on the beach; they were encountering heavy fire and taking numerous casualties. Extracting them was now the mission, but before a withdrawal could begin, the troops on the beach had to be reinforced.

By this time, five CH-53s had either been destroyed or put out of action by the enemy fire. The two remaining CH-53s joined three HH-53s in a reinforcement effort. One of the CH-53s experienced the same bad luck as its squadron mates – the helicopter took so many hits during the approach to the beach that the pilot had to break off and return to Thailand. The other CH-53 and the three HH-53s managed to land reinforcements then, after resistance from the Cambodians began to lessen, to withdraw what was left of the assault force.

The *MAYAGUEZ* rescue mission was solely a heliborne operation, except the initial movement of the Marines from Okinawa to Thailand by C-141. Seven C-130s were positioned at U Tapao loaded with BLU-82 bombs while others were loaded with supplies for possible airdrops. In the afternoon, four bomb-laden C-130s took off, along with a fifth airplane that was rigged for airdrop. They assumed an orbit in

Anything, Anywhere, Anytime

the vicinity of the island where the battle was taking place. Late in the afternoon, one of the BLU-82 crews dropped their giant bomb using the AWADS equipment on their airplane. It was the first time ever that a bomb had been dropped with the all-weather equipment. The *MAYAGUEZ* incident was America's last hostile action in Southeast Asia. The country was once again in a Cold War situation. Vietnam was a disaster for US foreign policy but there was one bright spot. Though very few Americans were aware of it, the Thai had, with US assistance, managed to defeat an insurgency within their own borders.

There have been numerous opinions offered as to why the United States lost the war in South Vietnam, and along with it, the similar conflicts in Cambodia and Laos. Some believe the effort was doomed to failure from the beginning, and there is some truth to this assertion. Many Vietnam veterans blame the defeat on Washington – "we would have won but the politicians wouldn't let us" is a common refrain. Yet, in truth, the military itself must bear the blame for the failure. Although American troops were engaged in combat from 1965 to 1970, and on a limited basis after that, no significant military gains were ever made. While it is true that the North Vietnamese were defeated at Khe Sanh, MACV abandoned the camp within a few weeks. The real reason for the loss of the war – and, ultimately, the region – is that the US and its allies failed to prevent North Vietnam from sending hundreds of thousands of troops into South Vietnam, Laos and Cambodia and keeping them supplied. Even while to some degree this was political, MACV failed to occupy and control the main infiltration route into South Vietnam, the A Shau Valley. The valley presented the perfect opportunity to use airlift to invade and occupy the main communist infiltration route into South Vietnam but MACV failed to exploit it. Instead of mounting an airborne operation to relieve the camp at A Shau in 1966, the camp was allowed to fall into communist hands and it was two years before MACV made another attempt to occupy the valley – and the occupation only lasted for a few weeks.

When American and South Vietnamese troops invaded Cambodia in 1970, no attempt was made to cut off the communist escape routes and the North Vietnamese withdrew into the Cambodian interior and back into Laos where they concentrated their efforts against the two national governments. South Vietnamese finally managed to capture the town of Tchepone, a major crossroads on the communist infiltration route, but no more had the town been captured than it was abandoned. The (not-so) "secret" war in Laos was a miserable failure, prompted to no small degree by the factionalism within the military between the "special operators," who thought they could defeat a major communist army using mostly illiterate rural tribesmen who had no loyalty to their country's government, and the rest of the services, which were focused on South Vietnam. A similar attitude was prevalent in South Vietnam, where US Army Special Forces attempted to use mountain tribes with no loyalty to the Saigon government to interdict the communist supply routes. By 1970 nearly all of the Special Forces camps had been overrun.

Over reliance on helicopters may have also been a contributing factor to the ultimate communist victory. While small helicopters, particularly the Bell UH-1, made light infantry forces more mobile, they also restricted their effectiveness. The loud noise of their rotors could be heard long before they arrived at their objective and any communist troops in the vicinity were alerted to expect them. The Bell's could only carry a maximum load of 12-14 troops and they were not capable of transporting vehicles or equipment. Their maximum payload was less than 4,000 pounds. MACV used them to insert troops into landing zones in forward areas then extracted them when their mission was over. Consequently, there was no permanency to US operations in the country – the Americans would arrive and search an area, then depart again, often within only a few days or even hours after they arrived – and the enemy controlled the countryside. MACV had the resources to establish large permanent bases deep in the interior of the country but failed to use them for that purpose. The few inland bases were at existing airfields such as Ban Me Thout. They were used primarily by Special Forces rather than as major bases for conventional infantry. Pleiku was the only major inland airbase but its importance lessened when the communists concentrated their efforts in other areas.

The post-Vietnam period was a time of peace but the US was still involved in some international crisis situations. In 1978, US airlifters returned to Africa. Armed guerrillas assaulted villages in the former Katanga Province in the new country of Zaire, which previously had been The Congo. France, Belgium and the United States intervened. The US contribution once again came in the form of airlift. MAC C-141s and C-5s moved troops to Africa from Europe while C-130s supported the peacekeeping force within Africa. In the past, C-130s involved in such operations had belonged to Tactical Air Command; after 1975 they belonged to MAC.

Anything, Anywhere, Anytime

Sam McGowan

Epilogue

In 1976 Georgia governor James Earl Carter, a US Naval Academy graduate and former submarine officer who had turned to near-pacifism, was elected president. Under Carter, the United States military forces entered a graveyard spiral in a time of little activity. Within the airlift community, changes were taking place as the tactical airlifters were absorbed into MAC. The terms of the arrangement for the transfer had stipulated that the C-130 squadrons would retain their tactical orientation. At the same time, the MAC C-141 and C-5 squadrons were to become more tactical. But the post-Vietnam military was undergoing other changes as well. A more politically progressive element in Congress, many of whom had campaigned on an antiwar platform, saw the military as a platform for social engineering. "Social actions" programs gained prominence as young, non-flying airmen and officers sought to place "blame" for problems in society on the "military establishment." The changes were more than many career military men could take – they opted for civilian life.

During the Carter years the United States military ate away inside itself to become a hollow shell. The post-Vietnam Congress reflected the antiwar attitudes which had come to prevail within the population as a whole. Congressional military appropriations were scaled down as spending on social programs increased and new government bureaucracies were created to administer them. The US military appeared to be a viable combat force but in reality it was mostly show, with little real substance. Many of the new weapons systems, such as the F-15 fighter, spent so much time out of commission that the fleet was hardly airworthy and definitely not combat ready. Congress cut funding for the military so much that spare parts were in short supply

Anything, Anywhere, Anytime

and training was practically nonexistent.

The Air Force lost its most experienced people in the years right after Vietnam, and nowhere was the loss more profound than within the tactical airlift community. Throughout the Vietnam period, the airlift squadrons had been staffed with a generally career-oriented cadre. With the exception of loadmasters, many of whom were young first-termers, and some pilots and navigators, airlift crewmembers were usually men who had been in their mid-twenties to early thirties in 1965 when the US combat role began and who were approaching retirement age as it drew to an end. They had been joined by many older officers who were brought back to the cockpit and who, in many cases, were already old enough to retire while others reached retirement age during the war years. Many of the younger officers and NCOs were frustrated with the changes in the military and the general attitude of the country as a whole, while at the same time the civilian aviation community was undergoing tremendous growth.

Within the airlift realm, the C-130, C-141 and C-5 offered unprecedented mobility but the combat ready status of the crews was in doubt. Even though the country had just come through a long war in which airlift had played a major part, few active duty military aircrew members of the second half of the 1970s had significant combat experience. Many of the pilots, navigators, flight engineers and loadmasters who had been part of TAC in the early 1960s had reached retirement age while the younger men had moved into staff positions away from the squadrons and operational flying. Large numbers of Vietnam airlift veterans had moved into C-141 and C-5 squadrons but although they had been promoted to higher rank, contributed little because they had been absorbed into the MAC heirarchy and were merely marking time until they could draw a retirement check. In 1962, when *MULE TRAIN* C-123s deployed to South Vietnam, Air Force officers in leadership positions and senior NCOs were men who had entered military service during World War II and many had gone on to fight in Korea. Consequently, the military was generally conservative with a strong emphasis on discipline. By 1975, the senior officers and NCOs had retired and more liberal attitudes were developing in the non-flying side of the Air Force in particular. "Social actions" had become a by-word and special sections had been set up on Air Force bases to "educate" military personnel and make them more socially aware.

Large numbers of younger men became fed up with the policies of the post-Vietnam military and took their discharges and resigned their commissions. Fortunately, many took their experience into guard and reserve units. Most of the few who remained on active duty with combat experience were either field grade officers and senior NCOs serving in management positions or they had gained their experience

Sam McGowan

during the final months of the war after US forces had been withdrawn and had never supported US troops in combat. Only a relative handful had seen combat in 1972. The majority of those who elected to remain in uniform were married men with families who could hardly afford to take their chances in the outside world for economic reasons.

One of the drawbacks of the post-Vietnam military was that Congress had become socially progressive and had turned the service into a social experiment. A new breed of politician with antiwar sentiments had risen to power; men and women with a social progressive outlook who saw government as a means of achieving social change. Because the military is a melting pot filled with men and women from all regions of the country and all ethnic groups, many social progressives saw the services as a medium for effecting the kind of changes they saw as necessary for the country as a whole. "Equality" was the byword of the day and not only racial but sexual as well. The feminist movement was in its heyday and its leaders, led by Colorado Congresswoman Patricia Schroeder, were pushing for "full equality for women," including within the military. For the first time in American history, military pilot and navigator training was opened up to women, with most graduates ending up in transport squadrons because women were barred from participating in combat. Because of the potential for combat operations by tactical airlift squadrons, women were not assigned to them as aircrew members.

Along with equality for women, other social agendas included the "homogenization of the military," particularly in the area of race relations. Although the Air Force was the first of the military services to fully integrate, racial problems that plagued the rest of the country were repeated within it in the 1960s although, as a general rule, they were not prevalent in operational squadrons. There were racial issues in support functions, however. Drug use had become common among younger airmen and even some officers and as the older men left the service, it became even more common, even among aircrew members. Social actions sections were established on all military bases and given unprecedented power to effect social change. Encounter sessions were the order of the day; sessions where rank had no meaning and enlisted men and women in the lower grades were encouraged to sound off to senior officers and NCOs about the "inequities" they faced. Military discipline all but ceased to exist while drug use was rampant among junior enlisted personnel as well as some officers, in reflection of conditions within the country as a whole. With such an attitude in the military, it is no wonder that *DESERT ONE* was the scene of disaster!

Anything, Anywhere, Anytime

The most serious crisis of the period – and one of the most serious since Vietnam – took place in Iran, a country that had been closely aligned with the United States since World War II. Iran's ruler, the Shah, who had been placed in power with CIA help in the 1950s, depended heavily on the United States for assistance in bringing his country into the modern world. An oil-rich economy allowed Iran to purchase the latest military and technological equipment from the United States and other western nations. Because of its location, Iran was considered to be a strategic asset to the US, which saw it as a buffer country between the Soviet Union and the Persian Gulf. In the early 1970s, Iran bought billions of dollar worth of US military equipment, including a fleet of C-130s and Boeing 707s in military configuration. Some of Iran's aircraft were later models than those in the US Air Force at the time. But while the Shah believed the influx of foreign technology was bringing his country into the Twentieth Century, Shiite Moslem religious leaders in the country declared the modernization effort to be the work of Satan. The Shah also faced unrest among the better-educated segment of his society, many of whom had been educated in the United States, who were upset because of the excesses of the Iranian secret police. With opposition to the government at several levels, Iran was ripe for revolution.

By the mid-1970s the Shah's health was failing, and the

Sam McGowan

opposition elements within the country took advantage of their leader's physical weakness to foment unrest. In January 1979, the Shah left Iran and as soon as he left, Iranians revolted against his regime. Two weeks after he left, the Shiite leader, Ayatollah Khomeini, who had been thrown out of Iraq and taken exile in Paris, returned to Iran aboard a chartered airliner to establish religious rule. At first, the revolution seemed to enjoy popular support but the Shiites soon took control. Some of their most loyal followers were young Iranian students who were themselves confused because of the unprecedented change in the youth cultures of the world, and who accepted the rigid positions of the Shiite Mullahs. On November 4, Shiite students took control of the United States Embassy in Tehran and placed all embassy personnel under their control. For more than a year, the Americans remained captives of the Iranian revolutionaries while the United States government was virtually powerless to act.

But even while the US government was seemingly doing nothing, the Joint Chiefs of Staff were planning a military rescue.[404] Six months after the seizure of the embassy, in April 1980, the world was shocked to learn that an attempted rescue by US military forces had turned into the most miserable of failures. Without ever reaching their objective in Tehran, the rescue force abandoned their mission in the Iranian desert and withdrew, leaving behind the burning remains of a USAF C-130 and a Navy helicopter and, even worse politically, the bodies of the crews. Operation *EAGLE CLAW* failed due to a combination of military politics and poor planning. The United States possessed the capability of such a mission in the Army's Special Forces and Air Force's special operations unit, but instead of seeking to guarantee the success of the mission, the Pentagon elected to make the rescue an all-service operation and include everyone.

The plan called for six Air Force C-130s to airlift an assault team from the Army's crack secret Delta Force to a point in the desert where they would link up with helicopters. The helicopters would fly the Delta Force troops to a point in the mountains; there they would switch to trucks for the journey into Tehran. Three special operations MC-130s would transport the troops while three EC-130s borrowed from an electronics warfare squadron were equipped with fuel bladders to refuel the helicopters. The MC-130s and EC-130s were crewed by personnel from the special operations squadrons at Hurlburt Field, Florida. The use of modified MC-130s[405] and EC-130s

---

[404] The USAF Chief of Staff was General Lew Allen, who had spent most of his career in space and science. His last operational assignment was during the Korean War when he flew B-29s.

[405] In 1977 the Air Force revised its aircraft designations. The former M designation, which had originally been used for missiles then was assigned to mine-

Anything, Anywhere, Anytime

instead of tactical airlift C-130s was justified because they had been equipped for aerial refueling and had the range to fly to the assembly point in the desert then return to a friendly air base. After an attack on the Embassy supported by AC-130 gunships, Delta Force would withdraw in trucks to a little-used airfield about an hour from Tehran with the captives. There they would link up with two C-141s, which would transport the entire force to a friendly country.

The rescue plan was lacking in vision due to the reliance of the Air Force portion on nothing but special operations forces with limited capabilities but the faulty link that finally doomed the mission was the helicopters.[406] Instead of using Air Force helicopters with the navigational and aerial refueling equipment necessary for long-range helicopter missions, US Navy mine-laying helicopters were substituted. The Pentagon reportedly was afraid the presence of USAF helicopters in the Middle East might tip off the Iranians that a rescue was underway. The Air Force helicopters allegedly were not equipped with folding rotor blades and could not be stored below decks on the aircraft carrier that would be needed to transport them to the launch point. If they were kept on deck, there was a possibility their presence would be detected by Soviet spy satellites and the Soviets would tip off the Iranian revolutionaries that a rescue effort was underway.[407] While the substitution of Navy helicopters may have been logical, the choice of pilots was not. The Air Force had a pool of experienced pilots with backgrounds in long-range night helicopter operations but the

---

laying aircraft, was changed to mean "multi-mission" and given mostly to special operations aircraft, including helicopters. The C-130E-(I)s were redesignated as MC-130Es.

[406] Early in the planning someone suggested using C-5s to fly Army helicopters into the same airfield where the C-141s were eventually planned to pick up the Delta Force team and the rescued hostages. A single C-5 could transport several smaller Army helicopters and a force of three could have probably carried the entire rescue force along with troops to defend the airfield. The plan was discounted by the officers from the special operations community as impractical, but the real reason was that had C-5s been used, there would have been no place for Air Force special operations forces, except for AC-130 gunships. After the mission failed, a new plan was developed which did, in fact, call for C-5s to fly into the abandoned airfield. Several crews were trained for night operations using night vision goggles. As it turned out, the hostages were released as a result of negotiations and the second rescue plan was never implemented.

[407] That the Air Force helicopter rotors did not fold is the excuse often given as the reason for the use of Navy helicopters. But the Air Force CH-53s were nearly identical to the Navy and Marine helicopters – except that they had been modified for aerial refueling. Another excuse given for not using Air Force helicopters and crews is that the losses during the *Mayaquez* incident had not been replaced. Critics assert that Navy helicopters were used as a means of making the operation a "joint-service" operation.

Joint Chiefs chose not to use them. At first, Navy pilots were assigned to the mission but their apparent lack of enthusiasm led to their replacement by Marines. Marine pilots in the 1970s were not trained for either long-range operations or for night flights in desert conditions but because there was no other Marine participation in the mission, USMC pilots were assigned to fly the Navy helicopters.

The C-130s arrived at the rendezvous site, *DESERT ONE*, without incident. The helicopters, on the other hand, met with numerous problems during their flight across the desert. First, the low-flying helicopters encountered a desert sandstorm that interfered with their navigation and caused problems with some of the engines. One pilot experienced a chip detector light that indicated a possible impending engine failure. Two of the eight helicopters eventually turned back, leaving only six to link up with the C-130s but one of those had developed a mechanical problem and was unable to fly the mission. Operational planning had called for a minimum of six helicopters for the mission. With the assault force down to five, the Pentagon ordered an abort. The mission had failed, but disaster lay only minutes away.

After the helicopters were refueled, the force prepared to depart. As one of the helicopters was air-taxiing in preparation for take-off, a team member who was giving directions to the pilot using electric wands – flashlights with yellow extensions – allowed it to drift too close to one of the EC-130s. A rotor-blade struck the C-130 fuselage causing the helicopter to go out of control and it came down on top of the airplane's cockpit. Both aircraft erupted in flames and although the troops, the radio operator and loadmasters escaped, the C-130 cockpit crew died in the resulting fire and explosion. Eight men died in the carnage; five C-130 crewmembers and three of the Marines on the helicopter. The rest of the force climbed aboard the remaining C-130s

Anything, Anywhere, Anytime

and departed the scene of disaster. When the public learned of the failed mission, President Jimmy Carter sank even lower in the eyes of his electorate then he already was. Eventually, the hostage crisis would play a major role in his defeat in the upcoming election. At the same time, the disaster at *DESERT ONE* was seen as an indication of the sorry state of the US armed forces in the wake of Vietnam.

The problems in the military were compounded because the career military personnel who had served in Vietnam were made to feel like second – or even third – class citizens. The civilian world looked down upon Vietnam veterans and members of the military in general. Those who had seen duty in Southeast Asia were seen by the population as potential weirdoes; men who could be capable of anything and who were subject to fly out of control at the slightest provocation. The psychiatric profession came up with a new term – PTSD for post-traumatic stress disorder – and soon all Vietnam veterans were seen by the public as suffering from it.[408] Serving or having served, in the military in the 1960s and 1970s was no honor.

There was one bright spot on the military horizon. While the active forces were losing their most experienced people in droves, the Reserves and Air National Guard were benefiting. Originally a sanctuary for students and others who were seeking to avoid active service in the sixties, the reserve components were becoming a more important feature of the American defense establishment as a whole. Experienced people were not leaving the military because they were disenchanted with the service in general but rather because they were disgusted with what the active duty military had become. Since both the Air Guard and Air Force Reserve were heavily slanted toward airlift, airlift squadrons turned away applicants with extensive airlift service, including combat service in Vietnam, because of a lack of slots.

At the same time that reserve units were attracting large numbers of former servicemen with extensive airlift service, their squadrons were receiving top-of-the-line equipment from the active forces. Prior to the 1960s, reserve units were given airplanes that had reached obsolescence. MAC, however, had begun a new phase in the late sixties as "associate" reserve units were established at its major bases. Reserve associate units at MAC bases flew the same airplanes as their active-duty counterparts in C-141 and C-5 wings on the bases at which they were co-located and with which they were associated. As the Air Force began reducing the number of active duty tactical airlift squadrons, reserve and guard units were given the older C-130As and

---

[408] The VA claims that as many as 30% of Vietnam veterans have suffered from PTSD at some point in their lifetimes. Vietnam veterans were often perceived as Looney-tunes who were prone to go off at the drop of a hat.

Bs, airplanes which, while they were technically approaching obsolescence because of their age, were little different from the Es and Hs in the active units.[409] Even though the active tactical airlift force had shrunk to three wings in the United States and one overseas, dozens of reserve squadrons were equipping with C-130s, and were airlift assets that could be counted on in the event of an emergency.[410]

After the transfer of the TAC C-130 squadrons to MAC, the strategic airlift squadrons adopted a more tactical role in addition to their deployment mission. As the transfer was underway, the MAC commander, General P.K. Carlton, who had spent his entire career in SAC bombers, began emphasizing that MAC was no longer an airline but was now a command with a combat mission. Signs began appearing on MAC C-141 and C-5 bases that read "Our mission is to fly and fight – and don't YOU forget it!" Within the C-141 squadrons, there was renewed emphasis on tactical training, not only in airdrop techniques but also on operations into forward fields. Previously, MAC airplanes had only operated into bases with MAC support facilities but the new emphasis included operations into airfields with limited facilities. Within the 437th Military Airlift Wing at Charleston, SC a special flight was created for support of special operations forces. (Ironically, as Special Operations Low Level – SOLL – qualifications were established for some C-141 crews, the same qualification was given to C-130 crews in squadrons where low-level tactical training had previously been standard for all combat-ready crews when they were part of TAC.)

There was a drawback to the new tactical emphasis in MAC. Women had been allowed into previously closed career fields as pilots, navigators, flight engineers and loadmasters but they were restricted by policy from combat flying. Consequently, female crewmembers in C-141 squadrons were not given tactical training and there was tacit understanding that should the country become involved in a war, the women would be shifted out of operational squadrons to duties in support flying. That women were even allowed to fly was a departure

---

[409] Up until the late 1960s, the military considered any airplane over ten years old to be obsolete. Once an airplane reached that age, a zero was added in front of the tail number. Many of the older C-130As had already reached obsolescence by 1965 and by 1968 some of the B-models had reached that mark.

[410] There was a downside to the reequipping of reserve units, and that was that the military began relying too much on them. Instead of considering the reserves as a standby force to supplement the active military in a major war, they came to be seen as merely an extension of the active duty forces, which resulted in their being assigned to perform missions reservists had not expected to be called on to perform when they enlisted for what they thought would be one weekend a month and two weeks active duty each year.

Anything, Anywhere, Anytime

from previous Air Force policy that every pilot was a potential combat pilot; a departure that had been forced upon the military in response to Congressional pressure prompted by feminist and civil rights groups.[411]

Yet, while the social changes in the military were here to stay, at least for an undetermined time, a new boost was in store for the military. Prompted in part by the fiasco in Iran, the American electorate rejected the Carter Administration in the 1980 election.[412] The new president, Ronald Reagan, was a firm believer in strong military forces. When Reagan came into office in January 1981, the former Roosevelt New Deal Democrat borrowed a page from 1939 and placed a new emphasis on military spending. The amiable president convinced key members of the Democratic Congress to support his military spending programs, which were designed not only to revitalize the military but also to boost a sagging economy. The "Reagan Years" were boom years in certain sections of the country, thanks largely to the flow of tax dollars into the national economy through the defense industry. And even though the emphasis of the Eighties was on high-tech equipment such as high performance fighters, electronic intelligence and the supersonic B-1 bomber, the generally low-tech airlift elements also got a shot in the arm.

Remembering Korea and the important role airlift had played in

---

[411] Women have been assigned to C-130 squadrons since the early 1990s but the US hasn't been involved in any conflicts with the intensity seen in World War II, Korea and Vietnam. No one really knows how they'll perform if exposed to intense combat.

[412] In a final insult to Carter, the Iranians released their hostages as soon as Reagan was sworn in.

Vietnam, military planners focused heavily on rapid deployment capabilities as a crucial element in future military operations. With the world still divided into two camps and with dozens of potential trouble spots scattered all around the globe, the military of the Reagan years was oriented toward meeting threats anywhere within a matter of hours instead of weeks. Because of the emphasis on rapid deployment forces, airlift was recognized as a major military responsibility. The importance of airlift and the lack of adequate resources to fill the country's military needs received special emphasis from the Pentagon, but there was disagreement over how best to accomplish it. A debate began within the military establishment and in Congress over the best means to alleviate the "airlift shortfall." While MAC was lobbying for a brand-new transport with both strategic range and short field capabilities, Boeing was trying to sell Congress on the idea of buying its huge 747 commercial transport for the Air Force.

Originally, Boeing had designed the 747 in a bid to win the contract that was ultimately awarded to Lockheed for the C-5A, but when the company lost the bid they decided to develop the airplane as a massive passenger transport for the airlines. While the 747 is an excellent airplane, like the militarized airliners of World War II and the 1950s, it lacks true military capabilities but the company had plans to adapt it as a military transport. Boeing's primary supporter was US Senator Henry Jackson of Washington State, where Boeing's headquarters were located in Seattle. Boeing tried to convince Congress that the 747 could become a military transport by simply adding forward cargo doors and beefed up floors to off-the-shelf commercial 747s. Lockheed and the Air Force stressed that the 747 was ill-suited for military use. Lockheed also pointed out that since it was going to be several years before a new-generation airlifter could be produced, the answer to the airlift problem was to replace the aging C-130 fleet with newer models and build more C-5s. The original C-5 order had been reduced; Lockheed proposed that the Air Force should return to the original plan and buy new airplanes incorporating all of the modifications that had been developed for the C-5As. Additional airlift capacity could be achieved by lengthening the fuselage of the existing C-141s and making other modifications – such as the addition of aerial refueling capabilities – to upgrade the Starlifter to B-model status.

Congress ultimately agreed with Lockheed; the Air Force contracted for continued production of the C-130H and for a new version of the C-5, the C-5B, which featured beefed-up wings and incorporated all of the fixes that had been developed to correct problems that had been found in the original C-5A. At the same time, MAC's C-141 fleet was upgraded to become C-141Bs and a proposed plan to re-wing the original C-5As was authorized. Additional airlift

Anything, Anywhere, Anytime

capabilities were gained as the Air Force began buying DC-10s from Douglas for use as tankers. Designated as the KC-10 Extender, the wide-bodied airplane could double as a transport while also providing fuel for C-5s and C-141s during deployments. SAC's KC-135s had long offered airlift capabilities because the fuel tanks were located only within the lower fuselage, leaving the upper floor available for cargo. The KC-10s could double as transports and tankers during long-range deployments.

As MAC received newer aircraft and its existing C-141 and C-5 fleet was modified, the command began developing new tactics to make itself into a command with true combat capabilities at all levels; not just within the C-130 squadrons. With new wings, the C-5 was once again capable of withstanding the prolonged flights at low altitudes that were necessary for tactical training so development of airdrop capabilities were resumed. Tactical training was given to both C-141 and C-5 crews; training that emphasized operations into airfields "as far forward as possible." Transport crews trained for night operations using night vision goggles; a mode of operation that proved very tricky to master. Tactical proficiency once again became primary for C-130 crews after a period when MAC's C-130 fleet had fallen into the airline role with the C-141s and C-5s. To allow survival in a high-threat environment, new equipment was added to new C-130s that were coming off the assembly lines. Decoy flare launchers became standard equipment, and crews were given training in dogfight techniques. Training operations conducted at Nellis AFB, Nevada indicated that the superior turning and maneuvering characteristics of the slower turboprops offered a significant advantage in the event a transport was attacked by fighters. *RED FLAG* combat training became a regular part of C-130 training, just as it already was for fighter pilots. Some C-130s were equipped with a special bubble on top of the fuselage to allow the loadmaster to scan for hostile aircraft and call out their maneuvers to the pilot in preparation for evasive action.

The failure of the Iranian rescue attempt prompted the Pentagon to place new emphasis on special operations. Special operations had long been part of the military but no real mission had been developed to fit the category. With the threat of hostage-takings throughout the world very real in the 1980s, the United States began developing a special force of highly trained military personnel who could go in fast and hit hard in a rescue effort.[413] To transport the special operations

---

[413] Veterans of the Air Force Special Operations Command and even the command's publicists claim that the failure of the Iranian rescue mission led to its establishment. In reality, the AFSOC, which was not established until 1990, eleven years after the disaster at *DESERT ONE*, came about after the hijacking of Trans

teams to their target and provide aerial firepower, the Pentagon decided to exploit the assets of the 1st Special Operations Wing at Hurlburt Field, Florida, which included MC-130s, AC-130 gunships and long-range helicopters. Eventually, a new special operations command would be created in the Air Force, but initially the mission fell under TAC. In the early 1980s, the mission transferred to MAC where the 2nd Air Division was established to control all Air Force special operations activities. Since 2nd Air Division did not include C-141s, the 41st MAS at Charleston AFB, South Carolina established a special flight for special operations activities.

Aircrews in the special operations units soon developed an air of superiority over their peers in conventional airlift squadrons – even though few of them had ever seen combat. MC-130 and AC-130 crews borrowed a slang term from Army aviation and began referring to conventional C-130s as "slicks" in a derogatory manner. The "special operations community" even went so far as to write their own version of history; a version that exaggerated the role of World War II air commando squadrons and US Army Rangers.[414] A successful Israeli operation to free hostages held on the airfield at Entebbe in Uganda was pointed to as an example of capabilities lacking in the US military; the equally successful *RED DRAGON/DRAGON ROUGE* operation in the

---

World Airlines Flight 847 after it took off from Cairo for a flight to Europe in 1985. Due to the inability of the US military to do anything about it, Congress authorized additional funding to develop a military capability to effect rescues of Americans held hostage in foreign countries. The US Special Operations Command came into being two years later in 1987.

[414] US Army Rangers were not involved with the air commando units in World War II at all.

Anything, Anywhere, Anytime

Congo in 1964 by TAC C-130 crews was ignored.[415] Such an attitude is not surprising – MAC historians simply ignored any US airlift operation that had not involved enough MATS participation to claim it as a MATS operation. "Special operators" were following MATS lead. It was no coincidence; Brigadier General Harry Aderholt, who had become the guru of special operations, had served on General William H. Tunner's staff in Europe in the 1950s. While Aderholt was quick to criticize airlifters, from whose ranks he had come, he did not hesitate to borrow Tunner's methodology of self-promotion to gain power and prestige for special operations.

In October 1983, MAC had its chance to prove what the command could do – and to learn that it still had a long way to go to become the real "combat command" it had been advertising itself as since the mid-1970s. The Air Force portion of Operation *URGENT FURY* was entirely a MAC operation. It was planned by the MAC staff, although resources were drawn in from all the services. The tiny island of Grenada in the southern Caribbean had fallen under the control of a communist-sympathetic government. With Cuban assistance, Grenada was building an airfield at one end of the island; an airfield with a runway long enough to accommodate high-performance military aircraft (although it could just as easily have handled large airline transports such as the 747.)

As the second southernmost island in the Caribbean, Grenada's military significance is questionable since it is over 1,500 miles from the US but the prospect of another Marxist government in the Western Hemisphere caused consternation in the Reagan White House. The airfield construction prompted the Reagan Administration to begin looking for an excuse to drive the Grenadian government out of power. American concern became even greater when rebels overthrew the current government and executed the prime minister. Grenada was the location for an American-run medical school. Because of quotas established in the United States under "affirmative action," many young Americans were denied admission to medical schools in the United States because they were of the wrong color and/or ethnicity. A school had been set up in the tropical setting of Grenada to accommodate such students. When Prime Minister Maurice Bishop's government was overthrown and he was subsequently executed, the White House felt that the lives of the American medical students were possibly endangered. To protect the students – at least that was the

---

[415] There's really no comparison between the two missions. The hostages in Stanleyville were held some distance from the airport while those at Entebbe were on the field. Stanleyville was a far more difficult operation. At Entebbe, all the Israelis had to do was land and capture the building where the hostages were being kept.

official reason given – the United States decided to invade the island.

In preparation for the invasion, MAC C-141s and C-5s began airlifting men and equipment to nearby Barbados. MC-130s and conventional C-130s were sent to Hunter Army Air Field outside Savannah, Georgia to pick up US Army Rangers who had been flown there from their base at Fort Lewis, Washington. Instead of following established troop carrier/tactical airlift doctrine of using lead crews in each squadron, MAC had adopted a policy that called for special operations MC-130s to lead formations of conventional C-130s. Prior to the assault on the airfield by the Rangers, special operations forces – US Navy SEALS and members of the Army's elite Delta Force – were to go ashore after being dropped from MC-130s.[416] A two-pronged assault on the island was planned. While the Rangers attacked and secured the nearly-completed airfield at Point Salines, Marines and other Rangers would land at other points on the island by helicopter. In the end, *URGENT FURY* was a success in that the island was eventually captured and the students were "rescued" before they fell into the hands of the Grenadians. But there were a lot of mistakes made along the way, including some major ones by airlifters.

Instead of a conventional airborne assault that would have overwhelmed the Cubans at Point Salines, the MAC planning staff instead opted for a small-scale operation that relied heavily on the new special operations forces. Two MC-130s were supposed to land a contingent of Rangers, whose job would be to help a Delta Force team that had landed earlier clear the runway and secure the airfield perimeter. Thirty minutes later, a third MC-130 and two conventional C-130s were to land with Ranger reinforcements. When the airfield was secure, C-141s would begin arriving with troops from the 82nd Airborne Division. The problems actually started the morning before the planned airborne assault when the Navy SEAL team that was supposed to go onto the island was lost. The four-man team and a boat were dropped from a C-130 and disappeared, evidently because they were too heavily laden with equipment and were pulled beneath the surface and drowned. Another SEAL team made a successful landing but they were unable to get their outboard motor started and drifted out to sea. A Delta Force team that arrived on the island during the night was unable to perform its assigned task of clearing the runway of construction vehicles so the C-130s could land. The Delta troops were

---

[416] The MC-130 was the C-130E-(I) with a new designation. The airplane had been developed to perform night insertions of agents into hostile territory then to resupply and finally retrieve them using the Fulton Recovery System. By the 1980s they were being used for missions that could have just as easily been performed by tactical airlifters; and would have been prior to the transfer of TAC's C-130s to MAC.

Anything, Anywhere, Anytime

supposed to hotwire the vehicles and drive them off the runway, but their presence was discovered and they were pinned down by fire from the Cuban construction battalion.

With the runway still completely blocked, the Air Mission Commander decided that the Rangers would have to be dropped instead of landed and the men struggled into their parachutes. As the first two MC-130s approached the island, the lead airplane experienced a failure of its AP-122 radar, an advanced system that had been developed as part of the Adverse Weather Airdrop System (AWADS), and of its inertial navigational equipment. The pilot aborted the drop because he didn't think he could find the drop zone and the two airplanes entered a holding pattern to await the arrival of the second element.[417] When the second element arrived, the first element fell in behind the third MC-130, which was carrying the headquarters company for the Ranger battalion, along with their equipment. The drop sequence had changed; now the troops who were supposed to land after the assault team had cleared the runway were going to be first to jump.

The second lead MC-130 came over the runway and dropped its troops. But as the second airplane which had been the original lead, came over the airfield, Cuban antiaircraft gunners opened fire on the formation. Once again the pilot aborted the drop; he turned out over the ocean and the other three C-130s followed. The forty Rangers from the headquarters company found themselves on the ground with only light weapons with which to defend themselves and no reinforcement. The pilot who aborted justified his actions by claiming he wanted to let the AC-130 gunships suppress the fire. Yet, in doing so, he placed the lives of the men on the ground in jeopardy. It was almost an hour before the other airplanes dropped their troops. Meanwhile, the lightly armed headquarters troops were fighting for their lives. Some of them had been hit while still hanging in their parachutes. Upon reaching the ground, they found themselves without the fire support teams who had been aboard the two MC-130s that were supposed to have been first to drop. The assault team was out orbiting over the ocean waiting for the gunships to silence the enemy guns while the men of the headquarters company were on the ground engaged in battle. It is no wonder the Ranger officers wanted to press charges of cowardice against the MC-130 pilot![418] Had it not been for the AC-130s to provide fire support, the Rangers would have been unlikely to have survived the battle.

---

[417] Really? Isn't that what navigators are far? The DZ was on a prominent landmark on an island!

[418] The Rangers' disgust and their threats of pressing charges against the lead pilot was reported by the news magazines.

Point Salines

After the rest of the Rangers jumped, they were able to relieve their comrades and secure the airfield. Once the runway was clear of obstacles, C-130s and C-141s began landing with troopers from the 82nd Airborne Division. A steady flow of transports continued throughout the day on October 25, 1983 as more 82nd personnel were brought in. Soon the Grenadians and Cubans fell back and began to surrender as they were overwhelmed in the face of sheer numbers and superior equipment. Nevertheless, it took several days for the Marines and paratroopers to secure the tiny island. Once the airfield was secured, a Ranger rescue force was able to make their way to the nearby True Blue Campus of the medical school. There they found the students unharmed but frightened because of the battle taking place nearby. Even though the first group of students was rescued, there were two other campuses that the Rangers were unaware of. It would be two days before all of the students were in American hands. As the students were located, they were brought to the airfield by helicopter and placed aboard C-141s and flown to Charleston.

The initial drop was not the only thing that was screwed up about the Grenada Invasion. Even before the invasion began, a team of Navy SEALs lost several members when they drowned after jumping into the water off the island because they were too heavily laden with equipment. The surviving SEALs were unable to complete their mission. A US Army Delta Force assault team ran into trouble when the helicopters that were bringing them in began receiving heavy fire from ZU-23 machineguns. One of the helicopters, from the super-secret Task Force 160 out of Fort Campbell, Kentucky, was shot down even before the team reached the vicinity of the prison they were attacking.

Anything, Anywhere, Anytime

As the elite Delta force team was rappelling from the helicopters, more fire raked the Blackhawk troop carriers. For several years, the Army denied that any helicopters were even lost in Grenada but eyewitnesses reported that as many as six out of the eight sent to attack the fort were shot down. The Delta Force attack was a failure. The fort was taken the next day by Marines.

Even though URGENT FURY was plagued by failure, the operation was a success because the Americans were rescued and the government of Grenada was restored. In the eyes of many of the students – especially the women – the paratroopers and Marines were heroes. With the successful invasion of Grenada and the rescue of the medical students, the US military was beginning to enjoy some measure of respect once more in the eyes of the American public. This respect in many ways insured the reelection of President Reagan.

Short C-23 Sherpa

During the Reagan years the US government engaged in a number of clandestine paramilitary operations along the lines of those that were initiated during the Kennedy Administration. When the Soviet Union sent troops to Afghanistan, the United States responded by providing supplies to the guerrillas who opposed the Marxist government. Long regarded as the toughest fighters in the world, the Afghans needed only to be supplied to eventually bring the Russians and their Afghani stooges to their knees. Just what role US airlift played in the war has yet to be fully revealed in detail, but there can be little doubt but that MAC transports were delivering cargo to bases within reach of the Afghani "freedom fighters." More than likely, airdrop missions were flown in support of the Afghan rebels, perhaps by civilian crews or maybe by special operations or even conventional C-130s. There are rumors that small twin-engine C-23 Sherpas flew supplies into close proximity to, if not into Afghanistan itself.[419]

---

[419] The C-23 is the military designation given to the Short 330 transport, which was originally developed for use as a commuter airliner. Due to the lack of a

Sam McGowan

While the American military role in the Afghan War still remains largely hidden, the whole world knows about the effort in Central America where US-backed rebels sought to drive the Nicaraguan Sandinistas from power. One of the most controversial political incidents of the 1980s involved the airlift of US-provided military supplies – including Stinger missiles – to Iran. Profits from the sale of parts for the country's fleet of US-built aircraft, which included several C-130s, and weapons were turned around and used to purchase supplies for the Contra rebels in an operation supervised by USAF Major General Richard Secord, who got his start in special operations in Laos, and USMC Lt. Col. Oliver North.[420] To preserve the clandestine nature of the resupply effort, arms and ammunition were delivered to the Contras in civilian transports flown by civilian crews. The operation was run by people with experience in clandestine operations during the Vietnam War.

The lid came off when a C-123 with a civilian crew was shot down by a missile over Nicaragua and the loadmaster/kicker, Eugene Hasenfus, was captured by the Sandinistas. Hasenfus, a former Marine, had worked for Air America in Southeast Asia as a cargo kicker. When his captors interrogated him, Hasenfus sang like a bird. The Hasenfus incident forced the US to use other means to get supplies to Central America. According to press reports at the time, USAF special operations MC-130s took over the supply role. This is not surprising since this is the mission the sophisticated airplanes were designed for. Eventually, as happened in Afghanistan, the rebel Contras wore down the Sandinista government to the point that legitimate elections were held. The communist-supported government was voted out of power and democracy returned to Nicaragua.

During the controversy over the Iran-Contra connection, both the Democrats on the Congressional committees investigating the episode and the media ignored the fact that such operations had long been a part of American foreign policy. It was ironic that while Democrats were chastising the Republican administration for "deceiving Congress," there were men present on both committees who were well aware that presidents from their own party, specifically Kennedy and Johnson, had done the same thing during their administrations. The whole issue of "plausible deniability" has long been a major factor in covert operations such as the sale of weapons to Iran and the resupply

---

small transport with short field capabilities, the Air Force purchased a number of the airplanes off the shelf with the intention of using them in Europe for aircraft parts runs between USAFE bases.

[420] Secord held considerable influence in Congress, particularly with Arizona Senator Barry Goldwater, and is largely responsible for Congressional action that increased the role of special operations forces.

missions to the Contras. Airlift, both overt and covert, has always been a part of such operations, both directly and indirectly.

In 1988, Vice President George Bush was elected President of the United States. The former Navy torpedo bomber pilot was the first American president since John Kennedy with combat experience and the first former military pilot to attain the office. As a combat veteran, President Bush appreciated the men and women in the military and, after long years of personal government service, he recognized that a strong military was essential to back up American foreign policy. During Christmas Week 1989, the Bush Administration launched another military operation in the western hemisphere. Operation *JUST CAUSE* was conceived to overthrow the Panamanian strong man, Manuel Noriega, and bring him to the United States to stand trial for drug trafficking. Justification for the invasion of Panama came when the Panamanian government declared war on the United States and began aggressive acts against American military personnel stationed in the Canal Zone. When a Marine lieutenant was killed by Panamanian soldiers and a Navy couple who witnessed the murder were abused, President Bush responded by launching an invasion of the country. *JUST CAUSE* relieved heavily on airlift just as had *URGENT FURY* and other similar operations of the past. The American military had learned from the mistakes in Grenada. Instead of being a small "surgical operation," the invasion involved a large-scale airborne assault on the Torrijos airfield. The airdrops involved both C-130s and C-141s, along with three special operations MC-130s, although just what role the *COMBAT TALONS* played is unclear since only three were involved in the whole operation. (The three MC-130s reportedly made a blacked-out landing on a Panamanian airfield in advance of the airdrop operation, possibly to bring in combat controllers to control the airdrops.) A second drop by twenty C-141s brought in reinforcements. When Manuel Noriega was finally located and forced to surrender, he was transported across the Gulf of Mexico to Miami aboard an MC-130.

Shortly after President Bush assumed the office, the entire world was stunned when the communist government in the Soviet Union fell out of favor and democracy was restored to Russia after nearly a century of communist rule. The Soviet Union was literally forced into bankruptcy as the country tried to outspend the United States during the Reagan years, while the war in Afghanistan took a terrible toll on the Soviet military after US-supplied shoulder-fired surface-to-air missiles began knocking down helicopters and low-flying aircraft. As a result, the Soviet government collapsed and the former Soviet Union was broken up. Suddenly, the United States found itself without an

Sam McGowan

enemy and the justification for the military procurement programs of the preceding fifty years was no longer existent. Members of Congress began talking about a "peace dividend' and how it could be used to alleviate the social ills of the nation. They did not seem to realize that the United States economy, indeed that of much of the world, had been fueled since the beginning of World War II by military spending and the so-called "peace dividend" did not exist.

Instead of an outbreak of world peace, as one enemy diminished to nonexistence another emerged. For more than a decade the countries of Iran and Iraq had been engaged in a prolonged conflict. The United States had, because of the country's enmity with Iran as a result of the hostage-taking in the 1970s, supported Iraq. Millions of dollars worth of military equipment had been sold to the Iraqi government of dictator Saddam Hussein. But while Hussein was at war with Iran, he also had his eyes on the oil reserves in neighboring Kuwait, which is one of the richest countries in the world and also offered something land-locked Iraq didn't have, access to the Persian Gulf. In August 1990, Hussein sent troops across the country's border with Kuwait and quickly occupied the oil fields.[421]

Whether or not Hussein intended to carry his advantage further and invade Saudi Arabia to the south of Kuwait will never be known but within hours of the occupation of Kuwait, President Bush set into motion the wheels of the first major military strategic airlift deployment in history. Had Iraq planned to invade Saudi Arabia, it is doubtful if the United States would have been able to stop it. As it was,

---

[421] It has been reported that Saddam notified the United States of his intentions to occupy a contested strip of land along the Iraq/Kuwaiti border, but then went further than expected and occupied the entire country. Saddam claimed Kuwait, which lies within the boundaries of the ancient Babylonian Empire. In the Twentieth Century the British made a deal with local sheiks and declared Kuwait to be an independent country. Iraq wanted to have more access to the Persian Gulf.

Anything, Anywhere, Anytime

it was almost six months from the time of the invasion before hostilities were opened against the Iraqi military. During the interim, the United States and several allied nations were able to pour thousands of troops, aircraft and ships into the region. A mountain of supplies was built-up in the Saudi desert. During the initial deployment, airlift was crucial. MAC's fleet of C-141s and C-5s was augmented by civilian airliners, just as the command and its predecessors had been in every conflict since World War II. Ironically, the crisis in the Gulf was the last gasp of a dying Pan American Airways, which was being forced out of business by the rising cost of jet fuel even as the company was proving to be a valuable national resource.

The first forces to deploy to the region were tactical fighter squadrons, which began deploying to Saudi Arabia on August 7, barely a week after the invasion and after several days of indecision in Washington. The fighters were refueled by SAC tankers while their support personnel and equipment were airlifted by MAC. Navy aircraft carriers were also on their way to stations within striking distance of Iraq. Within three days after the United States began reinforcing the Saudi government, a C-130 squadron from the 317th Tactical Airlift Wing at Pope AFB, NC arrived in the region for tactical airlift duty. The Pope C-130s brought troops of the 82nd Airborne Division to the desert with them and other 82nd personnel were arriving on MAC and contract transports. Other ground combat units in the United States were preparing to move to the region by ship but it would be three weeks or more before they could arrive. As the buildup continued, President Bush ordered the call-up of dozens of Air Force reserve units to active duty. Many were airlift units, both associate units at C-141 and C-5 bases and Air Force Reserve and Air National Guard C-130 units. Hundreds of reservist airlifters would see duty in the Gulf over the next several months.

MAC transports maintained an air bridge into the Gulf from the United States and Europe as more and more troops arrived in Saudi Arabia. The buildup was marred by the crash of a C-5 at Ramstein, Germany, which had become MAC's primary airlift base in Europe. While the airplane was an active duty transport assigned to the 60th Military Airlift Wing at Travis, the crew was made up of reservists from the 433rd MAW out of Kelly AFB, Texas. Thirteen of the seventeen crewmembers and passengers died in and as a result of the crash, which was determined to have been caused by an inadvertent thrust reverser deployment. The crash was the only airlift loss of the Gulf War and one of only about a dozen operational losses in MATS/MAC strategic airlift history (except for C-133s) and one of five C-5s that have been lost. The 433rd was a former reserve tactical airlift wing that had transitioned from C-130Bs to C-5s in 1985. The 433rd was the first reserve unit to equip with C-5s.

In January, almost six months after Iraq crossed the border into Kuwait, the Allied Coalition launched massive airstrikes against Iraqi targets. Fighters using sophisticated weapons struck key military installations such as radar sites, command centers and other targets in the vicinity of Baghdad. Other strikes were aimed at Iraqi military positions in the desert in Kuwait. For the first time in history, the American public witnessed airstrikes as they were happening, thanks to Cable News Network reporter Peter Arnett, who was in Baghdad when the war started. While AC-130 gunships, B-52s and fighters were maintaining a 24-hour campaign against Iraq, tactical airlifters in Saudi Arabia were doing what they had always done – flying supplies and equipment to theater forces throughout Saudi Arabia. This time, the C-130s were joined by C-141s once the huge military machine was in place in the Gulf region and the jet transports could be spared from deployment operations. *DESERT STORM* was a multinational effort with airlifters from several nations taking part. Most flew C-130s but some flew the Transvall C-160, a French and German design from the 1960s. Once again, American tactical airlifters worked with their British counterparts in an allied effort against a common enemy. Once again, the Americans and British were flying the same airplane, only this time it was the Lockheed workhorse Hercules instead of the Douglas C-47 or Dakota.

The war in the desert was different from Vietnam and Korea. The airlifters prepared for massive airdrop operations in support of the advancing ground forces once the ground war began but as the airstrikes continued it appeared more and more as if the ground war would not materialize. Iraq was holding its best troops in reserve well inside its borders while the defenders in Kuwait were made up for the most part of reservists who had little desire to be in the fight. The airstrikes were taking a tremendous toll on their morale. To further demoralize the Iraqi ground troops, the Air Force resurrected the BLU-82 15,000-pound bomb from Vietnam, only this time the mission was given to the special operations units whose role so far in the war had been limited. MC-130s dropped four of the huge weapons – allegedly the only ones still left in the US arsenal – on Iraqi positions where B-52 strikes were already taking a toll.

While the world waited for Coalition forces to launch an attack against the Iraqi lines, the military planners in the desert were preparing a secret end thrust to come in behind the lines from the west. Allied airmobile forces such as the 101st Division were shifted well to the west in preparation for an assault from behind the Iraqi rear. Airlift was crucial to the operation. Transports landed on long stretches of road to deliver fuel and other supplies to the deployed forces. When the long awaited ground assault finally came, it was brief.

Anything, Anywhere, Anytime

The Iraqi forces had already begun withdrawing from Kuwait and only a few Coalition forces ever engaged the enemy. Of the total Americans reported KIA in the short war, a large percentage lost their lives to "friendly fire." Fuel to support the advancing mechanized forces was airlifted into Kuwait aboard C-130s filled with fuel bladders. Refueling points were established along roadways in the desert and the C-130s linked up with the fuel trucks which were supporting the tanks and other vehicles.

Although the fighting came to an end when the last Iraqis left Kuwait, the airlifter's job was just beginning. There were thousands of refugees in the region and C-130s were put to work evacuating them from danger and airlifting supplies to refugee camps. A major crisis erupted when the Kurds, a tribe in northern Iraq who had helped the Coalition, were attacked by Saddam Hussein's forces after the fighting in Iraq came to an end. Many attempted to flee to Turkey but the Turkish government refused to let them in. Coalition C-130s and other transports airdropped supplies to Kurdish refugee camps in the mountains along the Turkish border.

The war in the Gulf was "won" by the Allied Coalition in the sense that the Iraqi forces withdrew from Kuwait. Although many politicians were in favor of continuing the war by invading Iraq, President George H.W. Bush declared a halt once Kuwait had been freed of the Iraqi occupying force. It was the first time since the Vietnam War that American military forces had met heavily armed enemy forces even though the action was very brief and Iraqi resistance was practically nonexistent. As for the airlifters, their exposure to enemy action was practically nil since the ground war only lasted for a few days and resupply was not crucial. However, even though the Allied Coalition won the Gulf War, there were consequences. The war provided the flame to light the fuse that would ultimately lead to direct confrontation between Islamic resistance movements and the United States.

At first, the US maintained a neutral state in the affairs of the Middle East even though there was a definite pro-Israel swing, but in 1973 it airlifted ammunition and other military supplies to Tel Aviv to replenish dwindling Israeli supplies during the Yom Kipper War. The US response infuriated much of the Arab world, and the Arab oil-producing countries announced an embargo on the sale of oil to the United States. The embargo created gasoline shortages and drove the price of petroleum products to record levels. When US "infidels" set foot in Saudi Arabia in 1990, their presence was seen as a travesty to the Islamic faithful since their faith had been born in the region; they considered the presence of foreign troops to be defiling the Islamic holy land. The continuing presence of US troops on Moslem holy ground after the Gulf War infuriated many Moslem religious leaders,

Sam McGowan

who were already upset at the role of Jewish-owned corporations in world trade. The World Trade Center in New York City became a focal point for their hostility because it was a center of commerce and closely connected to the American Jewish community. In February 1993, a truck bomb was set off in the parking garage in the basement. Five years later, coordinated attacks were carried out against US embassies in Africa and on October 12, 2000 suicide bombers detonated an explosive-laden raft adjacent to the USS *Cole*, a destroyer that was visiting the port at Aden in the Sudan. The attacks were a portent of things to come.

After the Gulf War concluded, the military took a look at itself. A number of problems were identified within the Air Force, particularly that some of the ideas of men like Hap Arnold, which led to the creation of the Strategic Air Command, and William H. Tunner, who advocated the consolidation of all military air transport, were ill-founded. Having fighters in one command, strategic bombers in another and tactical transports in still another led to numerous problems of command and coordination. Several high-ranking Air Force officers had long been concerned about the compartmentalization of the Air Force and the creation of numerous higher headquarters commands, each of which concentrated on its own turf.

In order to achieve a more streamlined service, the Department of the Air Force underwent a complete reorganization. Tactical Air Command, Strategic Air Command and the Military Airlift Command were all abolished and new commands were formed. The resources of Tactical Air Command and the bombers from SAC were combined into a new organization designated as the Air Combat Command, a move that was actually a return to the early days of World War II when the former Headquarters Air Force became the Air Force Combat Command. All combat functions would be the responsibility of ACC, including the tactical airlift mission. A new airlift organization was formed as the Air Mobility Command using the C-141 and C-5 wings from MAC and the air refueling wings that had previously been part of SAC. The new command would be responsible for logistical airlift and for refueling combat aircraft as well as its own transports. (After the Nickel Grass resupply mission of Israel, the Air Force had resumed aerial refueling training for C-5 crews and obtained funding to modify MAC's fleet of C-141s with refueling equipment. Special ops C-130s were also modified.) A few tankers went to ACC but most became part of the new command. However, with the exception of the 314th Tactical Airlift Wing at Little Rock, the C-130s became part of composite wings that included fighters or former SAC bombers.

The return of the C-130s to the successor to the command which

Anything, Anywhere, Anytime

had spawned them was hailed by many but opposed by the disciples of General Tunner, who had bought the singleness of purpose idea he had used throughout the 1950s in his attempts to elevate MATS to command status. Many C-130 crewmembers were not happy with the transfer. After almost two decades of enjoying the good life in MAC where the motto was "Anything, Anywhere, Anytime – for Per Diem", they were not thrilled at the prospect of once again being part of the combat element of the Air Force. The very thing that General William W. Momyer had feared would happen if all airlift resources were consolidated had occurred – the former TAC and PACAF tactical airlift units had lost their tactical orientation and attitude. To many post-Vietnam airlifters, "tactical" simply means airdrop.

That the C-130 squadrons were now part of composite wings that included fighter or bomber squadrons in addition to the tactical transports did not set well with many of the C-130 people. Having fighter and/or bomber crews on the same base with airlifters meant having to mingle in the on-base clubs as well as in the air around the bases. Complaints about "mixing" fighters with transports in traffic patterns were common – never mind that having fighters and transports flying off of the same airfields in wartime is routine. (There was a fighter wing of F-4s at Cam Ranh Bay as well as the 483rd TAW's C-7s and Det. 2, 834th Air Division's C-130s. In addition, C-123s and MAC transports were in the vicinity much of the time.) The C-130s would remain with the Air Combat Command for five years but in 1997 the single-manager airlift proponents won out and the tactical airlift squadrons transferred into the Air Mobility Command. However, there was still mixing of C-130s with other aircraft types. AMC merely activated airlift wings at Pope and Dyess, where the C-130 squadrons had been part of composite wings and the composite wing became a fighter wing at Pope and a bomber wing at Dyess.

The transfer of the tactical airlift units to AMC caused most of the units to lose their troop carrier lineage, at least at the wing level. The Pope wing was given the designation of the 43rd Bombardment Wing, a former SAC unit, while the Little Rock wing was redesignated as the 19th, which had also been a SAC unit. Both wings had fought in the Pacific during World War II but had never been associated with the air transport mission. The reason for the redesignation was that it was to preserve the lineage of historical units. Both of the two unit's predecessors had transferred to the Southwest Pacific in 1941 and 1942. The 19th had been active in SAC while the 43rd inactivated after the Korean War. The only former troop carrier wings still in existence were the 317th, which reactivated at Dyess; the 314th at Little Rock and the 374th in Japan. However, the 374th's former squadrons had all become associated with the 60th Airlift Wing at Travis. The 463rd reactivated at Little Rock as an airlift group; in 2008 it was inactivated when the 19th Airlift Group activated. However, the squadrons retained the identities of troop carrier squadrons. Lineages have become even more complicated by the activation of airlift groups as the operational unit within airlift wings. The original Army Air Corps groups included two or more squadrons to which maintenance personnel were assigned along with the aircrews. The modern group system establishes specialized groups within a wing. No doubt the Air Force will change its mind again in the future.[422]

Since 1990 and the Gulf War, the United States has been in a continual state of warfare; first with one country then another. In each case, the opposing country has been small with a military force incapable of standing up to US forces. After a series of small-scale conflicts with nations whose leaders were not acceptable to the US, the enemy became an enemy that cannot truly be defined – "global terrorism." In July 1992, several months before the US elections, President George H.W. Bush commenced humanitarian efforts in war-torn Bosnia, a country in the Balkans that had been formed when the Yugoslavian federation came apart as communism collapsed in Europe and the Soviet Union dissolved. The region has been characterized by ethnic strife since the Middle Ages when Muslim Turks advanced into the region around 1200 and practiced "conversion by sword" among the predominantly Christian population. Soviet domination of Eastern

---

[422] It already has. The three commands that deactivated after the Gulf War, SAC, TAC and MAC, have all been reactivated, SAC and TAC within the Air Combat Command and MAC within the Air Mobility Command.

Anything, Anywhere, Anytime

Europe put a temporary halt to the strife but as soon as the bounds of communism were cut, ethnic problems resurfaced and fighting broke out in early 1992. Aid initiated by President Bush came in the form of food and other humanitarian cargo delivered on July 3 when a C-130 landed at Sarejovo Airport, which had been cut off by Serbian forces from all ground contact. A French C-130 had landed the day before, commencing what would become a massive relief effort under the auspices of the United Nations. The airlift to Bosnia was well underway and was a factor in the US elections, although it was the declining economic situation in the United States prompted by the end of the Cold War that contributed the most to Arkansas Governor Bill Clinton's election. Although the Bosnian effort – Operation *PROVIDE PROMISE* – was a humanitarian effort, UN forces conducted airstrikes on Serbian positions to allow the airlift to continue. In December 1992, a new situation emerged when President Bush, who had become a lame-duck president, sent a US mission to Somalia, a mission including US Army soldiers and Marines. Air Force C-130s had become involved in the humanitarian airlift of supplies into Somalia from Kenya the previous August in Operation *PROVIDE RELIEF*, but the new mission escalated the relief effort to a major operation bordering on combat. The problem in Somalia was that rival warlords, who had gained control of the country after the former military government was defeated in a civil war, were controlling the delivery of humanitarian supplies. *PROVIDE RELIEF* was solely an airlift operation with Air Force C-130s delivering supplies and thus avoiding the rival forces. US Army Special Forces personnel accompanied the flights to provide security at the airfield and gather intelligence.(Stewart) The situation in Somalia became so desperate that on December 8, 1992 President Bush ordered a US military mission to the country as Operation *RESTORE HOPE*. President Bush's objectives in Somalia were merely to insure the delivery of humanitarian supplies to the people who needed them, and the presence of combat troops was to protect the distribution. The Clinton Administration elected to change the objectives to nation building, and set itself up for disaster.

The election of William Jefferson Clinton as the 42nd President of the United States in November 1992 once again ushered in change to the US military and it was not a positive one. Born in January 1946, the newly elected president was a member of the Vietnam Generation, the generation of young Americans who came of age during the Vietnam War and a generation that is largely divided because of their reaction to it. Like tens of thousands of other young men, Clinton chose to avoid military service by seeking a deferment for the military draft; a stand that did not make him popular with the men who either accepted their lot and were drafted or who enlisted or accepted commissions as officers. He was perhaps even less popular with the preceding generation who count military service as a patriotic duty. Yet even though his personal political views were akin to anti-military, he would preside over the beginnings of a period in US military history that has yet to end, a period of non-stop military action somewhere in the world.

During the Clinton administration, the United States enjoyed a period of strong economic growth, although the growth turned out to be due largely to a high-tech bubble that was bound to burst. The personal computer was becoming crucial to business as well as government, and companies and government agencies were purchasing millions of them and setting up internet technologies sections. Not only were they becoming essential to the business world and government, they were becoming popular with individuals as well. The Internet, a network of computers that had originally been setup for academics to communicate, developed rapidly and soon became available to the general public. The economic growth of the 1990s created hundreds of thousands of new job opportunities, including within the aviation industry, and thousands of highly trained military personnel who had originally planned to make a career of the military opted to take advantage of them. Vietnam Era airlifters were reaching retirement age as were the young men who had followed them in the 1970s. Airlift squadrons saw their experience level decline rapidly as the most experienced men opted for civilian life. Yet as the experience level was declining, the nation was entering a period of warfare that has yet to end.

President Clinton decided to use the young men now under his command to achieve political ends in the lawless country of Somalia. Although most of the conventional troops were withdrawn from Somalia a few months after Clinton assumed office, a number of special operations forces remained. They were given missions to capture various warlords who controlled the factions that kept the country in turmoil. The special operations forces in Somalia consisted primarily of aviation personnel from the Army's 160th Aviation Task Force, US Army Rangers, a detachment of Navy SEALs and Air Force combat controllers.[423] Disaster struck the force in October 1993, during a

---

[423] The combat control mission had changed drastically and the forces reorganized in the 1980s. Advances in navigational technology negated the need to have ground personnel to mark drop zones and the Air Force was considering doing away with the field. Maj. Gen. Robert Patterson, the commander of the newly activated Air Force Special Operations Command, suggested that combat controllers, tactical air control party personnel and pararescue technicians should be combined into what became "applied tactics." The combat control name remained. The new combat controllers were primarily equipped to accompany Army and Marine units into forward areas to control airstrikes using radios and to designate targets for laser-guided bombs with portable laser designators. Combat controllers

Anything, Anywhere, Anytime

mission to find and capture certain warlords who were in the city of Mogadishu. Two Blackhawk helicopters were shot down by rocket-propelled grenades and the troops that went in to attempt a rescue took heavy casualties. Nineteen were killed and some eighty wounded. Damage to US prestige was immeasurable, particularly photographs of the body of a US airman being dragged through the streets of the city.

In May 1994, US personnel were withdrawn from Somalia but the Bosnian airlift continued until 1996 when a ceasefire was negotiated and Serbian forces withdrew from their positions around the city of Sarajevo. Although the airlift was humanitarian in nature, for the aircrews it was like flying combat missions. Serbian soldiers frequently fired on the C-130s as they were on approach and during departure and the airport was the target of frequent shelling. Supplies were also delivered by parachute to other parts of the country, particularly in Eastern Bosnia where drops were made at night from high altitudes. Inexplicably, the Air Force had forgotten the lessons learned at the siege of An Loc and conventional CDS bundles and parachutes were used. Consequently, the bundles often landed thousands of feet from their intended destinations. Eventually, new airdrop methods were developed that allowed improved accuracy.

The situation in Bosnia had barely ended when a new situation developed in nearby Kosovo, a province of Yugoslavia that had declared itself to be an independent country in 1990. In 1996 an organization calling itself the Kosovo Liberation Army began attacking Yugoslavian police stations and other targets in Kosovo. Although the United States, at least officially, initially condemned the KLA, it eventually switched the national policy from condemnation to support. There are indications that the US supplied the KLA with arms delivered covertly by government contracted aviation companies. US support finally blossomed to full-scale military intervention. Clinton convinced the North Atlantic Treaty Organization, a 1950's era organization that had been created to defend against Soviet expansion in Europe, to intervene in the situation against Serbian Yugoslavia. US air forces were deployed to the region. Several squadrons of C-130s went along to provide logistical support. For a time it appeared that NATO troops – including American ground combat units – were going to enter the war. The Yugoslavian government finally decided it was unwilling to expose its citizens to what promised to be a very bloody conflict for all concerned and agreed to withdraw from Kosovo.

Clinton also inherited a situation in Iraq, where the UN had established "no-fly zones" patrolled primarily by US fighters and

---

were no longer involved with airlift operations but were primarily forward air controllers. The new mission made combat control even more glamorous than it already was.

airborne warning and control system (AWACS) aircraft. US and allied fighters patrolled the no-fly zones keeping watch for Iraqi aircraft that might be violating them. Tactical airlifters weren't directly involved in no-fly zone operations but they provided logistical support for the fighter squadrons.

With multiple military missions deployed in southern Europe and the Middle East, a shrunken US military was heavily taxed. Part of the burden was shared by reserve components, which sent squadrons or individual crews on overseas deployments. With a generally booming American economy, employment opportunities in the civilian sector were appealing, particularly in the airline industry, which had seen unprecedented growth by low-cost carriers and created a huge demand for pilots and mechanics. The policies of the Clinton Administration toward the military were largely unpopular with the young officers and enlisted men and they began leaving the service in droves. Consequently, the experience level in Air Force squadrons shrank to the lowest levels seen since the opening days of World War II. Sophisticated military equipment and aircraft were operated by young men – and women – with limited experience. Although the general public was not fully aware of the change, the Clinton Administration began placing its major emphasis on a new perceived threat of "international terrorism."

In 1998 at the graduation speech for the members of the graduating class of the US Naval Academy, at which the author was present, Clinton emphasized that future conflicts would be with terrorists. He stated that there was a world-wide network of terrorists at work and the United States was gearing up to fight them. It was not really a new threat; terrorist organizations have existed since the beginning of the Twentieth Century, particularly in the Middle East where European Jews had begun establishing communities in territory that belonged by treaty to local Palestinians.

In 1936, Palestinians revolted against the British in protest of the immigration of large numbers of Jews to the region from Germany and other European nations. The revolt lasted until 1939 when the outbreak of World War II and the basing of Allied troops in the region tempered Arab attitudes for a time. However, terrorism by Zionists increased during the war. Even though many Jews were enlisting in the British military services, some were living a double-life in the Zionist underground. Manachem Began, the leader of the Zionist paramilitary organization, the Irgun, would become prime minister of Israel in 1977. The influx of Jews into their ancestral land in Palestine during the aftermath of World War II led to an escalation of terrorist acts against the British troops and government personnel responsible for maintaining order in the region under a mandate given in 1917 by the Balfour Declaration and the subsequent Mandate for Palestine.

Anything, Anywhere, Anytime

Zionist terrorism increased to the point that the British decided to withdraw from the region, at which point the former terrorists proclaimed the Zionist State of Israel.

Almost immediately, the Arab inhabitants of the region began organizing to resist what they called the "Zionist occupation" of the land that had been inhabited by their nomadic ancestors for centuries.[424] The situation escalated when the Israelis occupied areas that had previously been designated as Palestinian territory by the mandate that recognized Israel as a nation in 1948. Immediately after Zionist leaders declared Israel to be a nation, armies from the surrounding nations attacked. The war lasted for fifteen months, until each of the attacking nations made its own armistice agreement with the Zionist State. However, there would be periodic flare ups that sometimes became outright war for the next thirty years. During this period, many Americans sided with Israel, thanks in large measure to fundamentalist Christian beliefs that Jews are God's chosen people. Yet, at the same time most senior military officers and many politicians were more inclined to support the Arab nations, at least in part to prevent them from turning toward the Soviet Union.

In 1956, Israel invaded the Suez region after Egyptian President Gamel Nassar declared that Egypt was nationalizing the Suez Canal, a canal connecting the Mediterranean with the Red Sea. Britain and France supported Israel, but the United States supported the rights of the Arab nations and put pressure on its allies to withdraw from the region. The crisis finally ended when Britain succumbed to US financial pressure. For two decades, the United States maintained a position of neutrality toward the conflict between the new nation of Israel and its neighboring states. Israel managed to procure some surplus World War II military aircraft by using backdoor channels but depended on France and the UK for most of its military equipment. Throughout the Truman, Eisenhower and Kennedy administrations, US aid to Israel came primarily in the form of low cost loans for the purchase of food and other humanitarian commodities. After Lyndon Johnson became president, the US switched to a pronounced pro-Israel position after almost twenty years of impartiality, particularly after the Six-Day War. However, even though Johnson opened the door for the sale of military equipment to Israel, the US continued to sell military equipment to Arab nations.

---

[424] Roman troops practically destroyed the Jews in the First Century and only one sect, the Pharisees, survived but they were dispersed mostly throughout Europe. Jewish Christians also survived because they had not been part of the rebellion that precipitated Rome's actions. Arabs migrated into the former land of Israel during the Middle Ages and their descendants came to be known as Palestinians.

July 1995, saw the delivery of the first operational McDonnell-Douglas C-17 Globemaster III transport to AMC's 17th Airlift Squadron at Charleston AFB, SC. The outgrowth of an Air Force plan to develop a replacement for the venerable C-130 stemming from the 1960s, the C-17 came about as a result of Military Airlift Command lobbying for a long-distance battlefield delivery capability. MAC had pressed for such an airplane throughout the 1980s. Originally, the only new airlifter proposed by the Air Force was a jet transport capable of landing on short, unimproved runways to replace the C-123 and C-130. Boeing and McDonnell-Douglas each produced prototypes as the YC-14 and YC-15. Boeing's YC-14 was a twin-engine transport while McDonnell-Douglas' YC-15 was four-engine. The end of the Vietnam War and subsequent transfer of TAC's tactical airlift squadrons killed the tactical transport program. However, MAC saw an opportunity to achieve the battlefield delivery capability that MATS leaders had advocated in the 1950s and started pressing for the development of a new transport capable of flying across the Atlantic and landing on an unpaved runway. McDonnell-Douglas decided to resurrect the YC-15 program but to redesign the airplane to turn it into a long-range transport. Boeing submitted a design based on its YC-14 while Lockheed submitted two proposals, one based on the C-5 and another based on the C-141, but with a larger fuselage.

One of the Army's requirements was for an airplane that could carry its larger rolling stock, including the new M-1 Abrams tank, across the Atlantic. MAC wanted tactical capabilities, including the ability to arrive over an airfield at 10,000 feet, then descend and land within two minutes. The new transport also had to be able to land on unimproved runways. After the 1973 airlift to Israel, MAC modified its C-141s to allow them to be refueled in the air. Its C-5As were produced with aerial refueling capabilities from the factory. The C-17 would be equipped for aerial refueling. MAC also used the short field takeoff and landing performance of the new transport, which was supposed to be equal to that of a C-130, as a selling point.[425] Another point was that new technology eliminated the need for a flight engineer – navigators had already been eliminated by Inertial Navigation Units on C-141 and C-5 crews – so the C-17 could be flown by a two-man crew of two pilots. A loadmaster was added to the flight crew to take care of cargo handling and perform scanner duties.

---

[425] In reality, although landing requirements for C-130s was established at 2,500 feet in Southeast Asia, actual landing distance was only 2,000. An additional 500 feet was added as a safety margin. C-130s routinely operated into 2,500 foot runways with 30,000 pound payloads. C-17s are limited to 3,000-foot runways.

Anything, Anywhere, Anytime

C-17

Although the idea of flying a large piece of military equipment such as a tank from the United States and landing on an overseas battlefield in order to affect the outcome of a battle is utter nonsense, Congress bought the concept and authorized the purchase of the new four-engine jet transport as a replacement for MAC's C-141s, which were reaching the end of their service life due to structural fatigue. The C-17 program soon ran into setbacks. The wings failed to pass structural tests. Cost overruns plagued the program while the actual airplane failed to live up to expectations. Takeoff performance was so poor that the airplanes were unable to take off with a full load of cargo and enough fuel to cross the Atlantic. In fact, the airplane failed to meet Air Force requirements. But even though it did not live up to its supporters' claims, the C-141s it was expected to replace were worn out and no other option was available so production continued. The first airplanes were delivered to the 437th Airlift Wing at Charleston and additional aircraft were put on order. The Secretary of the Air Force declared that the airplane's problems had been resolved.

During the debate over the wisdom of buying more C-17s or switching to production aircraft, the future of the C-130 also came into question. A product of the Korean War, C-130s were still in production after more than forty years of service. Active duty airlift squadrons at Pope AFB, NC were equipped with C-130Es that had been delivered thirty years previously. The Army made it clear that it wanted a new generation transport, not more C-130s. The special operations community and the Marine Corps were pushing for a tilt-wing STOL aircraft combining the capabilities of a helicopter with those of a turboprop airplane. Bell Helicopters and Boeing joined forces to develop a complex aircraft designated as the V-22 Osprey as a replacement for the heavy-lift helicopters that had come into service during the Vietnam War. The V-22 incorporates two large rotors that can be tilted ninety degrees to allow the aircraft to take off and land vertically, then to cruise like an airplane. Plagued by design problems that led to the loss of several during test and training flights, the V-22 program has managed to survive for three decades. The first flight was in 1989 but it wasn't until 2001 that Marine Corps crew training began. It took another six years before they were declared operational. The Air Force didn't receive its first aircraft until 2006. It wasn't until 2009 that they were deployed to squadrons in the Special Operations Command.

V-22

Lockheed Aircraft, which designed the C-130 during the Korean War and has been producing them ever since, offered a simple plan to replace their transports, which by the 1990s had proven to be the most reliable and versatile airplane ever developed – replace them with an advanced version of a tried and true airplane! Lockheed had offered just such a version to the Air Force in 1966, a new version of the C-130 – which had been designed to be a medium-range tactical transport – that incorporated lessons learned after several years of operations in Southeast Asia. The C-130J would allow the use of much shorter runways than the 2,500 feet that had been adopted as the standard in Southeast Asia, and feature improved performance. While the new version offered substantially improved performance, it also would come at a much higher cost than the existing E and H models so the Air Force elected to purchase H-models instead. Some of the new H

Anything, Anywhere, Anytime

models went directly to Reserve and Air Guard units to replace older A and B-models that were being permanently retired. Ironically, the older E-models that were delivered in the mid-1960s remained in active duty squadrons. Aircrews flew airplanes that were older than they were! This would continue to be the norm for years to come even though the C-130 had been designed at a time when an airplane was considered obsolete once it reached the ten-year mark in its lifespan.

Even though the Air Force turned the C-130J down in the 1960s, Lockheed kept the idea simmering on their back-burner. Over the next three decades, Lockheed engineers incorporated new technology into the design as it became available. By the 1990s, the C-130J had evolved into a truly high-performance airplane capable of taking off from short fields with a full payload, then climbing to fuel-saving upper-level altitudes and cruising at higher speeds. Yet, in spite of the C-130J's capabilities, neither the Air Force or Army wanted it. Both services were convinced that the C-130 had had its day and wanted an entirely new design. Retired Air Force tactical airlifters who had gone to work for Boeing and McDonnell-Douglas were also pushing for a new design to be produced by their employer. America's long-term British allies felt otherwise, and the Royal Air Force began purchasing C-130Js for its air transport squadrons in 1998. Finally, a few J-models were purchased for Air National Guard and Air Force Reserve units, including the Air Weather Service wing at Keesler AFB, Mississippi which saw the J-model's improved fuel consumption as a major plus for their long-range weather missions. The Weather Service airplanes were modified to include pylon tanks under the wings to give them extended range since they often operate at lower altitudes than airlift airplanes on long flights.

The Marine Corps began replacing its older KC-130s with C-130Js but the active duty Air Force wanted no part of it. The main opposition to the new J-model was that Lockheed had designed it to be flown by a two-man crew, which had become the standard for transport aircraft. Engineers and former engineers griped that the removal of the engineer would lead to accidents – even though six-engine B-47s and eight-engine B-52s had never had an engineer – while navigators were upset because they were being replaced by electronic navigational computers. It wasn't until 2009 that the Air Force – finally – began buying C-130Js to replace the aging C-130Es in the active duty squadrons. By that time the US had fought a war in Iraq and was engaged in another in Afghanistan where the C-130 had proven crucial. Although it took some time before the Air Force would allow them in Iraq, USAF Reserve C-130Js quickly proved that they were light-years beyond the H-models.

Sam McGowan

WC-130J – The weather version of the J-model has pylon tanks. (Author)

Yet even while the military was struggling with aircraft development problems for the combat airlift mission in the 1990s, the military itself was having major problems. President Clinton was hugely unpopular with the soldiers, sailors and airmen who served under him as commander-in-chief because of his status as a Vietnam Era draft-evader. His policies as the CIC added to his unpopularity. His Administration generally looked on the military as a necessary evil, but also saw it as a means of achieving political goals, particularly in the area of foreign policy. He involved US military forces in one conflict after another even though the size of the military was declining. Experience levels dropped as the airmen and officers who had come into the service in the 1970s reached retirement age.

In November 2000, Texas Governor George W. Bush was elected president in a controversial election. His opponent, Vice-President Al Gore actually received more votes in the meaningless national vote and the Electoral College came down to one state, Florida, where the results favored Bush by only a small margin. A recount still had Bush ahead. The final outcome of the election wasn't decided until December when the Supreme Court issued a ruling that one recount of votes in Florida was enough. The new president not only inherited an economy in decline, he also inherited a turbulent world situation. The Gulf War had ended in 1991 when his father halted Coalition Forces after Iraq abandoned Kuwait. A lot of Americans, particular former political progressives who had adopted conservative positions on international policy to become "neoconservatives," believed that the senior George Bush had ended the war too soon. They believed that Coalition Forces should have prosecuted the war until Saddam

Anything, Anywhere, Anytime

Hussein, the Iraqi dictator, was removed from office. Even before the new president took office, some of his staff was making plans to remove Hussein from office and establish a democratic government in Iraq.

The Bush Administrated inherited a new set of problems. The aftermath of the Gulf War led to rising tension in the Middle East and Central Asia in countries ruled by governments with strong ties to Islamic traditions. Many Moslems were incensed that American and European troops had intervened in a situation that they believed should have been handled without Western intervention. When the war ended, they were unhappy that infidels were still in the region.

There was also the threat of attack by so-called terrorists, particularly a mythical group called Al Qaeda, who was believed to have been responsible for the bombing of the USS *Cole* and the attack on the US Embassy in Kenya. Al Qaeda was alleged to be the name of a group of devout Muslims, mostly from Saudi Arabia, who had fought against the Soviets in Afghanistan then had remained in mountain camps where they trained young men and women to carry out suicide attacks in the name of Allah. Although the name has become a household word in the Western World, many intelligence specialists doubted if such an organization even existed. Al Qaeda was supposed to have connections to the Taliban, a group of devout Muslim clerics who believed in rule by rigid interpretation of the principles of the Koran. Taliban clerics had moved into Afghanistan after the Soviet defeat and established strict religious rule. Prominent Americans, including First Lady Laura Bush, began criticizing the Taliban for its strict adherence to Islamic law, particularly when it was applied to women and girls.

There was widespread fear that the training camps in the mountains of Afghanistan were being used to train terrorists who would stage terrorist attacks in the United States. Americans were calling for missile attacks on the camps, which were located in mountain valleys where they were practically impervious to the cruise missiles which had become a part of American reactions to terrorism. Volumes have been written linking Al Qaeda and the Taliban but the evidence is circumstantial. The name Al Qaeda, which means "the base," was rarely used by the Arabs who had set up camp in Afghanistan. Although the term was being used widely by the Western press, Osama Bin Laden never used the word in public until after 9/11.

September 11, 2001 became a red-letter day in history when four US airliners were hijacked by men reported to be of Middle Eastern origin and flown into the twin towers of the World Trade Center. The resulting fires completely destroyed the buildings and claimed just under 3,000 lives, including the passengers and crewmembers on the airplanes and people who had been working or visiting in the towers at the time of the attacks. One of the attacks and the resulting fires and collapse of the buildings was caught on camera and televised for all the world to see. Another airplane flew into the Pentagon and another that was on the way to Washington crashed in a mine in Pennsylvania. Although all of the attackers were killed in the attack, the new administration of George W. Bush connected the attacks to the shadowy organization known as Al Qaeda. Leadership of the organization was attributed to Osama Bin Laden, a wealthy Saudi businessman and devout Muslim who had gone to Afghanistan to fight against the Soviets in the 1980s. The Bush Administration announced that it was commencing a "war on terror" that commenced with a campaign against the Taliban, a religious council that "governed" Afghanistan, a remote, mountainous country in Central Asia that was believed to serve as a training ground for terrorists.

Initially, the Bush Administration made no overt moves toward Afghanistan. It appeared that the White House was taking a hard look at the events of 9/11 and seeking to determine who was responsible for them rather than taking immediate military action. The White House issued an ultimatum to the Taliban clerics to turn Osama Bin Laden over to the US so he could be tried for the 9/11 attacks. Although the Taliban leaders wished Bin Laden and his Arab followers would leave Afghanistan, local custom dictated that if a man seeks sanctuary, it is to be be given and he may remain as long as he wishes. The Taliban responded that they would try Bin Laden in Afghanistan if the US would provide evidence against him, to which the US refused. On October 7, less than a month since the attack on the World Trade Towers, the US launched Operation *ENDURING FREEDOM* and thus began the War on Terror.

The Afghan campaign was principally an air war, combined with the use of CIA operatives armed with millions in US funds to buy off the various warlords who actually controlled the country. Military participation included US Special Forces and Air Force combat controllers, whose primary mission was to use laser designators to pinpoint targets for bombs to guide on.[426] US-led forces quickly took control of most of the country and installed their own leaders. Although the Taliban was driven from power, devout Afghanis rebelled against the new regime and the US and began a new guerrilla war that rapidly increased in intensity and continues to this day. In March 2003, US and British troops invaded Iraq under the pretense of looking for "weapons of mass destruction" that were never found. The invading forces rolled across the border from Kuwait and headed

---

[426] The combat control mission had changed in the 1980s due to the proliferation of new generation navigational and airdrop equipment. The field was combined with the former tactical air control technician and pararescue fields.

Anything, Anywhere, Anytime

toward Baghdad but instead of the easy victory that had been forecast, they met stiff resistance from the Iraqi military. After the conventional Iraqi forces collapsed, the conflict turned into a guerrilla war.

From the end of the Vietnam War in 1975 to the invasion of Iraq in 2003 US Air Force airlifters had seen only limited combat in Grenada and Panama but the lineal descendants of the World War II troop carriers suddenly found themselves again in harm's way. In spite of strong resistance, the US and British forces were bound to eventually prevail over the Iraqi military, but then the conflict turned into a prolonged guerrilla war that kept US and British forces in constant danger. The inability of US forces to control the countryside led to a heavy dependence on airlift to maintain the supply lines from bases in Kuwait to the Iraqi interior. Airlift is also extremely important in Afghanistan, perhaps even more so than in Iraq. A remote, completely landlocked country characterized by rugged mountainous terrain, the only land route into the country is through the Khyber Pass, a high mountain pass that is blocked each winter by heavy snowfall. With no seaports in the vicinity of the country, the closest airport capable of handling large transports is at Peshawar, Pakistan. High elevations make helicopter operations difficult so the Army came to depend on airdrops by Air Force C-130s and C-17s to supply ground teams in the field.

Although airdrops in both Afghanistan and Iraq are common, they seem to be more for convenience than for military necessity since the conflicts in both countries are basically counterinsurgency operations. In March 2003, a formation of C-17s took off from Aviano AB, Italy with 1,000 paratroopers from the 173rd Airborne Brigade and dropped them onto an airfield at Bashur, in northern Iraq. Although the operation was hailed in the media as having been a military necessity, in reality the drop was onto an airfield in Kurdish northern Iraq and the troops could just as easily have been landed. What is even worse is that the C-17 crewmembers were awarded Distinguished Flying Crosses for a mission that was actually quite routine. The mission was only noteworthy in that the formation included Air Force reservists who had been called to active duty specifically for the mission – which had been planned weeks in advance – and the C-17s were sent to Europe from Stateside bases for what was essentially a media event.

If the US operations in Afghanistan and Iraq have accomplished anything, it is that they have demonstrated the need for tactical air transportation – specifically for more C-130s. After years of waffling, the Air Force finally began purchasing the latest version of the proven C-130, the C-130J, to replace the aging C-130Es and Hs that equip the active duty airlift squadrons. Opposition to the new model was widespread in the active duty Air Force, particularly among flight

Sam McGowan

engineers and navigators whose jobs were eliminated on the highly-automated C-130J. After the C-130J entered service with reserve units, it was several years before the Air Force incorporated them into overseas operations in Iraq. But once the C-130Js entered operations, their superior performance quickly demonstrated that they were far more capable than previous models. Hot desert temperatures severely restricted payloads on the older E and H-models but the more powerful power plants on the J allowed operations with considerably larger loads from high altitude airfields in temperatures that curtailed operations by older models.

The passing of seven decades has seen increasing use of technology in the US military, yet at the same time the basic mission has not changed. A high-tech military may devote billions of dollars to the development of remotely piloted aircraft equipped with sophisticated air-to-ground missiles designed for pinpoint accuracy, but they are of little use in attaining and maintaining air superiority in a war with another industrialized nation. Similarly, the air transport mission of 2014 is the same as that of 1942 – to move men and equipment into position to wage ground or air warfare and to keep them supplied with the material to do so, no matter where it might be.

The most heroic existing transport in USAAF and USAF history, C-130E 62-1787 was shot up over An Loc in April 1972 and the flight engineer was killed while most of the crewmembers were wounded. The pilot and one loadmaster received the Air Force Cross and the other crewmembers the Silver Star for their actions that day. The airplane was discovered to be in the inventory of the Arkansas Air Guard. Guard members proposed that it be sent to the US Air Force Museum at the end of its career. It was presented to the Museum in August 2010.

Anything, Anywhere, Anytime

Sam McGowan

Works Cited

(n.d.). *People Magazine* .
(1966). *The Airlifter* .
54th TCW Historians. *Moresby to Manila.*
(1945). *62nd TCS Mission Report.*
Aerial Delivery and Rigger History. (n.d.). Retrieved March 7, 2013, from http://www.qmfound.com/riggers.htm#World War II
Alternatt, M. R. (1945). *Aerial Delivery of Supplies.* Retrieved March 8, 2013, from http://www.qmmuseum.lee.army.mil/WWII/aerial_supplies.htm
Anderson, C. R. (1969). (S. McGowan, Interviewer)
Arnold, H. H. (1944, August). Aerial Invasion of Burma. *National Geographic* .
Berger, C. (1977). *The United States Air Force in Southeat Asia, 1961-1975.* Office of Air Force History.
Blanton, W. (1997). *Mill Hill Pilot.*
Bowers, R. (1986). *TACTICAL AIRLIFT, The United States Air Force in Southeast Asia.* Office of Air Force History.
Boyington, G. (1977). *Baa Baa Black Sheep.* Bantam.
Bradford, C. W. (1943). (W. Edmonds, Interviewer)
Brereton, L. H. (1946). *The Brereton Diaries.* New York, NY: William Morrow.
Butterfield, J. (1985). Personal Letter.
Caidin, M. (1963). *The Long Arm of America.* E.P. Dutton.
Copp, D. (2002). *Marshall's Airman.* Washington, DC: Air Force Office of History and Museums Program.
Craven & Cate. (1956). *The United States Army Air Forces in World War II.* Office of Air Force History.
Dabney, J. (1979). *Herk, Hero of the Skies.* Atlanta : Lighthouse Books.
Dengler, D. (1997). *Escape From Laos.* Presidio.
Edmonds, W. (1943). *Notes from Bradford Interview.* San Antonio, Texas.
Edmonds, W. *They Fought With What They Had.* Office of Air Force History (reprint).
Fall, B. *Hell in a Very Small Place.*
Ford, E. (2010). *My New Guinea Diary.*
Glasgow, W. (1965). *Operations Dragon Rouge and Dragon Noire.* Retrieved from United States Army Chief of Military History: http://www.history.army.mil/documents/glasgow/glas-fm.htm
Gropman, A. L. (1979). *Airpower and the Airlift Evacuation of Kham Duc.* Maxwell AFB, Alabama: Air Power Research Institute, Air University.
Gunn, N. *Pappy Gunn.* Author House.
Hansen, R. E. (1982). Flight of the Blind Bat. *Air University Review* .
Hoisington, R. (1988). Personal Communication.
Hospelhorn, C. W. (n.d.). *Quartermaster Aerial Supply.* Retrieved from http://www.qmfound.com/aerial_korea.htm
Investigators, A. (1963). *C-130 Defueling Fire at Naha AB, Okinawa.* Accident Report.

Anything, Anywhere, Anytime

Kenneth Conboy and Jim Morrison. (2002). *The CIA's Secret War in Tibet*. University Press of Kansas.
Kenney, G. C. *General Kenney Reports*.
Kenney, G. C. *The Saga of Pappy Gunn*.
Leary, W. (2000). Anything, Anywhere, Anytime: Combat Cargo in the Korean War. *Air Force History and Museums Program* .
Maurer, M. (1961). *Air Force Combat Units of World War II*. Washington, DC: US Government Printing Office.
McGowan, S. (1988). *The C-130 Hercules, Tactical Airlift Missions, 1956-1975*. TAB/Aero.
McLaughlin, B. (1968). Keeping An Outpost Alive. *Air University Review* .
Miller, C. E. (1988). *Airlift Doctrine*. Air University Press.
Miller, R. G. (2000). *To Save A City*. College Station, TX: Texas A&M University Press.
Mills, B. (2005). (S. McGowan, Interviewer)
Nalty, B. C. (1986). *Air Power and the Fight For Khe Sanh*. Office of Air Force History.
Porter, M. F. (1970). *Commando Vault*. US Air Force.
Prados, J. (2000). *The Blood Road*. Wiley.
Quartermaster Journal. (1944). Retrieved March 8, 2013, from http://www.qmfound.com/burma.htm
Reed, D. (1966). *111 Days in Stanleyville (Paperback - Save the Hostages)*. Colllins, Readers Digest.
Reed, D. (1966). *Save The Hostages! (Originally 111 Days in Stanleyville)*. Bantam Books.
Robbins, C. (1979). *Air America*. Putnam.
Scott, R. L. *God Is My Copilot*.
Secord, M. (1986). (S. McGowan, Interviewer)
Stewart, D. R. (n.d.). *U.S. Army in Somalia 1992-1994*. Retrieved March 20, 2013, from http://www.history.army.mil/brochures/Somalia/Somalia.htm
Strobaugh, D. (1964). *Mission Report on Congo Operation*.
Strobaugh, D. (1968). Personal Diary.
Thompson, A. G. *The Greatest Airlift - The Story of Combat Cargo*. Tokyo.
Thompson, A. G. *The Greatest Airlift - The Story of Combat Cargo*. Tachikawa, Japan: 315th Air Division.
TIME. (1964, December 4). Africa, The Congo Massacre. *TIME* .
Tolson, J. J. (1972). *Air Mobility 1961-1971*. Retrieved from US Army Historical Division: http://www.history.army.mil/books/vietnam/airmobility/airmobility-fm.html
Trest, W. (2000). *Air Commando One - Heinie Aderholt and America's Secret Wars*. Smithsonian Books.
Trest, W. (2000). *Air Commando One, Heinie Aderholt and America's Secret Air Wars*. Smithsonian Books.
Tunner, W. H. (1964). *Over the Hump*. New York: Duell, Sloan and Pierce.

Sam McGowan

Ulanoff, S. (1964). *MATS, the Story of the Military Air Transport Service.* Watts Aerospace Library.
US Army Historians. (1973). *US Army Special Forces 1961-1971.*
USAF Historians. (1975). *Air War, Vietnam.* Arno Press (for the Office of Air Force History).
Walker, F. K. (n.d.). *My Cousin Wally.* Retrieved April 8, 2013, from http://www.bufordfamilies.com/bufordwallacea.htm
Warner, W. A. (2012). *One Trip Too Many.* CreateSpace.
Warren, D. J. (1957). Airborne Operations in WW II, European Theater.
Westmoreland, W. C. (1976). *A Soldier Reports.* Doubleday.
WW 2 US Medical Research Center. (n.d.). Retrieved March 9, 2013, from http://med-dept.com/airEvac.php

Anything, Anywhere, Anytime

Sam McGowan

About the Author

(Ronda McGowan)

West Tennessee native Sam McGowan is a veteran of twelve years of Air Force service in the 1960s and 1970s, all of which was spent in airlift. After training as an aircraft mechanic, he was assigned to the 464th Troop Carrier Wing at Pope AFB, NC as a C-130 flight line mechanic. In the fall of 1964 he transferred to the 779th Troop Carrier Squadron and cross-trained to the aircraft loadmaster career field. During a year of Tactical Air Command troop carrier flying, he was TDY to France, Okinawa, the Congo and Mactan Island in the Philippines. In April 1965 he flew with his crew on missions to the Dominican Republic.

In early 1966 he transferred to Naha Air Base, Okinawa to the 35th Troop Carrier Squadron. During his 18-month tour, he flew FAC/flare missions over Laos and North Vietnam, leaflet missions over North Vietnam and against North Korea in addition to tactical airlift missions in South Vietnam and Thailand. After reenlisting, he returned to the US for an assignment with Military Airlift Command at Robins AFB, Georgia as a loadmaster on C-141s. Eighteen months later he returned to the Pacific, this time to the 29th Tactical Airlift Squadron at Clark Air Base, Philippine Islands and the C-130B. From February 1969 to August 1970 he flew tactical airlift missions in South Vietnam

Anything, Anywhere, Anytime

and COMMANDO VAULT bombing missions. He was then assigned to the 3rd Military Airlift Squadron at Charleston AFB, SC as a C-5A loadmaster. He was credited with more than 1,200 combat sorties in C-130As, Bs and Es and was awarded the Distinguished Flying Cross and the Air Medal with eleven oak leaf clusters.

After obtaining his FAA pilot ratings, he left the Air Force and spent the remainder of his working life as a flight instructor, air taxi pilot and corporate pilot. He began writing on military subjects in the 1980s and has since written numerous magazine articles and several books. He resides with his wife Ronda and their dogs in the Houston, Texas area.

Sam McGowan is a founding member of the Troop Carrier/Tactical Airlift Association, which is dedicated to the preservation of the troop carrier/tactical airlift heritage. The TC/TAA web site is at www.troopcarrier.org. Sam McGowan's personal web site is www.sammcgowan.com.

Sam McGowan